Michael Cooper's Buyer's Guide to New Zealand Wines 2004

Hodder Moa Beckett

A catalogue record for this book is available
from the National Library of New Zealand.

ISBN 1-86958-932-7

Text © Michael Cooper 2003
The moral rights of the author have been asserted.
Design and format © Hodder Moa Beckett Publishers Limited 2003

Published in 2003 by Hodder Moa Beckett Publishers Limited
[a member of the Hodder Headline Group]
4 Whetu Place, Mairangi Bay, Auckland

Designed and produced by Hodder Moa Beckett
Typeset by Jazz Graphics, Auckland
Printed by Griffin Press, Australia

All rights reserved. No part of this publication may be reproduced or transmitted in any form or by any means, electronic or mechanical, including photocopying, recording, or any information storage and retrieval system, without permission in writing from the publisher.

Contents

The Winemaking Regions of
   New Zealand 4

Preface 5

Classic Wines of New Zealand 6

Best Buys of the Year 11

2003 Vintage Report 14

Variety Focus:
   Chenin Blanc 22

Cellar Sense 24

Vintage Charts 26

How to Use this Book 27

White Wines _____ 30

Branded and Other White Wines ... 30

Breidecker 33

Chardonnay 34

Chenin Blanc 112

Gewürztraminer 114

Müller-Thurgau 125

Osteiner 127

Pinot Blanc 127

Pinot Gris 128

Riesling 144

Roussanne 173

Sauvignon Blanc 174

Sémillon 218

Verdelho 221

Viognier 222

Sweet White Wines _____ 224

Sparkling Wines _____ 239

Rosé and Blush Wines _____ 249

Red Wines _____ 254

Branded and Other Reds 254

Cabernet Franc 267

Cabernet Sauvignon and Cabernet-
   predominant Blends 270

Chambourcin 298

Gamay Noir 298

Grenache 299

Malbec 300

Merlot 302

Montepulciano 330

Pinotage 331

Pinot Noir 335

Sangiovese 384

Syrah (Shiraz) 385

Zinfandel 393

Index of Wine Brands 394

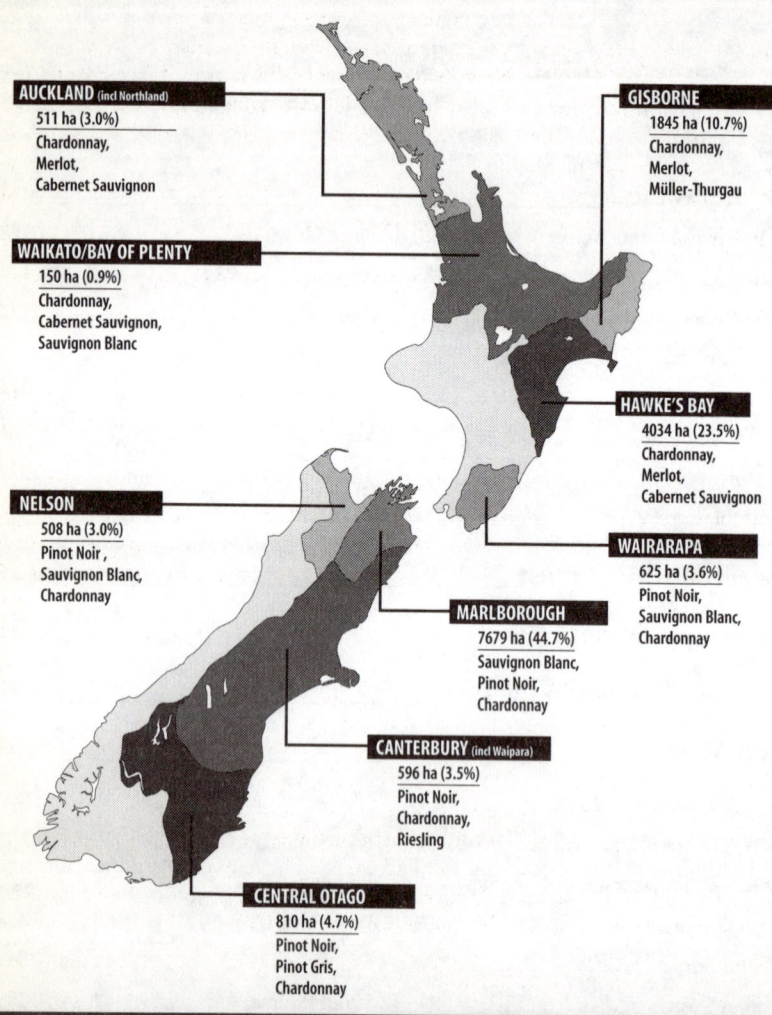

Preface

This twelfth edition of the *Buyer's Guide* will pass a memorable milestone — 100,000 copies sold.

In terms of the book's key goal, nothing has changed since the first 1992 edition, which I described as 'a guiding hand through the maze of New Zealand wines. Which are the finest New Zealand wines? Which offer the best value-for-money?' That early edition also identified those wines that had performed poorly in tastings, on the basis that 'readers are entitled to know the wines to avoid, as well as to pursue'.

Demand for the *Buyer's Guide* has risen over the years, as more and more New Zealanders who have discovered the pleasures of wine seek guidance through the 'maze'. You could choose from about 800 local wine labels in 1992; now there are at least 2000. Over 435 wineries are clamouring for your support. Among the latest arrivals are Destiny Bay, on Waiheke Island; Oasis Lodge, on Great Barrier Island; Blackenbrook Wines at Nelson; and Havoc Farms, in Central Otago.

The exceptionally low-cropping 2003 harvest will create gaps on the shelves, which wine importers will be happy to fill. Some local producers are restricting their supplies to the New Zealand market, in order to protect their hard-won export trade. Montana's steps to deal with the production shortfall will include 'a measure of substituting imported wines for New Zealand wines at the lower end of the price spectrum, changing the district of origin for some New Zealand blends, limiting the supply of certain wines, and, quite possibly, price increases'.

So what are we drinking? Gone are the days when white wines heavily outsold reds. In the year to July 2003, supermarkets sold nearly as many bottles of local or imported red wine (975,939 cases) as white (1,166,759 cases). Chardonnay (576,107 cases) and Sauvignon Blanc (364,177 cases) rule the white-wine roost, far ahead of Riesling (106,089 cases), Müller-Thurgau (38,993 cases), Pinot Gris (16,130 cases) and Gewürztraminer (11,588 cases.)

Among the reds, Cabernet Sauvignon (208,094 cases) is still the king, followed by Shiraz (169,370 cases), Cabernet/Merlot (162,597 cases), Merlot (151,808 cases), and Pinot Noir (42,755 cases). The majority of these white and red wines sold for less than $11; only one bottle in eight cost more than $15. For most New Zealanders, on most occasions, $10 to $12 is the limit for a bottle of wine.

— *Michael Cooper*

Classic Wines of New Zealand

A crop of one new Super Classic, nine Classics (all promoted from the Potential Classics category, including five Pinot Noirs), and seven Potential Classics, together with five deletions (of labels no longer at the very top of the tree), are the features of this year's revised list of New Zealand wine classics.

What is a New Zealand wine classic? It is a wine that in quality terms consistently ranks in the very forefront of its class. To qualify for selection, each label must have achieved an outstanding level of quality for at least three vintages; there are no flashes in the pan here.

By identifying New Zealand wine classics, my aim is to transcend the inconsistencies of individual vintages and wine competition results, and highlight consistency of excellence. When introducing the elite category of Super Classics in 1998, I restricted entry to wines that have achieved brilliance in at least five vintages (compared to three for Classic status). The Super Classics are all highly prestigious wines, with a proven ability to mature well (even the Sauvignon Blancs, compared to other examples of the variety).

The Potential Classics are the pool from which future Classics will emerge. These are wines of outstanding quality that look likely, if their current standards are maintained or improved, to qualify after another vintage or two for elevation to Classic status. All the additions and elevations on this year's list are identified by an asterisk.

An in-depth discussion of New Zealand's greatest wines (what they taste like, how well they mature, the secrets of their success) can be found in my book *Classic Wines of New Zealand* (Hodder Moa Beckett, 1999), which grew out of the *Buyer's Guide*'s annually updated list of New Zealand wine classics. A second, revised edition of *Classic Wines of New Zealand* will be published in 2004.

Super Classics

Chardonnay
*Ata Rangi Craighall
Clearview Estate Reserve
Kumeu River Kumeu
Kumeu River Mate's Vineyard
Morton Estate Black Label
Neudorf Moutere
Te Mata Elston

Gewürztraminer
Dry River

Pinot Gris
Dry River

Riesling
Dry River

Sauvignon Blanc
Cloudy Bay
Hunter's
Hunter's Winemaker's Selection (prev. Oak Aged)
Palliser Estate

Sweet Whites
Dry River Botrytis Bunch Selection Gewürztraminer and Riesling
Villa Maria Reserve Noble Riesling

Cabernet Sauvignon-predominant Reds
Goldwater Cabernet Sauvignon & Merlot
Stonyridge Larose Cabernets
Te Mata Coleraine Cabernet/Merlot

Merlot
Esk Valley Reserve Merlot-predominant blend

Pinot Noir
Ata Rangi
Dry River
Martinborough Vineyard

 # Classics

Chardonnay
Babich Irongate
Church Road Reserve
Cloudy Bay
Coopers Creek Swamp Reserve
Dry River
Esk Valley Reserve
Martinborough Vineyard
*Montana Ormond Estate
Palliser Estate
Pegasus Bay
Vidal Reserve
Villa Maria Reserve Marlborough
Wither Hills Marlborough

Chenin Blanc
Millton Te Arai Vineyard

Riesling
Palliser Estate
Pegasus Bay

Sauvignon Blanc
Grove Mill Marlborough
Isabel Marlborough
*Lawson's Dry Hills Marlborough
Nga Waka
*Seresin Marlborough
Villa Maria Reserve Clifford Bay
Villa Maria Reserve Wairau Valley
Wither Hills Marlborough

Sweet Whites
Ngatarawa Glazebrook Noble Harvest Riesling

Bottle-fermented Sparklings
Deutz Marlborough Cuvée
Pelorus

*New Classic

Branded and Other Reds
Esk Valley The Terraces

Cabernet Sauvignon-predominant Reds
Brookfields Reserve Vintage Cabernet/Merlot
Te Mata Awatea Cabernet/Merlot
Vidal Reserve Cabernet Sauvignon-predominant

Merlot
C.J. Pask Reserve

Pinot Noir
*Felton Road Block 3
*Fromm La Strada Fromm Vineyard
Gibbston Valley Reserve
*Neudorf Moutere
*Palliser Estate
*Pegasus Bay

Syrah
*Mills Reef Elspeth
Stonecroft

Potential Classics

Branded and Other White Wines
*Cloudy Bay Te Koko

Chardonnay
Isabel Marlborough
Millton Clos de Ste Anne
Sacred Hill Riflemans Reserve
*Seresin Reserve
Te Awa Farm Frontier
Trinity Hill Gimblett Road

Gewürztraminer
*Cloudy Bay
Stonecroft
Te Whare Ra Duke of Marlborough

Riesling
*Felton Road
Neudorf Moutere
Villa Maria Reserve Marlborough

Sauvignon Blanc
Goldwater New Dog Marlborough
Montana Brancott Estate
*Saint Clair Wairau Reserve
Thornbury Marlborough
Whitehaven Marlborough

Sweet White Wines
*Cloudy Bay Late Harvest Riesling

Bottle-fermented Sparklings
Elstree Cuvée Brut
Nautilus Cuvée Marlborough

Branded and Other Reds
Crossroads Talisman
Te Awa Farm Boundary
Unison Selection

Cabernet Sauvignon-predominant Reds
Babich The Patriarch Cabernet Sauvignon
Mills Reef Elspeth Cabernet/Merlot
Mills Reef Elspeth Cabernet Sauvignon
Newton/Forrest Cornerstone Cabernet/Merlot/Malbec

Merlot
Clearview Reserve
Matua Valley Ararimu Merlot/Cabernet Sauvignon
Villa Maria Reserve Merlot
Villa Maria Reserve Merlot/Cabernet Sauvignon

Pinot Noir
Greenhough Hope Vineyard
Kaituna Valley The Kaituna Vineyard
*Isabel Marlborough
Neudorf Moutere Home Vineyard
Pegasus Bay Prima Donna
Seresin
*Wither Hills Marlborough

*New Potential Classic

Best Buys of the Year

Six irresistible bargains, including the overall winner, are featured in this edition's Best Buy of the Year section.

In the past, I have compiled a shortlist of six great-value wines, from which the Best Buys of the Year was selected. The other five wines, although not highlighted in the front of the book, were presented at tastings held to celebrate the release of each new edition of the *Buyer's Guide*. Now, the shortlist is highlighted here, so that you can easily identify several of the best wine bargains around.

Best Buy of the Year

Nobilo Poverty Bay Chardonnay 2002
(★★★★☆ $15.95)

After tasting 303 Chardonnays, the judges at this year's Liquorland Top 100 International Wine Competition re-tasted the top wines side by side, before awarding a sprinkling of gold medals. Nestled among such prestigious labels as Villa Maria Reserve Hawke's Bay Chardonnay 2002 ($33), Wither Hills Marlborough Chardonnay 2002 ($29) and Esk Valley Reserve Chardonnay 2002 ($33) in the taste-off was a wine that cost only half the heavyweights. 'If it had gone gold, it would have caused a sensation,' recalls the show director, Kingsley Wood.

Some judges advocated giving the wine a gold medal, but more voted for a silver, and in the end that's what it got. A month earlier, I had encountered the same wine in another 'blind' tasting and enthused: 'Full, citrusy, balanced oak, very good depth, fleshy, ripe, slightly buttery, lovely balance.' Awarded a high silver medal at the Liquorland Top 100 and four and a half stars in *Winestate*'s annual Upper North Island tasting, at $15.95 Nobilo Poverty Bay Chardonnay 2002 is an irresistible buy (and can sometimes be found on special at $13.95).

Some past vintages of this softly seductive, affordably priced wine have been delightful, but the 2002 is the best yet. Freshly scented, with sweet-fruit delights and a strong surge of peachy, citrusy flavours, gently seasoned with oak, it's a classic Gisborne style, rich and rounded.

If you ask Katrina Sutherland, assistant winemaker for Nobilo Wine Group, why the wine is so good, she focuses immediately on the dream quality of the autumn, when Gisborne's vineyards basked in above-average sunshine hours and received less than half their average rainfall. 'It was warm and dry at the right times, with no disease pressure to pick, so we could wait until the grapes achieved optimum ripeness.'

The vintage produced an abundant supply of fine quality grapes, 'so although our cheaper wines are mostly handled in tanks, in 2002 we put a lot of wine into barrels. We need wood-aged wine for our premium Nobilo Icon Chardonnay and Selaks Founders Reserve Chardonnay labels, but there's a limit to how much wine you can sell at their relatively high prices. In 2002, we were able to blend some of the barrel-aged, lees-stirred wine into the Poverty Bay Chardonnay.'

Should you cellar the wine? 'I wouldn't keep it past 2005,' advises Katrina Sutherland. 'We make it to be accessible early.' Gisborne is renowned for the drink-young charm of its Chardonnays. Treat the classy, bargain-priced Nobilo Poverty Bay Chardonnay 2002 as the perfect wine for the summer of 2003–04.

Other Shortlisted Wines

Saints Marlborough Sauvignon Blanc 2003
(★★★★☆ $17.95)
This is a striking wine with an extra edge of intensity. Crammed with gooseberry, lime and green-capsicum flavours, beautifully fresh and vibrant, it's a racy, hugely drinkable style that shows far more class and personality than you'd expect at its moderate price (which on special drops to $14.95).

Made from the second crop off Montana's vineyards in the Awatere Valley, over the hills from the larger Wairau Valley, Saints Sauvignon Blanc shows the pungent aromas, brisk herbaceous edge, penetrating flavours, mouth-watering acidity and purity of varietal character that typify the Awatere's Sauvignon Blancs. A small proportion of the final blend was barrique-fermented and oak-aged, to add a touch of complexity, but the wine places its accent on its remarkable fruit flavours, which are notably fresh, pungent and long.

Collards Hawke's Bay Chenin Blanc 2002
(★★★☆ $12.75)
Collards has long produced some of the most sharply priced wines on the market, so the exceptional value offered by its 2002 Hawke's Bay Chenin Blanc will be no surprise to the supporters of this low-profile, but quality-focused, West Auckland-based winery.

Ripely scented, fleshy and rounded, it offers good depth of ripe, pineappley flavour, with a hint of honey, well-tamed acidity and a dry finish. Chenin Blanc is an unfashionable variety in New Zealand, but this wine shows that the famous Loire Valley variety can yield highly attractive wines here.

Lindauer Brut
(★★★☆ $13)
At the inaugural 2003 New World Wine Awards, devoted exclusively to sub-$20, widely available wines (minimum 500 cases), one sparkling wine stood out from the crowd by scoring the only silver medal – Montana's Lindauer Brut.

It's easy to take Lindauer for granted, but in blind tastings it performs consistently well – far better than you'd expect from its modest, sometimes almost give-away, price. The fresh, lively, non-vintage wine I tasted recently was straw-hued, with a moderately complex bouquet, plenty of fruity, yeasty flavour and a soft, smooth finish.

Don't let its huge production and low price blind you to its quality – it's a great buy.

Terrace Road Marlborough Pinot Noir 2002
(★★★★ $19)
Most four-star Pinot Noirs cost $35, often over $40. Terrace Road Pinot Noir 2002, from Cellier Le Brun, boasts a silver medal (the only one awarded in the Pinot Noir class at the 2003 New World Wine Awards) and a four-star rating from *Winestate* magazine, yet is widely available at $19.

Fullish in colour, with ripe-cherry and spice flavours and toasty oak adding complexity, it's a stylish and savoury wine, already delicious. Given its modest price, why is it so good?

'It's because our new, company-owned vineyards at Renwick have come on stream,' says winemaker Allan McWilliams. 'Previously, we relied on clones of Pinot Noir cultivated by contract growers for sparkling wine. Now we're using the far superior clone 5 ("Pommard") and Dijon clone 115.'

Matured in French oak casks (17 per cent new, but mostly two to five-year-old), Terrace Road Marlborough Pinot Noir has been deliberately made in a soft, forward style, for drinking during 2004. If there's a better sub-$20 Pinot Noir on the market, I haven't tasted it.

Villa Maria Cellar Selection Cabernet Sauvignon/Merlot 2001
(★★★★☆ $21.95)
Villa Maria Cellar Selection Merlot/Cabernet Sauvignon 2000 won the Best Buy of the Year award in last year's *Buyer's Guide*, and this densely coloured, concentrated and complex wine is another great buy.

Grown at the company's Ngakirikiri Vineyard, in the Gimblett Gravels District, and matured for 18 months in new and used French and American oak, it's a youthful wine with deep cassis, plum and spice flavours, sweet-fruit characters, toasty oak and a firm, lasting finish. Fragrant and ripe, slightly nutty and chocolatey, it's already highly enjoyable, but has the power to age long term.

Awarded a silver medal at the 2003 New Zealand Wine Society Royal Easter Wine Show, Villa Maria Cellar Selection Cabernet Sauvignon/Merlot 2001 has also won a top, five-star rating in *Winestate* magazine. If you can buy such a good Hawke's Bay claret-style red for a tad over $20, why pay more?

2003 Vintage Report

Jack Frost cut loose during the spring of 2002, launching a wave of attacks that left grape-growers reeling. At the end of the season, New Zealand's winemakers harvested their lightest crop on record – just 4.9 tonnes of grapes per hectare, barely half the average (9 tonnes per hectare) over the past decade.

At a time when the industry has been gearing up to expand its exports, New Zealand wine from the 2003 vintage will be in desperately short supply. At 76,400 tonnes of grapes, the harvest was 35 per cent down on 2002 and barely larger than the 1995 and 1996 vintages.

Of the major varieties, by far the worst hit was Chardonnay (down 54 per cent, compared to 2002), followed by Riesling (down 33 per cent), Cabernet Sauvignon (down 27 per cent) and Merlot (down 24 per cent). The two varieties enjoying growing export demand, Sauvignon Blanc (down 23 per cent) and Pinot Noir (down 10 per cent), were helped by extensive new plantings coming on stream and still managed to record their second-largest crops. Sauvignon Blanc (38 per cent), Chardonnay (21 per cent) and Pinot Noir (13 per cent), together accounted for over 70 per cent of the total 2003 harvest.

Over half of all New Zealand wine (54 per cent) flowed from the Marlborough region in 2003, followed by Gisborne (19 per cent) and Hawke's Bay (15 per cent). Nelson (the largest of the small regions, contributing 4 per cent of the national grape crop) and Central Otago were the only regions to produce a heavier crop than in 2002.

It was generally a cool growing season, with spring temperatures around the country the coldest for 20 years. Summer – the coolest for six years – brought no respite, although temperatures finally climbed above average in March, leading into the harvest.

The onslaught of frosts lasted for two months, from mid-September until mid-November. October, although exceptionally sunny, was the coldest for 20 years and November was windy and chilly. Squadrons of helicopters, wind machines, smudge pots and sprinkler systems were used in desperate bids to defend the vines' tender spring growth, but the damage to shoots and buds was widespread, wiping out the whole crop in some vineyards. 'Frosts on this scale have certainly not occurred before in my 25 years in the industry,' declared Tony Hoksbergen, national vineyards manager for Montana.

Steve Smith, of Craggy Range, pointed out that 'a year when frost hits in spring does not mean a bad year. If we get in and remove frosted shoots, remove late-ripening bunches at veraison [the start of the final stage of ripening], harvest in several passes, then we can still make some very good wines, even though our bank manager is a bit grumpy.'

After the ravages of the frosts, cool weather during the vines' flowering further inhibited the fruit set. Summer was dominated by a moderate El Niño weather pattern, which brought low temperatures (especially at night), sunny but unsettled weather and drought to eastern areas of the North and South Islands.

Temperatures finally rose in autumn, with very settled, extremely dry and sunny weather prevailing in the southern regions during March. However, the cool weather returned in April, with heavy rain in the first week of the month delaying the harvest in many vineyards.

Northland

Northland's harvest of 182 tonnes almost duplicated its 2002 record of 186 tonnes, but the region's vineyards produced just 0.2 per cent of the national grape crop.

During spring, a combination of high sunshine hours, below-average rainfall and strong south-westerly winds brought the region to the verge of a drought. Summer, however, brought heavy rains to eastern Northland, and in March some parts of the region experienced record rainfall.

'You could almost split the weather into east and west coast in Northland,' says grower spokesman Steve Nobilo. '[Heavy autumn rains] seemed to be the case right up to Kerikeri on the east coast, but further north again they had a lot less rain and were quite happy.' In the far north, Okahu Estate reported 'some very ripe fruit, especially Chambourcin and Pinotage'.

Auckland

'You're not going to get many gold medal wines, but it will be a pretty reasonable drop,' summed up grower spokesman Steve Nobilo, after a challenging season in Auckland.

Spring was the coldest in 30 years. During the flowering stage, the vines were 'chilled and stunted by cold conditions,' reported Nobilo. At 715 tonnes, the region's total grape harvest was the second smallest for the past decade and a massive 53 per cent below 2002.

Te Whau Vineyard, on Waiheke Island, noted 'the complete absence of spring. We went from winter to summer with a bang over the first weekend of December. January and early February brought long, hot days and brilliant sunshine, which later turned to a cooler, moister phase.'

March proved warmer and wetter than average. The Matakana sub-region had '300 millimetres or so of rain in the autumn harvest period, which made things very difficult,' reported Nobilo. Wine importer and retailer Paul Mitchell, who owns a small vineyard in West Auckland, described 2003 as 'a crap vintage ... our Cabernet Sauvignon eventually scraped over 20 brix!'

At Kumeu River, Michael Brajkovich reported 'not very high grape sugars, to say the least, but nothing really poor'. Inverness Estate, in Clevedon, chose to abandon rather than harvest its crop, 'our reasoning being that we couldn't afford to produce a sub-standard wine'.

However, others were more upbeat. Goldwater Estate, on Waiheke Island, reported 'one of our smallest vintages on record, but some beautiful grapes'. Te Whau picked 'very small Chardonnay berries with highly concentrated juice, which has made for a superb wine', and viewed 2003 as 'an excellent year for Merlot and Cabernet Franc'.

Waikato/Bay of Plenty

At a total of 497 tonnes – the third-smallest crop of the past decade – the Waikato/Bay of Plenty region harvested just 0.6 per cent of the national grape intake.

Spring was cool and frosty, but Te Kauwhata grower Ross Goodin later reported that 'the weather has been dry since late December. Forty millimetres of rain fell in mid to late February, but the grapes stood up well, with no splitting, and cool weather kept disease pressure low.'

Goodin later said that yields were down across all grape varieties, especially Chardonnay. 'Some vineyards reported good fruit, while others had to contend with low brix [sugar levels] and problems caused by rot.' However, Judge Valley, a red-wine specialist east of Te Awamutu, reported an 'excellent' 2003 harvest, with 'great balance, very high brix and awesome taste'.

Gisborne

After what the region's top winemaker, James Millton, called 'a difficult and challenging season', Gisborne's grape-growers processed a tiny crop of 14,350 tonnes – 46 per cent lighter than 2002 and the second-smallest harvest of the past decade.

After a very mild winter and a warm, early spring, bud-burst was 10 to 14 days earlier than usual. According to Montana viticulturist Warwick Bruce, 'the vines didn't get the winter hardening they did last year', which probably made the buds more susceptible to cold. During a series of three frosts over 20 days in September and early October, in some areas temperatures plummeted to –2.5°C. The impact of the frosts was felt in the Ormond, Hexton, Patutahi, Te Karaka and Tolaga Bay sub-regions, with some areas reporting spring frosts for the first time in memory.

At the end of a dry summer, some parts of Gisborne experienced a severe soil moisture deficit. 'The weather since Christmas has been fabulous – lovely hot days with a dry north-westerly wind,' reported grape-grower Doug Bell.

March, however, was overcast and rainy. Villa Maria noted that 'vintage was difficult, due to heavy rain and subsequent botrytis problems'. Doug Bell reported that 'through the ripening period we struck wet weather, so what little crop there was faced a real challenge'.

Yet Montana reported picking 'exceptionally good' Gewürztraminer and 'good parcels' of Chardonnay and Merlot. James Millton, initially less enthusiastic, described Chenin Blanc as 'coming through the best – it needs moisture and humidity to ripen with botrytis'.

However, after returning from an overseas trip, Millton declared he was 'quite surprised by the characters emerging. It's not such a bad vintage after all, it just needs time.'

Hawke's Bay

'It's been like the Battle of Britain – long and hard,' declared John Hancock, part-owner of Trinity Hill, after harvesting his 2003 crop. 'It's been my most difficult vintage in New Zealand so far [since arriving in 1979], in the sense of the frosts and fairly cool summer and fairly wet autumn. But it's not the worst in terms of quality.'

At 10,832 tonnes, the harvest was 42 per cent the size of the record 2002 crop, lighter than the frost-afflicted 2001 vintage, and the smallest of the past decade.

Steve Smith, chairman of the Gimblett Gravels Winegrowers Association, reported that 'three frosts hit us in the spring, the first nailing the Chardonnay, the second a gentle reminder, and the third severely hitting the remainder of the Chardonnay, Merlot and early crops of Cabernet Sauvignon and Syrah'.

Compared to the devastating but more localised frost of November 20, 2000, the 2002 frosts struck much earlier in the vines' vegetative cycle. Chardonnay, the first variety to go through bud-burst, was 'the worst hit', according to Stuart Devine, viticulturist for Villa Maria, but other white grapes – Sauvignon Blanc and Chenin Blanc – were also affected.

Red varieties, although later-budding, did not entirely escape the frosts. After a cold, wet and windy late spring, Devine described Merlot as 'whacked – I'd say 40 per cent is gone', but predicted Cabernet Sauvignon losses would only be 5–15 per cent.

Summer in Hawke's Bay was dry, with January rainfall less than half the normal, and fire bans were in place by early February. 'With summer slightly cooler than usual, we seemed to spend all of January and February in the vineyards leaf-plucking, removing late-ripening bunches and opening the canopy to maximise what sun there was,' reported Smith.

The harvest period was 'punctuated by moist easterlies', according to Ngatarawa Wines, which described the season as of average heat accumulation. Craggy Range views 2003 as 'an awkward, humid vintage that created real challenges in getting grapes fully ripe'. The Chardonnay crop was tiny. John Hancock, of Trinity Hill, reported harvesting only 20 per cent of his normal crop; Matariki, expecting 50 tonnes, harvested 4 tonnes.

Red-wine varieties fared better, displaying 'very low levels of herbaceousness and acid', according to Jeff Clarke, chief winemaker at Montana. 'We will get some excellent reds out of Hawke's Bay.' Hancock agreed, describing his red-wine grapes as 'fairly low sugar-wise, but the flavours are not green'.

Craggy Range described Merlot as the 'most seriously affected of the red grapes. Only about one-third of the crop shows the lusciousness required for the Craggy Range brand; the rest will be declassified.' Cabernet Sauvignon, however, was 'surprisingly good, with exceptional colour and ripe tannins'.

Winemakers in the Gimblett Gravels district predicted their reds would 'not be as lush as the 2002s or as big as the 1998s, but they have an inherent fineness and prettiness that is actually quite exciting'.

Wairarapa

Wairarapa wine, especially Martinborough Pinot Noir, will be in short supply, but most growers are predicting high quality from 2003. At 1311 tonnes, the region's crop was 35 per cent smaller than in 2002.

After a cool, windy spring brought a slow start to the growing season, vineyards in and around Martinborough were struck by frosts in October and November. Kai Schubert, who owns vineyards at Martinborough and near Masterton, reported 'more frosts than in all our past vintages [1999–2002] together'.

Summer, however, brought 'an extended spell of warm days, cool nights and very little rain', according to Christine Kernohan, of Gladstone Vineyard. Kernohan also reported 'average temperatures 0.5°C above normal for three months and a record maximum temperature for February of 35°C'.

In early April, Neil McCallum of Dry River reported his grapes looked 'outstanding, with low crops, open bunches and small berries'. Craggy Range viewed its Martinborough Riesling and Chardonnay crops as 'stunning' and Sauvignon Blanc as 'very smart, slightly softer in style than the cooler 2002 vintage, with slightly lower alcohol'.

At Gladstone Vineyard, the white-wine crop was down significantly and later-ripening than usual, but 'the flavours are excellent', reported Kernohan. 'Plus we have got the best Cabernet Sauvignon and Merlot for many years.'

Richard Riddiford, of Palliser Estate, estimated in early May that Pinot Noir from the Martinborough sub-region 'could be down in volume by two-thirds'. However, Craggy Range praised Pinot Noir as 'the real star' of its Martinborough crop, in its infancy looking 'unbelievable'.

Nelson

At 3149 tonnes, Nelson harvested by far its largest-ever grape crop, up 76 per cent on 2002. A week of heavy rain in early April caused some damage to Chardonnay, but expectations are for generally solid wines.

September, the warmest since 1997, was followed by unusually dry and sunny but cool weather during October and November. Bud-burst was early and even and there were no reports of frost damage. In early December, a grower on the Waimea Plains reported 'Chardonnay with good fruit set and a very healthy crop level – maybe too high.'

After a showery start to the summer in early December, both January and February were favourably dry and sunny (February's rainfall was just 7 per cent of the long-term average).

The dry, settled weather continued into autumn, with March sunshine hours the second highest on record, and temperatures above average. April, apart from a deluge on the night of April 5, was generally settled, sunny and cool, and May proved one of the mildest on record.

One grower on the Waimea Plains on April 20 reported harvesting grapes with 'slightly lower brix levels but acids also low. The fruit was in excellent condition despite the early April rains.' Agnes Seifried noted that the early April storm had 'hurried up the picking of the early grapes, especially Chardonnay, which showed a bit of botrytis, but most of the fruit was clean, with lovely sugars'.

Marlborough

After crippling spring frosts, Marlborough growers harvested 40,537 tonnes of grapes, down 26 per cent on 2002. A high incidence of uneven bunch ripeness is expected to cause unripe flavours and high acidity in some wines, but most winemakers reported picking grapes with excellent flavour intensity, including Sauvignon Blanc and Pinot Noir.

In spring, an unusually warm September was followed by a dry, sunny and cool October, with several ground frosts, and the pattern of below-average rainfall continued through November.

The big frost, on November 18, was 'the worst spring frost in the history of Marlborough viticulture', according to *Winepress*, the local growers' newsletter. Catching growers unaware, the unpredicted frost sent temperatures plunging to as low as –2.2°C, singeing leaves and damaging shoots and fruit. 'Some vineyards had superficial frostings; others were totally wiped out,' reported John Marris, of Wither Hills Vineyards. The worst-affected district was Rapaura, on the north side of the Wairau Valley, normally considered frost-free.

Above-average rainfall in December offered brief respite from the drought, but by the end of summer Marlborough was bone-dry again. During December, January and February, despite plentiful sunshine, temperatures stayed slightly below average. Only on one day (February 11) did the maximum daily temperature exceed 30°C.

Autumn brought no drought relief, with March, April (especially) and May all recording below-average rainfall. Although March was warmer than average, April was the coolest for 10 years. For the September-April growing season, Marlborough's heat summation total was exactly equal to the average for the past 16 seasons – warmer than 2000, but cooler than 2001 and 2002.

After a damp spell in early April delayed the harvest, 'some Chardonnay declined in quality', according to local grape-grower Stuart Smith. Winemaker John Forrest noted that the region's vineyards had a huge amount of 'second-set' fruit, which coupled with the presence of 'late first-set' fruit meant getting the bunches to ripen evenly was 'extremely difficult'. According to Hatsch Kalberer, of Fromm Vineyard, the impact of the late-ripening grapes would lead to 'unripe flavours and high acidities in some wines'. Quality-focused companies hand-harvested a higher proportion of their vineyards than usual, in a bid to select only premium grapes.

From the start, most winemakers claimed their 2003 wines would be more concentrated than the 2002s. 'Our Sauvignon Blanc is weightier and slightly riper and more intense than last year,' said Simon Nunns, winemaker at Coopers Creek. Villa Maria reported Sauvignon Blanc with 'high retention of acids, high sugars and great intensity of flavour'.

For Joe Babich, Pinot Noir was 'the highlight of the season'. Steve Bird, of Thornbury, reported harvesting Pinot Noir bunches with 'small berries, ripe and dark – a gem to work with'.

Steve Smith, of Craggy Range, crushed 'some stunning botrytised Riesling. From what I've heard, some of the stickies are going to be very, very good.'

Canterbury

After spring frosts in Waipara slashed yields, Canterbury growers harvested 1422 tonnes of grapes, down by 28 per cent on 2002 and their fourth-smallest crop in the past five years.

Mark Rattray, of Floating Mountain, reported four separate spring frosts at his Waipara vineyard. 'We ended up with two barrels of Chardonnay, compared to a dozen in the 2002 vintage.'

Christchurch vineyards basked in the sunniest summer for more than half a century, yet temperatures were generally lower than in 2002, and in late February the city recorded its lowest February temperature (1.5°C) since 1954. Drought conditions throughout the summer ensured a low level of disease pressure in the vineyards.

However, heavy rain in late March and early April took the edge off the harvest. Darjon Vineyard, at Swannanoa, reported a 'nightmare autumn with torrential rains'. Danny Schuster announced his company would not produce a 2003 Petrie Chardonnay from its Rakaia vineyard, south of Ashburton: 'Five inches of rain in seven days was simply too much.'

Pegasus Bay was more upbeat, describing its Pinot Noir as 'excellent', and Danny Schuster considers his Omihi Hills Pinot Noir to be 'as rich and concentrated as 2001'. However, another Waipara winemaker was less enthusiastic, describing his Pinot Noir as having 'satisfactory brixes, but it's certainly not on a par with 2001'.

Central Otago

The 2003 vintage was of variable quality in Central Otago, which harvested a record grape crop of 1825 tonnes – up 20 per cent on 2002.

After a very early bud-burst, a cold November (2°C below average) slowed the vines' growth. 'The warm days of early September lulled us into a false sense of security,' reported Black Ridge Winery, at Alexandra. 'Since then we've had a series of biting southerlies that have brought snow to the hilltops and wild fluctuations of temperature. Late frosts have taken their toll in some parts of the vineyard.'

Summer was highly variable, with alternating hot and cold spells. 'It's been warm, cold, warm, cold – up and down like a yo-yo!' declared David Grant, of William Hill Vineyard, in late January.

Settled weather finally arrived in March, with low rainfall (under 25 per cent of the long-term average) and warm temperatures (1.5°C above average). However, in early April some of the region's viticulturists were forced to battle frosts, as night temperatures plummeted. 'The cold nights usually start around 10 April, but this year they arrived during the third week of March, slowing ripening and delaying the harvest,' reported Rudi Bauer, of Quartz Reef.

In a growing season when the overall heat summation was not high, site selection and vineyard management were crucial influences on quality. One leading winemaker was 'pessimistic overall about Riesling, but those who managed their vineyards well will make good wines. Pinot Noir is the best variety, overall – lower in alcohol and less intense than the 2002s, but charming, with good varietal definition.'

'Some of the cooler districts had some ripening problems,' admitted another winemaker. 'But the quality of fruit from our Cromwell Basin vineyards was fantastic, with low crops, no disease and a wide range of flavours.'

Variety Focus

Chenin Blanc

Is Chenin Blanc our most unfashionable grape variety? 'No matter how many favourable reviews we get for our Chenin Blanc,' observes James Millton, the country's leading producer of the great French variety, 'it doesn't lead to extra sales. People just aren't interested in Chenin Blanc.'

A few years ago, Babich produced a convincingly full-flavoured and steely Chenin Blanc from its Gimblett Road plantings. At $13, it offered outstanding value, but after it languished on the shelves, the company abandoned the variety.

Yet Jancis Robinson, the English wine authority, believes Chenin Blanc should flourish here. 'Chenin Blanc seems to thrive best, and demonstrate its undoubted flair, in marginal climates. The Loire Valley is the most obvious example ... [but] the cool climate of New Zealand may well prove to have the most exciting potential outside France.'

From a position of prominence in New Zealand 20 years ago, Chenin Blanc has declined into near-obscurity. Corbans established the variety as a premium wine with their silver medal 1976 and 1977 vintages, grown at Tolaga Bay. By 1983, when it was seen as a usefully crisp blender for such naturally low-acid grapes as Müller-Thurgau, Chenin Blanc covered 372 hectares and accounted for 6.3 per cent of the country's total vine plantings.

Chenin Blanc's susceptibility to rot later led many growers to discard their vines. Today, with only 118 hectares established – almost entirely in the Hawke's Bay, Gisborne and Waikato regions – it forms a mere 0.7 per cent of the national vineyard. In the South Island, just 1 hectare is recorded.

A sure sign of the lowly stature of Chenin Blanc in New Zealand is the price paid for the grapes, of which 75 per cent are not cultivated by the wine companies themselves but purchased from growers (compared to 58 per cent of the total crop). In 2002, Sauvignon Blanc fetched an average price of $2144 per tonne; Riesling sold for $1520 per tonne; Chenin Blanc commanded just $763 per tonne.

Yet Chenin Blanc is a classic grape variety, arguably the most versatile of all. Around the world, it produces an array of sparkling wines, freshly acidic medium-dry whites and racy, rich, honey-sweet beauties.

In its Loire Valley homeland, notes Robinson, 'the very acid which makes tasting young Vouvray [based on Chenin Blanc] such a taxing experience is capable of masking youthful sweetness and sustaining the wines into a very ripe old age... The most prized Loire Chenin Blancs are late-picked and high in residual sugar, often further concentrated excitingly by botrytis.'

An ancient grape variety, Chenin Blanc was cultivated in the ninth century at Anjou, in the middle Loire Valley, and is now grown around the world. South Africa's extensive plantings of Steen – which probably arrived at the Cape in 1655 – were discovered in 1965 to be none other than Chenin Blanc.

However, in such New World countries as South Africa, the United States and Australia, Chenin Blanc is mostly treated as a workhorse variety, valued for its bumper crops. To coax out its greatness, low yields (as in the Loire Valley) are essential, and the French also believe that Chenin Blanc produces its most distinctive and exciting wines in calcareous soils.

One of the most uninspiring tastings I've ever plodded through was a line-up in 1991 of local Chenin Blancs from the 1988, 1989 and 1990 vintages. 'What a charmless lot!' I wrote later, put off by their tongue-curling acidity. The good news is that a new breed of New Zealand Chenin Blanc has since come on the market, far riper and more enjoyable, offering fresh, pure, pineappley flavours enlivened by appetising but not excessive acidity.

A small band of devotees keep Chenin Blanc's flag flying in New Zealand: James and Annie Millton at Gisborne; Esk Valley in Hawke's Bay; West Auckland-based Collards, who also draw their grapes from Hawke's Bay; Margrain in Martinborough, owners of a plot of Chenin Blanc established by the late Stan Chifney; and John Forrest in Marlborough.

James Millton, whose Millton Te Arai Vineyard Chenin Blanc enjoys a strong reputation in the UK, believes the essence of the variety's charm is 'its attack – its fine, tingling, mouth-watering, refreshing acidity... What other wines go with fresh fish to figs to fromage to foie gras to dried fruit?'

Site and soil both contribute to the ongoing success of his Chenin Blanc, Millton argues. 'Our vineyard at Manutuke [west of the city of Gisborne] is within 5 kilometres of the coast, so we get cooling sea breezes, which keeps up the acidity. Chenin Blanc needs that acidity for spine and longevity. And our soils are high in calcium, which Chenin Blanc likes. The calcium gives the wine backbone – like our skeleton – and upon that the acidity is built.'

To counter Chenin Blanc's tendency to crop heavily, Millton prunes his vines severely and discards some of their bunches, aiming for 5–10 tonnes of fruit per hectare. The grapes are picked by hand over a month, at three different stages of ripeness, culminating in a final harvest of botrytis-affected, nobly rotten fruit. Fermentation is partly in large, 620-litre French oak casks – used in the Loire for Chenin Blanc – to add complexity rather than obvious oak flavours.

By cultivating their vines in devigorating soils and reducing their yields, quality-focused growers will continue to upgrade the quality of New Zealand's Chenin Blancs. Small-bunched, earlier-ripening Loire Valley clones of Chenin Blanc, not yet planted commercially here, offer further scope for improvement.

The widely available Chenin Blancs from Collards, Esk Valley, Millton and others offer a welcome alternative to the countless Chardonnays and Sauvignon Blancs on the market. Let's hope more growers will accept the challenge of making top-flight wine from this unfashionable but aristocratic variety.

Is anyone interested in planting a plot of Chenin Blanc on the limestone-based hill country at Waipara?

Cellar Sense

Who doesn't relish the idea of a personal wine cellar, packed with vintage wines maturing slowly to their peak? Yet a 1999 survey of 1000 wine consumers by Montana found that 70 per cent of wine is drunk on the day it is bought and a further 20 per cent is consumed within a couple of days. Less than 1 per cent of all wine purchased in New Zealand is cellared for more than a year. So much for cellaring – we love contemplating it, but few of us actually do it.

It *is* worth the effort. To enjoy wine at the height of its powers, when its flavour is at its most complex, harmonious and downright enjoyable, you need to lay it down (in the case of screw-capped wines, standing upright is fine) for a few years. Keeping a stock of wine in the house is convenient and also economical: you can buy by the case at lower prices and it's the cheapest way to obtain mature vintages.

Which wines most repay cellaring? First, forget the idea that all wines improve with age. Much New Zealand wine is best drunk young, especially unoaked Sauvignon Blanc, which is typically at its aromatic and zesty best within 18 months of the vintage. Modest quality, low-priced Rieslings, Gewürztraminers, Pinot Gris and Chardonnays, specifically made for early consumption, after a year or two typically lose the fresh, vibrant fruit characters that are the essence of their appeal. Only superior examples of a few classic grape varieties blossom in the bottle for several years.

Chardonnay, Riesling, Pinot Noir, and Cabernet Sauvignon and Merlot-predominant reds should be the mainstays of your cellar. Chardonnay from top producers usually has the weight and richness to flourish for three or four years (the 2002s should be drinking well from 2004 onwards); fine-quality Riesling improves even longer. Premium-quality Pinot Noir, Merlot and Syrah should also flourish for at least three to five years. Top vintages of the best Cabernet Sauvignon-based reds from Hawke's Bay and Waiheke Island benefit from at least five years' cellaring and can age gracefully for a decade.

A sprinkling of other New Zealand varietal wines will add interest and diversity to your cellar: good Pinot Gris and Chenin Blanc (especially), Gewürztraminer, barrel-aged Sauvignon Blanc, Viognier and Sémillon will age well for at least a couple of years and often a lot longer.

Build your cellar in the coolest, darkest place you can find in (or under) the house. Start by buying full or half cases of your favourite wines, and monitor their development by broaching a bottle every six months or so. Many people with cellars make the mistake of keeping their wines too long. You'll get more pleasure from your wine when it's still a bit too young than when it's faded and dull.

Cellaring Guidelines

Grape variety   Best age to open

White
Sauvignon Blanc
    (non-wooded) .... 6–18 months
    (wooded) .... 1–3 years
Gewürztraminer .... 2–3 years
Viognier .... 2–3 years
Chenin Blanc .... 2–4 years
Sémillon .... 2–4 years
Pinot Gris .... 2–5 years
Chardonnay .... 3–5 years
Riesling .... 3–10 years

Red
Pinotage .... 1–3 years
Malbec .... 1–3 years
Cabernet Franc .... 1–4 years
Merlot .... 2–5 years
Pinot Noir .... 2–5 years
Syrah .... 2–5 years
Cabernet Sauvignon .... 3–7+ years
Cabernet/Merlot .... 3–7+ years

Other
Bottle-fermented sparklings ..... 3–5 years

Vintage Charts 1993–2003

	Auckland	Gisborne	Hawke's Bay	Wairarapa	Nelson	Marlborough	Canterbury	Otago
WHITES								
2003	5–6	4	3–4	6–7	5–6	5–6	4–6	5
2002	6	7	6	6	6–7	4–6	4–7	5–7
2001	3–5	4	4–5	6–7	6–7	6–7	6	4–6
2000	7	5	6	5–7	5–6	5–7	3–6	4–5
1999	6	5	5–6	5–7	5–6	6–7	5	5–6
1998	4–7	6	6	6–7	6–7	5	6	6–7
1997	5	5	4–6	6–7	6–7	6	5–6	4–5
1996	6	6	4–6	6–7	5	6	3–6	4–5
1995	4	4	3–7	5–6	2–4	2–3	6–7	5
1994	6	6	6–7	6	5–6	5–6	4	4
1993	7	4	3–4	4	4	3–4	3–4	5

	Auckland	Gisborne	Hawke's Bay	Wairarapa	Nelson	Marlborough	Canterbury	Otago
REDS								
2003	4–6	4	3–4	6–7	5–6	5–6	4–6	5
2002	6	7	5–6	4–6	5–7	4–7	4–7	6–7
2001	4–5	4	4	5–7	6–7	5–7	7	6
2000	7	5	5–7	5–7	5–6	5–7	4–6	4
1999	6	4	4–6	6–7	6	5–6	5–7	6
1998	4–7	6	7	6–7	6	6–7	6	6–7
1997	4–5	4	4	6	6–7	5	5–6	5–6
1996	6	5	4	7	5–6	4	4–6	5
1995	4	2	5–7	6	2–4	2–3	6–7	6
1994	6	6	5–6	6	5	5	4	5
1993	7	3	2	4–5	3–4	3–4	3–4	5

7=Outstanding 6=Excellent 5=Above average 4=Average 3=Below average 2=Poor 1=Bad

Note: these vintage charts are compiled with input from two leading winemakers in each region. They also reflect my general impressions of what counts most: what's in the glass.

How to Use This Book

It is essential to read this brief section to understand how the book works. Feel free to skip any of the other preliminary pages – but not these.

The majority of wines have been listed in the book according to their principal grape variety. Lawsons Dry Hills Marlborough Sauvignon Blanc, for instance, can be located simply by turning to the Chardonnay section. Non-varietal wines (with names that do not boldly refer to a grape variety or blend of grapes), such as Cloudy Bay Te Koko or Crossroads Talisman, can be found in the Branded and Other Wines sections for white and red wines.

Most entries are firstly identified by their producer's names. Wines not usually called by their producer's name, such as Church Road Cabernet Sauvignon/Merlot (from Montana) or Oyster Bay Marlborough Chardonnay (from Delegat's), are listed under their most common name.

The star ratings for quality reflect my own opinions, formed where possible by tasting a wine over several vintages, and often a particular vintage several times. THE STAR RATINGS ARE THEREFORE A GUIDE TO EACH WINE'S OVERALL STANDARD IN RECENT VINTAGES, rather than simply the quality of the latest release. However, to enhance the usefulness of the book, in the body of the text I have also given a QUALITY RATING FOR THE LATEST VINTAGE OF EACH WINE; sometimes for more than one vintage.

I hope the star ratings give interesting food for thought and succeed in introducing you to a galaxy of little-known but worthwhile wines. It pays to remember, however, that wine-tasting is a business fraught with subjectivity. You should always treat the views expressed in these pages for what they are – one person's opinion.

The quality ratings are:

★★★★★	Outstanding quality (gold medal standard)
★★★★☆	Excellent quality, verging on outstanding
★★★★	Excellent quality (silver medal standard)
★★★☆	Very good quality
★★★	Good quality (bronze medal standard)
★★☆	Average quality
★★	Plain
★	Poor
No star	To be avoided

These quality ratings are based on comparative assessments of New Zealand wines against one another. A five-star Merlot/Cabernet Sauvignon, for instance, is an outstanding-quality red judged by the standards of other Merlot/Cabernet Sauvignon blends made in New Zealand. It is not judged by the standards of overseas reds of a similar style (for instance Bordeaux), because the book is focused solely on New Zealand wines and their relative merits.

Where brackets enclose the star rating on the right-hand side of the page, for example (★★★), this indicates the assessment is only tentative, because I have tasted very few vintages of the wine. A dash is used in the relatively few cases where a wine's quality has oscillated over and above normal vintage variations (for example ★ – ★★★).

Super Classic wines, Classic wines and Potential Classic wines (see page 6) are highlighted in the text by the following symbols:

Super Classic   Classic   Potential Classic

Each wine has also been given a dryness-sweetness, price and value-for-money rating. The precise levels of sweetness indicated by the four ratings are:

DRY	Less than 5 grams/litre of sugar
MED/DRY	5–14 grams/litre of sugar
MED	15–49 grams/litre of sugar
SW	50 and over grams/litre of sugar

Less than 5 grams of sugar per litre is virtually imperceptible to most palates – the wine tastes bone-dry. With between 5 and 14 grams, a wine has a hint of sweetness, although a high level of acidity (as in Marlborough Sauvignon Blancs, which often have 4 to 7 grams per litre of sugar) reduces the perception of sweetness. Where a wine harbours over 15 grams, the sweetness is clearly in evidence. At above 50 grams per litre, a wine is unabashedly sweet.

Prices shown are based on the average price in a retail wine outlet (as indicated by the wine producer), except where most of the wine is sold directly to the public, either over the vineyard counter or by mail order.

The art of wine buying involves more than just discovering top-quality wines. The greater challenge – and the greatest satisfaction – lies in identifying wines at varying quality levels that deliver outstanding value for money. The symbols I have used are self-explanatory:

–V	=	Below average value
AV	=	Average value
V+	=	Above average value

The ratings discussed thus far are all my own. Many of the wine producers themselves, however, have also contributed individual vintage ratings of their own wines back to the early 1990s and the 'When to drink' recommendations. (The symbol **WR** indicates Winemaker's Rating, and the symbol **NM** alongside a vintage means the wine was not made that year.) Only the producers have such detailed knowledge of the relative quality of all their recent vintages (although in a very few cases, when the information was not forthcoming, I have rated a vintage myself). The key point you must note is that EACH PRODUCER HAS RATED EACH VINTAGE OF EACH WINE AGAINST HIS OR HER HIGHEST QUALITY ASPIRATIONS FOR THAT PARTICULAR LABEL, NOT AGAINST ANY ABSOLUTE STANDARD. Thus, a 7 out of 7 score merely indicates that the producer considers that particular vintage to be an outstanding example of that particular wine, not that it is the best quality wine he or she makes.

The 'when to drink' (**Drink**) recommendations (which I find myself referring to constantly) are largely self-explanatory. The **P** symbol for PEAKED means that a particular vintage is already at, or has passed, its peak; no further benefits are expected from aging.

Here is an example of how the ratings work:

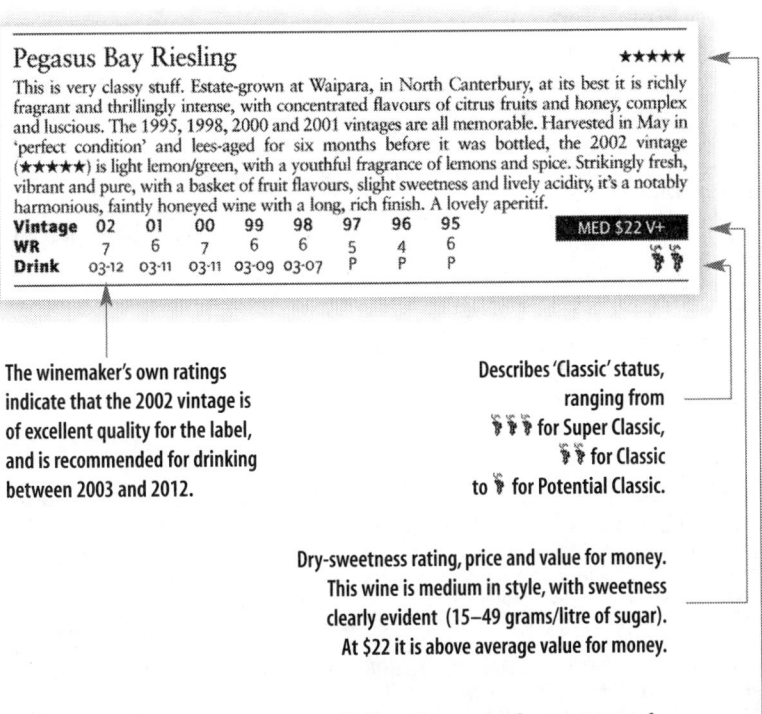

The winemaker's own ratings indicate that the 2002 vintage is of excellent quality for the label, and is recommended for drinking between 2003 and 2012.

Describes 'Classic' status, ranging from
🌿🌿🌿 for Super Classic,
🌿🌿 for Classic
to 🌿 for Potential Classic.

Dry-sweetness rating, price and value for money. This wine is medium in style, with sweetness clearly evident (15–49 grams/litre of sugar). At $22 it is above average value for money.

Quality rating, ranging from ★★★★★ for outstanding to no star (−), to be avoided. This is generally a wine of outstanding quality.

White Wines

Branded and Other White Wines

White Cloud, Kim Crawford Pia, Glenmark Waipara White, Black Ridge Otago Gold – in this section you'll find all the white wines that don't feature varietal names.

Lower-priced branded white wines can give winemakers an outlet for grapes like Chenin Blanc, Sémillon and (until recently) Riesling, that are otherwise hard to sell. They can also be an outlet for coarser, less delicate juice ('pressings'). Standing out from the bewildering array of varietal wines, strong, distinctive brands like White Cloud (New Zealand's answer to Blue Nun) have been hugely successful in attracting supermarket customers.

Most of the branded whites are quaffers, but such wines as Cloudy Bay Te Koko and Craggy Range Les Beaux Cailloux are highly distinguished.

Babich Fumé Vert ★★☆

In the past one of Babich's most popular wines – and with its easy-drinking style, it's easy to see why. Fumé vert means 'smoky green', which aptly sums up the wine's style. A 50/50 blend of Sémillon and Chardonnay, grown in Gisborne and the Henderson Valley, it typically offers lemony, gently herbaceous flavours, fractionally sweet, crisp and fresh. The 2002 vintage (★★★) is one of the best – very clean and vibrant, with lively, grassy aromas and flavours. (From 2003 onwards, the name Fumé Vert will disappear and the wine will be labelled as Babich Sémillon/Chardonnay.)

Vintage	02	01	00	99	98
WR	7	6	7	7	7
Drink	03-05	03-04	P	P	P

MED/DRY $13 AV

Black Ridge Otago Gold ★★☆

The Alexandra winery's estate-grown white for summer quaffing is usually pale, floral and light, its citrusy flavours harbouring a distinct splash of sweetness. Based on the Breidecker variety and vintage-dated since 2001, it's an enjoyable drop, but the big wineries churn out this sort of wine cheaper.

MED $12 AV

Cloudy Bay Te Koko ★★★★★

Te Koko o Kupe (the oyster dredge of Kupe) is the original name for Cloudy Bay; it is also the name of the famous Marlborough winery's exciting, innovative, oak-aged Sauvignon Blanc. The outstanding 2000 vintage (★★★★★) was made from mature vines grown adjacent to the winery, fermented with indigenous ('wild') yeasts and matured on its lees for 18 months in French oak barriques (10 per cent new), with full malolactic fermentation. Sturdy and rounded, it has an intriguing bouquet of smoky oak and ripe fruit, with slight minerally characters adding complexity. Tightly structured and intense, with an array of melon, fig, capsicum and oak flavours and a deliciously smooth texture, it offers great individuality and drinkability.

Vintage	00	99	98	97	96
WR	6	5	5	5	5
Drink	03-05	03-04	P	P	P

DRY $34 AV

Craggy Range Les Beaux Cailloux (★★★★★)

The debut 2001 vintage (★★★★★) is an unusually complex Hawke's Bay Chardonnay, with loads of personality. Based on first-crop, ultra low-yielding Gimblett Gravels vines, it was fermented with indigenous yeasts, lees-aged for over a year in French oak barriques (80 per cent new), with full malolactic fermentation, and bottled without fining or filtering. High-priced, but very classy, it shows great texture, mouthfeel and depth, with a complex, earthy rather than fruity bouquet, layers of grapefruit, peach and slight butterscotch flavours, finely balanced acidity and a rounded, rich finish.

Vintage 01
WR 7
Drink 05-09

DRY $60 AV

Glenmark Waipara White ★★☆

Pale, crisp and floral, this North Canterbury wine tastes like the Müller-Thurgau it basically is, with other grapes (including Breidecker, Sauvignon Blanc and Pinot Gris) accounting for 20 per cent of the blend. The 2001 vintage (★★☆) is fresh and light, with clean, lemony, appley flavours and a gently sweet finish.

MED $12 AV

Hatton Estate Gimblett Road EC2 ★★★

Designed as 'a delightful aperitif', the 2003 vintage (★★★☆) is made from clone 15 Chardonnay grapes (EC2 stands for 'Experimental Chardonnay 2'), grown in Gimblett Road, Hawke's Bay. Produced 'in the Chablis style' (read: without oak), it's a tangy wine with fresh, strong, lemony, appley aromas, good mouthfeel and depth of crisp, vibrant, citrusy flavour and a dry, slightly flinty finish.

Vintage 03 02
WR 7 7
Drink 03-05 03-04

DRY $25 -V

Kim Crawford Pia ★★★

Named after winemaker Kim Crawford's daughter, this is designed as an oak-aged dry white of varying regions and varieties, depending on the vintage. The 2000 (★★★) is a Hawke's Bay Chardonnay, grown at Te Awanga, fermented with natural yeasts and matured on its yeast lees for 11 months in one-year-old American oak barrels. It's a full-bodied, fairly complex wine with citrusy, slightly buttery flavours and a strong, biscuity oak influence, but is starting to taste a bit tired and past its best.

Vintage 00 99
WR 5 6
Drink 04-06 03-04

DRY $40 -V

Rippon Hotere White ★★☆

Cultivated on the shores of Lake Wanaka in the Southern Alps, this wine is made 'for summer drinking, not sipping'. Blended from such varieties as Müller-Thurgau, Breidecker and Chenin Blanc, it is typically a pale, light, appley, fractionally sweet wine, crisp and clean but lacking any real flavour depth. A solid quaffer, it's a bit high-priced for what it delivers.

MED/DRY $14 -V

St Aubyns Dry White ★★

This bottom-rung Villa Maria wine is ideal when you simply want a glass of no-fuss, off-dry white with reasonable body and flavour and a modest price-tag. It is grown principally in Gisborne, and tastes and smells like its predominant variety, Müller-Thurgau. A non-vintage wine, it's typically well-balanced, with citrusy, rounded flavours.

MED/DRY $7 AV

St Aubyns Medium White ★★

Villa Maria's low-priced, non-vintage quaffer is based largely on Müller-Thurgau, grown principally in Gisborne. It's typically a pleasant drop, with fresh, lemony, crisp flavours in a distinctly medium style.

MED $7 AV

St Helena Bernice (★★★★)

The 2002 vintage (★★★★) is the best wine I've tasted lately from this long-established Canterbury producer. Made from Pinot Blanc grapes, harvested at an ultra-ripe 27 brix (the highest sugar content since planting 22 years ago), with some noble rot, it was matured on its yeast lees for six months, but not oak-aged. Softly mouthfilling, with lovely richness of peachy, slightly spicy and honeyed flavour, gentle acidity and a medium-sweet finish, it has an Alsace-like weight and structure, and is already a delicious mouthful.

Vintage 02
WR 7
Drink 03-05

MED $28 -V

Schubert Tribianco ★★★☆

The 2002 vintage (★★★☆) is a distinctive Martinborough dry white, blended from Chardonnay, Pinot Gris and Müller-Thurgau. Fermented both in tanks and seasoned French oak hogsheads and puncheons, it's a bone-dry style, fresh and full-bodied, with citrus, pear and spice flavours, moderate acidity and some nutty, leesy complexity. Still coming together, it's a flavoursome wine with lots of interest, likely to be at its best during 2004–05.

Vintage 02 01 00
WR 6 6 5
Drink 03-08 03-07 03-06

DRY $20 -V

Stonecutter Topaz ★★★

Designed as an aperitif, this Martinborough white is an unusual blend of Gewürztraminer and Sauvignon Blanc, made in a distinctly medium style. Gently spicy on the nose, it's fresh and smooth, with ripe, citrusy, spicy flavours (much more Gewürztraminer than Sauvignon Blanc-like) and good weight on the palate. The 2002 vintage (★★★) is full-bodied (13 per cent alcohol), with a perfumed bouquet and fresh, spicy, slightly limey flavours, sweetish (40 grams/litre of sugar), crisp and lively.

MED $20 (500ML) AV

White Cloud ★★☆

Produced by Nobilo, this has long been a big seller in local supermarkets. Made from Gisborne Müller-Thurgau, sweetened with Muscat Dr Hogg juice, it is a very easy-drinking style, at its best fragrant, grapey and flavourful. The non-vintage wine (★★☆) I tasted in mid-2003 was not highly floral but pleasantly fresh and crisp, with lemony, appley flavours and more character than many Müller-Thurgaus.

MED/DRY $9 V+

Breidecker

A nondescript crossing of Müller-Thurgau (for which it is easily mistaken in a blind tasting) and the white hybrid Seibel 7053, Breidecker is rarely encountered in New Zealand, with 20 hectares planted in 2002. Its early-ripening ability is an advantage in cooler regions, but Breidecker typically yields light, fresh quaffing wines, best drunk young.

Hunter's Breidecker ★★★

This wine is made in a medium style, 'for those who are new to wine'. Grown in Canterbury, the 2002 vintage (★★★) has fresh lemon/apple aromas leading into a refreshing, light-bodied palate (only 11 per cent alcohol) with plenty of citrusy flavour and a slightly sweet, tangy finish. Very gluggable.

Vintage 02
WR 5
Drink P

MED $13 AV

Chardonnay

New Zealand Chardonnay has yet to make the international impact of our Sauvignon Blanc, accounting for 11 per cent of wine exports by volume, compared to 54 per cent for Sauvignon Blanc. Our Chardonnays are excellent, but so are those from several other countries in the Old and New Worlds.

Among recent overseas show successes, Matariki Hawke's Bay Chardonnay 2001 won the trophy for best Chardonnay at the 2003 Cool Climate Wine Show, staged in Australia but open to wines from cool-climate regions around the world. (Matariki Hawke's Bay Chardonnay 2000 scooped the same trophy in 2002.) Clearview Estate Reserve Chardonnay 2001, also from Hawke's Bay, won the prestigious trophy for Best Fuller Bodied Dry White Table Wine at the 2003 Sydney International Wine Competition. Yet another Hawke's Bay wine, the mid-priced Sacred Hill Barrel Fermented Chardonnay 2001, won a gold medal (awarded to only 4 per cent of entries) at the 2003 Chardonnay du Monde Competition, judged in Burgundy.

There's an enormous range of New Zealand Chardonnays to choose from. Almost every winery in the country makes at least one; many produce several and Montana makes dozens. The hallmark of New Zealand Chardonnays is their delicious varietal intensity – the leading labels show notably concentrated aromas and flavours, threaded with fresh, appetising acidity.

The price of New Zealand Chardonnay ranges from $9 to $80 per bottle (for Coniglio, from Morton Estate). The quality differences are equally wide, although not always in relation to their prices. Lower-priced wines are typically fermented in stainless steel tanks and bottled young with minimal oak influence; these wines rely on fresh, lemony, uncluttered fruit flavours for their appeal.

The 2002 and 2003 vintages have brought a surge of unoaked Chardonnays, as winemakers selling their Chardonnays in overseas markets strive to showcase New Zealand's fresh, vibrant fruit characters. However, as Stephen Brook, a UK wine writer who judged at the 2002 Air New Zealand Wine Awards, put it: 'They tend to be fairly simple wines ... so I think they have a limited place in the market.'

Mid-price wines may be fermented in tanks and matured in oak casks, which adds to their complexity and richness, or fermented and/or matured in a mix of tanks and barrels. The top labels are fully fermented and matured in oak barriques (normally French, with varying proportions of new casks); there may also be extended aging on (and regular stirring of) yeast lees and varying proportions of a secondary, softening malolactic fermentation (sometimes referred to in the tasting notes as 'malo'). The best of these display the arresting subtlety and depth of flavour for which Chardonnay is so highly prized.

Chardonnay plantings have been outstripped in the past few years by Sauvignon Blanc, as wine producers respond to overseas demand, and in 2004 will constitute 21 per cent of the bearing vineyard. The vines are spread throughout the major wine regions, particularly Marlborough (where almost 30 per cent of the vines are concentrated), Hawke's Bay (where it is still the number one grape, just ahead of Merlot), and Gisborne (where it now accounts for over half of all plantings).

Chardonnays of exciting quality are flowing from all of New Zealand's key wine regions, from Auckland to Otago. Of the three dominant regions, Gisborne is renowned for its deep-scented and soft Chardonnays, which offer very seductive drinking in their youth; Hawke's Bay yields sturdy wines with rich grapefruit-like flavours, power and longevity; and Marlborough's Chardonnays are leaner but stylish and mouth-wateringly crisp.

Chardonnay has often been dubbed 'the red-wine drinker's white wine'. Chardonnays are usually (but not always) bone-dry, as are all reds with any aspirations to quality. Chardonnay's typically mouthfilling body and multi-faceted flavours are another obvious red-wine parallel.

Broaching a top New Zealand Chardonnay at less than two years old is infanticide – the best of the 2000s are now at their peak and the 2002s will offer excellent drinking over the next couple of years. If you must drink Chardonnay when it is only a year old, it makes sense to buy one of the cheaper, less complex wines specifically designed to be enjoyable in their youth.

125 Gimblett Road Chardonnay (★★★★)

The powerful 2002 vintage (★★★★) is the first release from the Blake Family Vineyard in Gimblett Road, Hawke's Bay. Fermented with indigenous yeasts and matured in new French oak barriques, and bottled without fining or filtering, it's a weighty, richly flavoured wine with ripe, citrus and stone-fruit characters, but in its youth slightly dominated by a strong, toasty oak influence. Open mid-2004+.

DRY $28 AV

Akarua Central Otago Chardonnay ★★★★

The 1999 (★★★★) and 2000 (★★★☆) vintages were rewarding, and so is the 2001 (★★★★). Grown at Bannockburn, harvested at 24.5 brix and fermented and lees-aged for nine months in French oak barriques (35 per cent new), with full malolactic fermentation, it's a weighty, ripe-tasting wine with rich, buttery aromas, finely balanced acidity and excellent depth of peachy, mealy, toasty flavours.

Vintage	02	01
WR	6	6
Drink	03-08	03-05

DRY $25 AV

Akarua Unoaked Chardonnay (★★☆)

Slightly austere in its youth, the 2002 vintage (★★☆) of this Central Otago wine was handled in stainless steel tanks, with partial malolactic fermentation and extensive lees-stirring. It's a mouthfilling wine (14 per cent alcohol) with appley aromas, a hint of butterscotch and highish acidity in a crisp, simple style that lacks real ripeness and richness.

Vintage	02
WR	5
Drink	03-05

DRY $22 ·V

Alana Estate Martinborough Chardonnay ★★★★

This winery produces consistently stylish Chardonnays that mature well. Fermented with indigenous ('wild') yeasts in French oak barriques (27 per cent new), with malolactic fermentation and lees-aging, the 2001 vintage (★★★★) is deliciously soft and full, with strong peach, butterscotch and toast flavours, balanced acidity and a slightly creamy texture. The 2002

(★★★★) is again fleshy and creamy, with fresh, strong grapefruit characters, mealy, biscuity complexities and a rounded finish.

Vintage	01	00	99	98	97
WR	6	6	7	6	5
Drink	03-07	03-05	03-05	P	P

DRY $29 AV

Alexandra Wine Company Ferauds Chardonnay ★★★☆

This Central Otago wine is consistently enjoyable. The 2002 vintage (★★★☆), matured for 11 months in French oak barriques (30 per cent new), is a fleshy, flavoursome and toasty wine with mealy, creamy aromas, ripe-fruit characters, firm acidity and good potential.

Vintage	02	01	00	99
WR	5	6	5	5
Drink	04-06	03-05	03-04	P

DRY $21 AV

Alexia Nelson Chardonnay ★★★☆

Made by Jane Cooper, formerly winemaker at Seifried, the partly barrel-fermented 2001 vintage (★★★☆) is a full-bodied wine with ripe grapefruit and apple flavours and a touch of nutty oak. It's a finely balanced wine with very good depth.

Vintage	01	00
WR	5	5
Drink	04-05	P

DRY $18 V+

Allan Scott Marlborough Chardonnay ★★★★

This label began as a fruit-driven style, but in recent years has shown greater complexity and is now consistently satisfying. The 2001 vintage (★★★★), 75 per cent barrel-fermented, is a softly mouthfilling, strongly 'malo'-influenced wine with rich, ripe, citrusy, slightly toasty flavours.

Vintage	02	01	00	99	98
WR	6	7	6	6	7
Drink	03-06	03-05	03-05	03-04	P

DRY $22 V+

Allan Scott Prestige Chardonnay ★★★★☆

The debut 1998 vintage (★★★★★) was an outstanding Marlborough wine, robust, soft and lush, and the 1999 (★★★★★) was also memorable, with layers of peachy, figgy, nutty flavour, impressive harmony and a resounding finish. From a relatively cool vintage, the 2000 (★★★☆) is less exciting. Fermented and matured for 18 months in French oak casks, with 85 per cent malolactic fermentation, it's a light gold, crisp and mouthfilling wine with strong toast and butterscotch characters, but lacks the fruit ripeness and concentration – and therefore the balance – of its predecessors. Ready.

Vintage	01	00
WR	7	7
Drink	03-08	03-06

DRY $32 AV

Alpha Domus AD Chardonnay ★★★★☆

The 2000 vintage (★★★★☆) was grown in Hawke's Bay and fermented and matured for 10 months in French oak barriques. Light yellow, with a complex, slightly minerally and biscuity bouquet, it's a notably rich, strongly oaked wine with substantial body and impressively concentrated grapefruit, peach and butterscotch flavours. A tightly structured wine, it should be at its best during 2004.

Vintage	00	99	98	97	96
WR	6	7	6	6	5
Drink	03-06	03-05	P	P	P

DRY $32 AV

Alpha Domus Chardonnay ★★★

The 2002 vintage (★★★) of this Hawke's Bay wine was 15 per cent barrel-fermented, but it's basically a fruit-driven style with fresh, citrusy and appley flavours to the fore and a smooth finish.

Vintage	02	01	00
WR	6	7	7
Drink	03-07	03-06	03-05

DRY $18 AV

Artisan Waiohika Estate Chardonnay (★★★☆)

For drinking now or cellaring, the debut 2002 vintage (★★★☆) of this Gisborne wine was grown in the Waiohika Estate vineyard and barrique-fermented. Smooth and ripe, with fresh, attractive grapefruit and stone-fruit flavours, gentle acidity and a slightly buttery finish, it shows very good balance and depth.

DRY $23 AV

Ascension Matakana Chardonnay ★★★

Designed as an 'earlier-drinking style', the 2002 vintage (★★★) was harvested at a ripe 23.5 brix and partly handled in tanks, but 80 per cent was fermented in 'predominantly new' French and American oak barriques. It's a full-flavoured wine with ripe peach and grapefruit characters, buttery and toasty with a rounded finish.

DRY $22 -V

Ascension The Ascent Matakana Chardonnay ★★★☆

Estate-grown, the 2002 vintage (★★★★) was hand-harvested from low-yielding vines (4 tonnes per hectare) and fermented and matured for 10 months in French oak barriques (40 per cent new), with 40 per cent malolactic fermentation. It's an impressively weighty and rounded wine with an oaky bouquet, a full-bodied, creamy-rich palate showing good ripeness, harmony and length, and excellent structure and aging potential.

DRY $29 -V

Askerne Hawke's Bay Chardonnay ★★★★☆

Estate-grown on the banks of the Tukituki River, north of Te Mata Peak, this little-known wine has shown steadily rising form. Fermented in French oak barriques (40 per cent new), the 2001 vintage (★★★★☆) is a tightly structured, elegant wine with grapefruit, peach and cashew nut flavours showing good intensity. Maturing gracefully, it is now showing attractive, bottle-aged complexity. The 2002 (★★★★☆) is vibrant and fresh, full-bodied and creamy, with beautifully rich, ripe-fruit flavours and mealy, biscuity complexities. It should unfold splendidly; open mid-2004+.

Vintage	02	01	00	99	98	97
WR	6	6	NM	6	5	5
Drink	03-07	03-05	NM	03-04	P	P

DRY $24 V+

Ata Rangi Craighall Chardonnay ★★★★★

A consistently memorable Martinborough wine, since the 1996 vintage it has scaled great heights, with notable weight, richness, complexity and downright drinkability. Made from a company-owned block of low-yielding, Mendoza-clone vines in the Craighall vineyard, it is hand-picked, whole-bunch pressed and fully fermented in French oak barriques (25 per cent new). The elegant, tightly structured 2002 vintage (★★★★★) has lovely fullness and harmony, with sweet-fruit delights and rich stone-fruit, grapefruit and butterscotch flavours, threaded with fine acidity. Tasted alongside its 2002 Petrie stablemate (below), the Craighall is a more refined, less upfront style that needs a bit more time to unfold; open 2004+.

Vintage	02	01	00	99	98	97	96
WR	7	7	7	7	7	7	7
Drink	03-05	03-05	03-04	03-04	03-04	P	P

DRY $38 AV

Ata Rangi Petrie Chardonnay ★★★★

This single-vineyard wine is grown by Neil Petrie at East Taratahi, south of Masterton. It's not in the same class as its Craighall stablemate (above), but the price is lower. The 2002 vintage (★★★★), matured for a year in French oak barriques, has ripe peach/melon aromas leading into a fresh, creamy palate with rich peach and grapefruit characters, a distinct touch of butterscotch and a well-rounded finish. It's a full-flavoured wine with strong drink-young appeal.

Vintage	02	01	00	99	98
WR	7	7	7	7	7
Drink	03-06	03-05	03-04	03-04	P

DRY $25 AV

Babich East Coast Unoaked Chardonnay ★★★

This easy-drinking wine is grown in three North Island regions – Hawke's Bay, Gisborne and Auckland. In the past it was fully oak-aged, but from 2000 onwards was only partly handled in wood, and the 2002 vintage (★★★☆) was processed entirely in tanks. A full-bodied, citrusy, lively wine with fresh, vibrant fruit aromas and flavours and a fully dry finish, it's a fruit-driven style – with style.

Vintage	02	01	00	99	98
WR	7	6	7	7	7
Drink	03-06	03-05	03-04	P	P

DRY $15 V+

Babich Irongate Chardonnay ★★★★★

Now Babich's flagship Chardonnay, after the phasing-out of The Patriarch Chardonnay (last made in 2000). A stylish, taut wine, Irongate is typically leaner than other top Hawke's Bay Chardonnays, but a proven performer in the cellar. It is based on intensely flavoured, hand-picked fruit from the shingly Irongate vineyard in Gimblett Road, west of Hastings, whole-bunch pressed, fully barrel-fermented and lees-matured for up to nine months. Malolactic fermentation is rare. The 1992, 1995, 1996 and 1998 vintages are outstanding. The small-volume 2001 vintage (★★★★☆) has a youthful, minerally bouquet leading into a tightly structured palate with deep flavours of grapefruit and nuts and the steely finish typical of the label. It's more expressive in its youth than some past vintages, but bound to mature well for several years.

Vintage	01	00	99	98	97	96	95	94	93	92
WR	6	7	7	7	6	7	7	7	6	7
Drink	03-07	03-08	03-07	03-06	P	03-05	P	P	P	P

DRY $33 V+

Babich Winemakers Reserve Chardonnay ★★★☆

This is Babich's middle-tier Chardonnay, ranked below Irongate but above the East Coast label. Grown at Fernhill, in Hawke's Bay, and fully fermented in French oak barriques (20 per cent new), with some malolactic fermentation, the 2000 vintage (★★★☆) is a full, immaculate, finely balanced wine with strong citrusy fruit and some mealy, buttery complexities.

Vintage	02	01	00	99	98
WR	7	6	7	7	7
Drink	03-10	03-05	03-05	03-04	P

DRY $20 AV

Bilancia Chardonnay ★★★★

Pronouced 'be-larn-cha' (Italian for balance, harmony) this Hawke's Bay wine is made by Warren Gibson (full-time at Trinity Hill) and his partner, Lorraine Leheny. The 2002 vintage (★★★★☆) was grown at Glencoe Station, 10 kilometres south of Maraekakaho, fermented with indigenous yeasts, and lees-aged for 15 months in French oak barriques (50 per cent new), with full malolactic fermentation. It's a very elegant and harmonious wine, full-bodied and fresh, with grapefruit and peach characters, integrated oak and a hint of butterscotch. A refined, cool-climate style with a fully dry finish, it's already attractive, but should respond well to cellaring.

Vintage	02	01	00	99	98	97
WR	7	NM	6	6	6	5
Drink	03-07	NM	03-06	P	P	P

DRY $34 -V

Black Barn Barrel Fermented Chardonnay (★★★★)

Grown on the Havelock North hills and fermented and matured in French oak barriques (40 per cent new), the debut 2001 vintage (★★★★) is a substantial, ripe-tasting Hawke's Bay wine, peachy and citrusy, with a strong but not excessive seasoning of toasty oak. Maturing well, it shows good delicacy and concentration and offers highly satisfying drinking now to 2005.

DRY $26 AV

Black Barn Unoaked Chardonnay (★★☆)

A drink-young style, the debut 2002 vintage (★★☆) is a fresh, simple, briefly lees-aged Hawke's Bay wine with ripe melon/grapefruit flavours and a smooth, off-dry finish.

MED/DRY $19 -V

Black Estate Waipara Chardonnay ★★★★

The 2000 vintage (★★★★☆) of this estate-grown, North Canterbury wine is fragrant, plump and soft, with rich citrusy fruit flavours and integrated oak. The elegant 2002 (★★★★), fermented in French oak barriques (one-third new), is mouthfilling and rich, with strong grapefruit, peach and fig flavours wrapped in quality oak and fresh, lively acidity. It's still unfolding; open 2004+.

Vintage	02	01
WR	6	5
Drink	04-08	03-08

DRY $29 AV

Black Ridge Chardonnay ★★★

This Alexandra wine is generally attractive and one of the Central Otago region's more affordable Chardonnays. The 2002 vintage (★★★) is a more wood-influenced style than other recent vintages; 90 per cent of the blend was fermented in new oak barrels and 50 per cent was barrel-aged. Quite forward in its appeal, it's full-bodied and fresh, with lemony, appley, gently biscuity flavours showing good depth and a dry, rounded finish.

DRY $23 -V

Borthwick Estate Wairarapa Valley Chardonnay ★★★☆

The 2000 vintage (★★★★) was grown in Dakins Road, near Masterton, and fermented with indigenous and cultured yeasts in French and American oak casks. It's an upfront, toasty, high-flavoured wine, ripe and weighty, with good concentration and complexity and a soft, slightly creamy texture. The 2001 (★★★) is again bold and powerful, with cheesy, malolactic fermentation characters to the fore, but the fruit flavours are more restrained than in 2000.

DRY $20 AV

Brajkovich Kumeu Chardonnay ★★★

Kumeu River's lower-tier wine, designed for early consumption, is fermented with indigenous ('wild') yeasts in a mix of stainless steel tanks (principally) and seasoned French oak casks. Based on Chardonnay clones 4, 5 and 6 (all heavier-yielding than Mendoza), it is given a full, softening malolactic fermentation. Drinking well now, the 2002 vintage (★★★) is full-bodied, with plenty of peachy, lemony flavour, a hint of butterscotch and fresh acidity. (From the 2003 vintage, this wine will be rebranded as Kumeu River Village Chardonnay.)

DRY $18 AV

Brightwater Vineyards Nelson Chardonnay ★★★☆

Grown by Gary and Valley Neale at Hope and made by Sam Weaver, the 2001 vintage (★★★★) was mainly handled in tanks, but 25 per cent of the blend was French oak-aged. A stylish and immaculate wine, it's vibrantly fruity, with melon, citrus fruit and butterscotch flavours, refreshing acidity and a subtle oak influence. Slightly creamy, it shows good intensity.

Vintage	01	00	99
WR	6	6	6
Drink	03-06	03-04	P

DRY $21 AV

Brookfields Bergman Chardonnay ★★★

Named after the 'Ingrid Bergman' roses in the estate garden, this wine is grown alongside the winery at Meeanee. Hand-picked, whole-bunch pressed, and fermented and matured on its yeast lees for eight months in French and American oak casks, the 2002 vintage (★★★) is pale gold, with a minerally, toasty bouquet. It's a fleshy, upfront style with good body and depth of peachy, buttery flavour.

Vintage	02	01	00	99	98
WR	7	6	6	7	7
Drink	04-05	03-06	03-05	P	P

DRY $18 AV

Brookfields Marshall Bank Chardonnay ★★★★☆

Brookfields' top Chardonnay is named after proprietor Peter Robertson's grandfather's property in Otago. Grown in a vineyard adjacent to the winery at Meeanee and fermented in all-new French oak barriques, it is typically a rich, concentrated, strongly oak-influenced Hawke's Bay wine with peachy, toasty, buttery flavours, lush and complex. Already drinking well, the 2002 vintage (★★★★) is big-bodied, rich and rounded, with strong, well-ripened stone-fruit characters seasoned with toasty oak and a creamy-smooth finish.

Vintage	02	01	00	99	98	97	96
WR	7	7	7	7	7	7	7
Drink	05-07	04-07	04-07	04-06	03-05	P	P

DRY $30 AV

Burnt Spur Marlborough Chardonnay (★★★★)

Burnt Spur is a Martinborough-based company, but the 2001 vintage (★★★★) of this wine was mostly grown in Marlborough (apart from a small proportion of Martinborough fruit). Softly mouthfilling, it's an upfront style with a fragrant, creamy, oaky bouquet, strong, ripe, peachy flavours seasoned with toasty oak and a creamy-smooth finish. Delicious young.

Vintage	01
WR	6
Drink	03-04

DRY $27 AV

Burnt Spur Martinborough Chardonnay (★★★☆)

The peachy, slightly creamy 2002 vintage (★★★☆) was still coming together in mid to late 2003. Hand-picked and fully fermented and lees-aged in French oak barriques (30 per cent new), it's a pale straw wine with stone-fruit and butterscotch flavours, balanced acidity and good depth. Open mid-2004+.

DRY $26 -V

Cable Bay Waiheke Chardonnay (★★★☆)

The debut 2002 vintage (★★★☆) is a substantial wine with good mouthfeel, texture and length, but it needs time to unfold. Blended from six sites and fermented and matured for eight months in French oak barriques (30 per cent new), with no use of malolactic fermentation, it's a tightly structured wine with crisp grapefruit and fig characters and good weight. Open mid-2004.

Vintage	02
WR	7
Drink	03-07

DRY $33 -V

Cairnbrae Clansman Marlborough Chardonnay ★★★☆

This is typically a creamy-soft, generous wine in a very forward style. Estate-grown in Jacksons Road and handled in American oak, the 2001 vintage (★★★☆) is very typical – light yellow and buttery-soft, with citrusy fruit flavours, a sweet-oak influence and strong 'malo' characters in an upfront style with lots of drink-young appeal.

DRY $22 AV

Cairnbrae Unoaked Chardonnay ★★☆

Slightly honeyed on the nose, the 2002 vintage (★★☆) of this Marlborough wine is full-bodied (14 per cent alcohol) but simple, with citrusy, slightly green-edged flavours. Over-priced.

DRY $19 -V

Canadoro Martinborough Chardonnay ★★★☆

A little known but characterful Martinborough wine. Maturing well, the powerful 2001 vintage (★★★★) is a strapping wine (14.6 per cent alcohol), soft and creamy, with strong peach, butterscotch and toasty oak flavours, showing good harmony.

Vintage	01	00	99	98	97	96
WR	7	7	NM	7	6	5
Drink	03-06	03-04	NM	03-04	P	P

DRY $29 -V

Canterbury House Waipara Chardonnay ★★☆

Most vintages of this North Canterbury wine have been solid but plain. The 2001 (★★☆) has a slightly creamy texture, with very restrained oak (15 per cent of the blend was wood-aged), decent depth of lemony, appley flavours and firm acid spine.

DRY $19 -V

Cape Campbell Blenheim Point Chardonnay (★★☆)

The 2002 vintage (★★☆), handled with 'light American oak', has fresh, appley, lemony aromas leading into a fruit-driven, basically simple wine that lacks real richness and complexity.

DRY $22 -V

Carrick Central Otago Chardonnay ★★★★
From a region that often struggles with Chardonnay, the 2002 vintage (★★★★), grown on the Cairnmuir Terraces at Bannockburn, is an unusually successful wine, with real presence in the mouth. Fermented mostly (66 per cent) with indigenous yeasts in French oak barriques (20 per cent new), it is fragrant and mouthfilling, with complex grapefruit and nut flavours, mealy, buttery complexities and a freshly acidic, long finish.

Vintage	02	01
WR	6	7
Drink	04+	03+

DRY $24 V+

Chard Farm Closeburn Chardonnay ★★★
The winery's second-tier Chardonnay is typically a fresh, vibrant Central Otago wine with appetising acidity. The 2002 vintage (★★★), a blend of Bannockburn, Gibbston and estate-grown grapes, was handled entirely without oak. Full-bodied and tangy, with lemony, limey, slightly leesy and nutty flavours woven with fresh acidity, it's a drink-young style.

Vintage	02	01	00	99	98
WR	6	6	5	5	6
Drink	03-05	03-04	P	P	P

DRY $21 -V

Chard Farm Judge and Jury Chardonnay ★★★★
Named after a rocky outcrop overlooking the Kawarau River (Central Otago) vineyard, since 1994 this wine has been a blend of estate-grown (the best slopes) and Bannockburn (the best clones) fruit. The 2002 vintage (★★★☆) was fully barrel-fermented, but new oak was excluded from the recipe. Still developing, it offers strong citrusy flavours woven with fresh acidity, a seasoning of toasty oak and the slight herbal influence typical of the region's Chardonnays. Judge and Jury clearly rewards cellaring.

Vintage	02	01	00	99	98	97	96
WR	6	6	5	6	6	5	5
Drink	04-07	03-05	P	03-04	03-04	P	P

DRY $31 -V

Charles Wiffen Marlborough Chardonnay ★★★★
Charles and Sandy Wiffen own a vineyard in the Wairau Valley, but their wine is made at West Brook in Auckland. The 2002 vintage (★★★★) was matured in new and seasoned French oak barriques, with some lees-stirring and malolactic fermentation. Strong butterscotch and toast aromas lead into a bold (14 per cent alcohol), buttery wine with ripe, stone-fruit flavours, some mealy, oaky complexity and a rich finish. It's an upfront style, for drinking 2003-04.

DRY $22 V+

Church Road Chardonnay ★★★★
This typically full-bodied and richly flavoured Chardonnay is produced by Montana at the Church Road Winery. Showcasing the ripe, stone-fruit characters of Hawke's Bay fruit, the refined 2002 vintage (★★★★) was French oak-fermented (in one-third new barrels) and wood-aged for six months on its full yeast lees, with no use of malolactic fermentation. Fragrant, full-bodied and rounded, it offers strong, youthful, peachy flavours, with nutty, mealy characters adding complexity and good harmony. Delicious drinking from now onwards.

Vintage	02	01	00	99	98	97	96
WR	6	6	7	6	7	6	6
Drink	03-06	03+	P	P	P	P	P

DRY $23 V+

Church Road Cuve Series Chardonnay ★★★★★

The rare but outstanding 1994, 1995 and 1998 vintages are the result of Montana's decision to produce 'a more Burgundian, less fruit-driven, less oaky' style of Hawke's Bay Chardonnay than its lush, relatively fast developing Church Road Reserve wine. It is typically hand-picked, whole-bunch pressed, fermented and matured for a year in French oak barriques and given a full, softening malolactic fermentation. Light gold in hue, the 1998 vintage (★★★★★) is now at its peak, with a forthcoming, nutty, toasty bouquet leading into a rich, tightly structured palate showing crisp, strong grapefruit and peach characters, minerally, biscuity complexities and a slightly flinty finish. A wine of great finesse, harmony and depth, it's one of the most distinctive and classy Chardonnays on the market. Drink now.

Vintage 98
WR 7
Drink 03+

`DRY $33 AV`

Church Road Reserve Chardonnay ★★★★★

This opulent wine is based on the 'pick' of Montana's Hawke's Bay Chardonnay crop (always the shy-bearing Mendoza clone, but not always grown in the same vineyard). Given more skin contact than its Ormond Estate Chardonnay stablemate from Gisborne, and therefore more forward, it is fully fermented in French oak barriques (44 per cent new in 2002), and stays on its yeast lees for the total time in barrel (up to 10 months) with fortnightly lees-stirring. There was no 2001. The 2002 vintage (★★★★★) is deliciously soft, creamy and substantial (14 per cent alcohol), with integrated oak and a powerful surge of rich, ripe grapefruit and stone-fruit flavours. A top vintage, it's already delicious.

Vintage	02	01	00	99	98	97	96
WR	7	NM	7	6	7	NM	7
Drink	03-08	NM	04+	03+	03-05	NM	P

`DRY $30 V+`

C.J. Pask Gimblett Road Chardonnay ★★★☆

For her second-tier Chardonnay, chief winemaker Kate Radburnd emphasises Hawke's Bay's citrusy fruit characters ('the fruit should shine through') fleshed out with restrained wood. The 2002 vintage (★★★★), one of the best yet, shows greater complexity than most of its predecessors and was partly barrel-fermented. Instantly appealing, it is fresh and vibrant, with citrusy, slightly biscuity aromas and flavours, subtle oak handling and a creamy-smooth finish. Good weight, delicacy and length.

Vintage	02	01	00	99	98	97	96
WR	7	NM	6	7	6	6	7
Drink	03-08	NM	03-04	P	P	P	P

`DRY $23 AV`

C.J. Pask Reserve Chardonnay ★★★★

Grown in Gimblett Road, Hawke's Bay, this wine has shown good, occasionally outstanding, form since the 1994 vintage. Based on the company's oldest Chardonnay vines, planted in 1984, it has usually been fermented and matured in all-new French oak barriques, giving it a strong wood influence. Tasted in its infancy, the 2002 (★★★★☆) showed a finer fruit/oak balance than some past vintages, in a rich, mouthfilling style with deep, grapefruit-like flavours and a slightly creamy, long finish.

Vintage	02	01	00	99	98	97	96
WR	7	NM	7	7	6	6	7
Drink	04-07	NM	03-06	03-05	03-05	P	P

`DRY $30 -V`

C.J. Pask Roy's Hill Chardonnay ★★★

The 2002 vintage (★★☆) of this Hawke's Bay wine is fresh, lemony and uncomplicated, with very little if any oak showing. It's an easy-drinking style with a slightly honeyed, smooth finish.

Vintage 02
WR 6
Drink 03-05

DRY $16 AV

Clearview Beachhead Chardonnay ★★★

This small Hawke's Bay winery has a reputation for powerful Chardonnays, and in some years its second-tier label is no exception. The 2002 vintage (★★★) was grown on the coast, at Te Awanga, and 60 per cent barrel-fermented (in one-year-old French and American oak); the rest was handled in tanks. Youthful, with strong, citrusy flavours, balanced oak and acidity, it's a moderately complex style, probably at its best during 2004.

Vintage 02
WR 6
Drink 03-06

DRY $22 -V

Clearview Reserve Chardonnay ★★★★★

For his premium Chardonnay label, Te Awanga winemaker Tim Turvey aims for a 'big, grunty, upfront' style – and hits the target with ease. It's typically a hedonist's delight – an arrestingly bold, intense, savoury, mealy, complex wine with layers of flavour. Based on ultra-ripe fruit (always hand-harvested at 24+ brix), it is fermented in all-new French oak barriques, lees-stirred weekly, and about 25 per cent of the final blend undergoes a softening malolactic fermentation. The 1994 and subsequent vintages have all matured superbly. The 2002 vintage (★★★★★) is already an exciting mouthful. It's a strapping wine (14.5 per cent alcohol) with heaps of toasty oak, but its bold, peachy fruit characters are by no means overpowered, creating a deliciously high-flavoured style, complex and mealy, with fresh acidity enlivening the finish. Drink now or cellar.

Vintage	02	01	00	99	98	97	96
WR	6	7	7	7	6	6	6
Drink	03-10	03-10	03-08	03-07	03-06	03-07	03-04

DRY $35 AV

Clearview Unwooded Chardonnay ★★★

This Te Awanga, Hawke's Bay wine is a tank-fermented style, simple but full-flavoured. The 2002 vintage (★★★) is weighty (over 14 per cent alcohol) and vibrant, with satisfying depth of lemony, appley flavours, a sliver of sweetness and a fresh, lively finish.

Vintage 02
WR 5
Drink 03-05

MED/DRY $20 -V

Clifford Bay Marlborough Chardonnay ★★★

A single-vineyard Awatere Valley wine, made in a crisp, lively, fruit-driven style. Partly French oak-fermented, the 2002 vintage (★★☆) is citrusy and buttery, with a slightly green, limey edge and a tight finish.

Vintage	02	01	00	99	98
WR	6	6	6	6	6
Drink	03-06	03-05	03-04	P	P

DRY $19 AV

Cloudy Bay Chardonnay ★★★★★

A powerful Marlborough wine with an arresting concentration of savoury, lemony, mealy flavours, bold oak and alcohol, and a proven ability to mature well over the long haul (at least four years and up to a decade). The grapes are sourced from 10 estate vineyards and growers' vineyards, all located within the Wairau Valley. All of the wine is fermented (with some indigenous yeasts) in French oak barriques (20 to 25 per cent new) and lees-aged in oak for 15 months, and in the 2001 vintage, 65 per cent went through malolactic fermentation. The 2001 (★★★★☆) is a steely, minerally, biscuity style, complex and tightly structured. An elegant, multi-faceted, distinctly cool-climate style, it is richly flavoured and already very harmonious, but set for a long and graceful evolution in the bottle.

Vintage	01	00	99	98	97	96	95	94
WR	6	6	6	6	6	6	4	6
Drink	03-07	03-06	03-05	P	P	P	P	P

DRY $34 V+

Collards Blakes Mill Chardonnay ★★★

A good drink-young style, Collards' lightly oaked wine is named after the old Blakes Mill settlement, now the site of the company's Rothesay Vineyard in West Auckland, where most of the grapes are grown. It is oak-aged, says Bruce Collard, 'for flavour and style enhancement, rather than any noticeable oakiness'. The 2002 vintage (★★★) is an enjoyable, fruit-driven style, fresh, lemony and gently wooded, with plenty of flavour and a crisp, dry, slightly nutty finish. Ready.

Vintage	03	02	01	00	99	98
WR	NM	7	6	7	6	7
Drink	NM	03-04	P	P	P	P

DRY $13 V+

Collards Hawke's Bay Chardonnay ★★★★

This is Collards' middle-tier Chardonnay label and in favourable years it offers excellent value. Finely balanced for current drinking, the 2002 vintage (★★★★) is a creamy-smooth, fresh and vibrantly fruity wine with ripe, grapefruit-like characters to the fore, subtle use of oak and a deliciously rounded and harmonious finish.

Vintage	03	02	01	00	99	98
WR	NM	7	NM	6	6	7
Drink	NM	03-04	NM	P	P	P

DRY $19 V+

Collards Rothesay Vineyard Chardonnay ★★★★☆

Collards' flagship white is grown in Bruce and Geoffrey Collard's Rothesay Vineyard at Waimauku, in West Auckland. It is typically mouthfilling, richly flavoured and rounded, with sweet, ripe-fruit characters and impressive harmony. The 2002 vintage (★★★★☆) is still very youthful, with impressive weight and strong, ripe grapefruit and pear flavours, gently seasoned with French oak. Fresh, vibrant and finely balanced, it builds to a powerful finish; open mid-2004+.

Vintage	03	02	01	00	99	98	97	96
WR	NM	7	6	7	6	7	7	7
Drink	NM	03-05	03-04	P	P	P	P	P

DRY $29 V+

Coniglio Hawke's Bay Chardonnay (★★★★★)

Launched by Morton Estate in 2001 at $80, Coniglio is New Zealand's most expensive Chardonnay – by far. A Rolls-Royce version of the company's famous Black Label Chardonnay, it's an arresting wine that matches or surpasses the quality of imported Chardonnays at the same price. Grown in the cool, elevated Riverview vineyard at Mangatahi, Hawke's Bay, it was fermented and lees-aged for 11 months in all-new French oak barriques, with no malolactic fermentation. Youthful in colour, it has a rich, inviting bouquet, citrusy, mealy, minerally and very complex. The palate is very classy – refined, harmonious and highly concentrated, with layers of grapefruit and nut flavours, good acid spine and a wonderfully rich, resounding finish. Re-tasted in mid-2003, it is maturing very gracefully and probably at its peak now. There is no 1999 vintage, but the label reappears from 2000.

Vintage	98
WR	7
Drink	03-06

DRY $80 AV

Coopers Creek Fat Cat Chardonnay – see Fat Cat Chardonnay

Coopers Creek Hawke's Bay Chardonnay ★★★★

Coopers Creek's middle-tier Chardonnay is an upfront style, hard to resist in its youth. The 2001 vintage (★★★★) includes wine originally intended for the top Swamp Reserve label, which was declassified that year. Grown at two vineyards, in Havelock North and Meeanee, and fermented and matured for nine months in American oak casks, with a full, softening malolactic fermentation, the 2002 vintage (★★★★) is fleshy, rich and rounded, with ripe grapefruit and melon flavours, sweet, toasty oak and a deliciously creamy texture. A winning formula.

Vintage	02	01	00	99	98	97	96
WR	6	6	7	6	6	6	6
Drink	03-05	03-05	P	P	P	P	P

DRY $20 V+

Coopers Creek Reserve Gisborne Chardonnay (★★★★☆)

Made from 'super-ripe' (25 brix) grapes grown in the McLaurin vineyard, on the Slope of Gold, the 2002 vintage (★★★★☆), the first of this label, is Gisborne Chardonnay at its best. Fermented and aged for nine months in French (mostly) and American oak casks, with full malolactic fermentation, it's a fat, concentrated wine, sturdy (14.5 per cent alcohol), with strong, sweet-fruit flavours of grapefruit and fig and a deliciously rounded finish. Drink now to 2005.

DRY $25 V+

Coopers Creek SV Chardonnay ★★★★

The SV (Single Vineyard) Chardonnay sits immediately below the top Swamp Reserve Chardonnays in the Coopers Creek range. The 1999 vintage (★★★★) was grown near Havelock North, in Hawke's Bay, French oak-fermented and given a full malolactic fermentation. It's maturing gracefully, with strong, minerally, toasty flavours, complex and tight. The 2002 vintage (★★★★), the first since 1999, is a Marlborough wine, based on second-crop Wairau Valley vines. Fully French oak-fermented, it's a richly alcoholic wine (14.5 per cent), with well-ripened grapefruit, fig and pear flavours cut with fresh acidity, a distinct touch of butterscotch and good intensity.

Vintage	02	01	00	99	98	97
WR	6	NM	NM	7	7	6
Drink	03-04	NM	NM	03-04	P	P

DRY $24 V+

Coopers Creek Swamp Reserve Chardonnay ★★★★★

Based on the winery's best Hawke's Bay Chardonnay fruit, this is typically a lush, highly seductive wine with a finely judged balance of rich, citrusy, peachy fruit flavours and toasty oak. The 2002 vintage (★★★★★) was made from a 'tiny, tiny' crop of grapes in the company's Middle Road vineyard at Havelock North. Fully fermented and matured for nine months in French oak barriques (new and one-year-old), it's a robust (14 per cent alcohol) and

CHARDONNAY 47

concentrated wine with sweet, ripe-fruit characters, rich flavours of peach, grapefruit, toast and butterscotch and a long, well-rounded finish. A classic example of the style.

Vintage	02	01	00	99	98	97	96
WR	6	NM	6	6	6	6	6
Drink	04-05	NM	03-04	P	P	P	P

DRY $29 V+

Coopers Creek Unoaked Gisborne Chardonnay ★★★

Coopers Creek recently stopped wood-aging its popular, moderately priced Gisborne wine, but the recipe includes some lees-aging and malolactic fermentation. The 2002 vintage (★★★) is fleshy and ripe, with good depth of peachy, citrusy, slightly honeyed flavour and a very smooth finish.

Vintage	02	01
WR	7	5
Drink	03-04	P

DRY $16 AV

Corazon The Collective Chardonnay (★★★☆)

The debut 2002 vintage (★★★☆) is a single-vineyard (Waiohika Estate) Gisborne wine, fermented and lees-aged for 10 months in French oak barriques (20 per cent new), with 30 per cent malolactic fermentation. Mealy and buttery, with some richness, it's a full-bodied style with strong, ripe, grapefruit and peach flavours and finely integrated oak.

Vintage	02
WR	6
Drink	03-06

DRY $28 -V

Corbans Chardonnay ★★★

Designed to replace the Estate Chardonnay, last produced in 2000 (★★★), the 2002 vintage (★★☆) is a Gisborne wine, tank-fermented and 'matured on its lees in contact with new French and American oak for three months' (which is different to saying it was barrel-aged). It's a moderately ripe-tasting wine with fresh, citrusy and appley flavours and a sliver of sweetness on the finish. Smooth, easy drinking.

Vintage	03	02	01	00	99
WR	6	6	NM	NM	6
Drink	03-05	03+	NM	NM	P

DRY $14 V+

Corbans Cottage Block Marlborough Chardonnay ★★★★☆

The highly enjoyable 2001 vintage (★★★★☆) was hand-picked at 23.5 to 24 brix, whole-bunch pressed, and fermented and lees-aged for 10 months in new and one-year-old French oak barriques, with malolactic fermentation and lees-stirring to add textural complexity. A softly structured wine with buttery, 'malo' characters holding sway on the nose and palate, it offers sweet fruit delights and a medley of citrus fruit, pear, nut and butterscotch flavours, concentrated and creamy. The 2002 (★★★★) is also a soft, creamy-smooth style with ripe, citrusy fruit characters and fine-quality French oak (50 per cent new) adding complexity. It's a very harmonious wine, forward in its appeal.

Vintage	02	01	00	99
WR	6	7	NM	7
Drink	03-08	04+	NM	P

DRY $29 V+

Corbans Private Bin Marlborough Chardonnay (★★★★)

The instantly appealing, creamy-smooth 2001 vintage (★★★★) was fermented and matured on its yeast lees in French oak barriques (45 per cent new), and two-thirds of the blend had a softening

malolactic fermentation. Toasty and mealy on the nose, it's a full-flavoured wine with generous melon and grapefruit characters, good savoury, nutty complexity and a rich, rounded finish.
Vintage 01
WR 6
Drink 03-05

DRY $25 AV

Corbans White Label Chardonnay ★★☆

Easy to enjoy, the 2002 vintage (★★☆) is an unoaked Gisborne wine, fresh and simple, with ripe, peachy, citrusy fruit flavours holding sway and a slightly sweet (8 grams/litre of sugar), smooth finish. (The 2003 is a blend of Australian and New Zealand wine.)
Vintage 02
WR 5
Drink P

MED/DRY $9 V+

Cottle Hill Chardonnay (★★★)

The 2001 vintage (★★★) is not in the same class as the outstanding 2000 Reserve (★★★★★), but it's $10 cheaper. Blended from Northland and Hawke's Bay grapes and 80 per cent oak-aged for nine months, it's a full-bodied and flavourful wine, slightly honeyed, with fresh, citrusy, peachy flavours showing some complexity. Drink now onwards.

DRY $18 AV

Covell Estate Chardonnay ★★

Bob Covell and his family are to be saluted for pioneering winegrowing against high odds at Galatea, near Murupara, hard against the flanks of the Urewera Ranges. The 1999 vintage (★★), barrel-fermented and lees-aged for 15 months, is light/medium gold, with an austere, slightly honeyed, crisply acidic palate.

DRY $20 -V

Covell Estate Estate Chardonnay ★★

Grown near Murupara, in the inland, eastern Bay of Plenty, the non-vintage bottling (★★) on the market in 2003 is a lightly oaked, golden wine with a restrained bouquet and slightly buttery flavours threaded with firm acidity.

DRY $14 -V

Crab Farm Chardonnay (★★★☆)

High-flavoured, with lots of character, the 2002 vintage (★★★☆) from this Hawke's Bay winery was hand-picked and oak-aged for 10 months. It's a powerful, robust wine (14 per cent alcohol) with ripe, peachy fruit flavours, toast and butterscotch characters adding richness and a creamy-smooth finish.
Vintage 02
WR 6
Drink 03-04

DRY $17 V+

Crab Farm Reserve Chardonnay (★★★☆)

The 1999 vintage (★★★☆) from this small Bay View, Hawke's Bay winery was hand-picked and fermented and matured for a year in French oak casks (50 per cent new). It's a golden wine, nutty, peachy, toasty and minerally, with loads of character. Ready.

DRY $21 AV

Craggy Range Gimblett Gravels Vineyard Chardonnay (★★★★☆)

The debut 2002 vintage (★★★★☆) is an elegant Hawke's Bay wine, showing sophisticated winemaking. Fermented and matured for nine months in French oak barriques (60 per cent new), with 92 per cent of the blend going through malolactic fermentation, it has a stylish, citrusy bouquet with spicy, mealy notes. The palate is mouthfilling, with ripe grapefruit, peach and butterscotch flavours showing lovely softness, delicacy and complexity. Already delicious, it's come together very quickly.

Vintage 02
WR 6
Drink 04-06

DRY $26 V+

Craggy Range Les Beaux Cailloux – see the Branded and Other White Wines section

Craggy Range Seven Poplars Vineyard Chardonnay ★★★★☆

Grown on the banks of the Tutaekuri River in the lower Dartmoor Valley, this is typically a refined wine with lovely depth of flavour. The 2002 vintage (★★★★), based on 14-year-old vines, was fermented (with a 50/50 split of indigenous and cultured yeasts) and lees-aged for eight months in French oak casks (50 per cent new), with full malolactic fermentation. Light yellow, it's an excellent example of the Hawke's Bay regional style, fresh and mouthfilling, with rich, peachy, creamy, toasty flavours. It's arguably less intense than the 2001 (★★★★☆), but softer and more forward.

Vintage 02   01   00   99
WR   7   5   6   5
Drink   04-06 03-05 03-04 P

DRY $30 AV

Crossroads Classic Chardonnay ★★★

Up to and including the 1999 vintage, this wine was labelled as Crossroads Hawke's Bay Chardonnay. Oak-aged for seven months, the 2001 (★★★) is mouthfilling, with good depth of stone-fruit flavours and a fresh, dryish, distinctly crisp finish.

Vintage 01   00   99   98   97   96
WR   5   5   7   7   6   6
Drink   03-05 P   P   P   P   P

DRY $19 AV

Crossroads Destination Series Chardonnay (★★★☆)

The debut 2002 vintage (★★★☆) is described on the label as a 'fruit-driven' style, but the wine shows clear oak and malolactic fermentation influences. Matured for eight months in French and American oak, it's a weighty, smooth and creamy Hawke's Bay wine with grapefruit, pear and butterscotch flavours showing very good depth and harmony and some complexity. Drink now onwards.

Vintage 02
WR 6
Drink 03-08

DRY $24 AV

Crossroads Reserve Chardonnay ★★★

At its best, this is a full, elegant wine with excellent depth of grapefruit-like flavours and toasty oak, but it is not consistently impressive. The 2000 vintage (★★☆) was grown in the Dartmoor Valley and Gimblett Gravels areas and barrel-fermented. Re-tasted in 2003, it's a light gold wine with a restrained bouquet. Peachy, lemony and biscuity, with reasonable flavour depth but a slightly short finish, it lacks the freshness, vigour and intensity expected in its price range, and tastes past its best.

Vintage	00	99	98	97	96
WR	4	5	7	6	6
Drink	03	03	03-04	03	P

DRY $32 -V

Daniel Schuster Petrie Vineyard Selection ★★★★

Grown at Rakaia in Mid Canterbury, south of Christchurch, this is typically a Chablis-like wine with cool-climate freshness and crisp, savoury, concentrated flavours. The 2002 vintage (★★★★) was harvested from low-yielding vines (5 tonnes per hectare), handled in French oak barriques (20 per cent new), and given extended lees contact and stirring. The bouquet is citrusy and mealy; the palate is weighty and slightly buttery, with rich, sweet-fruit characters and firm acid spine. (The 2001 vintage was all exported, and the wine was not made in 2003.)

Vintage	03	02	01	00	99	98
WR	NM	6	7	7	7	7
Drink	NM	04-06	04-07	03-06	03-05	03-05

DRY $30 -V

Dashwood Marlborough Chardonnay ★★★☆

Vavasour's second-tier Chardonnay is a drink-young style with fresh, buoyant fruit flavours and appetising acidity. The 2002 vintage (★★★☆) is a blend of Wairau Valley (74 per cent) and Awatere Valley grapes, fermented and lees-aged in stainless steel tanks and French oak barrels of varying sizes. Pale lemon/green, it's fresh and weighty, with very good depth of ripe-fruit flavours, a hint of biscuity oak and a rounded, fractionally off-dry finish. Lots of pleasure here.

Vintage	02	01	00	99	98
WR	7	7	6	6	6
Drink	03-04	03-04	P	P	P

DRY $17 V+

Delegat's Hawke's Bay Chardonnay ★★★

For Delegat's bargain-priced, lower-tier Chardonnay, the goal is to 'let the fruit do the talking', with wood relegated to a minor role. The 2001 vintage (★★☆) was fermented in stainless steel tanks and then matured for six months in seasoned oak barrels. Light/medium yellow, it's a citrusy, slightly honeyed and minerally wine, with a buttery, flinty finish (reflecting the higher-acid year). The 2002 (tasted prior to bottling, and so not rated), is a noticeably riper and rounder wine, with plenty of soft, peachy flavour.

Vintage	02	01	00	99	98
WR	6	5	6	5	6
Drink	03-05	03-04	P	P	P

DRY $15 V+

Delegat's Reserve Chardonnay ★★★★

The launch of Delegat's $20 Chardonnay from the 1997 vintage was instantly successful. A deliciously easy-drinking style with a lot of class, it is generally at its best within two years of the harvest. The 2001 vintage (★★☆) was fermented and matured in French oak barriques (25 per cent new), with 'intensive' lees-stirring. From a difficult season, it's a light gold, slightly austere wine with minerally, toasty characters, a hint of botrytis and firm acid spine. Although attractive in its infancy, it is now past its best. The 2002 (tasted prior to bottling, and so not rated), promises to bring a return to form, with its generous stone-fruit flavours, ripe and creamy.

Vintage	02	01	00	99	98
WR	7	6	7	7	7
Drink	03-05	03-04	P	P	P

DRY $20 V+

Domaine Georges Michel Golden Mile Marlborough Chardonnay ★★★☆

Named after 'the central route of the Rapaura area', the 2002 vintage (★★★☆) is a fruit-driven style, French oak-aged for eight months. Full-bodied, fresh and vibrant, with ripe, pineappley characters, appetising acidity and a fractionally off-dry finish, it's a highly enjoyable, drink-young style.

Vintage	02
WR	6
Drink	03-06

DRY $22 AV

Domaine Georges Michel La Reserve Chardonnay ★★★☆

The 2001 vintage (★★★), grown at Rapaura, was tank-fermented and then matured for nine months in new French oak barriques, with regular lees-stirring. It's a full-bodied wine (14 per cent alcohol) with grapefruit-like characters and some complexity, but the bouquet is restrained and the acid level is high.

Vintage	01	00	99
WR	7	6	6
Drink	03-06	03-04	03-04

DRY $29 -V

Drylands Marlborough Chardonnay ★★★☆

No longer carrying the Selaks brand, this popular wine is made by Nobilo, the country's second-largest wine company. Fermented and matured in French and American oak casks, with regular lees-stirring, it is a drink-young style, typically punchy and vibrant. The 2002 vintage (★★★) has toasty oak aromas, grapefruit-like fruit flavours and a creamy finish. In a blind tasting, its cheesy, milky, malolactic fermentation-influenced characters were highly noticeable.

Vintage	02	01	00	99	98
WR	7	7	7	7	7
Drink	03-05	03-04	P	P	P

DRY $20 AV

Dry River Chardonnay ★★★★★

Elegance, restraint and subtle power are the key qualities of this distinctive Martinborough wine. It's not a bold, upfront style, but tight, savoury and seamless, with rich grapefruit and hazelnut flavours that build in the bottle for several years. Based on low-cropping (typically below 5 tonnes/hectare) Mendoza clone vines, it is hand-harvested, whole-bunch pressed and fermented in French oak barriques (averaging 24 per cent new). The proportion of the final blend that has gone through malolactic fermentation has never exceeded 15 per cent. The 2001 vintage (★★★★★), labelled 'Amaranth', meaning winemaker Neil McCallum sees it as especially suitable for cellaring, is fragrant, refined and immaculate, with intense grapefruit and nut flavours and a tight, crisp, minerally character that hints at riches to unfold. All delicacy and restraint in its infancy, the 2002 (★★★★☆) is finely poised, fresh and vibrant, with beautifully ripe grapefruit, melon and nut flavours and a rounded finish. It needs at least another couple of years to break into full stride.

Vintage	02	01	00	99	98	97	96
WR	7	7	7	7	7	7	6
Drink	04-09	03-07	03-05+	03-07	03-05	P	P

DRY $36 AV

🍇🍇

Equinox Hawke's Bay Barrel Fermented Chardonnay ★★★

The 2002 vintage (★★★☆) was fermented and lees-aged for six months in French oak barriques (50 per cent new), with partial malolactic fermentation. It's an upfront style, high-flavoured, with ripe grapefruit and butterscotch characters, fresh acidity and plenty of character.

Vintage	02	01
WR	5	5
Drink	03-05	03-04

DRY $19 AV

Eskdale Chardonnay ★★★★

Kim Salonius, founder of the deliberately low-profile Eskdale winery, aims 'to make wine a little differently'. In the case of his Chardonnay, this involves maturing the wine for up to two years in French oak casks. Fortunately, his Esk Valley, Hawke's Bay fruit has the richness to handle this extraordinarily long (by New Zealand standards) exposure to oak. Sold at several years old, when they are developed and mellow, the wines are typically full, peachy, nutty and complex, with excellent flavour depth. I haven't tasted the 1998 vintage, currently on sale, but Salonius describes it as 'good, current consumption'.

DRY $25 AV

Esk Valley Hawke's Bay Chardonnay ★★★★

Given its affordable price, the latest vintages of this 'black label' wine have been unexpectedly classy. An upfront style with strong, toasty oak aromas (77 per cent barrel-fermented), the 2002 vintage (★★★★) is mouthfilling and creamy, with ripe, concentrated grapefruit and stone-fruit flavours, a distinct touch of butterscotch and a rich, rounded finish. Fine value.

Vintage	03	02	01	00	99	98
WR	6	7	6	7	6	6
Drink	03-05	03-06	03-05	03-04	P	P

DRY $20 V+

Esk Valley Reserve Chardonnay ★★★★★

Since 1994, this has emerged as one of the most distinguished Chardonnays in Hawke's Bay. It is typically grown in several vineyards and fermented in French oak barriques (60 per cent new). There was no 2001 vintage, because the vineyard block designated to supply grapes for the Reserve Chardonnay was severely hit by frost. Pale yellow, the 2002 vintage (★★★★★) is a beauty – highly fragrant and softly structured, with substantial body (14.5 per cent alcohol), gentle acidity and layers of peach, grapefruit and butterscotch flavours, complex and deep.

Vintage	03	02	01	00	99	98
WR	NM	6	NM	6	7	6
Drink	NM	03-07	NM	03-06	03-05	P

DRY $33 V+

Fairhall Downs Marlborough Chardonnay ★★★☆

Grown in the Brancott Valley, this single-vineyard wine is designed as a 'robust, fruit-driven style with a subtle hint of oak' – which sums up the 2002 vintage (★★★☆) pretty well. Full-bodied (14 per cent alcohol), with sweet oak aromas, it's an upfront style with strong, ripe peach and grapefruit flavours, a hint of butterscotch and a creamy-smooth finish. Drink now onwards.

Vintage	02	01	00	99	98
WR	6	6	6	6	6
Drink	03-07	03-06	03-05	03-04	P

DRY $20 AV

Fairmont Estate Block One Chardonnay 2001 (★★★☆)

Grown at Gladstone, south of Masterton, in the Wairarapa, the 2001 vintage (★★★☆) has a rich, citrusy, toasty bouquet, quite voluminous. The palate is smooth and rich, with peachy, lemony flavours, a hint of butterscotch and a soft finish.

DRY $20 AV

Fat Cat Gisborne Chardonnay ★★★

Fat Cat is made by Purr Productions of Huapai, a division of Coopers Creek. The goal is 'a fat, alcoholic wine with lots of oak – a wine that's just what the name suggests' (an unspecified portion of the proceeds go to the SPCA). For the 2002 vintage (★★★), 70 per cent of the blend was fermented in contact with new American oak staves and given a softening malolactic fermentation. It's a bold, drink-young style, mouthfilling (14 per cent alcohol), with grapefruit and peach flavours strongly seasoned with sweet, toasty oak.

Vintage	02	01	00
WR	6	6	6
Drink	03-04	P	P

DRY $15 V+

Felton Road Barrel Fermented Chardonnay ★★★★☆

This highly impressive Bannockburn wine typically possesses greater richness and power than other Central Otago Chardonnays. The 2002 vintage (★★★★) was fermented with indigenous ('wild') yeasts in French oak casks, with a 'much lower' percentage of new oak than in the past. It's a youthful wine with fresh, intense grapefruit and lime aromas and flavours, threaded with cool-climate acidity and finely balanced with toast and butterscotch characters. Well worth cellaring.

Vintage	02	01	00	99	98
WR	7	7	6	6	6
Drink	03-08	03-05	03-04	03-05	P

DRY $30 AV

Felton Road Block 2 Chardonnay (★★★★)

Barrel-aged for 18 months, the 2001 vintage (★★★★) of this Bannockburn, Central Otago wine has fragrant, lemony aromas and a youthful, yellow/green hue. Full and fresh, it's an impressively rich wine with strong, citrusy, buttery flavours, subtle, well-integrated oak and acids well under control. Drink now onwards.

Vintage	02	01
WR	NM	6
Drink	NM	03-07

DRY $40 -V

Felton Road Chardonnay ★★★☆

Compared to its stablemates (above), this is a much more fruit-driven style. The 2002 vintage (★★★☆) was handled entirely without oak, but malolactic fermentation and lees-aging were used to add complexity. Estate-grown at Bannockburn, in Central Otago, it's a vibrantly fruity wine with crisp, citrusy flavours and a distinct hint of butterscotch. With its cool-climate freshness and vivacity, it's a delicious drink-young style.

Vintage	02	01	00
WR	6	6	6
Drink	03-08	03-05	03-04

DRY $21 AV

Fiddler's Green Waipara Chardonnay ★★★★
The 2001 (★★★★) is an elegant, cool-climate style with considerable richness. The 2002 vintage (★★★★) was fermented and matured for 10 months in French oak barriques (30 per cent new). It's a youthful, elegant wine with vibrant, ripe-fruit characters of peach and grapefruit, mealy, oaky complexities and a hint of butterscotch. Very fresh and crisp, it should be at its best from 2004 onwards.

Vintage	02	01
WR	6	6
Drink	03-06	03-05

DRY $30 -V

Floating Mountain Mark Rattray Vineyard Waipara Chardonnay ★★★★
Mark Rattray's Chardonnays are typically powerful and lush. Delicious now, the 2001 (★★★★) is a bold, upfront style, rich, smooth and full of character, with mouthfilling body, ripe, peachy flavours and plenty of toasty oak. Barrel-matured for 10 months, the more slowly evolving 2002 vintage (★★★☆) is a higher-acid style, weighty (14.5 per cent alcohol), with good depth of fresh, ripe, citrusy fruit flavours and a fractionally off-dry, crisp finish.

Vintage	02	01
WR	6	5
Drink	03-06	03-05

MED/DRY $25 AV

Forrest Marlborough Chardonnay ★★★★
John Forrest favours a gently oaked style, looking to very ripe grapes and extended lees-aging to give his wine character. The 2001 vintage (★★★★) was 50 per cent wood-aged (in French and American oak casks); the rest was handled in tanks. An easy-drinking style, it has substantial body (14.5 per cent alcohol), a hint of butterscotch and strong, citrusy flavours, fresh and smooth, with a slightly off-dry finish. A moderately complex style with excellent depth and harmony, it is maturing well.

Vintage	01	00	99	98	97	96
WR	6	5	6	6	5	5
Drink	03-05	03-04	03-04	P	P	P

MED/DRY $20 V+

Forrest Vineyard Selection Chardonnay (★★★★)
For the 2001 vintage (★★★★), John Forrest gave a visiting Spanish winemaker, Concha Vecino, 'free rein to choose a small parcel of our very best Chardonnay grapes and make it her way'. It's a more wood-influenced style than its stablemate (above), fully handled in French oak casks, new and seasoned. The bouquet is fresh and biscuity, the palate weighty and vibrant, with good concentration of peachy, citrusy flavours, loads of character and a smooth, off-dry finish.

Vintage	01
WR	6
Drink	03-07

MED/DRY $29 AV

Fossil Ridge Nelson Chardonnay ★★★★
Grown by the Fry family in the Richmond foothills, this is a consistently impressive wine. Still youthful, the 2002 vintage (★★★☆) has creamy, sweet oak aromas, good weight, and ripe grapefruit and toast flavours, with fresh acidity and some mealy complexity. Open mid-2004+.

DRY $25 AV

CHARDONNAY

Foxes Island Marlborough Chardonnay ★★★★☆

This richly flavoured, skilfully balanced Chardonnay is produced by John Belsham, a senior wine judge and vastly experienced winemaker. The 2001 vintage (★★★★☆) was hand-picked and fully fermented in French oak barriques (40 per cent new). Still developing, it has fragrant, toasty oak and ripe-fruit aromas. Full-flavoured, with crisp acidity, vibrant peach and melon characters, French oak complexity and a tight, rich finish, it's a very elegant and harmonious wine that should richly reward cellaring.

Vintage	01	00	99	98
WR	6	6	5	6
Drink	04-06	03-05	03-04	P

DRY $33 AV

Framingham Marlborough Chardonnay ★★★★

Framingham is best known for Riesling, but the Chardonnays are always attractive and the 2002 vintage (★★★★) offers good value. Partly (50 per cent) fermented in new and older French oak barriques, with 60 per cent malolactic fermentation, it's an elegant, slightly creamy wine with fresh, delicate grapefruit and apple flavours to the fore and substantial body. Delicious in its youth, it shows very skilful winemaking.

Vintage	02	01	00
WR	6	6	5
Drink	03-05	03-05	P

DRY $22 V+

Fromm La Strada Chardonnay ★★★★☆

The Fromm style is very different to the fresh, fruit-driven style of most Marlborough Chardonnays. Fully fermented with indigenous yeasts in French oak barriques (10 per cent new, to achieve a 'modest' wood influence), and barrel-aged for over a year, it is given a full, softening malolactic fermentation. The 2001 vintage (★★★★☆) is full of character and highly distinctive. Grown at two sites (including the company-owned Clayvin vineyard) in the Brancott Valley, it's a weighty, bone-dry wine, fresh, youthful, appley and mealy, with excellent mouthfeel and a slightly buttery, rounded finish.

Vintage	02	01	00	99	98	97	96
WR	6	6	6	5	NM	4	NM
Drink	03-07	03-06	03-05	P	NM	P	NM

DRY $38 -V

Fromm La Strada Clayvin Vineyard Chardonnay ★★★★★

Fromm's top Chardonnay, grown on clay soils in the Clayvin Vineyard, on the southern flanks of the Wairau Valley, was previously labelled Reserve, but from the 2001 vintage is called Clayvin Vineyard. The 2000 vintage (★★★★★) is a wine of real individuality, and so is the 2001 (★★★★★). Fermented with indigenous yeasts and matured for 18 months in French oak barriques (none new), it took two years to go through a full malolactic fermentation. The clay soils, says winemaker Hatsch Kalberer, give 'a less fruity, more minerally and tighter character'. The bouquet is mealy, the palate powerful (14.5 per cent alcohol), rich and savoury, with great complexity and a long, bone-dry but not austere finish. Worth tracking down.

Vintage	02	01	00	99	98	97	96
WR	6	7	6	7	6	NM	7
Drink	04-10	03-09	03-10	03-09	03-04	NM	03-08

DRY $48 AV

Gibbston Valley Greenstone Chardonnay ★★★

Oak is not part of the recipe for this Central Otago wine, but it's typically fresh and vibrant, with appetising acidity in a distinctly cool-climate style. The 2002 vintage (★★☆) is attractively scented, with lemony, appley aromas and flavours, lively and tangy. A simple but enjoyable style, it's pricey at $22.

Vintage	02	01	00
WR	5	5	5
Drink	03-05	03-04	P

DRY $22 -V

Gibbston Valley Reserve Chardonnay ★★★★

One of the top Central Otago Chardonnays, fermented and lees-aged in French oak casks, this is a far more complex wine than its Greenstone stablemate (above). Bright, light yellow/green, the 2002 vintage (★★★☆) is weighty (14.5 per cent alcohol), fresh and lemony, with finely balanced oak adding complexity and the appetising acidity typical of the region's Chardonnays.

Vintage	02	01	00	99
WR	7	6	6	7
Drink	04-08	03-07	03-06	03-08

DRY $32 -V

Giesen Marlborough Chardonnay ★★★

With its standard Chardonnay, Giesen aims for 'elegance rather than power'. The 2002 (★★★) is creamy and slightly nutty, with a strong 'malo' influence. It's less vibrantly fruity than most of the region's Chardonnays, but shows some crisp, grapefruit-like characters.

Vintage	02	01	00	99	98
WR	7	6	7	5	5
Drink	03-06	03-04	03-04	P	P

DRY $18 AV

Giesen Reserve Barrel Selection Marlborough Chardonnay ★★★☆

The strongly oaked 2001 vintage (★★★☆) is citrusy and slightly creamy in a cool-climate style with vigorous, citrusy, slightly minerally and toasty flavours showing some intensity and firm acid spine.

Vintage	01
WR	7
Drink	03-06

DRY $20 AV

Gladstone Wairarapa Chardonnay ★★★★

Typically a soft and creamy wine, delicious in its youth. Half tank, half barrel-fermented, the 2002 vintage (★★★★) has a pale straw hue, with good depth of fresh, lively peach and grapefruit flavours threaded with crisp acidity, some biscuity complexity and a seductively smooth finish.

Vintage	02	01	00	99	98
WR	6	6	NM	6	5
Drink	03-07	03-06	NM	03-04	P

DRY $23 V+

Goldwater Roseland Marlborough Chardonnay ★★★★

Typically a finely scented, weighty, vibrantly fruity wine with well-ripened, tropical-fruit characters and subtle use of oak in a moderately complex but highly attractive style. The skilfully crafted 2002 vintage (★★★★) was grown in two vineyards in the Wairau Valley and fermented and 'raised' for 10 months on its yeast lees in French oak barriques (20 per cent new). Full-bodied, with grapefruit and nut flavours, gentle acidity and a slightly buttery finish, it's a delicious drink-young style, with lots of character.

Vintage	02	01	00	99	98
WR	7	7	7	7	7
Drink	03-06	03-05	03-04	P	P

DRY $20 V+

Goldwater Zell Chardonnay ★★★★☆

Grown in the hillside, clay-based Zell vineyard on Waiheke Island, this is a rich, complex wine with the ripeness and roundness typical of northern Chardonnays. The 2002 vintage (★★★★) was hand-picked, whole-bunch pressed and fermented with indigenous yeasts in French oak casks (20 per cent new), with partial malolactic fermentation. Fleshy and well-rounded, with ripe flavours of stone-fruit, grapefruit and figs and a creamy texture, it's still unfolding but shows power through the palate; open mid-2004+.

Vintage	02	01	00	99
WR	7	6	7	7
Drink	03-08	03-06	03-05	03-05

DRY $38 -V

Gravitas Marlborough Chardonnay (★★★★☆)

Gravitas is the label of expatriate Kiwi Martyn Nicholls, whose company, St Arnaud's Vineyards, owns 30 hectares of vineyards in Marlborough. Fermented with indigenous yeasts, the 2002 vintage (★★★★☆) is highly impressive – strapping (14.5 per cent alcohol), lush and minerally, with lovely intensity of peach, butterscotch and nut flavours, mealy and very harmonious. It's a powerful yet delicate wine, dry and very concentrated.

DRY $30 AV

Greenhough Hope Vineyard Chardonnay ★★★★☆

Only produced in top years, this powerful wine is estate-grown at Hope, in Nelson. After the notably lush, concentrated 1998 vintage (★★★★★), there was no 1999 or 2000, but the 2001 (★★★★☆) is impressive. Fermented in tanks (60 per cent) and new French oak barriques, the wine was all aged on its gross lees after the completion of malolactic fermentation. A weighty (14.4 per cent alcohol), creamy wine with sweet-fruit characters, rich, citrusy flavours, finely integrated oak and a rounded finish, it's a very harmonious wine. The youthful 2002 (★★★★★) is refined and immaculate, with fresh, ripe grapefruit and slight butterscotch flavours, rounded and rich. Sensitively oaked, with notable delicacy and finesse and a very long finish, it looks great for 2004–06.

Vintage	02	01	00	99	98
WR	7	6	NM	NM	6
Drink	04-06	03-05	NM	NM	P

DRY $29 V+

Greenhough Nelson Vineyards Chardonnay ★★★☆

This is a consistently attractive wine. The 2001 vintage (★★★☆) was hand-harvested from two vineyards and fermented in a mix of tanks and French and American oak barrels. All of the wine was lees-aged and went through a softening malolactic fermentation. Pale, with a creamy, slightly biscuity fragrance, it's a smooth, citrusy, flavoursome wine in a forward style, very ripe and rounded. The instantly appealing 2002 (★★★★) has butterscotch and sweet oak aromas leading into a full-bodied, creamy wine with very ripe-fruit characters, peachy, toasty flavours and a rounded finish.

Vintage	02	01	00	99	98
WR	7	6	6	5	5
Drink	04-05	03-04	03-04	P	P

DRY $21 AV

Grove Mill Innovator Croft Chardonnay (★★★)

Named in honour of Peter Croft, a founder and long-serving director of the Marlborough winery, the 2002 vintage (★★★) was made from 'a specially selected parcel of ripe fruit', fermented and lees-aged for four months in tanks and French oak casks, and bottled young. Restrained on the nose, it is lemony, with good weight, some interesting minerally characters and a slightly austere, high-acid finish.

DRY $24 ·V

Grove Mill Marlborough Chardonnay ★★★★

Typically an attractive, skilfully balanced and flavourful wine with integrated oak, a hint of malolactic-derived butteriness and fresh acidity. The 2002 vintage (★★★★) was mostly (90 per cent) tank-fermented, but 10 per cent of the blend was French oak-fermented and half was matured in oak casks (20 per cent new). It's a tight, elegant wine with good weight (14 per cent alcohol) and fresh, grapefruit-like flavours showing lively acidity, good delicacy and depth.

Vintage	02	01	00	99	98
WR	7	6	6	6	6
Drink	04-08	03-05	03-04	P	P

DRY $23 V+

Gunn Estate Skeetfield Chardonnay (★★★☆)

The 2002 vintage (★★★☆) is the first since the established Gunn Estate brand was purchased by Sacred Hill. Grown in Hawke's Bay and fermented and matured for a year in French oak casks (new and one-year-old), it's an upfront style, deliciously drinkable in its youth, with ripe, faintly honeyed, stone-fruit characters, toasty oak and a well-rounded finish.

Vintage	02
WR	7
Drink	03-07

DRY $25 ·V

Gunn Estate Unoaked Chardonnay (★★☆)

Produced by the fast-growing Hawke's Bay company, Sacred Hill, the debut 2002 vintage (★★☆) is a fresh, simple wine with youthful lemon/apple flavours. A blend of Hawke's Bay (85 per cent) and Marlborough grapes, it's an easy-drinking style, priced right.

Vintage	02
WR	6
Drink	03-04

DRY $15 AV

Hanmer Junction, The, Lightly Oaked Chardonnay (★★☆)

'Lightly oaked' means 25 per cent of this Waipara wine was matured for nine months in old French oak casks; the rest was aged on its yeast lees in tanks. It's a lean, distinctly cool-climate wine with lemon and green apple flavours, still fresh and lively.

Vintage	01
WR	5
Drink	03-04

DRY $17 ·V

Hanmer Junction, The, Unwooded Chardonnay (★★★)

The 2002 vintage (★★★) of this Waipara wine was matured on its yeast lees for 10 months in tanks. Enjoyable in its youth, it offers plenty of fresh, crisp, citrusy flavour, with a sliver of sweetness (4.6 grams/litre) to smooth the finish.

Vintage	02
WR	6
Drink	03-04

DRY $16 AV

Heron's Flight Barrique Fermented Chardonnay ★★★☆

At its best, this Matakana Chardonnay is a classy wine with good weight and strong, ripe-fruit characters wrapped in toasty oak. Fermented and matured for a year in one-year-old French oak casks, the light yellow 2001 vintage (★★★★) is a big, generous wine with excellent depth of grapefruit and nut flavours.

Vintage 01
WR 6
Drink 03-06

`DRY $27 -V`

Heron's Flight La Volee Unoaked Chardonnay ★★★

This tank-fermented Matakana Chardonnay is typically fresh and lively, with good depth of melon and citrus-fruit flavours in a simple but enjoyable style. Verging on three-star quality, the 2002 vintage (★★☆) is a clearly varietal wine with firm acidity woven through its fresh, lemony flavours.

Vintage 02
WR 6
Drink 03-05

`DRY $18 AV`

Herzog Marlborough Chardonnay ★★★★☆

The 2001 vintage (★★★★★) is a notably powerful, strapping wine, complex and highly concentrated, with layers of peach, butterscotch, grapefruit and nut flavours and a long, rounded finish. Slightly less striking in its youth, the 2002 (★★★★) was lees-aged for a year in French oak barrels. Pale lemon, it's a robust wine (14 per cent alcohol) with well-ripened, sweet-fruit characters, strong grapefruit and peach flavours and a creamy, slightly off-dry finish. It needs time; open 2004+.

Vintage 02 01
WR 6 6
Drink 03-10 05

`MED/DRY $39 -V`

Highfield Marlborough Chardonnay ★★★★

Fermented and matured in French oak barriques, the 2000 vintage (★★★★) is drinking well now. Light/medium gold, it's a fleshy, firmly structured wine with grapefruit and toast flavours, strong, finely balanced and lingering. The very stylish 2001 (★★★★☆) has a youthful yellow/green hue, with good weight and concentrated, grapefruit-like flavours, slightly nutty and buttery. It's a classy, very harmonious and delicious wine for drinking now or cellaring.

Vintage 01 00 99 98
WR 7 6 6 5
Drink 04-06 P 03-04 P

`DRY $32 -V`

Himmelsfeld Moutere Chardonnay ★★★☆

This rare Nelson wine is grown in Beth Eggers' vineyard in the Upper Moutere hills, near the Tasman Bay winery. The 2000 (★★★☆), handled in American and French oak, has a creamy texture, with mouthfilling body and very good depth of peachy, smooth flavour. The 2001 vintage (★★★☆) is another substantial, rounded wine with toasty oak aromas, peach, grapefruit and oak flavours showing good depth and complexity and a tight, dry finish.

`DRY $26 -V`

Huia Marlborough Chardonnay ★★★★

The elegant 2001 vintage (★★★★) was hand-picked, fermented with indigenous yeasts and matured for 15 months, with weekly lees-stirring, in French oak barriques and puncheons; 60 per cent of the blend went through malolactic fermentation. Still fresh and youthful, with a light lemon/green hue, it's a tightly structured wine with crisp, strong grapefruit and apple flavours, subtle biscuity oak, good harmony and a dry finish.

Vintage	01	00	99
WR	6	6	7
Drink	03-05	03-05	03-04

DRY $26 AV

Huntaway Reserve Gisborne Chardonnay ★★★★

This former Corbans label, now a Montana brand, is made in a high-impact, creamy-rich style, delicious in its youth. The 2002 vintage (★★★★) was harvested (20 per cent by hand) at 23 brix, and fermented and matured for nine months, with weekly lees-stirring, in French (85 per cent) and American oak barriques. Very creamy and toasty on the nose, it's an upfront style, ripe and smooth, with good intensity of tropical-fruit characters seasoned with toasty oak. Fine value.

Vintage	02	01	00	99	98
WR	7	NM	7	6	7
Drink	03-06	NM	03-04	P	P

DRY $20 V+

Hunter's Marlborough Chardonnay ★★★★☆

Finesse is the key attribute of this consistently immaculate wine, which places its accent on fresh, vibrant, searching, citrusy flavours, overlaid with subtle, mealy barrel-ferment characters. About 40 per cent of the blend is fermented and lees-aged in new French oak barriques (medium toast); the rest is tank-fermented and then matured in one and two-year-old casks. It is a proven performer in the cellar. Delicious now, the 2001 vintage (★★★★☆) is a typically great buy. Fragrant, with grapefruit and butterscotch aromas, it has sweet-fruit delights, with ripe, peachy, citrusy flavours, a gentle, biscuity oak influence and a smooth, creamy texture.

Vintage	02	01	00	99	98	97	96
WR	5	6	6	5	6	6	5
Drink	04-07	03-06	03-05	03-05	04	P	P

DRY $22 V+

Hyperion Helios Chardonnay ★★★

The 2002 vintage (★★★) of this Matakana wine was hand-picked, whole-bunch pressed and fermented and lees-aged for six months in French oak casks. It's a substantial wine (14 per cent alcohol) with ripe, peachy, toasty flavours and a slightly honeyed finish. Drink now onwards.

Vintage	02	01	00
WR	7	6	7
Drink	03-07	03-06	03-04

DRY $25 -V

Hyperion Selene Chardonnay ★★☆

Labelled as a straight Chardonnay (unlike past vintages, labelled as a Chardonnay/Pinot Gris blend), the 2002 vintage (★★☆) of this unoaked Matakana wine is a medium-dry style, offering easy, no-fuss drinking. It's a full-bodied wine with lemony, appley, slightly spicy flavours and a smooth finish.

Vintage	02
WR	4
Drink	03-04

MED/DRY $20 -V

Inverness Estate Ness Valley Chardonnay (★★★★)

Estate-grown at Clevedon, in South Auckland, and made by Anthony Ivicevich at the West Brook winery, the 2000 vintage (★★★★) is light yellow, with lots of toasty French oak in evidence. It's a full-bodied wine (14 per cent alcohol) with strong, ripe, peachy fruit characters, plenty of flavour and a creamy-smooth finish.

DRY $20 V+

Isabel Marlborough Chardonnay ★★★★★

This prestigious producer is after 'a tight, restrained style [in] a deliberate move away from the somewhat overbearing, heavily oaked and fruity wines currently in vogue'. Better known in the UK than New Zealand, this is one of the region's most distinguished Chardonnays – notably complex and minerally rather than fruity, with very impressive subtlety, vigour and length. It is based on well-established Mendoza vines, fermented with a mix of indigenous and cultured yeasts in new and seasoned French oak barriques (60 per cent) and tanks (40 per cent), and given a full, softening malolactic fermentation. The 2001 vintage (★★★★★) has a powerful presence in the mouth. Rich, nutty, yeasty and harmonious, it's a mouthfilling and generous wine with deep grapefruit and nut flavours, a distinctly mineral streak and a long, refined finish. Tasted in mid to late 2003, the 2002 (★★★★) was very youthful, with a creamy texture and strong citrus fruit, nut and butterscotch flavours, still coming together. It needs time; open mid-2004+.

Vintage	02	01	00	01	99	98	97	96
WR	6	7	7	6	5	5	5	4
Drink	05-09	05-09	04-08	03-07	03-06	03-05	P	P

DRY $32 V+

Jackson Estate Chardonnay ★★★★

Although best known for its classy Sauvignon Blanc, this Marlborough producer's Chardonnay is consistently enjoyable. It is grown in the heart of the Wairau Valley and made by Australian consultant winemaker, Martin Shaw. Fully French oak-fermented, the 2000 vintage (★★★★) is a very harmonious wine with vibrant grapefruit, melon and peach flavours, a hint of butterscotch, fresh underlying acidity and mouthfilling body. Showing impressive complexity for its price, the 2001 (★★★★) is biscuity and buttery on the nose, with ripe citrus/melon flavours seasoned with French oak and a fully dry, rounded finish.

Vintage	01	00	99	98
WR	7	6	6	6
Drink	03-05	03-04	P	P

DRY $19 V+

Jackson Estate Chardonnay Reserve ★★★★

A consistently good wine, although the standard label (above) typically drinks well a year or two earlier, with greater emphasis on fresh, vibrant fruit characters. Based on grapes from older, crop-reduced vines, fully fermented in new French oak barriques and given a softening malolactic fermentation, the 1999 vintage (★★★☆) is light gold, with a toasty, slightly minerally, developed bouquet. Full-bodied, flavoursome and crisp, it's a powerfully wooded style, ready for drinking.

DRY $22 V+

Johanneshof Cellars Marlborough Chardonnay ★★★

This is consistently a tense, distinctly cool-climate style with taut acidity. Fermented with indigenous yeasts in new and old French oak casks, with lees-stirring, the 1999 vintage (★★☆) is pale yellow, with a taut, restrained palate. Outside the regional mainstream, it's a distinctive, slightly austere wine, but some earlier vintages have matured well.

DRY $22 -V

Kahurangi Estate Mt Arthur Chardonnay (★★★★)

The 2002 vintage (★★★★) was grown in the Upper Moutere hills of Nelson and barrel-fermented. It's a weighty wine with ripe, concentrated grapefruit and peach flavours, toast and butterscotch complexities and a well-rounded finish. Drink 2004–05.

DRY $21 V+

Kahurangi Estate Moutere Chardonnay (★★☆)

The 2002 vintage (★★☆) is a Chablis-like Nelson wine, based on the Mendoza clone and lightly oaked. Full-bodied, with appley aromas, it offers crisp grapefruit and green apple flavours, with a touch of biscuity oak, but also shows a slight lack of freshness and vibrancy.

DRY $20 -V

Kahurangi Estate Unwooded Chardonnay ★★★

The 2002 vintage (★★★) of this full-bodied Nelson wine is a good example of the unoaked style. Ripely scented, it's a crisp, full-bodied wine with fresh melon and lime flavours, attractively vibrant and zingy.

DRY $18 AV

Kaikoura Unoaked Marlborough Chardonnay (★★★)

The 2001 vintage (★★★) was grown in four Wairau Valley vineyards and handled entirely in stainless steel tanks. Still youthful in colour, it's a lemon-scented, vibrantly fruity wine with citrusy, appley flavours and a fresh, crisp finish.

DRY $20 -V

Kaimira Estate Brightwater Chardonnay ★★★★☆

This is a consistently classy wine. Deliciously robust (14.5 per cent alcohol), complex and rounded, the creamy 2002 vintage (★★★★☆) was estate-grown at Brightwater, in Nelson, barrel-fermented and lees-aged for eight months. Showing impressive flavour concentration and harmony, with rich, ripe peach and grapefruit characters, finely balanced oak and gentle acidity, it's sharply priced at $22.

Vintage	02	01	00
WR	6	6	6
Drink	03-06	03-04	P

DRY $22 V+

Kaimira Estate Nelson Chardonnay ★★★

Fermented and lees-aged in tanks, with 'light' oak treatment, the 2002 vintage (★★★) is a crisply mouthfilling wine with slightly creamy and mealy characters and decent depth of ripe, peachy fruit flavours.

Vintage	02	01	00
WR	5	4	6
Drink	03-06	03-04	P

DRY $18 AV

Kaimira Estate Unoaked Chardonnay ★★☆

The 2002 vintage (★★★), based on first-crop vines at Upper Moutere, in Nelson, is citrusy and crisp, with some fullness and richness. The 2003 (★★☆) is very fresh, lively and tangy, but green-edged. In its infancy, you could almost mistake it for a brisk, limey Sauvignon Blanc.

DRY $16 -V

Kaituna Valley Canterbury The Kaituna Vineyard Chardonnay ★★★★☆

The tightly structured 2000 (★★★★☆), based on first-crop Banks Peninsula vines and fermented and matured for a year in French oak barriques (60 per cent), has concentrated grapefruit and nut flavours and a long, rounded, slightly buttery finish. Even finer, the 2001 vintage (★★★★★) is a powerful wine with deep stone-fruit and butterscotch flavours seasoned with biscuity oak and firm underlying acidity. Tasted shortly after bottling, the 2002 (★★★★) is weighty and fresh, with sweet-fruit characters, rich, peachy, slightly toasty flavours and a finely balanced, bone-dry finish. This is clearly one of Canterbury's greatest Chardonnays.

Vintage	02	01	00
WR	5	6	5
Drink	04-06	03-06	03-05

DRY $22 V+

Kaituna Valley Marlborough The Awatere Vineyard Chardonnay ★★★★☆

Grown in Grant and Helen Whelan's vineyard in the Awatere Valley and fermented and matured for a year in French oak barriques (50 per cent new), the 2000 (★★★★☆) is a classy wine, smooth, mouthfilling and notably harmonious, with deep grapefruit and stone-fruit flavours, a strong seasoning of toasty oak and rounded acidity. For sheer drinkability, it scores 10 out of 10, and the 2001 vintage (★★★★☆) is a repeat performance. Light yellow/green in hue, it is richly fragrant, with deep, vibrant citrus and stone-fruit flavours, biscuity oak and a smooth, well-rounded finish. The 2002 (★★★★☆), tasted soon after bottling, is full-bodied (13.9 per cent alcohol) and vibrant, with fresh acidity, ripe, peachy, citrusy flavours shining through, slight mineral and butterscotch characters and a bone-dry finish. Drink mid-2004+.

Vintage	02	01	00
WR	7	6	6
Drink	04-06	03-05	03-04

DRY $24 V+

Karaka Point Vineyard Chardonnay (★★★☆)

Grown at Waiau Pa, south of the Manukau Harbour in South Auckland, the 2002 vintage (★★★☆) is a characterful, distinctive wine, mouthfilling and ripe, with concentrated, fresh peach and pear flavours, a buttery 'malo' influence and savoury, spicy oak adding complexity.

DRY $25 -V

Kawarau Estate Chardonnay ★★☆

Grown organically near Lowburn, in Central Otago, this is a fruit-driven style – about 15 per cent of the blend is fermented in French oak casks, with the rest handled entirely in stainless steel tanks. At its best, it is fresh and lively, with crisp, vibrant, lemony, appley flavours, but the 2001 (★★) is a lesser vintage. Full-bodied and citrusy, it lacks fragrance and is quite restrained in flavour. There is no 2002.

DRY $18 -V

Kawarau Estate Reserve Chardonnay ★★★☆

Grown organically at Lowburn, north of Cromwell in Central Otago, this is a consistently decent wine, full-flavoured and mouth-wateringly crisp. The 2002 vintage (★★★★) was fermented and matured for 10 months in French oak casks (20 per cent new), with full malolactic fermentation. Full-bodied, slightly creamy and toasty, with rich, ripe, citrusy characters, balanced acidity and well-integrated oak, it shows good weight, complexity and depth and should flourish with cellaring.

Vintage	02	01	00	99	98
WR	6	5	5	4	5
Drink	03-05	03-05	03-04	P	P

DRY $24 AV

Kemblefield The Distinction Chardonnay ★★★★

Previously labelled Hawke's Bay Chardonnay (the 2000 vintage has been marketed under both names), this is the key wine in the Kemblefield range. Estate-grown in the slightly elevated, relatively cool Mangatahi district, it is French oak-fermented and matured on its yeast lees for nine months. The 2000 vintage (★★★★) was handled in 25 per cent new oak casks, with partial malolactic fermentation. A stylish wine, maturing well, it offers good intensity of grapefruit-like flavours, finely integrated oak, a hint of butterscotch, fresh acidity and a lingering finish.

Vintage	00	99	98	97	96
WR	7	7	7	7	6
Drink	03-05	03-04	03-04	P	P

DRY $27 AV

Kemblefield The Reserve Chardonnay (★★★★★)

The highly distinguished 2000 vintage (★★★★★) was estate-grown at Mangatahi – a relatively cool area inland from Hastings in Hawke's Bay – and fermented and lees-aged for a year (with fortnightly lees-stirring) in French oak barriques (50 per cent new). Soft and creamy, it's a powerful, very weighty, concentrated and complex wine with layers of peachy, mealy, nutty flavours and loads of personality. You could cellar it, but why bother? It's already an exciting mouthful.

DRY $36 AV

Kemblefield Winemakers Signature Chardonnay ★★★

This is the Hawke's Bay winery's bottom-tier Chardonnay, despite its upmarket name. It is a further source of confusion that the words 'Winemakers Signature' appear solely on the back label, with winemaker John Kemble's signature on the front. Estate-grown at Mangatahi, tank-fermented and 'lightly' oaked, the 2002 vintage (★★★) is an attractive wine with vibrant fruit characters, peachy, citrusy and tangy. Showing good freshness and drive, it's a highly enjoyable drink-young style.

DRY $17 AV

Kerr Farm Hawke's Bay Chardonnay ★★☆

Fermented in tanks and French and American oak casks, the 2002 vintage (★★☆) has lemony, appley aromas leading into a slightly honeyed palate with a touch of sweet, toasty oak. Fruity and smooth, it's a pleasant, drink-young style.

Vintage	02	01
WR	6	6
Drink	03-04	03-04

DRY $20 -V

Kerr Farm Limited Release Kumeu Chardonnay ★★☆

The 2001 (★★☆) and 2002 (★★☆) vintages were estate-grown in West Auckland and fermented in new French and American oak casks. The golden 2001 is peachy, buttery and toasty, the 2002 lemony, appley and crisp, but both wines show a slight lack of freshness and vibrancy.

Vintage	02	01	00
WR	7	6	7
Drink	04-07	03-05	03-05

DRY $25 -V

Kim Crawford Doc's Block Hawke's Bay Chardonnay (★★★)

Weighty and creamy, with fullness of body and buttery, oaky flavours, the 2002 vintage (★★★) has plenty of drink-young appeal.

DRY $25 -V

Kim Crawford Te Awanga Vineyard
Hawke's Bay Chardonnay ★★★

The developed 2001 vintage (★★☆) is golden, with firm acidity and honeyed, botrytis characters showing. Likely to be much longer-lived, the clearly superior 2002 (★★★★) is weighty and generous, with peach, butterscotch and toasty oak flavours in an upfront style. Its ripe-fruit flavours are slightly overpowered by oak, but the wine has good mouthfeel and plenty of character.

DRY $30 -V

Kim Crawford Tietjen/Briant Gisborne Chardonnay ★★★★☆

Made in an upfront style, this is typically one of Gisborne's boldest Chardonnays, with rich, ripe citrus/melon flavours, strongly laced with oak. Lush and soft, the 2002 vintage (★★★★) was grown in the Tietjen and Briant vineyards, fermented in American oak barriques (half new) and given a full malolactic fermentation. It's a seductive style showing excellent body and flavour depth, with well-ripened fruit characters, heaps of sweet, toasty oak, mealy, biscuity complexities and a creamy-smooth finish.

Vintage	02	01	00	99	98
WR	7	NM	5	NM	7
Drink	03-06	NM	P	NM	P

DRY $30 AV

Kim Crawford Unoaked Marlborough Chardonnay ★★★☆

Given a full, softening malolactic fermentation, this is a very enjoyable drink-young style. The 2002 vintage (★★★☆) is full and smooth, with good depth of grapefruit, apple and butterscotch flavours in a forward style offering lots of pleasure.

Vintage	03	02	01	00	99	98
WR	6	6	6	6	5	6
Drink	03-08	03-05	P	P	P	P

DRY $20 AV

Koura Bay Mount Fyffe Chardonnay ★★★

Named after the peak overlooking the town of Kaikoura, the 2002 vintage (★★★) of this Marlborough wine is a straightforward wine with fresh, lively, appley flavours. Fermented in contact with American oak 'beans' and lees-aged, with 70 per cent malolactic fermentation, it's a simple but attractive wine.

DRY $20 -V

Kumeu River Kumeu Chardonnay ★★★★★

One of the country's most celebrated Chardonnays, this is typically a superbly constructed West Auckland wine, rich and powerful, with beautifully interwoven flavours and a seductively creamy texture. The key to its outstanding quality lies in the vineyards, says winemaker Michael Brajkovich: 'We manage to get the grapes very ripe.' Grown at five sites around Kumeu, fermented with indigenous yeasts and lees-aged (with weekly lees-stirring) in Burgundy oak barriques (typically 20–25 per cent new each year), the wine also undergoes a full malolactic fermentation (except in 2000, a warm, dry growing season). The 2002 vintage (★★★★★) is flintier than its Mate's Vineyard stablemate (below), with a fragrant, biscuity nose and tightly structured, very fresh and vibrant palate. Youthful and complex, with good acid backbone and strong, peachy, mealy, slightly buttery flavours, it needs another year or two to fully unfold; open mid-2004 onwards.

Vintage	03	02	01	00	99	98	97	96
WR	6	7	6	7	6	6	5	7
Drink	04-06	03-07	03-05	03-05	03-04	P	P	P

DRY $37 AV

Kumeu River Mate's Vineyard Kumeu Chardonnay ★★★★★

This extremely classy single-vineyard wine is Kumeu River's flagship. It is made entirely from the best of the fruit harvested from Mate's Vineyard, planted in 1990 on the site of the original Kumeu River vineyard purchased by Mate Brajkovich in 1944. Strikingly similar to Kumeu River Kumeu Chardonnay, but slightly more opulent and concentrated, it offers the same rich and harmonious flavours of grapefruit, peach and butterscotch, typically with a stronger seasoning of new French oak. For winemaker Michael Brajkovich, the hallmark of Mate's Vineyard is 'a pear-like character on the nose, with richness and length on the palate after two to three years'. An outstanding vintage, the bright, light lemon/green 2002 (★★★★★) is as usual slightly bolder than the Kumeu River Chardonnay, with a powerful palate showing lovely, ripe grapefruit, butterscotch and biscuit flavours, showing real concentration and harmony. Lush and well-rounded, with a very long finish, it's highly approachable in its youth, but worth cellaring for at least a couple of years.

Vintage	03	02	01	00	99	98	97	96
WR	6	7	6	7	6	6	5	6
Drink	04-08	03-09	03-06	03-05	03-04	P	P	P

DRY $48 AV

Lake Chalice Block Two Marlborough Chardonnay (★★★)

Despite the name, the 2002 vintage (★★★) was grown in several vineyards in the Wairau Valley. It was made in the same style (and at the same price) as the Vineyard Selection Chardonnay (below), but grown at different sites. Both tank and barrel-fermented, with full malolactic fermentation, it's a very easy-drinking wine with ripe, citrusy flavours, some leesy complexity and a creamy-smooth finish.

Vintage	02
WR	6
Drink	03-06

DRY $20 -V

Lake Chalice Platinum Marlborough Chardonnay ★★★★☆

This typically lush, rich and complex wine is estate-grown in the Falcon vineyard, hand-picked, whole-bunch pressed, fermented in French oak barriques (half new), lees-aged for eight months and given a full malolactic fermentation. It typically offers strong, nutty, mealy flavours and a very creamy texture in a fragrant, full-blown Chardonnay style. The 2002 vintage (★★★★) is weighty, with concentrated, ripe, citrusy, mealy, buttery flavours showing good complexity and fresh acidity. In its youth, it's slightly less opulent than some past vintages; open mid-2004+.

Vintage	02	01	00	99	98
WR	7	7	7	7	7
Drink	03-07	03-06	03-05	03-05	P

DRY $28 V+

Lake Chalice Unoaked Chardonnay ★★★

'Here is undiluted Chardonnay' declares the back label on this single-vineyard Marlborough wine. Made without any input from wood or malolactic fermentation, the 2002 vintage (★★★) offers vibrant lemon/apple aromas and flavours. It's a simple style, but fresh, crisp and lively, with plenty of drink-young charm.

DRY $19 AV

Lake Chalice Vineyard Selection Marlborough Chardonnay ★★★☆

This 'black label' wine is typically fresh and creamy, with drink-young appeal. Grown in the Falcon and Bryce vineyards, and both tank and barrel-fermented, with full malolactic fermentation, the 2002 vintage (★★★) is appley, lemony and buttery, with some oak complexity and a crisp, fractionally off-dry finish.

Vintage	02	01	00	99	98
WR	6	7	7	6	7
Drink	03-05	03-04	P	P	P

DRY $20 AV

Langdale Chardonnay ★★★

Fresh, lively and crisp, the 2001 vintage (★★★☆) is a South Island blend of Canterbury and Nelson grapes, made by Alan McCorkindale. Forty per cent of the blend was handled in tanks; the rest spent eight months in French (principally) and American oak casks. Showing good vigour and depth, it offers grapefruit and peach flavours, with hints of toast and butterscotch and a fractionally off-dry finish. (This wine was in 2002 re-released under the Waipara Hills label.)

Vintage	01
WR	6
Drink	03-05

DRY $18 AV

Lawson's Dry Hills Marlborough Chardonnay ★★★★

This is typically an impressively ripe and robust wine with concentrated, peachy, toasty, buttery flavours. The light yellow 2001 vintage (★★★★) was grown in the Wairau Valley, harvested at 24 brix and fermented in new to four-year-old French oak barriques (10 per cent was handled in tanks), with partial malolactic fermentation. Maturing well, it possesses punchy, well-ripened grapefruit and toast flavours, now starting to round out, with a backbone of fresh acidity and substantial body.

Vintage	02	01	00	99	98
WR	6	6	6	6	5
Drink	03-06	03-05	P	P	P

DRY $25 AV

Le Grys Unwooded Chardonnay (★★★)

Produced by Mud House Wine Company, the 2002 vintage (★★★) is fresh and light, with lemony, appley, rounded flavours. It lacks real complexity and concentration, but is enjoyable in a simple, fruit-driven style.

DRY $20 -V

Lincoln Heritage Patricia Chardonnay ★★★☆

Made in a rich, strongly oak-influenced, upfront style, Lincoln's middle-tier Chardonnay was named after the daughter-in-law of the founder, Petar Fredatovich. The powerful, youthful 2002 vintage (★★★★) is a Gisborne wine, grown in the Parklands Estate vineyard and fermented and lees-aged for nine months in American oak barriques. Full, fresh and creamy-smooth, with sweet, American oak aromas, ripe grapefruit and peach flavours and a long, well-rounded finish, it's a characterful, well-priced wine, likely to be at its best during 2003–04.

Vintage	02
WR	6
Drink	03-07

DRY $19 V+

Lincoln Reserve Chardonnay (★★★★)

The rich, rounded 2002 vintage (★★★★) replaces the President's Selection label (last made in 2000) as Lincoln's top Chardonnay. Grown in Chris Parker's vineyard at Gisborne and fermented and matured for a year in French oak barriques, it has toasty oak aromas leading into a fleshy, creamy-smooth palate with ripe-fruit flavours of peach, fig and grapefruit and a touch of butterscotch. A softly textured wine with good concentration, it's worth cellaring to 2004–05.

Vintage	02
WR	6
Drink	03-07

DRY $30 -V

Lincoln Winemakers Series Chardonnay ★★☆

Lincoln's bottom-tier Chardonnay offers fresh, simple fruit flavours and a smooth finish. The 2002 vintage (★★☆), grown in Gisborne and faintly oaked (5 per cent of the blend was wood-aged), is crisp, fruity and lively, delivering no-fuss, moderately priced drinking.

Vintage	02	01	00
WR	6	6	6
Drink	03-05	P	P

DRY $14 AV

Linden Estate Hawke's Bay Chardonnay ★★★☆

The 2001 vintage (★★★☆), from an extremely low-cropping year (below 2 tonnes/ha), was grown in the Esk Valley and fermented with indigenous yeasts in French oak casks (12 per cent new). Pale gold, it's a medium to full-bodied wine (below 12 per cent alcohol), showing good complexity and depth of peachy, buttery, biscuity, slightly honeyed flavour, with firm acid spine. Ready.

Vintage	01	00	99	98
WR	7	6	6	6
Drink	03-05	03-04	03-04	P

DRY $22 AV

Longridge Hawke's Bay Chardonnay ★★★

A former Corbans brand, now part of the Montana portfolio, this is a sound wine with a touch of quality. It typically showcases fresh, ripe-fruit characters, with a delicate oak underlay. The 2002 vintage (★★★), fermented and lees-aged in French (70 per cent) and American oak casks (20 per cent new), is flavoursome and forward in its appeal, with ripe, citrusy characters, a gentle seasoning of oak and a smooth finish.

Vintage	02	01	00	99	98
WR	6	NM	7	7	7
Drink	03+	NM	P	P	P

DRY $15 V+

Longview Estate Barrique Fermented Chardonnay (★★☆)

Estate-grown just south of Whangarei, the 2000 vintage (★★☆) was matured for 16 months in French oak casks. The bouquet is oaky, the palate full, creamy and assertively wooded, with ripe, melon-like fruit beneath. It's a wine of some complexity, but lacks balance.

Vintage	00
WR	5
Drink	03-05

DRY $19 -V

Longview Estate Unwooded Chardonnay ★★★

This Northland winery has produced attractive unoaked ('timber-free', as the winery puts it) Chardonnays since 1998. Estate-grown just south of Whangarei, the 2002 vintage (★★☆) is a solid wine, full-bodied, crisp, lemony and appley, but less aromatic and vibrantly fruity than in top years.

Vintage	02
WR	5
Drink	03-04

MED/DRY $18 AV

Loopline Vineyard Wairarapa Chardonnay ★★☆

Grown at Opaki, just north of Masterton, the 2002 vintage (★★★) was fermented and matured for nine months in French oak casks. It's a mouthfilling wine with a distinctly buttery bouquet, ripe peach and grapefruit flavours, strong butterscotch and toast characters and a fresh, crisp finish.

Vintage	02	01
WR	6	6
Drink	03-06	03-06

DRY $25 -V

Lucknow Estate Waihopai Valley Chardonnay (★★★)

The crisp, flinty 2001 vintage (★★★) from this Hawke's Bay winery was grown in Marlborough's Waihopai Valley and matured for five months in French oak casks, with partial malolactic fermentation. Its fresh, lemony, appley flavours show good depth, in a lively cool-climate style with minerally, slightly nutty characters.

DRY $19 AV

Lynskeys Wairau Peaks Reserve Marlborough Chardonnay ★★★★

This is a consistently impressive wine (labelled 'Reserve' since the 2001 vintage). The youthful 2002 vintage (★★★★) was estate-grown, harvested at 24 brix, fermented with indigenous and cultured yeasts in French oak barrels and lees-aged in wood for 10 months. It's a fragrant, generous, grapefruit and toast-flavoured wine showing good concentration, a delicious softness of texture (boosted by more than 4 grams per litre of residual sugar) and strong upfront appeal.

Vintage	02	01	00	99
WR	6	6	7	6
Drink	03-05	03-04	P	P

DRY $29 AV

Mahurangi Estate Mahurangi Chardonnay (★★★☆)

Mahurangi Estate lies near Warkworth, north of Auckland. Fermented and lees-aged for six months in one and two-year-old French and American oak barriques, the 2002 vintage (★★★☆) is pale lemon/green, creamy and sweetly oaked, with good weight and depth of peachy, citrusy, slightly mealy flavour and lots of upfront appeal. Good-value drinking during 2004.

DRY $18 V+

Main Divide Chardonnay ★★★★

The Main Divide range is from Pegasus Bay. The weighty, flavour-packed 2001 vintage (★★★★) is a blend of Canterbury and Marlborough grapes, fermented and lees-aged for 10 months in one-year-old French oak casks, with partial malolactic fermentation. It offers rich grapefruit, melon and slight butterscotch flavours, with a subtle backdrop of oak and fresh acidity on the finish. Delicious in its youth, it's a top buy at under $20.

Vintage	02	01	00	99
WR	6	7	6	6
Drink	03-05	03-05	03-04	P

DRY $19 V+

Margrain Martinborough Chardonnay ★★★★☆

This is typically a powerful, sophisticated wine with rich fruit wrapped in toasty, nutty oak and impressive weight and depth. French oak-fermented and wood-aged for 10 months, the 2002 vintage (★★★★) is a tight, elegant wine with good concentration of peachy, citrusy flavour, nutty oak, a hint of butterscotch and fresh acidity. It should mature gracefully; open mid-2004+.

Vintage	02	01	00	99	98
WR	6	6	6	7	6
Drink	03-06	03-06	03-05	03-05	03-04

DRY $32 AV

Marsden Black Rocks Chardonnay ★★★

This Kerikeri, Bay of Islands wine has shown varying form, but the very impressive 2000 (★★★★☆) was fleshy, rich and rounded. There is no 2001. Fermented in French (75 per cent) and American oak casks, the 2002 vintage (★★★) is a robust, oaky wine. The bouquet is toasty; the palate creamy and full-flavoured, with some concentration and potential to develop, but also rather heavy-handed use of wood.

DRY $30 -V

Marsden Estate Chardonnay ★★★

Estate-grown at Kerikeri, in the Bay of Islands, and fermented in French and American oak casks, the 2002 vintage (★★★☆) of this Northland wine is a strongly wooded style with lots of character. Bright, light lemon/green, it shows good body and fruit ripeness, with plenty of peachy, toasty flavour.

Vintage	02	01
WR	5	4
Drink	03-05	P

DRY $22 -V

Martinborough Vineyard Chardonnay ★★★★★

Mouthfilling, peachy, citrusy and mealy, this classic wine is typically powerful and harmonious, with concentrated flavours and rich, savoury characters. Made entirely from fruit grown on the gravelly Martinborough Terrace, it is fully fermented (with use of indigenous yeasts since 1997) in French oak barriques (25 to 30 per cent new each year). The 2000 vintage is drinking well now, with grapefruit, toast and nut flavours, deep and smooth. The 2001 (★★★★★), made with full malolactic fermentation and lees-aged for a year, is a tight, immaculate, Burgundian style with a fresh, mealy, citrusy bouquet. The palate is poised and slightly minerally, with intense grapefruit and biscuit flavours woven with fresh acidity and a hint of butterscotch. A great prospect for cellaring.

Vintage	01	00	99	98	97	96
WR	7	6	7	7	6	7
Drink	03-06	03-07	03-04	P	P	P

DRY $32 V+

Matakana Estate Chardonnay ★★★★

Estate-grown north of Auckland, this is typically a stylish wine with ripe, mealy, biscuity flavours and impressive complexity. The light gold 2000 vintage (★★★★), fermented and lees-aged for 11 months in French oak barriques (over 40 per cent new), is mouthfilling, with well-rounded grapefruit and toast flavours showing excellent depth and complexity. The 2002 (★★★★) is still youthful, with a slightly creamy texture, strong stone-fruit flavours and substantial body.

DRY $29 AV

Matariki Hawke's Bay Chardonnay ★★★★

This is a consistently rewarding wine. It is grown in Gimblett Road (principally), with a smaller portion of fruit cultivated in limestone soils on the east side of Te Mata Peak giving 'a flinty, lime character'. Fermented in French oak barriques and lees-stirred for 10 months, the 2001 vintage (★★★☆) is a tight, minerally, lively wine with grapefruit and toast flavours, fresh acidity and considerable depth and complexity. Slightly austere in its youth, it should mature well; open 2004+.

Vintage	01	00	99	98
WR	6	7	7	7
Drink	04-07	03-04	P	P

DRY $27 AV

Matariki Reserve Chardonnay ★★★★☆

This Hawke's Bay wine is grown at Gimblett Road and Te Mata Peak (see above) and fermented (partly with indigenous yeasts) in all-new French oak barriques. Bright, medium yellow, the 2001 vintage (★★★★) is a high-flavoured wine with grapefruit and slight honey characters, toasty oak and fresh acid spine, but slightly less rich, ripe and rounded than the 2000 (★★★★☆).

Vintage	01	00
WR	6	7
Drink	04-07	03-05

DRY $36 -V

Matawhero Reserve Chardonnay ★★★☆

The quality of this Gisborne label has varied. At its best, the wine is rewardingly robust, complex and rich-flavoured, and can age well (the 1994 was still drinking well in 2002), but some vintages have looked tired. Fermentation with indigenous yeasts and full use of malolactic fermentation gives a less fruit-driven style than is the norm with Gisborne Chardonnay. Toasty and nutty on the nose, the golden 1999 vintage (★★★★) shows excellent body and richness, with deep stone-fruit flavours and a hint of butterscotch. Drink now.

DRY $29 -V

Matua Valley Ararimu Chardonnay ★★★★☆

This is Matua Valley's premier Chardonnay, as its price underlines. The 2000 vintage (★★★★★), based on low-cropping vines (all clone 15) in the Judd Estate vineyard in Gisborne, was hand-harvested and matured, with regular lees-stirring, for 11 months in new French and American oak barriques. It's a gorgeous wine, softly textured and beautifully harmonious, with highly concentrated, citrusy, peachy flavours wrapped in quality oak. The 2001 vintage (★★★★) brought a switch to the Petrie vineyard, near Masterton. Light gold, it's a tightly structured wine with grapefruit-like flavours and some creamy richness, but less opulent than the 2000. Tasted very shortly after it was bottled (and not rated), the 2002 vintage was again grown in the Judd Estate vineyard in Gisborne. A powerful, fat, oily wine with rich grapefruit and toast characters, it should unfold into a classic Ararimu.

Vintage	02	01	00	99	98
WR	7	7	7	6	6
Drink	04-07	03-08	03-05	04+	04+

DRY $42 -V

Matua Valley Eastern Bays Chardonnay ★★★

This moderately priced wine is a fruit-driven style with fresh, crisp, citrusy flavours and a touch of French and American oak adding depth. The 2002 vintage (★★★), blended from Gisborne and Hawke's Bay grapes, is freshly scented and vibrantly fruity, with good depth of melon and pear-like flavours and a smooth finish. A good all-purpose white.

Vintage	02
WR	4
Drink	P

DRY $17 AV

Matua Valley Judd Estate Chardonnay ★★★★

Grown in the company-owned Judd Estate vineyard in Gisborne, this is a consistently delicious, softly mouthfilling, vibrantly fruity wine with considerable complexity. Over the past few years, its volume has gone down while the price and quality have moved up. The 2002 vintage (★★★★) was fermented and matured for eight months, with lees-stirring, in French and American oak barriques. A fresh, tight, complex wine with strong, youthful flavours of citrus fruits, pears and toast, a strong, sweet oak influence and lingering finish, it should mature well.

Vintage	02	01	00	99
WR	7	6	6	5
Drink	03-07	03-04	03-05	P

DRY $29 AV

Matua Valley Matheson Chardonnay ★★★★

This is one of the best Chardonnay buys around. It is grown in the company's Matheson Vineyard at Maraekakaho, in Hawke's Bay, and the 2002 vintage (★★★★) was fermented and lees-aged five months in French oak casks, with 15 per cent malolactic fermentation. A shining example of the fruit-driven style, it is full-bodied, finely balanced and moderately complex, with fresh fruit aromas, ripe grapefruit and peach flavours to the fore, a hint of butterscotch and a bone-dry, well-rounded finish. (The Museum Release 2000 [★★★★] is drinking well now, with grapefruit, butter and toast flavours, fresh and smooth.)

Vintage	02	01	00	99	98
WR	7	6	6	6	7
Drink	03-07	03-04	03-05	P	P

DRY $21 V+

Matua Valley Settler Chardonnay ★★☆

This low-priced, fruit-driven Chardonnay is a blend of Gisborne and Hawke's Bay grapes, with a hint of wood achieved by immersing oak staves in the wine in tank, rather than barrel-aging. Light lemon/green, the 2002 vintage (★★☆) is a very easy-drinking style with fresh, simple, lemony, appley flavours and a smooth, off-dry finish.

Vintage	03	02
WR	5	4
Drink	03-05	P

MED/DRY $13 AV

Matua Valley Shingle Peak Marlborough Chardonnay ★★★

Until recently, this wine was labelled solely as Shingle Peak, but now features the Matua Valley brand as well. It is typically a fresh, fruit-driven style with well-integrated oak and a smooth finish. The 2002 vintage (★★★) was fermented in French and American oak casks (20 per cent new). Vibrantly fruity, lemony and appley, it's a very easy-drinking style, with slight sweetness (5 grams/litre of sugar) adding smoothness, but for the price, I'd expect a bit more richness and complexity.

Vintage	02	01	00	99	98
WR	6	5	6	5	6
Drink	03-06	03-04	P	P	P

MED/DRY $21 -V

McCashin's Nelson Chardonnay (★★★☆)

The debut 2001 vintage (★★★☆) is a richly fragrant wine, fermented in new and one-year-old French oak barriques and given a full malolactic fermentation. It's a bold, high-flavoured style with grapefruit, peach and toast characters, a hint of honey and a dry, rounded finish.

DRY $20 AV

Melness Chatham Chardonnay ★★★☆

The 2001 vintage (★★★★) is a tightly structured, complex wine, grown at two Canterbury sites (in Waipara and Cust, near Rangiora) and fermented and lees-aged in American oak barriques (one-third new), with full malolactic fermentation. A full-bodied wine, it displays strong grapefruit and peach flavours, with finely integrated oak, balanced acidity and a slightly limey, buttery finish.

Vintage	01	00	99	98
WR	5	6	5	6
Drink	03-05	03-04	03-04	P

DRY $22 AV

Mill Road Hawke's Bay Chardonnay ★★☆

Morton Estate's bottom-tier, faintly oaked Chardonnay is typically fresh and lively, with lemony fruit characters in an uncomplicated style. The 2000 vintage (★★☆) is citrusy, appley, clean and simple, in a full-bodied style with crisp acidity. Re-tasted in 2003, it was still fresh, softening and maturing well.

Vintage	00	99	98
WR	6	6	6
Drink	03-04	P	P

DRY $12 V+

Mills Reef Elspeth Chardonnay ★★★★☆

Mills Reef's flagship Chardonnay, named in honour of owner and winemaker Paddy Preston's mother (who died in 2003), is consistently rewarding. It is grown in Mere Road, near Gimblett Road, in Hawke's Bay, hand-picked and fully French oak-fermented, with about 60 per cent of the final blend put through malolactic fermentation. The 2002 vintage (★★★★★) is a very sophisticated wine with a complex, nutty, minerally bouquet. Tightly structured, elegant and intense, with beautifully harmonious grapefruit, fig and butterscotch flavours, it is weighty, dry and persistent. An understated, rather than brash, style, it should be long-lived.

Vintage	02	01	00	99	98	97	96
WR	7	6	7	6	6	7	7
Drink	04-06	03-04	03-04	P	P	P	P

DRY $30 AV

Mills Reef Hawke's Bay Chardonnay ★★★

Mills Reef's bottom-tier Chardonnay is an easy-drinking, slightly off-dry wine, grown in the Meeanee district. About 60 per cent of the blend is oak-aged, and 20 per cent goes through a softening malolactic fermentation. The 2002 vintage (★★★) is tight and youthful, with crisp, delicate, lemony flavours, subtle oak and satisfying depth.

Vintage	02	01	00	99	98
WR	7	6	5	7	7
Drink	03-04	P	P	P	P

MED/DRY $16 AV

Mills Reef Reserve Cooks Beach Chardonnay ★★★☆

Grown at the Shakespeare Cliff vineyard, on the Coromandel Peninsula, the 2000 vintage (★★★☆) is a fat, rounded wine with ripe peach and grapefruit flavours, a soft middle palate and savoury, mealy characters adding complexity. Light/medium gold, the 2001 (★★★) looks quite developed for its age. The palate is plump and soft, with peachy, slightly honeyed characters in a forward style with very good depth of flavour. I see it as a drink-young rather than cellaring proposition.

DRY $20 AV

Mills Reef Reserve Hawke's Bay Chardonnay ★★★★

Mills Reef's middle-tier Chardonnay. Fermented and matured for nine months in French oak casks, it is typically excellent value (the unexpectedly classy 2000 vintage was one of the best buys on the market). The 2002 (★★★★) is still youthful, with rich butterscotch, peach and toast flavours, in a classic regional style. Full-bodied, with good acid balance and a tight finish, it should unfold well over the next couple of years.

Vintage	02	01	00	99	98
WR	7	6	7	5	7
Drink	03-05	03-04	P	P	P

DRY $20 V+

Mills Reef Reserve Te Horo Chardonnay ★★★★

Grown on the Kapiti Coast, north of Wellington, the straw-hued 2001 vintage (★★★★) is soft and rich, with stone-fruit and butterscotch flavours and lots of toasty oak. Full-bodied and creamy, it's delicious in its youth.

DRY $21 V+

Millton Clos de Ste Anne Chardonnay ★★★★★

Millton's memorable flagship Chardonnay, only made in top vintages (1992, 1995, 1998, 2002) is grown in the steep, north-east-facing Naboth's Vineyard in the Poverty Bay foothills, planted in loams overlying sedimentary calcareous rock. Fermented in all-new French oak barrels, then matured in older casks, it is deliberately not put through malolactic fermentation, 'to leave a pure, crisp mineral flavour'. The 2002 vintage (★★★★★) is stunning. Notably powerful, with a streak of minerality running through its stone-fruit and nut flavours, which show great depth, it's an unusually complex, distinctive, special wine. It's built to last (up to 10 years, according to James Millton), but its exceptional richness and harmony also give early appeal.

Vintage	02	01	00	99	98	97	96	95
WR	7	NM	NM	NM	7	NM	NM	7
Drink	03-11	NM	NM	NM	03-07	NM	NM	P

DRY $45 AV

Millton Gisborne Chardonnay Opou Vineyards ★★★★

This is Millton's middle-tier Chardonnay, in the past labelled as Barrel Fermented Chardonnay. Grown organically and fermented in French oak barriques, it is typically soft and ripe, with peach and citrus-fruit flavours and mealy, oaky characters adding richness in a very harmonious style with good mouthfeel and loads of personality.

DRY $22 V+

Millton Gisborne Vineyards Chardonnay ★★★

This is a drink-young style with its accent on ripe-fruit flavours. The 2002 vintage (★★★) was grown in the company's Riverpoint, Opou and Te Arai vineyards, tank-fermented and 50 per cent oak-aged. It's a mouthfilling wine with fresh, ripe grapefruit and peach flavours and a sliver of sweetness to smooth the finish.

DRY $18 AV

Mission Hawke's Bay Chardonnay ★★★

Winemaker Paul Mooney certainly knows how to make Chardonnay taste delicious at just a few months old, and his wine has shown distinct quality advances in recent vintages. The 2002 vintage (★★★), handled with some exposure to French and American oak, is fresh, smooth, lemony and slightly buttery in a fruit-driven style, crisp, ripe and flavoursome.

DRY $15 V+

Mission Jewelstone Chardonnay ★★★★★

The 2000 vintage (★★★★★), estate-grown at Greenmeadows, near Napier, was very complex and harmonious, and a great buy at under $30. Arguably Mission's greatest wine to date, the 2002 (★★★★★) was grown further south, at Patangata, in the Tukituki Valley of Central Hawke's Bay, fermented and matured for nine months in French oak casks (45 per cent new), and given a full, softening malolactic fermentation. Beautifully scented, with highly concentrated grapefruit and stone-fruit flavours, buttery, oaky complexities, fresh acidity and a rich, rounded finish, it's a strikingly good, very refined wine that could easily justify a much higher price. Not to be missed.

Vintage	02	01	00
WR	6	5	5
Drink	03-07	03-05	03-04

DRY $28 V+

Mission Moteo Reserve Chardonnay (★★★★)

Grown at Moteo in Hawke's Bay, given a full, softening malolactic fermentation and matured for nine months in French oak casks (30 per cent new), the 2001 vintage (★★★★) is a softly mouthfilling style with a creamy texture and generous palate showing some butterscotch characters and excellent flavour depth.

DRY $21 V+

Mission Reserve Chardonnay ★★★★

For Mission's middle-tier Chardonnay, the style goal is a wine that 'emphasises fruit characters rather than oak, but offers some of the benefits of fermentation and maturation in wood'. The 2002 vintage (★★★★) is a blend of grapes grown at Ngatarawa and Patàngata (a new limestone-based site above the Tukituki River, in Central Hawke's Bay). Fermented and matured for 10 months on its lees in French oak casks (25 per cent new), it's a weighty, nutty and toasty wine, fresh and immaculate, with strong malolactic fermentation characters, peachy fruit, and good texture and length.

Vintage	02	01	00	99
WR	5	5	5	6
Drink	03-05	03-05	03-04	P

DRY $21 V+

Mission Unoaked Chardonnay (★★★☆)

Delicious now, the debut 2002 (★★★☆) was grown at Patutahi, in Gisborne, and clearly reflects the region's outstanding vintage. Ripely scented, it's a weighty wine with good depth of fresh, tropical-fruit flavours and a seductively smooth finish.

DRY $15 V+

Moana Park Barrique Fermented Chardonnay (★★★)

Golden, with toast and butterscotch aromas, the 2001 vintage (★★★) is an upfront style of Hawke's Bay wine with plenty of peachy, slightly minerally and honeyed flavour and a crisp finish.

DRY $20 -V

Montana Gisborne Chardonnay ★★★

This hugely popular Chardonnay ('New Zealand's favourite since 1973', according to the back label) is typically an undemanding wine, fresh, fruity and smooth, although recent vintages are slightly more complex than the simple wines of the past. The 2002 vintage (★★★) was 'partly' (no doubt *very* partly) barrel-fermented, with 7 per cent malolactic fermentation. Re-tasted in August 2003, it has fresh fruit aromas leading into a full-bodied and flavourful wine with subtle oak (American) and a slightly buttery, dry, well-rounded finish.

Vintage	03	02	01	00
WR	5	7	4	6
Drink	03-05	03-04	P	P

DRY $15 V+

Montana Ormond Estate Chardonnay ★★★★★

This is Montana's flagship Gisborne Chardonnay, made for cellaring (more so than its Hawke's Bay equivalent, Church Road Reserve Chardonnay). Grown in the company's Ormond Estate vineyard, it is mostly (but not entirely) hand-harvested, whole-bunch pressed, fermented in French oak barriques (43 per cent new in 2002) and matured on its yeast lees, with regular stirring, for 10 months. The powerful 2002 vintage (★★★★☆) is fragrant, with substantial body (14 per cent alcohol), concentrated, ripe, tropical-fruit flavours, plenty of toasty oak and a deliciously creamy texture. It's still unfolding, but already a lovely mouthful.

Vintage	02	01	00	99	98
WR	7	NM	7	6	7
Drink	03-10	NM	03-06+	03+	03-05

DRY $29 V+

Montana Renwick Estate Chardonnay ★★★★☆

This is the company's top Marlborough Chardonnay. It is typically a tight, richly flavoured wine with citrusy characters and firm acidity in cooler years and creamy, tropical-fruit characters in warm years. The light yellow 2000 vintage (★★★★) was hand-picked in the centre of the

Wairau Valley and fermented and lees-aged for 10 months in French oak barriques (55 per cent new). It's a flinty but not austere wine with lemony, toasty flavours showing excellent depth. Complex and tautly structured, with firm acid spine and richness through the palate, it shows some maturity; drink now onwards.

Vintage	00	99	98	97	96
WR	6	7	7	7	6
Drink	03-06	03-06+	03-04	P	P

DRY $24 V+

Montana Reserve Marlborough Chardonnay ★★★★

A proven winner. The 1996 vintage (★★★★☆) rocketed off shelves in late 1997 after winning a Best White Wine of the Year trophy at the International Wine Challenge in London – an award reserved for fine-quality wines that must also be readily available and sharply priced. Then the smooth, harmonious and deliciously full-flavoured 2000 (★★★★★) won the Best Buy of the Year Award in the *Buyer's Guide*. Grown in Montana's Renwick and Brancott Vineyards, the wine is predominantly fermented and lees-aged for nine months in French and American oak barriques (22 per cent new in 2002). Already delicious, the 2002 vintage (★★★★) is fleshy and skilfully balanced, with loads of citrusy, toasty flavour, attractive mealy notes and a creamy-smooth finish. It's an upfront style, but matures well.

Vintage	02	01	00	99	98
WR	6	7	7	7	7
Drink	03-08	03-05	03-04	P	P

DRY $20 V+

Montana Timara Chardonnay – see Timara Chardonnay

Morton Estate Black Label Hawke's Bay Chardonnay ★★★★★

Grown at the company's cool, slightly elevated Riverview Vineyard at Mangatahi, this is one of the classiest of all New Zealand Chardonnays. It's typically a powerful wine, robust and awash with flavour, yet highly refined, with beautifully intense citrusy fruit, firm acid spine and the structure to flourish with age. It is fully barrel-fermented, and given the wine's concentrated fruit characters, the French oak barriques are 80 per cent new. Released at three and a half years old, the 2000 vintage (★★★★★) is a very elegant wine with a youthful, light yellow hue. Very typical of the label, it offers fresh, vibrant and rich grapefruit and nut flavours, with mealy, minerally complexities and a tautness, delicacy and intensity that promises further development in the bottle. Best drinking 2004–05.

Vintage	00	99	98	97	96	95	94
WR	7	NM	7	NM	6	6	6
Drink	03-06	NM	03-04	NM	P	P	P

DRY $35 AV

Morton Estate Boar's Leap Hawke's Bay Chardonnay ★★★

Named after a limestone cliff near the Riverview vineyard in Hawke's Bay and made without any wood-aging (although, unlike the 2000, it is not labelled as Boar's Leap Unoaked Chardonnay), the 2002 vintage (★★★☆) is a satisfying example of the fruit-driven Chardonnay style. Bright, light lemon/green, it is buoyantly fruity, with fresh, strong, citrusy flavours, showing considerable richness, appetising acidity and good body (reflecting a surprisingly high alcohol level of 14.5 per cent).

Vintage	02	01	00
WR	6	NM	6
Drink	03-05	NM	P

DRY $17 AV

Morton Estate Coniglio Chardonnay – see Coniglio Hawke's Bay Chardonnay

Morton Estate Riverview Hawke's Bay Chardonnay ★★★★

The 2000 vintage (★★★★) gives a rare opportunity to buy a mature, single-vineyard Hawke's Bay Chardonnay, approaching the peak of its powers. Grown at the same site at Mangatahi as the famous Black Label Chardonnay, and fermented and lees-aged for a year in French oak barriques, it's a very elegant, bright lemon/green wine with vibrant, grapefruit-like characters, slightly toasty and minerally, and the freshness and delicacy typical of wines from the cool, elevated Riverview site.

Vintage	00	99	98	97
WR	7	6	6	6
Drink	03-05	03-04	03-04	P

DRY $20 V+

Morton Estate Three Vineyards Hawke's Bay Chardonnay (★★★★)

The debut 1999 vintage (★★★★) is a blend of grapes from the elevated Riverview and Colefield vineyards, at Mangatahi (which give 'fine acidity'), and the newer Tantallon vineyard on State Highway 50, down on the Heretaunga Plains (which gives 'broader characters'). Fermented and matured for 11 months in French oak barriques, with partial malolactic fermentation, it's an elegant wine with tight, crisp, citrusy characters, well-integrated French oak and very good flavour length. Ready.

Vintage	00
WR	6
Drink	04-06

DRY $19 V+

Morton Estate White Label Hawke's Bay Chardonnay ★★★☆

Morton Estate's best-known Hawke's Bay Chardonnay is typically a fairly rich wine with ripe, citrusy fruit and gentle wood flavours. The 2000 vintage (★★★☆) was fully fermented and lees-aged in seasoned (one to five-year-old) French oak barriques, and 15 per cent went through a softening malolactic fermentation. Mouthfilling, fresh and rounded, its ripe, grapefruit-like characters are gently seasoned with biscuity oak, creating a moderately complex but full-flavoured and weighty wine with great drinkability.

Vintage	00	99	98	97	96
WR	6	6	6	5	6
Drink	03-05	03-04	P	P	P

DRY $17 V+

Morton Estate White Label Private Reserve Hawke's Bay Chardonnay (★★★☆)

The launch in 2002 of this label from the 1999 vintage (★★★☆) gave Morton Estate a total of 11 Chardonnays (under the Morton Estate, Coniglio and Nikau Point brands). It's a light gold, flavoursome wine with melon and grapefruit characters, buttery, biscuity complexities (from 11 months' maturation in French oak casks and lengthy bottle age) and a fully dry, slightly flinty finish. Ready.

Vintage	99
WR	6
Drink	03-04

DRY $19 V+

Morworth Estate Barrel Selection Chardonnay ★★★☆

The 2002 vintage (★★★☆) from this small Canterbury-based winery was grown in Marlborough and matured for 10 months in French oak barriques. A youthful wine with aging potential, it's citrusy, slightly toasty and creamy, with fresh acidity enlivening the finish.

DRY $24 AV

Moteo Terroire Reserve Chardonnay ★★☆

The 2002 vintage (★★★) of this Hawke's Bay wine ('terroire' is the winery's own spelling) is the best yet. Grown at Moteo, in the Omarunui Valley, hand-picked at 24 brix, and fermented with indigenous yeasts in French oak casks (40 per cent new), it was lees-aged in barrel for 10 months, with full malolactic fermentation. The bouquet is biscuity and mealy; the palate is robust (14.4 per cent alcohol) and rounded, with slightly honeyed, stone-fruit flavours and a strong, toasty oak influence. Drink now to 2004.

DRY $22 -V

Mount Cass Vineyards Waipara Valley Chardonnay (★★★☆)

Sharply priced, the 2001 vintage (★★★☆) shows good depth and harmony, with lively grapefruit and peach flavours, balanced acidity and mealy, toasty characters from fermentation and 15 months' aging in French oak casks.

Vintage 01
WR 5
Drink 03-04

DRY $19 V+

Mountford Chardonnay ★★★★☆

In top vintages, this rare Waipara wine offers splendidly rich melon, grapefruit and quality oak flavours, with a commanding mouthfeel. The 2001 vintage (★★★★☆) is light yellow, with a tight, nutty, mealy bouquet. A complex style, it shows excellent weight and intensity, with sweet, ripe-fruit flavours of grapefruit and peach mingled with butterscotch and mineral characters. The 2002 (★★★★★), fermented and matured for over a year in French oak barriques (30 per cent new), is a powerful, opulent wine with tremendous depth of stone-fruit and butterscotch flavours. Drink now to 2005.

DRY $39 -V

Mount Michael Central Otago Chardonnay ★★★★

Estate-grown on a site overlooking Cromwell, this is a consistently successful wine, one of the region's finest Chardonnays. Fermented and matured in French oak barriques (20 per cent new), the fragrant, mouthfilling 2002 vintage (★★★★) is a skilfully balanced wine with fresh, ripe grapefruit characters, good acid balance and finely integrated oak. It should age well.

Vintage 02 01 00
WR 6 6 5
Drink 03-06 03-04 P

DRY $23 AV

Mount Riley Marlborough Chardonnay ★★★

Mount Riley is named after the dominant peak in the Richmond Range, on the northern flanks of the Wairau Valley. The 2002 vintage (★★★) was fermented in a mix of stainless steel tanks (80 per cent) and new oak barriques (20 per cent), with full malolactic fermentation. A fresh, lively, fruit-driven style with a distinct touch of butterscotch, its grapefruit and apple flavours lack real complexity, but the wine is crisp and vibrantly fruity.

DRY $18 AV

Mount Riley Seventeen Valley Marlborough Chardonnay ★★★★★

The 2000 vintage (★★★★★), blended from several Wairau Valley vineyards, was fermented and matured for 11 months in French oak barriques (80 per cent new). Fragrant, rich and soft, it's creamy and concentrated in a notably generous and powerful style. The 2001 (★★★★★) is also a lush style, with well-managed use of barrel fermentation (French and American oak) and lees-aging adding a delicious creaminess of texture. Full-bodied, peachy, mealy and lingering.

DRY $30 V+

Moutere Hills Reserve Nelson Chardonnay (★★★☆)

The 2002 vintage (★★★☆) is one of the finest Chardonnays yet from this small Upper Moutere producer. It's an exuberantly oaked wine, full-bodied, with loads of peachy, toasty, buttery, slightly honeyed flavour in a very full-on style. The wood handling is a bit heavy-handed, but there's lots of character here.

Vintage 02
WR 7
Drink 03-04

DRY $27 -V

Mt Difficulty Central Otago Chardonnay ★★★☆

Grown at Bannockburn, this is typically a vibrantly fruity wine with subtle use of oak. The 2002 vintage (★★★☆) was 50 per cent oak-fermented; the rest was handled in tanks. Very fresh and buoyant, it's a distinctly cool-climate style with lively acidity, plenty of lemony, slightly nutty flavour and a crisp, flinty finish.

DRY $29 -V

Mt Difficulty Single Vineyard Mansons Farm Chardonnay (★★★★)

Fully barrel-fermented, the 2001 vintage (★★★★) was grown in the Mansons Farm Vineyard at the eastern end of the Kawarau Gorge, directly in the shadow of Mt Difficulty. It's a fresh and substantial wine (14.5 per cent alcohol), with good intensity of melon and citrus-fruit flavours, buttery, toasty characters adding complexity and an appetisingly crisp finish. Best drinking 2003-04.

DRY $29 AV

Mudbrick Vineyard Chardonnay ★★★☆

The 2002 vintage (★★★☆) was grown on Waiheke Island and fermented initially in stainless steel tanks, then in one and two-year-old French oak barriques. Bright, light yellow, with good weight and strong peach and lemon flavours, it's a gently wooded wine, balanced for early drinking.

Vintage 01 00
WR 5 5
Drink 03-04 04-05

DRY $29 -V

Muddy Water Waipara Chardonnay ★★★★☆

This is consistently one of Canterbury's finest Chardonnays. The intense, refined 2002 vintage (★★★★☆) was fermented with indigenous yeasts in French oak barriques (10 per cent new), with full malolactic fermentation. Light lemon/green, with a slightly nutty, complex bouquet, it has rich butterscotch and minerally characters on the palate, with fresh, balanced acidity and a long finish.

Vintage 02 01 00 99 98 97
WR 6 7 6 5 6 5
Drink 03-07 03-07 03-05 P P P

DRY $29 V+

Mud House Marlborough Chardonnay ★★★☆

The 2002 vintage (★★★☆) is a moderately complex style, French oak-aged for eight months, with toasty oak aromas and fresh, citrusy fruit flavours. Full and soft, it's a skilfully balanced wine with a slightly creamy texture.

DRY $20 V+

Murdoch James Martinborough Chardonnay (★★★☆)

An unoaked style, but not labelled as such, the 2003 vintage (★★★☆) was harvested at 24 brix and fermented dry. It's a mouthfilling wine (14 per cent alcohol) with fresh, vibrant grapefruit and peach flavours, showing balanced acidity and very good depth.

DRY $25 -V

Murdoch James Unoaked Chardonnay ★★★☆

This Martinborough wine is generally a high-alcohol style, fresh and crisp, with lemony, appley flavours and a dry finish. The 2002 vintage (★★★☆) is freshly scented and mouthfilling (14 per cent alcohol), with strong flavours of lemons and limes, vibrant and punchy. A very good example of the style.

DRY $25 -V

Mystery Creek Chardonnay (★★★)

Toasty and rounded, the 2002 vintage (★★★) is a blend of Waikato and Gisborne grapes, mostly (90 per cent) fermented in French and American oak barriques, with 50 per cent malolactic fermentation. Light yellow, it is fresh and weighty, with ripe, citrusy, buttery flavours, offering enjoyable drinking through 2004.

DRY $23 -V

Mystery Creek Reserve Chardonnay (★★★☆)

The weighty, high-flavoured 2002 vintage (★★★☆) was made from Waikato and Gisborne fruit, fermented in 'mostly new' French and American oak barriques, with full malolactic fermentation. Bright, light lemon/green, it shows very good body, with plenty of fresh, ripe, peachy, toasty flavour. Drink now onwards.

DRY $28 -V

Naked 17 Chardonnay (★★★)

Scantily dressed with a small, no-frills label giving only the barest details about the wine, the 2002 vintage (★★★) is available exclusively from Scenic Cellars in Taupo. Blended from Gisborne and Hawke's Bay grapes, it's a peachy, slightly buttery, toasty and honeyed wine, offering plenty of flavour for your dollar. An upfront style, it's now at its best.

DRY $10 V+

Nautilus Marlborough Chardonnay ★★★★

Typically a stylish wine with fresh, strong, citrusy flavours and finely integrated oak. The 2001 vintage (★★★★), fermented in French oak barrels (63 per cent) and tanks, is a refined wine, with fresh, slightly biscuity aromas leading into a finely balanced palate with smooth, delicate grapefruit and apple flavours, subtle mealy, leesy, oaky complexities and a long finish. The 2002 (★★★★) is tightly structured, with fresh, crisp grapefruit-like characters and a subtle, nutty oak influence in an elegant, fruit-driven style that should mature well.

Vintage	02	01	00	99	98
WR	7	6	6	6	6
Drink	04-06	03-05	03-04	P	P

DRY $27 AV

Neudorf Moutere Chardonnay ★★★★★

Superbly rich but not overblown, with arrestingly intense flavours enlivened with fine acidity, this rare, multi-faceted Nelson wine enjoys a reputation second to none among New Zealand Chardonnays. Grown in clay soils threaded with gravel at Upper Moutere, it is hand-harvested from old Mendoza clone vines, whole-bunch pressed, fermented with indigenous yeasts and lees-aged for a year in French oak barriques (half new, half one-year-old). Tasted in early 2003, the 1999 was light to medium yellow/green, with a Chablis-like nose – lemony and minerally – and tight, complex, slightly flinty palate. Only 300 cases were made of the opulent 2002 vintage (★★★★★). The bouquet is richly fragrant; the palate is seamless and superbly concentrated, with very deep stone-fruit and butterscotch flavours and a smooth, resounding finish. Hugely attractive in its youth, it's a drink-now or cellaring proposition.

Vintage	02	01	00	99	98	97	96
WR	6	6	6	6	7	6	6
Drink	03-13	03-10	03-09	03-08	03-08	03-07	03-05

DRY $45 AV

Neudorf Nelson Chardonnay ★★★★

Overshadowed by its famous stablemate (above), this regional blend is an excellent Chardonnay in its own right. The mouthfilling 2002 vintage (★★★★) was grown at four sites on the Waimea Plains and at Upper Moutere, and was fermented with indigenous yeasts in French oak casks (30 per cent new). An elegant, concentrated wine with ripe, citrusy flavours and mealy, toasty characters adding complexity, it's as good as many wineries' $30-plus labels, and already drinking well.

Vintage	02	01	00	99	98
WR	6	6	7	6	7
Drink	03-11	03-07	03-06	03-04	03-06

DRY $24 V+

Nevis Bluff Chardonnay ★★★

Grown at Gibbston, in Central Otago, the gently oaked 2001 vintage (★★★) is crisp, very lemony and buttery, with plenty of flavour in a moderately complex style with firm acid spine.

Vintage	02	01
WR	5	6
Drink	03-04	03-05

DRY $22 -V

Ngatarawa Alwyn Reserve Chardonnay ★★★★★

Based on 20-year-old vines in the estate vineyard in Hawke's Bay and fermented and lees-aged in all-new French oak barriques, with no malolactic fermentation, this is an arrestingly bold, highly concentrated wine. The tautly structured 2000 vintage (★★★★☆) is light yellow, with a toasty, mealy fragrance. The palate is rich, with intense grapefruit characters strongly seasoned with oak and firm acid spine. The 1998 and 1999 vintages took three years to reveal their full class and complexity. There is no 2001.

Vintage	01	00	99	98
WR	NM	6	7	6
Drink	NM	03-05	03-04	P

DRY $35 AV

Ngatarawa Glazebrook Chardonnay ★★★★

Ngatarawa's second-tier Chardonnay label is named after the Glazebrook family, formerly partners in the Hawke's Bay venture. Most – but not all – of the wine is fermented in new and older French and American oak barrels. Hard to resist in its youth, the 2000 vintage (★★★★) is fragrant and mouthfilling, with strong, ripe stone-fruit flavours and a deliciously creamy texture. Full-bodied, well-rounded and harmonious, it's a classic Hawke's Bay style. There is no 2001.

Vintage	01	00	99	98	97	96
WR	NM	6	7	6	6	6
Drink	NM	03-05	03-04	P	P	P

DRY $22 AV

Ngatarawa Stables Chardonnay ★★★

Ngatarawa's lower-tier Chardonnay is a mouthfilling, easy-drinking wine with some complexity; about half of the blend is fermented in French and American oak barrels. The 2002 vintage (★★★), grown in Hawke's Bay, is full-bodied and fresh, with plenty of peachy, slightly toasty flavour and a smooth finish.

Vintage	02	01	00	99	98
WR	5	6	6	6	6
Drink	03-06	03-05	03-04	P	P

DRY $16 AV

Nga Waka Martinborough Chardonnay ★★★★

The immaculate 2001 vintage (★★★★) was fermented and lees-aged for 10 months in French oak barriques (one-third new) and 20 per cent of the blend went through malolactic fermentation. It's a mouthfilling wine (14 per cent alcohol), light lemon/green in hue, with rich, grapefruit-like flavours, finely balanced acidity and mealy, buttery characters adding complexity. Re-tasted in August 2003, it's still youthful and maturing very gracefully.

Vintage 01
WR 6
Drink 03+

DRY $30 -V

Nikau Point Reserve Hawke's Bay Chardonnay (★★★☆)

In case you were wondering, the 'One Tree Hill Vineyards' in small print on the label is a division of Morton Estate. The debut 2000 vintage (★★★☆), hand-picked and French oak-fermented, offers good value. It's an elegant style, fresh and vibrant, with lively melon and grapefruit characters, some mealy, oaky complexity and good acid spine.

Vintage 00
WR 6
Drink 03-04

DRY $17 V+

Nikau Point Unoaked Hawke's Bay Chardonnay (★★★)

From Morton Estate, the 2000 vintage (★★★) is a good example of the style, with grapefruit and apple flavours and a crisp, tangy finish. Simple but youthful, fresh and lively.

Vintage 00
WR 6
Drink 03-04

DRY $14 V+

Nobilo Fall Harvest Chardonnay ★★☆

Grown in Gisborne, this is a dryish rather than bone-dry style, designed for easy drinking. The 2002 vintage (★★★) offers fine value. Smooth and full, with clean, ripe peach and melon fruit characters and a slightly buttery finish, it's not a complex wine, but offers some richness.

Vintage 02   01   00   99
WR 5   6   6   7
Drink 03-05 03-05 03-04 P

MED/DRY $13 AV

Nobilo Fernleaf Chardonnay ★★☆

Designed for easy drinking, the 2002 vintage (★★★) is a fleshy, creamy Gisborne wine, not complex but offering good depth of grapefruit-like flavours. It's a full, ripe, slightly honeyed wine in a forward style for current drinking. Great value.

Vintage 02
WR 5
Drink 03-04

MED/DRY $11 V+

Nobilo Icon Chardonnay ★★★★

Nobilo's middle-upper tier Chardonnay has been drawn from various regions since the first 1996 vintage, but the 2002 vintage (★★★★) is a blend of Gisborne and Hawke's Bay grapes. Oak-aged for 10 months, it's a light yellow wine with lots of toasty oak showing. Smooth, with loads of flavour, it's very much a style wine, with soft, peachy flavours and great immediacy and drink-young appeal. Drink 2003-04.

Vintage 02   01   00   99
WR 7   7   6   NM
Drink 03-06 03-04 P   NM

DRY $24 V+

Nobilo Poverty Bay Chardonnay ★★★☆

Top vintages are deliciously weighty, harmonious and well-rounded. French and American oak-aged, the 2002 (★★★★☆) is a freshly scented, peachy, citrusy Gisborne wine with finely balanced oak and acidity and strong, ripe-fruit flavours. Fleshy and slightly buttery, with lovely overall harmony, it's a wonderful bargain at $15.95 and the Best Buy of the Year (see page 11).

Vintage	02	01	00	99
WR	6	6	7	7
Drink	03-05	03-04	03-04	P

DRY $16 V+

Nobilo White Cloud Chardonnay – see White Cloud Chardonnay

Northrow Marlborough Chardonnay (★★★★)

Made by Villa Maria for on-premise (restaurant) consumption, the debut 2002 vintage (★★★★) is pale yellow, with a scented, mealy, sweetly oaked bouquet. Smooth, ripe peach/melon flavours hold sway, with gentle acidity and creamy, butterscotch-like characters giving a high level of drinkability. It's a drink-young style, probably at its best during 2004–05.

DRY $22 V+

Odyssey Gisborne Chardonnay ★★★

Odyssey is the personal label of Rebecca Salmond. A drink-young style, handled in a mix of tanks and seasoned oak casks, it's typically a crisp, fruit-driven, often slightly honeyed wine, flavoursome and smooth. The 2002 vintage (★★★) is a simple but well-made wine with fresh, crisp, lemony flavours.

Vintage	02	01	00	99	98
WR	5	5	6	5	5
Drink	03-06	03-05	03-04	P	P

DRY $18 AV

Odyssey Iliad Reserve Chardonnay ★★★★☆

The 2000 vintage (★★★★★) showed lovely delicacy and concentration, and the 2002 vintage (★★★★★) is another example of Gisborne Chardonnay at its finest. Hand-harvested in the Kawitiri vineyard in Gisborne, and fermented in French oak barriques (65 per cent new), it is richly fragrant, youthful and creamy, with a delicious array of ripe grapefruit, peach and fig flavours, very intense and long. A label worth discovering.

Vintage	02	01	00
WR	6	5	6
Drink	03-08	03-05	03-05

DRY $30 AV

Ohinemuri Estate Waihirere Reserve Chardonnay ★★★

The 2002 vintage (★★★☆) was 80 per cent barrel fermented, and half the final blend underwent a softening malolactic fermentation. Verging on four-star quality, it's a mouthfilling wine with beautifully ripe, melon/grapefruit flavours seasoned with biscuity oak, good delicacy and depth and a rounded finish. Drink now or cellar.

Vintage	02
WR	6
Drink	03-08

DRY $23 -V

Okahu Estate Clifton Chardonnay ★★★☆

The 2002 vintage (★★★) was produced from Hawke's Bay grapes (whereas the 2001 was a blend of Auckland [Te Hana, near Wellsford] and Hawke's Bay fruit). Fermented and lees-aged for nine months in American and French oak barriques, and given a full malolactic fermentation, it has strong drink-young appeal. Pale straw, it is smooth and creamy, with ripe, peachy fruit characters, a hint of butterscotch and a strong, toasty oak influence.

Vintage	02	01	00	99	98
WR	6	6	6	4	7
Drink	03-06	03-05	03-04	P	P

DRY $22 AV

Okahu Estate Clifton Reserve Chardonnay ★★★★

The lush, high-flavoured 2000 vintage (★★★★☆) is a blend of Northland (Okahu), Auckland (Te Hana) and Hawke's Bay grapes. Fermented and lees-aged for 15 months in new and one-year-old American (predominantly) and French oak barriques, with 60 per cent malolactic fermentation, it is fleshy, fragrant, smooth and concentrated, with rich, ripe, peachy fruit characters seasoned with sweet, toasty oak. It's a bold, softly seductive wine, drinking well now.

Vintage	00	99	98	97	96
WR	7	6	7	5	7
Drink	03-07	03-05	03-05	P	P

DRY $30 -V

Okahu Estate Ninety Mile Unoaked Chardonnay (★★★)

The 2002 vintage (★★★) is a full-bodied, smooth Gisborne wine with a lemon-scented bouquet, ripe, vibrantly fruity flavours and a well-rounded, off-dry finish.

MED/DRY $19 AV

Okahu Estate Shipwreck Bay Chardonnay ★★★

A fruit-driven style, 25 per cent oak-aged, the 2002 vintage (★★☆) is based mainly on grapes grown at Wellsford, north of Auckland. It's a crisp, lemony, appley wine, but lacks a bit of charm and richness.

Vintage	02	01	00
WR	6	6	7
Drink	03-05	03-04	03

DRY $18 AV

Old Coach Road Nelson Chardonnay ★★★☆

The 2002 vintage (★★★☆) from Seifried Estate is a great buy. Grown in Nelson and 40 per cent barrel-fermented (in one and two-year-old oak), it has toast, pineapple and butterscotch aromas leading into a mouthfilling, rich palate, mealy and slightly creamy. It's an upfront style, generous and long.

Vintage	02	01
WR	7	6
Drink	03-05	03-04

DRY $16 V+

Old Coach Road Unoaked Nelson Chardonnay ★★★

Seifried Estate's low-priced Chardonnay typically appeals strongly for its freshness and vigour. The 2001 vintage (★★★) is a citrusy, appley, cool-climate style, not complex but crisp and vibrantly fruity.

Vintage	01
WR	5
Drink	P

DRY $13 V+

Olsseń's of Bannockburn Barrel Fermented Chardonnay (★★★)

Maturing well, the 2000 vintage (★★★) is a robust (14.7 per cent alcohol) Central Otago wine, fermented in French oak barriques (20 per cent new). Bright, medium yellow/green, it offers strong lemon/grapefruit flavours, slightly appley and buttery, with a crisp, flinty finish.

DRY $27 -V

Olsseń's of Bannockburn Charcoal Joe Reserve Chardonnay ★★★★

Named after a nineteenth-century goldminer, the debut 2001 vintage (★★★★) is fresh, vibrant and strapping (14.5 per cent alcohol), with strong grapefruit and pear flavours. A youthful wine, fully fermented in French oak barriques (40 per cent new), it has ripe-fruit characters, excellent fruit/oak balance, a hint of butterscotch and good complexity. The 2002 (★★★☆) is citrusy, full-bodied and creamy, with considerable complexity and fresh acidity cutting in on the finish. It should open out well during 2004.

Vintage 01
WR 5
Drink 03-07

DRY $32 -V

Olsseń's of Bannockburn Chardonnay ★★★

This small Central Otago winery makes a consistently satisfying, barrel-fermented Chardonnay. The fragrant 2001 vintage (★★★☆) is a weighty wine (14.5 per cent alcohol), with ripe-fruit and oak aromas, showing good complexity, citrus and stone-fruit flavours, crisp, flinty acidity and a lingering finish.

Vintage 01 00 99 98
WR 5 4 4 5
Drink 03-06 03-05 03-04 03

DRY $27 -V

Olsseń's of Bannockburn The Bannockburn Club Chardonnay (★★★)

The unoaked 2002 vintage (★★★) is a Chablis-like wine from Central Otago with lemony, appley aromas, fresh and lively. It's a crisp, vibrantly fruity wine with cool-climate, green apple flavours, good freshness and vigour.

DRY $20 -V

Omaka Springs Marlborough Chardonnay ★★★

The latest vintages of this moderately priced wine are the best. The 2002 (★★★☆) is full-bodied and buttery-smooth, with good depth of fresh, citrusy flavour and a soft, creamy mouthfeel.

DRY $16 AV

Opihi South Canterbury Chardonnay ★★☆

The 2001 vintage (★★☆) was grown inland from Pleasant Point, near Timaru. Light lemon/green, with a slightly honeyed bouquet, it's a pleasant, medium-bodied wine, fresh and citrusy, but lacks any real weight and richness.

Vintage 01 00
WR 5 5
Drink 04-05 03-04

DRY $18 -V

Oyster Bay Marlborough Chardonnay ★★★☆

Made by Delegat's, this wine sets out to showcase Marlborough's pure, incisive fruit flavours. The 2001 (★★☆) was a lesser vintage, but the label is back on song from 2002 (★★★★). Past vintages were 75 per cent barrel fermented, but in 2002 this was cut back to 50 per cent, to achieve an even more fruit-driven style. Nevertheless, all of the final blend spent some time in casks, with 'heaps' of lees-stirring, but malolactic fermentation played no part in the recipe. It's an elegant wine, already drinking well, with fresh, ripe-fruit characters to the fore, finely integrated oak and a deliciously creamy texture.

Vintage	02	01	00	99	98
WR	7	6	6	6	7
Drink	03-04	P	P	P	P

DRY $20 AV

Palliser Estate Martinborough Chardonnay ★★★★★

Rather than sheer power, gracefulness, delicacy and finesse are the key attributes of this classic Martinborough wine. A celebration of strong, ripe, citrusy fruit flavours, it is gently seasoned with French oak, producing a delicious wine with subtle winemaking input and concentrated varietal flavours. It is barrel-fermented and lees-aged for nine months, but not lees-stirred, and the percentage of new wood is kept fairly low (25 per cent in 2002). The 2002 vintage (★★★★★) was partly (17 per cent) fermented with indigenous ('wild') yeasts and 14 per cent of the blend went through a softening malolactic fermentation. Astutely crafted, it has French oak aromas and notably concentrated, ripe citrus and stone-fruit flavours, delicately seasoned with toasty wood. Weighty and refined, with mealy, buttery characters adding complexity and a rich finish, it's a deliciously substantial, ripe and rounded wine. Drink now or cellar.

Vintage	02	01	00	99	98
WR	7	6	7	6	7
Drink	03-07	03-06	03-05	03-04	P

DRY $30 V+

Palliser Pencarrow Martinborough Chardonnay ★★★☆

Pencarrow is Palliser Estate's second-tier label, fermented and lees-aged in American and French oak casks. The easy-drinking 2002 vintage (★★★☆) is light yellow/green, full-bodied, citrusy, slightly honeyed and flavoursome, with some elegance and a slightly buttery finish. Drink now onwards.

Vintage	02
WR	6
Drink	03-04

DRY $18 V+

Park Estate Hawke's Bay Chardonnay ★★★

The American oak-matured 1999 vintage (★★★) matured very solidly, with lemony, toasty, bottle-aged characters and plenty of flavour and body. The 2001 (★★★) is a fleshy, slightly honeyed wine with some richness, drinking well now.

DRY $18 AV

Passage Rock Barrel Fermented Chardonnay ★★☆

The 2001 vintage (★★☆) is an assertively wooded, single-vineyard Gisborne wine, and the 2002 (★★★) is again a very upfront style (winemaker David Evans' goal is to make 'a big, luscious style of Chardonnay'). Grown in the Bridgewater Estate vineyard, it is light yellow/green, peachy, buttery, toasty and faintly honeyed, in a very full-flavoured style. Drink 2003–04.

Vintage	02
WR	5
Drink	03+

DRY $22 -V

Passage Rock Unoaked Chardonnay ★★★

The 2002 vintage (★★★) from this Waiheke Island winery is a single-vineyard, Gisborne wine. Handled entirely in tanks, it's a fresh, vibrant style with mouthfilling body (14 per cent alcohol), ripe citrusy, appley flavours, balanced acidity and a rounded finish.

DRY $17 AV

Pegasus Bay Chardonnay ★★★★★

Strapping yet delicate, richly flavoured yet subtle, this sophisticated wine is one of the country's best Chardonnays grown south of Marlborough. Muscular and taut, it typically offers a seamless array of fresh, crisp, citrusy, biscuity, complex flavours and great concentration and length. Estate-grown at Waipara, it is based on the shy-bearing Mendoza clone and fully fermented and lees-aged for a year in barrels (French oak, 25 per cent new in 2002). The 2002 vintage (★★★★★) is a fat, powerful, highly concentrated wine with rich, peachy, citrusy flavours seasoned with toasty oak and woven with fresh acidity. Robust (14.5 per cent alcohol), with commanding mouthfeel, it's a drink now or cellaring proposition.

Vintage	02	01	00	99	98	97	96
WR	6	6	5	7	6	6	6
Drink	03-09	03-08	03-06	03-08	03-06	P	P

DRY $33 V+

Peninsula Estate Anchorage Chardonnay ★★★

This rare Waiheke Island wine was formerly labelled 'Christopher'. Only 400 bottles were made of the 2001 vintage (★★★). Fermented in French oak barriques, it's a mouthfilling, strongly wood-influenced wine, citrusy, peachy and crisp.

Vintage	01	00
WR	6	5
Drink	03-05	03-05

DRY $28 -V

Peregrine Central Otago Chardonnay ★★★

The light yellow 2002 vintage (★★★☆) is the best yet. Fermented in stainless steel tanks (70 per cent) and French oak barriques, it's a characterful, full-bodied wine with balanced acidity and fresh, strong grapefruit, butterscotch and biscuit flavours.

Vintage	02
WR	5
Drink	03-04

DRY $23 -V

Phoenix Gisborne Chardonnay ★★★

Most of the Pacific winery's wines are labelled 'Phoenix'. The 2002 vintage (★★) was 60 per cent barrel-fermented, in a mix of American (two-thirds) and French oak. It's a robust but slightly heavy wine, lacking fruit sweetness and charm. I far prefer the Opaheke Chardonnay (below).

Vintage	02	01	00	99	98
WR	6	5	6	5	6
Drink	04+	03+	P	P	P

DRY $17 AV

Phoenix Opaheke Chardonnay (★★★☆)

The youthful, tightly structured 2002 vintage (★★★☆) was grown in South Auckland, lees-aged and 50 per cent barrel-fermented. Fresh and lively, with grapefruit, peach and slightly nutty and minerally aromas and flavours, it should age well; open 2004–05.

DRY $16 V+

Pleasant Valley Hawke's Bay Chardonnay (★★☆)

The 2002 vintage was aged on its yeast lees, with very little oak influence. Tasted the day before bottling (and so not rated), it looked promising, with fullness of body, fresh, vibrant fruit characters and a crisp, dry finish.

DRY $16 -V

Pukeora Estate San Hill Chardonnay (★★)

Grown near Hastings and made at the Pukeora Estate winery at Waipukurau, one hour south of Napier, the 2002 vintage (★★) is a light-bodied wine (11 per cent alcohol), aged briefly in new American oak barriques, with full malolactic fermentation. Light yellow, with a very oaky bouquet and flavour, it's a wood-dominated wine (at least at this stage), with lemony fruit flavours beneath and a crisp, dry finish.

DRY $15 -V

Ransom Barrique Chardonnay ★★★

Grown at Mahurangi, north of Auckland city, at its best this is a stylish wine with rich fig/melon flavours, fleshed out with subtle, mealy, nutty characters. The developed 2002 vintage (★★☆) was fermented and matured for 10 months in a mix of new and used French oak barriques. Golden, with a buttery, honeyed bouquet, it's a sturdy, peachy, toasty, obviously botrytis-influenced wine, with lots of flavour, but probably not for cellaring.

Vintage	02	01
WR	6	5
Drink	03-07	03-04

DRY $26 -V

Richmond Plains Nelson Chardonnay (★★★☆)

Grown organically, this is the company's 'most popular restaurant wine'. Full and fresh, with good depth of crisp, ripe citrus-fruit and melon flavours and subtle oak and malolactic fermentation influences, the 2001 vintage (★★★☆) offers plenty of character and is maturing solidly. Ready.

Vintage	01
WR	6
Drink	03-05

DRY $20 AV

Richmond Plains Reserve Chardonnay (★★★★)

Grown organically in Nelson and fully fermented in new French oak barriques, the 2001 vintage (★★★★) is a fat, robust, creamy-rich wine with impressive weight and flavour depth. Delicious drinking from now onwards.

Vintage	01
WR	6
Drink	04-08

DRY $25 AV

Ridgeview Estate Chardonnay (★★★)

Grown on Waiheke Island, the 2002 vintage (★★★) is light lemon/green, with plenty of citrusy, slightly mealy flavour and a slightly buttery finish. Good value by the island's standards.

DRY $17 AV

Rimu Grove Nelson Chardonnay (★★☆)

Grown in the Moutere hills, the 2001 vintage (★★☆) was hand-picked, whole-bunch pressed and 20 per cent French oak-fermented. Pale yellow, it's a dry, weighty, slightly minerally wine with grapefruit and pear characters and firm acid spine. Verging on three stars.

DRY $22 -V

Rimu Grove Reserve Chardonnay (★★★☆)

The 2001 vintage (★★★☆) is full of character. From a Mapua-based company, it was grown in heavy Moutere clays, hand-picked and whole-bunch pressed, and 60 per cent was fermented and lees-aged in French oak barriques (10 per cent new). Pale yellow, it's a tightly structured, slightly creamy, full-bodied wine with firm acidity and good flavour concentration.

DRY $32 -V

Rippon Chardonnay ★★★

Grown on the shores of Lake Wanaka, in Central Otago, this is typically a steely, Chablis-like wine with fresh, lingering, citrusy, appley flavours and a strong undertow of acid.

DRY $29 -V

Riverside Dartmoor Chardonnay ★★☆

This Hawke's Bay wine is typically a drink-young style with straightforward, lemony flavours. The faintly oaked 2002 vintage (★★☆) is light, appley and lemony, offering smooth, easy drinking. A solid but simple wine, priced right.

Vintage 02
WR 6
Drink 03-04

DRY $15 AV

Riverside Stirling Reserve Chardonnay ★★★★

Grown in the Dartmoor Valley of Hawke's Bay, top vintages of this wine are fragrant, intense and refined. Fermented and matured in new and seasoned French oak barriques, the 2000 (★★★★) is a beautifully harmonious wine with strong, ripe, citrusy fruit characters overlaid with biscuity, spicy oak. Fleshy and slightly buttery, with good complexity, it offers excellent drinking from now onwards.

Vintage 00 99 98
WR 7 6 6
Drink 04-05 03-04 P

DRY $30 -V

Robard & Butler Chardonnay ★★☆

Made by Montana, the 2002 vintage (★★★) is an unwooded style with an off-dry finish, blended from 'New Zealand's premier winegrowing regions'. Fresh and smooth, with good depth of ripe melon/peach flavours and a distinctly buttery finish, it's a fine-value quaffer.

Vintage 02
WR 5
Drink 03-04

MED/DRY $11 V+

Rockburn Central Otago Chardonnay (★★★☆)

From 'the best vintage in ten years', the 2002 (★★★☆) was principally handled in stainless steel tanks, but 35 per cent of the blend was barrel-fermented and 50 per cent went through malolactic fermentation. Grown at Gibbston (two-thirds) and Lowburn, in the Cromwell Basin, it's a crisp, lemony, nutty wine with a creamy 'malo' influence and some flavour richness.

DRY $30 -V

Rongopai Reserve Gisborne Chardonnay (★★★☆)

The creamy-smooth 2002 vintage (★★★☆) was grown at the Glencoe Estate vineyard and 75 per cent barrel-fermented (in new and older casks), with full malolactic fermentation. Sweetly oaked, it offers ripe grapefruit and peach flavours, slightly figgy and nutty, with a strong butterscotch influence and good depth. Drink now or cellar.

DRY $20 AV

Rymer's Change Chardonnay/Sauvignon Blanc ★★★

In the past (up to and including the 2001 vintage) known as Te Mata Oak Aged Dry White, this has typically been an easy-drinking Hawke's Bay wine, fresh and crisp, with moderate complexity, plenty of peachy, slightly buttery, limey flavour and satisfying body.

DRY $13 V+

St Francis Hawke's Bay Chardonnay ★★★☆

An easy-drinking, upfront style, the 2001 vintage (★★★☆) was grown near Taradale and handled in French and American oak, with 40 per cent malolactic fermentation. Light gold, with peachy, buttery, slightly honeyed flavours, it's full-bodied and forward, with good flavour depth and a smooth finish.

Vintage	01	00	99
WR	6	6	5
Drink	03-07	03-06	03-04

DRY $24 AV

Sacred Hill Barrel Fermented Chardonnay ★★★★

A typically delicious wine, robust, with rich, ripe, tropical/citrus-fruit flavours fleshed out with mealy, lees-stirred characters and toasty oak. The 2002 vintage (★★★★) is a Hawke's Bay blend of Ohiti Valley and estate-grown, Dartmoor Valley fruit, whole-bunch pressed and fermented and matured for six months in French and American oak barrels. It's a classic regional style, showing ripe grapefruit and stone-fruit characters, well-integrated toasty oak, a hint of butterscotch and a rich, rounded finish.

Vintage	02	01	00	99	98
WR	6	7	6	7	6
Drink	03-05	03-04	P	P	P

DRY $20 V+

Sacred Hill Riflemans Chardonnay ★★★★★

Sacred Hill's top Chardonnay is typically powerful and creamy, with lovely, ripe, very intense grapefruit and fig-like flavours (although the relatively lean, austere 2000 [★★★☆] is on a lower plane). Lush and lovely, the 2001 vintage (★★★★★) was grown in the Riflemans vineyard in the upper reaches of the Dartmoor Valley. Rich stone-fruit and toasty oak aromas, with minerally touches adding complexity, lead into a fleshy, rich, smooth and harmonious wine with intense peach, pear and butterscotch flavours.

Vintage	01	00	99	98	97
WR	7	5	7	7	7
Drink	03-08	03-06	03-05	03-04	P

DRY $35 AV

Sacred Hill Whitecliff Estate Unoaked Chardonnay ★★★

A fresh, smooth, flavoursome Chardonnay, made in a drink-young style. It is typically crisp and lively, with ripe, citrusy flavours and a slightly creamy finish. The 2002 vintage (★★☆), which makes no claims on the label about its region of origin, is lemony, appley and crisp, in a flavoursome, slightly honeyed, no-fuss style.

Vintage	02	01	00
WR	6	5	7
Drink	03-04	P	P

DRY $16 AV

Saint Clair Marlborough Chardonnay ★★★☆

Neal Ibbotson produces a smooth, full-flavoured wine with strong drink-young appeal. The 2002 vintage (★★★☆) was 50 per cent fermented in new and older American oak casks (the rest was handled in tanks), and two-thirds of the blend went through a softening malolactic fermentation. It's an instantly attractive, fresh, finely balanced wine with a slightly toasty nose,

CHARDONNAY

good depth of grapefruit-like, moderately complex flavour, and a fractionally off-dry (4.8 grams/litre of residual sugar) finish.

Vintage	02	01	00	99	98
WR	6	6	6	6	7
Drink	03-05	03-04	03-04	P	P

DRY $19 V+

Saint Clair Omaka Reserve Chardonnay ★★★★☆

A proven show-stopper, this is a fat, creamy Marlborough wine, weighty and rich, in a strikingly bold, upfront style. The 2002 vintage (★★★★☆) was fermented and lees-aged for 10 months in American oak casks (50 per cent new). Weighty and crisp, with sweet oak aromas, grapefruit and peach fruit characters and a sliver (4 grams/litre) of sweetness, in its youth it tasted slightly less seductive than the fleshy, lush, creamy-soft 2001 (★★★★★), but should come together well during late 2003 and 2004.

Vintage	02	01	00
WR	7	7	7
Drink	03-06	03-06	03-04

DRY $28 V+

Saint Clair Unoaked Chardonnay ★★★

Offering very easy drinking, this is typically a fruity Marlborough wine with simple but attractive tropical/citrus flavours. It is cool-fermented in tanks 'to maximise fruit flavours' and malolactic fermentation is used to 'add complexity and soften the acidity'. The 2002 vintage (★★★), grown in three vineyards, is fresh, lemony and appley, with a rounded finish and good drink-young appeal.

Vintage	02	01	00
WR	6	7	6
Drink	03-06	P	P

DRY $18 AV

Saints Gisborne Chardonnay ★★★☆

'Chardonnay is all about pleasure,' says the back label – and Montana's delicious wine delivers the goods. From one vintage to the next, this seductively smooth wine is one of the country's top Chardonnay bargains. It is typically grown in the company's vineyards at Patutahi and Ormond, and fermented and matured for six months in French and American oak barriques (20 per cent new). The 2002 vintage (★★★☆) is an upfront, creamy-smooth wine with lifted, toasty oak aromas and a deliciously well-rounded palate with strong, ripe peach/melon flavours and a buttery finish.

Vintage	02	01	00
WR	6	5	7
Drink	04	P	P

DRY $17 V+

Sanctuary Marlborough Chardonnay ★★★

A fruit-driven, 'lightly' oaked wine from Grove Mill that drinks well within a few months of the vintage. The 2002 (★★★) is a typically fresh, simple and vibrant wine with lemony, appley flavours, crisp and lively. Buoyantly fruity, the 2003 vintage (★★★) was mostly tank-fermented, with some malolactic fermentation, oak maturation and lees-aging. A full-bodied and rounded wine, it has citrusy, slightly limey flavours, fresh acidity and a dry, well-balanced finish.

Vintage	03	02	01
WR	7	7	6
Drink	03-05	03-04	P

DRY $15 V+

Sanderson Bellvine Chardonnay (★★☆)

The 2001 vintage (★★☆) is a Hawke's Bay wine, not oak-aged, with crisp, moderately ripe-fruit characters, lemony, appley and crisp.

DRY $14 AV

Schubert Hawke's Bay Chardonnay ★★★☆

Grown in Gimblett Road, the 2002 vintage (★★★☆) was fermented and aged for 10 months on its full ('gross') lees in French oak barriques and puncheons (50 per cent new), and then matured for another four months on its fine lees. Fresh and youthful, with the slight leanness typical of many of the district's Chardonnays, it's a citrusy, leesy, nutty, slightly limey wine, bone-dry, with lively acidity and good length. Open mid-2004+.

Vintage	03	02	01	00
WR	NM	6	NM	6
Drink	NM	03-10	NM	03-07

DRY $25 -V

Seifried Nelson Chardonnay ★★★☆

The quality of this wine has risen sharply in recent years. The fragrant 2001 vintage (★★★☆) was 50 per cent fermented in oak barriques; the rest was handled in tanks. The bouquet is peachy and toasty; the palate is mouthfilling, with ripe citrus and stone-fruit flavours, showing good depth and a slightly creamy texture.

Vintage	02	01	00	99	98
WR	7	6	6	6	6
Drink	04-06	04-05	03-06	03-04	P

DRY $19 V+

Seifried Winemaker's Collection Barrique Fermented Chardonnay ★★★★

This is a bold style, at its best concentrated and creamy-rich, with lashings of flavour, although some vintages have been American oak-dominated. Light gold, the 2001 (★★★☆) is a weighty Nelson wine with grapefruit and lemon flavours showing good ripeness, depth and roundness, balanced acidity, a hint of honey and plenty of toasty oak.

Vintage	01	00	99	98
WR	7	7	6	7
Drink	03-06	03-06	03-05	03-04

DRY $26 AV

Selaks Drylands Chardonnay – see Drylands Chardonnay

Selaks Founders Reserve Hawke's Bay Chardonnay (★★★★☆)

The beautifully fresh and rich 2002 vintage (★★★★☆) was hand-picked in the Pearce vineyard and fermented and lees-aged for 10 months in new and one-year-old French oak barriques, with full malolactic fermentation. Light lemon/green, with a fragrant, toasty bouquet, it's a tightly structured wine, mingling grapefruit, butterscotch and nutty oak flavours, very vibrant and concentrated. Drink now or cellar.

Vintage	02
WR	7
Drink	03-05

DRY $27 V+

Selaks Founders Reserve Marlborough Chardonnay (★★★★☆)

The classy 2001 vintage (★★★★☆) was hand-picked in the Woolley and Matador vineyards, and fermented – with some use of indigenous yeasts – and lees-aged for 10 months in new French oak casks. Light yellow, with a welcoming, biscuity fragrance, it is deliciously smooth, with rich citrus, stone-fruit and butterscotch characters and excellent depth, complexity and structure. Drink now or cellar.

Vintage	01
WR	7
Drink	03-04

DRY $27 V+

Selaks Premium Selection Marlborough Chardonnay ★★★☆

The 'standard' Chardonnay from Selaks usually shows a touch of class, and the 2002 vintage (★★★☆) is a top buy. Grown in the Rapaura and Renwick districts, tank-fermented and given 'a touch of oak', with full malolactic fermentation, it has butterscotch aromas leading into a very clean, vibrant and youthful palate, generous, peachy, mealy and rounded, with a smooth, lingering finish.

Vintage	02	01	00	99	98
WR	7	7	7	7	6
Drink	03-04	03-04	P	P	P

DRY $15 V+

Seresin Chardonnay ★★★★

This stylish Marlborough wine, estate-grown near Renwick, is designed to 'focus on the textural element of the palate rather than emphasising primary fruit characters'. It is typically a finely balanced, full-bodied and complex wine with good mouthfeel, ripe melon/citrus characters shining through, subtle toasty oak and fresh acidity. The 2002 vintage (★★★☆) was fermented (mostly with indigenous yeasts) in a mix of tanks and French oak barriques, with 60 per cent malolactic fermentation. The bouquet is fresh, youthful and buttery; the palate is vibrantly fruity, with strong grapefruit-like characters, cool-climate acidity and a slightly limey, nutty finish. Drink now onwards.

Vintage	02	01	00	99	98
WR	6	7	6	6	6
Drink	03-08	03-07	03-07	03-05	03-04

DRY $23 AV

Seresin Chardonnay Reserve ★★★★★

Finesse is the keynote quality of this classy Marlborough wine. Estate-grown near Renwick, hand-picked, French oak-fermented with mostly indigenous yeasts and lees-aged for over a year, it is typically a powerful wine, toasty and nutty, with citrusy, mealy, complex flavours of great depth. The 2001 vintage (★★★★★) has a beautifully fragrant and complex bouquet. Full of character, it is poised and vibrant, with grapefruit, fig and oak flavours, slightly minerally and buttery, and notable complexity and depth. Superb drinking from now onwards.

Vintage	01	00	99	98
WR	7	6	5	6
Drink	03-08	03-06	03-07	03-06

DRY $34 V+

Shepherds Point Chardonnay (★★★)

Made by the Mudbrick winery, the 2002 vintage (★★★) is based on first-crop vines at Onetangi, on Waiheke Island. Fermented initially in stainless steel tanks, then in seasoned French oak casks (where it was also matured on its yeast lees), it's a more woody wine than you'd expect (given the vinification details), with good body and crisp, dry, peachy, citrusy flavours. A moderately complex style, it needs time; open 2004 onwards.

DRY $29 -V

Sherwood Estate Chardonnay Reserve ★★★★

This is emerging as the small Waipara winery's top label. The 2000 vintage (★★★★), fermented in all-new French oak casks and matured for 11 months on its gross lees, is fresh and vibrant, with mouthfilling body and toasty, mealy, minerally complexities. It's a tautly structured wine with good potential. The 2001 (★★★☆) is the last vintage to be grown at West Melton, near Christchurch, where Sherwood was originally based. Matured in 50 per cent new oak, it's a weighty wine, citrusy, mealy and slightly creamy, with a crisp, slightly flinty finish.

DRY $30 -V

Shingle Peak Marlborough Chardonnay – see Matua Valley
Shingle Peak Marlborough Chardonnay

Sileni Cellar Selection Chardonnay ★★★☆

Designed for early drinking, the 2002 vintage (★★★☆) was blended from Hawke's Bay (55 per cent) and Gisborne grapes, and partly barrel-fermented. It's fresh and full-bodied, with crisp grapefruit and apple flavours and slightly buttery and leesy characters adding a touch of complexity.

Vintage	02	01
WR	7	7
Drink	03-06	03-04

DRY $22 AV

Sileni Estate Selection Chardonnay ★★★★☆

Since the debut 1998 vintage, Sileni has produced a consistently excellent Hawke's Bay Chardonnay. The 2000 vintage (★★★★☆) was the first to include grapes from the company's Plateau Vineyard at Maraekakaho. Hand-harvested, it got the works in the winery – whole-bunch pressing, fermentation (with some indigenous yeasts) in French oak barriques (65 per cent new), full malolactic fermentation and nine months' maturation on gross lees, with weekly lees-stirring. Slightly creamy, with a rich, mealy, biscuity bouquet and very good concentration, it's a powerful, multi-faceted wine with sweet, grapefruit-like characters, an impression of ripeness and harmony and a sustained finish. There is no 2001.

Vintage	02	01	00	99
WR	6	NM	7	6
Drink	04-08	NM	03-06	03-05

DRY $32 AV

Sleeping Dogs Chardonnay (★★★)

Grown in Roger Donaldson's vineyard at Gibbston, in Central Otago, and produced on his behalf by contract winemaker Dean Shaw, the 2001 vintage (★★★) is light yellow, robust and rounded, with peachy, strongly buttery flavours. It's an upfront style, ready for drinking.

DRY $20 -V

Soljans Barrique Reserve Chardonnay ★★★☆

The 2002 vintage (★★★☆) of Soljans' top Chardonnay, grown in Hawke's Bay, is fresh, vibrantly fruity and creamy, with grapefruit and pear flavours and integrated oak. It's a finely balanced wine, already drinking well.

DRY $20 AV

Soljans Hawke's Bay Chardonnay ★★☆

The 2002 vintage (★★☆) is a fruit-driven style, not wood-aged, but one-third of the blend went through a softening malolactic fermentation. Fresh and lively, with smooth, ripe, citrusy flavours, it's a no-fuss wine for current consumption.

DRY $16 -V

Solstone Estate Wairarapa Valley Chardonnay ★★★☆

Grown near Masterton, the 2001 vintage (★★★☆) was 50 per cent fermented in new French oak barriques. Fresh and weighty, it offers lemony, appley flavours, with subtle, spicy oak adding complexity and a rounded finish.

Vintage	01	00
WR	7	5
Drink	03-06	P

DRY $23 AV

Spencer Hill Coastal Ridge Nelson Chardonnay (★★★★★)

American Phil Jones built his Chardonnay reputation with a series of rich, creamy-smooth wines under the Tasman Bay label, based principally on Marlborough grapes. Now he's exploring the Chardonnay potential of his Coastal Ridge vineyard, just north of Nelson city, where the small Spencer Hill winery is based. The striking 2001 vintage (★★★★★) was French oak-matured for nine months, with full malolactic fermentation. Enticingly fragrant, with a bouquet of ripe-fruit and nutty oak, it's notably soft and rich, with great depth of peachy, mealy, buttery flavours, finely poised acidity and great power and presence through the palate. A top debut.

Vintage 01
WR 7
Drink 03-05

DRY $37 AV

Springvale Estate Chardonnay (★★☆)

American oak-aged, the 2001 vintage (★★☆) was grown at Alexandra, in Central Otago. It's a middleweight style with fresh, crisp acidity and lively, green-edged flavours, but lacks a bit of fruit sweetness and charm.

Vintage 01
WR 5
Drink 03-06

DRY $21 -V

Springvale Estate Unoaked Chardonnay (★★)

Grown at Alexandra, in Central Otago, the 2001 vintage (★★) is a simple style, crisp and lemony, but when tasted in early 2003, it lacked freshness and vibrancy.

Vintage 01
WR 6
Drink 03-05

MED/DRY $22 -V

Spy Valley Marlborough Chardonnay ★★★☆

The highly attractive 2002 vintage (★★★★) was harvested at over 24 brix in the Johnson Estate vineyard in the Waihopai Valley, and fermented and lees-aged for a year, with some use of indigenous yeasts, in French oak barriques (30 per cent new). Fresh, sturdy (14 per cent alcohol) and harmonious, it offers strong grapefruit and apple flavours and nutty oak complexities, with a creamy-smooth, yet bone-dry, finish.

Vintage 02 01 00
WR 6 6 5
Drink 03-06 03-06 03-05

DRY $20 AV

Squawking Magpie Chardonnay ★★★☆

Squawking Magpie is the label of Gavin Yortt, co-founder of the Irongate vineyard in Gimblett Road, Hawke's Bay. Also grown in Gimblett Road, the 2002 vintage (★★★☆) was hand-picked, whole-bunch pressed and fermented and lees-aged for 11 months in new French oak barriques. Fresh, nutty and creamy, it's a high-alcohol style (14.5 per cent), tight and youthful, needing at least another year to unfold, but with obvious potential.

DRY $33 -V

Squawking Magpie The Chatterer Chardonnay (★★★)

The 2002 vintage (★★★) was grown in Hawke's Bay and partly French oak-fermented, and 90 per cent of the blend went through malolactic fermentation. It's a much more forward style than its stablemate (above), fleshy and creamy, with citrusy, appley flavours showing moderate complexity. Drink 2003–04.

DRY $20 -V

Staete Landt Marlborough Chardonnay ★★★★

The 2001 vintage (★★★★) of this single-vineyard wine, grown in the Rapaura district, is very well crafted, with excellent depth of ripe, citrusy flavour, seasoned with quality oak, balanced acidity and a slightly creamy finish. The 2002 (★★★★) was hand-picked at 24.7 to 25 brix, whole-bunch pressed and fermented with some use of indigenous yeasts in French oak barriques (25 per cent new). Wood-aged for 15 months, with lees-stirring and full malolactic fermentation, it possesses rich, ripe, citrusy fruit flavours, integrated biscuity wood and a distinct touch of butterscotch. An elegant, concentrated and tightly structured wine, with a long finish, it should be at its best from mid-2004 onwards.

Vintage	02
WR	5
Drink	04-06

DRY $28 AV

Stonecroft Chardonnay ★★★★☆

Hawke's Bay winemaker Alan Limmer aims for a 'restrained style of Chardonnay with elegance and complexity which ages well'. His wine also has impressive weight and flavour richness. The 2002 vintage (★★★★☆) is one of the best yet. Fermented with indigenous yeasts and lees-aged for nine months in French oak barriques (50 per cent new), it's a fragrant, softly mouthfilling wine with sweet fruit characters of grapefruit and peach, a pronounced butterscotch influence and a long, rounded finish. Richly flavoured, it's still youthful; open mid-2004 onwards.

Vintage	02	01	00	99	98
WR	7	6	7	6	6
Drink	04-10	03-10	03-10	03-06	03-05

DRY $35 -V

Stoneleigh Marlborough Chardonnay ★★★

Now part of the Montana portfolio, Stoneleigh Chardonnays have typically displayed fresh, cool-climate, appley aromas, good weight, crisp, vibrant lemon/apple fruit flavours and a subtle oak and lees-aging influence. The easy-drinking 2002 vintage (★★★☆) is a full-bodied wine, handled in French (60 per cent) and American oak casks. Toasty, sweet oak aromas lead into a fresh and vibrant, citrusy wine with biscuit and butterscotch characters adding complexity and a creamy-smooth finish.

Vintage	02	01	00	99	98
WR	6	6	6	6	6
Drink	03-06	03-04	P	P	P

DRY $19 AV

Stoneleigh Vineyards Rapaura Series Marlborough Chardonnay ★★★★

The 2001 vintage (★★★★) is the first since the debut 1999. Fermented in French (85 per cent) and American oak barriques (25 per cent new), it's a deliciously full-flavoured and finely balanced wine, peachy, citrusy, mealy and toasty, drinking well from now onwards.

Vintage	02	01	00	99
WR	6	7	NM	7
Drink	03-07	03-04	NM	P

DRY $23 V+

Stony Bay Chardonnay ★★★

From the Matariki winery in Hawke's Bay, the 2002 vintage (★★★) has lots of drink-young appeal. Handled in French oak casks (50 per cent) and stainless steel tanks, it has ripe melon and citrus-fruit characters, cut with fresh acidity, and a slightly buttery finish.

Vintage	02
WR	7
Drink	03-05

DRY $20 -V

Stonyridge Row 10 Chardonnay ★★★★☆

Only 40 cases were produced of the highly impressive 2000 vintage (★★★★☆), sold exclusively at the Waiheke Island winery. It's a strapping, very mouthfilling wine with beautifully ripe, melon-like fruit characters seasoned with fine-quality oak. The 2002 (★★★★☆) was fermented and matured in French oak barriques (two-thirds new). Pale straw, with a complex bouquet of grapefruit, nuts and quality oak, it's a highly concentrated wine with figgy, nutty flavours, interesting minerally touches and loads of personality. It should mature well.

Vintage	02					DRY $49 ·V
WR	7					
Drink	04-06					

Stratford Martinborough Chardonnay ★★★★☆

Strat Canning (winemaker at Margrain Vineyard) also produces a consistently rewarding wine under his own Stratford label. The 2002 vintage (★★★★) was fermented and matured for 11 months in French oak barriques. It's a tight, youthful, elegant wine, built for cellaring, with strong citrusy and nutty flavours, minerally, crisp, dry and long. Open mid-2004+.

Vintage	02	01	00	99	98	DRY $32 AV
WR	6	6	6	6	6	
Drink	04-07	03-06	03-05	03-05	03-04	

Sunset Valley Chardonnay (★★★)

Pale yellow, the 2002 vintage (★★★) of this Nelson wine is full and citrusy, with ripe, grapefruit characters, a bare hint of sweetness and good depth.

DRY $19 AV

Tasman Bay Marlborough Chardonnay ★★★★

American Phil Jones, of the Tasman Bay (formerly Spencer Hill) winery at Upper Moutere, has built a glowing track record in comparative tastings around the world since his first Tasman Bay Chardonnay flowed in 1994. Seductively soft, rich and creamy-smooth, it is a hugely drinkable wine in its youth – it is typically irresistible at only 18 months old and peaks within two or three years. It is fermented entirely in stainless steel tanks, with full malolactic fermentation, and is not barrel-aged; instead, Jones immerses French and American oak staves in his wine. The 2002 vintage (★★★★) is an instantly engaging wine with mouthfilling body, rich, ripe citrus and peach flavours and a distinctly buttery, creamy-soft finish.

Vintage	02	01	00	99	98	DRY $19 V+
WR	6	6	7	6	6	
Drink	03-04	03-04	P	P	P	

Te Awa Farm Frontier Chardonnay ★★★★★

The 1996, 1998 and 2000 vintages (★★★★★) of this Hawke's Bay wine were all notably classy. Grown in the Gimblett Gravels district and fermented and lees-aged for a year in French oak barriques (30 per cent new), it displays intense grapefruit and nut characters, with excellent weight, texture and harmony. The yellow-hued 2001 vintage (★★★★) is more developed than the 2000 at a similar age, but complex, with very concentrated, peachy, mealy flavours, a distinct streak of minerality and good acid spine.

Vintage	01	00	99	98	97	96	95	DRY $35 AV
WR	7	7	7	7	NM	6	6	
Drink	03-08	03-06	03-06	03-04	NM	P	P	

Te Awa Farm Longlands Chardonnay ★★★★

Estate-grown in the Gimblett Road/Roys Hill area of Hawke's Bay, this is typically a fresh and harmonious, moderately complex wine, full-flavoured and rounded. The 2002 vintage (★★★★) is a fresh, vibrant, fruit-driven style, fermented and lees-aged for seven months in French and American oak casks. It's a satisfyingly full-bodied wine with ripe citrus and tropical-fruit aromas, with a subtle backdrop of oak, rich flavours of peach, fig and lemon, a hint of butterscotch and crisp finish. Delicious already.

Vintage	02	01	00	99	98
WR	7	7	7	7	6
Drink	03-06	03-04	03-04	P	P

DRY $20 V+

Te Kairanga Castlepoint Chardonnay ★★

The 2002 vintage (★★) is a simple, fruit-driven style made from Gisborne (65 per cent) and Wairarapa (35 per cent) grapes. Crisp and appley, it's strictly a quaffer, with a fractionally sweet, short finish.

MED/DRY $15 -V

Te Kairanga Gisborne Chardonnay ★★★

This is typically a drink-young style with fresh, vibrant fruit characters and restrained oak. The 2002 vintage (★★★), 30 per cent barrel-fermented, is lively and lemony, with a slightly creamy texture and some elegance.

Vintage	02	01	00	99
WR	6	NM	5	5
Drink	03-05	NM	P	P

DRY $20 -V

Te Kairanga Martinborough Chardonnay ★★★★

Te Kairanga's second-tier Chardonnay. The stylish, finely balanced and complex 2001 (★★★★) is scented and mouthfilling, with peachy, mealy flavours showing considerable richness. The elegant 2002 (★★★☆) was fully fermented and lees-aged for 10 months in French oak casks (20 per cent new), with 15 per cent malolactic fermentation. Fresh and vibrant, it has citrusy fruit flavours to the fore, with slightly creamy and nutty characters adding some complexity and a smooth, lingering finish.

Vintage	02	01	00	99	98
WR	6	7	7	NM	6
Drink	03-05	03-05	03-04	NM	P

DRY $25 AV

Te Kairanga Reserve Martinborough Chardonnay ★★★★☆

In top years, this is a distinguished wine with searching flavours and authoritative acidity. The 2001 (★★★) was hand-harvested at 25 brix and fermented and lees-aged for 10 months in French oak barriques (30 per cent new). It's a pale straw, very weighty wine (14.5 per cent alcohol), with concentrated, peachy, appley flavours and a slightly creamy finish. Slightly austere in its youth, less fresh and vibrant than the non-reserve model (above), it is not a long-term cellaring proposition. There is no 2002.

Vintage	02	01	00	99	98
WR	NM	7	7	7	5
Drink	NM	03-08	03-05	03-05	P

DRY $30 AV

CHARDONNAY   99

Te Mania Estate Reserve Chardonnay ★★★★☆

Typically a powerful, generous wine with heaps of oak seasoning, rich, concentrated, melon-like fruit and a long, silky finish. The 2002 vintage (★★★★☆) was fermented and matured for 10 months in French oak casks (40 per cent new). A substantial, weighty wine with very ripe, concentrated, citrusy fruit flavours wrapped in toasty oak, mealy, biscuity characters adding complexity and a distinct hint of butterscotch, it's well worth cellaring.

Vintage	02	01	00
WR	7	6	7
Drink	04-07	03-06	03-04

DRY $28 V+

Te Mania Nelson Chardonnay ★★★

The 2001 vintage (★★★) is a lightly oaked, moderately complex style with pleasing fullness of body, ripe grapefruit-like characters and a rounded finish. Both tank and barrel-fermented, the 2002 (★★★) is a gently wooded wine with ripe, grapefruit-like characters, fleshy and well-rounded.

Vintage	02	01	00	99	98
WR	6	6	5	6	6
Drink	03-06	03-05	P	P	P

DRY $19 AV

Te Mata Elston Chardonnay ★★★★★

One of New Zealand's most illustrious Chardonnays, Elston is a stylish, intense, slowly evolving Hawke's Bay wine. At around four years old, it is notably complete, showing concentration and finesse. The grapes are all grown in the Havelock North hills, and the wine is fully French oak-fermented and goes through full malolactic fermentation. The 2002 (★★★★★) is a wonderfully fragrant wine, creamy and nutty, with a distinct touch of butterscotch. The palate is weighty and well-rounded, with ripe grapefruit and peach flavours, mealy, toasty characters adding complexity and lovely depth and harmony.

Vintage	02	01	00	99	98	97	96
WR	7	7	7	7	7	7	7
Drink	05-08	05-07	03-07	03-05	03-05	03-04	03-04

DRY $35 AV

🍇 🍇 🍇

Te Mata Estate Woodthorpe Chardonnay ★★★☆

Formerly labelled as Te Mata Chardonnay, this Hawke's Bay wine is grown at the company's Woodthorpe Terraces vineyard in the Dartmoor Valley. Fermented in a mix of tanks and barrels, with full malolactic fermentation, the 2002 vintage (★★★★) showcases its beautifully ripe, citrusy fruit flavours, fleshed out with biscuity, buttery touches. Delicious drinking in its youth.

Vintage	02	01
WR	7	7
Drink	04-06	03-05

DRY $21 AV

Terrace Road Marlborough Chardonnay ★★★

Terrace Road is a Cellier Le Brun brand, reserved mainly for still (non-sparkling) wines, but also appearing on a mid-priced bubbly. The light yellow 2001 vintage (★★★☆) was fully fermented and lees-aged in French oak casks (20 per cent new). Fleshy and flavoursome, it shows ripe citrus-fruit characters woven with fresh acidity and some buttery, mealy complexity.

Vintage	01	00	99	98
WR	7	6	5	6
Drink	03-04	03-04	P	P

DRY $19 AV

Te Whare Ra Chardonnay ★★★

Estate-grown at Renwick, in Marlborough, the 2003 vintage (★★★☆) is a high-alcohol wine (14.5 per cent) with fresh, ripe flavours of pineapples, lemons and apples and a touch of butterscotch on the finish. It's a 'fruit-driven' style, already highly enjoyable.

Vintage 02 01
WR 6 5
Drink 03-06 03-05

DRY $18 AV

Te Whare Ra Duke of Marlborough Chardonnay ★★★☆

With winemaker Allen Hogan at the helm, Te Whare Ra produced distinctive, muscular, peachy-ripe Chardonnays. The wine went through a rough patch a few years ago, but it has been back on form since 1999. Already enjoyable, the 2002 vintage (★★★☆), based on the Mendoza clone, was fermented and matured on its gross lees in French oak casks, with partial malolactic fermentation. Slightly honeyed on the nose, it's a powerful and weighty (14 per cent alcohol) wine with ripe, peach and fig flavours showing some lushness and a moderate degree of complexity.

Vintage 02 01 00
WR 6 7 5
Drink 03-12 03-06 03-06

DRY $25 -V

Te Whau Vineyard Chardonnay ★★★★☆

Typically a very classy Waiheke Island wine with grapefruit and fig-like fruit characters showing good concentration, nutty oak and a long, finely poised finish. Fermented and matured for eight months in French oak barriques (one-third new), the 2002 (★★★★☆) is clearly a top vintage. Light yellow, with a nutty, minerally bouquet, it's an unusually complex wine with an array of peach, grapefruit, toast and nut flavours, youthful and intense. Already highly impressive, but with the structure to age, it's well worth cellaring for a year or two.

Vintage 02 01 00
WR 7 6 7
Drink 03-05 03 03-04

DRY $34 AV

Thornbury Marlborough Chardonnay (★★★★)

The richly flavoured, smooth 2001 vintage (★★★★) was grown in the company's Rapaura Road vineyard and fermented and matured for 10 months in French oak barriques (one-third new). The fragrant, biscuity nose leads into a refined, harmonious wine with strong, ripe citrus-fruit flavours, a hint of butterscotch and biscuity, nutty oak adding complexity.

Vintage 01
WR 7
Drink 03-06

DRY $24 AV

Three Sisters Clone 6 Chardonnay (★★★)

This rare wine flows from Central Hawke's Bay, 45 minutes' drive south of (and higher than) the Heretaunga Plains. The 2001 vintage (★★★), grown at Takapau and not wood-aged, has fresh, citrusy aromas. Balanced for easy drinking, it's a fruit-driven style, very clean, delicate and smooth, with lemony, appley flavours enlivened with crisp, lively acidity.

Vintage 01
WR 5
Drink 03-04

DRY $16 AV

Timara Chardonnay ★★☆
A decent quaffer, priced sharply. The 2002 vintage (★★☆) from Montana is an American oak-aged blend of New Zealand and Australian wines. Made in a 'soft, easy-drinking style', it is fresh, smooth and lively, with ripe citrusy flavours, well-balanced acidity, a hint of oak and a smooth, slightly sweet finish.

MED/DRY $11 V+

Tiritiri Chardonnay Reserve ★★★☆
Duncan and Judy Smith's tiny (0.27 ha), organically managed vineyard is in the Waimata Valley, 25 kilometres from the city of Gisborne. French oak-fermented and lees-aged for 10 months, the 2002 vintage (★★★☆) has a light gold colour, developed for its age. Fleshy and forward, with strong stone-fruit flavours seasoned with toasty oak, it's creamy and full of character, but may not be the long keeper the winery suggests (below).

Vintage	02	01	00	99	98
WR	7	5	NM	5	6
Drink	04-08	04-05	NM	03-04	P

DRY $28 -V

Tohu Gisborne Chardonnay ★★★
Made with 'a light touch of oak', the 2002 vintage (★★★☆) is more interesting than many of the region's Chardonnays, with some nutty, minerally characters surrounding its core of ripe, citrusy fruit. Slightly creamy and nutty, with good body and flavour depth, it offers very satisfying drinking from now onwards.

DRY $18 AV

Tohu Gisborne Reserve Chardonnay ★★★☆
The 2002 vintage (★★★★) was hand-picked and French oak-fermented. A youthful wine, full-bodied and ripe, with peachy fruit characters seasoned with toasty oak, it is fresh and full-flavoured, offering excellent drinking from mid-2004 onwards.

Vintage	02
WR	5
Drink	04-06

DRY $25 -V

Tohu Unoaked Chardonnay (★★★☆)
As a drink-young style, the 2002 vintage (★★★☆) works extremely well. Very fresh, vibrant and mouthfilling, it offers ripe, peachy flavours showing very good depth and a creamy-smooth finish.

DRY $18 V+

Torlesse Canterbury Chardonnay (★★☆)
The vibrantly fruity 2002 vintage (★★☆) was grown in Waipara and other parts of Canterbury and 25 per cent barrel-fermented, but most of the wine was handled in tanks. It's a medium-bodied wine, fresh and citrusy, with a slightly limey, appetisingly crisp finish. Priced right.

Vintage	02
WR	7
Drink	03-06

DRY $15 AV

Torlesse Waipara Chardonnay ★★★☆

The 2001 vintage (★★★★) is an excellent buy. Barrel-fermented, with 50 per cent malolactic fermentation, it's a fragrant wine with ripe stone-fruit and toasty oak aromas. Still youthful, it's a full-bodied wine, creamy and complex, with a sweet entry, balanced acidity and very good flavour depth.

Vintage	01	00	99	98
WR	7	6	6	6
Drink	03-07	03-05	03-04	P

DRY $20 AV

Trinity Hill Gimblett Road Chardonnay ★★★★★

The flagship Chardonnay from John Hancock is a very stylish, intense and finely structured wine that often needs two or three years to show its class. Grown in the Gimblett Gravels district of Hawke's Bay, it is hand-harvested, whole-bunch pressed, and fermented and matured on its yeast lees in French oak barriques. Opened in April 2003, the 1998 vintage (★★★★★) had matured superbly, with intense grapefruit and toast flavours, beautifully deep and harmonious. The 2002 vintage (★★★★☆) was grown in four vineyards and fermented and matured for 16 months in French oak barriques (30 per cent new oak), with partial malolactic fermentation. Already delicious, with a fragrant, toasty, creamy bouquet, in its youth it's a more open, forthcoming wine than some past vintages, with rich grapefruit, melon and toast flavours and a ripe, rounded finish.

Vintage	03	02	01	00	99	98
WR	NM	6	5	6	7	6
Drink	NM	03-08	03-06	03-06	03-05	03-05

DRY $30 AV

Trinity Hill Shepherd's Croft Chardonnay ★★★☆

The words 'by John Hancock' emblazoned across the label leave you in no doubt this Hawke's Bay wine is made by the high-profile winemaker who built his reputation at Morton Estate. The 2001 vintage (★★★) is a blend of Gimblett Road (80 per cent) and Bridge Pa grapes, fermented in a mix of tanks and French oak casks (mostly seasoned). A tight, minerally wine with fresh, grapefruit-like flavours and flinty acidity, it should age solidly.

Vintage	03	02	01	00	99	98
WR	5	6	6	5	6	5
Drink	04-06	03-06	03-06	03-05	03-05	03-04

DRY $20 AV

Trout Valley Nelson Chardonnay ★★★☆

The 2002 vintage (★★★☆) from Kahurangi Estate was grown in the Upper Moutere hills and on the Waimea Plains. Fresh, vibrant and tangy, it has strong drink-young appeal, with good body and depth of ripe, citrusy, slightly appley flavours.

DRY $19 V+

TW Gisborne Chardonnay ★★★★

'TW' stands for Tietjen and Witters, long-experienced Gisborne grape-growers. The excellent 2002 vintage (★★★★☆) was fermented and matured for 10 months in one and two-year-old oak casks, with partial malolactic fermentation. Bright, light lemon/green, it's a refined wine with very sweet, ripe-fruit characters, good weight, mealy, oaky touches and strong, fresh flavours of grapefruit, pears and butterscotch. Still unfolding, it should be at its best from mid-2004 onwards.

Vintage	02	01	00
WR	6	5	6
Drink	04-06	03-05	03-04

DRY $27 AV

TW Unoaked Chardonnay (★★★)
A drink-young charmer from Gisborne, the 2002 vintage (★★★) is a ripe style with grapefruit and pineapple characters, flavoursome and smooth, and good balance and palate weight.

DRY $18 AV

Twin Islands Marlborough Chardonnay ★★★
Produced by the wine distributor, Negociants, this is a lightly wooded, drink-young style. Pale lemon/green, the 2002 vintage (★★★☆) is fresh and lemon-scented, with citrusy, appley flavours, lively and crisp.

Vintage	02	01	00
WR	7	7	6
Drink	03-04	P	P

DRY $17 AV

Vavasour Awatere Valley Chardonnay ★★★★
At its best, this is a powerful wine with deep, citrusy, appley, creamy flavours. The 2001 vintage (★★★) was hand-picked and fermented and lees-aged for eight months in French oak casks (20 per cent new), with full malolactic fermentation. It's a softly mouthfilling wine with subdued fruit characters and a strong, creamy 'malo' influence, but in its youth lacked the intensity of past releases.

Vintage	01	00	99	98	97	96
WR	6	6	6	7	7	7
Drink	03-06	03-04	P	P	P	P

DRY $26 AV

Vidal Estate Hawke's Bay Chardonnay ★★★
This is typically a fruit-driven style with plenty of crisp, peachy, citrusy flavour. The 2002 vintage (★★★) was 40 per cent fermented and lees-aged for six months in oak casks; the rest was handled in stainless steel tanks. It's a very easy-drinking style, moderately complex, with good weight (14 per cent alcohol), ripe peachy flavours to the fore, a hint of honey, subtle oak and a smooth, rounded finish.

Vintage	02	01	00	99	98
WR	6	6	6	6	6
Drink	03-05	03-04	P	03-04	P

DRY $18 AV

Vidal Reserve Chardonnay ★★★★★
Clearly one of Hawke's Bay's finest Chardonnays, with a string of top wines stretching back to the mid-1980s. The 1998, opened in early 2003, offered no real delights (perhaps reflecting the unusually hot season) and was starting to dry out. The 2000 (★★★★★), fermented and matured for 11 months in French oak, is a classic expression of the regional style, with layers of beautifully ripe grapefruit, peach and oak flavours, concentrated, rounded and rich. There was no 2001. The 2002 (★★★★★) has a voluminous bouquet of toast and butterscotch. Seamless and soft, with substantial body and very ripe peach/grapefruit flavours, it is complex and creamy, and should reward cellaring to at least 2005.

Vintage	02	01	00	99	98	97	96
WR	7	NM	6	6	6	6	6
Drink	04-06	NM	03-04	03-04	P	P	P

DRY $32 V+ 🍇🍇

Vilagrad Chardonnay/Traminer ★★☆
For those with a sweeter tooth, this is an unusual marriage of 80 per cent Chardonnay and 20 per cent Gewürztraminer. Grown in the Waikato, it's a light, fresh wine with smooth, lemony, appley flavours and a distinct splash of sweetness. An easy to enjoy, no-fuss quaffer.

MED $17 -V

Vilagrad Mt Pirongia Chardonnay (★★★)

A fresh, uncomplicated Waikato wine, tank-fermented and half wood-aged. It typically offers decent depth of lemony, appley flavours, with a crisp finish.

DRY $18 AV

Vilagrad Reserve Chardonnay ★★★

This small Waikato winery has made some impressive Chardonnays over the years, although not all have matured well. The full, creamy 2000 (★★★★) was fermented in French oak barriques (75 per cent new). Tasted in mid-2001, it was savoury, with good complexity, offering strong grapefruit and stone-fruit flavours, seasoned with toasty oak.

Vintage	00	99	98	97	96
WR	7	6	6	7	5
Drink	03-04	P	P	P	P

DRY $26 -V

Villa Maria Cellar Selection Hawke's Bay Chardonnay ★★★★

Good value. The substantial, rich 2002 vintage (★★★★) was fermented and matured for nine months in French oak barriques, 60 per cent new, giving it a much stronger new oak influence than for its Marlborough stablemate (below). Toasty oak aromas lead into a full-bodied wine with ripe tropical-fruit flavours, well seasoned with oak, a hint of butterscotch and gentle acidity. It's a high-flavoured style, deliciously ripe and rounded, and builds to a powerful finish.

Vintage	02	01	00	99
WR	7	4	7	6
Drink	03-07	03	03	P

DRY $20 V+

Villa Maria Cellar Selection Marlborough Chardonnay ★★★★

A consistently elegant, good-value wine. The classy 2002 vintage (★★★★) was grown in vineyards in the Wairau and Awatere valleys, and two-thirds of the blend was fermented (with some use of indigenous yeasts) in French oak barriques (50 per cent new); the rest was handled in stainless steel tanks. It offers fresh, strong grapefruit and toast flavours and a hint of butterscotch in a vibrantly fruity, tight style woven with cool-climate acidity.

Vintage	02	01	00
WR	6	6	6
Drink	04-08	03-04	P

DRY $20 V+

Villa Maria Private Bin Chardonnay/Chenin Blanc (★★☆)

Grown on the east coast of the North Island, the budget-priced 2001 vintage (★★☆) is a lightly oaked wine. Fresh and crisp, with a hint of honey, green-edged flavours and a slightly short finish, it's a decent quaffer – but nothing more. (The 2002 vintage has been branded as Villa Maria Vintage Selection Chardonnay/Chenin Blanc.)

DRY $11 V+

Villa Maria Private Bin East Coast Chardonnay ★★★

At its best, this is an excellent wine and never less than enjoyable. It's a drink-young, fruit-driven style rather than a complex style for cellaring. The 2001 vintage (★★★) was grown in Gisborne and Hawke's Bay and given 'some' barrel fermentation, lees-stirring and malolactic fermentation. Fresh, with crisp, tangy flavours of lemons, apples and pears, a touch of biscuity oak and plenty of body, it's a good all-purpose Chardonnay, priced right. The 2002 (★★★☆), grown mostly in Hawke's Bay, but including parcels of fruit from Gisborne and Marlborough, is vibrantly fruity, with fresh, strong, grapefruit and peach flavours to the fore, hints of butter and toast and a very smooth (slightly off-dry) finish.

Vintage	02	01	00	99	98
WR	6	5	6	6	7
Drink	6	03-04	P	P	P

DRY $16 AV

Villa Maria Reserve Barrique Fermented Chardonnay –
see Villa Maria Reserve Gisborne Chardonnay

Villa Maria Reserve Gisborne Chardonnay (★★★★★)

Launched from the 2002 vintage (★★★★★), this superb wine effectively replaces the lush, multiple award-winning Villa Maria Barrique Fermented Chardonnay, last produced in 2000 and usually (but not always) made from Gisborne grapes. Fermented and matured for 10 months in French oak barriques (70 per cent new), it's a highly fragrant wine with beautifully fresh and vibrant, concentrated tropical-fruit flavours and a seductively smooth finish. Mealy and finely oaked, with a tight, complex palate showing very good delicacy and length, it should offer great drinking during 2004–05.

Vintage	02
WR	6
Drink	03-09

DRY $33 V+

Villa Maria Reserve Hawke's Bay Chardonnay ★★★★☆

A slightly creamy, delicious wine with lots of character, the powerful 2000 vintage (★★★★☆) offers rich, ripe, grapefruit-like flavours with a strong seasoning of toasty oak and a well-rounded finish. There is no 2001. The 2002 (★★★★★) was fermented and lees-aged for 10 months in French oak barriques, with a notably high (90 per cent) new oak influence. It's a strapping wine (14.5 per cent alcohol), yet very soft and delicate, with rich tropical-fruit flavours that have effortlessly soaked up the new oak. Deliciously creamy and smooth, with some butterscotch showing, it's a good cellaring prospect.

Vintage	02	01	00	99	98
WR	7	NM	7	6	7
Drink	04-10	NM	03-08	03-04	03-07

DRY $33 AV

Villa Maria Reserve Marlborough Chardonnay ★★★★★

With its rich, slightly mealy, citrusy flavours, this is a distinguished wine, very concentrated and finely structured. A marriage of intense, ripe Marlborough fruit with premium French oak, it is one of the region's greatest Chardonnays. Over the years, the Waldron and Fletcher vineyards in the Wairau Valley have been the major sources of fruit, now supplemented by grapes from Seddon Vineyards in the Awatere Valley. It is fully barrel-fermented, typically in 60 per cent new oak. The fragrant 2001 (★★★★★) is classy and seamless, with intense, ripe-fruit characters, finely integrated oak and lovely depth, harmony and softness. The 2002 vintage (★★★★☆) is a high-alcohol style (14.5 per cent), still very youthful, with rich grapefruit flavours, mealy, biscuity characters and impressive complexity.

Vintage	02	01	00	99	98	97	96
WR	7	7	7	7	6	7	6
Drink	04-10	03-09	03-08	03-05	P	P	P

DRY $33 V+

Villa Maria Single Vineyard Fletcher Chardonnay ★★★★

Grown and hand-picked in the Rocenvin vineyard in Old Renwick Road, Marlborough, and given 'the works' in the winery, the 2000 vintage (★★★★☆) is a sturdy (14.5 per cent alcohol) wine with highly concentrated, citrusy, peachy, mealy, toasty flavours, beautifully fragrant and rich. The 2002 (★★★★), fermented and matured for 10 months in French oak barriques (80 per cent new), is ripe and smooth, with grapefruit and pear flavours, good fruit/oak balance and mealy, biscuity complexities. In its youth, it's a more elegant but slightly less intense wine than the 2000.

Vintage 02
WR 6
Drink 04-08

DRY $35 -V

Villa Maria Single Vineyard Keltern Chardonnay (★★★★)

Grown at the Keltern vineyard, on State Highway 50, in Hawke's Bay, the 2002 vintage (★★★★) was fermented and matured for 10 months in French oak barriques (40 per cent new). Toasty oak aromas lead into a fresh, smooth and mouthfilling wine with strong, ripe, tropical-fruit flavours and some mealy complexity. It's a very harmonious wine, for drinking now or cellaring.

Vintage 02
WR 7
Drink 04-10

DRY $35 -V

Villa Maria Single Vineyard Taylors Pass Chardonnay (★★★★)

The 2002 vintage (★★★★) was grown in Marlborough's Awatere Valley and fermented and aged for 10 months in French oak barriques (60 per cent new). Showing a distinct, 'malo'-derived butterscotch character, it's a weighty, complex wine with rich melon and biscuit flavours, promising to mature well.

Vintage 02
WR 7
Drink 04-08

DRY $35 -V

Villa Maria Single Vineyard Waikahu Chardonnay ★★★★★

The classy 1999 vintage (★★★★★), grown on Maraekakaho Road, in Hawke's Bay, was a notably subtle and complex wine with rich, sweet grapefruit, fig and minerally characters and a well-rounded finish. The 2002 (★★★★★) is my pick of the five Single Vineyard wines from that vintage. Fermented and matured for 10 months in French oak barriques (60 per cent new), it's a highly complex wine, already lovely, with rich, ripe grapefruit, pear and fig flavours, mealy, biscuity characters and a creamy, sustained finish.

Vintage 02
WR 7
Drink 04-10

DRY $35 AV

Villa Maria Single Vineyard Waldron Chardonnay (★★★★☆)

Grown in Marlborough and fermented and matured in all-new French oak barriques, the 2002 vintage (★★★★☆) is light yellow, generous and rounded. It's a powerful, weighty wine with peach, melon and butterscotch flavours, showing lovely depth and harmony.

Vintage 02
WR 7
Drink 04-10

DRY $35 -V

Villa Maria Vintage Selection Chardonnay/Chenin Blanc (★★★)

It seems odd to brand a wine as 'Vintage Selection' and then not put the vintage on the label, but this is still a good buy. The wine on the market in late 2003 (★★★), in fact from the 2002 vintage, is a blend of Gisborne, Hawke's Bay and Marlborough grapes. It tastes more of Chenin Blanc than Chardonnay to me, with fresh, strong, pineappley, slightly honeyed flavours and a crisp finish. Good value.

DRY $11 V+

Vin Alto Chardonnay ★★★

Grown on the Clevedon hills in South Auckland, this easy-drinking wine is fermented in a mix of barriques (25 per cent) and tanks and given a full, softening malolactic fermentation. The 2000 vintage (★★★) is buttery, creamy and smooth, with good weight and sweet, ripe, peachy fruit characters in a moderately complex, forward style. Ready.

DRY $23 -V

Voss Estate Reserve Chardonnay ★★★★

Typically a powerful, richly flavoured Martinborough wine. Fermented and lees-aged for 10 months in French oak barriques, the 2002 vintage (★★★★☆) is softly mouthfilling, creamy and toasty, with strong, ripe peachy flavours and a good balance of fruit and oak. It's an instantly appealing wine, already delicious.

Vintage	02	01	00	99	98
WR	7	6	6	6	6
Drink	03-04	03-04	P	P	P

DRY $26 AV

Waimarie Gimblett Road Chardonnay ★★★☆

From Nicholas and Stephen Nobilo (third-generation members of the famous wine family), the 2001 vintage (★★★☆) was grown in Hawke's Bay and fermented and matured on its gross lees for 10 months in French oak casks (50 per cent new). Light yellow/green in hue, it's a well-balanced, richly flavoured (although strongly wooded) wine, full, fresh, peachy and toasty. Drink now or cellar.

Vintage	01
WR	6
Drink	03-06

DRY $22 AV

Waimarie Marlborough Chardonnay (★★★)

Released at two years old, the 2001 vintage (★★★) was hand-picked at 24 brix and fermented and matured for 10 months in new (50 per cent) and one-year-old French oak casks, with weekly lees-stirring. Light yellow, it's a full-bodied, citrusy, toasty wine, full-flavoured, with a strong oak influence and a crisp, off-dry finish.

Vintage	01
WR	6
Drink	03-05

MED/DRY $19 AV

Waimea Estates Bolitho Reserve Nelson Chardonnay ★★★★

Named after proprietors, Trevor and Robyn Bolitho, the 2001 vintage (★★★★☆) is a pale gold wine with a toasty, oaky bouquet. Fermented with indigenous yeasts and lees-aged for a year in French oak barriques, with 80 per cent malolactic fermentation, it's a fleshy and generous wine with tropical-fruit and strong toasty oak flavours.

Vintage	01	00
WR	7	6
Drink	03-05	03-05

DRY $30 -V

Waimea Estates Nelson Chardonnay ★★★☆

The 2002 vintage (★★★★) is a full, creamy wine with good weight, strong, ripe peach and grapefruit flavours and finely balanced acidity. A harmonious wine with subtle oak and malolactic fermentation influences, it was half tank, half barrel-fermented.

Vintage	02	01	00	99	98
WR	7	7	6	7	4
Drink	03-05	03-04	P	P	P

DRY $20 AV

Waipara Downs Barrel Fermented Chardonnay ★★★

This is generally the most successful wine grown at Keith and Ruth Berry's farm at Waipara. The 2001 vintage (★★★☆), harvested at over 24 brix, shows fresh, appley fruit characters and creamy, nutty touches. The 2002 (★★☆), harvested at 22 brix, is leaner and crisper, with a Chablis-like steeliness.

DRY $19 AV

Waipara Hills Barrel Fermented Canterbury Chardonnay (★★)

Light gold, with a developed colour and honeyed nose showing some botrytis influence, the 2002 vintage (★★) was lees-aged in French oak casks for six months. Peachy and honeyed on the palate, but also slightly dull, it's unlikely to be long-lived.

Vintage	02
WR	5
Drink	03-07

DRY $20 -V

Waipara Hills Marlborough Unoaked Chardonnay ★★★

Highly enjoyable in its youth, the 2002 vintage (★★★) is full-bodied and fresh, with citrusy, appley flavours showing good depth and an off-dry finish. The fully dry 2003 (★★★) was partly matured on its yeast lees and 50 per cent of the blend went through a softening malolactic fermentation. Freshly scented, it's a good example of the style, with satisfying depth of citrus and stone-fruit flavours, very clean and lively, with a dry finish.

Vintage	02
WR	5
Drink	03-05

DRY $17 AV

Waipara Hills Wickham Vineyards Marlborough Chardonnay (★★★☆)

Showing good potential, the youthful 2002 vintage (★★★☆) was grown in the Wickham vineyard at Grovetown and fermented and matured for a year in new French oak casks. Fresh and crisp, with grapefruit and nut flavours showing good concentration, it's a restrained, tightly structured wine, for opening mid-2004+.

Vintage	02
WR	7
Drink	04-10

DRY $37 -V

Waipara Springs Barrique Chardonnay ★★★☆

A full-flavoured North Canterbury wine with lots of character. Based on 19-year-old vines, the 2002 vintage (★★★☆) was fermented and lees-aged in French oak barriques. It's a full-bodied style (14 per cent alcohol), vibrantly fruity, with strong, ripe flavours of citrus fruits, toast and butterscotch.

Vintage	02	01	00	99	98
WR	7	6	6	6	6
Drink	03-09	03-08	03-08	03-06	P

DRY $24 AV

Waipara Springs Lightly Oaked Chardonnay ★★★

A fruit-driven style, grown at Waipara, the 2002 vintage (★★★) was fermented in stainless steel tanks (60 per cent) and well-seasoned barrels. It's a full, crisp and vibrant wine with lemony, peachy, appley flavours, fresh and punchy.

Vintage	03	02	01	00
WR	6	7	7	5
Drink	03-06	03-08	03-04	03-04

DRY $18 AV

Waipara West Chardonnay ★★★★

This label shows steadily rising form. The 2001 vintage (★★★★) was harvested from ultra low-cropping vines (2.7 to 4.7 tonnes/hectare), whole-bunch pressed and fermented and lees-aged for 10 months in French oak barriques (25 per cent new), with 45 per cent malolactic fermentation. It's a richly fragrant wine, weighty, with deep citrusy flavours, butterscotch and mineral characters adding complexity and fresh acid spine. The 2002 (★★★☆), tasted in May 2003, showed ripe, citrusy flavours seasoned with quality oak, but was still in its infancy.

Vintage	02	01	00	99	98
WR	6	6	6	7	6
Drink	03-06	03-05	03-04	03-05	P

DRY $24 AV

Wairau River Marlborough Chardonnay ★★★☆

This is a consistently attractive, tight, understated wine with the ability to age well. The 2000 vintage (★★★☆), matured for nine months in French oak casks (new and older), is an elegant, subtle style with gentle oak, crisp, citrusy flavours and some toasty complexity. Ready now onwards.

Vintage	00	99	98	97
WR	6	6	6	6
Drink	03-06	03-05	03-04	P

DRY $22 AV

Waitiri Creek Chardonnay ★★★

The 2001 vintage (★★★☆) of this Central Otago wine was grown and hand-harvested at Gibbston and about half the final blend was handled in new and one-year-old oak casks. A strapping wine (14.5 per cent alcohol), with creamy, buttery aromas and flavours, lemon/apple fruit characters and fresh acidity on the finish, it shows good body and concentration, and should be at its best during 2003–04. Bright, light lemon/green, the 2002 (★★☆) has a slightly honeyed nose and palate and crisp, green-edged flavours.

DRY $24 -V

West Brook Barrique Fermented Chardonnay ★★★☆

The 2001 vintage (★★★☆) was grown in Gisborne (with a small portion of Marlborough grapes) and fully barrel-fermented. Fragrant and fresh, it offers vibrant lemon and peach flavours with crisp underlying acidity and a smooth, fractionally off-dry finish. (Tasted prior to bottling, the 2002 was rich, citrusy and bone-dry.)

Vintage	01	00
WR	5	7
Drink	03-05	03-06

DRY $20 AV

West Brook Blue Ridge Marlborough Chardonnay ★★★★

West Brook Chardonnays are consistently distinguished. The 2001 vintage (★★★★) is a delicious wine, robust (14.5 per cent alcohol), with fresh, strong, vibrant fruit flavours enriched but not dominated by toasty oak. The 2002 (★★★★) is bright, light yellow, with a fragrant, citrusy, toasty bouquet. It's a high-alcohol style (14.5 per cent) with smooth, rich grapefruit flavours, sweet oak characters, a touch of butterscotch and good harmony.

Vintage	02	01	00	99	98
WR	6	7	7	7	7
Drink	03-07	03-07	03-06	03-05	03-05

DRY $25 AV

White Cloud Chardonnay ★★☆

Nobilo's easy-drinking, non-vintage wine is blended from grapes grown in Gisborne and Hawke's Bay. Fermented in tanks and not oak-aged, it is typically a slightly sweet (6 grams/litre of sugar), lemony, simple wine, clean and fresh. The wine I tasted in mid-2003 (★★★) was an unexpectedly good, upfront style with ripe, peachy flavours and a buttery, slightly sweet finish.

MED/DRY $9 V+

Whitehaven Marlborough Chardonnay ★★★

A fruit-driven style, the 2002 vintage (★★☆) was 50 per cent oak-matured. Pale, with lemony, appley flavours and a hint of butterscotch, it's an easy-drinking wine, but fairly simple, with a slightly off-dry finish.

Vintage	02
WR	6
Drink	03-05

DRY $22 -V

Whitehaven Reserve Marlborough Chardonnay ★★★☆

Made in a highly user-friendly style, the 2002 vintage (★★★☆) was fermented and matured for a year, with frequent lees-stirring, in French and American oak barriques (50 per cent new). The fragrant, sweetly oaked bouquet leads into a rich palate with strong, ripe peach, grapefruit and toasty oak flavours and a smooth finish. Delicious in its youth.

Vintage	02	01
WR	6	6
Drink	03-07	03-05

DRY $26 -V

William Hill Chardonnay ★★★

This is typically a good Central Otago wine, and the 2001 vintage (★★★☆) is one of the best yet. Estate-grown at Alexandra, it was fermented and lees-aged for six months in French oak casks (new to three-year-old), with full malolactic fermentation. Light yellow, with a citrusy, biscuity nose, it's a bold, upfront style with rich, citrusy, peachy flavours, a hint of butterscotch and fresh acidity.

Vintage	01	00
WR	5	4
Drink	03-05	03-04

DRY $20 -V

Winslow White Rock Barrique Fermented Chardonnay ★★☆

The single-vineyard 2002 vintage (★★☆) was harvested from low-cropping (3.5 tonnes/hectare) vines at Martinborough and matured for nine months in new French oak barriques, with 100 per cent malolactic fermentation. Light/medium yellow, it's a fleshy, very toasty wine, peachy and weighty, but (at least in its youth) oak-dominated.

DRY $28 -V

Wishart Barrique Fermented Chardonnay ★★★

The 2002 vintage (★★☆) was grown on the coast at Bay View, in Hawke's Bay, and fermented and matured on its yeast lees for three months in three-year-old barrels. The bouquet is fresh and appley; the palate is fruity but simple, with a splash of sweetness to smooth the finish. Past vintages offered greater complexity.

Vintage	01	00	99
WR	5	6	5
Drink	03-05	03-04	P

DRY $20 -V

Wishart Reserve Chardonnay ★★★★

Grown at Bay View, in Hawke's Bay, and fermented and lees-aged for 10 months in French and American oak casks (50 per cent new), with no malolactic fermentation, the 2002 vintage (★★★★) is ripe and rounded, with fullness of body, good depth of peach and grapefruit flavours and a slightly sweet oak influence.

DRY $25 AV

Wither Hills Marlborough Chardonnay ★★★★★

This is a classy wine with a formidable track record in shows. Powerful, with a mealy, biscuity complexity from fermentation and lees-aging in French oak casks (typically 60 per cent new), it offers the intense flavours of Marlborough fruit, with a long, creamy finish. The seductively full-bodied and rich 2002 vintage (★★★★☆) has strong toast and butterscotch aromas. A high-alcohol style (14.5 per cent) with a bold presence in the mouth, it offers deliciously lush grapefruit and peach-fruit characters, well-seasoned with toasty oak.

Vintage	02	01	00	99	98
WR	7	7	7	6	7
Drink	03-07	03-06	03-05	03-04	P

DRY $29 V+

Woollaston Estates Nelson Chardonnay (★★★)

Enjoyable in its youth, the 2002 vintage (★★★) is lemony, appley and moderately oaked, with fullness of body and slightly creamy, biscuity characters adding a touch of complexity.

DRY $18 AV

Chenin Blanc

Today's Chenin Blancs are far riper, rounder and more enjoyable to drink than the typically thin, sharply acidic and austere wines of a decade ago. Yet this great grape of the Loire Valley is still struggling for an identity in New Zealand. Over the last few years, several labels have been discontinued – not for lack of quality or value, but lack of buyer interest.

A good New Zealand Chenin Blanc is fresh and buoyantly fruity, with melon and pineapple-evoking flavours and a crisp finish. In the cooler parts of the country, the variety's naturally high acidity (an asset in the warmer viticultural regions of South Africa, the United States and Australia) can be a distinct handicap. But when the grapes achieve full ripeness here, this classic grape of Vouvray, in the Loire Valley, yields sturdy wines that are satisfying in their youth yet can mature for many years, gradually unfolding a delicious honeyed richness.

Only three wineries have consistently made impressive Chenin Blancs over the past decade: Millton, Collards and Esk Valley. Many growers, put off by the variety's late-ripening nature and the susceptibility of its tight bunches to botrytis rot, have uprooted their vines. Plantings have plummeted from 372 hectares in 1983 to an estimated 118 hectares of bearing vines in 2004.

Chenin Blanc is the country's fifteenth most widely planted variety, with plantings concentrated in Hawke's Bay and Gisborne. In the future, winemakers who plant Chenin Blanc in warm, sunny vineyard sites with devigorating soils, where the variety's vigorous growth can be controlled and yields reduced, can be expected to produce the ripest, most concentrated wines. New Zealand winemakers are still getting to grips with Chenin Blanc; the finest wines are yet to come.

Collards Hawke's Bay Chenin Blanc ★★★☆

Given a delicate touch of wood, at its best this is a rich, vibrantly fruity wine that can offer great value. Grown in the Gimblett Gravels district, the pale yellow 2002 vintage (★★★☆) is ripely scented, fleshy and rounded, with good depth of pineappley, faintly honeyed flavour and well-tamed acidity. It's a strongly varietal wine, already drinking well and – as usual – bargain-priced.

Vintage	03	02	01	00	99	98
WR	6	7	7	6	6	7
Drink	04-06	03-05	03-04	P	P	P

DRY $13 V+

Collards Summerfields Chenin/Sauvignon/Chardonnay ★★☆

This is the all-purpose dry white (or dryish white – there's a sliver of sweetness) in the Collards range. Blended from Hawke's Bay and Auckland fruit, it's typically an easy-drinking wine with plenty of fresh, crisp, citrusy, green-edged flavour. At below $10, a good buy.

Vintage	03	02	01	00
WR	6	7	6	6
Drink	03-04	03-04	P	P

DRY $9 V+

Esk Valley Hawke's Bay Chenin Blanc ★★★★

This is one of New Zealand's best (and few really convincing) Chenin Blancs, with the ability to mature well for several years. In the past, it was partly fermented in seasoned oak casks, but since 2001 has been handled entirely in stainless steel tanks. Richly scented, the 2002 vintage (★★★★)

is an intensely varietal wine with fresh, finely balanced acidity and strong, tropical-fruit aromas and flavours, pure and vibrant.

Vintage	02	01	00	99	98	97
WR	7	6	NM	6	6	6
Drink	03-07	03-05	NM	P	P	P

DRY $20 AV

Forrest Vineyard Selection Chenin Blanc ★★★★

Chenin Blanc is a rare beast in Marlborough, but the 2001 vintage (★★★★), handled in old oak barrels, is a unexpectedly good wine. Made in a medium style (28 grams/litre of sugar), it's smooth, peachy and mouthfilling, with good sugar/acid balance and faintly honeyed, concentrated, sweetly seductive flavours, now starting to unfold bottle-aged complexity.

Vintage	02	01
WR	5	6
Drink	03-10	03-05

MED $25 -V

Margrain Chenin Blanc Late Harvest ★★★★

When this small Martinborough producer purchased the neighbouring Chifney property, they acquired Chenin Blanc vines now over 20 years old. The 2002 (★★★), the first to be labelled as Late Harvest, is a weighty (14 per cent alcohol), distinctly medium style (24 grams/litre of sugar) with crisp, tight, lemony, appley flavours. In its youth, it lacks the richness of the 2000 and 2001 vintages, but may open out with time.

Vintage	02	01	00
WR	6	5	6
Drink	03-08	03-06	03-05

MED $24 -V

Millton Te Arai Vineyard Chenin Blanc ★★★★★

This Gisborne wine is New Zealand's top Chenin Blanc. It's a richly varietal wine with concentrated, fresh, vibrant fruit flavours to the fore in some vintages (2000, 2002), nectareous scents and flavours in others (1997, 1999). The grapes are grown organically and hand-picked over a month at three different stages of ripening, culminating in the final harvest of botrytis-affected fruit. About half of the final blend is fermented in large, 620-litre French oak casks, used in the Loire for Chenin Blanc, but all of the wine is barrel-aged. The 2002 vintage (★★★★★) is hard to resist, with strong personality and great cellaring potential (10 years, suggests James Millton). It shows lovely balance and richness, with refreshing acidity and tropical fruit, pear and honey flavours, very ripe and concentrated.

Vintage	02	01	00	99	98	97	96
WR	7	5	7	6	5	5	5
Drink	03-12	03-05	03-06	03-04	P	P	P

MED/DRY $22 AV

Terrace Road Marlborough Chenin Blanc ★★☆

The non-vintage wine (★★☆) on the market during 2003 was 50 per cent fermented in seasoned oak casks, with a softening malolactic fermentation; the rest was handled in tanks. It's a slightly austere wine from Cellier Le Brun, with tense, lemony flavours and some creamy, nutty complexity, but only moderate varietal character.

DRY $18 -V

Gewürztraminer

Only a few thousand cases of Gewürztraminer are exported annually, and most local bottlings lack the exciting weight and richness of the great Alsace model. Yet this classic grape is starting to get the respect it deserves from grape-growers and winemakers here.

For most of the 1990s, Gewürztraminer's popularity was on the wane. Between 1983 and 1996, New Zealand's plantings of Gewürztraminer dropped by almost two-thirds. A key problem is that Gewürztraminer is a temperamental performer in the vineyard, being particularly vulnerable to adverse weather at flowering, which can decimate grape yields. Now there is proof of a strong renewal of interest: the area of bearing vines is surging from 85 hectares in 1998 to 247 hectares by 2005. Most of the plantings are in Marlborough and Hawke's Bay, with other significant pockets in Gisborne and Central Otago.

Slight sweetness and skin contact have been commonly used in the past to boost the flavour of Gewürztraminer, at the cost of flavour delicacy and longevity. Such outstanding wines as Dry River have revealed the far richer, softer flavours and greater aging potential that can be gained by reducing crops, leaf-plucking to promote fruit ripeness and avoiding skin contact.

Gewürztraminer is a high-impact wine, brimming with scents and flavours. 'Spicy' is the most common adjective used to pinpoint its distinctive, heady aromas and flavours; tasters also find nuances of gingerbread, freshly ground black pepper, cinnamon, cloves, mint, lychees and mangoes. Once you've tasted one or two Gewürztraminers, you won't have any trouble recognising it in a 'blind' tasting – it's one of the most forthright, distinctive grape varieties of all.

Amor-Bendall Gisborne Gewürztraminer ★★★☆

The 2002 vintage (★★★☆) has a fresh, rich, musky perfume. It's a mouthfilling wine with strong pear, lychees and spice flavours and a crisp, slightly sweet finish. The 2003 (★★★☆) is highly aromatic, with fullness of body (13.4 per cent alcohol) and good depth of fresh, slightly sweet, spicy, peachy flavour.

MED/DRY $23 -V

Artisan Sunvale Estate Gewürztraminer ★★★

The 2002 vintage (★★★) is a Gisborne wine, based on 'very old' vines at Tolaga Bay. Balanced for easy drinking, it's a clearly varietal wine with good depth of lychees and spice flavours, slightly sweet, crisp and lively.

MED/DRY $17 AV

Askerne Gewürztraminer ★★★★

The 2002 vintage (★★★★☆) from this small Hawke's Bay winery, partly (25 per cent) fermented in old French oak casks, has a heady, intensely varietal perfume. Substantial in body, it's a dryish style (around 5 grams/litre of residual sugar) with lovely depth of fresh, vibrant lychees and spice flavours and a rounded finish. The 2003 (★★★☆) has a perfumed, spicy, musky bouquet. It's a crisp, medium-bodied style (11.5 per cent alcohol) with plenty of citrusy, spicy flavour, but less lush and rich than the 2002.

Vintage	03	02	01	00
WR	6	6	5	6
Drink	03-05	03-04	P	P

DRY $20 V+

Babich Winemakers Reserve Gewürztraminer ★★★★

This consistently stylish Gewürztraminer is from a small (1.2-hectare) plot in the company's Gimblett Road vineyard, in Hawke's Bay. It's typically a sturdy wine, designed for cellaring, with deep yet delicate lemon/spice flavours. The exotically perfumed, soft and substantial 2001 (★★★★☆) is a classy, beautifully ripe-tasting wine with a rich array of lychees, peach, ginger and spice flavours and a dryish, rounded finish. The 2002 vintage (★★★☆), from a heavier-yielding year, is weighty, with delicate flavours of lychees, spice and pears and gentle acidity, but less striking than the 2001.

Vintage	02	01	00	99	98
WR	6	7	7	7	7
Drink	03-08	03-08	03-07	03-06	03-04

MED/DRY $25 -V

Black Ridge Gewürztraminer ★★★

The Gewürztraminer style at this Alexandra vineyard has varied over the years, but the wines are always interesting, with a cool-climate, appley edge. It is typically flavoursome, with good weight, firm acidity and a fractionally sweet, gently spicy finish.

DRY $19 -V

Bladen Marlborough Gewürztraminer ★★★☆

Grown and hand-picked in a single vineyard near Renwick, the generously flavoured, seductively soft 2001 vintage (★★★★☆) is rich and weighty, with a full-bloomed, musky perfume and concentrated lychees and spice characters, slightly sweet and rounded. The 2002 (★★★) displays lemony, slightly earthy and spicy flavours of decent depth, with a dry finish, but lacks the intensity of the 2001.

DRY $23 -V

Brookfields Hawke's Bay Gewürztraminer ★★★★

Powerful, richly flavoured Gewürztraminers are rare in New Zealand, which makes Brookfields' all the more welcome. Grown in stony soils in Ohiti Road, inland from Fernhill, it's a weighty wine with deep, lingering flavours. The 2002 vintage (★★★☆) was picked at 24 brix and made in a fractionally off-dry style. Minerally rather than spicy on the nose, it's a substantial (14 per cent alcohol) wine with very good depth of peach, pear and slightly earthy flavours and an oily, spicy finish.

Vintage	01	00	99	98	97	96
WR	6	7	7	7	7	6
Drink	03-07	03-06	03-05	03	03	P

MED/DRY $22 AV

Chard Farm Central Otago Gewürztraminer ★★★☆

The weighty 2001 vintage (★★★☆) is an unusually dry style (just 3 grams/litre of sugar), with fresh, ripe, delicate flavours of lychees and spice, balanced acidity and a lingering finish. Drink now onwards.

Vintage	01
WR	5
Drink	03-04

DRY $24 -V

Clearview Estate Gewürztraminer (★★★☆)

The powerful, robust 2003 vintage (★★★☆) needs time to unfold its full potential. Grown at Te Awanga, on the Hawke's Bay coastline, it has a well-spiced, slightly gingery bouquet and strong lychees and spice flavours, finishing slightly sweet and crisp. Open mid 2004+.

Vintage	03
WR	6
Drink	03-07

MED/DRY $20 AV

Cloudy Bay Marlborough Gewürztraminer ★★★★★

To experience the Cloudy Bay magic at its most spellbinding, try the rare, less fashionable wines, made in small volumes. The stunning 2001 vintage (★★★★★), grown at Rapaura and in the Brancott Valley, was harvested at an average of over 25 brix, and fermented with indigenous yeasts and lees-aged in old French oak barrels. Robust (14.8 per cent alcohol) and well-rounded, it's an opulent, lush wine with seductive depth of citrus, pear and spice flavours and a slightly earthy complexity. It offers the substantial body weight and deliciously soft texture found in the classic Gewürztraminers of Alsace.

Vintage	01	00	99	98	97
WR	6	6	4	NM	5
Drink	04-06	04	P	NM	P

MED/DRY $29 V+

Collards Hawke's Bay Gewürztraminer (★★★☆)

The smartly priced 2002 vintage (★★★☆) is the first Gewürztraminer for many years from a firm that once pioneered the variety in New Zealand. Perfumed and mouthfilling, it offers very good depth of ripe lychees, ginger and spice flavours, with a soft, basically dry finish.

Vintage	03	02	01
WR	NM	7	NM
Drink	NM	03-04	NM

DRY $15 V+

Coopers Creek Gisborne Gewürztraminer (★★★)

A single-vineyard wine, fermented close to dryness (5 grams/litre of residual sugar), the 2003 vintage (★★★) has rose-petal and spice aromas, leading into a softly mouthfilling wine with fresh lemon, lychees and spice flavours. Tasted soon after bottling, it looked promising.

MED/DRY $16 AV

Crab Farm Gewürztraminer ★★★

Ready now, the 2000 vintage (★★★) of this Hawke's Bay wine is golden, spicy and peachy, with some richness. It's an earthy, honeyed wine with a slight lack of delicacy on the finish, but shows lots of character.

Vintage	00
WR	5
Drink	P

DRY $15 AV

Crossroads Destination Series Gewürztraminer (★★★☆)

The 2002 vintage (★★★☆) of this Hawke's Bay wine has a well-spiced, full-bloomed bouquet. It's an easy-drinking wine with good weight, strong, ripe lychees and spice flavours, a hint of ginger and a fractionally off-dry, rounded finish. Drink now onwards.

Vintage	02
WR	7
Drink	03-06

DRY $20 AV

Dry River Gewürztraminer ★★★★★

This intensely perfumed and flavoured Martinborough Gewürztraminer is the country's finest, in terms of its gorgeous quality from one vintage to the next. Medium-dry or medium in most years, in top vintages it shows a power and richness comparable to Alsace's *vendange tardive* (late-harvest) wines. Always rich in alcohol and exceptionally full-flavoured, it is also very delicate, with a tight, concentrated, highly refined palate that is typically at its most seductive at two to four years old. Exotically perfumed, weighty and soft, the 2002 vintage (★★★★★) offers a lovely concentration of peach, spice, lychee and honey flavours. Showing great delicacy, intensity and length, it's already impossible to resist (winemaker Neil McCallum serves it as an aperitif and with cheeses).

Vintage	02	01	00	99	98	97	96
WR	7	7	7	7	6	7	6
Drink	04-08	03-07	03-04	P	P	P	P

MED $40 AV

Eskdale Winegrowers Gewürztraminer ★★★☆

Winemaker Kim Salonius prefers a low profile, but his wine (usually several years old) is worth searching for. Typically made from very ripe, late-harvested fruit grown in the Esk Valley, his wine bursts with character. Most vintages display mouthfilling body and a pungent, lingering spiciness; in some years botrytis adds a honeyish intensity. In mid to late 2003, the 1999 vintage was still on sale.

DRY $20 AV

Forrest Marlborough Gewürztraminer ★★★★

The excellent 2002 vintage (★★★★) is richly perfumed, with concentrated flavours of pears, lychees and spice. It's a mouthfilling, very ripe-tasting wine with gentle acidity and a slightly sweet, soft, lingering finish. The 2003 (★★★★) is a weighty wine with fresh, strong lychees and spice aromas and flavours. An intensely varietal wine with a long, slightly sweet, well-spiced finish, it's already delicious.

Vintage	03	02	01
WR	6	5	5
Drink	04-07	03-04	P

MED/DRY $24 AV

Framingham Marlborough Gewürztraminer ★★★★

This label has shown steadily rising form in recent vintages and the 2002 (★★★★) is one of the best. Estate-grown at Renwick, harvested at over 24 brix from low-cropping vines (4.5 tonnes/hectare) and lees-aged in tanks, it's a medium/dry style with gentle acidity. Pale lemon/green, with lychees and spice aromas, it's a softly substantial wine with ripe pear, lychees and spice flavours, deliciously rounded and rich.

Vintage	02	01	00	99
WR	6	7	6	5
Drink	03-05	03-05	03-04	03-04

MED/DRY $27 -V

Fromm La Strada Gewürztraminer (★★★★)

'A pet variety on the sideline,' is winemaker Hatsch Kalberer's description of Gewürztraminer, which occupies a tiny, 0.1-hectare plot in the estate vineyard. The 2002 vintage (★★★★) is richly perfumed, with loads of spicy, gingery flavour, in a leaner, much drier style than most of Marlborough's top examples of the grape.

DRY $33 -V

Glenmark Waipara Gewürztraminer ★★☆

The dry, lemony 2001 vintage (★★☆) is less attractive and clearly varietal than the 2002 (★★★), a crisp, fresh and lively wine with good depth of citrusy, gently spiced flavour.

DRY $24 -V

Grove Mill Winemakers Reserve Gewürztraminer (★★☆)

The 2001 vintage (★★☆) is a single-vineyard Marlborough wine, grown in the Waihopai Valley and stop-fermented with a distinct splash (22 grams/litre) of residual sugar. It's a solid, lemony, appley wine, but lacks the exotic aromas and flavours of this variety at its best.

MED $20 -V

Huia Marlborough Gewürztraminer ★★★☆

This is a consistently characterful wine that rewards cellaring. The 2002 vintage (★★★☆) was harvested at 23.5 brix from 23-year-old vines in the Fell vineyard, one of the oldest in the Wairau Valley. It's a substantial (14 per cent alcohol), almost fully dry wine with ripe lychees and spice flavours and a rounded finish. Still youthful, it's maturing well.

Vintage	03	02	01
WR	6	6	7
Drink	03-06	03-05	03-05

DRY $23 -V

Huntaway Reserve Gisborne/Marlborough Gewürztraminer (★★★☆)

Verging on four-star quality, the 2002 vintage (★★★☆) is a ripely aromatic wine from Montana, full-bodied and slightly sweet, with good palate weight, varietal character and depth of lychees, spice and ginger flavours. Lush and exotically perfumed, it has strong upfront appeal.

Vintage	02
WR	7
Drink	03-10

MED/DRY $20 AV

Hunter's Marlborough Gewürztraminer ★★★★

Hunter's produces an excellent Gewürztraminer, with good weight and clearly defined varietal character. Harvested at 24 brix, the 2002 vintage (★★★★) is a rich, powerful wine (14.5 per cent alcohol), enticingly perfumed, with deep flavours of lychees, lemons and spice and a slightly sweet, lasting finish.

Vintage	02	01	00	99	98
WR	5	6	6	5	5
Drink	05	04-05	03-04	P	P

MED/DRY $19 V+

Kahurangi Estate Gewürztraminer ★★★☆

This Nelson winery produces an attractive Gewürztraminer. The 2002 vintage (★★★), grown in the Moutere hills and on the Waimea Plains, is a slightly sweet and smooth wine with pear, lychees and spice flavours, showing some intensity.

MED $19 AV

Kaikoura Marlborough Gewürztraminer ★★★☆

Offering immediate enjoyment, the 2002 vintage (★★★☆) was grown on the south side of the Wairau Valley. It's a slightly sweet style, richly perfumed, with substantial body and very good depth of citrusy, spicy flavour.

MED/DRY $19 AV

Kemblefield The Distinction Hawke's Bay Gewürztraminer (★★★)

Blended from estate-grown and other grapes, and bottled after extended aging on its yeast lees, the 2002 vintage (★★★) is a pale yellow wine, citrusy, spicy and gingery, with a slightly off-dry finish. Less striking than some of this winery's past releases.

MED/DRY $19 -V

Lawson's Dry Hills Marlborough Gewürztraminer ★★★★★

This is consistently one of the country's most impressive Gewürztraminers. Grown near the winery in the Lawson and Woodward vineyards, at the foot of the Wither Hills, the 2003 vintage (★★★★★) is highly distinguished. It was mostly cool-fermented in stainless steel tanks, but a small percentage was given 'the full treatment, with a high-solids, wild ferment in French oak, malolactic fermentation and lees-stirring'. The richly spiced bouquet leads into a weighty (14 per cent alcohol), softly structured wine with a lovely concentration of lychees and spice flavours, notable harmony and a rich, dryish (6 grams/litre of sugar) finish.

Vintage	02	01	00	99	98
WR	7	6	6	6	5
Drink	03-06	03-05	03-04	P	P

MED/DRY $22 V+

Leaning Rock Gewürztraminer ★★★

Some past vintages of this Alexandra, Central Otago wine were oak-aged, but the 2001 (★★★) was handled in stainless steel tanks. It's a crisp, slightly sweet wine (11 grams/litre of residual sugar), floral and weighty (13 per cent alcohol), with appley, gently spicy flavours of decent depth.

Vintage	01
WR	5
Drink	03-04

MED/DRY $19 -V

Longridge Vineyards Gewürztraminer ★★★☆

From one vintage to the next, this is a bargain. As a long-popular Corbans brand, it was always a Hawke's Bay wine, but the 2002 vintage (★★★☆) from Montana is blended from Hawke's Bay (46 per cent), Gisborne (38 per cent) and Marlborough (16 per cent) grapes. It's an aromatic, characterful wine, weighty, with strong, spicy, peachy flavours and a slightly sweet, rounded finish.

Vintage	02	01
WR	6	NM
Drink	03-07	NM

MED/DRY $15 V+

Longview Gewürztraminer (★★)

Grown in Northland, just south of Whangarei, the 2002 vintage (★★) lacks the perfume typical of Gewürztraminer. It's a crisp, slightly sweet wine with some varietal spiciness, but the flavour is also restrained.

Vintage	02
WR	5
Drink	04-05

DRY $21 -V

Lynskeys Wairau Peaks Marlborough Gewürztraminer ★★★

Estate-grown in the Wairau Valley, the 2002 vintage (★★★) was fermented in stainless steel tanks, but a small percentage was oak-aged and given a softening malolactic fermentation. Delicate rose-petal aromas lead into a fresh, weighty wine (14 per cent alcohol) with lychees, apple and spice flavours, a slightly oily texture and a rounded, dry finish. It should mature well.

Vintage	02	01	00
WR	7	7	6
Drink	03-04	P	P

MED/DRY $25 -V

Margrain Martinborough Gewürztraminer ★★★★

Sturdy and impressively concentrated, the 2002 vintage (★★★★) is a late-harvest style, picked at 26.5 brix and stop-fermented with 33 grams per litre of residual sugar. It's a medium-sweet style with noticeably high alcohol (14.5 per cent), an aromatic, intensely varietal bouquet, strong lychees and spice flavours, gentle acidity and a soft finish.

Vintage	02	01	00
WR	7	7	6
Drink	03-06	03-05	P

MED $30 -V

Matawhero Reserve Gewürztraminer ★★★★

An acclaimed Gisborne wine in the late 1970s and early 1980s, when it was arrestingly perfumed and concentrated, since then its style has been slightly less pungent, with a soft finish. The use of indigenous yeasts and malolactic fermentation has toned down the varietal character, but the wine is impressively weighty and flavoursome. The golden 1999 vintage (★★★☆), recently on sale, is full-bodied, with strong, gingery, slightly honeyed and toasty flavours. I'd prefer greater delicacy and freshness, but it's a characterful dry wine, now ready.

DRY $28 -V

Mills Reef Reserve Gewürztraminer ★★★★

The 2002 (★★★★), matured on its full ('gross') lees for four months, is an exotically perfumed, mouthfilling, slightly sweet Hawke's Bay wine with ripe lychees, pear and spice flavours and a rounded, lingering finish. For the 2003 vintage (★★★☆), the fruit supply switched to Gisborne. It's a weighty, strongly varietal wine with ripe lychees and spice characters and a dry finish. Tightly structured, it should open up well during 2004.

MED/DRY $22 AV

Millton The Growers Series Gisborne Gewürztraminer ★★★

Launched from 2001 (★★★), this wine is grown in the McIldowie vineyard, which is not managed organically. The 2002 vintage (★★★☆) is mouthfilling and rounded, with ripe, citrusy, peachy flavours in a forward style, highly enjoyable in its youth.

MED/DRY $20 -V

Mission Hawke's Bay Gewürztraminer ★★★☆

Typically an easy-drinking style, fruity, fresh and flavoursome. The 2002 vintage (★★★☆), grown at Greenmeadows (Taradale) and Bay View, is a slightly sweet style with ripe citrusy, spicy flavours, a slightly oily texture, good depth and a rounded finish.

Vintage	02
WR	5
Drink	03-05

MED/DRY $16 V+

Montana Patutahi Estate Gewürztraminer ★★★★☆

Full of character, at its best this is a mouthfilling wine with a musky perfume and intense pepper and lychees-like flavours, delicate and lush. Grown hard against the hills inland from the city of Gisborne, it is harvested very ripe, with some botrytis-affected, nobly rotten grapes, picked at a super-ripe 28 to 30 brix, imparting an apricot-like lusciousness to the final blend. There was no 1999 or 2001, but a small supply was released from 2000 (★★★★). Full yellow/light gold in hue, it's a good but not great vintage, full of character, in a relatively forward style with rich, slightly honeyed flavour. I also found the 2002 vintage (★★★☆) slightly disappointing in mid to late 2003. Grown 'predominantly' at the company's Patutahi Estate, it's a yellow-hued wine with a richly spicy bouquet, mouthfilling body and ripe, gingery flavours, but in its infancy it also showed a slight lack of delicacy and softness.

Vintage	02	01	00	99	98
WR	7	NM	6	NM	6
Drink	03-06	NM	03+	NM	03-04

MED/DRY $24 V+

Morworth Estate Canterbury Gewürztraminer (★★★)

The 2001 vintage (★★★) is a fruity, medium style with moderately varietal, lemony, appley flavours and a slightly phenolic, gently spicy finish.

MED $19 -V

Mount Maude Gewürztraminer (★★★)

The 2001 vintage (★★★) is a bone-dry wine from low-cropping vines (2.5 tonnes/hectare) at Lake Wanaka, in Central Otago. The finish is slightly hard, but it's a full-bodied, gingery and spicy wine with clearcut varietal character.

DRY $18 AV

Ohinemuri Estate Gisborne Gewürztraminer ★★★

The 2001 vintage (★★★) is a pleasantly rounded wine with ripe, peachy, lemony, spicy flavours and a slightly sweet, smooth finish. Grown at Ormond, the 2002 (★★★) is a gently sweet wine (15 grams/litre of sugar), crisp and flavoursome, with lychees and spice characters showing some richness.

Vintage 02 01
WR 6 6
Drink 03-06 03-05

MED $20 -V

Olssen's of Bannockburn Gewürztraminer ★★★★

Mouthfilling and delicate, with tight lychees and spice flavours showing excellent depth, the 2001 vintage (★★★★) is a dryish style from Central Otago. The 2002 (★★★★) was 15 per cent barrel-fermented in seasoned French oak barriques. Weighty, rich and rounded, it's a ripely scented and flavoured wine with a floral bouquet, strong pear, lychees and spice characters, a slightly oily texture, gentle acidity and an off-dry finish.

MED/DRY $24 AV

Peregrine Central Otago Gewürztraminer ★★★☆

The powerful, lush 2001 (★★★★☆) was grown at Gibbston and Lowburn (in the Cromwell Basin), harvested at a very ripe 25 brix, stop-fermented in a medium-dry style (with 8 grams/litre of residual sugar) and lees-aged before bottling. It's a distinguished wine with substantial body (13.5 per cent alcohol) and a lovely surge of ripe, concentrated ginger, lychees, pear and spice flavours. Much more restrained in its youth, the 2002 vintage (★★★) is a fully dry wine, mouthfilling (14.5 per cent alcohol) and rounded, with peachy, spicy flavours now starting to open out.

Vintage 02
WR 4
Drink 03-04

DRY $20 AV

Phoenix Gisborne Gewürztraminer ★★★☆

This Gisborne wine stands out in the Pacific range. Grown in the Butler (previously Thomas) vineyard and made in a slightly sweet style, top vintages are pungently spiced, with a full-bloomed fragrance and concentrated flavour, although the quality is variable. Perfumed, with a strongly spicy bouquet, the 2002 (★★★★) is a full-bodied, medium style (stop-fermented at 16 grams/litre sugar), with rich, ripe lychees and spice flavours and a well-rounded finish. It's a luscious wine with good intensity.

Vintage 02 01
WR 6 NM
Drink 03+ NM

MED $19 AV

Pleasant Valley Marlborough Gewürztraminer (★★★)

The 2001 vintage (★★★) is gently perfumed, with ripe, delicate citrus/spice flavours in a full-bodied, fruity, slightly sweet and smooth style, offering very easy drinking.

MED/DRY $15 AV

Revington Vineyard Gewürztraminer ★★★★

The Revington Vineyard in Gisborne's Ormond Valley yields a rare wine that has ranked among the country's finest Gewürztraminers. No wine was made in 1999 or 2000, because the fruit quality was not good enough. Ross Revington and John Thorpe (of Longbush) have made the 2001 and 2002 vintages in a slightly sweeter style than the dry wines of the past. From 'an awful year', the 2001 (★★★☆) is light gold, with honey and spice aromas. Gingery and soft, with a clear botrytis influence, it's full of personality and drinking well now. The 2002 (★★★★) was harvested from low-cropping young vines (2.5 tonnes/hectare) at a ripe 23.8 brix and fermented in old oak casks. Fractionally pink-hued, it's soft and harmonious, with good weight, more complexity than most Gewürztraminers and rich lychees, pear and spice flavours.

DRY $22 AV

Rossendale Reserve Canterbury Gewürztraminer (★★★)

A perfumed, clearly varietal wine, the 2001 vintage (★★★) is slightly sweet, with ripe citrus-fruit, lychees and spice flavours showing good depth and a fresh, crisp finish. It's still youthful; drink now or cellar.

MED $18 AV

Saints Gisborne Gewürztraminer ★★★★

Grown at Patutahi, Montana's wine is consistently rich and flavour-packed, with loads of varietal character. The 2002 vintage (★★★★) was harvested at a ripe 23 brix and the juice was given brief skin contact to increase aroma and flavour extraction. Stop-fermented in a slightly sweet style, it is perfumed, spicy and slightly honeyed on the nose, with mouthfilling body (13.5 per cent alcohol) and rich flavours of lychees, spice, ginger and tropical fruits. Very harmonious and soft, with a slightly oily texture, it's already delicious.

Vintage	03	02	01	00
WR	6	6	NM	7
Drink	03-08	03-07	NM	P

MED/DRY $18 V+

Seifried Nelson Gewürztraminer ★★★★

Gewürztraminer is represented in the Seifried range in two styles: medium-dry and the sweet Ice Wine. This is typically a floral, well-spiced, crisp wine, very easy-drinking, and recent vintages have been of excellent quality. The 2002 (★★★★) is exotically perfumed and weighty, soft and ripe, with a distinct splash of sweetness amid its pear, lychees and spice flavours, which show good concentration.

Vintage	02	01	00	99	98
WR	7	6	6	6	6
Drink	03-06	03-05	03-05	P	P

MED $18 V+

Seifried Winemaker's Collection Nelson Gewürztraminer ★★★★

Drier than the standard label (above), this is typically a well-ripened wine with good body and a rich, rounded finish. The 2002 vintage (★★★★), grown in the Redwood Valley, has some distinctly Alsace-like qualities. The bouquet is spicy, gingery and exotically perfumed; the palate is rich, with gentle acidity, ripe ginger and spice flavours, a slightly oily texture and a slightly sweet finish. The 2003 vintage scored a silver medal at the 2003 Liquorland Top 100 International Wine Competition.

Vintage	02	01	00	99
WR	7	6	6	6
Drink	03-08	03-07	03-06	03-04

DRY $23 AV

Soljans Gisborne Gewürztraminer ★★★

Drinking well from the start, the 2002 vintage (★★★) is ripely scented, fruity and vibrant, with mouthfilling body, lychees and spice flavours and a slightly sweet, smooth finish. An earthy character gives it a slightly European feel.

MED/DRY $16 AV

Spy Valley Marlborough Gewürztraminer ★★★★

Already hard to resist, the 2002 vintage (★★★★) was estate-grown in the Waihopai Valley, picked at a ripe 24.5 brix and stop-fermented with a splash (9 grams/litre) of residual sugar. It's a sturdy wine (14 per cent alcohol) with attractive rose-petal aromas, concentrated citrus-fruit, lychee and spice flavours and a soft, rich finish. The 2003 vintage scored a gold medal at the 2003 Liquorland Top 100 International Wine Competition.

Vintage 03
WR 6
Drink 03-06

MED/DRY $20 V+

Stonecroft Gewürztraminer ★★★★★

The Gewürztraminers from this tiny Hawke's Bay winery are striking and among the finest in the country. Not oak-aged, the 2002 vintage (★★★★★) is an opulent wine, muscular and creamy-rich. Robust, with concentrated pear, lychees and spice flavours and a slightly gingery, dryish (5 grams/litre of sugar) finish, it's a highly characterful wine with richness right through the palate.

Vintage	02	01	00	99	98
WR	6	6	6	6	6
Drink	04-10	03-06	03-10	03-06	03-10

MED/DRY $30 AV

Te Whare Ra Duke of Marlborough Gewürztraminer ★★★★★

Arrestingly powerful and rich, this hedonistic wine usually crams more sheer flavour into the glass than most other Gewürztraminers from the region – or anywhere else. Made from 24 year-old vines, the 2003 vintage (★★★★★) is pale, musky and slightly sweet, with beautifully ripe, exotic fruit flavours, good weight, gentle acidity and a distinctly spicy finish.

Vintage	02	01	00	99	98
WR	7	7	6	7	7
Drink	03-12	03-05	03-04	03-04	P

MED $25 V+

Torlesse Waipara Gewürztraminer (★★☆)

Made in a fully dry style, the 2002 vintage (★★☆) is youthful and crisp, with lemony, slightly spicy and gingery, green-edged flavours. It's a moderately varietal wine that lacks a bit of richness and softness, but may need more time to show its best.

Vintage 02
WR 7
Drink 03-05

DRY $17 -V

Villa Maria Private Bin East Coast Gewürztraminer ★★★☆

This popular wine is fruity and well-spiced, with a sliver of sweetness. Delicious in its youth, the 2002 vintage (★★★★) is a blend of Gisborne, Hawke's Bay and Marlborough grapes. The bouquet is lifted and full-spiced; the palate is mouthfilling (13.5 per cent alcohol), with good sugar/acid balance (8 grams/litre of residual sugar) and loads of flavour, citrusy, spicy and lingering. The 2003 scored a silver medal at the 2003 Liquorland Top 100 International Wine Competition.

Vintage	03	02	01	00	99	98
WR	6	6	6	6	5	7
Drink	03-05	03-04	P	P	P	P

MED/DRY $18 V+

Villa Maria Reserve Gewürztraminer ★★★★☆

The 2002 vintage (★★★★☆) was grown in the company's Katoa vineyard, near Manutuke, south of the city of Gisborne, hand-picked and whole-bunch pressed. Almost bone-dry (harbouring 4 grams/litre of sugar), it's weighty and ripe-tasting, with excellent mouthfeel and youthful, delicate lychees and spice flavours. It shows strong potential; open 2004+.

DRY $25 AV

Waipara Hills Marlborough Gewürztraminer ★★★★

Maturing very gracefully, the 2001 vintage (★★★★) is a fresh, mouthfilling, well-rounded wine with a slightly oily texture and rich, ripe flavours of lychees and spice. A slightly sweet style, it shows excellent varietal character, delicacy and depth. The 2003 (★★★★) is again rewarding. A single-vineyard wine, it has a gently musky, perfumed bouquet, good weight, strong, ripe flavours of pears, lychees and spice, and good varietal character and texture.

Vintage 01
WR 6
Drink 03-07

MED $22 AV

Wairau River Marlborough Gewürztraminer (★★★☆)

A medium-dry style with a full-spiced bouquet, the debut 2002 vintage (★★★☆) is mouthfilling and fresh, with a slightly oily texture, plenty of citrusy, gingery flavour and a distinctly spicy finish.

Vintage 02
WR 7
Drink 03-06

MED/DRY $25 ·V

Waitiri Creek Gewürztraminer ★★★☆

Worth tracking down, the 2002 vintage (★★★★) was harvested at Gibbston, in Central Otago, in April and early May. Full and rounded, it has highly attractive, ripe lychees and spice flavours, and shows good weight, texture and depth. If you enjoy the classic Alsace style of Gewürztraminer, try this (winery sales only).

MED/DRY $26 ·V

Whitehaven Single Vineyard Reserve Gewürztraminer ★★★★

Grown in the Two Ponds vineyard at Grovetown and 30 per cent oak-aged (in seasoned casks), the 2001 (★★★★☆) is mouthfilling (14 per cent alcohol) and smooth, with a distinct splash of sweetness and strong lemon/spice flavours. Rich and oily, with good intensity, it's a sweetly seductive Marlborough wine, lovely and lingering. The 2003 vintage scored a bronze medal at the 2003 Liquorland Top 100 International Wine Competition.

Vintage 01 00
WR 6 5
Drink 03-04 P

MED/DRY $21 V+

William Hill Gewürztraminer ★★★☆

Gewürztraminer is a minor variety in Central Otago, but the William Hill winery at Alexandra has long crusaded on its behalf. Estate-grown and hand-picked at 23 brix, the 2002 vintage (★★★★) is a perfumed and weighty wine (although only 12.5 per cent alcohol), with gentle acidity and a delicious delicacy and depth of ripe lychees and spice flavours, fractionally sweet and smooth.

Vintage 02 01
WR 5 6
Drink 03-05 03-04

MED/DRY $20 AV

Müller-Thurgau

Every country has had its 'vin ordinaire' grape varieties: the south of France its endless tracts of red Carignan and white Ugni Blanc; Australia its ubiquitous Sultana and Trebbiano (Ugni Blanc); New Zealand its highly prolific Müller-Thurgau.

Professor Hermann Müller, a native of the Swiss canton of Thurgau, who worked at the Geisenheim viticultural station in Germany, wrote in 1882 of the benefits of 'combining the superb characteristics of the Riesling grape with the reliable early maturing qualities of the Sylvaner'. The variety Müller created (most likely a crossing of Riesling and Sylvaner, as he intended, but possibly of two different Rieslings) became extremely popular in Germany after the Second World War. Müller-Thurgau was prized by German growers not for the Riesling-like quality of its wine (it is far blander) but for its ability to ripen early with bumper crops.

In New Zealand, where plantings started to snowball in the early 1970s, by 1975 the same qualities had made it our most widely planted variety. Today, Müller-Thurgau is only number eight in terms of its area of bearing vines, and between 2000 and 2005 its plantings are projected to contract from 430 hectares to 256 hectares.

The grape's rapid decline reflects New Zealand's success with far more prestigious white-wine varieties like Sauvignon Blanc and Chardonnay. Montana also now finds it much cheaper to import the bulk wine it needs to fill its highly price-sensitive casks. The remaining Müller-Thurgau vines are concentrated in three regions: Gisborne (with almost half of all plantings), Hawke's Bay and Marlborough.

Müller-Thurgau should be drunk young, at six to 18 months old, when its garden-fresh aromas are in full flower. To attract those who are new to wine, it is typically made slightly sweet. Its fruity, citrusy flavours are typically mild and soft, lacking the intensity and crisp acid structure of Riesling.

Corbans White Label Müller-Thurgau ★★☆

This cheap wine is typically smooth and lemon-scented, with moderate sweetness balanced by crisp acidity in a light-bodied style with mild, appley flavours.

MED/DRY $9 AV

Jackman Ridge Müller-Thurgau ★★☆

Produced by Montana, this regional blend offers pleasant, lemony, appley flavours and a distinct splash of sweetness (it is markedly sweeter than its stablemate, the Corbans White Label [above]). Not vintage-dated, it is typically medium-bodied, with a soft finish.

MED $8 AV

Opihi Vineyard Müller-Thurgau ★★★

Müller-Thurgau is out of fashion in New Zealand, but of those still around this is one of the best. Grown at Pleasant Point in South Canterbury, it is typically fresh and floral, light and easy, with soft, ripe, lemony fruit characters. A good lunch wine.

MED/DRY $11 AV

Villa Maria Private Bin Müller-Thurgau ★★★

Top vintages of this wine are scented and lively – as Müller-Thurgau must be to have any appeal. Totally undemanding, the 2002 (★★★) is a medium style (with 22 grams/litre of sugar), blended from Hawke's Bay and Gisborne grapes. It's fresh and smooth, with delicate, ripe, lemony flavours, refreshing and floral.

Vintage 02
WR 7
Drink P

MED $9 V+

Wohnsiedler Müller-Thurgau ★★

Wohnsiedler won a gold medal or two for Montana decades ago, when Müller-Thurgau ruled the roost in New Zealand. Now a non-vintage regional blend, it's typically light, fruity, lemony and soft. Made in a medium style, it is fractionally sweeter than its Jackman Ridge stablemate (above).

MED $8 AV

Osteiner

This crossing of Riesling and Sylvaner is a rarity not only in New Zealand (with less than 2 hectares planted) but also in its native Germany. Only Rippon, at Lake Wanaka, has shown long-term interest in this obscure variety.

Rippon Osteiner ★★☆
This fragile Lake Wanaka wine tastes like a restrained Riesling. It is typically pale and tangy, with light body and lemon, apple and lime flavours cut with fresh acidity.

DRY $17 -V

Pinot Blanc

If you love Chardonnay, try Pinot Blanc. A white mutation of Pinot Noir, Pinot Blanc is highly regarded in Italy and California for its generous extract and moderate acidity, although in Alsace and Germany the more aromatic Pinot Gris finds greater favour.

With its fullness of weight and restrained, appley aroma, Pinot Blanc can easily be mistaken for Chardonnay in a blind tasting. The variety is still rare in New Zealand, but between 2002 and 2005, the area of bearing vines will expand from 8 to 12 hectares, mostly in Canterbury and Central Otago.

Gibbston Valley Central Otago Pinot Blanc (★★★★☆)
Arguably the finest Pinot Blanc yet made in New Zealand, the 2002 vintage (★★★★☆) was oak-aged and lees-stirred for 11 months. Pale straw, it is fat and rich, with a strong surge of fresh, peachy, appley, spicy flavours, impressive weight (14.5 per cent alcohol) and a dry finish. It tastes like a cross between Chardonnay and Gewürztraminer.

Vintage 02
WR 6
Drink 03+

DRY $32 AV

Waipara Hills Pinot Blanc ★★★
The 2001 vintage (★★★☆) was grown in the Tuscany Downs vineyard at West Melton, near Christchurch, and 30 per cent barrel-fermented. It's a lemony, full-flavoured wine with toasty, buttery characters adding complexity and firm acid spine. The 2002 (★★★), grown in the same vineyard and 10 per cent oak-aged, has a slightly honeyed nose and palate, with lemony, slightly buttery flavours and a crisp, off-dry finish.

MED/DRY $20 -V

Pinot Gris

Pinot Gris has soared in popularity in recent years, making this one of the fastest growing sections of the *Buyer's Guide*. It will account for only 2 per cent of the total producing vineyard area in 2004, but the vine is spreading swiftly – from 130 hectares of bearing vines in 2000 to 379 hectares in 2005. Pinot Gris is now the country's fourth most widely planted white-wine variety, behind only Sauvignon Blanc, Chardonnay and Riesling.

A mutation of Pinot Noir, Pinot Gris has skin colours ranging from blue-grey to reddish-pink, sturdy extract and a fairly subtle, spicy aroma. It is not a difficult variety to cultivate, adapting well to most soils, and ripens with fairly low acidity to high sugar levels. In Alsace, the best Pinot Gris are matured in large casks, but the wood is old, so as not to interfere with the grape's subtle flavour.

What does Pinot Gris taste like? Imagine a wine that couples the satisfying weight in the mouth of Chardonnay with some of the rich spiciness of Gewürztraminer. If you like substantial, refined dry whites that enhance food and can flourish long-term in the cellar (the Germans recommend drinking the wine when it has 'grey hairs'), Pinot Gris is well worth getting to know.

In terms of style and quality, New Zealand Pinot Gris vary widely. Many of the wines lack the mouthfilling body, flavour richness and softness of the benchmark wines from Alsace. These lesser wines, probably made from heavily cropped vines, are lean and crisp – more in the tradition of cheap Italian Pinot Grigio.

Popular in Germany, Alsace and Italy, Pinot Gris is now playing an important role here too. Over half of all plantings are concentrated in Marlborough and Otago, but there are also significant pockets of Pinot Gris in Gisborne, Hawke's Bay, Martinborough and Canterbury.

Akarua Pinot Gris ★★★☆

Grown at Bannockburn, in Central Otago, and 15 per cent oak-aged for three months, the 2002 vintage (★★★☆) is slightly pink-hued, sturdy, peachy and spicy, with ripe stone-fruit flavours and a slightly oily texture. It's a fresh, characterful wine with some leesy complexity and an off-dry finish.

Vintage	02	01
WR	6	5
Drink	03-07	03-05

MED/DRY $22 AV

Alan McCorkindale Waipara Valley Pinot Gris (★★★★☆)

Fleshy and rounded, the distinctly Alsace-like 2002 vintage (★★★★☆) was partly estate-grown. It's a mouthfilling, slightly sweet wine with rich, ripe pear, quince and spice flavours, a touch of complexity, gentle acidity and a long finish. Well worth cellaring.

MED/DRY $29 AV

Amisfield Central Otago Pinot Gris (★★★★)

The pale, faintly pink, debut 2002 vintage (★★★★) was grown at Amisfield vineyard, in the Cromwell Basin, and 20 per cent of the blend was fermented and lees-aged for five months in large (600-litre) French oak casks. Spice and stone-fruit aromas lead into a fresh, full-bodied (13.9 per cent alcohol), slightly oily and rounded wine with peach, lemon and distinctly spicy flavours, subtle oak and lees-aging characters and a fractionally sweet finish.

MED/DRY $30 -V

Amor-Bendall Gisborne Pinot Gris (★★★☆)

Tasted in its extreme youth, the 2002 vintage (★★★☆) was a fresh, tight, unwooded wine with vibrant pear and spice flavours, restrained and delicate, and good body.

DRY $19 AV

Ascension Matakana Pinot Gris (★★★★)

The 2002 vintage (★★★★) is a richly varietal wine, grown north of Auckland, harvested ripe (at 25 brix) and fermented and lees-aged in seasoned French oak barriques. It's full and rounded, with excellent depth of clearly delineated stone-fruit, pear and spice flavours, subtle oak adding complexity and a well-rounded, lingering finish.

DRY $25 AV

Ata Rangi Lismore Pinot Gris ★★★★☆

Grown in Ro and Lyle Griffiths' Lismore vineyard in Martinborough and 20 per cent barrel-fermented, the 2002 vintage (★★★★☆) is a strapping, highly concentrated wine with rich, slightly sweet peach, pear and spice flavours. The highly refined 2003 vintage (★★★★★) is remarkably attractive in its youth. Not oak-aged and a slightly sweeter style than the 2002, it shows lovely fullness, richness and roundness, with very ripe pear, melon and lychees flavours, lowish acidity and a gently sweet (15 grams/litre of residual sugar) finish. Showing great beauty and harmony, it's hard to resist.

Vintage	03	02	01	00
WR	7	7	6	6
Drink	03-05	03-04	P	P

MED $28 AV

Babich Marlborough Pinot Gris ★★★☆

Grown in the Pigou vineyard, on the Rapaura (north) side of the Wairau Valley, the 2002 vintage (★★★★) was mostly handled in tanks, but 20 per cent of the blend was fermented in seasoned French oak casks. Building up well with bottle age, it's a fleshy, smooth, dry wine with good body, texture and depth of ripe, peachy, lemony flavour and slightly leesy, nutty characters adding richness. The 2003 (★★★★) shows good varietal character, ripeness and texture. Full and fresh, with strong peach, pear and spice flavours and a fractionally sweet finish, it should be at its best from mid-2004 onwards.

Vintage	02	01	00	99	98
WR	7	7	7	7	7
Drink	03-04	03-05	03-05	03-04	P

MED/DRY $19 AV

Bald Hills Pigeon Rocks Pinot Gris (★★★☆)

From the Hunt family's vineyard at Bannockburn, in Central Otago, the debut 2003 vintage (★★★☆) is a dry style, fresh and lively, with soaring alcohol (14.5 per cent), very good depth of lychees and apple flavours and a well-spiced finish. Open mid-2004 onwards.

DRY $23 -V

Bilancia Pinot Grigio ★★★☆

Bilancia is a Hawke's Bay-based company, but the grapes for this wine are grown in Marlborough. Hand-harvested, it is fermented and matured on its yeast lees in stainless steel tanks. The 2002 vintage (★★★☆), re-tasted in late 2003, showed some leesy complexity in a crisp, appley, distinctly cool-climate style. Tasted in its infancy, the 2003 (★★★★) is floral, mouthfilling and vibrantly fruity, with very pure, citrusy, spicy flavours and a dry (4 grams/litre of residual sugar), long finish.

Vintage	03	02	01
WR	6	7	6
Drink	03-06	03-06	03-04

DRY $28 -V

Bilancia Reserve Pinot Grigio ★★★★

The full, weighty 2002 vintage (★★★☆) was grown in Hawke's Bay and matured for five months in old oak casks. It's a flavoursome wine with grapefruit and slight honey characters, showing some complexity and a crisp finish, but past vintages (especially the trophy-winning 1999) have been more distinguished.

Vintage	02
WR	6
Drink	03-06

DRY $33 -V

Bladen Marlborough Pinot Gris ★★☆

The 2001 vintage (★★★☆), a single-vineyard wine, not wood-aged, is the best yet – gently perfumed, full-bodied and rounded, with fractionally sweet stone-fruit, pear and spice flavours showing good depth. However, the 2002 (★★) is less attractive, lacking fresh, vibrant fruit aromas and flavours.

DRY $23 -V

Brick Bay Matakana Pinot Gris ★★★★

Grown at Matakana, north of Auckland, this is one of the country's finest Pinot Gris, rich and rounded. Hand-picked and mostly cool-fermented in tanks, with a small proportion briefly oak-aged, the 2002 vintage (★★★★) is a slightly sweet style, fresh, full-bodied and finely balanced, with rich, slightly honeyed stone-fruit flavours, good mouthfeel and length.

Vintage	02	01	00	99	98
WR	7	6	7	6	7
Drink	03-07	03-06	03-05	03-04	P

MED/DRY $25 AV

Brookfields Pinot Gris ★★★☆

Peter Robertson's Hawke's Bay wine is typically sturdy, with plenty of fresh, peachy, slightly earthy and spicy flavour. Grown at Ohiti Estate, near Fernhill, the 2002 vintage (★★★★) is a strongly varietal, dryish wine, mouthfilling and well-rounded, with good mouthfeel and texture and deep peach, pear and spice flavours.

MED/DRY $22 AV

Canterbury House Waipara Pinot Gris ★★★

Mouthfilling and slightly creamy, with fresh lemon and spice flavours and an underlying crispness, balanced by faint sweetness, the 2002 vintage (★★★) of this North Canterbury wine is a cool-climate style, for drinking now or cellaring. Visiting the winery, I was told: 'It's what the staff drink.'

MED/DRY $18 AV

Carrick Pinot Gris ★★★

Not oak-matured, the 2001 vintage (★★★) is a fresh, full-bodied (13.5 per cent alcohol) Central Otago wine. It's a distinctly cool-climate style with crisp, appley flavours and yeasty, lees-aging characters adding interest. The 2002 (★★★) is slightly creamy and mouthfilling, with tight, lemony flavours and a freshly acidic finish.

Vintage	02
WR	6
Drink	04

DRY $23 -V

Chard Farm Central Otago Pinot Gris ★★★★

Matured on its yeast lees but not oak-aged, the 2002 vintage (★★★★) is a basically dry style (4 grams/litre of sugar) with fresh, strong lemon, pear and spice flavours, balanced acidity and good length. It should age well. The 2001 (★★★★) was equally impressive, with excellent mouthfeel and depth.

Vintage	02	01
WR	6	6
Drink	03-06	03-04

DRY $24 AV

Coopers Creek Huapai Pinot Gris (★★★)

A good debut, the 2003 vintage (★★★) was estate-grown in West Auckland and handled entirely in tanks, with brief lees-aging. Fresh and lively, it has ripe pear and spice aromas and flavours, with a slight earthy character, and an off-dry (5 grams/litre of sugar), soft finish.

MED/DRY $16 V+

Corbans Pinot Gris ★★★

A slightly sweet Gisborne style with citrus fruit, pear and spice flavours offering good depth, the 2002 vintage (★★★) is a sharply priced wine from Montana. The 2003 (★★★) is very similar, with a full, smooth palate offering slightly sweet pear and spice flavours, showing good varietal character.

Vintage	03	02
WR	6	6
Drink	03-05	03+

MED/DRY $14 V+

Drylands Marlborough Pinot Gris ★★☆

The smooth, slightly bland 2001 vintage (★★☆) is onion skin-coloured, with slightly earthy characters and a medium-dry finish. It's an easy-drinking wine, but shows only limited varietal character. The 2002 (★★☆) is slightly pink-hued, with strawberry and spice flavours, but lacks real richness and varietal definition.

Vintage	02	01	00
WR	7	7	7
Drink	03-06	03-04	03-04

MED/DRY $20 -V

Dry River Pinot Gris

★★★★★

Since its first vintage in 1986, Dry River has towered over other New Zealand Pinot Gris, by virtue of its exceptional body, flavour richness and longevity. It's a satisfyingly sturdy Martinborough wine with peachy, spicy characters that can develop great subtlety and richness with maturity (at around five years old for top vintages, which also hold well for a decade). To avoid any loss of varietal flavour, it is not oak-aged. The 2002 vintage (★★★★★) is labelled 'Amaranth', indicating it is especially recommended for cellaring. It's a softly substantial, medium wine (18 grams/litre of residual sugar) with lovely ripeness of peach, quince and spice flavours, lush and rounded. A fleshy, rich wine, it's quite open and forthcoming in its youth.

Vintage	02	01	00	99	98	97	96	95	94
WR	7	NM	6	7	6	7	NM	5	6
Drink	03-10	NM	04-07	03-07	03-06	03-05	NM	P	P

MED/DRY $39 AV

Escarpment Martinborough Pinot Gris

★★★★☆

A top debut, the 2001 vintage (★★★★★) from Larry McKenna was grown 'in town' at the Station Bush vineyard, hand-picked from first-crop vines and fermented in seasoned oak barrels. The bouquet is fresh, spicy and floral; the palate is rich and round, with beautifully fresh, concentrated flavours of pears and spice fleshed out with subtle oak. The creamy-textured 2002 (★★★★) is smooth and full, with strong, peachy, spicy, slightly honeyed, nutty and mealy flavours in a complex style with loads of character.

Vintage	02	01
WR	6	6
Drink	04-05	03-04

MED/DRY $29 AV

Esk Valley Hawke's Bay Pinot Gris

★★★★

A blend of Esk Valley and Te Awanga fruit, not oak-aged, the 2002 (★★★★☆) is a very impressive wine with fragrant, rich aromas of stone-fruit, pears and spice. Softly mouthfilling, it shows beautifully ripe fruit characters, with gentle acidity and commanding mouthfeel. Tasted before it was bottled (and so not rated), the 2003 vintage looked potentially outstanding – rich and soft, with concentrated pear and spice flavours and a lovely, Alsace-like texture.

Vintage	02	01
WR	6	5
Drink	03-06	03-05

MED/DRY $23 AV

Fairhall Downs Marlborough Pinot Gris

★★★★☆

This Brancott Valley vineyard produces a weighty style with an appealing, floral bouquet and deep stone-fruit, pear and spice flavours, typically threaded with crisp Marlborough acidity. The initial releases were robust, dry and richly alcoholic, but the 2001 (★★★★) and outstanding 2002 (★★★★★) vintages have a touch of residual sugar. Notably rich, ripe and rounded, with strikingly deep flavours and a slightly sweet finish, the 2002 is a finely balanced wine with highly impressive weight, richness and harmony. Drink now onwards.

Vintage	02	01
WR	7	7
Drink	03-05	P

MED/DRY $28 AV

Framingham Marlborough Pinot Gris ★★★★

Mostly estate-grown at Renwick, harvested at a ripe 24 brix and aged on its lees in tanks, with no oak-aging, the 2002 vintage (★★★★) is a mouthfilling, medium-dry style with pronounced varietal character. It has a slightly oily texture, with excellent depth of fresh apple, pear and peach flavours, showing some lushness, and gentle acidity giving a well-rounded finish.

Vintage	02	01	00	99
WR	6	6	5	6
Drink	03-05	03-06	03-05	P

MED/DRY $23 AV

Gibbston Valley Central Otago Pinot Gris ★★★☆

This wine is typically full of personality and the 2000 (★★★★) and 2001 (★★★☆) vintages both show good intensity. The 2002 (★★★☆) has candied aromas, with lemony, peachy flavours, slightly sweet, fresh and vibrant. It's a high-alcohol style (14.5 per cent), crisp and distinctly spicy, that should unfold well with cellaring. The 2003 scored a bronze medal at the 2003 Liquorland Top 100 International Wine Competition.

Vintage	02	01	00	99	98
WR	6	6	6	6	6
Drink	03-10	03-10	03-08	03-06	P

DRY $27 -V

Gladstone Pinot Gris ★★★

The easy-drinking 2002 vintage (★★★) of this Wairarapa wine is a slightly sweet style (7 grams/litre of sugar), blended from estate-grown grapes and fruit from the McGovern vineyard at Opaki, north of Masterton. Matured on its yeast lees for four months, it has a gently spicy bouquet, fullness of body, decent depth of lemon, pear and spice flavours, gentle acidity and a soft finish.

MED/DRY $25 -V

Goldridge Estate Pinot Gris ★★☆

Partly matured in French oak barriques, the 2001 vintage (★★☆) from Matakana Estate is pale gold, with developed colour for its age. Medium-full in body, with a honeyed bouquet, it offers plenty of citrusy, slightly pineappley flavour, with a slightly sweet (8 grams/litre of sugar), crisp finish. Drink now.

Vintage	01	00	99
WR	6	NM	5
Drink	P	NM	P

MED/DRY $19 -V

Grove Mill Marlborough Pinot Gris ★★★★

Grove Mill is a key pioneer of Pinot Gris in Marlborough, since 1994 producing a richly flavoured style with abundant sweetness. The fleshy 2002 vintage (★★★★☆) was grown principally in the Omaka Valley, stop-fermented in a distinctly medium style (with 17 grams/litre of sugar), and given a full malolactic fermentation. Deliciously mouthfilling, rich and rounded, it has good mouthfeel and texture, and a strong surge of peach, lemon and spice flavours.

Vintage	02	01	00	99	98
WR	7	6	7	7	NM
Drink	03-06	03-05	03-05	03-04	NM

MED $25 AV

Hanmer Junction Waipara Valley Pinot Gris ★★★☆

A pale, distinctly cool-climate style from a single vineyard at Waipara, the 2002 vintage (★★★) is a medium-dry style (7 grams/litre of sugar) with lemony, spicy flavours showing some delicacy and a fresh, crisp finish.

Vintage 02 01
WR 5 6
Drink 03-04 P

MED/DRY $17 V+

Hay's Lake Pinot Gris (★★★★)

Grown in Central Otago, the powerful 2001 vintage (★★★★) shows good body and richness, with slightly sweet flavours of stone-fruit and spice, balanced acidity and a long finish.

MED/DRY $24 AV

Herzog Marlborough Pinot Gris ★★★★☆

Grown alongside the Wairau River and harvested at a very ripe 26 brix, the 2002 vintage (★★★★☆) is a sturdy (14 per cent alcohol) wine. It was fermented and lees-aged in new French oak casks, and 50 per cent of the wine went through a softening malolactic fermentation. Rich and robust, with loads of peach, lychees and spice flavours and a lasting, bone-dry finish, it should mature splendidly.

Vintage 02 01
WR 6 6
Drink 03-06 03-04

DRY $39 -V

Huia Marlborough Pinot Gris ★★★☆

Drinking well now, the 2002 vintage (★★★☆) was harvested in the Anderson vineyard in the Brancott Valley, whole-bunch pressed and fermented with indigenous yeasts in stainless steel tanks. A dry style (4.8 grams/litre of sugar), it's full-bodied (13.5 per cent alcohol), fresh and harmonious, with good texture, faintly honeyed, pear and spice flavours and a well-rounded finish.

Vintage 02 01 00
WR 6 7 6
Drink 03-06 03-07 03-05

DRY $25 -V

Huntaway Reserve Marlborough Pinot Gris (★★★☆)

The very easy-drinking 2002 vintage (★★★☆) from Montana was hand-picked at over 23 brix, tank-fermented and matured on its yeast lees for three months. Pale straw, it's a freshly aromatic, slightly sweet style with smooth pear, lychees and spice flavours, mouthfilling body and a slightly creamy texture. The 2003 scored a silver medal at the 2003 Liquorland Top 100 International Wine Competition.

Vintage 03
WR 5
Drink 03-06

MED/DRY $20 AV

Hyperion Phoebe Pinot Gris ★★☆

Estate-grown at Matakana, north of Auckland, the easy-drinking 2002 vintage (★★☆) is a medium-bodied, slightly sweet style, clean and fresh, with moderate depth of citrusy, gently spicy flavour and a crisp finish.

Vintage 02
WR 5
Drink 03-05

MED/DRY $21 -V

Isabel Marlborough Pinot Gris ★★★★☆

The sturdy, rich 2002 vintage (★★★★☆) was harvested at 22 to 24 brix and most of the wine was handled in tanks, but a minority was barrel-fermented and given a softening malolactic fermentation. Pale, with delicate, spicy aromas, it's a weighty wine with excellent intensity of pear, lychees and spice flavours in a dryish style (5 grams/litre of sugar) with a slightly oily texture and excellent varietal character. It's well worth cellaring; open 2004+.

MED/DRY $25 AV

Johanneshof Marlborough Pinot Gris ★★★☆

Perfumed and spicy, the 2001 vintage (★★★★☆) is soft and dryish (5 grams/litre of sugar), with lovely fruit characters of pears, lychees and spice and mouthfilling body. The 2002 (★★☆) is less impressive – faintly pink, with lemony, spicy flavours that slightly lack freshness and a soft finish.

MED/DRY $25 -V

Kim Crawford Boyszone Vineyard Marlborough Pinot Gris ★★★

The 2002 vintage (★★★) includes 10 per cent Gewürztraminer and 3 per cent Chardonnay. A single-vineyard wine, it was partly (15 per cent) fermented in one-year-old American oak casks, with some malolactic fermentation. A dryish style (5 grams/litre of sugar), it is freshly aromatic and vibrantly fruity in an easy-drinking style with lemony, appley, slightly spicy flavours and a smooth finish. The 2003 scored a bronze medal at the 2003 Liquorland Top 100 International Wine Competition.

Vintage	03	02	01
WR	6	7	6
Drink	04-05	03-05	P

MED/DRY $20 -V

Koura Bay Shark's Tooth Marlborough Pinot Gris ★★★

The skilfully crafted, very easy-drinking 2002 vintage (★★★☆) was estate-grown in the Awatere Valley and lees-aged in tanks, with no oak handling. It's a medium-dry style with good body and depth of ripe pear and lychees flavours, a hint of honey, gentle acidity and a well-rounded finish.

Vintage	02
WR	6
Drink	04-05

MED/DRY $20 -V

Kumeu River Pinot Gris ★★★★

This is a consistently attractive wine. Grown at Kumeu, in West Auckland, matured on its yeast lees but not oak-matured (future releases will be fermented in large, 600-litre oak casks), the 2002 vintage (★★★★) is weighty, with a fresh, floral bouquet, peach and pear flavours showing excellent richness, a slightly oily texture and a long, slightly sweet, crisp finish. It's still youthful; open 2004 onwards.

Vintage	03	02	01	00	99	98
WR	6	6	6	5	5	5
Drink	03-05	03-05	P	P	P	P

MED/DRY $25 AV

Lawson's Dry Hills Marlborough Pinot Gris ★★★

The 2001 vintage (★★★) was grown in the Hutchison vineyard and 10 per cent of the final blend was fermented with indigenous ('wild') yeasts in barrels. It's an easy-drinking, slightly sweet style with a subtle wood influence and decent depth of peach, pear and spice flavours. The 2002 (★★★), also 10 per cent wood-matured, is a mouthfilling wine with a restrained oak influence and decent depth of lemon and spice flavours.

Vintage 02
WR 6
Drink 03-05

MED/DRY $19 -V

Loopline Vineyard Wairarapa Pinot Gris (★★★)

Faintly pink-hued, the 2002 vintage (★★★) is a dry style, full-bodied and crisp, with strongly spicy, gingery, citrusy flavours that could almost be mistaken for Gewürztraminer.

Vintage 02
WR 6
Drink 03-06

DRY $25 -V

Lucknow Estate QBV Pinot Gris (★★☆)

'QBV' on the label stands for the Quarry Bridge Vineyard, in Hawke's Bay. Fermented and lees-aged for five months in older French oak casks, with weekly lees-stirring, the 2002 vintage (★★☆) shows restrained varietal character in a full-bodied, dry style, peachy, nutty, buttery and flavoursome. Verging on three stars.

Vintage 03
WR 6
Drink 08

DRY $28 -V

Margrain Martinborough Pinot Gris ★★★☆

Lees-aged but not matured in oak, the 2001 (★★★☆) is full-bodied (14 per cent alcohol), lemony and slightly spicy, with firm acidity woven through its bone-dry flavours. The 2002 (★★★☆) is very similar. It's a robust (14.5 per cent alcohol) wine, lemon-scented, with strong citrusy, spicy, slightly minerally flavours and a tight, dry finish. Still youthful, it's best cellared to mid-2004+.

Vintage 02 01 00 99 98
WR   7   6   6   7   7
Drink 03-07 03-06 03-06 03-05 03-04

DRY $28 -V

Marsden Bay of Islands Pinot Gris ★★★

Grown further north than any other New Zealand Pinot Gris, the light gold 2002 vintage (★★★) has a slightly honeyed bouquet, reflecting some botrytis influence. Fleshy and flavoursome, it shows good varietal character, with ripe, stone-fruit characters, gentle acidity and a slightly sweet finish. It's ready for drinking now.

Vintage 02
WR 5
Drink 03-05

MED/DRY $22 -V

Martinborough Vineyard Pinot Gris ★★★★★

Since its launch from 1996, this powerful, concentrated wine has emerged as one of the finest Pinot Gris in the country. It is fermented with a high percentage of indigenous yeasts, and lees-aged, partly in seasoned oak casks, in a bid to produce a 'Burgundian style with complexity, texture and weight' (small pockets of Pinot Gris can be found in Burgundy). The 2001

(★★★★★) is a very satisfying and weighty wine with rich stone-fruit, citrus and spice flavours and subtle oak adding complexity. The 2002 vintage (★★★★☆) was grown in the McCreanor vineyard at Martinborough and the St Francis vineyard, in central Wairarapa. Showing good weight and complexity, with strong peachy, nutty flavours and a slightly buttery finish, it could probably be mistaken in a blind tasting for Chardonnay, but the pear and spice characters of Pinot Gris are also in evidence.

DRY $35 AV

Matakana Estate Pinot Gris ★★★★

Estate-grown north of Auckland, the 2000 vintage (★★★★) is a stylish wine with a slightly nutty bouquet and strong melon and pear flavours, soft, fractionally sweet and spicy. It was mostly handled in tanks, but 30 per cent was fermented and matured for three months in French oak barriques (half new). The fleshy, slightly sweet 2002 vintage (★★★★) is again highly attractive – ripely scented, with good weight and plenty of well-rounded, citrusy, peachy flavour.

MED/DRY $26 -V

Matua Valley Shingle Peak Pinot Gris – see Shingle Peak Pinot Gris

Mills Reef Reserve Pinot Gris (★★★★)

Launched from the 2002 vintage (★★★★), this Hawke's Bay wine is weighty, with ripe aromas of lemons, pears and spice. Highly attractive in its youth, it is vibrantly fruity and full-flavoured, with a slightly oily texture and good mouthfeel.

DRY $20 V+

Mission Hawke's Bay Pinot Gris ★★★☆

The Mission has long been a standard-bearer for Pinot Gris. The 2002 vintage (★★★) was grown in three vineyards at Greenmeadows, Havelock North and Patangata (Central Hawke's Bay). Lees-aged, with some malolactic fermentation but no oak handling, it's a ripe, lemony and spicy wine with fresh acidity, vibrant fruit characters, a slightly oily texture and a rounded finish.

Vintage	02	01	00	99	98
WR	6	5	6	7	6
Drink	03-08	P	03-04	03-06	03-05

MED/DRY $16 V+

Morton Estate White Label Hawke's Bay Pinot Gris ★★★☆

Grown in the elevated, inland Riverview and Colefield vineyards at Mangatahi, the 2002 vintage (★★★☆) was fermented and lees-aged in old French oak barrels. It's a weighty, youthful wine with peach, lemon and spice flavours, slightly nutty and honeyed, and a crisp finish. Good value.

Vintage	02
WR	6
Drink	03-05

DRY $16 V+

Murdoch James Martinborough Pinot Gris (★★★★)

An auspicious debut, the 2003 vintage (★★★★) was harvested at 23 brix in the Blue Rock vineyard, south of Martinborough, and fermented dry. Weighty (14 per cent alcohol) and soft, it's a strongly varietal wine with ripe pear, lychees and spice flavours showing excellent depth and a well-rounded finish. It should mature well.

DRY $29 (500ML) -V

Mt Difficulty Pinot Gris ★★★☆

Grown at Bannockburn, in Central Otago, this is typically a substantial, citrusy and spicy, tightly structured wine. Slight nutty, yeasty characters – derived from varying degrees of lees-aging, barrel fermentation and malolactic fermentation – add a touch of complexity, and most vintages show good depth, cool-climate freshness and drive.

MED/DRY $22 AV

Nautilus Marlborough Pinot Gris ★★★☆

The skilfully crafted 2002 vintage (★★★★), a blend of Awatere Valley and Wairau Valley grapes, was 20 per cent barrel-fermented and all of the wine was lees-aged for three months. It's a highly fragrant, generous, full-flavoured wine with lemony and spicy characters and a slightly sweet (6.5 grams/litre of sugar), lingering finish. An immaculate wine with lots of personality, it's maturing well. Tasted prior to bottling (and so not rated), the 2003 showed balanced acidity and fresh, strong pear and spice flavours.

Vintage	03	02	01	00
WR	6	7	6	5
Drink	04-06	03-05	P	P

MED/DRY $25 -V

Neudorf Moutere Pinot Gris ★★★★☆

The floral, softly textured 2002 vintage (★★★★☆) was harvested at 24 brix from ultra low-cropping vines (below 4 tonnes/hectare) in the Home Vineyard at Upper Moutere, fermented with indigenous yeasts in old French oak barrels and stop-fermented with 16 grams per litre of residual sugar (making it a medium style). It's a highly scented, beautifully rounded wine, weighty, fresh and vibrant, with rich peach, pear and spice flavours. Delicious in its youth, it also invites cellaring.

MED $28 AV

Neudorf Nelson Pinot Gris (★★★★)

Worth cellaring, the finely balanced 2003 vintage (★★★★) was handled entirely in stainless steel tanks and made in a dryish (5 grams/litre of residual sugar) style. It's a weighty wine (14 per cent alcohol), very fresh and vibrant, with good varietal character and excellent depth of pear, lychees and spice flavours.

Vintage	03
WR	5
Drink	03-07

MED/DRY $25 AV

Nevis Bluff Pinot Gris ★★★★☆

This Central Otago wine is always full of character. The richly flavoured 2002 vintage (★★★★) was grown at Nevis Bluff Estate and the neighbouring Pociecha vineyard at Gibbston. Fermented and lees-aged for nine months in tanks, it is fleshy and ripe, with concentrated stone-fruit flavours, hints of honey and spice and a deliciously soft, smooth finish.

Vintage	02
WR	6
Drink	04-07

MED/DRY $30 AV

Omaka Springs Marlborough Pinot Gris ★★★

Grown in the Omaka Valley, the 2002 vintage (★★★) is weighty and rounded, with good depth of peach, lemon and spice flavours in a slightly sweet style. Balanced for easy drinking, the 2003 (★★★☆) is a mouthfilling wine (14 per cent alcohol), with strong, ripe, peachy, slightly honeyed flavours, a slightly oily texture, fresh acidity and a sliver of sweetness. Great value.

MED/DRY $16 V+

Opihi Pinot Gris ★★★☆

Grown on a north-facing slope inland from Timaru, in South Canterbury, this is typically a highly attractive wine, hand-picked and made with some use of indigenous yeasts and lees-stirring. It's a fresh and lively style, fractionally sweet, with ripe peach, melon and spice flavours, slightly nutty and leesy, and a smooth finish.

MED/DRY $20 AV

Palliser Estate Martinborough Pinot Gris ★★★★☆

The 2001 (★★★★☆) was cool-fermented and lees-aged for four months in tanks, and stop-fermented with 7 grams/litre of residual sugar. Weighty and rounded, it shows clearly defined varietal characters, with fresh, strong grapefruit, lychees and spice flavours and the combination of gentle acidity and slight sweetness giving a seductively smooth finish. The 2002 vintage (★★★★) is a full-bodied wine with good mid-palate weight and richness, fresh pear and spice characters and a dryish, lingering finish.

MED/DRY $26 AV

Peregrine Central Otago Pinot Gris ★★★★

Grown at Gibbston and matured on its yeast lees, although not oak-aged, this is one of the region's top Pinot Gris. The 2002 vintage (★★★☆) is a dry style with strong stone-fruit and spice flavours and substantial body. There's a touch of phenolic hardness on the finish, but that's unlikely to bother most drinkers.

Vintage 02
WR 6
Drink 03-06

DRY $23 AV

Porters Martinborough Pinot Gris ★★★☆

The 2002 vintage (★★★☆) was harvested from ultra low-cropping vines (2.5 tonnes/hectare) and lees-aged in tanks. The bouquet is spicy and slightly earthy; the palate is strongly spiced and nutty, with good weight, a slightly oily texture and a dryish finish.

Vintage 02 01 00 99 98
WR 7 6 7 6 7
Drink 03-06 03-07 03-06 03-05 03-04

MED/DRY $40 -V

Quartz Reef Central Otago Pinot Gris ★★★★☆

Past vintages were grown entirely at Gibbston, but the 2002 (★★★★) also includes grapes from the company's much earlier-ripening Bendigo Estate vineyard, in the Cromwell Basin. Fermented to dryness and lees-aged for five months in tanks, it's a weighty wine (14 per cent alcohol) with strong pear and spice flavours and a rounded finish. Refined and delicate, and still very fresh and youthful, it should mature well.

Vintage 02 01 00 99
WR 6 6 7 6
Drink 03-05 03-04 03-04 P

DRY $28 AV

Ransom Clos De Valerie Pinot Gris ★★★

Estate-grown at Mahurangi, near Warkworth, north of Auckland, this wine is named after the road on which the vineyard lies – Valerie Close. The fully dry 2002 vintage (★★☆) is crisp and lemony, with slightly high acidity for the variety. Medium-bodied, with a slight lack of lushness and fruit sweetness, it's much more in the mould of northern Italian Pinot Grigio than Alsace Pinot Gris.

Vintage 02 01 00 99
WR 6 5 6 5
Drink 03-08 03-06 P P

DRY $23 -V

Ridgeview Estate Pinot Gris (★★☆)

Grown on Waiheke Island, the yellow-hued 2002 vintage (★★☆) shows a slight hardness, or lack of delicacy, on the palate, but offers plenty of citrusy, peachy, slightly spicy and honeyed flavour.

MED/DRY $23 -V

Rockburn Central Otago Pinot Gris ★★★☆

The pale, green-tinged 2002 vintage (★★★☆) is a substantial wine (14.5 per cent alcohol) with fresh, strong, pear and spice flavours and a crisp and lively finish. A blend of grapes grown at Lowburn, in the Cromwell Basin (two-thirds) and Gibbston, it's a bone-dry wine, maturing well. (Earlier releases were labelled as Hay's Lake.)

MED/DRY $27 -V

St Francis Marlborough Pinot Gris (★★☆)

Verging on three-star quality, the 2002 vintage (★★☆) was grown in the Schoolhouse Vineyard, in the Omaka Valley. Light yellow/green, it's a dry style with plenty of peachy, spicy flavour and mouthfilling body (14 per cent alcohol), but lacks real delicacy, with a crisp, slightly hard finish.

Vintage 02
WR 6
Drink 03-07

DRY $24 -V

St Helena Canterbury Pinot Gris ★★☆

Estate-grown on the northern outskirts of Christchurch, the 2002 vintage (★★☆) shows only moderate varietal character. A medium-bodied style, it is pale and crisp, with strongly spiced flavours and a slightly sweet finish.

MED/DRY $16 AV

St Helena Reserve Pinot Gris ★★★

Faintly pink, the 2002 vintage (★★☆) of this Canterbury wine shows some ripe-fruit characters, but also a slight lack of freshness, delicacy and roundness.

DRY $19 AV

Sacred Hill Marlborough Vineyards Pinot Gris (★★★)

The 2002 vintage (★★★) was grown in the company's Jacksons Road vineyard and partly French oak-fermented. Fragrant, pear/spice aromas lead into a full-bodied wine with strong pear, herb and spice flavours, restrained oak and a crisp, dryish, green-edged finish.

MED/DRY $23 -V

Saint Clair Godfrey's Creek Pinot Gris (★★★☆)

Mostly grown in the Walsh vineyard, at the head of the Brancott Valley, in Marlborough, the debut 2003 vintage (★★★☆) was mainly handled in tanks, but 10 per cent was fermented in seasoned oak casks and all of the blend went through a softening malolactic fermentation. It has good mouthfeel, with fresh citrus-fruit, pear and spice flavours, a touch of complexity and a slightly sweet (7 grams/litre of sugar), crisp finish.

MED/DRY $24 -V

Saint Clair Marlborough Pinot Gris (★★★)

The debut 2002 vintage (★★★) was partly fermented with indigenous yeasts in old oak casks; the rest was handled in stainless steel tanks and given a softening malolactic fermentation. It offers smooth, slightly sweet pear, lemon and spice flavours, with a slightly creamy texture and good body.

MED/DRY $18 AV

Seresin Pinot Gris ★★★★☆

One of the country's top Pinot Gris. The 2002 vintage (★★★★★) was hand-harvested in Marlborough at a high sugar level of 23.8 brix, began its ferment in tanks, but was then transferred to old French oak barriques to complete its fermentation and age on its yeast lees, with regular lees-stirring. Ripe, stone-fruit aromas lead into a powerful wine (14.5 per cent alcohol) with rich pear, peach and spice flavours, a slightly oily texture and a rounded, dry finish. A strongly varietal wine, it should be long-lived.

Vintage	02	01	00	99	98
WR	6	6	6	7	6
Drink	03-07	03-08	03-07	03-05	03-04

DRY $24 V+

Shingle Peak Marlborough Pinot Gris ★★★☆

Balanced for easy drinking, the 2002 vintage (★★★☆) from Matua Valley was 50 per cent handled in tanks; the rest was fermented or matured in oak barrels. It's a mouthfilling, lemony, appley wine with slight sweetness and good texture, with some creamy, lees-aging influence adding complexity.

Vintage	02
WR	5
Drink	03-06

MED/DRY $21 AV

Spy Valley Marlborough Pinot Gris (★★★★)

Showing excellent weight, depth and balance, the 2002 vintage (★★★★) was estate-grown in the Waihopai Valley, picked at 24 brix, tank-fermented and lees-aged. It's a full-bodied style (14 per cent alcohol) with strong, peachy, lemony, spicy flavours and a rounded, rich finish. The 2003 scored a bronze medal at the 2003 Liquorland Top 100 International Wine Competition.

Vintage	03	02	01
WR	7	7	6
Drink	03-06	03-07	03-06

MED/DRY $20 V+

Staete Landt Marlborough Pinot Gris ★★★★☆

A rare, single-vineyard wine, well worth tracking down. The 2002 vintage (★★★★☆) was hand-picked at 24.9 brix, whole-bunch pressed, and fermented and matured on its light yeast lees for four months in six-year-old French oak puncheons. A dry style (3 grams/litre of residual sugar), it is weighty and concentrated, with sweet-fruit delights, citrus and stone-fruit flavours, a slightly nutty complexity and a long, tight finish. It should really blossom with cellaring; open 2005+.

Vintage	02
WR	6
Drink	03-05

DRY $34 -V

Stonecutter Martinborough Pinot Gris ★★★☆

Handled entirely in stainless steel tanks, the 2001 vintage (★★★☆) is full-bodied, with a slightly oily texture and lemony, peachy, spicy flavours showing good varietal character and depth.

Vintage 01
WR 4
Drink 03-04

DRY $23 -V

Tasman Bay Marlborough Pinot Gris ★★★

The 2002 vintage (★★★) is a medium-bodied style with drink-young charm. Twenty per cent French oak-aged, it is smooth and fresh, with a slightly oily texture and decent depth of lemony, appley, spicy flavour.

MED/DRY $18 AV

Three Sisters Pinot Gris (★★)

Grown at altitude in Central Hawke's Bay, the 2001 vintage (★★) is lemon-scented, fresh and clean, but lacks real weight and richness. Pale, it offers light, citrusy, appley flavours with restrained varietal character.

Vintage 01
WR 4
Drink 03-06

MED/DRY $16 -V

Torlesse Pinot Gris (★★★)

Grown at West Eyreton in Canterbury, the 2002 vintage (★★★) is a tight, appley, lemony, slightly minerally wine with a bone-dry finish. Fresh, with good delicacy and depth, it's worth cellaring. (The 2003 is a 50/50 blend of Waipara and other Canterbury grapes.)

Vintage 02
WR 6
Drink 03-06

DRY $16 V+

Trinity Hill Gimblett Gravels Pinot Gris ★★★★

The 2003 vintage (★★★★) was hand-picked in Hawke's Bay and fermented and matured for five months in seasoned French oak barrels. A medium-dry style, it is mouthfilling, with strong pear and spice characters, a hint of honey, very subtle oak and loads of character. Drink now or cellar.

Vintage 03 02 01 00 99
WR 6 5 5 5 6
Drink 03-08 03-05 03-05 03-04 P

MED/DRY $30 -V

Vavasour Awatere Valley Marlborough Pinot Gris (★★★)

A good but not great debut, the 2002 vintage (★★★) is a distinctly cool-climate style, full and fresh, with pear, spice and apple flavours and a crisp finish.

Vintage 02
WR 7
Drink 03-06

MED/DRY $20 -V

Villa Maria Private Bin Pinot Gris ★★★

The 2002 vintage (★★★), grown in Marlborough, is a sturdy (14.5 per cent alcohol) wine with pear, spice and lime aromas and flavours in a crisp and lively, green-edged, cool-climate style.

Vintage	02	01	00	99
WR	5	NM	5	4
Drink	P	NM	P	P

MED/DRY $16 V+

Vin Alto Pinot Grigio ★★★

Grown in the Clevedon hills, in South Auckland, but 'made in the European tradition', the 2001 vintage (★★★) is a bone-dry wine, designed to accompany food. Light straw, with a vinous, lemony bouquet, it's less vibrantly fruity than most New Zealand Pinot Gris, but shows good weight and complexity, with fresh, rounded grapefruit and slightly spicy flavours, showing good depth.

DRY $28 -V

Waimea Estates Bolitho Reserve Pinot Gris (★★☆)

The 2002 vintage (★★☆) was hand-picked in Nelson from low-yielding vines (below 5 tonnes/hectare), and fermented with some use of indigenous yeasts in a 50/50 split of tanks and barrels. In its youth, its crisp, citrusy flavours are overpowered by wood, but the wine shows good body and with time should achieve a finer balance.

DRY $25 -V

Waipara Hills Pinot Gris (★★★)

Restrained in its youth, but well-structured, the 2002 vintage (★★★) is a fresh, crisp, cool-climate style with citrusy, appley flavours and a slightly sweet finish.

MED/DRY $20 -V

Wairau River Marlborough Pinot Gris (★★★☆)

Estate-grown, the 2002 vintage (★★★☆) is a distinctly medium style, delicious in its youth. Soft and fleshy, it offers good depth of stone-fruit and pear flavours, abundant sweetness (26 grams/litre of sugar) and a well-spiced finish.

Vintage	02
WR	7
Drink	03-06

MED $25 -V

Riesling

Riesling isn't yet one of New Zealand's major international wine successes – the 69,680 cases shipped in the year to June 2003 accounted for only 2.3 per cent of our total wine exports. Yet overseas acclaim is starting to flow. UK wine writer Stephen Brook reported tasting some 'absolutely delicious' Rieslings at the 2002 Air New Zealand Wine Awards, and Waipara Hills Riesling 2002 won the trophy for Best Aromatic Wine at the Sydney International Wine Competition 2003.

Captivated by Chardonnay and Sauvignon Blanc, Kiwi wine lovers until a few years ago ignored this country's equally delightful Rieslings. At last, Riesling is slowly growing in popularity and starting to achieve the profile it richly deserves.

Scentedness and intense lemon/lime flavours enlivened by fresh, appetising acidity are the hallmarks of the top New Zealand Rieslings. Around the world, Riesling has traditionally been regarded as Chardonnay's great rival in the white-wine quality stakes, well ahead of Sauvignon Blanc. So what took New Zealand wine lovers so long to appreciate Riesling's lofty stature?

Several factors tethered Riesling's popularity. A long-lived confusion over names (with 'Riesling-Sylvaner' used as an alternative to Müller-Thurgau and 'Rhine Riesling' as a synonym for the true Riesling) hardly helped Riesling build a distinctive identity. Riesling is typically made in a slightly sweet style to balance the grape's natural high acidity, but this gentle sweetness runs counter to the fashion for bone-dry wines. And fine Riesling demands time to unfold its full potential; drunk in its infancy, as it often is, it lacks the toasty, minerally, honeyed richness that is the real glory of Riesling.

Riesling ranks as New Zealand's third most extensively planted white-wine variety. Between 2000 and 2005, the total area of bearing vines is expanding slowly, from 503 to 628 hectares. The great grape of Germany, Riesling is a classic cool-climate variety, particularly well suited to the cooler growing temperatures and lower humidity of the South Island. Its stronghold is Marlborough, where over half of all the vines are clustered, but the grape is also extensively planted in Nelson, Canterbury and Central Otago.

Riesling styles vary markedly around the world. In the past, New Zealand's Rieslings veered mainly towards the light German style, relying on their garden-fresh, summery scents and exquisite balance of fruit, sweetness and acidity for their appeal. Now, a new breed of more powerful, richer, drier wines is starting to emerge – more likely to appeal to wine drinkers raised on Chardonnay and Sauvignon Blanc.

Alana Estate Martinborough Riesling ★★★☆

Light and lovely, the 2002 vintage (★★★★) is a distinctly medium style (18 grams per litre of residual sugar) with fresh, strong flavours of citrus fruits, limes and even pineapple. Highly scented, it's a tangy, finely poised wine, vivacious and harmonious.

Vintage	02	01
WR	6	6
Drink	03-06	03-05

MED $18 AV

Alan McCorkindale Waipara Valley Dry Riesling (★★★★★)

The 2002 vintage (★★★★★) is a very classy wine with a youthful, pale lemon/green hue and pure, lemony, appley aromas. Slightly minerally, with a deliciously well-rounded texture, it possesses deep, delicate lemon/lime flavours, moderate acidity for South Island Riesling and a very rich, harmonious finish. High-priced, but worth it.

DRY $26 AV

Alexandra Wine Company Crag An Oir Riesling ★★★

The 2002 vintage (★★★☆) of this Central Otago wine is a zesty, medium style (16 grams/litre of sugar). It's a youthful wine with fresh, crisp lemon/lime flavours showing good balance and intensity.

Vintage	02	01	00	99
WR	5	5	5	6
Drink	04-06	03-05	03-05	03-04

MED $18 AV

Alexia Nelson Riesling ★★★☆

The 2002 vintage (★★★★) from winemaker Jane Cooper shows good richness and delicacy, with fresh, strong citrus/lime flavours, balanced acidity and a slightly sweet, sustained finish. The 2003 (★★★☆) is also fresh, vibrant and tangy, with ripe lemon/lime aromas and flavours showing very good depth. Open mid-2004+.

Vintage	02
WR	6
Drink	03-07

MED/DRY $17 V+

Allan Scott Marlborough Riesling ★★★☆

Top vintages of this wine are impressive. Made from vines averaging 20 years old, the richly scented 2002 (★★★★☆) offers intense but delicate lemon and lime flavours. Full-bodied and vibrantly fruity, with fresh acidity and a long, slightly sweet finish, it's a finely poised wine, with bottle-aged toasty characters just starting to unfold. The 2003 scored a silver medal at the 2003 Liquorland Top 100 International Wine Competition.

Vintage	03	02
WR	7	7
Drink	03-08	03-06

MED/DRY $17 V+

Amor-Bendall Gisborne Riesling (★★★)

The fresh-scented 2003 vintage (★★★) shows good varietal character, with vibrant, pure lemon/apple flavours, firm acidity and a slightly sweet finish. A flavoursome, finely balanced wine, it should open up well during 2004.

MED/DRY $18 AV

Ascension Marlborough Riesling ★★★

The attractively floral 2002 vintage (★★★☆) is a crisp, medium-bodied wine with slightly sweet lemon/lime flavours showing good freshness, delicacy and depth.

MED/DRY $20 -V

Askerne Hawke's Bay Riesling ★★★

Estate-grown near Havelock North, the light yellow/green 2001 vintage (★★★) is a citrusy, slightly honeyed wine with an off-dry finish. It's a finely balanced wine, drinking well now.

Vintage	01	00
WR	6	5
Drink	03-08	03-05

DRY $16 AV

Babich Marlborough Riesling ★★★★
This is typically a beautifully crafted, ripe, flavour-packed wine with great drinkability. A medium-dry style, grown in the Pigou vineyard at Rapaura, in the Wairau Valley, the 2002 vintage (★★★★) shows lovely harmony. Full-bodied, with strong, ripe flavours of citrus fruits, lime and passionfruit, it is fresh, lively and slightly honeyed, with good richness through the palate. The 2003 (★★★★) is scented, lively and immaculate, with fresh, strong lemon/lime flavours and good sugar/acid balance. It needs another year to show its best; open late 2004+.

Vintage	02	01	00	99	98
WR	7	7	7	7	7
Drink	03-09	03-08	03-06	03-05	03-04

MED/DRY $18 V+

Black Ridge Riesling ★★★
Grown in rocky terrain in one of the world's southernmost vineyards, at Alexandra in Central Otago, this is typically a green-appley wine with a crisp, fresh, Mosel-like delicacy. Still youthful, the 2002 vintage (★★★) is light lemon/green, with strong lemon, lime and apple flavours in a cool-climate style with firm acidity and a tight, slightly minerally finish. Open late 2004+.

DRY $18 AV

Bladen Marlborough Riesling ★★☆
The 2002 vintage (★★) of this single-vineyard wine is restrained on the nose, with crisp, appley, slightly sweet flavours that lack a bit of vibrancy and depth.

MED/DRY $19 -V

Borthwick Estate Wairarapa Riesling ★★★
Estate-grown in Dakins Road, near Masterton, the 2002 vintage (★★★) is a slightly sweet style, appley, lemony and limey, with a hint of honey and a freshly acidic finish. Best drinking 2004+.

MED/DRY $18 AV

Brightwater Vineyards Nelson Riesling ★★★☆
Estate-grown on the Waimea Plains, this wine is always full of personality. The 2002 vintage (★★★★), picked with no botrytis influence and fermented to full dryness, should mature well for years. Bright, light lemon/green, it is tight, intense and zingy, with penetrating lemon/lime flavours threaded with appetising acidity. Open mid-2004 onwards.

Vintage	02	01	00
WR	6	6	7
Drink	03-06	03-05	03-04

DRY $18 AV

Brookfields Ohiti Estate Riesling ★★★☆
Peter Robertson's Hawke's Bay wines are full of interest. Grown on the Ohiti Estate, inland from Fernhill, the 2002 vintage (★★★★) has fresh, strong lemon/apple aromas. A slightly sweet style, it shows good freshness, vigour and varietal character, with tangy, limey flavours, finely balanced and lingering. Drink now onwards.

Vintage	02	01	00	99	98	97
WR	7	6	6	6	6	6
Drink	04-05	03-07	03-05	03-04	P	P

MED/DRY $16 V+

Burnt Spur Martinborough Riesling (★★★)

Bright, light lemon/green, the 2002 vintage (★★★) is a ripely scented, slightly honeyed wine with citrusy, limey flavours of good depth, fresh acidity and a bone-dry finish. Drink now or cellar.

Vintage 02
WR 6
Drink 03-10

DRY $21 -V

Canterbury House The Good Times Riesling (★★★)

The 2002 vintage (★★★) won a gold medal at that year's Air New Zealand Wine Awards, but wasn't that exciting by mid-2003. Grown at Waipara, it has a lightly floral bouquet, with slightly sweet, lemony flavours, smooth and forward.

MED/DRY $14 V+

Canterbury House Waipara Riesling ★★★☆

Estate-grown in North Canterbury, the 2001 (★★★★) is a floral wine with good intensity of lemon/apple flavours and a sliver of sweetness balanced by fresh acidity. Showing some botrytis influence, the slightly honeyed 2002 (★★★) offers decent depth of citrusy, limey flavours, but lacks the richness of the 2001.

MED/DRY $15 V+

Cape Campbell Blenheim Point Riesling (★★★)

Balanced for easy drinking, the 2002 vintage (★★★) is a full-bodied, medium style with firm acid spine and a touch of honey.

MED $18 AV

Carrick Central Otago Riesling (★★★)

Slightly austere in its youth, the 2002 vintage (★★★) offers tight, lemon and green apple flavours in a crisp, dryish style. A tautly structured wine with good intensity, it needs time; open mid-2004+.

Vintage 02
WR 6
Drink 04+

MED/DRY $19 -V

Chard Farm Central Otago Riesling ★★★☆

The standard of this Central Otago wine varies, reflecting the marginal growing climate, but is typically high. The 2002 vintage (★★★★), grown in the Cromwell Basin, is a tangy, youthful, slightly sweet wine with strong lemon/lime flavours, punchy, vibrant and long. It's a delicious wine, for drinking now onwards.

Vintage	02	01	00	99
WR	6	6	5	6
Drink	04-07	03-05	P	P

MED/DRY $19 AV

Charles Wiffen Marlborough Riesling ★★★☆

Drinking well now, the 2002 vintage (★★★☆) is a honeyed wine with ripe pineapple and lime flavours, slightly sweet and strong. The 2003 (★★★☆) is floral, fresh and tangy, with citrusy, limey, pineappley flavours, slightly sweet and finely balanced for early drinking.

MED/DRY $17 V+

Christina Estate Riesling ★★★

The 2001 vintage (★★★★) of this Martinborough wine is fleshy and slightly honeyed, with good concentration, some development showing and lots of character. The 2002 (★★★) is crisp and lemony, with decent flavour depth, but less intense than the 2001.

MED/DRY $20 -V

Clifford Bay Marlborough Riesling ★★★☆

This single-vineyard Awatere Valley wine matures well. Already highly attractive, the 2002 vintage (★★★★) shows good weight and intensity, with fresh, ripe-fruit aromas and punchy lemon/lime flavours, slightly sweet and zingy.

Vintage	02	01	00	99
WR	6	6	6	6
Drink	03-08	03-07	03-05	03-04

MED/DRY $17 V+

Coney Ragtime Riesling ★★★★

Grown a few kilometres south of Martinborough, the 2002 vintage (★★★★) is a full-bodied, medium style with ripe citrusy flavours and a hint of honey. It's a fragrant, fleshy and forward wine, with gentle acidity, loads of flavour and a rich finish.

Vintage	02
WR	4
Drink	03-05

MED/DRY $19 V+

Coney Rallentando Riesling ★★★☆

Grown in Martinborough, the 2002 vintage (★★★★) is a slightly sweet style (the 2001 was fully dry). It's a youthful, finely balanced wine with strong, zingy, lemony flavours, a hint of passionfruit and good length. Drink now or cellar.

Vintage	02
WR	5
Drink	03-05

DRY $19 AV

Coopers Creek Marlborough Riesling ★★★

Enjoyable now, the 2002 vintage (★★★) is a single-vineyard wine, with slightly honeyed, botrytis characters enriching its fresh lemon and apple flavours and a slightly sweet finish.

MED/DRY $16 AV

Corbans Marlborough Riesling ★★★

Designed for drink-young appeal, the debut 2001 vintage (★★★☆) was a surprisingly rich, finely balanced wine with good intensity of ripe, limey flavour and a crisp acid finish. The 2002 (★★☆) is solid but on a lower plane. It's a medium-bodied, slightly sweet style (12 grams/litre of sugar) with reasonable depth of lemony, appley flavours and a crisp finish.

Vintage	03	02	01
WR	5	6	6
Drink	03-06	04+	P

MED/DRY $14 V+

Corbans Private Bin Amberley Riesling (★★★★)

The tangy, limey, minerally 2002 vintage (★★★★) is the first vintage of this once-famous label since 1996. Grown at Waipara (rather than Amberley) in North Canterbury, it is light and lively, with good flavour intensity, a splash of sweetness and a tight, slightly flinty finish. A fresh, youthful, medium-dry style, it's balanced for early enjoyment but best cellared until mid-2004+.

Vintage 02
WR 5
Drink 03-10

MED/DRY $22 AV

Craggy Range Rapaura Road Vineyard Marlborough Riesling (NR)

The 2002 vintage (tasted shortly after bottling, and so not rated), is based on 23-year-old vines. A dry style (with just 3 grams/litre of residual sugar), good weight (13.5 per cent alcohol) and fresh lime, spice and green apple flavours, it is crisp, delicate, slightly minerally and long. It needs at least a couple of years to unfold its potential.

Vintage 02
WR 6
Drink 03-07

DRY $25 V?

Crossroads Destination Series Riesling (★★★)

Full-bodied, with youthful lemon/lime flavours, the 2002 vintage (★★★) of this Hawke's Bay wine is less scented and vibrant than the better South Island Rieslings, but offers some richness, with a hint of honey and a dryish, crisp finish.

Vintage 02
WR 6
Drink 03-06

MED/DRY $20 -V

Darjon Swannanoa Riesling (★★☆)

Still quite restrained in mid-2003, the 2002 vintage (★★☆) of this Canterbury wine is lemony, appley and slightly sweet, with an appealing lightness and crispness. It's a clearly varietal wine, but needs time; open mid-2004 onwards.

MED/DRY $18 -V

Drylands Marlborough Dry Riesling ★★★

The 2001 vintage (★★★) is a slightly austere wine from Nobilo, dryish (5 grams/litre of sugar), with good depth of lemony, appley flavours and firm acid spine. The light yellow 2002 (★★☆) is lemony and minerally, with some development showing and a slightly hard finish.

Vintage 02 01 00
WR 7 7 7
Drink 03-05 03-04 P

MED/DRY $20 -V

Dry River Craighall Riesling ★★★★★

Winemaker Neil McCallum believes that, in quality terms, Riesling is at least the equal of Pinot Noir in Martinborough. His Craighall Riesling, one of the finest in the country, is a wine of exceptional purity, delicacy and depth, with a proven ability to flourish in the cellar for many years: 'It's not smart to drink them at less than five years old,' says McCallum. The grapes are grown in a part of the Craighall vineyard now owned by Dry River, with yields limited to an average of 6 tonnes per hectare. The 2002 vintage (★★★★★) impresses with its unusual complexity and smoothness of texture, with distinct minerally touches adding interest to its deep lemon, lime and green apple characters and a dryish, rounded, lasting finish. Still a baby, the pale lemon/green 2003 (★★★★☆) is finely scented, with very impressive delicacy and harmony of citrusy, slightly sweet flavours. It needs years to unfold: McCallum's suggestion is to 'drink from about three years and evaluate'.

Vintage	02	01	00	99	98	97	96
WR	6	7	7	6	7	7	7
Drink	04-07	05-11	04-10	03-10	03-04	03-06	03-04

MED/DRY $33 AV

Esk Valley Hawke's Bay Riesling ★★★☆

This label ranks among the finest Rieslings in the Bay. The 2002 vintage (★★★★), picked from 21-year-old vines at Clive and stop-fermented in a medium-dry style, is a youthful wine with pure lemon/lime flavours cut with fresh acidity, and good balance and intensity. Tasting the very charming 2003 (★★★★) is like biting a Granny Smith apple. It's a light-bodied, gently sweet wine with good sugar/acid balance, strong appley flavours and a long finish.

Vintage	03	02	01	00	99	98	97
WR	6	7	6	7	NM	7	6
Drink	04-07	03-07	03-05	03-05	NM	P	P

MED/DRY $20 AV

Fairmont Estate Riesling ★★☆

Grown at Gladstone, in the Wairarapa, the 2002 vintage (★★☆) is a crisp, moderately ripe-tasting wine with appley, limey flavours showing reasonable depth.

MED/DRY $15 AV

Felton Road Block 1 Riesling – see Sweet White Wines

Felton Road Dry Riesling ★★★★☆

Based on low-yielding vines in schisty soils at Bannockburn, in Central Otago, this is a consistently classy wine. The 2002 vintage (★★★★☆) is still in its infancy. Hand-picked, whole-bunch pressed and fermented with indigenous yeasts, it's a crisp, tightly structured wine, punchy and zingy, with lemony, limey, minerally flavours cut with fresh acidity and a fractionally off-dry (5 grams/litre of sugar) finish. It needs time – at least a couple of years.

Vintage	02	01	00	99	98
WR	7	6	7	6	6
Drink	03-12	03-10	03-10	03-10	03-09

MED/DRY $21 V+

Felton Road Riesling ★★★★★

Estate-grown at Bannockburn, this is typically a gently sweet wine with deep flavours cut with fresh acidity. It offers more drink-young appeal than its Dry Riesling stablemate, but still needs cellaring. Fermented with indigenous yeasts, the 2002 vintage (★★★★★) was stop-fermented with an alcohol level of 10 per cent and 35 grams per litre of residual sugar, making it a truly medium style. A notably fresh, intense and zingy wine, it reveals minerally, appley aromas and flavours, with mouth-watering acidity and lovely lightness and vivacity. A great aperitif.

Vintage	02	01	00	99	98
WR	7	6	6	6	7
Drink	03-15	03-12	03-11	03-12	03-09

MED $21 V+

Fiddler's Green Waipara Riesling ★★★★

A consistently rewarding North Canterbury wine. Bright, light yellow/green, the 2002 vintage (★★★★) offers strong lemon/lime flavours in a gently sweet style, fresh and lively. Easy drinking in its youth, it also has obvious aging potential.

Vintage	02	01	00	99	98
WR	6	6	6	6	5
Drink	03-06	03-05	03-05	P	P

MED/DRY $20 AV

Forrest Estate Dry Riesling ★★★★☆

This is proprietor John Forrest's 'personal favourite', at its best dry but not austere, with intense, limey flavours and slatey, minerally characters adding complexity. The 2002 vintage (★★★★☆) is a very refined and immaculate Marlborough wine, highly scented, with rich flavours of citrus fruits and limes, finely balanced acidity and a long finish. Weighty and ripe, and not at all austere in its youth, it should flourish with cellaring.

Vintage	03	02	01	00
WR	5	6	6	6
Drink	04-10	05-10	05	04

DRY $24 AV

Forrest Marlborough Riesling ★★★☆

John Forrest believes Riesling will one day be Marlborough's greatest wine, and his own wine is helping the cause. The finely scented 2003 vintage (★★★☆) shows good intensity of citrusy flavour, with a distinct splash of sweetness to balance its high acidity. It's drinking well already.

Vintage	03	02	01	00	99	98
WR	4	4	5	5	6	6
Drink	04-05	03-04	P	P	P	P

MED/DRY $16 V+

Framingham Classic Riesling ★★★★

Estate-grown at Renwick, top vintages of this Marlborough wine are deliciously aromatic, richly flavoured and zesty. The lovely 2002 vintage (★★★★☆) has a Germanic lightness (11 per cent alcohol), sweetness and intensity. The bouquet has interesting minerally characters; the palate is tightly structured, with deep lemon/lime flavours, spot-on sugar/acid balance and a lasting finish.

Vintage	02	01	00	99	98	97
WR	6	7	6	6	7	5
Drink	03-06	03-05	P	P	P	P

MED $20 AV

Framingham Dry Riesling ★★★★☆

This is the Marlborough winery's flagship. Estate-grown in the Front Block of the company's Conders Bend vineyard, at Renwick, the 2002 vintage (★★★★) is a finely poised, distinctly minerally wine, threaded with fresh acidity. Slightly off-dry, with strong melon/lime characters, it's a finely balanced, tightly structured wine, still unfolding.

Vintage	02	01	00	99
WR	6	7	7	7
Drink	03-08	03-10	03-08	03-06

DRY $28 -V

Fromm La Strada Dry Riesling ★★★★☆

Typically a beautifully poised and delicate Marlborough wine with lemony, slightly minerally flavours and a zingy, lasting finish. Fresh, vibrant and youthful, the 2002 vintage (★★★★☆) is already a lovely drink, with crisp lemon/apple flavours showing excellent intensity and a crisp, long, not quite bone-dry finish. Obvious cellaring potential.

Vintage	03	02	01	00
WR	6	6	6	6
Drink	03-13	03-12	03-11	03-10

DRY $27 -V

Fromm La Strada Riesling – see Sweet White Wines

Gibbston Valley Central Otago Riesling ★★★☆

At its best, this is a deliciously zingy wine, awash with lemon and lime-like flavour. Grown at four sites in the region, the rich 2002 vintage (★★★★) is garden-fresh, with strong, tangy lemon/lime flavours, a gentle splash of sweetness (9 grams/litre of residual sugar) and good drink-young appeal.

Vintage	02	01	00	99	98	97	96
WR	6	6	6	6	7	5	3
Drink	03-08	03-06	03-10	03-10	03-05	P	P

MED/DRY $24 -V

Giesen Marlborough/Canterbury Riesling ★★★☆

From one vintage to the next, this is one of the best-value Rieslings around. Early releases were based solely on Canterbury grapes, but the 2003 vintage (★★★☆) is a blend of fruit from Marlborough and Canterbury. A distinctly medium style (20 grams/litre of sugar), with 'a hint of noble rot', it has a slightly honeyed bouquet. Tangy and full-flavoured, it has pungent lemon/lime characters and more obvious sweetness than most New Zealand Rieslings, balanced by lively acidity.

Vintage	03
WR	7
Drink	04-10

MED $15 V+

Giesen Reserve Selection Riesling – see Sweet White Wines

Gladstone Wairarapa Riesling ★★★

After a flat patch a few years ago, this label has bounced back to form. The scented and punchy 2002 vintage (★★★★) was grown at Gladstone and Waipipi. Dry but not austere, with good cellaring potential, it displays fresh lemon/lime aromas and flavours, showing a slightly minerally character and good intensity.

DRY $18 AV

Glenmark Proprietors Reserve Waipara Riesling ★★★

Labelled in different vintages as 'Dry' or 'Medium', this North Canterbury wine is always full of interest. The slowly evolving 1999 Dry (★★★) has firm, steely acidity and kerosene and toast characters emerging. The 2000 Medium (★★★☆), the pick of recent releases, is drinking well now, with a good balance of sweetness and acidity and strong, lemony, slightly minerally flavours. Offering more drink-young appeal than the 1999, the 2002 Dry is citrusy, limey, fresh and flavourful, with a dry but not austere finish.

DRY-MED $21 -V

Glover's Dry Riesling (★★☆)

The 2002 vintage (★★☆) of this Nelson wine is lean and austere, with green apple flavours and high acidity.

DRY $17 -V

Greenhough Nelson Vineyards Dry Riesling ★★★★

Andrew Greenhough produces a classy Riesling, at its best strikingly perfumed, incisively flavoured and zesty. The 2002 vintage (★★★★) is a full, dryish style, impressively weighty (13 per cent alcohol) and full-flavoured, with ripe citrus/lime characters, balanced acidity and a long finish. The 2003 (★★★★★) is even better. Pale lemon/green, tight and intense, it is full of youthful promise. An immaculate wine with the structure of fine Riesling, it shows a very fine balance of slight sweetness (6 grams/litre) and refreshing acidity, and concentrated, classic lemon/lime flavours, poised, delicate and sustained. It should be long-lived; open mid-2004+.

Vintage	03	02	01	00	99	98
WR	6	6	5	6	6	5
Drink	03-07	03-06	03-05	P	P	P

MED/DRY $18 V+

Grove Mill Innovator Riesling (★★★☆)

The 2002 vintage (★★★☆) from this Marlborough winery is a Canterbury wine, harvested on 22 May and stop-fermented with 5.8 grams per litre of residual sugar. Light yellow/green, it is quite Germanic on the nose, minerally, earthy and slightly honeyed, with a light (11 per cent alcohol), lemony palate, quite developed for its age, a sliver of sweetness and firm acid spine. Drink now to 2004.

DRY $20 AV

Grove Mill Marlborough Riesling ★★★★☆

At its best highly perfumed, with intense lemon/lime flavours, this is a classy wine. It typically harbours 15 to 20 grams per litre of residual sugar, but that plentiful sweetness is finely balanced with lush, concentrated fruit characters and appetising acidity. Some botrytis has been present in most vintages and, unusually for New Zealand, winemaker Dave Pearce puts about half the final blend through malolactic fermentation, 'not to modify acidity but to enhance the wine's texture'. The 2003 vintage (★★★★) was stop-fermented in a medium/dry style. From a low-cropping season (5 tonnes/hectare), it is pale, light (11 per cent alcohol) and tangy, with lemon and green apple flavours showing good sugar/acid balance, varietal character and intensity.

Vintage	03	02	01	00	99	98	97	96
WR	6	6	6	7	6	6	7	7
Drink	04-10	03-06	03-06	03-05	03-06	03-04	03-04	P

MED/DRY $18 V+

Hanmer Junction, The, Waipara Valley Riesling ★★★

The 2001 vintage (★★★), labelled 'Tricina's', is a youthful, cool-climate style from North Canterbury, pale and delicate. It's a medium-dry style (14 grams/litre of sugar) with light body and decent depth of smooth, appley flavours. The 2002 (★★★) is a full-bodied, slightly sweet style (14 grams/litre of residual sugar) with ripe, lemony, slightly honeyed flavours.

Vintage	02	01
WR	5	6
Drink	03-04	03-04

MED/DRY $17 AV

Highfield Marlborough Riesling ★★★☆

Still on sale, the 2000 vintage (★★★☆) was hand-harvested, whole-bunch pressed and stop-fermented in a medium-dry style (8 grams/litre sugar). Re-tasted in mid-2003, it's an elegant, finely balanced wine, still youthful in colour and developing well, with good depth of crisp, lemony flavour, now developing toasty, minerally, bottle-aged notes. Drink now onwards.

Vintage	00	99	98
WR	6	6	5
Drink	04-08	03-04	03-05

MED/DRY $23 -V

Huia Marlborough Riesling ★★★

Claire Allen's wines can take time to show their best, but typically open up well after a year or two in the bottle. However, the 2002 vintage (★★) is disappointing. Grown in the Pukenga vineyard, north of Blenheim, and fermented with indigenous yeasts, it lacks fresh, lifted aromatics and the lemony, appley flavours are not vibrant.

Vintage	02	01	00	99
WR	7	6	7	7
Drink	03-08	03-08	03-10	03-08

DRY $23 -V

Hunter's Marlborough Riesling ★★★★

This wine is consistently good and in top vintages beautifully poised, with lovely depth of citrusy flavours, some riper tropical-fruit characters and a long, dryish finish. The 2002 vintage (★★★☆) is an almost fully dry style (3.7 grams/litre of residual sugar), with strong lemony, appley flavours, fresh and tight. Attractively scented, it's a slightly austere wine in its youth, needing time to unfold; open mid-2004+.

Vintage	02	01	00	99	98	97	96
WR	6	5	4	5	5	6	5
Drink	05-06	04-05	03-04	P	P	P	P

DRY $18 V+

Hurunui River Riesling (★★★☆)

Light and lively, the 2002 vintage (★★★☆) was grown at Hawarden, north-west of Waipara in North Canterbury, and stop-fermented with plentiful (20 grams/litre) residual sugar. Pale lemon/green, it's a light-bodied wine (11 per cent alcohol) with zingy, vibrant lemon/lime flavours showing well-defined, cool-climate varietal characters, fresh acidity and good vigour.

MED $18 AV

Isabel Marlborough Dry Riesling ★★★★☆

The 2002 vintage (★★★★☆) has minerally aromas and a tight, intense palate with crisp, vibrant, citrusy, appley flavours, beautifully balanced and long. It's potentially outstanding. Tasted soon after bottling, the 2003 vintage (★★★★☆) is minerally and limey, with notable vigour and intensity. Crisp and tight, with racy acidity, locked-in power and a lasting finish, it should be at its best from 2005 onwards.

Vintage	02	01	00	99
WR	6	6	6	5
Drink	03-08	03-10	03-08	03-05

DRY $20 V+

Jackson Estate Marlborough Dry Riesling ★★★★

Proprietor John Stichbury took some convincing that Riesling is fashionable, so until a few years ago this wine was labelled Marlborough Dry, with the name of the variety in small print. From a difficult vintage for Riesling, the 2001 (★★★☆) shows good vigour and freshness. Full-bodied, it offers strong, citrusy, slightly minerally flavours, with a tight, dry finish. Drinking well now, it's a quietly classy wine, verging on four-star quality.

Vintage	01	00	99	98
WR	5	6	6	5
Drink	03-05	03-05	03-04	P

DRY $16 V+

Johanneshof Marlborough Riesling ★★★☆

The 2000 vintage (★★★) from this tiny Koromiko winery is minerally and limey, with a rather European feel. It's a medium style (15 grams/litre of sugar) with good body and complexity and a rounded finish.

MED $18 AV

Jules Taylor Marlborough Riesling ★★★★☆

The 2001 vintage (★★★★★) is a beautifully refined dry Riesling, with great delicacy and purity of flavour. Grown on the Ellin Estate, in Dog Point Road, the slightly sweeter 2002 (★★★★☆) was hand-picked, whole-bunch pressed and stop-fermented with 8 grams per litre of sugar, making it a medium-dry style. More forward than the 2001, it's a highly characterful, full-bodied wine (13 per cent alcohol), with excellent intensity of citrusy, minerally flavour.

MED/DRY $23 AV

Kahurangi Estate Moutere Dry Riesling (★★★☆)
Slightly austere in its youth, the 2002 vintage (★★★☆) is an almost fully dry style (4.9 grams/litre of sugar). Flinty and appley, lemony and slightly minerally, it has good potential but needs time; open 2004 onwards.

DRY $18 AV

Kahurangi Estate Moutere Reserve Riesling (★★★★☆)
The refined 2002 vintage (★★★★☆) was hand-picked in the Upper Moutere hills, whole-bunch pressed and stop-fermented with 13 grams per litre of residual sugar, making it a medium-dry style. It shows excellent weight and intensity, with rich, ripe passionfruit/lime flavours, real delicacy and softness through the palate and impressive length. A good bet for the cellar.

MED/DRY $19 V+

Kahurangi Estate Moutere Riesling ★★★☆
The classy 2002 vintage (★★★★) was produced 'from the South Island's oldest Riesling vines' (planted by the Seifrieds in the 1970s). Fresh, immaculate and tight, it's a slightly sweet style with rich lemon/lime flavours and lovely sugar/acid balance. Well worth cellaring.

MED/DRY $18 AV

Kahurangi Estate Nelson Riesling (★★★★)
The intensely varietal 2002 vintage (★★★★), estate-grown at Upper Moutere, is a medium-dry style (11 grams/litre of sugar). Very fresh and lively in its youth, it has good intensity of lemon/lime flavours, a lovely balance between slight sweetness and crisp acidity and a lingering finish.

MED/DRY $18 V+

Kaimira Estate Brightwater Dry Riesling ★★★
Estate-grown at Brightwater, in Nelson, the 2001 vintage (★★★) is a virtually bone-dry style (3 grams/litre of sugar). It's a medium-bodied wine with lifted, lime-juice aromas, plenty of flavour and a crisp, lemony finish. The 2003 (★★★☆) is tight and zesty, with very good depth of lemony, appley flavour, refreshing acidity and plenty of cellaring potential. Open late 2004+.

DRY $17 AV

Kaimira Estate Marlborough Riesling (★★★☆)
The 2002 vintage (★★★☆) is a single-vineyard wine, made in a slightly sweet style (12 grams/litre of sugar). An immaculate wine, lively and well-balanced, it's scented and springy, with strong, lemony, limey flavours and an appetisingly crisp finish.

MED/DRY $15 V+

Kaimira Estate Nelson Riesling ★★★★☆
The 2002 vintage (★★★★☆) is fresh and immaculate. Slightly sweet (12 grams/litre of sugar), it shows lovely lightness, delicacy and vigour, with an extra degree of intensity than its Marlborough stablemate (above) and a rich finish.

MED/DRY $17 V+

Kim Crawford Marlborough Dry Riesling ★★★★

The fragrant 2002 vintage (★★★★) shows good ripeness and intensity, with a dryish, long finish. Punchy and rich, with citrus and tropical-fruit flavours, it has good palate weight and cellaring potential. The 2003 scored a bronze medal at the 2003 Liquorland Top 100 International Wine Competition.

Vintage	03	02	01	00	99	98
WR	4	6	7	5	7	5
Drink	03-06	03-10	03-06	03-06	03-05	P

MED/DRY $20 AV

Koura Bay Barney's Rock Awatere Valley Riesling ★★★

Re-tasted in mid-2003, the 2001 vintage (★★★) shows a lot of development for its age, with crisp, minerally, toasty characters. The 2002 (★★☆), a medium-dry style, is a slightly austere wine with green apple aromas and flavours.

Vintage	02
WR	6
Drink	06-08

MED/DRY $17 AV

Lake Chalice Marlborough Riesling ★★★★

The 2002 vintage (★★★★☆) is a highly refined wine, beautifully scented, with strong yet delicate flavours of lemons and limes, a hint of passionfruit and a slightly sweet finish, balanced by mouth-watering acidity. The 2003 (★★★☆), grown at the Falcon Vineyard and other sites, is skilfully balanced for early drinking, with fresh, vibrant lemon/apple flavours showing good delicacy and depth and a slightly sweet, crisp finish.

Vintage	03
WR	6
Drink	03-08

MED/DRY $18 V+

Lake Hayes Riesling (★★★☆)

A tightly structured wine, maturing gracefully, the 2001 vintage (★★★☆) was grown at Bannockburn and Gibbston, in Central Otago. Light, youthful lemon/green in hue, it is lemon-scented, with good intensity and varietal character, fresh acidity and a dry, minerally finish. Drink now or cellar.

DRY $20 AV

Lawson's Dry Hills Marlborough Riesling ★★★☆

Charming in its youth, the 2002 vintage (★★★★) is a scented and refined wine with good harmony of lemon/lime flavours, slight sweetness and crisp, lively acidity. Grown in the Wairau and Waihopai valleys, and harvested with a small amount of botrytis infection, the 2003 (★★★) is a more austere, high-acid wine with strong, lemony, faintly honeyed flavours and a splash of sweetness (12 grams/litre of sugar) to balance its steely acidity.

Vintage	02	01	00	99	98
WR	6	5	5	6	6
Drink	03-06	03-06	03-05	03-04	03-04

MED/DRY $18 AV

Leaning Rock Riesling ★★★

Grown at Alexandra, in Central Otago, the 2001 vintage (★★★) is light (10.7 per cent alcohol) and racy. It's a slightly sweet style (12 grams/litre of sugar) with good depth of lemony, appley flavours and high acidity giving it a slightly tart finish. Best drinking 2004+.

Vintage	01
WR	5
Drink	03-06

MED/DRY $19 -V

Le Grys Marlborough Riesling (★★★★)

The richly flavoured 2001 vintage (★★★★) is a slightly sweet style (7 grams/litre of sugar), with tropical-fruit flavours, a hint of honey and a powerful finish. Balanced for easy drinking, it's full of character.
Vintage 01
WR 6
Drink 03-05

MED/DRY $19 V+

Linden Estate Riesling Dry (★★☆)

The debut 2002 vintage (★★☆) was harvested from over 20-year-old vines in the Yates vineyard at Clive, in Hawke's Bay, and fermented with indigenous yeasts to near dryness (6 grams/litre of sugar). Light yellow/green, it's light and lemony, limey and rounded, with a fairly short finish.

MED/DRY $19 -V

Loopline Vineyard Reserve Riesling (★★★☆)

Grown at Opaki, north of Masterton in the Wairarapa, the 2002 vintage (★★★☆) is not highly scented, yet zingy and intense, with ripe, citrusy flavours, appetising acidity and a slightly sweet (12 grams/litre of sugar), lingering finish. Verging on four stars.
Vintage 02
WR 6
Drink 03-08

MED/DRY $20 AV

Lucknow Estate Waihopai Valley Marlborough Riesling (★★☆)

Slightly austere in its youth, with a restrained bouquet, the 2002 vintage (★★☆) is a dry style (4.5 grams/litre of sugar) that should open up with more bottle age. Pale lemon/green, it's a tangy, appley, lemony wine with a freshly acidic finish.
Vintage 02
WR 6
Drink 05

DRY $17 -V

Mahurangi Selection Marlborough Riesling (★★★)

The 2002 vintage (★★★) from this north-of-Auckland producer is a Marlborough wine with taut, appley, minerally flavours, firm acid spine and some bottle-aged toasty characters emerging. Drink now to 2004.

DRY $17 AV

Margrain Proprietors Selection Riesling ★★★☆

The 2002 vintage (★★★), grown in Martinborough, lacks the striking intensity and poise of the beautifully perfumed, rich 1999 (★★★★★), but shows some promise. Pale lemon/green, it's still youthful, with tight, limey flavours showing some richness and a slightly sweet, tangy finish.
Vintage 02
WR 6
Drink 03-08

MED/DRY $23 -V

Martinborough Vineyard Jackson Block Riesling ★★★★☆

This is one of the jewels of the Martinborough Vineyard range. Full of promise, the 2003 vintage (★★★★☆) is based on 13-year-old vines in Bernie and Jane Jackson's vineyard, just 'around the corner' from the winery. Tight and youthful, dryish but not austere, it shows good weight and intensity of delicate grapefruit and lime flavours, with fresh acidity and a long finish. A top candidate for cellaring.

Vintage	02	01	00	99	98	97	96
WR	6	7	7	5	7	6	6
Drink	03-09	03-08	03-07	03-05	03-05	P	P

MED/DRY $23 AV

Martinborough Vineyard Manu Riesling (★★★★☆)

Already a delicious mouthful, the 2003 vintage (★★★★☆) was hand-picked from 13-year-old vines in the Jackson Block, left to develop 'a touch' of noble rot. A medium-sweet style (harbouring 28 grams/litre of residual sugar), it has fresh, vibrant passionfruit and lime flavours, crisp, intense and lingering. Drink now or cellar.

MED $28 -V

Matua Valley Innovator Petrie Riesling (★★★★☆)

The bone-dry 2001 vintage (★★★★☆) was grown in the Petrie vineyard, near Masterton, in the Wairarapa. It's an immaculate, finely balanced wine, carrying the dry style well, with good weight and intense, refined lemon, apple and spice flavours showing great length. A top choice for the cellar.

DRY $20 V+

McCashin's Waipara Riesling ★★★☆

The 2002 vintage (★★★☆) is steely and slightly honeyed, with high acidity but good concentration and persistence. It's a dryish style (6.5 grams/litre of sugar) with lots of flavour and character.

MED/DRY $17 V+

Melness Riesling ★★★★

The lovely 2001 vintage (★★★★) is a crisp, light (9 per cent alcohol), intensely aromatic wine with fine sugar/acid balance and delicious depth of lemony, limey flavour. The 2002 (★★★★), grown in several North Canterbury vineyards, is a fuller-bodied style (12.5 per cent alcohol), picked with some noble rot. Matured on its yeast lees for six months, it's a medium style (26 grams/litre of residual sugar) with excellent depth of crisp, lemony, limey, slightly honeyed flavour and lots of personality in its youth.

Vintage	02	01
WR	7	6
Drink	03-07	03-06

MED $23 -V

Mills Reef Hawke's Bay Riesling ★★★

This is a slightly sweeter style than its stablemate (below), produced in an easy-drinking style. The 2002 vintage (★★☆), grown at Meeanee and lees-aged for three months, is a medium-bodied style. It's not intense, but fresh, crisp and lively, with drink-young appeal. (The 2003 vintage is a Marlborough wine.)

Vintage	03	02	01	00	99	98
WR	7	7	7	6	6	6
Drink	03-06	03-05	P	P	P	P

MED $16 AV

Mills Reef Reserve Riesling ★★★☆

The 2002 vintage (★★★☆) was grown in Hawke's Bay and matured on its gross lees for four months. Punchy and tangy, with tight lemon/lime flavours and a persistent, dryish finish, it should be at its best from 2004 onwards.

Vintage	02	01	00	99	98	97	96
WR	6	NM	6	NM	6	NM	5
Drink	03-05	NM	P	NM	P	NM	P

MED/DRY $19 AV

Millton Opou Vineyard Riesling ★★★★☆

Typically finely scented, with rich, lemony, often honeyed flavours, this is the country's northernmost fine-quality Riesling. Grown in Gisborne, it is slightly sweet, in a softer, less racy style than the classic Marlborough wines. The grapes, grown organically in the Opou vineyard at Manutuke, are hand-harvested over a month at three stages of ripening, usually culminating in a final pick of botrytis-affected fruit. The 2002 vintage (★★★★) is finely scented, fresh and slender (10.5 per cent alcohol), with a musky perfume, crisp, delicate, slightly honeyed flavours of citrus fruits and apples and a distinct minerally character adding complexity. A medium style (19 grams/litre of residual sugar), it's already delicious, but likely to be at its best from 2005 onwards.

Vintage	02	01	00	99	98	97	96
WR	7	NM	7	5	7	5	6
Drink	03-15	NM	03-12	03-05	03-10	P	P

MED $22 AV

Mission Riesling ★★★☆

Mission's Rieslings are typically more lively than most Hawke's Bay Rieslings. Offering lots of drink-young charm, the 2002 vintage (★★★☆) is a medium-dry wine (10 grams/litre of sugar), blended from Hawke's Bay (85 per cent) and Waipara, North Canterbury grapes. Pale lemon/green, it is freshly scented, with finely balanced lemon/apple flavours showing very good depth.

Vintage	02	01	00	99	98	97	96
WR	6	5	7	5	7	5	6
Drink	03-06	P	03-05	P	03-04	P	P

MED/DRY $15 V+

Moana Park Hawke's Bay Riesling (★★★)

Maturing gracefully, the full-bodied 2001 vintage (★★★) has strong lemon/apple flavours in a medium-dry style with good sugar/acid balance and a fresh, lively finish.

MED/DRY $18 AV

Montana Marlborough Riesling ★★★☆

One of New Zealand's best wine buys, this old favourite can mature well for a decade or longer. It is typically full-bodied and slightly sweet, with strong lemon and lime flavours hinting of tropical fruits. The 2002 vintage (★★★☆) was grown mainly in the company's Brancott Estate vineyard, and after the grapes were crushed the juice was briefly held in contact with the skins to maximise flavour extraction. It's a freshly scented wine, full-bodied, with very satisfying depth of slightly sweet (10 grams/litre of sugar), lemony, limey flavours, balanced for easy, characterful drinking.

Vintage	03	02
WR	5	6
Drink	03-09	04+

MED/DRY $16 V+

Montana Reserve Marlborough Riesling ★★★★

Released after a couple of years in the bottle, this is a slightly drier style than its cheaper stablemate (above). The 2001 vintage (★★★★★) was a great buy during 2003, with a lovely intensity of ripe grapefruit/lime characters and toasty, bottle-aged characters contributing richness and complexity. The 2002 vintage (★★★★) possesses rich, ripe citrus and tropical-fruit flavours, with a sliver of sweetness (7 grams/litre of sugar) and good intensity, freshness and vigour.

Vintage	02	01	00	99	98
WR	5	7	7	7	6
Drink	04-09	04+	04+	03+	P

MED/DRY $20 AV

Morton Estate Stone Creek Marlborough Riesling (★★★☆)

Recommended for cellaring 'up to 10 years', the single-vineyard 2002 vintage (★★★☆) is a full-bodied, medium-dry style (6 grams/litre of residual sugar), with strong citrus/lime flavours, good acid spine and a lingering finish. It's a finely poised, elegant wine, for drinking now or laying down.

Vintage	02
WR	7
Drink	03-10

MED/DRY $18

Morton Estate White Label Marlborough Riesling ★★★☆

A consistently good buy. The 2001 vintage (★★★☆) is crisp and lively, with good depth of lemon/lime flavour and a fresh, slightly sweet finish.

Vintage	02	01	00	99	98	97	96
WR	6	6	6	6	6	NM	6
Drink	03-08	03-05	03-04	P	P	NM	P

MED/DRY $17 V+

Morworth Estate Vineyard Selection Riesling ★★★☆

Showing some bottle-aged complexity, the estate-grown 2000 (★★★☆) is a medium style (18 grams/litre sugar), light in body (only 10.5 per cent alcohol), with very good depth of lemony, slightly honeyed flavour. The 2002 vintage (★★★★) has a floral bouquet, with a touch of honey. It's a medium-dry style from Canterbury with limey, gently honeyed flavours showing good richness and a steely, long finish.

MED/DRY $18 AV

Mount Cass Waipara Valley Dry Riesling (★★★)

A full-flavoured dry style (harbouring only 3.7 grams/litre of residual sugar), the 2001 vintage (★★★) shows good vigour, with fresh, lemony, limey flavours and steely, minerally characters emerging. Drink now or cellar.

Vintage	01
WR	6
Drink	03-04

DRY $18 AV

Mount Edward Central Otago Riesling ★★★☆

Alan Brady's wine is a poised, lively medium-dry style with lemony, crisp flavours, zesty and lingering. Grown entirely in the Gibbston sub-region, the 2002 vintage (★★★★) offers strong, lemony, appley flavours, showing good freshness, varietal character and depth, with refreshing acidity, slight sweetness and a long finish.

Vintage	02	01	00	99	98
WR	6	6	6	5	6
Drink	03-07	03-06	03-05	P	P

MED/DRY $18 AV

Mount Maude Central Otago Riesling ★★★
Grown at Lake Wanaka, the 2002 vintage (★★☆) is a lean wine with dryish, lemony, appley flavours and a flinty finish.

DRY $19 -V

Mount Riley Marlborough Riesling ★★★
Grown in the Rapaura district, the 2002 vintage (★★★) is full-bodied and juicy, with a fresh, floral bouquet, ripe, appley flavours showing some concentration and a slightly sweet (9.5 grams/litre of sugar), crisp and lively finish.

MED/DRY $16 AV

Moutere Hills Dry Riesling ★★★
The 2002 vintage (★★★) is a slightly rustic, but honest and characterful, Nelson wine. It's a powerful wine with apple, mineral and slight 'kerosene' notes on the nose, good weight, flavour depth and ripeness, and a firm, dryish finish.

Vintage	01	00	99
WR	5	6	5
Drink	03-05	P	P

MED/DRY $20 -V

Mt Difficulty Dry Riesling ★★★
The slightly austere 2001 vintage (★★★) is a single-vineyard wine from Bannockburn, in Central Otago, with a slightly honeyed fragrance, strong, dry, lemony flavours and firm acidity. The 2002 (★★★) is tangy, dryish (5 grams/litre of residual sugar) and incisive, with tight lemon/lime flavours and appetising acidity. It shows good intensity, but lacks a bit of charm in its youth; open 2005+.

MED/DRY $21 -V

Mt Difficulty Target Gully Riesling ★★★☆
Grown in the Target Gully vineyard in Felton Road, Bannockburn, Central Otago, the 2002 vintage (★★★) is a freshly scented wine with strong, delicate lemon/apple flavours, steely acidity and a lingering finish A medium style (with 25 grams/litre of residual sugar), it needs more time; open mid-2004+.

MED $21 -V

Mudbrick Vineyard Nelson Riesling (★★★☆)
Labelled as a 'zingy expression of lime, lemon and song', the 2002 vintage (★★★☆) from this Waiheke Island winery is fresh and lively, with strong, tangy, slightly sweet flavours of lemons and limes. Drink now or cellar.

MED/DRY $17 V+

Muddy Water James Hardwick Waipara Riesling ★★★★
Showing lovely lightness and freshness, the 2002 vintage (★★★★) was stop-fermented in a medium style (15 grams/litre sugar). A pale, green-tinged wine, it is finely balanced, with strong lemon/apple flavours, crisp and vivacious. (Note: the Riesling Dry was not produced in 2002 or 2003.)

Vintage	03	02	01	00	99
WR	NM	7	7	7	7
Drink	NM	03-13	03-12	03-10	03-06

MED $22 AV

Muddy Water Riesling Unplugged (★★★★)

A medium-sweet style (40 grams/litre residual sugar) from Waipara, the 2002 vintage (★★★★) is a light (11.5 per cent alcohol) and lively wine, late-harvested at 23–27 brix with some noble rot. The floral, lemony bouquet leads into a penetratingly flavoured, luscious wine, lemony and appley, with a hint of honey and good sugar/acid balance. It needs time to show its best, but is already highly enjoyable.

Vintage	03	02
WR	6	6
Drink	03-13	03-12

MED $22 AV

Mud House Marlborough Riesling (★★★★)

Bargain-priced, the 2002 vintage (★★★★) is a full-flavoured, slightly sweet style with very good weight on the palate and ripe, slightly honeyed, stone-fruit flavours showing impressive richness. It's a delicious mouthful, full of character.

MED $16 V+

Murdoch James Martinborough Riesling ★★★☆

The 2002 vintage (★★★☆) is full-bodied (13 per cent alcohol), with punchy lemon and lime characters and a tangy, slightly sweet (6 grams/litre of sugar) finish. The 2003 (★★★), harvested at 20 brix, is a slender wine (only 9 per cent alcohol) with abundant sweetness (over 20 grams/litre) and appetising acidity. Pale, with fresh, strong, green apple flavours, it is light and lively, with good sugar/acid balance, but needs time; open 2005+.

MED $19 AV

Neudorf Brightwater Riesling ★★★★☆

The 2002 vintage (★★★★★) was harvested from young vines at Brightwater, on Nelson's Waimea Plains. Made in a dryish style, it's an immaculate wine, richly scented, with rich, ripe flavours of lemons and limes, lively acidity and notable intensity, poise and charm. A great buy. The 2003 (★★★★☆) also shows excellent depth, delicacy and vivacity. Fresh lemon/lime aromas lead into a tangy, slightly sweet wine (7 grams/litre of sugar) with a burst of lemon and green apple flavours, crisp acidity and a lingering, harmonious finish.

Vintage	03	02
WR	5	6
Drink	03-08	03-08

MED/DRY $19 V+

Neudorf Moutere Riesling ★★★★★

This is a copybook cool-climate style, with exciting flavour intensity. The 2001 vintage (★★★★☆), made with a high degree of residual sugar, is a light (10 per cent alcohol), tightly structured wine with good intensity of delicate lemon/lime flavours and racy acidity. The 2002 (★★★★☆), made from ultra low-cropping vines (less than 1.5 tonnes per hectare) and fermented with indigenous yeasts, is a pale, light (10 per cent alcohol), tightly structured wine with zesty lemon/lime flavours and mouth-watering acidity. A finely poised, delicate wine with good intensity, it is crying out for more time; open mid-2004+.

Vintage	03	02	01	00	99	98	97	96
WR	6	5	6	5	6	7	6	6
Drink	04-12	03-09	03-08	03-06	03-05	03-09	03-07	03-04

MED $28 AV

Nga Waka Martinborough Riesling ★★★★

A consistently powerful wine, with mouthfilling body and deep, bone-dry flavour. The 2001 vintage (★★★★) is maturing well. Pale lemon/green, it is tight and minerally, with strong lemon/lime flavours, a touch of bottle-aged toastiness, refreshing acidity and a long finish. Made with no concessions to drink-young charm, it's still youthful and should be very long-lived.

DRY $25 -V

Ohinemuri Estate East Coast Riesling ★★★

German winemaker Horst Hillerich makes a consistently attractive Riesling. The 2001 vintage (★★★), grown in Gisborne, is a distinctly medium style, stop-fermented with 20 grams per litre of residual sugar. Light gold, it offers plenty of citrusy, slightly honeyed flavour in a well-rounded style, very easy to enjoy. Ready.

Vintage	01	00	99	98	97	96	95
WR	5	6	NM	6	NM	6	5
Drink	03-06	03-06	NM	P	NM	P	P

MED $18 AV

Olssen's of Bannockburn Riesling ★★★☆

The 2002 vintage (★★★★) of this Central Otago wine is the finest yet. Fermented to an almost bone-dry style (3.5 grams/litre of sugar), it is full-bodied (13 per cent alcohol), with ripe, citrusy flavours, moderate acidity and excellent depth and harmony. It's a generous, finely balanced wine, for drinking now or cellaring.

DRY $20 AV

Omaka Springs Marlborough Riesling ★★★

The 2002 vintage (★★★☆) is fresh-scented, with good intensity of lemony, slightly sweet flavours. Pale lemon/green, the 2003 (★★☆) is fresh and lively, but less ripe than the 2002, with appley, green-edged flavours of decent depth.

MED/DRY $13 V+

Opihi Riesling ★★★☆

The youthful, green-tinged 2002 vintage (★★★☆) was grown near Pleasant Point, 30 km inland from Timaru in South Canterbury. Scented, with a sliver of sweetness amid its crisp, lively lemon/lime flavours, it's a distinctly cool-climate style, with good delicacy and depth. Sharply priced, it's worth cellaring.

Vintage	02	01
WR	5	5
Drink	04-07	03-06

MED/DRY $16 V+

Palliser Estate Martinborough Riesling ★★★★★

Allan Johnson's Rieslings are typically beautifully scented, with intense, slightly sweet lemon and lime flavours and a long, racy finish. Top vintages mature well, for up to a decade. The very easy-drinking 2002 vintage (★★★☆) is highly fragrant, with fullness of body (13 per cent alcohol) and loads of fresh, vibrant flavour. A medium-dry style (7 grams/litre of sugar), it is weighty and rounded, with strong limey characters showing good intensity and vigour, but the green edge to the flavours suggests a slight lack of ripeness.

Vintage	02	01	00	99	98	97	96
WR	6	7	5	6	7	7	6
Drink	03-13	03-10	03-06	03-05	03-07	03-06	03-06

MED/DRY $19 V+

Park Estate Riesling (★★☆)

The 2001 vintage (★★☆) of this Hawke's Bay wine, grown at Pakowhai, is developed in colour, with reasonable depth of lemony, limey, slightly honeyed flavour and a slightly hard finish.

Vintage	01
WR	5
Drink	03-05

MED/DRY $15 AV

Pegasus Bay Aria Late Harvest Riesling – see Sweet White Wines

Pegasus Bay Riesling ★★★★★

This is very classy stuff. Estate-grown at Waipara, in North Canterbury, at its best it is richly fragrant and thrillingly intense, with concentrated flavours of citrus fruits and honey, complex and luscious. The 1995, 1998, 2000 and 2001 vintages are all memorable. Harvested in May in 'perfect condition' and lees-aged for six months before it was bottled, the 2002 vintage (★★★★★) is light lemon/green, with a youthful fragrance of lemons and spice. Strikingly fresh, vibrant and pure, with a basket of fruit flavours, slight sweetness and lively acidity, it's a notably harmonious, faintly honeyed wine with a long, rich finish. A lovely aperitif.

Vintage	02	01	00	99	98	97	96	95
WR	7	6	7	6	6	5	4	6
Drink	03-12	03-11	03-11	03-09	03-07	P	P	P

MED $22 V+

Peregrine Central Otago Riesling ★★★☆

The 2002 vintage (★★★☆) was fermented to a dryish style (6 grams/litre of sugar). Pale lemon/green, it is tight and youthful, with fresh, lemony, limey, slightly spicy flavours threaded with crisp acidity and very good depth. It needs more time; open mid-2004+.

Vintage	02
WR	6
Drink	03-06

MED/DRY $20 AV

Phoenix Canterbury Dry Riesling (★★★)

Slightly Germanic in style, the 2002 vintage (★★★) is light (11.5 per cent alcohol) and crisp, with honeyed characters on the nose and palate and a fractionally sweet (5 grams/litre of residual sugar), freshly acidic finish. Drink now to 2004.

Vintage	02
WR	6
Drink	03+

MED/DRY $15 AV

Phoenix Marlborough Riesling ★★★☆

The Pacific winery's 2002 vintage (★★★☆) is a good buy. Made in a distinctly medium style (17 grams/litre of sugar), it is fresh and tangy, with punchy lemon/lime flavours showing good sugar/acid balance. A vivacious wine with lots of character, it's drinking well already.

Vintage	02	01	00	99
WR	6	6	5	6
Drink	03+	03+	P	P

MED $13 V+

Pukeora Estate San Hill Riesling (★★☆)

Pukeora Estate is near Waipukurau, an hour's drive south of Napier, but the grapes for the 2002 vintage (★★☆) were grown near Hastings. It's a light wine (10.5 per cent alcohol) with fresh, lemon/apple aromas and a crisp, dry palate showing good balance and moderate flavour depth.

DRY $14 AV

Rippon Riesling ★★★☆

In its youth, this Lake Wanaka wine is typically restrained, with invigorating acidity, but it can flourish with bottle-age. The impressive 2001 vintage (★★★★) is finely scented and intensely varietal, with fresh, zingy lemon/lime flavours and a steely, rich finish. The 2002 (★★★) is tautly structured, crisp and appley, with a dry, steely finish. Austere in its youth, it needs time; open 2005+.

DRY $21 -V

Riverby Estate Marlborough Riesling (★★)

Grown in Jacksons Road, in the heart of the Wairau Valley, the 2001 vintage (★★) is a dry style (3.3 grams/litre of residual sugar) with green-edged, appley flavours that lack real ripeness and richness.

DRY $19 -V

Rockburn Central Otago Riesling (★★☆)

Released far too early, the 2003 vintage (★★☆) was grown at Lowburn, in the Cromwell Basin. Harvested on 12 May from low-cropping (5 tonnes/hectare) vines, it's a light-bodied wine (11.5 per cent alcohol) with fresh, green apple aromas and flavours, crisp acidity and a dry (4 grams/litre of residual sugar) finish. Open 2005+.

DRY $27 -V

Rossendale Marlborough Riesling ★★☆

A slightly sweet style, the 2002 vintage (★★☆) has lemony, appley aromas and flavours, with a crisp, slightly hard finish. It's a reasonably flavoursome wine, but lacks real delicacy and finesse.

MED/DRY $16 -V

St Francis Marlborough Riesling ★★★

Described on the label as 'Hugely Riesling', the 2001 vintage (★★★) is a full-flavoured wine, stop-fermented in a medium-dry style (8 grams/litre of sugar). Light lemon/green, with lemon and apple aromas, it shows good body, with fresh, strong lemon/lime characters and firm acid spine.

Vintage	01	00	99
WR	6	5	4
Drink	03-07	03-06	03-06

MED/DRY $19 -V

St Helena Riesling ★★★

In top vintages, St Helena produces a Mosel-like wine, fresh, vibrant and racy. The 2002 (★★☆) doesn't identify a region of origin on the label, except for 'South Island', but the winery says it was grown in Canterbury. A lemony, appley wine with firm acidity, a splash of sweetness and decent depth, it's verging on three-star quality.

Vintage	02
WR	5
Drink	04-06

MED $16 AV

Sacred Hill Marlborough Vineyards Riesling (★★★)

The 2002 vintage (★★★) is a single-vineyard (Jacksons Road) wine. Tangy, with very good depth of lemon/lime flavours, it is fresh and tight, with a dryish (5.7 grams/litre of residual sugar) finish and biting acidity. It demands time; open 2005+.

MED/DRY $22 -V

Saint Clair Marlborough Riesling ★★★☆

This is typically a delicious wine, priced sharply. The 2002 vintage (★★★★) has a fragrant, ripe, slightly honeyed bouquet. Forward in its appeal, it's a gently sweet style with ripe lemon/lime flavours, showing very good depth, and lots of character.

Vintage	02	01	00	99	98
WR	6	6	6	6	6
Drink	03-07	03-05	03-05	03-04	P

MED/DRY $17 V+

Sanctuary Marlborough Riesling ★★★☆

From Grove Mill, the 2002 vintage (★★★☆) is ripely scented, fresh and vivacious, with plenty of lemony, limey flavour and a distinct splash of sweetness. A good buy. The 2003 (★★★) is light-bodied (11 per cent alcohol) and lively, in a distinctly medium style (15 grams/litre of sugar) with lemony, appley flavours showing good delicacy and sugar/acid balance.

Vintage	03	02	01	00	99	98
WR	6	6	6	6	6	6
Drink	03-05	03-04	P	P	P	P

MED $17 V+

Seifried Nelson Riesling ★★★☆

Seifried whites are reliable and well-priced. The 2002 vintage (★★★★) is fresh, light and lively, with strong lemon/lime flavours, some residual sugar balanced by crisp acidity, and excellent varietal character and intensity. The 2003 scored a gold medal at the 2003 Liquorland Top 100 International Wine Competition.

Vintage	02	01	00	99	98	97	96
WR	7	7	6	5	6	5	5
Drink	03-06	03-05	03-06	03-05	P	P	P

MED/DRY $17 V+

Seifried Riesling Dry ★★★☆

The 2001 vintage (★★★☆) is the first wine under this label for several years. It's a dryish rather than bone-dry Nelson wine with good depth of limey, appley flavours and a freshly acidic finish. The 2003 scored a bronze medal at the 2003 Liquorland Top 100 International Wine Competition.

MED/DRY $16 V+

Seifried Winemaker's Collection Riesling ★★★★

The 2000 vintage (★★★★★) is an intense, punchy and zesty wine, with tremendous vigour and drive. The slightly sweet 2002 (★★★) is less distinguished, with appley, lemony characters of decent but not outstanding depth.

MED/DRY $20 AV

Selaks Premium Selection Marlborough Riesling ★★★

The Selaks brand (now part of the Nobilo stable) is best known for Sauvignon Blanc, but the Rieslings are also typically good. The 2002 vintage (★★☆) is a slightly sweet wine (9 grams/litre of residual sugar) with decent depth of crisp, passionfruit and lemon flavours and balanced acidity.

Vintage	03	02	01	00
WR	7	7	7	7
Drink	03-06	03-05	03-04	03-04

MED/DRY $15 AV

Seresin Riesling ★★★★☆

The 2001 vintage (★★★★★) was harvested from very low-yielding Marlborough vines (4 tonnes/hectare) with no botrytis, whole-bunch pressed and fermented to dryness. It's a classic dry Riesling with tight, youthful, intense lemon/lime flavours, minerally, flinty characters and a long-lasting finish. Dry but not austere, with crisp, balanced acids, it's a natural for the cellar.

Vintage	02	01
WR	5	6
Drink	04-08	03-10

DRY $22 AV

Sherwood Estate Reserve Riesling (★★★★☆)

An almost fully dry style (with 4.5 grams/litre of sugar), the 2002 vintage (★★★★☆) is full-bodied and intense, with ripe passionfruit, lemon and lime flavours and a rich, rounded finish. Grown in the Whitestone vineyard at Waipara, it's already delicious.

Vintage	02
WR	7
Drink	03-05

DRY $20 V+

Sherwood Estate Riesling (★★★)

Grown 'principally' at Waipara, in North Canterbury, the 2002 vintage (★★★) is a very easy-drinking style. Strong, citrusy, slightly limey aromas lead into a full-bodied (13 per cent alcohol), slightly sweet wine (14 grams/litre of residual sugar), with moderate acidity and good depth of flavour, fresh and vibrant.

MED/DRY $16 AV

Shingle Peak Marlborough Riesling ★★★☆

Matua Valley's Riesling is consistently attractive. The 2002 vintage (★★★☆) is garden-fresh, with strong, vibrant lemon/lime flavours and a slightly sweet (11 grams/litre of residual sugar), mouth-wateringly crisp finish.

Vintage	02	01	00	99	98
WR	6	6	7	6	6
Drink	03-06	03-06	03-06	03-05	03-05

MED/DRY $17 V+

Soljans Marlborough Riesling ★★☆

The 2002 vintage (★★☆) is a fresh, lively, medium-bodied wine with lemony, appley flavours, a sliver of sweetness and a slightly short finish. Verging on three-star quality.

MED/DRY $16 -V

Solstone Classic Riesling (★★★☆)

The floral, slightly honeyed 2001 vintage (★★★☆) from this Wairarapa-based winery was made from Canterbury grapes. It's a medium-bodied, slightly sweet wine, attractively balanced, with fresh acidity and citrusy, slightly honeyed flavours of good depth.

Vintage 01
WR 6
Drink 03-04

MED $18 AV

Spy Valley Marlborough Riesling (★★★)

A dry style (4 grams/litre of sugar), the 2002 vintage (★★★) of this Waihopai Valley wine is floral and lemon-scented, with plenty of citrusy, limey flavour and a crisp, tangy finish. The 2003 scored a bronze medal at the 2003 Liquorland Top 100 International Wine Competition.

Vintage 03 02 01
WR 6 6 5
Drink 03-06 03-07 03-06

DRY $17 AV

Stoneleigh Marlborough Riesling ★★★★

Deliciously fragrant in its youth, this is typically a refined wine from Montana with good body, excellent depth of lemon/lime flavour and a crisp, impressively long finish. The wine's style is evolving towards more sheer varietal character, less sweetness and less botrytis than in the past. Already drinking well, the 2002 vintage (★★★★) is a scented and zingy, finely balanced wine (8 grams/litre of sugar) with a lifted, floral bouquet, strong, fresh lemon/lime flavours cut with fresh acidity and a slightly sweet, sustained finish.

Vintage 02 01 00 99 98
WR 6 6 6 5 7
Drink 03-10 04-10 03+ 03-06 03-08

MED/DRY $19 V+

Stratford Riesling ★★★☆

Stratford is the personal label of Strat Canning, winemaker at Margrain Vineyard in Martinborough. Crisp and zingy, the 2002 vintage (★★★☆), stop-fermented with 7 grams per litre of sugar, offers fresh, vibrant, lemon/lime fruit characters, showing good balance and depth. It's still youthful and should mature well.

Vintage 02 01 00
WR 6 5 7
Drink 03-08 03-07 03-06

MED/DRY $22 -V

Te Kairanga Martinborough Riesling ★★★☆

The 2001 vintage (★★★★) was an impressive debut for this label. It's a finely scented wine with ripe, lemony flavours showing good concentration, balanced sweetness (13 grams/litre of sugar) and a rich finish. The 2002 (★★★☆) is tangy and fresh, with strong lemon/lime flavours in a full-bodied, slightly sweet style. Drink now or cellar.

MED/DRY $20 AV

Te Whare Ra Duke of Marlborough Riesling ★★★★

The latest vintages of this wine are the best. Estate-grown at Renwick, the 2003 (★★★★) is a beautifully harmonious wine, slightly sweet (14 grams/litre of residual sugar) with rich, delicate flavours of lemons and limes, showing good ripeness, and a long, lively finish. The 2002 (★★★★) is equally attractive.

Vintage 02 01 00
WR 7 6 6
Drink 03-12 03-11 03-05

MED/DRY $18 V+

Three Sisters Riesling ★★★
Grown at Takapau, in Central Hawke's Bay, the 2001 vintage (★★★) is a dry style (4 grams/litre of sugar), clean and steely, with firm acidity woven through its lemon and green apple flavours and a slightly tart finish. Attractively scented, with fresh, lemony aromas, the 2002 (★★★) is a crisp, clearly varietal wine, slightly honeyed, with lively lemon/lime flavours and racy acidity.

Vintage 02 01
WR 6 5
Drink 03-06 03-05

DRY $16 AV

Timara Riesling ★★☆
The 2002 vintage (★★☆) is a good buy. Blended by Montana from New Zealand and Australian wines, it's a ripe-tasting, slightly sweet wine with decent depth of lemony, limey flavours and a fairly crisp finish. A decent drink-young style.

MED $10 V+

Torlesse Canterbury Riesling (★★★)
Floral and citrusy on the nose, the 2002 vintage (★★★) is a blend of grapes from Waipara (50 per cent) and the Canterbury Plains. It's a medium style (15 grams/litre of residual sugar) with good acid balance and depth of lemon/lime flavours and a crisp finish. A pleasant drink-young style, it's priced sharply.

Vintage 02
WR 7
Drink 03-06

MED $14 V+

Torlesse Waipara Riesling ★★★
The characterful 2001 vintage (★★★☆) displays strong, limey, appetisingly crisp flavours and toasty, bottle-aged complexity. It's a dryish style, maturing well. The 2002 (★★★) has a slightly honeyed bouquet leading into a fleshy (13 per cent alcohol) palate with citrusy, limey flavours showing some richness and an off-dry (5.7 grams/litre of residual sugar) finish.

Vintage 02 01
WR 7 6
Drink 03-06 03-05

MED/DRY $17 AV

Trinity Hill Wairarapa Riesling ★★★☆
Trinity Hill is a Hawke's Bay-based winery, but this wine is grown at the Petrie vineyard, near Masterton. The 2003 vintage (★★★☆) is tight and youthful, with good intensity of lemon, lime and passionfruit flavours and a slightly sweet, finely balanced finish. It's a light-bodied wine (11.5 per cent alcohol) with good potential; open mid-2005+.

Vintage 03 02 01 00 99 98 97
WR 5 6 6 5 5 6 5
Drink 04-10 03-10 03-08 03-08 03-06 03-06 03-05

MED/DRY $20 AV

Trout Valley Nelson Riesling ★★★
Grown at Upper Moutere by Kahurangi Estate, the 2002 vintage (★★★) includes a splash (10 per cent) of Sauvignon Blanc and Chardonnay. Full-bodied, with a rounded finish, it's a flavoursome wine with fresh lemon, apple and lime characters, slightly sweet and crisp.

MED/DRY $17 AV

Vidal Estate Marlborough Riesling ★★★☆

Full-bodied and dryish (5 grams/litre of sugar), the 2002 vintage (★★★★) is an attractively weighty and rounded wine with smooth, ripe passionfruit, lemon and apple flavours. Showing good richness, it's quite forward in its appeal.

Vintage	03	02	01	00	99
WR	6	6	5	6	6
Drink	04-07	03-06	03-04	03-04	P

MED/DRY $18 AV

Villa Maria Cellar Selection Marlborough Riesling ★★★☆

Grown in the Wairau and Awatere valleys, the mouthfilling, full-flavoured 2002 vintage (★★★★) is an almost-dry style (below 5 grams/litre of sugar). It shows good weight on the palate, with ripe, delicate flavours of stone-fruit and limes, rich and lingering. The 2003, tasted prior to bottling (and so not rated) is ripely scented, with lemon and passionfruit flavours, crisp and strong.

Vintage	03	02	01
WR	6	6	6
Drink	03-09	03-08	03-08

DRY $20 AV

Villa Maria Private Bin Marlborough Riesling ★★★☆

A consistently enjoyable wine, priced right. The 2002 vintage (★★★) is finely balanced, with crisp grapefruit and apple flavours showing good depth and vigour in a fresh, appealing style. Tasted before bottling (and so not rated), the 2003 showed crisp, tropical-fruit flavours, ripe and lively.

Vintage	03	02	01	00
WR	6	5	6	7
Drink	03-07	03-06	03-05	03-04

MED/DRY $16 V+

Villa Maria Reserve Marlborough Riesling ★★★★★

This label is an emerging classic. The 2001 vintage (★★★★☆) was grown in the Fletcher vineyard, in the Wairau Valley, and fermented to near dryness (5 grams/litre of sugar). It's a youthful, tightly structured wine, slightly minerally, with good intensity and a long, freshly acidic finish.

Vintage	01	00	99	98	97	96
WR	6	6	7	6	7	7
Drink	03-10	03-08	03-07	03-06	03-05	P

MED/DRY $23 V+

Voss Riesling ★★★☆

This Martinborough wine is usually full of character. The 2002 vintage (★★★☆) has fresh, lemony aromas leading into a full-bodied, slightly sweet and crisp palate with strong lemon, apple and lime flavours.

Vintage	03	02	01	00
WR	6	6	5	6
Drink	04-08	05-08	03-07	03-09

MED/DRY $19 AV

Waimea Estates Classic Riesling ★★★★

This Nelson wine is consistently excellent and offers great value. Perfumed and slightly musky, the 2001 (★★★★) is weighty and rich, with ripe, tropical-fruit aromas and flavours, strong personality and wide appeal. The 2002 vintage (★★★★) is strongly flavoured and slightly sweet, with ripe, lemony, limey characters and good sugar/acid balance. A bargain.

Vintage	02	01	00
WR	7	7	6
Drink	03-05	03-04	P

MED/DRY $17 V+

Waimea Estates Dry Riesling ★★★☆

Less memorable than the intense, racy 2001 vintage (★★★★☆), the 2002 (★★★) is a limey, appetisingly crisp Nelson wine with green-edged fruit characters. Still youthful, it shows good depth and obvious aging potential.

Vintage 02 01
WR 6 7
Drink 03-06 03-06

DRY $17 V+

Waipara Hills Dry Riesling (★★★)

A blend of Canterbury and Marlborough grapes, the 2002 vintage (★★★) is a medium-dry style (7 grams/litre of sugar), tight and flavoursome, with lemon, apple and lime characters and a firm, crisp finish.

MED/DRY $18 AV

Waipara Hills Riesling ★★★

More forward in its appeal than its stablemate (above), the 2002 vintage (★★★) is a blend of Canterbury and Marlborough grapes, made in a distinctly medium style (16 grams/litre of sugar). It's a fresh, crisp wine, lemony and limey, with good sugar/acid balance and plenty of flavour. The 2003 (★★★), blended from grapes grown in eight vineyards in Canterbury and Marlborough, is again a medium style, with good depth of appley flavours, fresh, slightly sweet and crisp.

MED $20 -V

Waipara Springs Riesling ★★★★

Delicious in its youth, the 2002 vintage (★★★★) has a floral, lemony bouquet and intense, citrusy, limey flavours, slightly sweet, fresh and lively. A medium-dry style (with 8 grams/litre of residual sugar), it shows good richness and harmony.

Vintage 02
WR 7
Drink 03-10

MED/DRY $17 V+

Waipara West Riesling ★★★★

The latest vintages of this flinty, dry and punchy North Canterbury wine are the finest yet. The 2002 vintage (★★★★) is virtually bone-dry (3 grams/litre of residual sugar), with incisive lemon/lime flavours woven with racy acidity. It's definitely a cellaring style; open 2005+.

Vintage 02 01 00 99 98 97
WR 6 6 6 6 6 6
Drink 04-06 03-05 03-04 P P P

DRY $20 AV

Wairau River Marlborough Riesling ★★★☆

The 2001 vintage (★★★★☆) is a full-bodied and fleshy, ripe-tasting wine with very good depth of citrus-fruit and passionfruit flavours and a rounded finish. Still youthful, the pale lemon/green 2002 (★★★) is a dryish wine (5.7 grams/litre of sugar) with fresh, citrusy, limey flavours showing good vigour and depth.

Vintage 02 01
WR 7 7
Drink 03-06 03-06

MED/DRY $20 AV

West Brook Marlborough Riesling ★★★☆

The 2001 vintage (★★★) is a high-acid, slightly tart wine but offers good depth of citrusy, limey flavours. Delightful in its infancy, the slightly sweet 2002 (★★★★☆) is crisp and intense, with rich, ripe tropical-fruit and honey flavours, very concentrated and harmonious. The 2003 scored a silver medal at the 2003 Liquorland Top 100 International Wine Competition.

Vintage	02	01	00
WR	7	5	6
Drink	03-06	03-05	03-05

MED/DRY $17 V+

Whitehaven Marlborough Riesling ★★★

This is typically a lively and flavourful wine, slightly sweet and zesty. The 2002 vintage (★★★) is a full-flavoured, medium-dry wine (7.5 grams/litre of sugar), lemony, appley and crisp. Fresh and vibrant, it's finely balanced for easy drinking.

Vintage	02	01	00
WR	6	6	6
Drink	03-07	03-06	03-04

MED/DRY $18 AV

William Hill Riesling ★★★

This Alexandra, Central Otago wine has shown rising quality in recent years. Estate-grown and stop-fermented in a medium-dry style (12 grams/litre of residual sugar), the 2002 vintage (★★★) is a medium-bodied wine (11.5 per cent alcohol) with decent depth of lemony, appley flavours, delicate and floral.

Vintage	02	01	00	99	98
WR	5	4	4	4	3
Drink	03-07	03-04	P	P	P

MED/DRY $18 AV

Winslow St Vincent Riesling ★★★☆

At its best, this Martinborough wine is chock full of flavour. The 2002 vintage (★★★★) is a fresh, tightly structured, slightly sweet wine with rich, ripe citrus and passionfruit characters showing good intensity.

Vintage	02	01	00	99	98	97	96
WR	7	NM	7	6	7	6	5
Drink	03-06	NM	P	P	P	P	P

MED/DRY $25 -V

Woollaston Estates Nelson Riesling ★★★★

Racy and rich, the 2001 vintage (★★★★) is a delicious mouthful. Grown on the Waimea Plains, it is a distinctly medium style (15 grams/litre of sugar) with strong passionfruit, pineapple and lime flavours, vibrant, punchy and tangy, and a slightly minerally, flinty finish. The 2002 (★★★★) is also impressive. Pale, tangy, slightly minerally and flinty, it shows excellent freshness and vigour, with citrusy, slightly sweet flavours, crisp and penetrating.

MED $18 V+

Roussanne

Roussanne is a traditional ingredient in the white wines of France's northern Rhône Valley, where typically it is blended with the more widely grown Marsanne. Known for its fine acidity and 'haunting aroma', likened by some tasters to herb tea, it is also found in the south of France, Italy and Australia, but this late-ripening variety is extremely scarce in New Zealand.

Grove Mill Winemakers Reserve Roussanne (★★)

Grove Mill makes consistently excellent white wines, but the 2001 vintage (★★) suggests Roussanne will not have a strong future in Marlborough. Harvested at 21 brix from low-yielding vines (2.5 tonnes/hectare) adjacent to the winery and fermented and matured for four months in six-year-old French oak barrels, it's a bone-dry, austere wine with lemony, sharp, almost searing acidity.

DRY $20 ·V

Sauvignon Blanc

Sauvignon Blanc is New Zealand's key calling card in the wine markets of the world. At the 2003 International Wine and Spirit Competition, judged in London, the Silverado Trophy for the champion Sauvignon Blanc was awarded (yet again) to a New Zealand wine – Saint Clair Wairau Reserve Sauvignon Blanc 2002. At the 2003 Sydney International Wine Competition, Saints Marlborough Sauvignon Blanc 2002 scooped the trophy for Best Medium Bodied Dry White Table Wine.

Yet Kiwi Sauvignon Blanc has also attracted criticism during the past year. UK wine writer Stephen Brook, who judged at the 2002 Air New Zealand Wine Awards, found the Sauvignon Blancs 'a touch disappointing overall'. Jancis Robinson, the influential British commentator, declared in the *Financial Times* in May 2003 that she has recently found herself 'almost more impressed by Sauvignons from Australia's newer, cooler regions than New Zealand's offerings, most of which have become rather formulaic (take a bunch of grass, add a drop of sweetness, a dollop of canned asparagus, a feline whiff, and bottle early).'

The rise to international stardom of New Zealand Sauvignon Blanc was swift. The variety was first introduced to the country in the early 1970s; Matua Valley marketed the first varietal Sauvignon Blanc in 1974. Montana then planted sweeping vineyards in Marlborough, allowing Sauvignon Blanc to get into a full commercial swing in the early 1980s. In the year to June 2003, 65.6 per cent by volume of all New Zealand's wine exports were based on Sauvignon Blanc.

Sauvignon Blanc is New Zealand's most extensively planted variety, in 2002 (the latest figures available) comprising 31 per cent of the national vineyard. Over 85 per cent of all vines are concentrated in Marlborough, with Hawke's Bay the other significant stronghold. Plantings are expanding like wildfire: between 2000 and 2005, the area of bearing Sauvignon Blanc vines is projected to increase from 2485 hectares to 5519 hectares.

The flavour of New Zealand Sauvignon Blanc varies according to fruit ripeness. At the herbaceous, under-ripe end of the spectrum, vegetal and fresh-cut grass aromas hold sway; riper wines show capsicum, gooseberry and melon-like characters; very ripe fruit displays tropical-fruit flavours.

Intensely herbaceous Sauvignon Blancs are not hard to make in the viticulturally cool climate of the South Island and the lower North Island (Wairarapa). 'The challenge faced by New Zealand winemakers is to keep those herbaceous characters in check,' says Kevin Judd, chief winemaker at Cloudy Bay. 'It would be foolish to suggest that these herbaceous notes detract from the wines; in fact I am sure that this fresh edge and intense varietal aroma are the reasons for its recent international popularity. The better of these wines have these herbaceous characters in context and in balance with the more tropical-fruit characters associated with riper fruit.'

There are two key styles of Sauvignon Blanc produced in New Zealand. Wines fermented and matured in stainless steel tanks (by far the most common) place their accent squarely on their fruit flavours and are usually labelled as 'Sauvignon Blanc'. Wood-fermented and/or wood-matured styles are often called 'Sauvignon Blanc Oak Aged' or 'Reserve Sauvignon Blanc'.

Another major style difference is regionally based: the crisp, incisively flavoured wines of Marlborough contrast with the softer, less pungently herbaceous Hawke's Bay style. These are wines to drink young (within 18 months of the vintage) while they are irresistibly fresh, incisive and tangy, although the more complex, oak-aged Hawke's Bay wines (currently an endangered species, despite their quality), can mature well for several years.

Alana Estate Martinborough Sauvignon Blanc ★★★★

This wine is consistently attractive. The 2002 vintage (★★★★) shows excellent weight, ripeness and vibrancy, with a fresh, herbaceous edge to its rich tropical-fruit flavours and a finely balanced, lingering finish.

Vintage	02	01	00
WR	6	6	6
Drink	03-04	P	P

DRY $20 AV

Alexia Nelson Sauvignon Blanc ★★★★

A low-volume wine from Jane Cooper with loads of character. Grown on the Waimea Plains, the 2003 vintage (★★★★) is full-bodied and immaculate, with freshly herbaceous aromas, appetising acidity and vibrant, tropical-fruit and green capsicum flavours, deliciously well balanced.

Vintage	02
WR	6
Drink	03-04

DRY $17 V+

Allan Scott Marlborough Sauvignon Blanc ★★★★

The Scotts aim for a 'ripe, tropical-fruit' Sauvignon – a style typical of the Rapaura area of the Wairau Valley, where the company's vineyards are clustered. The 2003 vintage (★★★★) is a tangy, lively wine with well-ripened flavours of passionfruit and limes, a gently herbaceous edge and a long finish. It's a sophisticated wine, less aggressive than many Marlborough Sauvignons.

DRY $19 AV

Allan Scott Prestige Marlborough Sauvignon Blanc (★★★★☆)

The rich and zingy 2003 vintage (★★★★☆) is a single-vineyard wine, barrel-fermented and briefly oak-aged. It's a full-bodied wine with fresh, ripe, incisive melon/lime flavours, a subtle seasoning of wood and a long finish.

DRY $30 -V

Alpha Domus Hawke's Bay Sauvignon Blanc ★★★

The 2003 vintage (★★★) is attractive in its youth – crisp and lively, with passionfruit and lime flavours showing good freshness and zing and a fully dry finish.

Vintage	03	02	01	00	99	98
WR	5	6	6	7	7	6
Drink	03-04	03-05	03-04	P	P	P

DRY $17 AV

Amisfield Central Otago Sauvignon Blanc (★★★★☆)

One of the region's finest Sauvignon Blancs yet, the debut 2003 vintage (★★★★☆) was picked at over 23 brix from the estate vineyard in the Cromwell Basin. It was mostly fermented in tanks, but a small part of the crop, retained on the vines for an extra 10 days, was fermented with indigenous yeasts and lees-aged in old French oak barriques. The bouquet is lovely – fresh, lifted and intensely varietal. Dry but not austere, it's an immaculate wine with concentrated, well-ripened gooseberry and lime flavours, a touch of complexity and a notably persistent finish.

DRY $23 AV

Artisan Marlborough Sauvignon Blanc (★★★☆)

Showing good freshness and vivacity in mid-2003, the 2002 vintage (★★★☆) is a single-vineyard wine, grown at Valley East Estate. Punchy, with melon and green capsicum characters, it is crisp and lively, with a slightly off-dry finish.

MED/DRY $19 AV

Ashwell Sauvignon Blanc/Sémillon ★★★☆

The 2001 vintage (★★★☆) of this Martinborough wine has good weight, rounded acidity and sweet, ripe tropical-fruit flavours showing plenty of depth. Blended with 15 per cent Sémillon, the 2002 (★★★☆) is fresh and weighty, with ripe, 'sweaty armpit' aromas, tropical-fruit flavours and a well-rounded finish.

Vintage 02
WR 6
Drink 03-04

DRY $20 -V

Askerne Hawke's Bay Sauvignon Blanc ★★★☆

This small Havelock North winery makes a consistently good Sauvignon. The 2002 vintage (★★★★) shows excellent weight and depth. Partly (20 per cent) oak-matured, it is fresh and crisp, with strong herbal, guava and pawpaw flavours and a long, dry finish. The 2003 (★★★☆) is fresh and ripe, with good varietal character. Partly (7.5 per cent) oak-matured, it offers delicate melon and lime flavours, with a touch of complexity and crisp, lively acidity.

Vintage 03 02 01 00
WR 6 6 6 5
Drink 03-05 03-04 P P

DRY $18 AV

Ata Rangi Sauvignon Blanc ★★★★

A consistently attractive Martinborough wine, with ripe, tropical-fruit flavours. The 2003 vintage (★★★★) was mostly handled in tanks, but 15 per cent of the blend was fermented in seasoned oak barrels. Showing strong melon/lime flavours cut with fresh acidity and a smooth, slightly off-dry finish, it's a delicious wine in its youth.

Vintage 03
WR 6
Drink 03-04

DRY $20 AV

Awarua Terraces Goldstones Sauvignon Blanc (★★★★)

The impressive 2002 vintage (★★★★) was grown in the elevated, inland Mangatahi district of Hawke's Bay, hand-picked, whole-bunch pressed and matured on its yeast lees for five months before bottling. Weighty and rich, with lees-aging complexity, it has strong, ripe, tropical-fruit flavours, fresh acid spine and a finely balanced finish.

DRY $22 -V

Babich Marlborough Sauvignon Blanc ★★★★

The 2002 (★★★★) is rich and zingy. Showing good intensity, it's a finely scented wine with impressive delicacy and depth of tropical-fruit and herbaceous characters, enlivened by mouth-watering acidity. The 2003 vintage (★★★☆) is a 50/50 blend of Wairau Valley and Awatere Valley grapes. It has very good mouthfeel, ripeness and texture, with fresh melon/lime flavours showing plenty of depth and a dry, rounded finish.

DRY $18 V+

Babich Winemakers Reserve Sauvignon Blanc ★★★★☆

A top example of gently wooded Marlborough Sauvignon Blanc, with ripely herbaceous flavours and lovely poise and intensity. Grown in the Wairau and Awatere valleys and 10 per cent barrel-fermented, the 2002 vintage (★★★★) has the touch of complexity typical of the label in a generous, weighty style, ripe, rich, delicate and rounded, with a lingering finish.

Vintage 02
WR 7
Drink 03-05

DRY $23 AV

Black Barn Hawke's Bay Sauvignon Blanc (★★★)

A good example of the regional style, the 2002 vintage (★★★) was grown on the Havelock North hills and handled in stainless steel tanks. Maturing well, it's an immaculate and clearly varietal wine, fresh and lively, with melon and green capsicum flavours and a crisp, fully dry finish.

DRY $18 -V

Bladen Marlborough Sauvignon Blanc ★★★

The 2002 vintage (★★★) of this single-vineyard wine was very enjoyable in its youth, with tropical-fruit and herbaceous characters and a smooth finish, but with bottle-age it looks plainer, with green asparagus characters emerging.

DRY $19 -V

Brightwater Vineyards Nelson Sauvignon Blanc ★★★★

Grown on the Waimea Plains, this is a consistently impressive wine, made in a powerful, dry style. The 2002 vintage (★★★★☆) is a hugely drinkable wine in a non-herbaceous style with rich tropical-fruit flavours of passionfruit and melon, a rounded finish and good weight. The 2003 (★★★★) is again fleshy, generous and ripely flavoured, with a touch of complexity and zingy finish.

Vintage 02　01　00　99
WR　　 6　 6　 6　 5
Drink　03-04　03　P　P

DRY $19 AV

Burnt Spur Martinborough Sauvignon Blanc (★★★☆)

Fleshy and weighty, the 2002 vintage (★★★☆) is a partly barrel-aged wine (20 per cent of the blend was matured in old oak casks). It offers strong melon/capsicum flavours, fresh, crisp, slightly nutty and dry.

Vintage 02
WR 6
Drink 03-06

DRY $21 -V

Cable Bay Marlborough Sauvignon Blanc (★★★★)

Waiheke Island-based winemaker Neill Culley aims for a Sauvignon Blanc with 'restraint and textural interest, to enjoy with food'. The debut 2002 vintage (★★★★) was grown in the Brancott Valley. Most of the blend was tank-fermented and lees-aged, but 5 per cent was fermented in new barrels. It's a sophisticated, weighty wine with fresh, clearly herbaceous but not aggressive flavours, some complexity and good length.

Vintage 02
WR 6
Drink 03-04

DRY $21 -V

Cairnbrae The Stones Marlborough Sauvignon Blanc ★★★☆

A consistently attractive wine, now part of the Sacred Hill stable. The 2002 (★★★☆) is a medium to full-bodied style, still fresh and lively in mid to late 2003, with melon, pineapple and lime characters showing good ripeness, delicacy and length. The 2003 vintage (★★★) is full-bodied and vibrantly fruity, with firm acidity woven through its melon and lime flavours, which show good depth.

DRY $19 AV

Canterbury House Waipara Sauvignon Blanc ★★★★

Estate-grown, this is Canterbury House's biggest success – Sauvignon Blanc suits the company's cool grape-growing climate and warm, shingly soils. In most years it is fresh and strongly varietal, with grassy, nettley aromas and excellent depth of lively, crisply herbaceous flavour. The 2002 vintage (★★★★) is an intensely varietal wine with nettley aromas and crisp, punchy flavours of passionfruit and lime, fresh and zingy.

DRY $18 V+

Cape Campbell Marlborough Sauvignon Blanc ★★★

The 2003 vintage (★★★☆) from Murray Brown (who formerly owned the Cairnbrae winery) is very fresh, crisp and lively, with melon/lime flavours showing good varietal character and intensity.

DRY $18 -V

Carrick Sauvignon Blanc ★★★

Grown at Bannockburn, in Central Otago, this is a distinctly cool-climate style, fresh and strongly herbaceous. The 2002 vintage (★★★) is vibrant and zingy, with citrusy, grassy flavours, lively acidity and good length.

Vintage 02
WR 6
Drink P

DRY $18 -V

Cat's Pee on a Gooseberry Bush East Coast Sauvignon Blanc (★★☆)

From 'Purr Productions' (a division of Coopers Creek), the 2002 vintage (★★☆) is an easy-drinking blend of Hawke's Bay and Marlborough grapes. Restrained on the nose, it's a medium-bodied style with reasonable depth of fresh, crisp gooseberry and lime flavours and a fractionally sweet (5 grams/litre of sugar) finish.

MED/DRY $13 AV

Charles Wiffen Marlborough Sauvignon Blanc ★★★☆

The 2003 vintage (★★★) is full-bodied and crisp, with appley, slightly honeyed aromas and flavours, firm acidity and some richness.

DRY $19 AV

Church Road Sauvignon Blanc ★★★★☆

Aiming for a wine that is 'more refined and softer than a typical New Zealand Sauvignon Blanc, with restrained varietal characters', in 2002 (★★★★☆) Montana blended Marlborough (57 per cent) and Hawke's Bay (43 per cent) fruit and fermented and lees-aged 40 per cent of the blend in mostly seasoned French oak barriques. Only free-run juice was used (with minimal skin contact), giving the wine delicacy and the potential for greater longevity. It's a weighty, smooth, full-flavoured wine with well-ripened fruit characters and a clear emphasis on delicacy, complexity and texture. A gently herbaceous style, it's drinking well now.

Vintage 02
WR 7
Drink 03+

DRY $23 AV

C.J. Pask Roys Hill Sauvignon Blanc ★★☆

Winemaker Kate Radburnd aims for 'an easy-drinking style with its emphasis on tropical-fruit flavours and a tangy lift'. Verging on three-star quality, the 2002 vintage (★★☆), grown in Hawke's Bay, is a freshly aromatic, bone-dry wine with crisp, clean, citrusy, appley flavours showing moderate length.

DRY $16 AV

Claddagh Martinborough Sauvignon Blanc (★★★)

The robust 2002 vintage (★★★) is a moderately varietal wine with substantial body (14.5 per cent alcohol), ripe, concentrated flavours and a strong, creamy oak influence.

DRY $? V?

Clearview Estate Reserve Sauvignon Blanc ★★★☆

Grown in the Wilkins vineyard, close to the sea at Te Awanga, the 2002 vintage (★★★☆) of this Hawke's Bay wine was barrel-fermented and oak-aged for eight months. Toasty and oaky on the nose, it's a powerful wine, robust, rich and rounded, with strong, ripe, guava-like flavours, but would have been even better with a more restrained wood influence.

Vintage 02
WR 6
Drink 04-09

DRY $22 -V

Clifford Bay Estate Marlborough Sauvignon Blanc ★★★★

A consistently impressive single-vineyard wine, grown in the Awatere Valley. The 2003 vintage (★★★★) is vibrantly fruity and freshly herbaceous, with good intensity. Intensely varietal, it's balanced for easy drinking, with lively acidity, a sliver of sweetness (4.2 grams/litre) and a lingering finish.

Vintage 03 02
WR 7 6
Drink 03-06 P

DRY $18 V+

Cloudy Bay Sauvignon Blanc ★★★★★

New Zealand's most internationally acclaimed wine is highly sought after from Sydney to New York and London. Its irresistibly aromatic and zesty style and rapier-like flavours stem, chief winemaker Kevin Judd is convinced, from 'the fruit characters that are in the grapes when they arrive at the winery'. It is sourced from company-owned and contract growers' vineyards in the Rapaura, Fairhall, Renwick and Brancott districts of the Wairau Valley. The juice is cool-fermented in stainless steel tanks; the wine does not have any significant oak maturation. The 2003 vintage (★★★★☆) is the first to be closed with a screw-cap, rather than a cork. In the classic Cloudy Bay style, it is full-bodied (13.5 per cent alcohol) and fresh, with good vigour and excellent depth of clearly herbaceous, melon and lime flavours.

Vintage	03	02	01	00	99	98
WR	6	6	6	6	6	5
Drink	04	P	P	P	P	P

DRY $26 AV

Cloudy Bay Te Koko – see Branded and Other White Wines

Collards Rothesay Sauvignon Blanc ★★★☆

Who says you can't make good Sauvignon Blanc in Auckland? Grown in the company's Rothesay Vineyard at Waimauku, in West Auckland, and made with some use of barrel fermentation, malolactic fermentation and lees-aging, at its best it shows the weight and ripe tropical-fruit flavours of North Island grapes, with good acidity keeping things fresh and lively, and subtle oak adding richness. The 2002 vintage (★★★) is full-bodied, with gently herbaceous, slightly nutty and leesy flavours and a rounded finish.

Vintage	03	02	01	00	99	98
WR	6	6	6	7	6	7
Drink	04-06	03-05	03-04	P	P	P

DRY $16 V+

Coopers Creek Marlborough Sauvignon Blanc ★★★☆

A consistently good wine, bargain-priced. Balanced for easy drinking, the 2002 (★★★☆) is a vibrantly fruity wine with plenty of gooseberry and capsicum-like flavour and a crisp, racy finish. Even better, the 2003 vintage (★★★★) is ripely scented and punchy, with fresh, zingy melon, passionfruit and lime flavours showing excellent balance and intensity.

Vintage	03	02	01	00
WR	6	6	6	6
Drink	03-04	P	P	P

DRY $16 V+

Coopers Creek Reserve Marlborough Sauvignon Blanc ★★★★

The 2001 vintage (★★★★☆), based on the 'most intense fruit', was grown at Rapaura and in the Brancott Valley, and 40 per cent of the blend was wood-fermented (in two and four-year-old barrels). It's a tightly structured wine with rich, ripe, tropical-fruit flavours, a very subtle seasoning of oak and a long finish. There is no 2002. The 2003 (★★★★) is very fragrant and appealing, with strong melon/lime flavours and a slightly creamy texture.

Vintage	03	02	01	00	99
WR	7	NM	7	NM	7
Drink	03-04	NM	P	NM	P

DRY $20 AV

Corbans Cottage Block Marlborough Sauvignon Blanc ★★★★☆

The searching and complex 2000 vintage (★★★★★) was outstanding, with a very subtle oak influence (15 per cent of the final blend was oak-aged for eight months) and lovely, ripe, intense passionfruit and lime fruit characters. The 2002 (★★★★☆), only 8 per cent oak-aged, has fresh, nettley aromas leading into a mouthfilling palate with a touch of complexity, ripely herbaceous flavours and a deliciously rounded finish.

Vintage 02 01
WR 6 7
Drink 03-05 03+

DRY $29 -V

Corbans Private Bin Marlborough Sauvignon Blanc ★★★★

The 2002 vintage (★★★★) is the first since 1999. Partly (6 per cent) French oak-aged, it's an intensely aromatic, strongly varietal wine with rich tropical-fruit and herbaceous flavours and a fresh, rounded finish.

Vintage 02
WR 6
Drink 03-04

DRY $22 -V

Corbans Sauvignon Blanc ★★☆

The 2002 vintage (★★☆) doesn't state any particular region of origin on the label, but was made from Hawke's Bay grapes. It's a solid wine with good body, ripe, tropical-fruit flavours and a slightly off-dry (4 grams/litre of sugar) finish. The 2003 (★★☆), a blend of Chilean (54 per cent) and Hawke's Bay wine, is crisp and lively, with tropical-fruit/lime flavours showing decent depth.

Vintage 03 02 01
WR 5 6 6
Drink 03-04 03+ P

DRY $14 AV

Corbans White Label Sauvignon Blanc ★★☆

This low-priced quaffer is no longer solely from New Zealand – the 2002 vintage (★★☆) is a blend of Marlborough and Chilean wines. It's an easy-drinking style with smooth melon and cut-grass flavours in a weighty, rounded, slightly sweet style.

MED/DRY $9 V+

Cottle Hill Sauvignon Blanc (★★★)

The 2002 vintage (★★★) from this Northland winery was grown in Gisborne. It's a clearly varietal wine with fresh, ripe-fruit aromas leading into a crisp and lively palate with citrus fruit, melon and lime flavours showing good depth.

DRY $16 AV

Crab Farm Sauvignon Blanc ★★☆

The 2003 vintage (★★☆) of this Hawke's Bay wine is an off-dry style (5 grams/litre of sugar), with citrusy, slightly honeyed flavours and a crisp, green-edged finish.

Vintage 03
WR 5
Drink 03-04

MED/DRY $15 AV

Craggy Range Avery Vineyard Marlborough Sauvignon Blanc ★★★★

Grown in Richard and Linda Avery's vineyard, a slightly cooler site in the Wairau Valley than the Old Renwick Vineyard (below), the 2003 vintage (★★★★) was matured on its light yeast lees in stainless steel tanks for four months before bottling. It has a restrained bouquet in its youth, but shows good weight and intensity, with ripe, citrusy, appley, limey flavours, fresh acidity and a tight, smooth, sustained finish.

Vintage	03	02
WR	7	5
Drink	03-05	03-04

MED/DRY $19 V+

Craggy Range Old Renwick Vineyard Sauvignon Blanc ★★★★☆

Based on mature, 15 year-old vines in the heart of the Wairau Valley, the 2003 vintage (★★★★☆) was bottled after four months' aging in tanks on its light yeast lees. It's a fresh, tight, intensely flavoured wine with crisp, limey, slightly minerally characters, crisp and punchy.

Vintage	03	02	01	00	99
WR	6	6	6	6	6
Drink	03-05	03-04	P	P	P

DRY $19 V+

Craggy Range Te Muna Road Vineyard Martinborough Sauvignon Blanc (★★★★★)

Grown at the company's site a few kilometres south of Martinborough, the 2003 vintage (★★★★★) was mostly fermented and lees-aged in tanks, but 11 per cent of the blend was barrel-fermented with indigenous yeasts. Notably weighty and concentrated, it's a non-herbaceous style with very rich, ripe flavours of pears, apples and grapefruit, lively acidity, a slightly minerally streak and excellent vigour and depth.

Vintage	03	02
WR	6	6
Drink	03-05	03-04

DRY $19 V+

Crossings, The, Catherine's Run Reserve Sauvignon Blanc (★★★☆)

Grown in the Medway vineyard, at 200 metres above sea level in the Awatere Valley of Marlborough, and 20 per cent fermented in old barrels, the 2002 vintage (★★★☆) is fresh, crisp and lively, with fullness of body, a hint of oak and very good length of melon/lime, slightly chalky, minerally flavours.

DRY $22 -V

Crossings, The, Marlborough Sauvignon Blanc (★★★☆)

The punchy 2002 vintage (★★★☆) was grown in the Awatere Valley and lees-aged for three months. It's a fully dry wine with fresh gooseberry, passionfruit and lime flavours and a tight, minerally finish.

DRY $19 AV

Crossroads Destination Series Sauvignon Blanc (★★★★)

Hawke's Bay Sauvignon at its best, the weighty, zingy 2002 vintage (★★★★) was based principally on grassy Dartmoor Valley grapes, blended with riper fruit from the coastal Te Awanga district. It's a satisfyingly full-bodied wine with a strong surge of pineappley, limey flavours and a crisp, sustained finish.

Vintage 02
WR 7
Drink 03-06

DRY $20 AV

Dashwood Marlborough Sauvignon Blanc ★★★★

The Vavasour winery's drink-young, unwooded Sauvignon Blanc is typically great value. The 2003 vintage (★★★★) is a blend of Awatere Valley (55 per cent) and Wairau Valley grapes. Showing good intensity, it is freshly herbaceous, with vibrant melon and green capsicum flavours and a zingy, dryish (4.8 grams/litre of sugar) finish.

Vintage 03 02 01 00
WR 6 7 6 7
Drink 03-04 P P P

DRY $17 V+

De Gyffarde Berekah Estate Sauvignon Blanc (★★★★)

A single-vineyard wine grown in the Rapaura district of Marlborough's Wairau Valley, the 2002 vintage (★★★★) shows good concentration and zing. Freshly herbaceous on the nose, it's a gooseberry and capsicum-flavoured wine with crisp, lively acidity and good intensity and punch. Tasted before it was bottled (and so not rated), the 2003 was very promising – weighty and vivacious, with strong, appetisingly crisp gooseberry/lime flavours.

Vintage 02
WR 7
Drink 03-04

DRY $17 V+

Delegat's Hawke's Bay Sauvignon Blanc ★★★

This unwooded wine places its accent on ripe, rounded, tropical-fruit flavours in a very easy-drinking style. The delicious 2002 vintage (★★★☆) was grown mainly on relatively heavy soils at Meeanee and Havelock North. A dry style (3 grams/litre of sugar), it is ripely aromatic, with full body, vibrant, gently herbaceous, melon-like flavours and a well-rounded finish. However, the 2002 vintage was the last; this wine has been replaced by the Marlborough Sauvignon Blanc (below).

Vintage 02 01 00
WR 7 7 6
Drink P P P

DRY $15 V+

Delegat's Marlborough Sauvignon Blanc ★★★

Winemaker Michael Ivicevich is aiming for 'a tropical-fruit-flavoured style, a bit broader and softer than some'. The debut 2002 vintage (★★★) is ripely aromatic, with pineappley flavours and a rounded finish. The 2003 (★★★) is again great value. Tangy and ripe, with good depth of gooseberry, lime and pineapple flavours, it is very fresh and vibrant, with moderate acidity (less than in the company's Oyster Bay Sauvignon Blanc) giving an easy-drinking character.

Vintage 03 02
WR 7 6
Drink 03-04 P

DRY $15 V+

Domaine Georges Michel Marlborough Sauvignon Blanc ★★★

Grown in the Rapaura ('golden mile') district of the Wairau Valley, this wine has been of uneven quality since it was launched in 1998. The 2002 vintage (★★) is not one of the best. It lacks fresh fruit aromas, and the palate, although not fully dry (5 grams/litre of sugar) is austere, with high acidity.

MED/DRY $20 -V

Drylands Marlborough Sauvignon Blanc ★★★★

This is typically an upfront style from Nobilo with strong, crisply herbaceous flavours. Punchy and clearly herbaceous on the nose, the 2002 (★★★★) is a melon and capsicum-flavoured wine with excellent depth and zest. The 2003 vintage (★★★☆) was cool-fermented and lees-aged for three months in tanks. Freshly herbaceous, it has lively, green capsicum and slightly grassy flavours showing good depth and a smooth (fractionally off-dry) finish.

Vintage	03	02	01	00
WR	7	7	7	7
Drink	03-05	03-04	P	P

MED/DRY $19 AV

Dry River Sauvignon Blanc ★★★★

Estate-grown in Martinborough, this is typically a sturdy, notably ripe-tasting wine. Neil McCallum aims to 'minimise herbaceous and vegetal flavours and provide a wine with attractive aging qualities'. The 2002 (★★★★) is a mouthfilling, bone-dry wine with strong melon, fig and capsicum flavours, fresh, crisp and lively, and good mouthfeel. More restrained in its youth, the 2003 vintage (★★★☆) is weighty, with fresh grapefruit and apple flavours and a dry finish. It may develop well, but at this stage is less rich and concentrated than this label at its best.

Vintage	02	01	00	99	98	97	96
WR	6	6	7	6	6	7	7
Drink	03-13	03-12	03-10	03-05	03-04	P	P

DRY $23 -V

Equinox Hawke's Bay Sauvignon Blanc (★★)

It's not high-priced, but the 2002 vintage (★★) is still disappointing. Briefly wood-aged, it lacks fragrance, with moderate flavour depth and an overall lack of freshness, delicacy and charm.

Vintage	02
WR	3
Drink	03-04

DRY $14 -V

Esk Valley Hawke's Bay Sauvignon Blanc ★★★★

In warm vintages this is a robust wine with rich, ripe, tropical-fruit flavours; cooler years produce a less powerful but zesty wine. The 2002 (★★★☆) was grown in two vineyards, at Eskdale and Meeanee, and principally handled in tanks, but 10 per cent of the blend was barrel-fermented. It's a fresh, full-bodied wine with ripe melon and lime-evoking flavours, a touch of oak/lees complexity and a smooth, dry finish. Tasted prior to bottling (and so not rated), the 2003 vintage was full, crisp and clearly varietal, with melon/lime flavours, a touch of complexity and a smooth finish.

Vintage	03	02	01	00
WR	6	6	6	7
Drink	03-05	03-05	P	P

DRY $20 AV

Fairhall Downs Marlborough Sauvignon Blanc ★★★★
Estate-grown at the head of the Brancott Valley, this is a consistently classy wine. Finely scented, the 2002 vintage (★★★★) is full-bodied and smooth, with a basket of sweet, ripe-fruit flavours and a fresh, herbaceous edge. The 2003 (★★★★) is full and fresh, with rich, ripe passionfruit and lime flavours, pure and zesty, lively acidity and an easy-drinking balance.

DRY $18 V+

Fairmont Estate Sauvignon Blanc ★★★☆
This Wairarapa wine is grown at Gladstone, between Masterton and Martinborough. The 2002 vintage (★★★★★) is highly impressive and the best I've tasted. Instantly attractive, with fresh, ripe melon/capsicum aromas and flavours threaded with lively acidity, it shows excellent balance and varietal intensity, with a rich, smooth finish. A great buy at $15.

DRY $15 V+

Fiddler's Green Waipara Sauvignon Blanc ★★★☆
A distinctly cool-climate style, typically with good vigour and intensity. Estate-grown, hand-picked and tank-fermented, the full-bodied 2002 vintage (★★★☆) is fresh and vibrant, with crisp, almost fully dry (3 grams/litre of sugar) melon and green capsicum-like flavours showing very good delicacy and depth.

Vintage 02 01 00
WR 6 6 6
Drink 03-04 P P

DRY $20 -V

Forefathers Marlborough Sauvignon Blanc ★★★
The Forefathers label is owned by Kiwi winemaker Nick Goldschmidt, now based in the US, where most of this wine is sold. The 2002 vintage (★★★☆) is the best yet. A single-vineyard wine (in Hawkesbury Road, near Renwick), it is ripe and rounded, with very good depth of tropical-fruit flavours, fresh and vibrant.

DRY $17 AV

Forrest Marlborough Sauvignon Blanc ★★★☆
John Forrest's wine is fresh, fragrant and full-flavoured in a smooth, easy-drinking style that offers good value. The punchy 2003 vintage (★★★★) is one of the best yet. A slightly off-dry (4.5 grams/litre of sugar) style, it is scented, finely balanced, fresh and lively, with tropical-fruit and lime flavours showing excellent intensity.

Vintage 03 02 01 00
WR 7 5 6 7
Drink 04-05 03-04 P P

DRY $16 V+

Forrest Vineyard Selection Sauvignon Blanc ★★★★
The 2002 vintage (★★★★) is strongly aromatic, fresh, vibrant and ripe, with good intensity of melon and passionfruit flavours, a sliver of sweetness (4 grams/litre) and crisp Marlborough acidity.

Vintage 02 01
WR 5 6
Drink 03-04 P

DRY $22 -V

Framingham Marlborough Sauvignon Blanc ★★★★☆

This label has recently emerged as one of the most finely crafted Sauvignon Blancs in the region. Andrew Hedley makes a bone-dry style with no use of oak: 'Complexity comes from different sites [five] and levels of fruit maturity.' A worthy follow-up to the stylish and concentrated 2002 (★★★★★), the 2003 vintage (★★★★★) is very delicate, with a hint of 'sweaty armpit' on the nose and a lovely spread of flavours, pure and intense. Ripe, with sweet-fruit characters and fresh, finely balanced acidity, it's a sophisticated wine that carries the dry style superbly, with a very long finish.

Vintage	02	01	00	99
WR	7	6	5	6
Drink	03-04	03-04	P	P

DRY $20 AV

Gibbston Valley Central Otago Sauvignon Blanc ★★★

The 2003 vintage (★★★) is attractive in its youth, with ripe, citrusy, limey flavours, well balanced, lively and freshly scented.

DRY $23 -V

Giesen Marlborough Sauvignon Blanc ★★★☆

This is by far the largest-volume wine from the Canterbury-based Giesen brothers. The 2003 vintage (★★★) is fresh and mouth-wateringly crisp, with strong, citrusy, appley flavours and a dry finish.

Vintage	03	02	01	00
WR	7	7	7	7
Drink	03-06	03-04	03-04	P

DRY $15 V+

Gladstone Wairarapa Sauvignon Blanc ★★★★

Grown at Gladstone, south of Masterton, the 2002 vintage (★★★★★) is a fleshy, slightly creamy wine, 10 per cent barrel-fermented. Aromatic and punchy, it's a generous wine with fresh, clearly varietal aromas, searching gooseberry/lime flavours, a touch of oak and lees-aging complexity and a slightly off-dry, lingering finish. The 2003 (★★★☆) needs time to unfold, but is weighty, with firm acidity and ripe, concentrated, tropical-fruit flavours.

MED/DRY $20 AV

Glover's Moutere Sauvignon Blanc ★★

Estate-grown at Upper Moutere, this is a bone-dry style with flinty, nettley flavours and biting acidity. The 2001 vintage (★★) is an austere wine, lacking fresh fruit characters, liveliness and charm.

DRY $17 -V

Goldridge Premium Reserve Marlborough Sauvignon Blanc ★★☆

Grown in the Wairau Valley and to the south in the smaller Waihopai Valley, the 2001 vintage (★★☆) is a slightly austere wine with firm acidity and moderately ripe, green apple flavours. The fleshy 2002 (★★★) is ready now, with herbaceous aromas and flavours, now showing a developed, 'canned peas' character.

DRY $19 -V

Goldwater New Dog Marlborough Sauvignon Blanc ★★★★★

Bold and weighty, with a striking intensity of pineapple and passionfruit-like flavour, enlivened with fresh acidity, this is an exceptionally power-packed Sauvignon Blanc. The grapes were in the past grown mainly in the Dog Point vineyard in the Brancott Valley, but in 2003 were drawn principally from a vineyard in St Leonard's Road, in the heart of the Wairau Valley (hence the label change from 'Dog Point' to 'New Dog'). The wine is fermented almost to full dryness (the 2003 vintage has 3.5 grams/litre of residual sugar) and lees-aged for three months, with frequent stirring, in stainless steel tanks; a small percentage is barrel-fermented. The 2003 vintage (★★★★) has good weight, a freshly herbaceous bouquet and strong, tangy gooseberry/lime flavours. Woven with lively acidity, it's a tightly structured wine that should open out well during 2004.

Vintage	03	02
WR	7	7
Drink	03-05	03-04

DRY $20 V+

Gravitas Reserve Sauvignon Blanc (★★★★★)

The arresting 2002 vintage (★★★★★) was produced by St Arnaud's Vineyards, which owns 30 hectares of vineyards near Renwick, in Marlborough. One of the most powerful and intense Sauvignon Blancs I've tasted from the region, it's a robust wine (14.5 per cent alcohol), richly fragrant, with bold, highly concentrated gooseberry/lime flavours, fine acidity and a resounding, fully dry finish. Well worth tracking down, it's a wine of great depth and individuality.

DRY $22 V+

Greenhough Nelson Sauvignon Blanc ★★★★☆

Andrew Greenhough aims for a 'rich Sauvignon Blanc style with ripe, creamy mouthfeel' – and hits the target with ease. The pungently aromatic 2002 vintage (★★★★★) was grown at two sites at Hope. Mostly handled in tanks, but with 5 per cent of the blend fermented in new American oak casks, it's a richly scented, mouthfilling wine with excellent weight and rich tropical-fruit and herbaceous flavours, intense and lingering. The 2003 (★★★★☆) is fresh, ripely fragrant, weighty and dry, with good intensity of melon/lime flavours, lively acidity and a long finish.

Vintage	03	02
WR	6	6
Drink	03-05	03-04

DRY $18 V+

Grove Mill Marlborough Sauvignon Blanc ★★★★★

With a shower of awards around the world in the past few years, this label has established itself as a regional classic. Concentrated, rich and lush, it's a powerful Sauvignon Blanc, opulent and weighty, with huge drinkability. The grapes are drawn from vineyards (both company-owned and growers') scattered across the Wairau Valley. In most years, the blend includes minor portions of Sémillon and (unusually) Chardonnay, and since 1995, around 20 per cent has gone through malolactic fermentation to 'improve the wine's complexity and texture'. Lees-aged prior to bottling, the light lemon/green 2003 vintage (★★★★) is full and crisp, with searching melon/capsicum flavours and a slightly flinty, long finish. It should be at its best from early 2004 onwards.

Vintage	03	02	01	00	99
WR	6	5	7	7	6
Drink	03-05	03-04	P	P	P

DRY $20 V+

Gunn Estate Sauvignon Blanc (★★★)

From Sacred Hill (which now owns the Gunn Estate brand), the debut 2002 vintage (★★★) is a blend of Hawke's Bay (64 per cent) and Marlborough grapes. It has the restrained aromas typical of Hawke's Bay Sauvignon Blanc, strong, ripe, grapefruit and lime flavours, good weight and a crisp, dry finish.

Vintage	02
WR	6
Drink	03-04

DRY $15 V+

Highfield Marlborough Sauvignon Blanc ★★★★

Typically a classy wine – freshly scented and finely balanced, with rich, limey fruit characters and very good vigour and depth. Partly (below 5 per cent) barrel-fermented, the fleshy 2002 vintage (★★★★) is fragrant, with a very subtle seasoning of oak and well-ripened melon/lime flavours showing excellent delicacy and softness.

Vintage	02	01	00
WR	7	7	7
Drink	03-05	P	P

DRY $22 -V

Himmelsfeld Moutere Sauvignon Blanc ★★★☆

From a small vineyard in the Upper Moutere hills, the 2002 (★★★☆) is freshly aromatic, weighty and lively, with good varietal character and strong, lingering melon/capsicum flavours. The 2003 vintage (★★★★) is scented and full-bodied, with good intensity of ripely herbaceous, gooseberry/lime flavours, fresh, vibrant and punchy.

DRY $18 AV

Huia Marlborough Sauvignon Blanc ★★★☆

This is typically a restrained style of Sauvignon Blanc (by Marlborough standards), yet substantial and satisfying. Grown in six vineyards spread around the Wairau Valley, and 20 per cent fermented with indigenous yeasts, the 2003 vintage (★★★☆) is full-bodied, with very good depth of citrus-fruit, melon and lime flavours, fresh, ripe and lively.

Vintage	03	02	01	00	99
WR	6	7	6	7	6
Drink	03-05	03-05	03-05	P	P

DRY $21 -V

Hunter's Marlborough Sauvignon Blanc ★★★★★

Hunter's fame rests on the consistent excellence of this wine, which exhibits the intense aromas of ripe, cool-climate grapes, uncluttered by any oak handling. The style goal is 'a strong expression of Marlborough fruit – a bell-clear wine with a mix of tropical and searing gooseberry characters'. The grapes are sourced from vineyards in the Wairau (mostly) and Awatere valleys, and to retain their fresh, vibrant characters, they are processed quickly, with protective anaerobic techniques and minimal handling. The wine usually takes a year to break into full stride. The typically classy 2003 vintage (★★★★☆) is weighty and soft (in the sense of great delicacy through the palate, rather than any lack of acidity). A dry style (2.8 grams/litre of sugar), it offers good intensity of melon/capsicum flavours, with a long, lively finish.

Vintage	03	02	01	00
WR	6	5	6	5
Drink	04	03-04	P	P

DRY $18 V+

Hunter's Single Vineyard Sauvignon Blanc ★★★★☆

Grown 'predominantly' in the Spelsbury vineyard, in the Wairau Valley of Marlborough, the 2002 vintage (★★★★☆) shows impressive delicacy and finesse. Pale lemon/green, it is fragrant, with ripe melon and passionfruit flavours, a touch of minerality, gentle herbaceous characters and a fully dry, rounded finish. It's the sort of Sauvignon Blanc that keeps drawing you back for another glass.

Vintage	03	02
WR	6	5
Drink	05	04

DRY $22 AV

Hunter's Spring Creek Sauvignon Blanc/Chardonnay ★★★

As an all-purpose white, this works well. A distinctive Marlborough blend of Sauvignon Blanc and Chardonnay, with some exposure to French oak, it typically offers good depth of ripe, melon-like, gently herbaceous flavours in a crisp, lively style with plenty of interest.

Vintage	02
WR	5
Drink	04

DRY $15 V+

Hunter's Winemaker's Selection Sauvignon Blanc ★★★★★

Up to and including the 1998 vintage, this regional classic was labelled Sauvignon Blanc Oak Aged (and long ago, Fumé Blanc). It is based on Hunter's ripest, least-herbaceous Marlborough grapes, grown usually in the early-ripening estate vineyard in Rapaura Road, adjacent to the winery. Part of the blend is handled entirely in stainless steel tanks; another portion is barrel-fermented; another is tank-fermented but barrel-aged. It typically offers pure, deep, incisive fruit flavours, plenty of body and acidity, and well-judged, subtle wood-handling. The 2002 vintage (★★★★) has toasty oak aromas leading into a robust, creamy palate with ripely herbaceous flavours, a stronger than usual seasoning of wood and a rounded finish. It needs time to achieve a finer fruit/oak balance; open 2004+.

Vintage	02	01	00	99	98
WR	6	5	5	5	4
Drink	04-05	03-04	P	P	P

DRY $22 V+

🍇 🍇 🍇

Hurunui River Sauvignon Blanc (★★★)

Showing good freshness and depth, the 2002 vintage (★★★) was grown at Hawarden, north-west of Waipara, in North Canterbury. The bouquet is fresh and grassy; the palate is vibrant and zesty, with strongly varietal, green-edged flavours and a sliver of sweetness (5 grams/litre) to balance its mouth-watering acidity.

MED/DRY $18 -V

Huthlee Sauvignon Blanc ★★★

This small Hawke's Bay winery often makes a good Sauvignon Blanc, especially in cool, low-cropping years. The 2002 vintage (★★☆) is an easy-drinking, citrusy, appley wine with solid depth of flavour and a rounded finish.

Vintage	02
WR	6
Drink	03-04

DRY $16 AV

Isabel Estate Marlborough Sauvignon Blanc ★★★★★

Grown in the Tiller family vineyard near Renwick, this is a consistently stunning wine. It is harvested at a range of ripeness levels and a small portion of the blend (15 per cent) is fermented with indigenous yeasts in French oak barriques; the rest is tank-fermented and lees-aged. It is typically finely scented, fresh, crisp and punchy, but not one-dimensional, with lovely passionfruit, lychee and pineapple flavours, tight and long, and the barest hint of oak. The 2003 vintage (★★★★★) is pale lemon/green, with a very forthcoming, limey bouquet. Weighty and dry, with very intense, vibrant gooseberry/lime flavours, it shows great purity and depth, with a distinct minerally touch and racy acids. Full of personality, this is one of the region's greatest wines.

Vintage	03	02	01	00	99
WR	6	6	6	7	6
Drink	03-06	03-04	03-04	P	P

DRY $25 AV

Jackman Ridge Sauvignon Blanc (★★)

The non-vintage wine (★★) released by Montana in mid-late 2003 is a blend of Chilean and New Zealand wines. The bouquet is subdued; the flavours are ripe, citrusy and vaguely herbaceous, with fresh acidity. It's a solid but plain wine with limited varietal character.

MED/DRY $9 AV

Jackson Estate Sauvignon Blanc ★★★★

Grown in John Stichbury's vineyards in the heart of the Wairau Valley, this is typically a lush, ripe and rounded, fully dry wine with good concentration and huge drinkability. The stylish 2003 vintage (★★★★) is full-bodied, well-ripened and rounded, with tropical-fruit flavours showing excellent depth and a dry, lingering finish. It's not a 'leap out of the glass' style, but quietly satisfying.

Vintage	03	02
WR	6	7
Drink	03-04	P

DRY $19 AV

Johanneshof Marlborough Sauvignon Blanc ★★★☆

The 2002 (★★★★☆) from this small Koromiko producer is the best yet. Rich, ripe-fruit aromas lead into a fleshy palate with concentrated tropical-fruit flavours. The 2003 vintage (★★★) is vibrantly fruity, with plenty of fresh, ripely herbaceous flavour and a smooth finish.

DRY $19 AV

Kahurangi Estate Moutere Sauvignon Blanc ★★★☆

The fresh, punchy 2002 (★★★☆) was briefly lees-aged and part of the blend was aged in French oak casks, with malolactic fermentation. Aromatic, with melon and green capsicum flavours, it's a strongly varietal wine with a touch of complexity and good depth. The 2003 vintage (★★★) is scented and crisp, with lively acidity and plenty of freshly herbaceous flavour.

DRY $18 AV

Kaikoura Marlborough Sauvignon Blanc ★★★☆

From a small winery overlooking the ocean at Kaikoura, the 2002 vintage (★★★☆) is very ripely scented, with good depth of passionfruit/lime flavours in a full-bodied, smooth style, lively and balanced for easy drinking.

DRY $17 AV

Kaimira Estate Nelson Sauvignon Blanc ★★★☆

A freshly herbaceous wine, typically crisp, full-flavoured and zesty. The 2003 vintage (★★★☆) is a distinctly cool-climate style, intensely varietal, with grassy, tangy flavours showing good intensity and a dry, flinty finish.

DRY $17 AV

Kaituna Valley Marlborough Sauvignon Blanc ★★★★

Grown in the company's closely planted vineyard in the Awatere Valley, the 2002 vintage (★★★★) is weighty, fresh and rounded, with deliciously strong tropical-fruit flavours (much riper than is usual in the Awatere). The 2003 (★★★★☆) was mostly handled in tanks, but 5 per cent was barrel-fermented (in old casks) and 12 per cent underwent a softening malolactic fermentation. Ripely scented and weighty, it offers rich passionfruit/lime flavours, with lovely body, depth and roundness.

Vintage	03	02	01
WR	7	7	6
Drink	03-06	03-05	03-04

MED/DRY $19 AV

Kemblefield The Distinction Sauvignon Blanc ★★★☆

Fragrant, slightly minerally and oaky on the nose, the 2002 vintage (★★★★) was estate-grown in the relatively cool, elevated Mangatahi district of Hawke's Bay. A blend of Sauvignon Blanc (80 per cent) and Sémillon, it was fermented and lees-aged in stainless steel tanks and French oak barrels. Offering greater complexity than most Sauvignon Blancs, it is buoyant and penetrating, with tropical-fruit characters, a subtle seasoning of oak and crisp acidity keeping things lively.

DRY $20 -V

Kemblefield Winemakers Signature Sauvignon Blanc ★★★

The 2002 vintage (★★☆) of this unoaked Hawke's Bay wine developed well with bottle-age. It's a typical regional style, not highly aromatic but showing good body, with ripe, tropical-fruit flavours. The 2003 (★★★), estate-grown at Mangatahi, is a youthful wine with plenty of fresh passionfruit and lime-evoking flavour and a dry finish.

DRY $16 AV

Kennedy Point Vineyard Berekah Estate Sauvignon Blanc ★★★

Fresh, with tropical-fruit characters, the 2003 vintage (★★★☆) from this Waiheke Island-based producer is a single-vineyard wine, already attractive. Passionfruit, lime and pineapple flavours hold sway, with good intensity and a crisp, lively finish.

DRY $18 -V

Kerr Farm Kumeu Sauvignon Blanc ★★☆

Estate-grown in West Auckland, the 2002 vintage (★★★) is not a 'show style', but makes an interesting change from the Marlborough model. Bright, light yellow/green in hue, it has a minerally rather than herbaceous bouquet. Full-bodied and ripe-tasting, with tropical-fruit characters, balanced acidity and a dry finish, it's worth trying.

Vintage	02
WR	7
Drink	03-04

DRY $16 -V

Kim Crawford Flowers
Marlborough Sauvignon Blanc (★★★★★)

The notably ripe 2002 vintage (★★★★★) has strong, herb and melon aromas and flavours in a rich, concentrated style that retains good acid spine. Made from first-crop, Awatere Valley vines, it is deliciously vibrant and punchy.

DRY $25 AV

Kim Crawford Marlborough Sauvignon Blanc ★★★★

At its best, this is a punchy style with deliciously strong, fresh, tropical-fruit and capsicum flavours. The 2002 (★★★☆) is an attractive wine (10 per cent Chardonnay) with fresh, lifted, ripely herbaceous aromas. It's smooth and fresh, with an easy-drinking balance and ripe, rounded melon/capsicum flavours. The 2003 vintage (★★★★☆) is scented, ripe and tangy, with buoyant melon/lime flavours showing excellent intensity and a long finish.

Vintage	03	02	01	00
WR	5	6	6	6
Drink	03-04	03-04	03-04	P

DRY $20 AV

Kim Crawford Sauvignon Blanc ★★★

The 2002 vintage (★★★☆), with no region of origin stated on the front label, is a blend of 75 per cent Sauvignon Blanc and 25 per cent Sémillon, grown at Te Awanga, in Hawke's Bay. Herbaceous on the nose, it's a fresh, crisp wine with vibrant, lingering melon and cut-grass flavours. (The 2003 vintage is a blend of Marlborough, Nelson and Hawke's Bay grapes.)

DRY $17 AV

Konrad Marlborough Sauvignon Blanc ★★★☆

The 2002 vintage (★★★☆) is a finely balanced wine, grown in the Wairau and Waihopai valleys. Freshly scented and vibrantly fruity, it's a full-bodied wine with strong, ripe melon/lime flavours and a rounded finish. The 2003 (★★★☆) is crisp and tangy, with lively passionfruit/lime flavours showing very good depth.

Vintage	03	02	01	00
WR	6	6	6	6
Drink	03-05	03-04	P	P

DRY $20 -V

Koura Bay Whalesback Marlborough Sauvignon Blanc ★★★☆

This single-vineyard wine is grown in the Awatere Valley. The 2002 (★★★☆) has grassy aromas leading into a lively, melon and lime-flavoured palate, moderately intense, with a crisp, dry finish. The 2003 vintage (★★★☆) is aromatic, with fresh, strong, ripely herbaceous flavours, showing good delicacy and purity, and a smooth finish.

Vintage	03
WR	7
Drink	04-05

DRY $19 AV

Lake Chalice Marlborough Sauvignon Blanc ★★★★

The 2002 vintage (★★★★) was grown in the Wairau and Awatere valleys. Very fresh and aromatic, it is vibrant, zingy and incisively flavoured, with rich melon and capsicum characters, good weight and a long finish. The fleshy, finely balanced 2003 (★★★★☆) is even better. Grown at five sites (including the estate Falcon vineyard), it is beautifully scented and weighty, with loads of passionfruit/lime flavour and a sliver of sweetness (4.5 grams/litre) balanced by appetising acidity. A delicious mouthful.

Vintage	03	02	01	00
WR	7	6	7	7
Drink	03-04	P	P	P

DRY $19 AV

Lake Chalice The Raptor Sauvignon Blanc (★★★★)

The 2002 vintage (★★★★) is a single-vineyard Marlborough wine, grown in the Awatere Valley and fermented and lees-aged for seven months in French oak barriques, with full malolactic fermentation. Fragrant, with nutty oak aromas, it is weighty, with strong, ripe, passionfruit and herb fruit flavours, gentle acidity, a deliciously creamy texture and a slightly buttery finish.

Vintage	02
WR	7
Drink	03-07

DRY $29 -V

Lake Hayes Sauvignon Blanc (★★★)

The crisply herbaceous 2002 vintage (★★★) is a blend of grapes grown at the Amisfield vineyard, in the Cromwell Basin of Central Otago, and at Renwick, in Marlborough. It was mostly tank-fermented and lees-aged, but 5 per cent of the blend was matured in old French oak casks. Pale, with fresh, grassy aromas, it shows a touch of complexity, with fresh, vibrant, grassy flavours and a bone-dry finish.

DRY $20 -V

Lawson's Dry Hills Marlborough Sauvignon Blanc ★★★★★

Consistently among the region's finest Sauvignon Blancs, this is a powerful and stylish wine, vibrantly fruity, intense and structured. (In blind tastings, it can remind me of Cloudy Bay.) The 2003 vintage (★★★★☆) was grown in 10 vineyards in the Wairau Valley (and its southern off-shoots, the Brancott and Waihopai valleys). It includes 10 per cent Sémillon, and to add a subtle extra dimension, 8 per cent of the blend was fermented in French oak casks (one to five years old). Lifted, zesty aromas of gooseberry and lime lead into a vibrant and punchy wine with a basket of fruit flavours, as usual showing impressive freshness, richness and complexity.

Vintage	03	02	01	00
WR	6	6	6	7
Drink	03-05	03-04	P	P

DRY $20 V+

🍇🍇

Le Grys Marlborough Sauvignon Blanc ★★★☆

Produced by Mud House, this is a lightly wooded style. The fresh, punchy 2002 vintage (★★★☆) is a 50/50 blend of Wairau Valley and Awatere Valley grapes, 10 per cent oak-aged for three months. The bouquet is strongly herbaceous; the palate is lively, with gooseberry and lime flavours and a crisp finish.

Vintage	02
WR	6
Drink	03-04

DRY $19 AV

Lincoln Heritage Collection Lukrica Marlborough Sauvignon Blanc ★★★

Named after Lukrica Fredatovich, the wife of the founder, Petar, the 2002 vintage (★★★) is a crisp, green-edged wine with a freshly herbaceous bouquet and good depth of lively, tangy flavour.

Vintage	02	01
WR	5	6
Drink	03-04	P

DRY $17 AV

Lincoln Winemakers Series Sauvignon Blanc ★★★

Grown at Te Kauwhata, in the Waikato, the 2002 vintage (★★★☆) is a ripe-tasting wine with balanced acidity, tropical-fruit characters showing some lushness and plenty of flavour. Good value.

Vintage 02
WR 6
Drink 03-04

DRY $14 V+

Linden Estate Hawke's Bay Sauvignon Blanc ★★★

The 2002 vintage (★★★) is a blend of tank-fermented Sauvignon Blanc (92 per cent) and barrel-fermented Sémillon (8 per cent), grown in the Esk Valley and Dartmoor Valley. Fully dry, it's a mouthfilling wine, not pungent but satisfying, with ripe tropical-fruit flavours and a hint of oak adding complexity.

DRY $18 -V

Linden Estate Reserve Sauvignon Blanc (★★★★)

(The word 'reserve' appears only on the back label.) An excellent example of the regional style, the 2002 vintage (★★★★) is a single-vineyard wine from the Esk Valley of Hawke's Bay, and was partly barrel-fermented. Still fresh, it's a complex style with strong, ripe tropical-fruit flavours, finely integrated toasty oak and a tightly structured, dry finish. Drink now or cellar.

DRY $19 AV

Longridge Vineyards Sauvignon Blanc ★★★

Under Corbans' direction, this traditionally Hawke's Bay wine was a lightly oaked style, typically full-bodied, with fresh, limey, tangy flavours. Now, as a Montana brand, the wood influence has been dropped. The 2003 vintage (★★★), a blend of Chilean (54 per cent) and Hawke's Bay wine, is full-bodied and fresh, with good depth of tropical-fruit/lime flavours and a touch of lees-aging complexity.

DRY $16 AV

Lynskeys Wairau Peaks Marlborough Sauvignon Blanc ★★★

The 2002 (★★★) offers ripe melon/lime flavours, gently grassy, fresh and lively. Tasted in its infancy, the 2003 vintage (★★★) was pale, with citrusy, limey characters, crisp acidity and decent flavour depth.

DRY $19 -V

Mahi Sauvignon Blanc ★★★☆

Mahi ('your work, your craft') is the personal brand of Brian Bicknell, chief winemaker at Seresin Estate. The 2001 vintage (★★★☆) was tight and reserved in its youth, with tense, limey flavours, but the 2002 (★★★★) is a different beast. Grown in the Byrne vineyard at Conders Bend, near Renwick, it was mostly tank-fermented and lees-aged for six months, but 12 per cent of the blend was French oak-fermented with indigenous yeasts. Instantly appealing, it's a richly scented wine with ripe-fruit aromas, tropical-fruit flavours and a soft, well-rounded finish.

Vintage 02 01
WR 6 6
Drink 03-07 03-08

DRY $22 -V

Mahurangi Estate Selection Marlborough Sauvignon Blanc ★★★

Still drinking well, the 2002 vintage (★★★) is a strongly varietal wine, crisp and lively, with herbaceous aromas, firm acid spine and good depth of melon and green capsicum flavours.

DRY $18 -V

Main Divide Sauvignon Blanc/Sémillon ★★★☆

From Pegasus Bay, the 2002 vintage (★★★★) is a highly characterful blend of tank-fermented, lees-aged Marlborough Sauvignon Blanc and Waipara Sémillon, fermented in old French oak barriques. Fragrant and full-bodied, with strong, ripe, tropical-fruit flavours and a herbal undercurrent, it shows good intensity and complexity, with a slightly flinty finish. Great value.

Vintage	02
WR	6
Drink	03-04

DRY $17 V+

Martinborough Vineyard Sauvignon Blanc ★★★★

The 2003 vintage (★★★★) was grown in the Pirinoa Block, at Martinborough, and a small portion was fermented in old French oak barriques. Fresh and lively, with ripe melon, lime and capsicum flavours and a slightly flinty finish, it shows good delicacy, complexity and length. Open early 2004 onwards.

DRY $20 AV

Matariki Hawke's Bay Sauvignon Blanc ★★★★

An unoaked style, grown in Gimblett Road, the 2002 vintage (★★★★) has strong, sweet-fruit characters of passionfruit and red capsicum, showing good richness. It's a very fresh and vibrant wine, with lively acidity and a fully dry finish.

Vintage	02	01
WR	6	5
Drink	03-06	03-04

DRY $20 AV

Matariki Reserve Sauvignon Blanc ★★★★

This is generally among Hawke's Bay's richest, most satisfying Sauvignon Blancs. The 2002 vintage (★★★☆) was grown in Gimblett Road and 40 per cent barrel-fermented and lees-aged, with some malolactic fermentation. The bouquet is slightly toasty; the palate is fresh, ripe and vibrantly fruity, with good acidity, a strong seasoning of wood and passionfruit, nectarine and lime flavours showing very good depth.

Vintage	02	01	00	99	98
WR	6	5	7	6	7
Drink	04-07	03-05	03-04	P	P

DRY $25 -V

Matawhero Reserve Sauvignon ★★★

The distinctive 1999 vintage (★★★) from Denis Irwin is a golden Gisborne wine, soft and slightly honeyed, with dry, developed, pineappley flavours and mouthfilling body. Ready.

DRY $20 -V

Matua Valley Hawke's Bay Sauvignon Blanc ★★★

This isn't a pungent, 'leap-out-of-the-glass style', but it delivers easy, moderately priced drinking. The 2002 vintage (★★★) has good body and citrusy, ripely herbaceous flavours. The 2003 (★★★), handled entirely in stainless steel tanks, is full-bodied, fresh and vibrant, with citrusy, appley, limey flavours and a smooth (off-dry) finish.

MED/DRY $17 AV

Matua Valley Matheson Sauvignon Blanc ★★★★

Since the first 1986 vintage, this classy wine has ranked among the country's finest oak-aged Sauvignons. In the past, it was usually estate-grown at Waimauku in West Auckland, but since 1998 the fruit supply has switched to the Maraekakaho district in Hawke's Bay. It is typically a beautifully harmonious and subtle wine, with good body and excellent depth of fresh, ripe passionfruit and melon-like flavours, lightly seasoned with oak. The 2002 vintage (★★★☆) is a blend of 90 per cent Sauvignon Blanc and 10 per cent Sémillon, matured for eight months in one and two-year-old French and American oak casks. Less lush, ripe and concentrated than some past releases, it's a full-bodied wine with pear, gooseberry and grapefruit flavours, firm acidity, a gentle oak influence and smooth finish.

Vintage	02	01	00	99	98	97	96
WR	6	NM	6	6	7	6	6
Drink	03-06	NM	03-05	03-04	03-04	P	P

DRY $19 AV

Matua Valley Shingle Peak Marlborough Sauvignon Blanc ★★★☆

The Shingle Peak label is reserved by Matua Valley for its Marlborough wines. The fresh, limey aromas on the 2002 vintage (★★★☆) lead into a crisp, clearly herbaceous but not grassy wine with pure, zingy melon/lime flavours. The 2003 (★★★☆) is full, fresh and smooth, with good depth of melon and lime flavours, lively and zingy, and a well-rounded finish.

Vintage	03	02	01	00
WR	7	6	6	5
Drink	03-05	P	P	P

DRY $18 AV

McCashin's Nelson Sauvignon Blanc ★★★☆

Grown in the company's vineyard at Hope, the 2001 (★★★☆) is a punchy, herbaceous wine with substantial body, strong varietal character and plenty of crisp, capsicum-like flavour. The 2002 vintage (★★★☆) is similar: freshly herbaceous, with crisp gooseberry/lime flavours, vibrant and tangy.

DRY $19 AV

Mebus Estate Sauvignon Blanc ★★

Grown at East Taratahi, south of Masterton, in the Wairarapa, the 2001 vintage (★★☆) is a full-bodied, smooth wine but it lacks real freshness and intensity. The 2002 (★☆), tasted in 2003, was again dull and plain.

DRY $18 -V

Melness Marlborough/Canterbury Sauvignon Blanc ★★★☆

The 2002 vintage (★★★★) is a weighty, deeply flavoured regional blend, principally cool-fermented in tanks but with a small portion of barrel-fermented Sémillon. It's a fleshy wine with ripe gooseberry and crisp herbal flavours showing excellent depth and subtle oak and lees-aging characters adding complexity.

Vintage	02
WR	6
Drink	03-06

DRY $22 -V

Mills Reef Hawke's Bay Sauvignon Blanc ★★★

The lower-tier Sauvignon Blanc in the Mills Reef range is grown in Hawke's Bay and made in an off-dry, easy-drinking style. Fresh and limey on the nose, the 2002 vintage (★★★) is frisky and flavoursome, with lemon, melon and lime characters and a slightly sweet, smooth finish.

Vintage	03	02	01	00
WR	6	7	7	6
Drink	03-04	P	P	P

MED/DRY $16 AV

Mills Reef Reserve Sauvignon Blanc ★★★★

The 2002 vintage (★★★★) of this Hawke's Bay wine was 30 per cent fermented in French oak barriques (one and two-year-old). Fresh, full-bodied and ripely herbaceous, with a very subtle oak influence, it shows good weight and palate richness, with deep tropical-fruit flavours. The 2003, tasted just prior to bottling (and so not rated), offers melon and green capsicum flavours, with a slightly yeasty, nutty complexity. Fresh and crisp, with greener-edged flavours than in 2002, but excellent freshness and intensity, it should age well.

Vintage	02	01	00
WR	7	7	6
Drink	03-04	P	P

DRY $19 AV

Mission Sauvignon Blanc ★★★

The 2002 vintage (★★★) is a blend of Marlborough (60 per cent) and Hawke's Bay grapes, and includes 10 per cent Sémillon. It's a ripe, full-bodied wine, balanced for easy drinking, with melon/capsicum characters, fresh and flavoursome, and a smooth, fractionally off-dry (3 grams/litre sugar) finish. The 2003 (★★★), a 2:1 blend of Hawke's Bay and Marlborough fruit, is a slightly herbaceous wine with tropical-fruit and green capsicum flavours, fresh, crisp and lively.

DRY $15 V+

Moana Park Pascoe Series Sauvignon Blanc (★★☆)

Verging on three-star quality, the 2002 vintage (★★☆) is a solid Hawke's Bay wine, full-bodied, with melon and capsicum flavours and a crisp, green-edged finish.

DRY $14 AV

Montana Brancott Estate Sauvignon Blanc ★★★★★

Promoted as a 'complex style of Sauvignon Blanc', this wine lives up to its billing. It is grown in the company's sweeping Brancott Estate vineyard in Marlborough and a small portion of the final blend (15 per cent in 2002) is fermented and lees-aged in French oak barriques (half new). The 2002 vintage (★★★★☆) is ripely herbaceous, with a slightly creamy texture. Weighty and lively, with rich tropical-fruit characters and subtle oak adding complexity, it offers top drinking during 2004.

Vintage	02	01	00	99	98
WR	7	6	7	7	6
Drink	03-05	03-04	P	P	P

DRY $24 V+

Montana Marlborough Sauvignon Blanc ★★★☆

This famous, bargain-priced label rests its case on the flavour explosion of slow-ripened Marlborough fruit – a breathtaking style of Sauvignon Blanc which this wine, more than any other, has introduced to wine lovers in key markets around the world. Recent vintages are less lush, more pungently herbaceous than some other Marlborough labels; 'this is the style we can sell locally and the UK wants,' reports Montana. It lives forever – the 1984 vintage, opened in September 2003, was golden, toasty, herbal and honeyed. The 2002 vintage (★★★☆) was grown in the company's Brancott Estate (on the south side of the Wairau Valley), Squire Estate (at Rapaura), and Kaituna Estate (inland from Renwick). Citrusy, grassy and lively, the 2003 (★★★☆) shows good balance and depth, with strongly herbaceous characters, satisfying body and a crisp, dry (4 grams/litre of sugar) finish.

Vintage	03	02	01	00
WR	7	7	7	7
Drink	03-05	03-04	P	P

DRY $16 V+

Montana Reserve Marlborough Sauvignon Blanc ★★★★☆

This is a richer, riper, less pungently herbaceous style of Marlborough Sauvignon Blanc than its stablemate (above). The grapes are grown mainly at Brancott Estate, on the south side of the Wairau Valley, blended with fruit from Squire Estate, at Rapaura. Weighty and rounded, the 2002 (★★★★☆) offers a strong surge of passionfruit, melon and green capsicum flavours, deliciously fresh, vibrant, smooth and long. The 2003 vintage (★★★★☆) is powerful and punchy, with good weight, a gentle herbaceous influence and strong, ripe tropical-fruit flavours, crisp and lively.

Vintage	03	02	01	00	99	98
WR	6	7	7	7	6	6
Drink	03-04	P	P	P	P	P

DRY $20 AV

Morton Estate Stone Creek Marlborough Sauvignon Blanc ★★★

The 2002 vintage (★★★☆) of this single-vineyard wine is fleshy and ripe, with good concentration of tropical-fruit flavours, balanced acidity and a rounded, off-dry finish.

Vintage	02	01	00	99
WR	7	6	6	6
Drink	03-05	03-04	P	P

MED/DRY $18 -V

Morton Estate White Label Hawke's Bay Sauvignon Blanc ★★★

Morton's 'white label' wine was traditionally a slightly off-dry style, but the 2002 vintage (★★★☆) is fully dry. Full-bodied (13.5 per cent alcohol) and ripe-tasting, it shows very good depth of melon/lime flavours and good acid balance. It's a more restrained style than the classic Marlborough model, but crisp, dry and lively, with satisfying flavour depth. The 2003 (★★★), grown at two elevated sites, is fresh and full-flavoured, with melon and capsicum characters, lively and tangy.

Vintage	03	02	01	00	99
WR	6	7	6	6	5
Drink	03-05	03-05	03-04	P	P

DRY $15 V+

Morton Estate White Label Marlborough Sauvignon Blanc ★★★

The 2002 vintage (★★★) is fresh and lively, with passionfruit/lime flavours showing solid depth and a sliver of sweetness (4 grams/litre of sugar) to smooth the finish. The 2003 (★★★☆) shows good varietal character, freshness and depth, with ripely herbaceous flavours, crisp and punchy.

Vintage	03	02	01
WR	6	7	6
Drink	03-05	03-05	03-04

DRY $17 AV

Mount Cass Vineyards Waipara Valley Sauvignon Blanc (★★★☆)

Made from grapes harvested at 18 and 22 brix (sugar levels) to capture grassy and tropical-fruit flavours, the 2002 vintage (★★★☆) shows good flavour intensity, with herb and passionfruit characters on the palate and a crisp, lively, off-dry finish.

Vintage	02
WR	6
Drink	P

MED/DRY $18 AV

SAUVIGNON BLANC 199

Mount Nelson Marlborough Sauvignon Blanc ★★★★★
Mount Nelson is owned by Lodovico Antinori, of the famous Tuscan winemaking family, who with his brother, Piero, is establishing vineyards in Marlborough and Waipara and a winery that will focus exclusively on Sauvignon Blanc. Since the first 1998 vintage, the wine has been based on high-quality batches purchased from other companies, blended by Antinori and Waipara-based winemaker Danny Schuster, and sold mainly in Italy. Fermented to full dryness and matured on its yeast lees for up to 15 months, with no exposure to oak, it is typically a rich yet subtle, tautly structured wine with excellent mouthfeel and slightly flinty, minerally characters adding complexity. The 2002 vintage (★★★★☆) shows good weight, strong, ripe flavours, finely balanced acidity and a long, tight, bone-dry finish. It should mature gracefully, and won't be released in Italy until May 2004.

DRY $30 AV

Mount Riley Marlborough Sauvignon Blanc ★★★
The 2002 vintage (★★★) is freshly herbaceous, with grassy aromas and crisp, lemony, appley flavours showing good length. The 2003 (★★★) is full-bodied and smooth, with melon/capsicum flavours cut with fresh acidity.

DRY $17 AV

Mount Riley Seventeen Valley Sauvignon Blanc (★★★★★)
The debut 2002 vintage (★★★★★) is a superb example of oak-aged Marlborough Sauvignon Blanc. Weighty, non-aggressive and complex, it was grown in the Wairau Valley, fermented with indigenous yeasts and matured on its yeast lees in old oak barriques. It's a delicious, very finely balanced wine with excellent concentration of ripe, tropical-fruit flavours, good texture, well-integrated oak and a lasting finish.

DRY $22 V+

Mud House Marlborough Sauvignon Blanc ★★★☆
Grown in the Wairau Valley, the 2002 vintage (★★★☆) offers fresh, strong melon/lime aromas and flavours, crisp, lively and balanced for easy, enjoyable drinking. Ripely scented, the 2003 (★★★☆) has strong tropical-fruit and gently herbaceous flavours, showing good freshness and length.

Vintage	03	02	01
WR	6	6	7
Drink	03-05	03-04	P

DRY $19 AV

Murdoch James Estate Martinborough Sauvignon Blanc ★★★★
This is Murdoch James' best white wine – incisive and racy. The 2002 vintage (★★★☆) is so punchy and zingy, it could easily pass for a Marlborough wine. Freshly herbaceous on the nose, it's a distinctly cool-climate style with incisive melon and green capsicum flavours cut with fresh acidity. The 2003 (★★★★) is similar, with pungent flavours of passionfruit and limes, fresh, vibrant and tangy.

DRY $23 V

Murray Ridge Sauvignon Blanc (★★☆)
Restrained on the nose, the 2003 vintage (★★☆) from Montana is a blend of Chilean and New Zealand wine. It's a slightly sweet, rounded wine with ripe, tropical-fruit flavours, gentle acidity and a soft finish. An easy-drinking quaffer, it tastes more of Chile than New Zealand, lacking the pungency typical of local Sauvignon Blanc.

MED/DRY $9 V+

Nautilus Marlborough Sauvignon Blanc ★★★★

Typically a richly fragrant wine with mouthfilling body and a surge of ripe, passionfruit and lime-like flavours, enlivened by fresh acidity. Oak plays no part in the wine, but it is briefly matured on its yeast lees. Based on fruit grown in the company's own Awatere River vineyard and by Wairau Valley growers, the 2003 vintage (★★★☆) is smooth and ripe, with tropical-fruit and green capsicum flavours, showing good freshness, delicacy and roundness. (The wine can certainly mature well. The 1998 vintage, from a hot, dry season, was very alive when tasted in September 2003, with an array of toast, tropical-fruit and herb flavours reminiscent of a Barossa Valley Sémillon.)

Vintage	03	02	01	00
WR	6	7	7	7
Drink	03-04	P	P	P

DRY $22 -V

Neudorf Nelson Sauvignon Blanc ★★★★☆

An immaculate, intensely flavoured wine, aromatic, fresh and zippy. The 2002 (★★★★★) is a blend of fruit from first-crop vines in the company's Brightwater vineyard and other young vines at Motueka. It is a richly scented, fleshy and lush wine with lovely intensity of ripe tropical-fruit flavours enlivened by fresh acidity. A fractionally off-dry style, it shows great overall balance and richness. The 2003 vintage (★★★★), 15 per cent matured in old oak casks, is a weighty, finely balanced wine with crisp melon and green capsicum flavours, fresh and punchy.

Vintage	03	02	01	00
WR	5	6	6	6
Drink	03-05	03-04	P	P

DRY $19 V+

Ngatarawa Glazebrook Vineyard Selection Sauvignon Blanc ★★★☆

Full-bodied and smooth, the 2002 vintage (★★★☆) of this Hawke's Bay wine was 50 per cent barrel-fermented; the rest was handled in tanks. Ripely scented, with melon/passionfruit flavours, very subtle oak influence and a rounded finish, it should be at its peak during 2004. The 2003 vintage won a bronze medal at the 2003 Liquorland Top 100 International Wine Competition.

DRY $19 AV

Ngatarawa Stables Sauvignon Blanc ★★★

Balanced for easy drinking, the 2002 vintage (★★★) of this Hawke's Bay wine is a full-bodied style with lively mango and lime flavours, ripe and smooth. The 2003 (★★★) is fresh and lively, with crisp, citrusy, appley flavours.

Vintage	02	01	00	99	98
WR	6	NM	6	6	5
Drink	03-04	NM	P	P	P

DRY $15 V+

Nga Waka Martinborough Sauvignon Blanc ★★★★★

Roger Parkinson's wine stands out for its substantial body and highly concentrated, ripe, bone-dry flavour. A cool-climate style of Sauvignon Blanc, it is an immaculate wine, always highly aromatic and zingy. Power and intensity are its key attributes, with an ability to age gracefully for several years. The 2002 vintage (★★★★☆) is mouthfilling (13.5 per cent alcohol), with strong, ripe tropical-fruit flavours, fresh, punchy, crisp and dry. Still youthful, it should be at its best during 2004–05.

DRY $25 AV

Nikau Point Hawke's Bay Sauvignon Blanc ★★★☆

The debut 2002 vintage (★★★★) from One Tree Hill Vineyards (owned by Morton Estate) offers great value. Grown in 'elevated and well inland vineyards', it is a freshly scented, smooth, lively wine with ripe, zingy flavours of passionfruit and lime, showing excellent balance and depth. Less striking but still enjoyable, the 2003 (★★★) is a full-bodied wine with good depth of tropical-fruit flavours and a smooth, rounded finish.

Vintage 02
WR 6
Drink 03-04

DRY $15 V+

Nobilo Fall Harvest Sauvignon Blanc – no longer a New Zealand wine (the 2002 vintage was grown in the south of France)

Nobilo Fernleaf Sauvignon Blanc ★★☆

A blend of fruit from Gisborne and Hawke's Bay, the 2002 vintage (★★☆) is a solid quaffer, fresh, citrusy and gently herbaceous in a moderately varietal style with a crisp, fractionally sweet (5 grams/litre of sugar) finish. Priced right.

Vintage 02
WR 6
Drink 03-04

MED/DRY $11 V+

Nobilo Icon Marlborough Sauvignon Blanc ★★★★

Nobilo's top Sauvignon Blanc. Briefly lees-aged, the richly scented 2002 vintage (★★★★☆) is a finely structured wine that flows and grows across the palate. It has a persistent sense of ripeness, with excellent flavour depth and a delicate, well-rounded finish. The 2003 scored a bronze medal at the 2003 Liquorland Top 100 International Wine Competition.

Vintage 03 02 01
WR 7 7 7
Drink 03-06 03-05 03-04

DRY $24 -V

Nobilo Marlborough Sauvignon Blanc ★★★

The 2002 vintage (★★★) is a ripe yet still herbaceous style with gooseberry and melon flavours showing good depth. It offers fresh, lively fruit characters, with a hint of sweetness to balance its appetising acidity. The 2003 (★★★) is ripely flavoured, with fresh, vibrant passionfruit/lime characters, balanced for easy drinking.

Vintage 03 02 01 00
WR 7 7 7 7
Drink 03-05 P P P

DRY $16 AV

Northrow Marlborough Sauvignon Blanc (NR)

From Villa Maria, the debut 2003 vintage is aimed at the restaurant trade. Tasted prior to bottling (and so not rated), it is finely scented, beautifully ripe and delicate, with intense passionfruit and lime flavours, zingy and long.

DRY $20 V?

Odyssey Marlborough Sauvignon Blanc ★★★★

A very non-herbaceous style, the 2003 vintage (★★★★) was grown in the Odyssey vineyard in the Brancott Valley and 35 per cent of the blend was oak-aged. Weighty and ripely scented, it has passionfruit and lime flavours showing impressive freshness, vibrancy and intensity, with a crisp, fully dry finish.

DRY $22 -V

Okahu Estate Shipwreck Bay Sauvignon Blanc ★★☆

Grown at Te Kauwhata, in the Waikato, and fermented in stainless steel tanks, the 2002 (★★☆) is a full-bodied, rounded wine with melon-like, gently herbaceous flavours and a smooth, off-dry finish. The easy-drinking 2003 vintage (★★☆), also from Te Kauwhata, is a solid, clearly varietal wine with fresh tropical-fruit and herbal flavours and a slightly sweet, crisp finish.

MED/DRY $17 -V

Old Coach Road Nelson Sauvignon Blanc ★★☆

Seifried Estate's lower-tier Sauvignon. The 2003 vintage (★★☆) is full-bodied, with ripe fruit flavours of moderate depth and a very smooth finish. Moderately priced, easy drinking.

DRY $15 AV

Olssen's of Bannockburn Sauvignon Blanc ★★★

The 2002 vintage (★★★) is a cool-climate style from Central Otago. More restrained than the Marlborough model of Sauvignon Blanc, it's a mouthfilling white with green apple and slightly grassy flavours, fresh and crisp, with a tight, dry finish.

DRY $19 -V

Omaka Springs Marlborough Sauvignon Blanc ★★★☆

The 2000 and subsequent vintages have seen a big jump in quality. The 2002 (★★★☆) is fresh, punchy and zingy, with a sliver of sweetness (5.5 grams/litre of sugar) amid its crisp, forthright melon/capsicum flavours. The 2003 (★★★☆), which includes 10 per cent Sémillon, has fresh, direct, grassy aromas in a traditional style of Marlborough Sauvignon Blanc with incisive, zesty, strongly herbaceous flavours.

MED/DRY $16 V+

Origin Marlborough Sauvignon Blanc (★★★★)

Blended from Wairau Valley and Awatere Valley grapes, the 2002 vintage (★★★★) is a fresh, crisp and punchy wine, showing good weight and intensity. Freshly herbaceous on the nose, it offers strong, fractionally sweet gooseberry/lime flavours, threaded with appetising acidity.

DRY $19 AV

Oyster Bay Marlborough Sauvignon Blanc ★★★★

Oyster Bay is a Delegat's brand, reserved for Marlborough wines. Handled entirely in stainless steel tanks, the wine is typically zesty and flavour-packed, with strong melon and capsicum characters. It is grown at dozens of vineyards around the Wairau Valley, from the coast to the Oyster Bay vineyard in the west (the furthest inland), and from the Omaka Valley in the south to the banks of the Wairau River at Rapaura. The 2002 vintage (★★★★) is maturing well, with fresh, ripe melon, lime and capsicum flavours, strong and zingy. Tasted prior to bottling (and so not rated), the 2003 is crisp and penetrating, with a delicious array of fruit flavours and good structure and length.

Vintage	03	02	01	00
WR	7	7	7	7
Drink	03-04	P	P	P

DRY $20 AV

Palliser Estate Martinborough Sauvignon Blanc ★★★★★

This wholly seductive wine is one of the greatest Sauvignon Blancs in the country. A distinctly cool-climate style, it offers an exquisite harmony of crisp acidity, mouthfilling body and fresh, penetrating fruit characters. The grapes give the intensity of flavour – there's no blending with Sémillon, no barrel fermentation, no oak-aging. The 2002 vintage (★★★★★) is ravishingly scented, with beautifully ripe fruit aromas showing a hint of 'sweaty armpit'. Very fresh, mouthfilling, crisp and punchy, it's a fractionally sweet wine (4 grams/litre of sugar) with a basket of fruit flavours – melons, limes, passionfruit – showing all their customary delicacy, vibrancy and intensity. Showing lovely harmony in its youth, the 2003 (★★★★☆) is weighty and lively, with fresh, strong tropical-fruit flavours, rich and rounded.

DRY $20 V+

Palliser Pencarrow Martinborough Sauvignon Blanc ★★★★

Pencarrow is the second-tier label of Palliser Estate, but this is typically a fine wine in its own right. The 2002 vintage (★★★★) has fresh, ripe aromas and strong, vibrant tropical-fruit flavours, crisp and lingering. The 2003 (★★★☆) is fresh and lively, with strong, limey flavours, a hint of passionfruit and a rounded finish.

DRY $18 V+

Pegasus Bay Sauvignon/Sémillon ★★★★☆

At its best, this North Canterbury wine is strikingly lush and concentrated, with loads of personality. The 2002 vintage (★★★★★) is a blend of Sauvignon Blanc (70 per cent) and Sémillon (30 per cent). Fermented with indigenous yeasts, it was matured on its yeast lees for 10 months (the Sémillon component in old oak barriques) and underwent a full, softening malolactic fermentation. An unusually complex wine, it is weighty and rounded, with a strong surge of tropical-fruit flavours, minerally touches and a subtle twist of oak. It's a distinctive and extremely satisfying wine, drinking well now.

Vintage	02	01	00	99	98	97
WR	7	7	6	7	7	7
Drink	03-09	03-08	03-07	03-06	03-05	03-04

DRY $23 AV

Peregrine Central Otago Sauvignon Blanc ★★★☆

This single-vineyard wine is grown at Gibbston. The strongly herbaceous 2002 vintage (★★★☆) has loads of gooseberry, lime and green capsicum flavour, finishing crisp and fully dry.

Vintage	02
WR	4
Drink	03-04

DRY $19 AV

Pleasant Valley Hawke's Bay Sauvignon Blanc ★★☆

Typically a solid but not intense wine, offering easy, smooth drinking. The 2002 vintage (★★☆) is fresh and crisp, with moderate depth of citrusy, appley flavours.

MED/DRY $14 AV

Quarry Road Sauvignon Blanc ★★☆

Grown at Te Kauwhata, in the Waikato, the 2003 vintage (★★☆) is an enjoyable but not intense wine with citrusy, appley flavours and a smooth finish.

DRY $14 AV

Ra Nui Marlborough Wairau Valley Sauvignon Blanc (★★★★)

From Steve Hotchin, formerly a partner in Mount Riley, the 2003 vintage (★★★★) is an auspicious debut. Grown and hand-picked in the Roughan-Lee vineyard, near Renwick, it was fermented and lees-aged for two months in a single stainless steel tank. Fresh, ripe, limey aromas lead into a crisp and lively wine with good weight and mouthfeel and passionfruit/lime flavours showing impressive intensity.

DRY $20 AV

Richmond Plains Nelson Sauvignon Blanc ★★★☆

The Holmes Brothers vineyard at Richmond in Nelson is one of the few in New Zealand to enjoy full Bio-Gro (certified organic) status. This is a consistently attractive wine, full-bodied and lively, with zesty, ripely herbaceous flavour. The 2002 vintage (★★★☆) is mouthfilling, with strong, citrusy and herbal aromas and flavours and a mouth-wateringly crisp finish.

DRY $19 AV

Rippon Sauvignon Blanc ★★★

This estate-grown, partly barrel-fermented wine from Lake Wanaka is typically a grassy style with some complexity, crisp, herbaceous flavours gently seasoned with oak and a freshly acidic finish.

DRY $22 -V

Riverby Estate Marlborough Sauvignon Blanc ★★★

A single-vineyard wine, grown in the heart of the Wairau Valley, the 2002 vintage (★★★) is weighty (14 per cent alcohol) and dry, with strong, ripe tropical-fruit flavours and a rounded finish.

DRY $19 -V

Riverside Dartmoor Sauvignon Blanc ★★☆

Grown in the Dartmoor Valley, this is typically a solid Hawke's Bay wine with moderate depth of smooth, citrusy, green-edged flavours in an easy-drinking style.

Vintage	03	02
WR	6	6
Drink	03-04	P

DRY $14 AV

Robard & Butler Sauvignon Blanc (★★☆)

A blend of Chilean and New Zealand wine, the 2002 vintage (★★☆) from Montana is subdued on the nose, but the palate offers decent depth of melon and green capsicum flavour, with a slightly sweet, crisp finish.

MED/DRY $11 V+

Rockburn Central Otago Sauvignon Blanc (★★★★)

Showing lovely delicacy and length, the 2003 vintage (★★★★) is a single-vineyard wine from the Gibbston district, ultra low-cropped (2.5 tonnes/hectare) and fermented almost to full dryness (3 grams/litre of residual sugar). Tank-fermented, it is very fresh and vibrant, with intense melon and green capsicum flavours, long and racy. Delicious in its youth, it's one of the region's best Sauvignon Blancs yet.

DRY $25 -V

Rongopai Reserve Marlborough Sauvignon Blanc (★★★☆)

Oak-aged for eight months, the 2002 vintage (★★★☆) is an easy-drinking style, very fresh and lively, with ripe melon/capsicum flavours showing good delicacy and depth and a very smooth finish.

DRY $20 -V

Rongopai Sauvignon Blanc ★★★

This is typically a distinctly northern style of Sauvignon Blanc, with very non-herbaceous flavours, ripe and rounded. The 2002 vintage (★★★) was blended from equal proportions of Te Kauwhata (Waikato) and Gisborne grapes. Ripely herbaceous aromas, with a touch of 'sweaty armpit', lead into a medium-bodied and lively palate with rounded melon/capsicum flavours.

DRY $14 V+

Rossendale Marlborough Sauvignon Blanc ★★★☆

The 2002 vintage (★★★) is a slightly sweet wine with gooseberry, apple and lime flavours, balanced for easy drinking. Now softening and developing mature, 'canned peas' characters, it tastes ready.

MED/DRY $18 AV

Ruben Hall Sauvignon Blanc (★★☆)

Ruben Hall is a Villa Maria brand. The non-vintage wine (★★☆) on the market in late 2003 is a slightly sweet style with solid depth of lemony, appley flavours, ripe and rounded.

MED/DRY $10 V+

St Francis Marlborough Sauvignon Blanc (★★★☆)

'Best consumed within the next 3–5 minutes', the 2002 vintage (★★★☆) has fresh, grassy aromas leading into a full-bodied, strongly herbaceous wine with gooseberry and capsicum characters showing good vigour and depth and a smooth finish.

Vintage 02
WR 6
Drink 03-04

DRY $22 -V

St Helena Marlborough Sauvignon Blanc ★★☆

The green-edged 2001 (★★☆) is a reasonably flavoursome wine with firm acidity, clearly herbaceous flavours and a slightly tart finish. The 2002 vintage (★★) is plain, crisp and dry, lacking freshness and charm.

Vintage 02
WR 5
Drink 03-05

DRY $20 -V

Sacred Hill Barrel Fermented Sauvignon Blanc ★★★☆

At its best, this Hawke's Bay wine is deliciously rich, with strong, ripe, non-herbaceous fruit flavours and complexity from partial fermentation and lees-aging in French oak barriques. The ripely scented 2002 vintage (★★★★) is full-bodied, youthful, fresh and vibrant, with strong melon/lime flavours, a twist of oak and finely balanced acidity. Excellent drinking 2004–05.

Vintage 02 01 00 99 98
WR   7   NM 7   NM 6
Drink   03-05 NM 03-04 NM P

DRY $20 -V

Sacred Hill Marlborough Vineyards Sauvignon Blanc ★★★☆

The debut 2002 vintage (★★★☆) is a fresh, buoyantly fruity wine with very good depth of crisp melon/capsicum flavours and a smooth finish. The 2003 (★★★★) is full-bodied and smooth, with the slight 'armpit' aromas of ripe fruit and excellent intensity of gently herbaceous, tropical-fruit flavours.

DRY $20 -V

Sacred Hill Sauvage ★★★★☆

One of the country's most expensive and complex Sauvignon Blancs. The 2002 vintage (★★★★★) is an absorbing example of the widely underrated, barrel-matured Hawke's Bay Sauvignon Blanc style. Fermented with indigenous ('wild') yeasts in one-year-old French oak barriques, followed by a year's lees-aging in wood, it is bright, light lemon/green in hue, with mouthfilling body (14 per cent alcohol) and a fresh, tight, still youthful palate. Complex and creamy, with rich grapefruit and guava characters, mealy, nutty notes adding complexity and layers of flavour, it offers outstanding drinking from 2004 onwards.

Vintage 02
WR 6
Drink 04-08

DRY $30 -V

Sacred Hill Whitecliff Estate Sauvignon Blanc ★★★☆

This is the junior partner in the winery's quartet of Sauvignons, but it offers great value. The 2003 vintage (★★★☆) is a blend of Marlborough and Hawke's Bay grapes. Pale lemon/green, with lifted, limey aromas, it is fresh, punchy and tangy, with very good depth and zest.

DRY 16 V+

Saint Clair Marlborough Sauvignon Blanc ★★★★

This label has shown great form lately. The 2002 vintage (★★★★) is richly scented and weighty, with strong, zingy melon/capsicum flavours and a crisp, very finely balanced finish. The 2003 vintage (★★★★), blended from grapes grown in the Wairau and Awatere valleys, is attractively scented, with good intensity of ripe passionfruit, melon and green capsicum flavours, cut with fresh acidity.

Vintage 02 01
WR 7 7
Drink 03-04 P

DRY $19 AV

Saint Clair Wairau Reserve Sauvignon Blanc ★★★★★

The 2001 to 2003 vintages are all exceptional, in a deliciously ripe and concentrated style, lush and rounded, that has enjoyed glowing success on the show circuit. Based on young, first-crop vines at Rapaura, on the north side of the Wairau Valley, the 2003 (★★★★★) is fleshy and bold, with the 'sweaty armpit' aromas of super-ripe fruit and an explosion of melon, passionfruit and green capsicum flavours, deliciously smooth and rich.

Vintage 03 02
WR 7 7
Drink 03-04 P

DRY $25 AV

Saints Marlborough Sauvignon Blanc ★★★★☆

The 2003 vintage (★★★★☆) was made from Montana's second-crop vines in the Awatere Valley. It's a faintly oaked style – 10 per cent of the blend was matured for up to three months in 10,000-litre French oak cuves and 2 per cent was barrique-aged. Green-tinged, it's an intensely aromatic wine with lovely freshness and pungency of gooseberry, lime and capsicum flavours, woven with racy acidity. An immaculate wine, delicate yet intense, it's a great buy.

Vintage 03 02
WR 5 7
Drink 03-05 03-04

DRY $18 V+

Sanctuary Marlborough Sauvignon Blanc ★★★☆

Grove Mill's lower-tier label. The 2003 vintage (★★★☆) is an instantly appealing, finely balanced wine with gooseberry/lime flavours, showing good freshness, vibrancy and harmony.

Vintage	03	02	01	00
WR	7	6	6	6
Drink	03-04	P	P	P

DRY $17 AV

Schubert Hawke's Bay Sauvignon Blanc ★★★

The crisp, bone-dry 2002 vintage (★★★) was grown in Gimblett Road and lees-aged for 14 months, with no oak. Very fresh and tangy, with crisp grapefruit and lime flavours and a flinty, nutty finish, it's a slightly austere style in its youth, worth cellaring to at least mid-2004.

Vintage	03	02	01	00
WR	NM	6	6	6
Drink	NM	03-07	03-06	03-05

DRY $20 -V

Seifried Brightwater Sauvignon Blanc (★★★☆)

Based on first-crop vines grown in stony soils at Brightwater, on the Waimea Plains of Nelson, the 2003 vintage (★★★☆) is a highly appealing wine with fresh, lively melon/lime flavours showing good ripeness, length and zing.

DRY $21 -V

Seifried Nelson Sauvignon Blanc ★★★☆

From a low-yielding vintage in Nelson, the 2002 (★★★★) is a highly characterful wine with pleasing fullness of body, a strong surge of ripe, tropical-fruit flavours, lively acidity and a rich finish. The 2003 (★★★) is crisp and green-edged in an appetisingly crisp, clearly herbaceous style.

Vintage	03	02	01	00
WR	6	7	6	5
Drink	03-04	P	P	P

DRY $18 AV

Seifried Winemakers Collection Sauvignon Blanc ★★★

The 2003 vintage (★★★☆) was made from the 'very best fruit' and matured on its yeast lees before bottling. It's a strongly flavoured, herbaceous Nelson wine with some riper, melon and pineapple characters in a crisp, lively, cool-climate style.

DRY $22 -V

Selaks Drylands Sauvignon Blanc – see Drylands Sauvignon Blanc

Selaks Founders Reserve Oak Aged Sauvignon Blanc ★★★★

One of the flagship Sauvignons from the Nobilo Group (which owns Selaks). The 2002 vintage (★★★★) was grown in the Awatere and Wairau valleys, fermented in new French barriques and wood-matured for five months, with weekly lees-stirring. It's a complex style, with toasty oak in balance with ripe, tropical-fruit and herbaceous flavours, good weight, texture and intensity, and a smooth finish.

Vintage	02	01	00	99	98	97
WR	6	6	NM	7	7	7
Drink	03-05	P	NM	P	P	P

MED/DRY $27 -V

Selaks Premium Selection Marlborough Sauvignon Blanc ★★★☆

This is Selaks' lower-tier Sauvignon Blanc, fermented in stainless steel tanks and bottled early. Designed as an 'intensely herbaceous' style, in contrast to its riper, rounder stablemate under the Nobilo brand, from one vintage to the next, it offers top value. Full of character and drink-young appeal, the 2003 vintage (★★★☆) is fresh and crisply herbaceous, with strong, tangy melon/lime characters and a finely balanced, smooth finish.

Vintage	03	02	01	00
WR	7	7	7	6
Drink	03-05	P	P	P

MED/DRY $15 V+

Seresin Marama Sauvignon Blanc ★★★★☆

A 'style' rather than pungently 'varietal' wine, the 2001 vintage (★★★★☆) was grown in Marlborough, fermented with indigenous yeasts in seasoned French oak barrels, wood-aged for 14 months and given a full, softening malolactic fermentation. Still youthful in colour, it's a very non-herbaceous style with good mouthfeel and texture, intense fig, grapefruit and lime flavours with a slightly nutty complexity and a crisp, slightly minerally finish.

DRY $25 AV

Seresin Marlborough Sauvignon Blanc ★★★★★

One of the region's most sophisticated, subtle and satisfying Sauvignons. It's a complex style; the 2002 vintage (★★★★★), fermented with indigenous and cultured yeasts, includes 8 per cent Sémillon, and 7 per cent of the blend was fermented and lees-aged in seasoned French oak casks. The grapes were grown mostly in the estate vineyard at Renwick, but a small portion came from the cooler Tatou vineyard, further inland. Grassy and nettley on the nose, it is weighty, dry, punchy and incisive, with intense melon and fresh-cut grass flavours, slightly nutty, flinty and tight. A Sauvignon Blanc to ponder over, it offers loads of individuality and interest.

Vintage	01	00	99	98	97	96
WR	6	7	7	6	7	6
Drink	03-06	03-04	P	P	P	P

DRY $23 V+

Sherwood Estate Marlborough Sauvignon Blanc ★★★☆

Grown in the company's jointly owned vineyards in the Wairau Valley, the 2002 vintage (★★★☆) is fresh, crisp and lively, with very satisfying depth of melon and green capsicum flavours.

DRY $16 V+

Shingle Peak Marlborough Sauvignon Blanc – see Matua Valley Shingle Peak Marlborough Sauvignon Blanc

Solstone Wairarapa Valley Sauvignon Blanc ★★★☆

Maturing well, the concentrated and vibrantly fruity 2002 vintage (★★★★) was grown at Masterton. The bouquet is fresh and fragrant, with a clear herbaceous edge; the palate is full-bodied, with crisp acidity woven through its punchy, ripe melon, passionfruit and lime flavours.

DRY $25 -V

Spy Valley Marlborough Sauvignon Blanc ★★★☆

Estate-grown in the Waihopai Valley, on the south side of the Wairau Valley, the freshly herbaceous, strongly varietal 2002 vintage (★★★☆) is weighty and dry, with crisp, lively acidity and plenty of gooseberry, melon and green capsicum flavour. The 2003 (★★★☆) is ripely scented and mouthfilling, with fresh, smooth, green-edged flavours, showing good delicacy and length.

Vintage	03
WR	6
Drink	03-05

DRY $17 AV

Squawking Magpie Premium Reserve Marlborough Sauvignon Blanc (★★★★)

The 2002 vintage (★★★★) from this Hawke's Bay-based winery is very fresh and refined, with beautifully ripe melon/lime flavours, showing excellent delicacy and depth, and a crisp, dry finish.

DRY $20 AV

Staete Landt Marlborough Sauvignon Blanc ★★★★☆

Ripely scented, rich and zingy, this single-vineyard wine is grown at Rapaura and mostly handled in tanks, with some fermentation in seasoned (at least six-year-old) French oak casks. Showing lovely texture, the 2003 vintage (★★★★) is a fully dry but not austere wine with tropical-fruit flavours to the fore, a touch of lees-derived complexity, good weight and roundness and a persistent finish.

Vintage	03
WR	7
Drink	04-05

DRY $23 AV

Stoneleigh Marlborough Sauvignon Blanc ★★★★

Once a famous Corbans wine, now part of the Montana stable. It is grown in the shingly Rapaura district of the Wairau Valley, which produces a relatively ripe style, yet retains good acidity and vigour. Harvested at 23–24 brix, the 2003 vintage (★★★★) is pale lemon/green, fresh, punchy and vibrant, with strong melon/capsicum flavours and a zingy finish.

Vintage	03	02	01	00	99	98
WR	6	6	7	6	6	5
Drink	03-04	P	P	P	P	P

DRY $19 AV

Stoneleigh Vineyards Rapaura Series Marlborough Sauvignon Blanc ★★★★☆

A richly flavoured wine, seasoning ripe, tropical-fruit flavours with a touch of oak. Most of the 2002 vintage (★★★★) was handled in tanks, but 7 per cent was fermented and lees-aged in French oak barriques. It shows lovely weight and depth of ripely herbaceous flavour, with subtle oak adding a toasty, nutty complexity, crisp acidity and a strong finish.

Vintage	02	01	00
WR	6	7	6
Drink	03-05	03-04	P

DRY $23 AV

Stony Bay Sauvignon Blanc ★★★

Made by Matariki Wines, the 2002 vintage (★★★☆) is a crisp and lively Hawke's Bay wine with good varietal character and ripe melon/lime flavours, slightly minerally, punchy and tangy.

Vintage	02	01	00	99
WR	6	5	6	5
Drink	03-05	P	P	P

DRY $17 AV

Sunset Valley Vineyard Sauvignon Blanc ★★★
Grown organically at Upper Moutere, in Nelson, the 2002 vintage (★★★★) was harvested at a very ripe 24 brix and stop-fermented with a splash of residual sugar (8 grams/litre), which sits very easily with its ripe-fruit characters and fresh acidity. Full-bodied, crisp and lively, it shows excellent depth of tropical-fruit and herbaceous flavours, fresh, vibrant and long. A distinctive and vivacious wine, it's well worth trying. (The 2003 vintage has also been made in a medium-dry style.)

Vintage 03
WR 6
Drink 03-04

MED/DRY $18 -V

Tasman Bay Marlborough Sauvignon Blanc ★★★☆
Showing good intensity, the 2002 vintage (★★★★) was mostly fermented and lees-aged in tanks, but 15 per cent of the blend was briefly oak-matured. It's a weighty, ripe style with passionfruit and lime flavours to the fore, a subtle twist of oak and a smooth, sustained finish. Highly enjoyable.

DRY $16 V+

Tasman Bay Nelson Sauvignon Blanc ★★★
Partly oak-aged, this is typically a restrained wine, with gently herbaceous characters and a touch of oak/lees complexity. The 2003 vintage (★★★) is not a pungently varietal style, but shows ripe fruit flavours, with a slightly creamy texture.

DRY $16 AV

Te Awa Farm Frontier Sauvignon Blanc ★★★☆
This is a worthy attempt at a rich, complex style of Hawke's Bay Sauvignon. The 2002 vintage (★★★☆) was fermented and matured for eight months in French oak casks. Still fresh and youthful, it is full-bodied and crisp, with tropical-fruit characters and a slightly creamy texture. A tightly structured, potentially complex wine, it's worth cellaring to mid-2004+.

Vintage 02 01 00
WR 7 7 6
Drink 03-07 03-05 03-04

DRY $24 -V

Te Awa Farm Longlands Sauvignon Blanc ★★★
Grown in the Gimblett Gravels district of Hawke's Bay, the 2002 vintage (★★★☆) is a fresh, vibrant wine, full-bodied, crisp and dry, with ripe flavours of melon, passionfruit and lime showing good intensity.

Vintage 03 02 01 00
WR 7 6 6 7
Drink 03-05 03-04 P P

DRY $18 AV

Te Kairanga Martinborough Sauvignon Blanc ★★★
Up to and including the 2001 vintage, this was a slightly sweet, oak-aged style, but 2002 brought a change of direction – no oak, less residual sugar. The 2002 (★★☆) is weighty and rounded, with ripe gooseberry, pineapple and lime flavours and a slightly off-dry (4 grams/litre of sugar) finish, but lacks fresh, clean fruit aromas.

DRY $20 -V

Te Mania Nelson Sauvignon Blanc ★★★☆

Typically a fresh, crisply herbaceous style of Sauvignon from the Waimea Plains. The 2003 vintage (★★★☆) is freshly scented and zingy, with grapefruit and herb flavours showing good depth and a fractionally sweet (4 grams/litre of sugar), crisp finish.

Vintage	03	02	01	00
WR	6	6	6	6
Drink	04-05	03-05	P	P

MED/DRY $17 AV

Te Mata Cape Crest Sauvignon Blanc ★★★★☆

This Hawke's Bay label is impressive for its ripely herbal, complex, sustained flavours. The grapes are grown in the company's Woodthorpe Terraces vineyard in the Dartmoor Valley and at Havelock North, with fermentation and maturation in French oak barriques, mostly seasoned, adding depth and clearly differentiating the wine from its stablemate under the Woodthorpe label. The 2002 vintage (★★★★☆) is a mouthfilling wine with ripe, tropical-fruit flavours seasoned with toasty oak in a complex style with balanced acidity and a rich finish.

Vintage	02	01	00	99	98	97	96
WR	7	7	7	7	7	7	6
Drink	04-06	03-06	03-05	03-04	P	P	P

DRY $24 AV

Te Mata Woodthorpe Sauvignon Blanc (★★★☆)

Grown at the company's inland Woodthorpe Terraces vineyard, in the Dartmoor Valley of Hawke's Bay, the 2003 vintage (★★★☆) was handled entirely in tanks and fermented to dryness. Light lemon/green, it is fresh and tangy, with citrus fruit, lime and pineapple flavours showing good ripeness, vigour and length.

Vintage	03
WR	7
Drink	P

DRY $19 AV

Terrace Heights Estate Marlborough Sauvignon Blanc (★★★☆)

The 2002 vintage (★★★☆) has fresh, strongly herbaceous, nettley aromas and melon and green capsicum flavours showing very good depth.

DRY $17 AV

Terrace Road Marlborough Sauvignon Blanc ★★★★

The latest vintages of Cellier Le Brun's wine are the best. The 2002 (★★★★) is an elegant wine with fresh, lively melon and lime flavours, building across the palate to a lingering finish. The 2003 vintage (★★★★) is again impressive – ripely scented, with very good depth of melon, passionfruit and lime flavours, fresh and appetisingly crisp. An excellent buy.

MED/DRY $17 V+

Thornbury Marlborough Sauvignon Blanc ★★★★★

Made by Steve Bird, for many years winemaker at Morton Estate, this wine has enjoyed high critical acclaim in the United States. Grown mostly in the shingly, relatively early-ripening Rapaura district of the Wairau Valley, in terms of style it places its accent on palate weight and texture, rather than pungent herbaceous characters. Top vintages are weighty and concentrated, with deep tropical-fruit flavours and a deliciously well-rounded finish. In its infancy, the 2003 (★★★★) was freshly scented and finely balanced, with strong, lively melon/capsicum flavours.

Vintage	03	02
WR	6	5
Drink	03-05	03-04

DRY $20 V+

Three Sisters Central Hawke's Bay Sauvignon Blanc ★★★
Fully dry, the 2001 vintage (★★★) was grown at altitude in Central Hawke's Bay. A fresh, crisp, cool-climate style, it is clearly herbaceous, with some ripe, tropical-fruit notes and good weight and depth. The slightly austere 2002 (★★☆) is crisp and clean, green-edged and racy, with flinty acidity. Unlike most New Zealand Sauvignon Blancs, it needs cellaring; open mid-2004+.

DRY $16 AV

Tohu Marlborough Sauvignon Blanc ★★★☆
Tohu is a joint venture between three Maori land incorporations. This is a consistently good wine and the 2002 (★★★☆) is highly attractive – fragrant, fresh and lively, with good body and ripe tropical-fruit flavours, rich and lingering. The 2003 vintage (★★★☆) shows good balance and liveliness, with vibrant flavours of passionfruit, melons and limes and a crisp finish.

DRY $17 AV

Torlesse Waipara Sauvignon Blanc ★★★
Woven with fresh acidity, the 2002 vintage (★★★) of this North Canterbury wine is a pale, grassy, clearly varietal wine, fresh and weighty, with good flavour depth. The 2003 (★★★) is similar: pale, with satisfying depth of lively, herbaceous flavour and a crisp, fractionally off-dry finish.

Vintage 02
WR 7
Drink 03-04

DRY $16 AV

Trinity Hill Shepherds Croft Sauvignon Blanc ★★★
Grown in the Shepherd's Croft vineyard in the Ngatarawa district of Hawke's Bay, the 2002 vintage (★★☆) is a medium-bodied wine with green apple and lime flavours, fresh and crisp. The 2003 (★★★) is a very easy-drinking style with ripe flavours of grapefruit, melon and lime, good weight, balance and freshness, and a dry, well-rounded finish.

DRY $20 -V

Twin Islands Marlborough Sauvignon Blanc ★★★
Negociants' wine is finely balanced for easy drinking and priced right. The 2002 vintage (★★★) is fresh and vibrant, with good depth of gooseberry and lime flavours and a smooth finish. Attractive in its youth, the 2003 (★★★☆) is full-flavoured and zingy, with good weight and depth of passionfruit/lime characters and fresh acid spine.

Vintage 03 02 01 00
WR 6 6 6 6
Drink 03-04 P P P

DRY $17 AV

Vavasour Awatere Valley Marlborough Sauvignon Blanc ★★★★☆
A consistently classy, high-impact wine, with flinty acidity underpinning its penetrating tropical-fruit and green-edged flavours, which always show impressive delicacy and length. The 2003 vintage (★★★★), sourced entirely from Awatere Valley vineyards, was mostly handled in tanks, but a portion was lees-aged in a large oak vat. It's very fresh and vibrant in its youth, with good weight, ripe melon and green capsicum flavours and a lingering finish.

Vintage 03 02
WR 6 7
Drink 03-05 P

DRY $20 AV

Vavasour Single Vineyard Awatere Valley Sauvignon Blanc ★★★★★

The outstanding 2002 vintage (★★★★★) is the first time Vavasour's premier Sauvignon Blanc has appeared since 1999. Grown at the Vavasour vineyard in the Awatere Valley, it was hand-picked and fermented and matured for nine months, with weekly lees-stirring, in seasoned French oak barriques. The bouquet is complex, mingling ripe-fruit aromas with subtle oak; the palate is mouthfilling and rounded, with sweet-fruit delights, ripe tropical-fruit flavours, lovely weight and texture and a fully dry, rounded finish. Delicious now.

DRY $30 AV

Vidal Estate Hawke's Bay Sauvignon Blanc ★★★

The 2002 vintage (★★★) is a typical northern style of Sauvignon Blanc with ripe, gently herbaceous, tropical-fruit flavours, good body and a dry, rounded, lingering finish. There is no 2003 (but the vintage has produced a Marlborough Sauvignon Blanc – see below).

Vintage	03	02	01	00
WR	NM	6	6	6
Drink	NM	03-04	P	P

DRY $18 -V

Vidal Estate Marlborough Sauvignon Blanc (NR)

Tasted before it was bottled (and so not rated), the 2003 vintage is an intensely varietal wine, freshly herbaceous, with green capsicum and melon-evoking flavours showing good depth.

Vintage	03
WR	6
Drink	03-05

DRY $18 V?

Villa Maria Cellar Selection Marlborough Sauvignon Blanc ★★★★☆

An intense, fruit-driven style, this is typically of a very high standard. Scented, weighty, rich and rounded, the 2002 vintage (★★★★★) is a blend of grapes grown in the Wairau and Awatere valleys. It offers excellent depth of zingy, ripe, tropical-fruit flavours, with a herbal undercurrent and long, smooth finish. The 2003 (★★★★☆) shows good body and punch, with lovely depth of melon, passionfruit and lime flavours building across the palate to a rich, zingy finish.

Vintage	03	02	01	00
WR	6	6	7	6
Drink	03-05	P	P	P

DRY $20 AV

Villa Maria Private Bin Sauvignon Blanc ★★★★

A very user-friendly wine, Villa Maria's third-tier label offers impressive quality and top value. The 2002 vintage (★★★★) has freshly herbaceous aromas leading into a strongly varietal wine with rich melon and green capsicum flavours and a crisp, fractionally off-dry (4 grams/litre of sugar) finish. The 2003, tasted just before bottling (and so not rated), has ripe, sweet-fruit aromas and a full palate with tropical-fruit and herbaceous flavours, strong and zingy.

Vintage	03	02	01	00
WR	6	6	6	7
Drink	03-04	P	P	P

DRY $16 V+

Villa Maria Reserve Clifford Bay Sauvignon Blanc ★★★★★

Grown in the Awatere Valley (although the label refers only to 'Clifford Bay', into which the Awatere River empties), this is an exceptional Marlborough wine. Most of the fruit comes from Seddon Vineyards, a large block of vines in the Awatere Valley not owned but managed by Villa Maria. Handled entirely in stainless steel tanks, it typically exhibits the leap-out-of-the-glass fragrance and zingy, explosive flavour of Marlborough Sauvignon Blanc at its inimitable best. The 2003 vintage (★★★★★) is intense, limey and zingy, with the flinty character typical of the Awatere Valley and lovely concentration and freshness. A bone-dry wine with great delicacy and depth, it should be at its best during 2004.

Vintage	03	02	01	00	99	98
WR	7	6	7	6	6	5
Drink	04-05	P	P	P	P	P

DRY $25 AV

Villa Maria Reserve Wairau Valley Sauvignon Blanc ★★★★★

An authoritative wine with tremendous depth and drive, it is typically ripe and zingy, with marvellous weight and length of flavour, and tends to be fuller in body, less herbaceous and rounder than its Clifford Bay stablemate (above). In the past, a small proportion of the final blend (up to 10 per cent) was oak-aged, but the 2001 and subsequent vintages have been handled entirely in tanks. Grown in four vineyards in the Wairau Valley, the 2002 (★★★★★) is a weighty, richly flavoured wine, bursting with sweet-fruit characters. It's a fully dry, beautifully ripe wine with passionfruit-like flavours showing great freshness and intensity. In its infancy, the 2003 vintage (★★★★☆) is ripely scented and powerful, with good weight, deep melon/capsicum flavours threaded with fresh acidity and a rich, fully dry yet rounded finish.

Vintage	03	02	01	00	99	98
WR	7	7	7	6	5	5
Drink	04-05	P	P	P	P	P

DRY $25 AV

Villa Maria Single Vineyard Seddon Sauvignon Blanc (NR)

Showing an extra edge of intensity, the 2003 vintage was tasted just before bottling, and so not rated. Grown in the Awatere Valley, it's a full-bodied Marlborough wine with strong, vibrant melon and green capsicum flavours, fresh, crisp and sustained.

DRY $25 V?

Villa Maria Single Vineyard Taylors Pass Sauvignon Blanc (NR)

The pungently varietal 2003 vintage, grown in Marlborough's Awatere Valley, was tasted prior to bottling and so not rated. Richly scented, it's an incisively flavoured wine with crisp, herbaceous characters.

DRY $25 V?

Waimea Estates Bolitho Reserve Sauvignon Blanc ★★★☆

The 2002 vintage (★★★) is a Nelson wine, mostly fermented and lees-aged in tanks, but 30 per cent of the blend was fermented with indigenous yeasts in one-year-old French oak casks. It's a ripely flavoured, gently herbaceous wine, but less impressive than the very aromatic and intense 2001 (★★★★).

DRY $22 -V

Waimea Estates Nelson Sauvignon Blanc ★★★
Grown near Richmond, the 2002 (★★★) is weighty and smooth, with ripely herbaceous flavours showing good depth. In its youth, the 2003 (★★☆) looks like a lesser vintage, with high acidity and a lack of real richness and charm.

Vintage	02	01	00
WR	7	7	7
Drink	03-04	P	P

DRY $17 AV

Waimea Estates Winemakers Selection Sauvignon Blanc (★★★)
Grown at two vineyards at Hope, in Nelson, and 5 per cent oak-aged, the 2002 vintage (★★★) shows some concentrated, sweet-fruit characters, but also a slight lack of softness and charm.

DRY $17 AV

Waipara Hills Marlborough Sauvignon Blanc ★★★★☆
The 2002 vintage (★★★★☆) is strongly herbaceous, fresh and lively, with nettley aromas and flavours, a hint of passionfruit and a crisp, dryish finish (5 grams/litre of sugar). The 2003 (★★★★☆) is similar: intensely varietal, deliciously fresh, vibrant and punchy, with rich melon and green capsicum flavours and a smooth, lasting finish.

MED/DRY $18 V+

Waipara Springs Sauvignon Blanc ★★★★
This North Canterbury wine is a very lightly oaked style of consistently high quality and good value. The 2002 vintage (★★★★) was mostly handled in tanks, but 5 per cent was barrel-fermented. Rich, ripely herbaceous aromas lead into a smooth, weighty wine with excellent depth of tropical-fruit flavours, fresh, vibrant and punchy, and a crisp, bone-dry finish. The 2003 (★★★★) is ripely scented, fresh, pure and zingy, with good intensity of melon, passionfruit and lime flavours and a rich, long finish.

Vintage	03	02	01	00
WR	6	7	7	6
Drink	03-05	03-05	03-04	P

DRY $18 V+

Waipara West Sauvignon Blanc ★★★★
An intensely flavoured North Canterbury wine with racy acidity. The 2002 vintage (★★★★) was made from very low-cropped vines (4.5 tonnes/hectare). Freshly scented, it is a strongly herbaceous style with excellent weight and depth of gooseberry/lime flavours, bone-dry, crisp and lively.

Vintage	02	01
WR	6	6
Drink	03-04	P

DRY $21 -V

Wairau River Marlborough Sauvignon Blanc ★★★★
Phil and Chris Rose produce a substantial style of Sauvignon Blanc, at its best offering a tantalising interplay of rich, lush, tropical-fruit flavours and pungent, zingy, herbaceous characters. The grapes are grown in the Roses' Giffords Road vineyard alongside the Wairau River, on the north side of the valley. The 2002 vintage (★★★☆) is a crisp and lively wine with good but not great depth of fresh, tropical-fruit and herbaceous flavours and a tight, dry finish.

Vintage	02	01	00	99	98
WR	7	7	7	7	7
Drink	03-05	03-04	P	P	P

DRY $20 AV

Wairau River Reserve Sauvignon Blanc ★★★★

The Marlborough winery's top wine is based on low-cropping vines and fermented and matured for nine months in seasoned French oak casks. The 2002 vintage (★★★★) is a tight and immaculate wine with good weight, fresh, strong gooseberry and capsicum flavours, a hint of nutty oak adding complexity and a well-rounded finish.

Vintage	02	01
WR	7	7
Drink	03-06	03-05

DRY $25 -V

West Brook Blue Ridge Marlborough Sauvignon Blanc ★★★★☆

A consistently impressive wine. The 2002 vintage (★★★★☆) is weighty (13.5 per cent alcohol), with fresh, concentrated tropical-fruit flavours, a touch of complexity and a sustained finish.

DRY $22 AV

West Brook Marlborough Sauvignon Blanc ★★★☆

The 2002 vintage (★★★☆) is a well-ripened wine with fairly rich melon/lime flavours and a seductively smooth finish. The 2003 (★★☆) was less impressive in its extreme infancy, but a bit of bottle-age can work wonders.

DRY $18 AV

Whitehaven Marlborough Sauvignon Blanc ★★★★★

Whitehaven adopts a low profile, but this is a consistently impressive wine. Grown in the Wairau and Awatere valleys, the 2002 vintage (★★★★) is fresh and immaculate, with a lifted, ripely herbaceous bouquet. Offering melon/capsicum flavours enlivened by fresh acidity, it's a deliciously well-balanced wine, although slightly less concentrated than the 2001 (★★★★★). In its infancy, the 2003 (★★★★☆) looked excellent, with fresh, strong melon/lime flavours, delicate, smooth and long.

Vintage	02	01
WR	6	7
Drink	03-04	P

DRY $20 V+

White Rock Wairarapa Sauvignon Blanc (★★★)

From Capricorn Wine Estates, a division of Craggy Range, the 2003 vintage (★★★) is an easy-drinking, fresh, citrusy and limey wine with clear varietal character, decent depth and a slightly sweet, crisp finish.

MED/DRY $17 AV

Wishart Estate Sauvignon Blanc ★★★

Grown on the coast at Bay View, the 2002 vintage (★★★) is an enjoyable example of the Hawke's Bay regional style. Lees-aged for two months, it is weighty, vibrant and soft, with strong, ripe tropical-fruit flavours and a smooth, off-dry (6 grams/litre of sugar) finish.

Vintage	02	01	00	99
WR	5	6	6	5
Drink	03-04	P	P	P

MED/DRY $18 -V

Wither Hills Marlborough Sauvignon Blanc ★★★★★

This is typically a striking wine, with a voluminous fragrance, mouthfilling body and very rich, sweet-tasting fruit flavours. Winemaker Brent Marris says he's not after 'a high-acid, steely wine; I want a fleshy, ripe, weighty style with charm and elegance'. There's a subliminal oak influence (3 to 5 per cent of the final blend is barrel-fermented), but maturation on yeast lees (and regular lees-stirring) play a much more significant role in the wine's style, 'adding to the layers of complexity, without interfering with the fruit'. The 2003 vintage (★★★★☆) is pale lemon/green, with the 'sweaty armpit' aromas of very ripe fruit. Smooth and vibrantly fruity, with tropical-fruit and green capsicum flavours, it shows good weight, depth and roundness, with fresh acidity and a fractionally off-dry (4 grams/litre of sugar), sustained finish.

Vintage	03	02	01	00	99	98
WR	6	7	7	7	6	5
Drink	04-05	03-04	P	P	P	P

DRY $20 V+

Woollaston Estates Nelson Sauvignon Blanc (★★★)

The 2002 vintage (★★★) is a briskly herbaceous wine, grown in the Moutere hills (60 per cent) and on the Waimea Plains (40 per cent). It's a fresh, lively wine with melon/lime flavours threaded with crisp, racy acidity.

DRY $17 AV

Sémillon

You'd never guess it from the small selection of labels on the market, but Sémillon is New Zealand's fifth most widely planted white-wine variety. The few New Zealand winemakers who a decade ago played around with Sémillon could hardly give it away, so aggressively stemmy and spiky was its flavour. Now, there is a new breed of riper, richer, rounder Sémillons emerging – and they are ten times more enjoyable to drink.

The Sémillon variety is beset by a similar problem to Chenin Blanc. Despite being the foundation of outstanding white wines in Bordeaux and Australia, Sémillon is out of fashion in the rest of the world, and in New Zealand its potential is still largely untapped.

Sémillon is highly prized in Bordeaux, where as one of the two key varieties both in dry wines, most notably white Graves, and the inimitable sweet Sauternes, its high levels of alcohol and extract are perfect foils for Sauvignon Blanc's verdant aroma and tartness. With its propensity to rot 'nobly', Sémillon forms about 80 per cent of a classic Sauternes.

Cooler climates like those of New Zealand, Tasmania and Washington state, however, bring out a grassy-green character in Sémillon which, coupled with its higher acidity in these regions, can give the variety strikingly Sauvignon-like characteristics. Sémillon's plantings in New Zealand are expanding slowly.

Grown predominantly in Gisborne, Marlborough and (to a lesser extent) Hawke's Bay, Sémillon is commonly used in New Zealand as a minor (and anonymous) partner in wines labelled Sauvignon Blanc, contributing complexity and aging potential. By curbing the variety's natural tendency to grow vigorously and crop bountifully, winemakers are now overcoming the aggressive cut-grass characters that in the past plagued the majority of New Zealand's unblended Sémillons. The recent arrival of clones capable of giving riper fruit characters (notably BVRC-14 from the Barossa Valley) is also contributing to quality advances. You'll hear a lot more about this grape in the future.

Alpha Domus AD Sémillon ★★★★

The 2000 vintage (★★★★) is impressively weighty, ripe and rich. Estate-grown at Maraekakaho and fermented and lees-aged for 10 months in French oak barriques, it's a light yellow Hawke's Bay wine with a strongly oak-influenced bouquet. The palate is powerful and concentrated, with strong, ripe, tropical-fruit flavours seasoned with biscuity oak. There is no 2001.

Vintage	02	01	00	99
WR	7	NM	7	NM
Drink	04-10	NM	03-05+	NM

DRY $28 -V

Alpha Domus Sémillon ★★★

The 2002 vintage (★★★☆) is a fruit-driven style; most of the wine was handled in tanks, but 15 per cent was barrel-fermented. Fresh and lively, with grassy aromas, it's a fairly herbaceous style with punchy flavours, a bare hint of oak and a bone-dry, crisp finish. It should age well.

Vintage	02	01	00	99	98
WR	7	NM	7	6	6
Drink	04-08	NM	03-05	03-04	P

DRY $17 AV

Askerne Sémillon ★★★☆

Still youthful, with good complexity, the 2002 vintage (★★★☆) of this Hawke's Bay wine is bright, light yellow/green, with fresh, lemony, grassy aromas. Estate-grown near Havelock North, it's a medium-bodied style (11.5 per cent alcohol), fresh, crisp and tight, with a touch of nutty oak and good varietal character and intensity. The 2001 (★★★), labelled Barrel Fermented, is full-bodied and creamy, with oak slightly subduing its varietal character but some complexity.

Vintage	02	01
WR	6	5
Drink	03-07	03-07

DRY $18 AV

Askerne Sémillon/Sauvignon Blanc ★★★☆

This is a clearly but not pungently herbaceous Hawke's Bay wine with satisfying weight and depth. Still on sale at the winery in mid to late 2003 (and bargain-priced), the 1999 vintage (★★★★) is a partly barrel-fermented blend, with 20 per cent Sauvignon Blanc. Showing the benefits of lengthy bottle-age, it's a dry wine with bright, lemon/green colour, good mouthfeel and highly attractive, limey, toasty, minerally aromas and flavours.

Vintage	99	98	97	96
WR	5	5	5	5
Drink	03-05	03-04	P	P

DRY $12 V+

Awarua Terraces Goldstones Sémillon (★★★☆)

Needing time to open out, the 2002 vintage (★★★☆) is a fresh, tightly structured wine, grown at Mangatahi in Hawke's Bay and fermented and lees-aged in new French oak barriques. It shows good concentration of ripe-fruit flavours (nectarines and limes) strongly seasoned with oak, and lively acidity. Best drinking mid-2004+.

DRY $27 -V

Clearview Sémillon (★★★★)

The richly flavoured 2002 vintage (★★★★) was grown at Te Awanga, on the Hawke's Bay coast, blended with 20 per cent Sauvignon Blanc and handled without oak. It's a fresh, weighty wine, intensely varietal, with strong, lemony, grassy aromas and flavours and a slightly buttery, long finish. 'It'll be unbelievable in four years,' says winemaker Tim Turvey.

DRY $20 AV

Inverness Estate Sémillon ★★☆

The 2001 vintage (★★★) was estate-grown at Clevedon, in South Auckland, and made by Anthony Ivicevich at the West Brook winery. Light gold, it's a crisp, dry, clearly varietal wine with limey, minerally, slightly nutty flavours. Ready.

DRY $18 -V

Kerr Farm Kumeu Sémillon ★★★

Estate-grown in West Auckland, the 2000 vintage (★★☆) was fermented and matured in seasoned French and American oak casks. Still youthful in colour, it is crisp and dry, with restrained fruit characters and nutty, minerally flavours in a slightly austere style, maturing solidly.

Vintage	00
WR	7
Drink	03-06

DRY $17 AV

Matakana Estate Sémillon ★★★☆

Sémillon is a variety 'we have a real passion for', say the proprietors. The 2000 vintage (★★★☆) was partly (28 per cent, to be precise) fermented and matured for seven months in French oak barriques (half new); the rest was handled in tanks, with some lees-aging. It has a broad, rounded palate, with ripe tropical-fruit flavours, delicate herbal characters, a touch of oak/lees-aging complexity and good varietal definition. The 2002 (★★★) shows good potential, with well-ripened fruit characters and powerful, toasty oak aromas and flavours. It needs time to achieve a better balance between fruit and oak; open mid-2004+.

DRY $24 -V

Montana Gisborne Sémillon ★★★☆

The launch of the easy-drinking 2000 vintage helped to introduce Sémillon to a wider audience in New Zealand. Bright, full yellow, the 2001 (★★★) has citrusy, grassy, slightly minerally flavours, with a touch of oak adding complexity and some bottle-aged characters emerging. The 2002 (★★★☆) was mostly handled in tanks, but 15 per cent of the blend was barrel-fermented. Full-bodied, it has ripe, tropical-fruit flavours, showing good depth, with a smooth, fractionally off-dry finish.

Vintage	02	01	00
WR	6	6	6
Drink	03-04	P	P

DRY $14 V+

Okahu Estate Kaz Sémillon ★★★☆

Estate-grown near Kaitaia, the 1999 vintage (★★★☆) is a yellow-hued, mouthfilling wine with a strong oak influence on the nose. The well-ripened fruit characters are wrapped in nutty wood, creating a flavoursome, Chardonnay-like style with balanced acidity and a dry, tight finish. Ready. (This label is being phased out, due to Sémillon's lack of popularity.)

Vintage	99	98
WR	6	6
Drink	03-06	03-05

DRY $28 -V

Sanderson Hawke's Bay Sémillon ★★★☆

Grown organically at Mangatahi, inland from Hastings, and not oak-matured, the 2001 vintage (★★★☆) is a weighty, well-balanced wine with fresh, lemony, grassy varietal characters, showing some richness, and a fractionally sweet finish.

Vintage	01	00
WR	6	5
Drink	03-06	03-04

MED/DRY $20 AV

Sileni Estate Selection The Circle Sémillon ★★★☆

Full-bodied, ripe-tasting and rounded, the 2002 vintage (★★★★) of this Hawke's Bay wine offers very good depth of tropical-fruit/lime flavours, with a subtle seasoning of oak and a smooth, fractionally sweet, lingering finish. An immaculate, finely balanced wine, it's opening out well with age. The 2003 (★★★) was mostly fermented and lees-aged in tanks, but 20 per cent of the blend finished its fermentation in barrels. Fresh and crisp, slightly sweet and appley, it tastes less ripe than the 2002, but needs time to show its best; open 2005+.

Vintage	03	02	01	00
WR	5	6	5	5
Drink	04-07	03-06	03-05	03-05

MED/DRY $24 -V

Te Whare Ra Duke of Marlborough Sémillon ★★☆
This label has shown varying form in recent vintages, but the 2001 (★★) is disappointing. It's a very simple wine with under-ripe, green apple aromas and flavours and a slightly sweet finish. There is no 2002 or 2003.

Vintage	03	02	01	00
WR	NM	NM	4	5
Drink	NM	NM	03-04	P

MED/DRY $16 -V

Verdelho

Verdelho is a Portuguese variety, traditionally grown on the island of Madeira. It preserves its acidity well in hot regions, yielding enjoyably full-bodied, lively, lemony table wines in Australia, but is extremely rare in New Zealand.

Esk Valley Hawke's Bay Verdelho (★★★)
Described as an 'early-ripening' variety with 'built-in resistance to botrytis', the rare 2002 vintage (★★★) was grown in the Gimblett Gravels district, hand-picked, whole-bunch pressed and 15 per cent barrel-fermented. A distinctly medium style, with plenty of residual sugar (2.5 grams/litre) to balance its highish acidity, it offers fresh, lemony, appley flavours, balanced for easy drinking, but in its youth doesn't show a lot of personality. Tasted prior to bottling (and so not rated), the moderately characterful 2003 was pale and weighty, with restrained, citrusy, gently spicy flavours.

MED $20 AV

Viognier

Viognier is a classic grape of the northern Rhône, where it is renowned for its exotically perfumed, substantial, peach and apricot-flavoured dry whites. A delicious alternative to Chardonnay, Viognier (pronounced *vee-yon-yay*) is an internationally modish variety, now starting to pop up in shops and restaurants here.

Viognier accounts for only 0.2 per cent of the national vineyard, but the area of bearing vines is expanding swiftly, from 15 hectares in 2002 to 39 hectares in 2005. As in the Rhône, Viognier's flowering and fruit 'set' have been highly variable here. The deeply coloured grapes go through bud-burst, flowering and 'veraison' (the start of the final stage of ripening) slightly behind Chardonnay and are harvested about the same time as Pinot Noir.

The wine is generally fermented in seasoned oak barrels, yielding scented, substantial, richly alcoholic wines with gentle acidity and subtle flavours. If you enjoy mouthfilling, softly textured dry or dryish white wines, but feel like a change from Chardonnay and Pinot Gris, try Viognier. You won't be disappointed.

Ascension Matakana Viognier (★★★★)

The instantly attractive 2002 vintage (★★★★) has the scentedness and seductively soft texture of this increasingly popular variety. Fermented in seasoned French oak barriques, it offers deep yet delicate pear and lychees flavours, with leesy characters adding complexity and a well-rounded finish.

DRY $25 AV

Babich Winemakers Reserve Viognier ★★★☆

Sold only at the winery in Henderson, the 2002 vintage (★★★★) is a bone-dry Hawke's Bay wine, grown at Fernhill and fermented and matured in a mix of old French oak barriques (60 per cent) and tanks. It's a very weighty wine (14 per cent alcohol) with an oily texture and strong peach, pear and fig flavours, with a slightly honeyed richness.

Vintage	02	01
WR	7	7
Drink	03-04	03-04

DRY $24 AV

Collards Rothesay Viognier ★★★☆

The 2002 vintage (★★★☆) was grown at the Rothesay Vineyard in Waimauku, West Auckland and matured on its yeast lees in old oak barriques. Light lemon/green, it's a subtle wine, lightly floral, full-bodied and soft, with gentle peach, pear and spice flavours showing great delicacy and a lingering finish.

Vintage	03	02	01	00
WR	NM	6	NM	6
Drink	NM	03-04	NM	P

DRY $25 -V

Coopers Creek Gisborne Viognier (★★★)

Handled entirely in tanks, the debut 2003 vintage (★★★) is based on first-crop vines in the Bell vineyard at Hexton. It's a fresh, clean, vibrantly fruity wine, full-bodied, with lemony, appley, slightly spicy flavours and a crisp, dry finish. It's less powerful and lush than the country's top Viogniers, but the price is right.

DRY $20 AV

Herzog Marlborough Viognier ★★★★

The 2002 vintage (★★★★☆) was picked at a ripe 25 brix and fermented and lees-aged for a year in a single, 500-litre French oak cask. Floral, with good freshness and varietal character, it's a full-bodied wine (14 per cent alcohol) with delicate peach, pear and spice flavours, good fruit/oak balance and a lingering, rounded finish.

Vintage	02	01
WR	6	7
Drink	03-08	03-05

DRY $39 -V

Millton Growers Series Tietjen Vineyard Viognier ★★★★☆

Fermented in old barrels with indigenous yeasts, but not grown organically, the 2002 vintage (★★★★☆) is a powerful, floral Gisborne wine, rich and rounded, with very ripe tropical-fruit, lemon and pear flavours, fresh, slightly spicy and showing excellent depth. It's a complex wine, robust and concentrated.

DRY $28 V+

Passage Rock Viognier (★★★☆)

The robust 2002 vintage (★★★☆) from this small Waiheke Island winery is a promising debut. Fermented but not matured in barrels, it's a very substantial wine (14.4 per cent alcohol), with strongly varietal, pear and spice flavours and a crisp, bone-dry finish.

DRY $24 AV

Te Mata Woodthorpe Viognier ★★★★☆

This single-vineyard wine is grown at Te Mata's Woodthorpe Terraces property, on the south side of the Dartmoor Valley in Hawke's Bay, whole-bunch pressed and fermented and lees-aged in seasoned French oak barriques. Robust and fleshy, with a powerful surge of peachy, pineappley, gently honeyed flavours, the light yellow 2002 vintage (★★★★★) is one of the finest Viogniers yet produced here.

Vintage	02	01	00	99	98
WR	7	6	6	6	5
Drink	04-05	03-04	P	P	P

DRY $29 V+

TW Viognier ★★★☆

Fresh, mouthfilling and finely balanced, the 2002 vintage (★★★☆) of this Gisborne wine is vibrantly fruity, with delicate pear and spice flavours and a smooth finish. The 2003 (★★★☆) was fermented and aged for three months in old French oak casks. Fresh and full-bodied, with clearcut varietal character, it's a subtly wooded wine with pear, citrus fruit and spice flavours, a touch of complexity and good length.

DRY $27 -V

Sweet White Wines

The ravishing beauty of New Zealand's top sweet wines is winning international acclaim. At the 2003 Sydney International Wine Competition, the trophy for champion dessert wine was awarded to the breathtakingly beautiful Konrad & Co Sigrun Marlborough Noble Riesling 2001, with Wither Hills Marlborough Noble Riesling 2001 one of the joint runners-up.

New Zealand's most luscious, concentrated and honeyish sweet whites are made from grapes which have been shrivelled and dehydrated on the vines by 'noble rot', the dry form of the *Botrytis cinerea* mould. Misty mornings, followed by clear, fine days with light winds and low humidity, are ideal conditions for the spread of noble rot, but in New Zealand this favourable interplay of weather factors occurs irregularly.

Some enjoyable but rarely brilliant dessert wines (often labelled Ice Wine) are made by the freeze-concentration method, whereby a proportion of the natural water content in the grape juice is frozen out, leaving a sweet, concentrated juice to be fermented.

Marlborough has so far yielded a majority of the finest sweet whites. Most of the other wine regions, however – except Auckland (too wet) and Central Otago (too dry and cool) – can also point to the successful production of botrytised sweet whites in favourable vintages.

Riesling has been the foundation of the majority of New Zealand's most opulent sweet whites, but Müller-Thurgau, Sauvignon Blanc, Sémillon, Gewürztraminer, Pinot Gris, Chenin Blanc and Chardonnay have all yielded fine dessert styles; the Rongopai winery even conjured up a sticky from Pinot Noir. With their high levels of extract and firm acidity, most of these wines repay cellaring.

Alan McCorkindale Waipara Valley Noble Riesling (★★★☆)

Light green/gold in hue, the 2002 vintage (★★★☆) has a minerally, rather than floral, bouquet leading into a citrusy, honeyed palate with good sugar/acid balance and rich flavour. Drink now onwards.

SW $25 (375ML) -V

Alpha Domus Leonarda Late Harvest Sémillon ★★★☆

The 2002 vintage (★★★☆) of this Hawke's Bay wine is a gently oaked style (20 per cent barrel-fermented). Green/gold, it's a sweet but not super-sweet wine (120 grams/litre of residual sugar) with good body and concentration of ripe, honeyed flavour and a well-rounded finish.

Vintage	02	01	00	99	98
WR	7	NM	7	5	5
Drink	03-08	NM	03-06	P	03-05

SW $19 (375ML) V+

Alpha Domus Noble Selection Sémillon ★★★★★

A lush, oily Sauternes style, the gorgeous 1998 vintage (★★★★★) was estate-grown at Maraekakaho, in Hawke's Bay, and fermented and matured in all-new French oak barrels. The 2000 (★★★★★), also fully barrel-fermented, is gold/amber, with a strongly honeyed fragrance.

It's a classy, weighty wine with abundant sweetness (220 grams/litre of residual sugar), a deliciously oily texture and rich, ripe, honeyed, complex flavours.

Vintage 00
WR 7
Drink 03-14

SW $30 (375ML) AV

Askerne Botrytised Riesling (★★)

Still on sale, the 2000 vintage (★★) of this Hawke's Bay wine was harvested in two picks, at 30 and 35 brix, partly fermented in old French oak casks, and stop-fermented with 134 grams per litre of residual sugar. It's a golden wine with botrytis-derived honey characters, but slightly dull, lacking real freshness.

Vintage 00
WR 5
Drink 03-06

SW $17 (375ML) -V

Askerne Botrytised Sémillon ★★★☆

The 2002 vintage (★★★★☆) is by far the best yet. Grown in Hawke's Bay and matured in old oak casks, it's a golden wine with a rich, honeyed, complex bouquet. Oily and sweet (180 grams/litre of residual sugar), it's very lush and concentrated, with substantial body (despite being only 10 per cent alcohol), good sugar/acid balance and a powerful botrytis influence. Classy stuff.

Vintage 02 01
WR 7   NM
Drink 03-08 NM

SW $30 (375ML) -V

Ata Rangi Kahu Botrytis Riesling ★★★★

Grown in the Hensley vineyard, near the Ata Rangi winery in Martinborough, the 2003 vintage (★★★☆) is a light-bodied wine (9 per cent alcohol), with 150 grams per litre of residual sugar. Slightly less concentrated than the lovely 2002 (★★★★☆), it offers ripe, apricot and honey flavours showing some richness, with strong drink-young appeal.

Vintage 03
WR 6
Drink 03-05

SW $28 (375ML) -V

Babich Mara Estate Botrytised Sauvignon Blanc (★★☆)

Still on sale in 2003, the 1996 vintage (★★☆) of this Hawke's Bay wine is golden, with sweet tea and honey flavours now tasting a bit tired.

SW $16 (375ML) -V

Babich Winemaker's Reserve Late Harvest Riesling (★★★☆)

The 1999 vintage (★★★☆), grown in the Pigou vineyard in Marlborough, is drinking well now, although it looked even better a year or two ago. Golden, with citrusy, honeyed flavours and firm acid spine, it's showing minerally, toasty, bottle-aged characters.

SW $29 (375ML) -V

Cairnbrae Late Harvest Riesling (★★☆)

Estate-grown in the Wairau Valley, Marlborough, the 2001 vintage (★★☆) is a solid but plain dessert wine, lacking scentedness, with sweet, lemony flavours of moderate depth.

SW $20 (375ML) -V

Canterbury House Late Harvest Pinot Gris (★★★☆)

Smooth and sweet, the 2002 vintage (★★★☆) is an elegant wine with ripe aromas and flavours of citrus fruits, pears and spice. It shows good weight, delicacy, length and roundness, with slight honey characters adding richness.

SW $29 (375ML) -V

Canterbury House Noble Riesling ★★★★☆

Estate-grown at Waipara and fermented in old oak casks, the exquisite 2000 vintage (★★★★★), champion wine at the 2001 Air New Zealand Wine Awards, offered ravishingly pure and intense scents and flavours, enriched but not dominated by botrytis. The light yellow 2002 (★★★★) is less arresting, but still highly attractive, with a floral, scented bouquet and citrusy, gently honeyed flavours, sweet, rounded and rich.

SW $29 (375ML) AV

Chancellor Waipara Valley Late Harvest Chardonnay (★★☆)

Harvested in June at a soaring 39 brix and fermented in old oak barrels, the 2001 vintage (★★☆) is weighty (14 per cent alcohol), golden and concentrated, with sweet flavours of apricot and honey, but a slight dullness on the nose and palate detracts from its overall quality.

Vintage 01
WR 5
Drink 03-04

SW $21 (375ML) -V

Charles Wiffen Dessert Riesling ★★★☆

Packaged in a 500 ml bottle, the 2001 vintage (★★★☆) of this Marlborough wine is light yellow, crisp and slightly honeyed, with sweet, lemony, limey flavours gently enriched by noble rot. The 2002 (★★★★), partly oak-aged, is deep gold, oily and concentrated, with sweet apricot and honey flavours and good acid spine. It's already delicious.

SW $30 (500ML) AV

Church Road Reserve Noble Sémillon ★★★★☆

The 1997 vintage (★★★★), still on sale in 2003, was harvested in Hawke's Bay as late as mid-June at 31 to 37 brix and matured for 19 months in all-new French oak barriques. Weighty and rich, with sweet, lush flavours of stone-fruits, honey and tea, it shows good complexity, concentration and acid backbone. The 1999 (★★★★☆), also made from individually selected, botrytised berries, is amber-hued, with a richly honeyed and complex bouquet. Weighty and sweet, it's a powerful Sauternes style with a deliciously oily texture and concentrated apricot and honey flavours.

Vintage 99
WR 6
Drink 03-06

SW $33 (375ML) -V

Clearview Estate Late Harvest Chardonnay (★★★☆)

The robust (14.5 per cent alcohol), gently honeyed 2002 vintage (★★★☆) was grown at Te Awanga, in Hawke's Bay, hand-picked at 36 brix, and fermented and matured for 11 months in oak casks (50 per cent new). Light gold, it offers rich, well-ripened grapefruit and peach flavours, strongly seasoned with toasty oak, and a sweet, crisp finish.

Vintage 02
WR 6
Drink 03-07

SW $35 (375ML) -V

Cloudy Bay Late Harvest Riesling ★★★★★

Cloudy Bay only makes this Marlborough dessert wine occasionally (the 1996, reports winemaker Kevin Judd, 'is still great'), but it's well worth waiting for. The light gold 2000 vintage (★★★★★) has a gorgeous balance of rich, citrusy fruit flavours, botrytis-derived honey characters, sweetness (122 grams/litre) and acidity. It was harvested in early May at Fairhall, in the Wairau Valley, when the grape sugar levels had reached an average of 30.1 brix and over half of the berries were botrytis-affected. Fermented in a mix of tanks and barrels, then matured on its yeast lees in old French oak casks for 18 months, it's a very classy, intense and complex wine – an exquisite sweet Riesling, still unfolding.

Vintage	00	99	98	97	96
WR	6	6	NM	NM	6
Drink	04-05	03-04	NM	NM	P

SW $29 (375ML) V+

Collards Botrytis Riesling (★★★)

The amber-hued 1999 vintage (★★★) is a sweet (92 grams/litre of sugar) but not super-sweet Marlborough wine with good depth of lemony, honeyed flavours cut with firm acidity and toasty, bottle-aged characters. Ready.

Vintage	99
WR	7
Drink	03-04

SW $19 (375ML) AV

Coopers Creek Late Harvest Riesling ★★★

The 2000 vintage (★★★) is a botrytis-affected Marlborough wine, picked at 27 brix. It's a light wine (8.5 per cent alcohol) with lemon, lime and pear-like flavours and a green-edged finish. Light yellow, the 2002 (★★★☆) is an elegant late-harvest style. Harvested in the Wairau Valley at 30 brix, with a 'moderate' level of botrytis, and stop-fermented with 150 grams per litre of residual sugar, it's a light-bodied wine (9 per cent alcohol), with lemony, gently honeyed aromas and flavours, fresh, sweet and lively.

Vintage	02	01	00	99	98	97	96
WR	6	NM	6	NM	NM	5	7
Drink	03-05	NM	03-04	NM	NM	P	P

SW $20 (375ML) AV

Cottle Hill Late Harvest Estate Chardonnay (★★☆)

Estate-grown at Kerikeri, in the Bay of Islands, and briefly oak-aged, the 2000 vintage (★★☆) is a lemon-hued wine with a restrained bouquet. A full-bodied, gently sweet wine (80 grams/litre of sugar) with soft, peachy, lemony flavours, it's a pleasant mouthful, although not rich.

SW $16 (375ML) -V

Dry River Arapoff Selection Gewürztraminer (★★★★★)

The seductive 2002 vintage (★★★★★) of this Martinborough wine harbours over 60 grams per litre of residual sugar, but you hardly notice it, the palate is so full and creamy-rich. Weighty (but only 11.5 per cent alcohol), with a bouquet of fruit and flowers, it shows lovely fullness and softness, with beautifully deep lychees, pear and spice flavours, possessing great delicacy and richness.

Vintage	02
WR	7
Drink	03-08

SW $36 (750ML) AV

Dry River Late Harvest Craighall Riesling ★★★★★

Dry River produces breathtakingly beautiful botrytised sweet wines in Martinborough – sometimes light and fragile, sometimes high in alcohol and very powerful – from a range of varieties. For winemaker Neil McCallum, Riesling is the queen of dessert wines, and his wines are made for cellaring, rather than drink-young appeal. The 2002 vintage (★★★★★) was hand-picked in mid-May, after most of the leaves had fallen, 'with a sprinkling of botrytis and berry shrivel'. It's a light lemon/green, beautifully harmonious wine, finely scented and rich, with intense, ripe, faintly honeyed flavours of lemons and apples, showing great delicacy and length. Likened by McCallum to a Mosel spatlese, 'for its clarity of expression, but with greater weight and concentration overall', it is already hugely drinkable, but best cellared to 2005+. (The Super Classic designation applies to Dry River's range of sweet whites from different varieties.)

Vintage 02
WR 7
Drink 03-08

SW $41 (750ML) AV

Felton Road Block 1 Riesling ★★★★★

Grown on a 'steeper slope' which yields 'riper fruit' without noble rot, this Bannockburn, Central Otago wine is made in a style 'similar to a late-harvest, Mosel spatlese', says winemaker Blair Walter. Very youthful, the 2002 vintage (★★★★★) is a classic aperitif style, delicate and racy, with green apple and lemon aromas, a distinct minerally streak, and searching flavours of lemons and limes, sweet (60 grams/litre of residual sugar) and tangy. It should be very long-lived; open 2005+.

Vintage 02
WR 6
Drink 03-15

SW $26 (375ML) V+

Firstland Glacier Ice Wine (★★★)

The 2001 vintage (★★★) is a Marlborough Riesling, late-harvested in a Renwick vineyard with 'very little' botrytis and then freeze-concentrated. Lemon/green, with fresh lemon/lime aromas and flavours, it is sweet, simple and crisp, although not honeyed, with good depth.

SW $30 (375ML) -V

Forrest Botrytised Riesling ★★★★☆

Always impressive. The 2002 vintage (★★★★★) is a light gold, very elegant Marlborough wine with lovely, pure honey characters enriching but not swamping its ripe, citrusy fruit flavours. It's a deliciously sweet style (170 grams/litre of sugar) with excellent acid balance, intensity and scentedness.

Vintage 03 02
WR 7 6
Drink 04-10 03-05

SW $35 (375ML) -V

Framingham Noble Selection ★★★★

The golden 2002 vintage (★★★★) is Framingham's first botrytised Riesling since 1999. Already delicious, it's a mouthfilling (13 per cent alcohol), strongly botrytis-affected wine with apricot and honey flavours and a sweet but not super-sweet finish (95 grams/litre of sugar).

Vintage 02
WR 5
Drink 03-04

SW $27 (375ML) -V

Fromm La Strada Riesling (★★★★☆)

The light and vivacious 2002 vintage (★★★★☆) is 'basically our late-harvest style', says Marlborough winemaker Hatsch Kalberer. Light-bodied (only 9 per cent alcohol) with lemony, appley flavours showing lovely delicacy and freshness, it's a moderately sweet style (70 grams/litre of residual sugar) with appetising acidity and no sign of botrytis. 'Drink it on a Sunday afternoon, with a slight breeze from the sea,' suggests Kalberer.

SW $27 (750ML) V+

Fromm La Strada Riesling Auslese ★★★★☆

The 2001 vintage (★★★★★) is one of the best yet. Made from late-harvested grapes, it is light (7.5 per cent alcohol) and lovely, with intense lemon/lime flavours, showing no sign of botrytis. Very delicate, with a harmonious balance of sweetness (87 grams/litre of sugar) and fresh, tense acidity, and slightly slatey, minerally characters to add complexity, it's a delicious aperitif. The whole point of wine like this is to cellar it, for the complexity that comes with bottle-age.

Vintage	03	02	01	00	99	98
WR	6	7	7	6	5	7
Drink	03-13	03-14	03-13	03-12	03-09	03-13

SW $26 (375ML) AV

Fromm La Strada Riesling Beerenauslese (★★★★★)

Showing exceptional richness, the 2001 vintage (★★★★★) was made from individually selected, botrytis-free, slightly shrivelled berries, harvested in four separate sweeps through the Marlborough vineyard within a 12-day period. Only 7.5 per cent alcohol, with a high residual sugar level (180 grams/litre) balanced by high acidity, it has a lovely light-to-medium yellow/green hue. Rich, ripe-fruit aromas lead into an instantly seductive palate, lemony, sweet and crisp, with outstanding concentration and harmony. Expensive but memorable.

Vintage	01
WR	7
Drink	03-20

SW $90 (375ML) -V

Giesen Late Harvest Riesling Reserve Selection (★★★★)

The golden 2002 vintage (★★★★) is a bargain. Grown in Canterbury, it's a strongly botrytised style with a honeyed bouquet and a rich, sweet palate (harbouring 95 grams/litre of sugar), with grapefruit, lime and honey flavours and refreshing acidity. Delicious now, it should be long-lived, and at $20 for a full (750 ml) bottle, it offers irresistible value.

Vintage	02
WR	7
Drink	04-15

SW $20 (750ML) V+

Glover's Late Harvest Riesling (★★★)

Grown in Nelson, the 2002 vintage (★★★) is pale, light and crisp, with youthful, sweet apple flavours. It's still very youthful; open 2005+.

SW $21 (750ML) AV

Greenhough Hope Vineyard Riesling Botrytis Selection (★★★★☆)

The golden 2000 vintage (★★★★☆) was made from late-harvested, raisined grapes, partly botrytis-affected. Fermented and matured for a year in French oak casks, it has a lovely, rich, complex and honeyed fragrance. Offering Sauternes-style complexity, but with the lower alcohol (11 per cent) typical of sweet Rieslings, it is a beautifully poised, sweet (147 grams/litre of sugar) and honeyed Nelson wine, with good acid spine.

SW $25 (375ML) AV

Hunter's Late Harvest Sauvignon Blanc (★★★★)

The rich, gently honeyed 2002 vintage (★★★★) was picked at 36.8 brix in Marlborough in early June. Bright, light lemon/green, it is citrusy, sweet (143 grams/litre of residual sugar) and slightly honeyed in a fresh and lively style with lovely depth, ripeness and roundness. Drink now onwards.

SW $27 (375ML) -V

Jackson Estate Botrytis Riesling ★★★★☆

The oak-aged 1995 vintage (★★★★★) was gorgeously treacly, oily and honey-sweet, and the 1999 (★★★★☆) isn't far behind. Golden, with a scented bouquet of citrus fruits and honey, it's a rich, softly seductive wine, sweet, concentrated and lovely. Re-tasted in 2003, it's still drinking well.

Vintage	99	98	97	96	95
WR	5	NM	NM	NM	5
Drink	03-04	NM	NM	NM	03-05

SW $30 (375ML) AV

Johanneshof Riesling Auslese (★★★☆)

The bargain-priced 2001 vintage (★★★☆) is a floral, elegant Marlborough wine, worth cellaring. Light lemon/green, it is a late-harvest style rather than a full-on botrytised Riesling, with gentle honey characters and fresh acidity woven through its pure, ripe lemon/lime fruit flavours.

SW $25 (750ML) V+

Kahurangi Estate Nelson Late Harvest Riesling (★★☆)

Grown in the Upper Moutere hills, the 2002 vintage (★★☆) is a slightly austere wine in its infancy, with plentiful sweetness (140 grams/litre of sugar) and steely acidity. Lemony and appley, with a hint of honey, it should be long-lived; open 2005+.

SW $25 (375ML) -V

Kim Crawford Reka ★★★★

The region and variety for Kim Crawford's sweet white (Reka means 'sweet') may vary with the vintage, but the 2002 (★★★★) is a Marlborough Riesling. Light yellow, with a fresh, lemony bouquet, it's a very elegant late-harvest style with well-ripened, citrusy flavours and a gentle botrytis influence.

SW $35 (500ML) AV

Konrad & Co Sigrun Noble Riesling ★★★★☆

The golden, richly honeyed 2001 (★★★★★) is a ravishingly beautiful and intense wine. The 2002 (★★★★☆) was grown in the Waihopai Valley of Marlborough and matured in French oak casks, new and old. Golden and nectareous, with a strong botrytis influence, it's a light-bodied (8.5 per cent alcohol) but richly flavoured wine, lemony, sweet and rounded, with lovely purity and freshness.

Vintage	02	01
WR	6	7
Drink	03-10	03-10

SW $33 (500ML) AV

Lake Chalice Botrytised Riesling ★★★★☆

The 2002 vintage (★★★★) was made from individually selected, late-harvested bunches of botrytis-affected grapes in the Falcon vineyard. Light-to-medium yellow/green, it is full-bodied (13 per cent alcohol), fresh and very youthful, with strong lemon, lime and honey characters and a slightly oily richness. It needs time; open 2004+.

SW $25 (375ML) AV

Lawson's Dry Hills Late Harvest Sémillon ★★★☆

Harvested in Marlborough at close to 30 brix and handled in a mix of tanks (90 per cent) and seasoned French oak barrels, the 2001 vintage (★★★☆) is a smooth, sweet (106 grams/litre of sugar) dessert wine. It is not a Sauternes style, but shows very ripe, non-herbaceous fruit flavours, fresh, light (10 per cent alcohol) and lovely.

Vintage	01	00
WR	5	5
Drink	03-04	P

SW $19 (375ML) V+

Leaning Rock Late Harvest Riesling (★★☆)

Grown at Alexandra, in Central Otago, harvested in May with some noble rot and partly oak-aged, the 2001 vintage (★★☆) is a slightly austere wine with a restrained bouquet, lemon and green apple characters, ample sweetness (120 grams/litre of sugar), and high acidity giving a slightly tart finish.

Vintage	01
WR	5
Drink	03-07

SW $34 (750ML) -V

Lincoln Ice Wine ★★☆

The 2002 vintage (★★☆) is a freeze-concentrated wine, made from Chardonnay (55 per cent) and Chenin Blanc grapes grown at Te Kauwhata. It's a light-bodied wine (10 per cent alcohol) with lemony, slightly appley flavours, sweet (105 grams/litre of sugar), simple, fresh, crisp and lively.

Vintage	03	02
WR	5	6
Drink	03-06	03-06

SW $18 (500ML) AV

Margrain Botrytis Selection Chenin Blanc (★★★☆)

Grown in Martinborough, the 2002 vintage (★★★☆) is fresh, lush and sweet (180 grams/litre of residual sugar) in a lightly botrytised style. Light gold, with gentle acidity for Chenin Blanc, it's a full-bodied wine (although only 10 per cent alcohol) with ripe peach, pear and honey flavours and a rounded finish. Drink now onwards.

Vintage	02
WR	6
Drink	03-07

SW $27 (375ML) -V

Martinborough Vineyard Late Harvest Riesling ★★★★☆

The rich, elegant 2002 vintage (★★★★☆) offers intense lemon, lime and honey flavours, with lovely balance and concentration and loads of cellaring potential. The 2003 (★★★★) was harvested at over 36 brix from 13-year-old vines in the Jackson Block and stop-fermented with 170 grams per litre of residual sugar. Light lemon/green, with lemony, appley, gently honeyed aromas and flavours, it shows lovely poise, but in its infancy looked less concentrated than top past vintages.

SW $35 (375ML) -V

Matariki Late Harvest Riesling ★★★☆

The 2001 vintage (★★★☆) is an attractive late-harvest style, harvested in Hawke's Bay at 32 brix with a 30 per cent botrytis infection. Light-medium yellow, with a citrusy, slightly honeyed bouquet, it's a gently botrytised wine, sweet, crisp and well-balanced, with good intensity. The 2002 (★★★), which shows little botrytis influence, offers fresh lemon and lime flavours in a true late-harvest style with ripe-fruit characters, gentle sweetness (100 grams/litre of residual sugar) and lively acidity.

Vintage	02	01	00	99
WR	7	6	6	7
Drink	03-06	03-06	03-04	P

SW $30 (375ML) -V

Matua Valley Late Harvest Muscat ★★★

The heady perfume is a highlight of this low-priced dessert wine. Made from Early White Muscat grapes and freeze-concentrated, it is typically fruity, sweet and smooth, with clearcut citrus/orange varietal characters in an enjoyable although not luscious style. The 2002 vintage (★★★), grown in Gisborne, is floral and deliciously soft and sweet (114 grams/litre of sugar) – like Asti Spumante without the bubbles. (The 2003 is a blend of Muscat and Riesling, grown in Gisborne and Marlborough.)

SW $13 (375ML) V+

Matua Valley Shingle Peak Botrytis Riesling (NR)

Tasted at the winery before it was bottled (and so not rated), the 2003 vintage looked outstanding. Harvested in Marlborough at 43 brix, it's a golden wine with a richly honeyed bouquet and pure, searching Riesling flavours, fresh, crisp, citrusy and honey-sweet.

SW $30 (375ML) V?

Mission Ice Wine ★★★

The 2002 vintage (★★☆) is pale gold, with a restrained bouquet. It's a simple wine with lemony, appley flavours, plentiful sweetness (90 grams/litre of sugar) and firm acidity cutting in on the finish.

SW $15 (375ML) AV

Montana Late Harvest Selection (★★★☆)

Made from 'botrytised Marlborough grapes' (Müller-Thurgau and Riesling), the yellow-hued 2002 vintage (★★★☆) is a ripely scented wine with lemony, gently honeyed flavours and plentiful sweetness (140 grams/litre of residual sugar). An elegant late-harvest style, it's drinking well now and priced sharply.

Vintage	02
WR	5
Drink	03-08

SW $15 (375ML) V+

Montana Virtu Noble Sémillon ★★★★★

The 1998 vintage (★★★★★) is arguably the best Sauternes-style wine yet made in New Zealand. Made from botrytised grapes grown in Hawke's Bay and fermented in new French oak barriques, it is golden, with a rich, complex, honeyed, oak-influenced bouquet. The palate shows a lovely concentration of very ripe-fruit, botrytis-derived honey characters and oak. The pale gold 2000 (★★★★) is concentrated, with crisp, honey-sweet flavours, toasty, minerally complexities and some development showing; drink now onwards.

Vintage	02	01	00
WR	7	NM	7
Drink	03-08	NM	03-10+

SW $40 (375ML) AV

Morton Estate Black Label Hawke's Bay Sémillon/Chardonnay (★★★☆)

The golden 2000 vintage (★★★☆) was made from botrytised grapes grown in the company's elevated Riverview and Colefield vineyards, and French oak-aged for a year. Rich, lemony, sweet (180 grams/litre of sugar) and crisp, with some green, limey Sémillon characters, it shows finely integrated oak and good intensity.

Vintage 00
WR 7
Drink 03-06

SW $30 (375ML) -V

Mount Cass Vineyards Waipara Valley Late Harvest Selection (★★★★)

Honey-sweet, golden, oily and rich, the 2002 vintage (★★★★) is a good buy. A blend of Chardonnay (83 per cent) and the German variety Optima (17 per cent), it was harvested in July at 42 brix and slow-fermented in seasoned French oak barrels. It's a weighty wine with abundant sweetness (174 grams/litre of sugar), good acidity and concentrated, apricot-like flavours. Drink now onwards.

Vintage 02
WR 6
Drink 03-05

SW $22 (375ML) V+

Ngatarawa Alwyn Reserve Noble Harvest Riesling ★★★★★

'Botrytis plays a huge part in this wine,' says Hawke's Bay winemaker Alwyn Corban. The estate-grown 2002 vintage (★★★★☆), made from bunches that had more than 80 per cent of their berries raisined by botrytis, was hand-harvested at 43.5 brix and fermented and matured for eight months in seasoned French oak barriques. Amber-green, with rich honey and apricot aromas, to which the oak adds complexity, it's an abundantly sweet wine (189 grams/litre of sugar), full-bodied and very concentrated, with high acidity giving a slightly tart finish.

Vintage	02	01	00	99	98	97	96	95	94
WR	7	NM	7	NM	NM	NM	NM	NM	7
Drink	03-10	NM	03-10	NM	NM	NM	NM	NM	03-04

SW $60 (375ML) -V

Ngatarawa Glazebrook Noble Harvest Riesling ★★★★★

Typically a richly botrytised, honey-sweet wine, concentrated and treacly. The grapes are estate-grown at the Ngatarawa winery in Hawke's Bay, in a block in front of the winery specially dedicated to the production of nobly rotten grapes. The deep gold 2002 vintage (★★★★) was late-harvested at 41.5 brix, but unlike its Alwyn stablemate (above), not cask-aged. It's a full-on, rampantly botrytised style with 155 grams per litre of residual sugar, richly honeyed aromas and flavours and firm acid spine.

Vintage	02	01	00	99	98	97	96	95	94
WR	7	NM	6	NM	NM	6	7	NM	6
Drink	03-10	NM	03-07	NM	NM	03-06	03-07	NM	03-05

SW $32 (375ML) AV

Ngatarawa Stables Late Harvest ★★★

This Hawke's Bay wine is called 'a fruit style' by winemaker Alwyn Corban, meaning it doesn't possess the qualities of a fully botrytised wine. The 2000 vintage (★★★) is a blend of Riesling (90 per cent) and Muscat. Light yellow/green, with interesting, minerally notes on the nose, it has an appealing lightness and harmony, with citrusy, gently sweet flavours (90 grams/litre of sugar). It's drinking well now.

Vintage 00
WR 7
Drink 03-05

SW $17 (375ML) AV

Okahu Estate Chardonnay Desserte Reserve (★★★)

Fleshy and soft, the 1999 vintage (★★★) was still on sale in 2003. A blend of Chardonnay (90 per cent) and Sémillon, hand-picked in Northland and matured for a year in French and American oak barriques, it's a light gold wine, weighty and sweet, with grapefruit and slight honey flavours showing some complexity and richness.

SW $22 (375ML) -V

Olssen's of Bannockburn Desert Gold Late Harvest Riesling ★★★☆

The 2001 vintage (★★★★) is a very refined late-harvest style from Central Otago, showing excellent depth of pure lemon/apple flavours, cut with fresh acidity. The 2002 (★★★☆) has fresh, elegant, citrusy aromas and flavours, with good sugar/acid balance, refreshing acidity and satisfying depth.

SW $35 (375ML) -V

Pegasus Bay Aria Late Picked Riesling ★★★★☆

After 'the most perfect, lingering autumn, the 2002 vintage (★★★★★) was harvested in late June at Waipara in multiple stages, each time selecting only berries which were 'fully ripened, shrivelled and in perfect condition'. Bright, light yellow/green, it's beautifully fresh, poised and concentrated, with lively acidity and intense, ripe, lemony, honeyed flavours, sweet but not super-sweet (160 grams/litre of residual sugar). A ravishingly beautiful wine, it shows great harmony and richness, and at $30 for a full-size bottle delivers fine value.

Vintage	02	01	00	99	98	97	96	95
WR	7	6	6	7	6	NM	5	4
Drink	03-12	03-11	03-10	03-10	03-05	NM	P	P

SW $30 (750ML) V+

Pegasus Bay Finale ★★★★☆

The rich, golden 1999 vintage (★★★★☆) was made from botrytised Chardonnay grown at Waipara, and fermented and aged on its yeast lees in seasoned French oak barriques for over two years. Fresh and smooth, with a strong noble rot influence, it's a lush, weighty and rounded wine with concentrated flavours of apricots and peaches and complexity from the long oak maturation. Drink now onwards.

SW $35 (375ML) -V

Richmond Plains Nelson Ice Wine (★★)

Grown in Nelson, the 2001 vintage (★★), made from Riesling, has green-edged, high-acid flavours that lack real ripeness and richness.

SW $19 (375ML) -V

Rongopai Reserve Special Late Harvest (★★★)

The gently botrytised 2002 vintage (★★★) is a blend of Riesling and Chardonnay, grown in the company's vineyards at Te Kauwhata, in the Waikato. Light/medium yellow, it's not highly fragrant, but the palate shows good depth of pear and honey flavours, with some complexity and moderate sweetness (72 grams/litre of sugar) balanced by crisp acidity.

SW $26 (375ML) -V

Sacred Hill Halo Botrytis Sémillon ★★★★

The green-gold 2002 vintage (★★★★) was harvested in Hawke's Bay at 52 brix and fermented and matured for a year in new French oak barriques. A very sweet wine (220 grams/litre of sugar) with a relatively low alcohol content (10 per cent), it is smooth, rich and oily, with concentrated, honeyish flavours and firm acidity cutting in on the finish. Delicious drinking now onwards.

Vintage 02
WR 7
Drink 03-08

SW $40 (375ML) -V

Sacred Hill XS Noble Selection ★★★★

A strongly botrytised Riesling, harvested at 32 brix in George Gunn's vineyard in the Ohiti Valley of Hawke's Bay, the 2000 vintage (★★★★) is golden, with concentrated apricot and honey flavours and a slightly limey, sweet, crisp finish.

SW $25 (375ML) AV

Saints Gisborne Noble Sémillon ★★★☆

The great-value 2002 vintage (★★★★) is a light gold, 'Sauternes-style' wine from Montana, grown at Patutahi in Gisborne and matured in French oak casks. Lush, with a honeyed fragrance and powerful surge of sweet apricot and honey flavours, beautifully fresh, rich and rounded, it's a pleasure to drink from now onwards.

Vintage 03 02
WR 5 6
Drink 03-10 03-10

SW $18 (375ML) V+

Schubert Dolce ★★★★

Named after the Italian viticulturist who planted the vineyard a decade earlier, the 2000 vintage (★★★☆) is based principally on Müller-Thurgau, grown at Martinborough. A golden, honeyed wine with a slight herbaceous edge, it is soft and rich, with some developed, bottle-aged characters.

Vintage 00 99
WR 6 6
Drink 03-20 03-10

SW $25 (375ML) AV

Seifried Winemakers Collection Riesling Ice Wine ★★★☆

The 2001 vintage (★★★) was made from raisined grapes grown in the company's vineyard at Redwood Valley, in Nelson. Freeze-concentrated and briefly oak-aged, it's a pale gold, citrusy, flavoursome wine, sweet and crisp.

SW $19 (375ML) V+

Selaks Premium Selection Ice Wine ★★★☆

This low-priced Marlborough wine is popular in supermarkets – and it's easy to see why. A blend of Gewürztraminer and Riesling, made by the freeze-concentration technique, the 2002 vintage (★★★☆) has a perfumed, spicy bouquet and flavour, with no botrytis influence. It's a simple but pretty wine, sweet (118 grams/litre of sugar), very fresh, vibrantly fruity and floral, offering delicious, bargain-priced drinking.

Vintage	02	01	00	99	98
WR	7	7	7	7	7
Drink	03-06	03-05	03-04	P	P

SW $15 (375ML) V+

Sileni Estate Selection Late Harvest Sémillon ★★★☆

Forward in its appeal but well worth cellaring, the 2002 (★★★☆) was grown in Hawke's Bay and stop-fermented with plenty of residual sugar (150 grams/litre). It's a smooth, sweet wine, weighty and rounded, with ripe, pear-like flavours enriched by a touch of honeyed botrytis. The 2003 vintage (★★★) has a faintly honeyed bouquet. Fresh and vibrant, citrusy and limey, with hints of apricot and honey, moderate acidity and a rounded finish, it should age well.

Vintage	03	02
WR	6	5
Drink	03-06	03-06

SW $22 (375ML) AV

Sileni Pourriture Noble ★★★★

The 2001 vintage (★★★★) was made from 100 per cent botrytis-affected Hawke's Bay Sémillon. Not oak-aged, it's a golden, sturdy (14 per cent alcohol) wine with fresh, smooth, concentrated peach, apricot and honey flavours in a sweet (95 grams/litre of sugar) but not super-sweet style.

Vintage	01
WR	5
Drink	03-05

SW $32 (375ML) -V

Stratford Noble Riesling ★★★★

Picked in late May at 48.5 brix, with a high level of botrytis shrivel, the 2002 vintage (★★★★☆) is golden, with a full-bloomed, honeyed fragrance. It's a deliciously concentrated Martinborough wine with apricot and honey flavours, rich, sweet (280 grams/litre of residual sugar) and lingering.

Vintage	02
WR	7
Drink	03-07

SW $27 (375ML) -V

Torlesse Waipara Late Harvest Riesling (★★★)

Weighty, with a high alcohol level for the variety (14 per cent), the 2001 vintage (★★★) was harvested at over 30 brix and matured in old oak barrels. The bouquet is restrained but the palate is substantial, with citrusy, lemony, late-harvest characters holding sway – rather than botrytis-derived honey flavours – and a moderate degree of sweetness (90 grams/litre of residual sugar).

SW $17 (375ML) AV

TW Botrytis Chardonnay (★★☆)

'A surprising gem from a challenging vintage' in Gisborne, the 2003 (★★☆) is a lemon-hued wine with a restrained bouquet, gentle pear, apple and honey flavours, a hint of botrytis and crisp acidity. Briefly oak-aged, it needs time; open mid-2004+.

SW $27 (375ML) -V

TW Botrytis Sémillon (★★★☆)

Late-harvested at Gisborne in May at 48 brix, the light gold 2003 vintage (★★★☆) is full of character. Matured for four months in old oak casks, it's rich and creamy, with very sweet pear and apricot flavours, honeyed, concentrated and soft.

SW $27 (375ML) -V

Villa Maria Reserve Noble Riesling ★★★★★

New Zealand's top sweet wine on the show circuit. It is typically stunningly perfumed, weighty and oily, with intense, very sweet honey/citrus flavours and a lush, long finish. The grapes are grown mainly in the Fletcher vineyard, in the centre of Marlborough's Wairau Plains, where sprinklers along the vines' fruit zone create ideal conditions for the spread of noble rot. The 2001 vintage (★★★★★) is typically outstanding. Golden, with a richly botrytised fragrance, it's a classic sweet Riesling, with a lovely intensity and purity of fruit and botrytis adding a honeyed, marmalade-like lusciousness. Benchmark stuff.

Vintage	01	00	99	98	97	96	95	94
WR	5	7	7	7	NM	7	NM	7
Drink	03-08	03-10	03-08	03-08	NM	03-05	NM	P

SW $50 (375ML) AV

Virtu Noble Sémillon – see Montana Virtu Noble Sémillon

Voss Late Harvest Riesling (★★★☆)

A true late-harvest style, the 2002 vintage (★★★☆) is a gently sweet Martinborough wine. Freshly scented, it is ripe-tasting, citrusy and limey, with good balance, freshness and aging potential, but also lots of drink-young charm.

SW $19 (375ML) V+

Waimea Estates Bolitho Reserve Noble Riesling (★★★★)

The golden 2001 vintage (★★★★) was harvested in Nelson at 47 brix and French oak-fermented (only one barrel made). It's a finely scented wine with a lovely richness of sweet, citrusy flavours and a luscious botrytis influence.

SW $45 (375ML) -V

Waimea Estates Late Harvest Riesling ★★★

The 2001 vintage (★★★) was picked in mid-May in Nelson at 26.8 brix, stop-fermented at 72 grams/litre of sugar, and 30 per cent of the blend was matured in one and two-year-old French and American oak casks. Light yellow/green, it's a medium-bodied wine (11 per cent alcohol), with ripe lemon/lime flavours woven with crisp acidity and a very restrained botrytis influence.

Vintage	01	00
WR	6	5
Drink	03-04	P

SW $16 (375ML) AV

Waipara Springs Botrytised Riesling ★★★

Still on sale, the golden, honeyed 2000 vintage (★★★☆) was late-harvested in North Canterbury at over 36 brix, with 70 per cent botrytis infection of the berries. It shows good palate weight, with strong, apricot-like flavours, sweet (95 grams/litre of sugar), crisp and raisiny.

Vintage	00	99
WR	6	5
Drink	03-08	03-06

SW $28 (375ML) -V

Wairau River Reserve Botrytised Riesling ★★★★★

The 1999 vintage (★★★★★) is very classy. A light gold Marlborough wine, it's fairly low in alcohol (10.5 per cent), with rich, delicate fruit characters of pears and apples, enriched by strong, botrytis-derived honey. Intense and perfectly balanced, with fresh, lively acidity and a sweet, very rich finish, it's drinking superbly now.

Vintage	99	98	97
WR	7	7	7
Drink	03-10	03-08	03-07

SW $40 (375ML) AV

West Brook Blue Ridge Late Harvest Riesling ★★★★

Still fresh and youthful, the 2000 vintage (★★★★) is golden, with pure, scented fruit aromas. Perfect for a lazy Sunday afternoon, it's a stylish Marlborough wine with lovely, lemony, gently honeyed flavours, sweet and rounded.

Vintage	00	99
WR	7	7
Drink	03-11	03-10

SW $28 (500ML) V+

Whitehaven Single Vineyard Reserve Noble Riesling ★★★★

The concentrated 2000 vintage (★★★★☆), grown in the Rapaura district of Marlborough, was hand-picked in stages over several weeks. Light gold, it's a powerful, mouthfilling style, sweet and rich, with a delicious surge of lemon and apricot flavours and a honey-sweet, lasting finish.

Vintage	00
WR	5
Drink	P

SW $20 (375ML) V+

Sparkling Wines

Fizz, bubbly, 'méthode traditionnelle', sparkling – whatever name you call it by (the word Champagne is reserved for the wines of that most famous of all wine regions), wine with bubbles in it is universally adored.

How good are Kiwi bubblies? Good enough for the local industry to have shipped 217,343 cases of bubbly in the year to June 2003 – mostly Lindauer to the UK – and for Deutz Marlborough Cuvée to win the trophy for Best Value Sparkling Wine of the Year at the 2002 International Wine Challenge in London. In the past year, sparkling wine accounted for 7.2 per cent of New Zealand's wine exports.

Yet the range of New Zealand sparklings is not expanding swiftly. Most small wineries view the production of fine, bottle-fermented sparkling wine as too time-consuming and costly, and the domestic demand for premium bubbly is limited. Of the total volume of sparkling wines (local and imported) sold in supermarkets in the past year, only 7.6 per cent retailed at over $15.

New Zealand's sparkling wines can be divided into two key classes. The bottom end of the market is dominated by extremely sweet wines which acquire their bubbles by simply having carbon dioxide pumped into them. Upon pouring, the bubbles race out of the glass.

At the middle and top end of the market are the much drier, bottle-fermented, 'méthode traditionnelle' (formerly 'méthode Champenoise', until the French got upset) labels, in which the wine undergoes its secondary, bubble-creating fermentation not in a tank but in the bottle, as in Champagne itself. Ultimately, the quality of any fine sparkling wine is a reflection both of the standard of its base wine, and of its later period of maturation in the bottle in contact with its yeast lees. Only bottle-fermented sparkling wines possess the additional flavour richness and complexity derived from extended lees-aging.

Pinot Noir and Chardonnay, both varieties of key importance in Champagne, are also the foundation of New Zealand's top sparkling wines (Pinot Meunier, the least prestigious but most extensively planted grape in Champagne, is still rare here). Marlborough, with its cool nights preserving the grapes' fresh natural acidity, has emerged as the country's premier region for bottle-fermented sparkling wines.

The vast majority of sparkling wines are ready to drink when marketed, and need no extra maturation. A short spell in the cellar, however, can benefit the very best bottle-fermented sparklings.

Alan McCorkindale Blanc de Noir (★★★★)

Estate-grown at Waipara, the biscuity, high-flavoured and smooth 1999 vintage (★★★★) is based entirely on Pinot Noir. Straw-hued, it's a very easy-drinking wine with a steady 'bead', strong, citrusy, yeasty, toasty flavours and a dryish, slightly creamy finish.

MED/DRY $38 -V

Allan Scott Blanc de Blancs ★★★☆

Based entirely on Chardonnay, this non-vintage Marlborough wine is typically fresh and harmonious. Its quality and style have varied slightly between batches (oak dominated on one occasion), but at its best it shows refined fruit characters and well-developed yeastiness.

MED/DRY $25 AV

Aquila ★★☆

This Asti-style bubbly is just what you'd expect – fresh, fruity and flavoursome, with a sweetish, soft finish. Within Montana's range of bubblies, in terms of sweetness Aquila (which has 50 grams/litre of sugar) sits between the medium Lindauer Sec and the unabashedly sweet Bernadino Spumante.

SW $9 AV

Arcadia Brut NV ★★★☆

This bottle-fermented bubbly is produced by Amisfield Vineyards in Central Otago. The non-vintage wine (★★★☆) currently on the market is a crisp, vivacious blend of Chardonnay (55 per cent) and Pinot Noir. Pale straw, it has lemony, gently yeasty, moderately complex flavours and a slightly toasty finish.

MED/DRY $24 AV

Arcadia Lake Hayes Central Otago Cuvée Brut Vintage (★★★★)

The stylish 1998 vintage (★★★★) is a 2:1 blend of Pinot Noir and Chardonnay, with 15 per cent of the base wine aged in old French oak casks. Drier than its non-vintage stablemate (above), it's pale straw, with strong, smooth, lemony, biscuity flavours, good yeast autolysis and a slightly creamy, very harmonious finish.

Vintage 98
WR 6
Drink 03-04

MED/DRY $30 AV

Bernadino Spumante ★★★☆

What great value! Montana's popular Asti-style wine is an uncomplicated bubbly based on Muscat grapes, traditionally grown in Gisborne but now also Australia. It's a higher-alcohol style (10 per cent) than most true Asti Spumantes (which average around 7.5 per cent) and less ravishingly perfumed, but it's still delicious, with a light, grapey, well-balanced palate, fresh, distinctly sweet (75 grams/litre of sugar), vibrantly fruity and smooth.

SW $7 V+

Canterbury House Méthode Traditionnelle ★★★★

The non-vintage wine (★★★★) on the market in 2002 was a stylish Waipara blend of 50 per cent Pinot Noir and 50 per cent Chardonnay. Light straw, with a bready bouquet and creamy, biscuity palate, it shows developed yeast autolysis characters and a lingering finish. On sale at the winery in 2003, the very attractive 1998 vintage (★★★★) is crisp, light and vivacious.

MED/DRY $24 AV

Coopers Creek First Edition ★★★☆

The current release is a non-vintage wine (★★★★), based entirely on Pinot Noir grown in Marlborough. Fermented and aged for a year on its gross lees in old hogsheads, then bottled and matured 'en tirage' for a further three years, it's light yellow, refined and lively, with crisp, lemony, yeasty flavours showing good vigour and yeast-derived complexity. The best wine yet under this label.

MED/DRY $24 AV

Corbans Diva ★★☆

This popular bubbly is fresh, crisp and simple in a light, medium-sweet style (28 grams/litre of sugar). It tastes like a sparkling Müller-Thurgau, but the blend includes Riesling and Muscat.

MED $10 AV

Corbans Diva Brut ★★☆

The drier model of Diva is based on 'various grape varieties', including Chenin Blanc and Riesling. Its scented bouquet reminded me of Muscat. It's a simple, slightly sweet (13 grams/litre of sugar) bubbly in a fruity, middle-of-the-road style.

MED/DRY $10 AV

Corbans Verde – see Verde

Daniel Le Brun Blanc de Blancs ★★★★

Some of the early vintages of this entirely Chardonnay-based Marlborough wine were outstanding, especially the 1991 (★★★★★). The 1997 (★★★☆), based on low-cropping vines and disgorged after five years on its yeast lees, is light gold, with plenty of crisp, citrusy flavour and gentle yeast characters. It's a moderately complex wine with good length.

Vintage	97	96	95	94	93	92	91
WR	6	7	5	NM	NM	5	7
Drink	03-07	03-05	03-04	NM	NM	P	P

MED/DRY $38 -V

Daniel Le Brun Brut NV ★★★★

The latest release (★★★★) is a Pinot Noir-dominant blend (60 per cent), with smaller portions of Chardonnay and Pinot Meunier. Disgorged after four years 'en tirage', it is toasty and high-flavoured, with a mealy, yeasty bouquet. Crisp, clean and dryish (only 6 grams/litre of sugar), it has very attractive, biscuity flavours showing good complexity, maturity and length.

MED/DRY $28 AV

Daniel Le Brun Brut Taché ★★★☆

This non-vintage sparkling rosé is *taché* (stained) with the colour of red grapes. The latest release (★★★☆), blended from Pinot Noir, Chardonnay and Pinot Meunier, is salmon pink, dryish (only 5 grams/litre of sugar) and lively, with strawberryish, slightly yeasty and earthy flavours and a crisp, lively finish.

MED/DRY $28 AV

Daniel Le Brun Vintage Brut ★★★★☆

Over the years, this has been the most distinguished Le Brun bubbly. A 50/50 blend of Pinot Noir and Chardonnay, matured for up to five years on its yeast lees, it is a high-flavoured style with loads of character. From 'the New World's premier wine region, Marlborough', the 1997 vintage (★★★★) shows good fragrance, intensity and vigour, with yeasty, toasty, complex flavours and a notably (for sparkling wine) dry finish (only 4 grams/litre of sugar).

Vintage	97	96	95	94	93	92	91
WR	7	7	6	NM	NM	4	7
Drink	03-08	03-06	03-04	NM	NM	P	P

DRY $38 -V

Daniel No 1

★★★☆

This is a non-vintage *blanc de blancs* style, based entirely on Marlborough Chardonnay. Made by Daniel Le Brun (in his family company) and matured for two years on its yeast lees, the latest batch (★★★★) is crisp and lively, with fine, small bubbles, intense, citrusy flavours with well-balanced yeast characters and a slightly toasty, long finish.

MED/DRY $36 -V

D Cuvée Number Eight

★★★★

This 'easy-drinking aperitif style' (from Daniel and Adele Le Brun's No. 1 Family Estate) is a blend of Pinot Noir (70 per cent) and Chardonnay, grown in Marlborough and disgorged after three years on its yeast lees. The bouquet is rich and yeasty, the palate tight and citrusy, with strong yeast characters. Fresh and lively, with lemony, biscuity flavours, it's a tight-knit wine with good intensity.

MED/DRY $28 AV

Deutz Marlborough Cuvée

★★★★★

The marriage of Montana's fruit at Marlborough with the Champagne house of Deutz's 150 years of experience created an instant winner. Bottled-fermented and matured on its yeast lees for at least two years, this non-vintage wine has evolved over the past five years into a less overtly fruity, more delicate and flinty style. The Pinot Noir and Chardonnay grapes are drawn from Montana's own vineyards throughout the Wairau Valley, and before being bottled, the base wine is lees-aged for up to three months and given a full malolactic fermentation. Ten per cent of the final blend is reserve wine, a year or two older than the rest. Faintly pink-hued, with a fine, small 'bead', the latest release (★★★★☆) has a fresh, moderately complex bouquet. It's a very delicate and harmonious style, with intense flavours, crisp, yeasty, slightly sweet and lingering.

MED/DRY $28 V+

Deutz Marlborough Cuvée Blanc de Blancs

★★★★☆

Matured for several years on its yeast lees, this Chardonnay-dominated blend is typically an elegant cool-climate style with delicate, piercing, lemon/apple flavours, well-integrated yeastiness and a slightly creamy finish. The vivacious 1999 vintage (★★★★★) is fragrant, tightly structured and complex, its lemony, appley fruit flavours enriched with strong, bready yeast characters. Intensely flavoured, with a long, yeasty, creamy-smooth finish, it's the finest wine yet under this label.

Vintage	99
WR	7
Drink	03+

MED/DRY $37 -V

Elstree Cuvée Brut

★★★★★

This is a distinguished wine from Highfield, guided since 1993 by Michel Drappier, from Champagne, and typically one of the most Champagne-like New Zealand sparklings, intense and tight-knit. The 1998 vintage (★★★★) is a 50/50 blend of Marlborough Chardonnay and Pinot Noir, given its primary alcoholic fermentation in a mix of old barrels (50 per cent) and tanks and disgorged after three years' maturation on its yeast lees. Broader, less flinty than usual, it is light gold, fragrant, rich and smooth, with citrusy, toasty, yeasty aromas and flavours showing very good complexity.

Vintage	98	97	96
WR	6	6	6
Drink	03-05	P	P

MED/DRY $29 V+

Fusion ★★★

Soljans produces this delicious bubbly from Muscat grapes grown in Hawke's Bay. It's a perfumed, sweetly seductive wine, light (10.5 per cent alcohol) and lively, with a steady stream of bubbles and plenty of lemony, appley flavour, fresh and smooth. A good Asti Spumante copy, it's full of easy-drinking charm.

SW $11 V+

Heron's Flight Blanc de Blancs (★★★☆)

One of the country's northernmost sparklings, the 2000 vintage (★★★☆) was grown at Matakana, north of Auckland. Pale yellow, it is crisp and lean, with citrusy, moderately yeasty flavours showing good vigour and length.

Vintage	00
WR	6
Drink	03-05

MED/DRY $32 -V

Huia Marlborough Brut ★★★☆

The 1999 vintage (★★★☆) is a marriage of Chardonnay and Pinot Noir with 29 per cent Pinot Meunier – an unusually high proportion by New Zealand standards of a variety grown widely in Champagne, but little used here. The base wine was fermented and matured for seven months in old French oak casks and the wine spent 42 months on its yeast lees before it was disgorged. Pink-hued, it's a mellow, developed wine with strawberryish, yeasty, complex flavours, nutty, crisp and dry.

Vintage	99	98	97
WR	7	6	6
Drink	03-05	03-04	03-05

DRY $36 -V

Hunter's Brut ★★★★

Full and vigorous, broad and generous, with loads of citrusy, yeasty, nutty flavour and a creamy, lingering finish, this is one of Marlborough's finest sparklings. The typical blend in recent years has been 55 per cent Pinot Noir, 35 per cent Chardonnay and 10 per cent Meunier, and the wine is matured on its yeast lees for an average of three and a half years. The 1999 vintage (★★★☆) is fresh, crisp and lively, with moderate yeastiness and good harmony and length.

Vintage	99	98	97	96	95	94
WR	6	5	6	6	6	6
Drink	03-06	03-05	P	P	P	P

MED/DRY $29 AV

Johanneshof Emmi ★★☆

The 1995 vintage (★★☆) from this tiny Koromiko (Marlborough) winery is a blend of 60 per cent Chardonnay and 40 per cent Pinot Noir, disgorged after four years on its yeast lees. Still on the market in 2003, it's a light gold, austere, very mature-tasting wine, crisp, dry, lemony and toasty, but lacks real finesse and charm.

MED/DRY $33 -V

Laverique (★★☆)

Although named after a bay on Banks Peninsula in Canterbury, the bottle-fermented 1996 vintage (★★☆) from Sherwood Estate was made from Marlborough Pinot Noir. It's a dryish, citrusy, yeasty, slightly appley and limey wine, but the fruit characters are now starting to dry out. Drink up.

MED/DRY $20 -V

Le Brun Cuvée Virginie (★★★★☆)

Designed as a tribute to Daniel and Adele Le Brun's daughter, Virginie, the vivacious 1997 vintage (★★★★☆) is a Marlborough blend of equal parts of Pinot Noir and Chardonnay, lees-aged for three years. Pale straw, with fine, steady bubbles, it is refined, fragrant, nutty and yeasty, with a fresh, crisp, tight palate showing excellent intensity, elegance and harmony.

Vintage 97
WR 6
Drink 03-06

MED/DRY $48 -V

Lindauer Brut ★★★☆

Given its high quality, low price and huge volumes, this non-vintage bubbly is one of the miracles of modern winemaking. The recipe is Pinot Noir (50 per cent), Chardonnay (30 per cent) and Chenin Blanc (20 per cent), grown in Marlborough, Hawke's Bay and Gisborne, and 15 months' maturation on yeast lees. It's a fractionally sweet style (12 grams/litre of sugar) with good vigour and flavour depth in a refined style, crisp and finely balanced. The wine I tasted in mid to late 2003 was straw-hued, with fresh, attractive, moderately yeasty aromas. Showing good balance of fruitiness and yeastiness, it's a flavoursome, smooth wine with lots of character. At $13 or less (often under $10 and even down to $7.95), it offers unbeatable value.

MED/DRY $13 V+

Lindauer Fraise (★★☆)

Launched in late 2002, 'strawberry Lindauer' is 'aimed at the RTD [ready-mixed drinks] market', according to one major wine retailer. Made 'with an added touch of natural strawberry', it has a pink/onion skin colour and a fruity, rather than yeasty, bouquet. The flavours are crisp and – well – strawberryish, in a fresh, light and lively, fairly simple style with gentle yeast characters and quite high acidity, balanced by ample sweetness (at 24 grams/litre of sugar, twice as sweet as Lindauer Brut). It's unlikely to appeal to regular wine drinkers, but we are obviously not the target market.

MED $14 AV

Lindauer Grandeur ★★★★★

The vivacious Rolls-Royce version of Lindauer is a non-vintage (★★★★★) blend of Pinot Noir (70 per cent) and Chardonnay, grown in Marlborough (90 per cent) and Hawke's Bay. Sixty per cent of the wine is from the 1998 vintage, supplemented by reserve stocks from 1991, 1994, 1996 and 1997 (giving an average period of maturation on yeast lees of four years). Pale straw, with an enticingly fragrant and complex bouquet, it is rich, strawberryish and intensely yeasty. It floats very smoothly across the palate, with lovely freshness, texture, vigour and intensity. Classy stuff.

MED/DRY $40 AV

Lindauer Rosé ★★★☆

Montana's bottle-fermented rosé is blended from Pinot Noir, Chardonnay, Chenin Blanc and Pinotage, grown in Marlborough, Gisborne and Hawke's Bay. The non-vintage wine (★★★☆) I tasted in mid to late 2003 was salmon-pink, with fresh, strawberryish, yeasty aromas and flavours and a smooth, dryish, lingering finish. A great buy.

MED/DRY 13 V+

Lindauer Sec ★★★☆

The medium version of Montana's bestseller is exactly twice as sweet (24 grams/litre of sugar) as its Brut stablemate (which has 12 grams/litre). A bottle-fermented blend of Pinot Noir (40 per cent), Chardonnay (40 per cent) and Chenin Blanc (20 per cent), it's a refined wine, straw-hued, with fragrant, citrusy, strongly yeasty aromas and flavours and a smooth finish. Top value.

MED $13 V+

Lindauer Special Reserve ★★★★

Montana's vivacious, immensely drinkable bubbly is a non-vintage blend of Pinot Noir (70 per cent) and Chardonnay (30 per cent), grown in Hawke's Bay and Marlborough, given a full malolactic fermentation and matured *en tirage* (on its yeast lees) for two years. Re-tasted in mid to late 2003 (★★★★), it is fresh and dryish, with pink/onion skin colour, highly fragrant strawberry and yeast aromas and a soft, flavoursome palate with loads of character.

MED/DRY $16 V+

Morton Premium Brut ★★★★

This has long been a deliciously easy-drinking, creamy-smooth, bottle-fermented bubbly. Blended from Pinot Noir and Chardonnay, grown in Hawke's Bay and Marlborough and disgorged after a year on its yeast lees, it's a straw-hued, delicate and complex wine with an eruption of tiny bubbles. Smooth, biscuity and strongly yeasty, with a slightly creamy, rounded finish, it's a vivacious mouthful and bargain-priced.

MED/DRY $19 V+

Mount Riley Savée ★★★

This is a rarity – a sparkling Sauvignon Blanc, intended to be 'a fruit-driven style with bubbles … a taste of summer'. A bottle-fermented Marlborough wine, briefly lees-aged, it has fresh, green, herbaceous characters on the nose and palate. Simple, lively and tangy, it's a fun wine.

MED/DRY $20 -V

Nautilus Cuvée Marlborough ★★★★★

The latest releases of this non-vintage, bottle-fermented sparkling reveal an intensity and refinement that positions the label among the finest in the country. A blend of Pinot Noir (75 per cent) and Chardonnay (25 per cent), it is blended with older, reserve stocks held in old oak barriques and disgorged after five years aging on its yeast lees. Lean and crisp, piercing and long, it's a beautifully tight, vivacious and refined wine, its Marlborough fruit characters subjugated by intense, bready aromas and flavours. One of the most Champagne-like of New Zealand sparklings.

MED/DRY $34 AV

Palliser Estate Martinborough Méthode Champenoise ★★★★☆

This is easily Martinborough's finest sparkling (although few have been produced). The 1998 vintage (★★★★) is a blend of Chardonnay (57 per cent) and Pinot Noir (43 per cent). Pale straw, with a fine 'bead', fragrant, fresh, very yeasty bouquet and dry finish, it has an attractive lightness and vivacity, with good complexity and lingering, citrusy, yeasty flavours.

MED/DRY $36 -V

Park Estate Cuvée Sauvignon (★★)

This plain, non-vintage bubbly is a sparkling Sauvignon Blanc, grown in Hawke's Bay and not bottle-fermented. Light gold, it has no obvious varietal character on the nose, with a lack of lightness and vivacity on the palate.

MED $14 -V

Pelorus ★★★★★

Cloudy Bay's bottle-fermented sparkling is typically a very powerful wine, creamy, nutty and superbly full-flavoured. A blend of Pinot Noir and Chardonnay – with always a slightly higher proportion of Pinot Noir – it is given its primary alcoholic fermentation in a mixture of stainless steel tanks, large oak vats and oak barrels, followed by complete malolactic fermentation. Once bottled it is matured for at least three years on its yeast lees before it is disgorged. The 1998 vintage (★★★★★) is a typically powerful and richly flavoured wine, notably complex, lively and yeasty, with a deliciously long, rounded finish. The 1999 (★★★★☆) is straw/pink, with punchy, very yeasty flavours, strawberryish, citrusy, toasty and long.

Vintage	99	98	97	96	95	94
WR	6	6	NM	6	5	4
Drink	03-06	03-04	NM	P	P	P

MED/DRY $42 AV

Pelorus NV (★★★★)

Cloudy Bay's non-vintage Marlborough bubbly is a Chardonnay-dominant style, matured for at least two years on its yeast lees (a year less than for the vintage). Fresh and lively, soft and creamy, it's typically a gently yeasty wine with lots of flavour. It is deliberately made in a more fruit-driven style than the vintage, and so less complex, but still very refined and refreshing.

MED/DRY $35 -V

Quartz Reef Chauvet NV ★★★★

This consistently impressive non-vintage bubbly is from a small Central Otago company involving Rudi Bauer and Clotilde Chauvet (whose family own the Champagne house of Marc Chauvet). The latest release (★★★★) is a blend of Chardonnay (53 per cent) and Pinot Noir, grown in Central Otago and Marlborough. Bottle-fermented and disgorged after two years aging on its yeast lees, it's very fresh and lively, with a lemony, biscuity, yeasty fragrance, a steady 'bead', crisp, strong grapefruit, lime and nut flavours and a rich finish.

MED/DRY $30 AV

Quartz Reef Chauvet Vintage (★★★★)

Drier than its non-vintage stablemate (above), the 1998 (★★★★) is a blend of Chardonnay (93 per cent) and Pinot Noir, grown entirely in Central Otago and disgorged in late 2002. Pale straw, with a steady stream of tiny bubbles, it's an elegant wine with citrusy, slightly limey and buttery flavours, integrated yeast characters, good complexity and a smooth, lingering finish.

MED/DRY $42 -V

St Aubyns Black Label Dry Sparkling Wine (★★☆)

Made by Villa Maria for the cheap and cheerful market, this is a simple, plain and fruity, Muscat-based Gisborne wine with light, limey, lemony flavours, a gentle stream of bubbles and a slightly sweet finish.

MED/DRY $8 AV

St Aubyns Gold Label Medium Sparkling Wine (★★☆)

Marketed by Maison Vin, a Villa Maria subsidiary used for bottom-tier wines, this simple bubbly is based on Muscat grapes, grown in Gisborne. At its best, it's full of charm, but this light, unabashedly sweet wine (50 grams/litre of sugar) can also lack the perfume and richness of fine Muscat. No complaints about the price.

SW $8 AV

Selaks Premium Selection Marlborough Brut NV ★★☆

This non-vintage wine (★★☆) is made entirely from Chardonnay. Light and smooth, it offers straightforward, lemony, appley flavours in a no-fuss, easy-drinking style.

MED/DRY $15 AV

Seresin Moana (★★★★)

The stylish 1996 vintage (★★★★) is a Marlborough blend of Pinot Noir (60 per cent) and Chardonnay. Half the base wine was matured in new French oak barrels before its second fermentation in the bottle, and the wine was disgorged after three years on its yeast lees. The yeasty, slightly toasty and limey bouquet leads into a crisp, elegant, slightly lean, bone-dry wine with good yeast autolysis and vigour.

Vintage 96
WR 6
Drink P

DRY $40 -V

Sienna (★★★)

This 'méthode traditionnelle rouge' from Soljans is an unusual beast – it's red rather than white. Full of plummy, blackcurrant and spice flavour, with a hint of dark chocolate and a slightly sweet finish, it's a fun wine which Tony Soljan suggests serving with roasted vegetable tart or chocolate cake.

MED/DRY $16 AV

Soljans Legacy ★★★☆

Lemony and lively, the 1998 vintage (★★★☆) is a blend of Chardonnay (60 per cent) and Pinot Noir, grown in Auckland and Marlborough and lees-aged for three years. The bouquet is fresh, with moderately intense, biscuity yeast autolysis characters; the palate is attractively balanced, with some nutty, bready complexity and a smooth finish.

MED/DRY $21 AV

Terrace Road Classic Brut NV ★★★★

From Cellier Le Brun, this bargain-priced bubbly is based on grapes from young vines, bottle-fermented and lees-aged for up to two and a half years before it is disgorged. The non-vintage wine (★★★★) on the market in 2003 is a great buy. A Pinot Noir-dominant style, with smaller amounts of Chardonnay and Pinot Meunier, it has a fine 'bead', yeasty fragrance and tight, lemony, yeasty flavours showing good intensity.

MED/DRY $19 V+

Verde NV ★★★☆

A good aperitif, this is a fresh, elegant Marlborough bubbly from Montana, based on Chardonnay (60 per cent) and Pinot Noir (to provide a style contrast to the Pinot Noir-dominant Lindauer Special Reserve). Matured on its yeast lees for 18 months, the wine I tasted in mid to late 2003 was light yellow, with citrusy, gently yeasty flavours, strong and smooth.

MED/DRY $18 V+

Voyage Special Cuvée Brut ★★★☆

Giesen's non-vintage, bottle-fermented sparkling is made from Pinot Noir, grown in Canterbury and Marlborough. Matured on its yeast lees for two years, it's fresh, crisp and lively, with lemony, appley flavours and good yeast-derived complexity. It's a stylish wine, priced right.

DRY $21 AV

White Cloud (Sparkling) ★★☆

From Nobilo, this blend of Müller-Thurgau and Muscat, grown in Gisborne, is just what you'd expect – totally undemanding, with fruity, medium-sweet flavours (34 grams/litre of sugar), lemony, simple, fresh, lively and crisp.

MED $9 AV

Rosé and Blush Wines

Pink wines attract little attention in New Zealand, from winemakers, wine judges or wine lovers. At the 2001 and 2002 Air New Zealand Wine Awards, the judges chose not to award the trophy for champion rosé or blush wine – which was no surprise, given the complete absence of gold or silver medal winners.

What is the difference between a rosé and a blush wine? There is a style divergence, at least in theory, but in the glass it can be fun and games trying to tell them apart.

In Europe many pink or copper-coloured wines (like the rosés of Provence, Anjou and Tavel) are produced from red-wine varieties. Dark-skinned grapes are even used to make white wines: Champagne, heavily based on Pinot Meunier and Pinot Noir, is a classic case.

To make a rosé, after the grapes are crushed, the time the juice spends in contact with its skins is crucial: the longer the contact, the greater the diffusion of colour and other extractives from the skins into the juice. A rosé is typically held longer on the skins than a blush wine, picking up more colour, tannin and flavour. (The organisers of the New Zealand Wine Society Royal Easter Wine Show stipulate that blush wines ought to be 'made in the white-wine style from varieties with some red pigmentation', whereas rosés should exhibit 'red varietal character, and not just be coloured versions of white wine, e.g. blush'.)

Cabernet Sauvignon, Pinot Noir and (more and more) Merlot are the grape varieties most commonly used in New Zealand to produce rosé and blush wines. These are typically charming, 'now-or-never' wines, peaking in their first six to 18 months with seductive strawberry/raspberry-like fruit flavours and crisp, appetising acidity. Freshness is the essence of the wines' appeal.

Ata Rangi Summer Rosé ★★★☆

The 2003 vintage (★★★) is a blend of Cabernet Sauvignon and Merlot grapes, grown in Hawke's Bay (75 per cent) and Martinborough. Cool-fermented in tanks and bottled with a sliver of sweetness (7 grams/litre of sugar), it's a pink/light red, buoyantly fruity wine, fresh and lively, with slightly grassy aromas and flavours, light, berryish and smooth.

Vintage 03
WR 6
Drink 03-04

MED/DRY $18 AV

Christina Estate Rosé (★★☆)

Grown in Martinborough, the 2002 vintage (★★☆) is a crisp, onion skin-coloured wine with strawberryish, green-edged flavours.

MED/DRY $20 -V

Clearview Estate Blush ★★★

This dryish, flavoursome wine is a bargain. Based on the Chambourcin variety (a deeply coloured French hybrid) grown in Hawke's Bay, with 'hints of Merlot and Cabernet Franc', it's typically a pink/red or pink/orange, full-bodied wine, fresh, crisp and lively, with good depth of raspberryish, slightly earthy and spicy flavours. A characterful wine, it's strong enough to accompany food.

MED/DRY $12 V+

Cottle Hill Sailor's Sky (★★★)

Bright, light pink in hue, the 2002 vintage (★★★) is a blend of Northland and Hawke's Bay grapes, made in a medium (15 grams/litre of sugar) style. Fresh, lively and crisp, it's a strawberryish, slightly earthy wine with refreshing acidity and good body.

MED $15 AV

Esk Valley Rosé ★★★★

This is New Zealand's best widely available rosé. The 2002 (★★★★), blended from Merlot (73 per cent) and Malbec, grown in Hawke's Bay, is a bone-dry, substantial (14 per cent alcohol) wine with strong raspberryish and strawberryish flavours, a hint of spice and a well-rounded finish. The bright pink 2003 vintage (★★★★) has fresh, berryish aromas and a smooth, rich palate with gentle acidity and cherryish, raspberryish flavours, full of drink-young charm.

Vintage	03	02	01	00	99	98
WR	6	7	NM	7	6	6
Drink	03-04	P	NM	P	P	P

DRY $18 V+

Felton Road Vin Gris (★★★☆)

This Bannockburn (Central Otago) wine is 'bled' from the Pinot Noir fermenter before the juice has a chance to pick up much colour and aged for six months in old oak casks. Slightly pink, with a spicy, earthy bouquet, it's a full-bodied wine with strawberry and spice flavours, gentle tannins and good depth.

DRY $22 AV

Forrest Marlborough Rosé ★★★☆

At its best, this is an enticingly fragrant Marlborough rosé, fresh and charming. 'I aim it to be perfect on New Year's Day [after the vintage],' says John Forrest. The 2002 vintage (★★★☆) is a buoyantly fruity wine, blended from Cabernet Sauvignon and Pinot Noir (40 per cent each), with small amounts of Merlot and Syrah. It's fresh and summery, crisp and raspberryish, with good flavour depth and a smooth, nearly dry (5 grams/litre of sugar) finish. The 2003 (★★★) is light pink/red, fresh and smooth, with raspberryish, slightly spicy flavours, crisp and lively.

Vintage	03	02	01
WR	5	6	6
Drink	04	P	P

MED/DRY $15 V+

Gibbston Valley Blanc de Pinot Noir ★★★

Drained from its skins after overnight contact, the 2002 vintage (★★★☆) of this Central Otago wine is one of the best. It's a full-bodied, dry wine with a pink/light red colour. Fresh and buoyantly fruity, with raspberryish, slightly earthy and spicy flavours and a tangy finish, it shows very good depth.

MED/DRY $27 -V

Lake Chalice Black Label Rosé (★★☆)

Designed for 'fun brunches, leisurely lunches or barbecues', the simple, pleasant 2003 vintage (★★☆) is a blend of Merlot, Pinot Noir and Cabernet Franc, grown in Hawke's Bay and Marlborough. Light pink/red, it is lively and berryish, with moderate flavour depth and a freshly acidic finish.

Vintage 03
WR 5
Drink 03-04

DRY $19 -V

Linden Estate Merlot Rosé (★★★)

Grown in Hawke's Bay and fermented with indigenous yeasts, the 2002 vintage (★★★) is an almost dry style (6 grams/litre of sugar) with pink/light red colour and fresh, crisp, berryish flavours, showing good depth.

MED/DRY $18 AV

Margrain Pinot Rosé (★★★☆)

Grown in Martinborough, the attractive 2002 vintage (★★★☆) is distinctly Pinot Noir-ish, with onion-skin colour from 24 hours' skin contact, fresh, crisp, strawberryish flavours and a smooth, slightly sweet (12 grams/litre of residual sugar) finish.

MED/DRY $26 -V

Marsden Bay of Islands Rosé (★★★)

Still fresh and lively, the 2002 vintage (★★★) is a blend of Cabernet Sauvignon and Merlot, grown in Northland and given brief skin contact. Light pink/red, it is crisp, with raspberry and strawberry flavours showing good depth and a slightly sweet, smooth finish.

Vintage 02
WR 5
Drink 04

MED/DRY $18 AV

Martinborough Vineyard Rosé ★★★★☆

This ranks among the country's finest rosés. Ensconced in a 500 ml bottle ('designed for two'), the pink/light red 2003 vintage (★★★★☆) was made from Pinot Noir grapes grown in Martinborough, fermented in tanks and drained from its skins after 24 hours' contact. Smooth, with strong raspberry, cherry and spice flavours woven with fresh acidity, it shows good body and richness. Great drinking during the summer of 2003–04.

MED/DRY $16 (500ML) AV

Mills Reef Rosé (★★★)

Full of drink-young charm, the 2003 vintage (★★★) is a Hawke's Bay blend of Pinot Noir and Merlot. Bright, light pink/red, it's a buoyantly fruity wine, fresh, raspberryish and slightly earthy, with appetising acidity and an off-dry finish.

MED/DRY $16 AV

Millton Merlot Rosé (★★★)

Enjoyed during summer in 'bars, cafés and back gardens all around the country', this very easy-drinking wine is grown organically in the company's Te Arai Vineyard at Gisborne. Stop-fermented in a slightly sweet style (12 grams/litre of sugar), the pink/light red 2002 vintage (★★★) is fresh and full-bodied, with vibrant plum and red-berry flavours, finely balanced acidity and a very smooth finish.

MED/DRY $18 AV

Neudorf Kina Merlot Rosé (★★★★)

Already delightful, the 2003 vintage (★★★★) was grown in the Moutere Hills of Nelson. An attractive pink/light red, it is berryish and plummy, fresh and smooth, with loads of flavour and a long, dry finish.

Vintage 03
WR 6
Drink 03-07

`DRY $23 AV`

Okahu Estate Shipwreck Bay Rosé ★★☆

The pale pink 2003 vintage (★★☆) was blended from Cabernet Sauvignon (80 per cent), Merlot and Pinotage, grown at Te Kauwhata, in the Waikato. It's a pleasant, light-bodied wine with raspberryish, slightly earthy and spicy aromas and flavours and a freshly acidic finish.

`MED/DRY $17 -V`

Putiki Bay Pinot Noir Rosé (★)

Matured in seasoned oak barrels, the 2002 vintage (★) was grown on Waiheke Island and made in an off-dry style. Slightly amber-hued, it lacks fresh, vibrant fruit characters, softness and charm.

`MED/DRY $33 -V`

Redmetal Vineyards Rosé ★★★★☆

This distinguished Hawke's Bay wine is designed 'more in the style of a Mediterranean light red wine than a typical rosé'. A serious style of rosé, it is barrel-fermented, dry and mouthfilling, with a strong surge of berry-fruit flavours, crisp and lively, and oak adding complexity and nuttiness. The 2003 vintage (★★★★) reveals a youthful, light red colour. Offering strong berry and plum characters, subtle oak and balanced acidity, it has a lot more flavour interest than most rosés, with a fully dry finish.

Vintage 03 02 01
WR 6 6 5
Drink 03-05 P P

`DRY $23 AV`

Riverside Dartmoor Rosé ★★☆

At its best, this is an attractive Hawke's Bay rosé, fresh, light, raspberryish and smooth. However, the 2002 vintage (★★) is simple and a bit rustic, lacking real freshness and charm.

Vintage 03 02
WR 6 5
Drink 03-04 P

`DRY $12 AV`

Rymer's Change Rosé ★★★☆

Designed as 'a verandah wine for alfresco dining', this Hawke's Bay rosé was previously called Te Mata Rose. Blended from Merlot and Cabernet Sauvignon, it typically offers fresh, strong, raspberryish aromas and flavours, deliciously lively, dry and smooth.

Vintage 03 02
WR 7 7
Drink 03-04 P

`DRY $16 V+`

Sileni Cellar Selection Saignée Rosé ★★★★☆

The 2002 (★★★★★) is a serious, unusually satisfying rosé. It's a Merlot-based blend, grown in Hawke's Bay. The juice spent 48 hours on its skins, then was run off to barrels for fermentation and three months' oak-aging. Bright pink, with strawberryish, slightly earthy aromas and flavours, it is fresh, vibrant, dry and flavoursome, with as much character as you could hope to find in a rosé. The 2003 vintage (★★★★), labelled Saignée (the French term for bleeding unfermented juice off red-wine ferments), was fully barrel-fermented. Light pink/red, with berryish, slightly earthy aromas, it is smooth, raspberryish and slightly nutty, with a dry, rounded finish. A delicious wine for this summer.

Vintage	03	02
WR	6	6
Drink	03-05	P

DRY $20 V+

Te Kairanga Castlepoint Rosé ★★☆

Light pink/red, the 2002 vintage (★★☆) was blended from Martinborough Pinot Noir (80 per cent) and Gisborne Merlot (20 per cent). Still fresh, it's a solid wine with smooth, strawberryish flavours and a slightly sweet, crisp finish.

MED/DRY $15 -V

Trinity Hill Hawke's Bay Rosé (★★★)

Easy summer sipping, the light-bodied 2003 vintage (★★★) is light pink/red, with pleasant flavours of raspberries and strawberries, smooth and refreshing.

MED/DRY $19 -V

Unison Rosé ★★★☆

Only sold directly from the winery, the attractive and satisfying 2002 vintage (★★★★) is a mouthfilling, fully dry Hawke's Bay rosé, blended from Syrah (80 per cent) and Merlot (20 per cent). Not oak-aged, it's a full-bodied wine with strong strawberry and spice flavours and a crisp, lingering finish.

DRY $19 AV

Waipara Hills Pinot Rosé (★★★)

The smooth, raspberryish 2003 vintage (★★★) was made entirely from Marlborough Pinot Noir. A slightly sweet style, it is pink-hued, with red-berry and spice flavours, balanced for early appeal.

MED/DRY $17 AV

Winslow Rosetta Cabernet Rosé ★★★★

This Martinborough wine is one of New Zealand's few classy rosés, although its quality took a dip in 2000 (★★☆). The 2002 vintage (★★★★) is back on form. Made from estate-grown, 'super-ripe' Cabernet Sauvignon, picked at 25 brix and fermented in seasoned French oak barriques, it's a bright pink, full-bodied wine (13.5 per cent alcohol) with fresh, strong, raspberryish flavours, a touch of complexity and a long, slightly sweet (12 grams/litre of sugar) finish.

MED/DRY $27 -V

Red Wines

Branded and Other Reds

The vast majority of New Zealand red wines carry a varietal label, typically Pinot Noir, Merlot or Cabernet Sauvignon (or blends in varying proportions of the last two). Those not labelled prominently by their principal grape varieties – often prestigious wines such as Esk Valley The Terraces, Unison Selection and Crossroads Talisman, but also a few basic reds – can be found here.

Although not varietally labelled, these wines are mostly of high quality and sometimes outstanding.

Alpha Domus AD The Aviator ★★★★★

The 2000 vintage (★★★★★) is a triumph for Hawke's Bay claret-style reds. A blend of Cabernet Sauvignon, Merlot, Malbec and Cabernet Franc, it shows striking all-round intensity, with impenetrable colour and bottomless depth of blackcurrant, nut and spice flavours. Even an Aussie red-wine lover would be forced to sit up and pay attention. There is no 2001.

Vintage	01	00	99
WR	NM	7	6
Drink	NM	03-10	03-08

DRY $48 AV

Alpha Domus The Navigator ★★★★☆

The firm, rich, complex 2000 (★★★★☆) is a blend of four Bordeaux varieties: Merlot, Cabernet Sauvignon, Cabernet Franc and Malbec. From a year in which the top label, The Aviator, was not produced, the 2001 (★★★★) is full-coloured and sturdy. Matured for 18 months in oak casks (50 per cent new), it's a concentrated Hawke's Bay red with deep blackcurrant, spice and nut flavours, firm tannins and obvious cellaring potential.

Vintage	01	00	99	98
WR	6	7	6	7
Drink	03-10	03-08	03-06	03-06

DRY $28 V+

Artisan Dominic (★★☆)

Grown in Rex Sunde's vineyard at Oratia, in west Auckland, the 2001 vintage (★★☆) is a blend of Gamay Noir and Pinot Noir, matured in French oak casks (20 per cent new). Ruby-hued, with a spicy, slightly earthy bouquet, it's a middleweight, berryish wine with a gentle oak influence and firm tannins. Verging on three stars.

DRY $20 -V

Ata Rangi Célèbre ★★★★☆

Pronounced *say-lebr*, this distinctive Martinborough red blends Cabernet Sauvignon with Merlot and Syrah. Robust and vibrantly fruity, it's typically tinged with the leafy character that cool-climate conditions accentuate in Merlot and Cabernet-based reds, but also displays impressive weight and depth of plummy, minty, spicy flavour in a complex style that matures well. Less impressive than the dark, deliciously weighty and concentrated 2000 vintage (★★★★☆), the 2001 (★★★☆) is a blend of 40 per cent Merlot, 30 per cent Syrah and 30 per cent Cabernet Sauvignon. Matured for 18 months in French and American oak barriques (25 per cent new), it has a distinct herbal streak on the nose and palate. Mouthfilling, with very good depth of plummy, spicy flavour, quality oak and rounded tannins, it's drinking well in its youth.

Vintage	01	00	99	98	97	96	95	94
WR	6	6	7	7	6	7	6	6
Drink	03-05	03-04	03-04	03-04	P	P	P	P

DRY $32 AV

Benfield & Delamare ★★★★☆

Bill Benfield and Sue Delamare specialise in claret-style reds of very fine quality and impressive longevity at their tiny Martinborough winery. Benfield & Delamare is typically slightly leaner than the leading Hawke's Bay reds, yet intensely flavoured and complex. From a 'cool, very dry year in which Merlot performed brilliantly', the classy, dark, fleshy 2001 vintage (★★★★★) caresses the mouth with rich, sweet-fruit flavours. A blend of Merlot (85 per cent) and equal portions of Cabernet Sauvignon and Cabernet Franc, it was matured in French oak barriques (half new). A lush, rich wine, crammed with plummy, spicy and nutty flavour, it's the best vintage since the beautifully ripe, densely packed 1998 (★★★★★) and already dangerously drinkable.

DRY $52 -V

Benfield & Delamare A Song For Osiris ★★★☆

Dedicated to Osiris, an ancient patron of the grape and wine, this Martinborough red is designed as a 'lively, fruit-driven style, suitable for early drinking'. Made from barrels excluded from the premium blend (above), it is typically vibrantly fruity, with strong, fresh, plummy, spicy flavours, gently oaked and smooth. Blended from Cabernet Sauvignon, Merlot and Cabernet Franc, the 2002 vintage (★★★☆) is fullish in colour, with considerable depth and complexity, moderate tannins and lots of drink-young appeal.

DRY $25 AV

Bilancia (★★★★☆)

Simply labelled 'Bilancia', the generous 2001 vintage (★★★★☆) is a Merlot-based blend, with smaller portions of Malbec, Cabernet Franc and Cabernet Sauvignon. Grown in Gimblett Road, Hawke's Bay, and matured for two years in predominantly French oak barriques (40 per cent new), it is deep and still youthful in colour, with impressively concentrated cassis, spice and mint chocolate flavours, warm and complex. Still fresh and vibrant, it shows good cellaring potential; open 2005+.

Vintage	01
WR	6
Drink	04-08

DRY $39 -V

Brick Bay Pharos (★★★)

Brick Bay's second red-wine release, from the 2000 vintage (★★★), is named after the famous lighthouse off the coast of Alexandria. A blend of Cabernet Sauvignon (60 per cent), Cabernet Franc (30 per cent) and Malbec (10 per cent), it was French oak-aged for a year. Grown at Sandspit, north of Auckland, it's a brambly, leafy, flavoursome wine, distinctly herbaceous, but nutty and firm, with good depth.

Vintage	00
WR	7
Drink	03-08

DRY $26 -V

Christina Estate Declaration ★★★☆

The powerful, gutsy 2000 vintage (★★★☆) is based principally on an unidentified grape variety, with 8 per cent Pinot Noir and Syrah. It's a full-coloured, warm and concentrated Martinborough red with a hint of rusticity but spicy oak adding complexity. The 2001 (★★★), matured for a year in one-year-old barrels, shows rich, youthful colour and generous, plummy, spicy flavour, with a slightly high-acid finish.

DRY $25 AV

C.J. Pask Reserve Declaration (★★★★☆)

The 1999 vintage (★★★★☆) is a powerful Hawke's Bay blend of Cabernet Sauvignon (48 per cent), Malbec (39 per cent) and Merlot (13 per cent), matured for 19 months in new French and American oak barriques. Dark, with a warm, nutty, perfumed bouquet, it's a concentrated wine with blackcurrant, spice and nut flavours, firm, balanced tannins and good complexity, but arguably over-oaked. There's some development showing, but it should be long-lived.

Vintage 99
WR 7
Drink 03-05

DRY $48 -V

Clearview Estate Enigma (★★★★)

The deeply coloured 2001 vintage (★★★★) is a Merlot-predominant red (57 per cent) with equal portions of Malbec, Cabernet Franc and Cabernet Sauvignon. Grown at Te Awanga, in Hawke's Bay, and matured for 15 months in French oak barriques (mostly new), it's fragrant and fleshy, with warm, generous plum, spice and nut flavours, oak complexity and supple tannins. Drink now or cellar.

Vintage 01
WR 6
Drink 04-10

DRY $40 -V

Craggy Range Sophia (★★★★★)

The bold, brambly, densely coloured 2001 vintage (★★★★★) is a Gimblett Gravels, Hawke's Bay blend of Merlot (61 per cent), Cabernet Franc (23 per cent) and Malbec (14 per cent), with a splash of Cabernet Sauvignon. It was matured for 19 months in French oak barriques (70 per cent new), then for a further six months in older barrels, and bottled unfiltered. A 10-year cellaring proposition, yet already delicious, it offers densely packed blackcurrant, plum and spice flavours seasoned with new French oak, with leathery, nutty characters adding complexity and very substantial mouthfeel.

Vintage 01
WR 6
Drink 06-11

DRY $40 AV

Craggy Range The Quarry (★★★★★)

Recommended for cellaring 'for at least a decade', the inky-black 2001 vintage (★★★★★) is a Cabernet Sauvignon-based Hawke's Bay red (71 per cent), with Merlot (24 per cent), Cabernet Franc (4 per cent) and Malbec (1 per cent). Grown in the stoniest part of the company's Gimblett Gravels vineyard, matured for 20 months in French oak barriques (70 per cent new), and bottled unfiltered, it has a youthful, fragrant bouquet of berries, blackcurrants and spice. Still a baby, it's a powerful, superbly concentrated (but not tough) wine, packed with brambly, spicy, nutty flavour, warm and chewy. It needs at least another two or three years to open out, but shows huge potential.

Vintage 01
WR 6
Drink 06-13

DRY $60 AV

Crossroads Talisman ★★★★★

A blend of up to six red grapes whose identities the winery delights in concealing (I see Malbec as a prime suspect), Talisman is grown in the estate vineyard at Fernhill in Hawke's Bay and matured for two years in French and American oak barriques, with a high percentage of new wood. Typically a boldly coloured, highly fragrant, voluptuous red, it bursts with sweet, ripe-fruit flavours. The 1999 vintage (★★★☆) is a powerful red with oodles of blackcurrant, redberry and plum flavour, strongly seasoned with sweet, perfumed oak, but a slight whiff of volatility detracts from the bouquet. A big, upfront style, it's ready for drinking now.

Vintage	99	98	97	96	95	94
WR	6	7	6	6	6	7
Drink	03-06	03-07	03-05	03-05	03-04	03-06

DRY $38 AV

Dog Rock (★★☆)

Labelled as 'a fun, full-bodied red', the 2001 vintage (★★☆) is a Marlborough blend of Gamay Noir, Merlot and Pinot Noir, from the Omaka Springs winery. It's a fruit-driven style with youthful, purple-flushed colour and crisp, plummy, berryish, slightly spicy flavours that lack real warmth and roundness.

DRY $17 -V

Esk Valley The Terraces ★★★★★

Grown on the steep terraced hillside flanking the winery at Bay View, Hawke's Bay, this is a strikingly bold, dark wine with bottomless depth of blackcurrant, plum and spice flavours. Merlot and Malbec are typically the major ingredients, supplemented by Cabernet Franc; the Malbec (45 per cent in 1998) gives 'perfume, spice, tannin and brilliant colour'. The vines' yields are very low, averaging only 5 tonnes per hectare, and the wine is matured for 15 to 18 months in all-new French oak barriques. The 2000 vintage (★★★★★) is powerful and intense, but slightly more elegant than earlier releases and more approachable in its youth. Boldly coloured but not opaque, it is beautifully fragrant and supple, with deep cassis, plum and spice flavours, very fresh and vibrant, sweet-fruit characters and finely balanced tannins. It needs less cellaring time than past vintages; open 2004+. There is no 2001.

Vintage	02	01	00	99	98	97	96	95
WR	7	NM	7	NM	7	NM	NM	7
Drink	03-12	NM	03-10	NM	03-10	NM	NM	03-08

DRY $90 AV

Fenton The Red ★★★☆

This is the second-tier red from Fenton Estate, on Waiheke Island. The 2000 vintage (★★★☆) is a blend of Bordeaux varieties – Cabernet Sauvignon, Merlot and Cabernet Franc – matured in a mix of seasoned French and new American oak casks. It's a full-coloured wine with satisfying weight, firm tannins and red-berry and spice flavours showing very good depth.

Vintage	01	00
WR	5	5
Drink	03+	P

DRY $30-V

Glenmark Waipara Red ★★☆

This North Canterbury red is typically crisp, berryish and leafy. The 2001 vintage (★★☆) is a blend of Cabernet Sauvignon (70 per cent), Merlot, Cabernet Franc and Pinot Noir. Fullish in colour, it's fruity, plummy and smooth, with distinctly herbaceous aromas and flavours. You could call it an 'old-style New Zealand red', but it has a certain gutsy, flavoursome appeal.

DRY $18 -V

Glover's Lionheart (★★★☆)

Deeply coloured, the 2001 vintage (★★★☆) of this Nelson red is youthful, with strong, plummy, peppery flavours, a hint of dark chocolate and a firm tannin grip. It shows a slight lack of warmth and softness, but also good depth and complexity and should develop well.

DRY $40 -V

Harrier Rise Bigney Coigne ★★★★

If you like Bordeaux, you'll love the 2000 vintage (★★★★☆). A Kumeu, West Auckland blend of Merlot (60 per cent) and Cabernet Franc, it was matured for a year in French oak casks (30 per cent new). A floral, fleshy and sensuous wine, it's still unfolding, with sweet-fruit delights, an abundance of plummy, berryish flavour and good backbone. From 'the best vintage since 1993', this is Tim Harris' finest red yet.

Vintage	00	99
WR	7	6
Drink	03-08	03-06

DRY $35 -V

Harrier Rise Monza ★★★★

Kumeu-grown, the 2000 vintage (★★★★) is based almost entirely on Cabernet Franc, with a splash (4.5 per cent) of Merlot. Matured for nine months in French and American oak casks (20 per cent new), it's a vibrantly fruity red with the geniality of Cabernet Franc, but also a firm underlay of tannin. It offers strong blackcurrant and spice flavours, with savoury, nutty complexities adding interest.

Vintage	00
WR	7
Drink	03-08

DRY $28 AV

Harrier Rise Uppercase ★★★

A characterful West Auckland red, previously based on Merlot. The 2000 vintage (★★★), the first to include Cabernet Franc (16 per cent) in the blend, is gamey, spicy, earthy and leathery, with a firm underlay of tannin. It tastes ready. The 2001 (★★☆) clearly reflects the challenging season. Made principally from Cabernet Franc (60 per cent), blended with Merlot (32 per cent) and Cabernet Sauvignon (8 per cent), it was matured for 10 months in new and seasoned French oak barriques. Lightish in colour, it lacks real fruit sweetness and concentration, but shows some coffee and spice complexity, with a firm finish. Ready.

DRY $18 AV

Hatton Estate Gimblett Road Tahi (★★★★)

Tahi (Maori for 'number one') is a Bordeaux-style red, grown in Gimblett Road, Hawke's Bay. The 1998 vintage (★★★★), based principally (75 per cent) on Cabernet Sauvignon and matured for up to 18 months in all-new French and American oak barriques, is a powerfully wooded wine, dark, concentrated, nutty and firm. The more supple 2000 (★★★★) has a stronger Merlot (33 per cent) and Cabernet Franc (17 per cent) influence, with 50 per cent Cabernet Sauvignon. It's an oaky, plummy, spicy wine with good intensity and slightly chewy tannins; open 2003–04.

Vintage	00	99	98
WR	7	NM	6
Drink	03-10	NM	03-08

DRY $70 -V

Kim Crawford Tane ★★★★

This Hawke's Bay blend of Merlot and Cabernet Franc is typically dark and bold, with a perfumed bouquet and lush, concentrated flavours seasoned with sweet, toasty oak. It's an upfront, delicious style. The 2000 vintage (★★★★), a blend of Merlot (69 per cent) and Cabernet Franc (31 per cent), was matured for 14 months in all-new American oak barriques. The colour is dense and the palate is substantial, soft and rich, with lashings of oak and impressive warmth and concentration.

Vintage	00
WR	6
Drink	06-08

DRY $40 -V

Kumeu River Melba ★★★★

Kumeu River's top claret-style red is named in honour of the company matriarch, Melba Brajkovich. The 2000 vintage (★★★★☆), blended from Merlot (70 per cent) and Malbec (30 per cent) and matured for 20 months in French oak barriques (25 per cent new), is a richly coloured, beautifully fragrant wine with concentrated spice, leather and chocolate characters and warm, ripe tannins. The best Melba yet, it should be long-lived. The 2001 (★★★★) is a worthy successor. From 'an incredibly low-yielding season', it shows good colour depth, ripe-fruit characters and strong berry/plum flavours, with a firm foundation of tannin. There is no 2002 or 2003.

Vintage	03	02	01	00	99	98
WR	NM	NM	6	7	6	6
Drink	NM	NM	04-08	05-10	03-08	03-05

DRY $25 AV

Mad Red (★★★☆)

From the Margrain winery at Martinborough, the 2002 vintage (★★★☆) has promisingly deep, youthful colour. The bouquet is herbaceous; the palate is full and smooth, with strong blackcurrant, plum and herb flavours. It tastes like cool-climate Cabernet Sauvignon to me. Spicy, with oak complexity and moderate tannins, it's already drinking well.

Vintage	02
WR	5
Drink	03-04

DRY $22 AV

Matariki Quintology ★★★★☆

The 2000 vintage (★★★★★), grown in Gimblett Road, Hawke's Bay, is a complex blend of Cabernet Sauvignon (40 per cent), Merlot (24 per cent), Cabernet Franc (20 per cent), Syrah (10 per cent) and Malbec (6 per cent). After a year's maturation in French (principally) and American oak casks, it was blended and then returned to barrels for another eight months. Densely coloured, fragrant, smooth and complex, with a lovely surge of blackcurrant and plum flavours seasoned with cedary oak, it's deliciously drinkable – rich, harmonious and long. The 2001 (★★★★) has full but not dense colour. The bouquet is spicy, earthy, nutty and slightly leafy; the palate is plummy and spicy, firmly structured and complex, with very good complexity in a Bordeaux style with a distinct nod at the Rhône. However, it's less concentrated than the 2000.

Vintage	01	00	99	98	97
WR	6	7	6	7	6
Drink	04-08	03-12	03-05	03-04	03-04

DRY $36 -V

Miller's Serious One (★★★★)

The debut 2000 vintage (★★★★) was grown by Craig Miller (of Miller's Coffee) at his tiny Garden of Dreams vineyard on the Awhitu Peninsula, overlooking Auckland's Manukau Harbour. A blend of Merlot (principally) and Cabernet Franc, matured in one-year-old French oak barriques, it has good colour depth and a fragrant, spicy bouquet. Warm and generous, it's a concentrated wine, already delicious, with mouthfilling body, sweet-fruit characters, strong blackcurrant, spice and dark chocolate flavours and a smooth finish. Only 47 cases were made (sold at Serious Espresso, in Swanson Street). The 2001 vintage was released as Miller's Merlot (see the Merlot section).

Vintage	00
WR	6
Drink	03-07

DRY $60 -V

Mills Reef Elspeth One ★★★★★

Named after Elspeth Preston (mother of winemaker Paddy Preston), who died at the age of 94, two days after the launch of the debut 2000 vintage (★★★★★), this is a highly distinguished Hawke's Bay red. A complex marriage of Merlot (40 per cent), Cabernet Franc, Malbec, Syrah and Cabernet Sauvignon, it's an extremely classy wine, deep and youthful in colour, with densely packed blackcurrant and spice flavours to which the Syrah adds a distinctive twist of black pepper. Fragrant and beautifully structured, with a firm underlay of tannin, it's clearly one of Hawke's Bay's most stylish reds and should reward cellaring for several years. The 2001 (★★★★★) is again unusually complex and complete. Densely coloured, it offers rich blackcurrant, plum and spice flavours, with hints of dark chocolate and leather and lovely harmony, warmth and length.

Vintage 00
WR 7
Drink 03-08

DRY $50 AV

Morton Estate White Label The Mercure ★★★☆

Promisingly full-coloured, the 2000 vintage (★★★★) is a blend of Merlot (principally) and Cabernet Sauvignon, grown in Hawke's Bay and matured for 14 months in French and American oak casks. Full of character, it's a rich, mouthfilling (14 per cent alcohol) and smooth wine with ripe berry and spice flavours and savoury, earthy touches adding complexity. The 2001 (★★★) is fullish in colour, berryish and smooth, with a sweet oak influence and moderately firm tannins. It's a lighter style than the 2000, with blackcurrant and plum characters and some complexity.

Vintage 01 00
WR 6 6
Drink 03-06 03-05

DRY $19 V+

Muddy Water Waipara Laborare ★★★

The 2000 vintage (★★☆) is a North Canterbury blend of Pinotage, Cabernet Sauvignon, Cabernet Franc and Merlot. Lightly coloured, with the distinctive, slightly meaty bouquet of Pinotage, it's a smooth, savoury wine, more flavoursome than its colour suggests, with some fruit sweetness and a slightly crisp finish.

Vintage 01 00 99 98
WR 5 5 5 6
Drink 03-05 P P P

DRY $20 -V

Nobilo Fernleaf Vintage Red ★☆

The 2001 vintage (★) is light and charmless. The 2002 (★★), not oak-aged, is a North Island blend of Pinotage (principally) and Cabernet Sauvignon, made in a 'soft, accessible, fruity style'. It's a ruby-hued wine, fruity and simple, with plummy, berryish flavours and a very smooth finish.

Vintage 02 01
WR 5 6
Drink 03-05 03-04

DRY $11 -V

Obsidian ★★★★

The Obsidian vineyard at Onetangi is the source of one of the finest Cabernet Sauvignon and Merlot blends on Waiheke Island. Matured in French and American oak barriques (two-thirds new), the 2000 vintage (★★★★) was made from Cabernet Sauvignon (63 per cent) and Merlot (30 per cent), with a splash of Cabernet Franc and Malbec. Already a pleasure to drink, with excellent harmony, it's a distinctly Bordeaux-like wine with a moderate level of alcohol (12.5 per cent), ripe tannins and impressive depth of blackcurrant, plum and green-leaf flavours, seasoned with spicy oak.

Vintage	00	99	98	97
WR	7	6	6	5
Drink	04-10	03-08	03-06	03-04

DRY $49 -V

Olssen's of Bannockburn Robert The Bruce (★★★★)

The densely coloured, soft, rich 2001 vintage (★★★★) is a Central Otago blend of Pinotage (40 per cent), Syrah (40 per cent) and Cabernet Sauvignon (20 per cent). Showing good texture, concentration and length, it has a strong surge of plummy, spicy flavours, with sweet, ripe-fruit characters, integrated oak and fine tannins.

DRY $28 AV

Passage Rock Forte ★★★★☆

The 2000 vintage (★★★★★) is a highly impressive Waiheke Island red, dark, mouthfilling and supple, with excellent depth of warm, ripe blackcurrant, plum and spice flavours and a firm backbone of tannin. The 2002 (★★★★) is a blend of Merlot (40 per cent), Cabernet Sauvignon (30 per cent), Cabernet Franc (20 per cent) and Malbec (10 per cent), matured in French and American oak casks (30 per cent new). Boldly coloured, it is rich, plummy and spicy, with the herbal character of Cabernet Sauvignon, but also impressive intensity and complexity and a firm tannin grip. Open 2005+.

DRY $35 AV

Passage Rock Sisters ★★★

Labelled as 'our earlier drinking style of Bordeaux wine', the 2002 vintage (★★★) is a gutsy Waiheke Island blend of Cabernet Sauvignon (predominantly), Cabernet Franc, Merlot and Malbec, matured for a year in oak casks (35 per cent new). It's a slightly herbaceous wine, full-coloured, with mouthfilling body, oak complexity and firm blackcurrant, plum and green-leaf flavours. The 2001 (★★★☆), which includes 25 per cent Sangiovese (grown at Matakana), is robust (14.4 per cent alcohol) and flavour-packed, with cassis, plum, spice and green-leaf characters and a firm tannin grip.

Vintage	01
WR	5
Drink	03-09

DRY $27 -V

Pegasus Bay Maestro ★★★★★

The 1998 (★★★★★) and 1996 vintages (★★★★★) rank as the finest claret-style reds yet from Canterbury. Re-tasted in 2003, the 1998 has a complex bouquet of cigar-box, spice and chocolate and a very powerful palate, concentrated, savoury and firm. Grown at Waipara and matured for 18 months in French oak barriques (40 per cent new), the 2001 (★★★★★) is a blend of Merlot and Malbec, with 5 per cent Cabernet Sauvignon. The colour is bold and bright; the palate fleshy, with deep, warm plum and spice flavours that build across the palate to a firm, resounding finish.

Vintage	01
WR	7
Drink	04-06

DRY $40 AV

Peninsula Estate Hauraki ★★★★

In the past labelled as a Cabernet Sauvignon/Merlot, this Waiheke red is typically robust, complex and firmly structured, but less opulent and sweet-fruited than the island's most famous wines. The 1998 vintage (★★★★) French oak-aged for 18 months, was blended from Cabernet Sauvignon (62 per cent), Merlot (20 per cent), Cabernet Franc (14 per cent) and Malbec (4 per cent). It's a substantial, brambly, spicy red showing good complexity and concentration.

Vintage	98	97
WR	7	5
Drink	03-08	03-10

DRY $45 -V

Pleiades Vineyard Maia ★★★★☆

Grown in the Waihopai Valley of Marlborough, this is a consistently impressive red. The 2001 vintage (★★★★★), the finest yet, is a blend of Malbec (55 per cent) and Merlot (45 per cent), matured in half new, half one-year-old oak casks. The colour is bold purple/black; the palate is very warm and concentrated, plummy, spicy and nutty. Already delicious, with a seductively soft finish, it offers great drinking now and during the next several years. If you like full-on reds, this is for you.

Vintage	01	00	99	98
WR	6	6	5	6
Drink	04-07	03-08	03-05	03-08

DRY $31 AV

Providence ★★★★★

This is New Zealand's most expensive wine, sold in a dozen overseas markets but rarely seen here. The 2.5-hectare vineyard at Matakana is close-planted in Merlot (principally), Cabernet Franc and Malbec, and the wine is matured for up to two years in all-new French oak barriques. With its beguiling fragrance, lush fruitiness and sweet, silky, sustained finish, the 1993 stood up well against the other (and cheaper) top Auckland reds of the vintage, but did not overshadow them. The 1998 vintage (★★★★★) is a perfumed and graceful red that impresses not with sheer power, but with its harmony, complexity and silky elegance. If you're a Bordeaux fan, you'll love it.

DRY $185 -V

Red Rock Gravel Pit Red (★★★★)

From Capricorn Wine Estates, a division of Craggy Range, the gutsy 2001 vintage (★★★★) is a flavour-packed Hawke's Bay blend of Malbec and Merlot. The colour is bold and purple-flushed; the palate is muscular and tannic, with concentrated, brambly, plummy, spicy flavours and a firm finish.

DRY $20 V+

Richmond Plains Escapade (★★☆)

Grown organically in Nelson, the 2000 vintage (★★☆) is a single-vineyard blend of Domina (a German variety), Cabernet Sauvignon, Cabernet Franc, Syrah, Merlot and Malbec. Matured in new French oak puncheons, it's a full-coloured wine with a slightly rustic bouquet. It's a reasonably flavoursome wine, but green-edged, and lacks real ripeness and warmth.

DRY $25 -V

Rippon Jeunesse (★★★)

Based on young vines ('jeunesse' is French for youthful) at Lake Wanaka, the debut 2001 vintage (★★★) is an attractive Central Otago red, ruby-hued, fresh and buoyantly fruity, with ripe raspberry and spice flavours and gentle tannins. Ready.

DRY $30 -V

Solstone Petit Rouge (★★☆)

A decent quaffer, the 2001 vintage (★★☆) is a Wairarapa blend of Cabernet Sauvignon, Cabernet Franc, Malbec and Merlot. Lightly oaked, it is fullish in colour, with fresh plum, green-leaf and spice flavours in a medium-bodied style with a slight lack of softness and warmth.

Vintage 01
WR 5
Drink 03-05

DRY $16 -V

Solstone Quartet (★★★)

The sturdy, honest 2001 vintage (★★★) is a Wairarapa blend of four Bordeaux varieties – Cabernet Sauvignon, Cabernet Franc, Merlot and Malbec. French oak-aged for over a year, it is full-coloured, with plenty of plummy, slightly leafy flavour and balanced tannins. Ready.

Vintage 01
WR 6
Drink 03-08

DRY $25 -V

Stonecroft Crofters ★★★☆

The Hawke's Bay winery's lower-priced red is made from fruit off young vines, together with wine which, at blending, winemaker Alan Limmer prefers to omit from his top Ruhanui label. Each release is numbered rather than vintage-dated. Crofters V (★★★) is a blend of Syrah (40 per cent), Cabernet Sauvignon (38 per cent) and Merlot (22 per cent), matured for 18 months in French oak barriques (40 per cent new). Medium-full in colour, with spice and black pepper aromas, it has berryish, green-edged flavours, some savoury, spicy complexity and a firm tannin grip.

DRY $19 V+

Stonecroft Ruhanui ★★★★☆

Ruhanui is a blend of Cabernet Sauvignon, Syrah and Merlot, grown in the stony soils of Mere Road, near Hastings. (Opened in 2002, the 1991 vintage, labelled Cabernet/Merlot, was richly coloured, brambly and spicy in a powerful Bordeaux style, savoury, complex and firm.) French oak-aged, the 2001 vintage (★★★☆) is based principally on Cabernet Sauvignon (43 per cent) and Merlot (40 per cent), with 17 per cent Syrah. Full but not dense in colour, with a spicy bouquet, it offers firm, tautly structured, plum and black pepper flavours, with a slightly high-acid finish. It lacks the generosity and warmth of a top year, but shows very good depth.

Vintage 01 00 99 98 97
WR 6 5 6 6 NM
Drink 04-10 03-10 03-10 03-10 NM

DRY $30 AV

Te Awa Farm Boundary ★★★★★

This is typically a Hawke's Bay red of rare breed. Grown at the Lawson family's vineyard near Gimblett Road, it is made by Jenny Dobson, who was once *maitre d'chais* at a well-respected Haut-Médoc *cru bourgeois*, Château Senejac. Subtle, multi-faceted and beautifully harmonious, it is more complex and savoury than most New Zealand reds. The 2000 (★★★★☆) is a blend of Merlot (85 per cent), Cabernet Sauvignon (11 per cent) and Cabernet Franc (4 per cent), matured for 18 months in French oak barriques (30 per cent new). Deeply coloured, it's a fleshy, generous wine with rich, plummy flavours, sweet-fruit characters, spicy, savoury, earthy touches adding complexity and a firm tannin grip. It's still youthful; open 2004+.

Vintage 00 99 98 97 96 95
WR 7 6 7 6 6 6
Drink 03-08 03-06 03-05 P 03-04 03-04

DRY $50 AV

Te Mania Three Brothers ★★★

The richly coloured 2002 vintage (★★★) is a blend of Merlot, Malbec and Cabernet Sauvignon, grown in Nelson, Marlborough and Hawke's Bay. Barrel-aged for 10 months, it has blackcurrant and plum flavours, with subtle oak and a cool-climate freshness. Smooth and flavoursome, it's a moderately complex style.

Vintage	02	01
WR	6	6
Drink	04-07	03-06

DRY $20 AV

Te Whare Ra Sarah Jennings ★★★

For the first time in 2002 (★★★), the principal variety in this Marlborough red is Cabernet Franc (38 per cent), with smaller amounts of Malbec (28 per cent), Merlot (26 per cent) and Cabernet Sauvignon (8 per cent). Estate-grown at Renwick, it's a deeply coloured, purple-flushed wine with berry and spice aromas and a vibrantly fruity palate with cool-climate freshness, moderately ripe flavours and gentle tannins.

Vintage	03	02	01	00
WR	NM	6	6	5
Drink	NM	06-10	05-12	05-10

DRY $22 -V

Te Whau The Point ★★★★★

This very classy Waiheke Island red flows from the steeply sloping Te Whau vineyard at Putiki Bay. Re-tasted in late 2003, the totally satisfying 2000 vintage (★★★★★) is distinctly Bordeaux-like, with an array of cassis, spice, herb and nut flavours and savoury, earthy characters adding complexity. The highly characterful 2002 (★★★★★) is a Merlot-dominant blend (50 per cent), with Cabernet Sauvignon (25 per cent), Cabernet Franc (15 per cent) and Malbec (10 per cent). Matured for 15 months in French oak barriques (30 per cent new), it's distinctly Merlot-ish – plummy, spicy, earthy and savoury, with sweet, ripe-fruit characters, firm, balanced tannins and notable complexity.

Vintage	02	01	00	99
WR	7	NM	6	7
Drink	04-08	NM	03-07	03-06

DRY $39 AV

Tom ★★★★★

Montana's super-premium red, launched from the 1995 vintage (★★★★★), honours pioneer winemaker Tom McDonald, the driving force behind New Zealand's first prestige red, McWilliam's Cabernet Sauvignon. The 1998 vintage (★★★★★), grown principally in the company's McDonald Estate vineyard at Moteo, in the lower Dartmoor Valley, Hawke's Bay, is a blend of Merlot (50 per cent), Cabernet Sauvignon (28 per cent) and Cabernet Franc (22 per cent), matured for 18 months in all-new French oak barriques. Densely coloured and perfumed, with a lovely array of blackcurrant, spice, nut and dark chocolate flavours, concentrated and firm, it's a more intense and tightly structured wine than the 1995, which is now savoury and mellow. I have never tasted the 1996 – people I know who have were not wildly excited – and there is no Tom from 1997 and 1999, but the 1998 is clearly one of New Zealand's greatest claret-style reds. You can drink it with great pleasure now, but it won't reach its peak for several years. The 2000 vintage is currently in the wings.

Vintage	00	99	98
WR	7	NM	7
Drink	04-15	NM	03+

DRY $99 AV

BRANDED AND OTHER REDS 265

TW Makauri (★★★★)

The vibrantly fruity 2002 vintage (★★★★) is a blend of Malbec (two-thirds) and Merlot, named after the Makauri district in Gisborne. Purple-flushed, with a sweet oak perfume, it's a ripe-tasting wine with rich berry, plum and dark chocolate flavours, firm tannins and substantial body.

DRY $27 AV

Unison ★★★★★

Husband and wife team, Bruce and Anna-Barbara Helliwell, own a block of densely planted vines in an old river bed near Hastings. A blend of Merlot, Cabernet Sauvignon and Syrah, matured for a year in large, 3000-litre Italian oak casks and 225-litre oak barriques, it is typically boldly coloured and highly concentrated, with rich flavours of cassis, plum and spice and a long, firm finish. The 2002 (★★★★★) is described by the Helliwells as 'the most exciting and rewarding vintage we have ever had'. Boldly coloured, it has the distinctive bouquet of cassis, black pepper and slight earthiness, so typical of the label. The palate is weighty, warm and multi-faceted, with deep plum, spice and dark chocolate flavours and noble tannins. Already delicious, it's a great cellaring prospect.

Vintage	02	01	00	99	98	97	96
WR	7	6	7	6	6	6	6
Drink	04-12	03-09	03-08	03-08	03-08	03-06	03-06

DRY $28 V+

Unison Selection ★★★★★

Designed for cellaring and oak-matured longer than the above wine, this is a consistently outstanding Hawke's Bay red. The 2000 vintage (★★★★★) is a vineyard (rather than barrel) selection of Merlot, Cabernet Sauvignon and Syrah, matured initially for a year in French and American oak barriques (half new), then (for 'harmonising') for a further eight months in large Italian casks of French and Slavonian oak. Deep and youthful in colour, warm and tightly structured, it offers rich blackcurrant, plum and spice flavours, with ripe, chewy tannins and a very persistent finish. The 2001 (★★★★☆) is boldly coloured, with a complex, peppery, earthy bouquet. It's a very generous and complex wine, full of character, but compared to the finest vintages, shows a slight lack of softness on the finish.

Vintage	01	00	99	98	97
WR	6	7	6	6	6
Drink	03-13	03-13	03-10	03-10	03-07

DRY $44 AV

Vin Alto Celaio (★★★☆)

Only made in top vintages, this Clevedon, South Auckland red is a reserve version of Di Sotto (see below). The 1998 vintage (★★★☆) is a blend of Sangiovese, Cabernet Franc, Merlot and Montepulciano, oak-aged for two years. Fullish in colour, with some development showing, it has a savoury, herbal, spicy bouquet. Full-bodied, spicy and mellow, with evidence of lengthy barrel-aging, it shows lots of character, while being well outside the New Zealand mainstream, in terms of style. Drink now.

Vintage	98
WR	6
Drink	03-09

DRY $38 -V

Vin Alto Di Sotto ★★★☆

This Clevedon, South Auckland red was previously labelled as Ordinario. The 1998 vintage (★★★) is a blend of Cabernet Franc, Cabernet Sauvignon, Merlot, Sangiovese and a touch of Nebbiolo. Oak-aged for a year, it is fullish and mature in colour, with a leathery, spicy bouquet. Mellow and flavoursome, spicy and slightly herbal, it's a characterful wine with a firm, slightly chewy finish. Ready.

Vintage 98
WR 5
Drink 03-07

DRY $29 -V

Vin Alto Retico ★★★★

In hill country at Clevedon, in South Auckland, Enzo Bettio has set out 'to make traditional Italian-style wines in New Zealand'. His most prized wine, Retico, based on air-dried, highly concentrated grapes, is Clevedon's equivalent of the prized *amarones* of Verona. Based on Italian (70 per cent) and French grape varieties, the 1998 vintage (★★★★) is tawny-hued, with very leathery, nutty, spicy, raisiny, almost porty flavours. A muscular wine with a touch of residual sugar, it's best served at the end of a meal, 'with cheese, in front of the fire'.

DRY $89 -V

Vin Alto Ritorno ★★★★

Created in the Veronese *ripasso* tradition, the 1998 vintage (★★★★) was grown at Clevedon in South Auckland. A blend of Italian (70 per cent) and French grape varieties, fermented on the skins of the air-dried Retico grapes (above), it is full in colour, with a bouquet of leather and spice. The palate is substantial (14.5 per cent alcohol), lively and complex, with sweet-fruit characters and strong, plummy, spicy flavours, braced by firm tannins. It's a much more conventional style (to Kiwi palates) than Retico, and drinking well now.

DRY $65 -V

Waimarie Testament ★★★

The 2000 vintage (★★★) is a Kumeu, West Auckland blend of Cabernet Sauvignon (92 per cent) and Cabernet Franc, matured for 20 months in a 50/50 split of American and French oak barriques, all new. Garnet in colour, with a hint of development, it's a full-flavoured wine with sweet-fruit characters and some savoury, spicy complexity. The 2001 (★★★) is a Hawke's Bay red, matured for 19 months in new and one-year-old French oak casks. A Dartmoor Valley blend of Merlot (65 per cent) and Malbec, it's a smooth, middleweight wine with plum, raspberry and spice flavours and gentle tannins.

Vintage 01
WR 6
Drink 04-08

DRY $28 -V

Waipara West Ram Paddock Red ★★★

Blended from Cabernet Sauvignon (45 per cent), Cabernet Franc (45 per cent) and Merlot (10 per cent), the 2001 vintage (★★★) of this North Canterbury red is richly coloured, with a slightly herbaceous bouquet. A fresh, vibrantly fruity wine with strong blackcurrant and plum flavours seasoned with French oak, it needs a bit more time; open mid-2004+.

DRY $21 -V

Cabernet Franc

Cabernet Franc is New Zealand's fourth most common red-wine variety, although its plantings are much smaller than those of the big three: Pinot Noir, Merlot and Cabernet Sauvignon. Cabernet Franc is probably a mutation of Cabernet Sauvignon, the much higher-profile variety with which it is so often blended. Jancis Robinson's phrase, 'a sort of claret Beaujolais', aptly sums up the nature of this versatile and underrated red-wine grape.

As a minority ingredient in the recipe of many of New Zealand's top reds, Cabernet Franc lends a delicious softness and concentrated fruitiness to its blends with Cabernet Sauvignon and Merlot. However, admirers of Château Cheval Blanc, the illustrious St Émilion (which is two-thirds planted in Cabernet Franc) have long appreciated that Cabernet Franc need not always be Cabernet Sauvignon's bridesmaid, but can yield fine red wines in its own right. The supple, fruity wines of Chinon and Bourgueil, in the Loire Valley, have also proved Cabernet Franc's ability to produce highly attractive, soft light reds.

The 2002 national vineyard survey predicted the bearing area of Cabernet Franc will rise from 121 to 202 hectares between 2000 and 2005. Almost 70 per cent of the vines are in Hawke's Bay. As a varietal red, Cabernet Franc is lower in tannin and acid than Cabernet Sauvignon; or as Michael Brajkovich of Kumeu River puts it: 'more approachable and easy'.

Alexander Vineyard Reserve Cabernet Franc (★★★★)

Well worth cellaring, the 2001 vintage (★★★★) of this Martinborough red was low-cropped (under 4 tonnes/hectare) and matured in French oak barriques (30 per cent new). Full-coloured, with fresh, red-berry aromas, it has strong, ripe, plummy, spicy flavours, oak complexity and a tight finish.

DRY $28 AV

Clearview Estate Reserve Cabernet Franc ★★★★★

Te Awanga winemaker Tim Turvey produces a bold Cabernet Franc – one of the most powerful in the country. The 2000 vintage (★★★★★), which includes 5 per cent Cabernet Sauvignon and 5 per cent Merlot, was matured for 14 months in new oak barrels – 85 per cent French and 15 per cent American – and bottled without filtering. Deeply coloured, it's a very generous red, mouthfilling, plummy and spicy, with nutty, leathery, savoury complexities and a seductively smooth finish.

DRY $35 AV

Crab Farm Cabernet Franc ★★★

The 2000 vintage (★★★) was matured for 18 months in French and American oak casks. The colour is full and youthful; the palate is berryish, plummy and slightly earthy, with integrated oak and a slightly crisp finish.

DRY $22 -V

Inverness Estate Cabernet Franc ★★★

A very good debut, the 1999 vintage Reserve Cabernet Franc (★★★☆) was grown at Clevedon, in South Auckland, and made by Anthony Ivicevich at the West Brook winery. French oak-aged, with the spicy, earthy bouquet characteristic of Auckland reds, it's a slightly Bordeaux-like wine, warm, spicy and savoury, with some complexity and supple tannins. The 2001 (★★☆), not labelled Reserve, is lightish in colour, with some development showing. A middleweight red, it lacks real ripeness and stuffing, reflecting the difficult season, but has some mellow, earthy appeal, with slightly chewy tannins. Drink now.

DRY $27 -V

Judge Valley Cottage Block Cabernet Franc/Merlot/Malbec ★★★★

Well worth discovering, this rare wine is grown at Puahue, midway between Cambridge and Te Awamutu, in central Waikato. The youthful, exuberantly fruity 2002 vintage (★★★★) is promisingly dark, with a fragrant, spicy bouquet. On the palate, there's loads of ripe, brambly, spicy fruit flavour, seasoned with French oak, to which the Malbec adds a distinctly gamey element. Enjoyable now, with moderate tannins, it should be at its best around 2005.

DRY $54 -V

Kim Crawford Wicken Vineyard Hawke's Bay Cabernet Franc ★★★

Grown in the Wicken vineyard in Omahu Road, on the edge of the Gimblett Gravels area, the 2001 vintage (★★★) has an enticing bouquet, with toasty oak aromas. It has some fruit sweetness, with good depth of berryish, spicy flavours, but the finish is slightly green.

DRY $30 -V

Lucknow Estate Cabernets/Merlot (★★☆)

The 2002 vintage (★★☆) is a full-coloured blend of Cabernet Franc (60 per cent), Merlot (30 per cent) and Cabernet Sauvignon (10 per cent), grown in Hawke's Bay and matured for five months in seasoned oak casks. It's a vibrantly fruity wine with raspberry and plum flavours and a fresh, crisp finish.

DRY $16 -V

Matakana Estate Cabernet Franc/Cabernet Sauvignon/Malbec/Merlot (★★★)

The 2000 vintage (★★★) has medium-full colour, showing some development. It's a gutsy wine, slightly herbaceous, but offers plenty of blackcurrant, spice and green-leaf flavour, with some savoury complexity.

DRY $32 -V

Mills Reef Elsepth Cabernet Franc (★★★★)

The notably concentrated 2000 vintage (★★★★) was grown in Mere Road, on the edge of the Gimblett Gravels district in Hawke's Bay, and French oak-matured for 18 months. Richly coloured, with a perfumed, floral bouquet of raspberries and cedary oak, it's a serious, firmly structured red with deep, spicy, berryish flavours, fresh acidity and chewy tannins. It's a very intense wine, but slightly lacks softness and warmth.

Vintage 00
WR 7
Drink 03-05

DRY $40 -V

Mission Reserve Cabernet Franc ★★★★

The 2000 vintage (★★★★) is a dark, rich wine with fragrant, berryish aromas seasoned with quality French oak (40 per cent new). The slightly lighter 2002 (★★★☆), estate-grown at Greenmeadows, in Hawke's Bay, shows spicy, earthy, Bordeaux-like characters and good complexity. Drink now or cellar.

Vintage	02	01	00	99	98
WR	6	NM	5	6	6
Drink	04-08	NM	03-05	03-05	03-04

DRY $25 AV

Moana Park Cabernet Franc (★★★)

Fresh and vibrantly fruity, the 2001 vintage (★★★) was grown in the Dartmoor Valley of Hawke's Bay. Deeply coloured, with perfumed, sweet oak aromas, it's a plummy, spicy, green-edged wine with slightly high acidity but also some complexity and plenty of flavour.

DRY $24 -V

Murdoch James Cabernet Franc ★★★

The 2001 vintage (★★★☆) of this Martinborough red is the best yet. Richly coloured, with strong raspberry, herb and plum flavours, seasoned with spicy, nutty oak, it's a distinctly cool-climate style, fresh and crisp, with good intensity and some cellaring potential. The 2002 (★★★) was harvested at over 23 brix and matured in French oak barriques (30 per cent new). Deeply coloured, with green-leaf aromas, it offers strong blackcurrant, herb and mint flavours, but lacks real ripeness, with a slightly high-acid finish.

Vintage	01	00
WR	6	6
Drink	04-08	04-07

DRY $30 -V

Solstone Cabernet Franc Reserve (★★★☆)

The 2000 vintage (★★★☆) of this Wairarapa red was matured for 16 months in French oak barriques. It's a firm, mouthfilling, slightly herbal wine with fresh, strong, plum/spice flavours seasoned with quality oak and good length.

Vintage	00
WR	6
Drink	03-07

DRY $40 -V

Voss Waihenga
Cabernet Franc/Syrah/Cabernet Sauvignon ★★★☆

Estate-grown in Martinborough (Waihenga), this is one of the district's most convincing claret-style reds, although the blending of about 20 per cent Syrah with Cabernet Franc and Cabernet Sauvignon reduces any comparison with traditional 'claret'. French and American oak-aged for over a year, it is typically richly coloured, with concentrated red-berry, spice and mint flavours, oak complexity and a solid backbone of tannin.

Vintage	02	01	00	99	98	97	96
WR	5	6	5	6	6	4	7
Drink	04-07	04-07	03-05	03-04	03-04	P	P

DRY $28 -V

West Brook Cabernet Franc/Merlot/Shiraz ★★★

The 2001 vintage (★★★), grown 'predominantly' in Auckland, is fullish in colour, with a distinctly spicy, peppery bouquet. It offers decent depth of moderately ripe plum/pepper flavours, to which the Shiraz makes a clear contribution, with a firm tannin grip.

DRY $19 AV

Cabernet Sauvignon and Cabernet-predominant Blends

Cabernet Sauvignon has proved a tough nut to crack in New Zealand. Mid-priced New Zealand Cabernet Sauvignon is typically of lower quality than a comparable offering from Australia, where the relative warmth suits the late-ripening Cabernet Sauvignon variety. Yet a top New Zealand Cabernet-based red from a favourable vintage can hold its own in all but the most illustrious company.

At a tasting by top wine writers and sommeliers of some of the 30,000 wines on display at Vinexpo 2003 in Bordeaux, Te Mata Estate Coleraine Cabernet/Merlot 2000 was voted the second best red, behind a super-Tuscan, Testa Matta 2001, and ahead of Poeira 2001, from the Duoro Valley of Portugal, in third place. (Only one of the top ten wines, white and red, was French.)

Cabernet Sauvignon was first planted here in the nineteenth century. By the 1890s, this most famous variety of red Bordeaux was well-respected throughout the colony. The modern resurgence of interest in Cabernet Sauvignon's potential was led by Tom McDonald, the legendary Hawke's Bay winemaker, whose string of elegant (though, by today's standards, light) Cabernet Sauvignons under the McWilliam's label, from the much-acclaimed 1965 vintage to the gold-medal winning 1975, proved beyond all doubt that fine-quality red wines could be produced in New Zealand. With the growing selection of fine claret-style reds that has emerged from the region in the past 20 years, Hawke's Bay has established itself as the country's major source of Cabernet-based reds.

A decade ago, Cabernet Sauvignon ruled the red-wine roost in New Zealand. Since then, it has been pushed slightly out of the limelight by Pinot Noir and Merlot. Winemakers are searching for red-wine varieties that will ripen more fully and consistently than Cabernet Sauvignon in our cool growing environment. Between 2000 and 2005, the country's total area of bearing Cabernet Sauvignon vines will grow from 671 to 779 hectares. During the same period, Pinot Noir plantings will skyrocket from 1126 to 3282 hectares and Merlot plantings will surge from 674 to 1433 hectares.

Only in Hawke's Bay (where nearly 70 per cent of the vines are clustered) is Cabernet Sauvignon expanding significantly. In Marlborough, where most of the Cabernet-based reds have lacked warmth and richness, during the past decade Cabernet Sauvignon plantings have nose-dived. This magnificent, late-ripening variety's future in New Zealand clearly lies in the warmer vineyard sites of the north.

What is the flavour of Cabernet Sauvignon? When newly fermented a herbal character is common, intertwined with blackcurrant-like fruit aromas. New oak flavours, firm acidity and taut tannins are other hallmarks of young, fine Cabernet Sauvignon. With maturity the flavour loses its aggression and the wine develops roundness and complexity, with assorted cigar-box, minty and floral scents emerging. It is infanticide to broach a Cabernet Sauvignon-based red with any pretensions to quality at less than three years old; at about five years old the rewards of cellaring really start to flow.

Alexander Vineyard Reserve Cabernet/Merlot (★★★★☆)

The 2001 vintage (★★★★☆) is one of the best claret-style reds yet from Martinborough. Made from low-cropped vines (under 4 tonnes per hectare), it is densely coloured, supple, and crammed with cassis, plum and spice flavours. A 4:1 blend of Cabernet Sauvignon and Merlot, it is entirely free of herbaceous characters, with hints of dark chocolate, cedary French oak and a resounding finish.

DRY $34 AV

Archipelago Waiheke Cabernets (★★★)

From Miro Vineyard, on Waiheke Island, the 2000 vintage (★★★) is a decent red with full colour, showing some development. Flavoursome, spicy, slightly herbaceous and earthy, it's ready for drinking.

DRY $22 -V

Ashwell Cabernet/Merlot ★★★☆

The 2001 vintage (★★★☆) of this Martinborough red is a full-coloured blend of Cabernet Sauvignon (70 per cent), Cabernet Franc (20 per cent) and Merlot (10 per cent), matured in French oak casks for 18 months. Smooth and rich, with sweet, ripe-fruit characters, blackcurrant and plum flavours and gentle tannins, it's a moderately complex style, for drinking now onwards.

Vintage 01
WR 6
Drink 03-06

DRY $29 -V

Askerne Cabernet Sauvignon/Merlot/Malbec/Franc ★★★☆

The 2002 vintage (★★★☆) is a deeply coloured Hawke's Bay red. It's a bit leafy on the nose, but offers strong blackcurrant, plum, spice and herb flavours, with some attractive, savoury notes and good tannin balance. A generous wine with considerable complexity, it's already drinking well.

Vintage 02
WR 6
Drink 04-08

DRY $22 AV

Awarua Terraces Cabernet/Merlot/Franc ★★★

Enjoyable now, the 2001 vintage (★★★) is a blend of Cabernet Sauvignon (40 per cent) with equal portions of Merlot and Cabernet Franc, grown at Mangatahi, in Hawke's Bay, and oak-aged for nine months. Fullish but not dense in colour, with a fragrant, slightly leafy bouquet, it's a flavoursome wine with plum, red-berry and herb characters and some savoury, spicy complexity.

DRY $27 -V

Awarua Terraces Foundation Cabernet Sauvignon/Merlot/Franc (★★★★★)

The beautiful 2000 vintage (★★★★★) is one of the best claret-style reds yet from the inland Mangatahi district, in Hawke's Bay. Grown on a river terrace with red metal soils, it's a blend of Cabernet Sauvignon (45 per cent), Merlot (30 per cent) and Cabernet Franc (25 per cent), oak-aged for a year. Boldly coloured, with a classy, fragrant, spicy bouquet, it shows lovely concentration of vibrant berry, plum and blackcurrant flavours, with well-integrated oak and ripe, supple tannins. Sweet-fruited, with a long finish, it's already delicious, but should mature very gracefully.

DRY $45 AV

Babich Hawke's Bay Cabernet/Merlot ★★☆

Typically a decent quaffer, matured in seasoned American and French oak casks. The 2002 vintage (★★☆), grown at Fernhill, is a slightly herbaceous, middleweight wine, fruity and berryish, with a slightly spicy, smooth finish.

Vintage	02	01	00	99	98
WR	6	6	7	7	7
Drink	03-07	03-05	03-05	03-04	P

DRY $15 AV

Babich Irongate Cabernet/Merlot ★★★★☆

Grown in the Irongate vineyard in Gimblett Road, Hawke's Bay and matured in French oak, this is typically a deeply flavoured, complex and firmly structured red, built to last. The 2000 vintage (★★★★☆) is richly coloured, with a lifted bouquet of blackcurrants, spice and cedary oak. A refined, elegant wine, it's still youthful, with rich, well-ripened blackcurrant/plum flavours overlaid with spicy French oak. A classic claret style with balanced acidity and supple tannins, it should unfold gracefully for several years.

Vintage	01	00	99	98	97	96	95	94
WR	6	7	7	7	6	6	7	6
Drink	03-07	03-07	03-05	03-07	03-06	P	03-04	P

DRY $33 AV

Babich The Patriarch Cabernet Sauvignon ★★★★★

This is Babich's best red, regardless of the variety or vineyard, and only produced in top vintages. All the releases so far, however, have been unblended Cabernet Sauvignons grown in the company's shingly vineyards in Gimblett Road, Hawke's Bay. Dark and lush, with the aromas of blackcurrants and spicy oak, it is typically a seductively warm, ripe and complex red with deliciously rich flavour. The early vintages were American oak-aged, to give The Patriarch a more upfront style than Irongate Cabernet/Merlot, but the wine is now matured in French oak barriques. Built for cellaring, the 2000 vintage (★★★★★) is deeply coloured, robust and concentrated, with warm, ripe blackcurrant, plum and dark chocolate characters, spicy oak, firm tannins and good mouthfeel. There is no 2001.

Vintage	01	00	99	98	97	96	95	94
WR	NM	7	NM	7	NM	7	7	7
Drink	NM	03-10	NM	03-07	NM	03-05	03-05	P

DRY $40 AV

Borthwick Cabernet/Merlot ★★★

The 2001 vintage (★★★☆), grown near Masterton, in the Wairarapa, is a blend of 70 per cent Cabernet Sauvignon and 30 per cent Merlot. Matured in French oak casks (30 per cent new), it's a dark, quite gutsy red with blackcurrant and plum flavours, a distinctly leafy streak, hints of prunes and dark chocolate, and a firm finish.

DRY $20 AV

Brookfields Ohiti Estate Cabernet Sauvignon ★★★

Hawke's Bay winemaker Peter Robertson believes that Ohiti Estate produces 'sound Cabernet Sauvignon year after year – which is a major challenge to any vineyard'. The 2002 vintage (★★★), matured in French oak casks, is a mouthfilling, deeply coloured wine with fresh, vibrant plum, blackcurrant and green-leaf flavours, smooth tannins and good depth.

Vintage	02	01	00	99	98
WR	7	6	7	6	7
Drink	05-08	03-06	03-05	03-05	03-05

DRY $18 AV

Brookfields Reserve Vintage Cabernet/Merlot ★★★★★

Brookfields' 'gold label' Cabernet/Merlot is one of the most powerful and long-lived reds in Hawke's Bay. At its best, it is a thrilling wine – robust, tannin-laden and overflowing with very rich cassis, plum and mint flavours. The grapes are cultivated in an old river bed in Ohiti Road, behind Roys Hill, and the wine is matured for 18 months in French oak barriques (95 per cent new). The muscular 2000 vintage (★★★★★) is based on Cabernet Sauvignon (85 per cent) with minor portions of Merlot and Cabernet Franc. Dark, with a welcoming fragrance of ripe fruit and cedary French oak, it is generous and rounded on the palate, with good extract and gentle acidity in a very warm, spicy and complex style. There is no 2001.

Vintage	01	00	99	98	97	96	95
WR	NM	7	NM	7	7	NM	7
Drink	NM	05-12	NM	03-08+	03-07	NM	03-05

DRY $55 AV

Canadoro Cabernet Sauvignon ★★★

Typically a gutsy, full-flavoured Martinborough red. The 2001 vintage (★★★) is dark, in a high-extract style with strong, crisp plum and blackcurrant flavours with a green edge. It needs cellaring; open 2004+.

Vintage	01	00	99	98	97	96	95
WR	6	6	NM	7	6	5	5
Drink	03-08	03-08	NM	03-10	P	P	P

DRY $30 -V

Church Road Cabernet Sauvignon/Merlot ★★★☆

For sheer drinkability, Montana's high-profile Hawke's Bay wine, produced at the Church Road Winery with technical input from the Bordeaux house of Cordier, is hard to beat. The 2001 vintage (★★★☆) is a blend of Cabernet Sauvignon (45 per cent) and Merlot (44 per cent), with minor parcels of Malbec, Syrah and Cabernet Franc. It was matured for 14 months in French oak barriques (30 per cent new). A mouthfilling wine with concentrated black fruits, complex, nutty characters and a firm tannin structure, it shows the benefits of the low-yielding year, although the finish is green-edged. (The 2002 vintage is a Merlot/Cabernet Sauvignon; see that section.)

Vintage	01	00	99	98	97	96	95	94
WR	6	6	6	7	5	6	7	6
Drink	03+	03+	03+	03-05	P	P	P	P

DRY $22 AV

C.J. Pask Gimblett Road Cabernet/Merlot ★★★★

Made from vines mostly over 15 years old, the 2000 vintage (★★★★) of this Hawke's Bay red is a Cabernet Sauvignon-predominant blend (70 per cent), matured for 14 months in French and American oak casks. It's a richly coloured and fragrant wine with impressive weight, ripeness and flavour depth and a firm, spicy, powerful finish. Well worth cellaring, it's an excellent vintage of this label.

Vintage	00	99	98	97	96	95	94
WR	6	6	7	6	6	7	6
Drink	03-04	03-05	03-05	P	P	P	P

DRY $25 AV

C.J. Pask Roys Hill Cabernet/Merlot ★★★

A 'fruity, soft, easy-drinking' style is the goal for this mid-priced red. It is normally grown in Hawke's Bay, but the 2002 vintage (★★☆) was made from 'East Coast' grapes. Fullish but not deep in colour, it's a fruity, slightly herbaceous wine with moderate depth and a berryish, smooth finish. Not a top vintage of this label.

DRY $16 AV

Clearview Estate Cape Kidnappers Cabernet/Merlot ★★★☆

Grown at Te Awanga, on the Hawke's Bay coast, and matured for 15 months in seasoned oak casks, this is typically a sturdy red with sweet-fruit characters and plenty of savoury, spicy flavour. The 2002 vintage (★★★☆) is deeply coloured, weighty and generous, with strong, smooth blackcurrant and plum flavours and a sweet oak influence. It's an instantly likeable wine, already drinking well.

Vintage 02
WR 6
Drink 03-06

DRY $20 AV

Clearview Reserve Old Olive Block Cabernet Sauvignon/Merlot/Franc ★★★★☆

This Hawke's Bay red is a Cabernet Sauvignon-centred blend, grown in the estate vineyard at Te Awanga, which has a 60-year-old olive tree in the centre. The 2000 vintage (★★★★☆) is a blend of Cabernet Sauvignon (45 per cent), Cabernet Franc (23 per cent), Merlot (20 per cent) and Malbec (12 per cent), matured for 14 months in French (85 per cent) and American oak barriques. The colour is deep and youthful; the palate is generous, fresh and warm, with spicy, complex flavours and slightly chewy tannins. It's approachable now, but best cellared to 2004+.

Vintage 01
WR 5
Drink 04-08

DRY $30 AV

Collards Cabernet/Merlot ★★☆

A pleasantly smooth, fruity, gently oaked quaffer. Grown in Auckland, the Waikato and Hawke's Bay, it's typically a berryish, supple red with soft tannins. The 2001 vintage (★★☆) is a medium-bodied, slightly herbaceous wine with plummy, spicy flavours and gentle tannins. It's an easy-drinking wine, priced right.

Vintage	02	01	00	99	98
WR	6	5	6	6	7
Drink	03-05	03-04	03	P	P

DRY $13 AV

Collards Rothesay Cabernet Sauvignon ★★★

Collards' vineyard at Waimauku in West Auckland yields a characterful wine with strong blackcurrant/spice flavours in good years, but in other vintages it is distinctly herbaceous. The 2000 vintage (★★☆) is fullish in colour, with plenty of blackcurrant/plum flavour seasoned with French oak, but also a leafy bouquet and slight lack of warmth on the finish.

Vintage	01	00	99	98	97	96
WR	7	6	6	7	6	6
Drink	03-05	03-05	03-04	P	P	P

DRY $19 AV

Coopers Creek Hawke's Bay Cabernet Sauvignon/Franc ★★☆

The 2001 (★★☆), a blend of Cabernet Sauvignon (95 per cent) and Cabernet Franc (5 per cent), was grown at Havelock North (principally) and in the Dartmoor Valley. It's a distinctly green-edged wine with red-berry and plum flavours and a crisp finish.

Vintage	01	00	99	98	97
WR	5	6	5	7	NM
Drink	03-05	03-04	P	P	NM

DRY $16 -V

Corbans Cabernet Sauvignon/Merlot (★★☆)

A decent quaffer, the 2002 vintage (★★☆) from Montana is a vibrantly fruity Hawke's Bay red with fresh red-berry and green-leaf flavours. It's a lightly oaked style, flavoursome and smooth.

DRY $14 AV

Corbans Cottage Block Marlborough Cabernet Sauvignon/Merlot (★★★☆)

Released in 2002, the 1996 vintage (★★★☆) is a mature red with a leathery, developed bouquet. A blend of 60 per cent Cabernet Sauvignon and 40 per cent Merlot, it was matured for 18 months in new and one-year-old French and American oak casks. An old-style New Zealand red, with a strongly herbal thread on the palate, it also has good flavour concentration and some fruit sweetness. Overall, however, it shows why Cabernet Sauvignon is no longer a major variety in Marlborough and struggles to justify its high price.

DRY $35 -V

Corbans Private Bin Hawke's Bay Cabernet Sauvignon/Cabernet Franc/Merlot (★★★★)

Re-released in late 2002 with new packaging, the 1998 vintage (★★★★) is richly coloured, with some development showing. A blend of 75 per cent Cabernet Sauvignon, 15 per cent Cabernet Franc and 10 per cent Merlot, matured in French and American oak (new and one-year-old) for 15 months, it's a mature wine with a lifted, plummy, cedary bouquet. Firm and well-structured, with sweet-fruit characters and good flavour concentration, it's drinking well now.

DRY $25 AV

Cornerstone Cabernet/Merlot – see Newton/Forrest Estate
Cornerstone Cabernet/Merlot

Crab Farm Cabernet/Merlot (★★☆)

Described on the label as possessing 'a soft, young, ripe body', the 2001 vintage (★★☆) is a 60/40 blend, grown in Hawke's Bay and oak-aged for 15 months. It's a full-coloured wine, buoyantly fruity, with berryish, plummy flavours, but lacks real warmth, with a slightly high-acid finish.

Vintage	01
WR	4
Drink	P

DRY $22 -V

Crab Farm Cabernet Sauvignon (★★★☆)

The dark 2000 vintage (★★★☆) is superior to its identically priced stablemate (above). A gutsy wine with strong personality, it was grown in Hawke's Bay and oak-matured for 15 months. It offers concentrated, blackcurrant-like flavours with a herbal edge, oak complexity and a firm tannin grip. Worth cellaring.

DRY $22 AV

Crossroads Reserve Cabernet/Merlot ★★★

The 1999 vintage (★☆) of this Hawke's Bay red was grown at Bay View and Fernhill, and matured for 22 months in French and American oak barrels (40 per cent new). It shows good concentration of colour and strong, blackcurrant-like flavours, but has not matured well, now tasting slightly sharp and piquant.

Vintage	99	98	97	96	95	94
WR	6	7	5	6	6	6
Drink	03-04	P	P	P	P	P

DRY $32 -V

Dashwood Marlborough Cabernet Sauvignon (★★☆)

Ripening Cabernet Sauvignon grapes in the Awatere Valley is a battle, as demonstrated by the 2000 vintage (★★☆) from Vavasour. Fullish in colour, with a leafy bouquet, it's a fruity, flavoursome wine but lacks real warmth and generosity, with a slightly high-acid finish.

DRY $19 -V

Delegat's Gimblett Gravels Cabernet Sauvignon/Merlot (★★★★★)

The densely coloured 2000 vintage (★★★★★) is a 3:1 blend, matured for two years in oak barriques, new and one-year-old. Plump, with sweet-fruit characters, it is still fresh and youthful, with beautifully ripe, blackcurrant, plum and spice flavours, good complexity and long, firm tannins. Drink now or cellar. The 2001, tasted prior to bottling (and so not rated), is a more herbaceous style, but still promisingly rich and complex.

DRY $? V?

Delegat's Cabernet/Merlot ★★☆

Two blends were released from the 2001 vintage. One, labelled as Hawke's Bay/Gisborne Cabernet/Merlot (★★☆), is a solid, spicy, flavoursome red, but lacks real warmth and softness. The other, labelled as Hawke's Bay/Marlborough Cabernet/Merlot (★★★), is a blend of Hawke's Bay Cabernet Sauvignon and Marlborough Merlot, matured in old oak casks. It's a more generous and riper wine than its stablemate, with plenty of plummy, spicy flavour.

Vintage	02	01
WR	6	6
Drink	03-05	03-04

DRY $15 AV

Delegat's Reserve Cabernet Sauvignon/Merlot ★★★★

This Hawke's Bay red typically offers good value (up to and including the 2000 vintage, it was a straight Cabernet Sauvignon). The 2001 vintage (★★★★), only 7 per cent Merlot, was matured for a year in new and one-year-old French oak barriques. Densely coloured, oaky and tannic, it's a very youthful wine with concentrated, brambly, spicy, nutty flavours. Tasted from the barrel (and so not rated), the 2002 looked very promising – dark and highly concentrated.

Vintage	02	01	00	99	98	97
WR	6	6	6	6	7	6
Drink	03-05	03-04	P	P	P	P

DRY $20 V+

De Redcliffe Hawke's Bay Estates Cabernet/Malbec (★★☆)

The 2000 vintage (★★☆) is a blend of Cabernet Sauvignon (84 per cent) and Malbec (16 per cent). Full coloured, it's a berryish, plummy, green-edged, smooth red with a gentle oak influence and a slightly high-acid finish. Ready.

DRY $16 -V

Dunleavy Cabernet/Merlot ★★★☆

The second-tier red from Waiheke Vineyards, best known for Te Motu Cabernet/Merlot. The 2000 vintage (★★★☆) is like a minor Bordeaux – savoury and leafy, with plummy, spicy flavours, balanced for early consumption. Ready.

DRY $35 -V

Fenton Cabernet Sauvignon/Merlot/Franc ★★★★

Fenton is a little-known Waiheke Island producer, but in 1993 and 1994 it made magical reds. It is grown at Barry Fenton's Twin Bays vineyard at Oneroa, where Cabernet Sauvignon is the principal variety, supplemented by Merlot and Cabernet Franc. The 2000 vintage (★★★☆), matured in 'newish' French oak barriques, is smooth and forward, with blackcurrant and spice flavours, oak complexity and very good depth.

Vintage	00	99	98	97	96
WR	6	NM	7	6	7
Drink	04	NM	P	P	P

DRY $50 -V

Ferryman Cabernet Sauvignon/Merlot ★★★

Grown on Waiheke Island, and matured in French oak casks, the 2001 vintage (★★☆) is a full-coloured, slightly rustic wine with a high-acid finish. Overpriced.

DRY $40 -V

Firstland Cabernet Sauvignon (★★★)

The green-edged 2000 vintage (★★★) is a blend of 90 per cent Hawke's Bay Cabernet Sauvignon and 10 per cent Te Kauwhata Malbec. The colour is deep; the palate is full-flavoured, with blackcurrant and green-leaf characters seasoned with spicy French oak and a firm tannin grip.

DRY $24 -V

Foreman's Vineyard Cabernet Sauvignon/Merlot ★★★

Grown at Onetangi, on Waiheke Island, the 2000 vintage (★★★) is a richly coloured wine with strong berry/plum flavours braced by firm tannins. It's fresh and vibrant, with good concentration, but the finish shows a slight lack of warmth and softness.

DRY $30 -V

Glover's Moutere Cabernet Sauvignon ★★★☆

Dave Glover's Nelson red is typically sturdy, with strong cassis/plum flavours laden with tannin. It *demands* time. Power, rather than finesse, is the key attribute, but if you're prepared to wait, it can be rewarding. The 1999 vintage (★★★★) ranks among the best yet. Bold in colour, with blackcurrant and red-berry aromas, it has buckets of fruit and chewy tannins. Spicy and ripe, with sweet, ripe-tasting fruit, as usual it lacks some of the finer touches, but there's no denying the raw power, and it does have loads of character.

Vintage	00	99	98	97	96	95	94
WR	6	7	7	7	NM	NM	7
Drink	03-07	04-10	03-10	03-07	NM	NM	03-04

DRY $40 -V

Goldridge Estate Barrique Matured Cabernet/Merlot ★★☆

Estate-grown at Matakana Estate, the 2000 vintage (★★☆) was matured for 15 months in new and one-year-old casks, mostly French. It's a slightly old-fashioned New Zealand red (and certainly not as good as the back label suggests), with lightish colour showing some development. Leafy on the nose, it's a medium to full-bodied wine, moderately ripe-tasting, with berry, spice and nut flavours, firm tannins and a slightly high-acid finish.

Vintage 00
WR 6
Drink 03-05

DRY $20 -V

Goldwater Cabernet Sauvignon & Merlot ★★★★★

Kim and Jeanette Goldwater's stunning Waiheke Island wine is one of New Zealand's greatest reds. 'To begin with, we were preoccupied with enormity,' recalls Kim Goldwater after 22 vintages. 'Now we aim for elegance.' The vines are cultivated in sandy clay soils on the hillside overlooking Putiki Bay and vinification is based on classic Bordeaux techniques, including maturation for 12 to 21 months in Nevers oak barriques (typically half new). The lighter wines drink well at six or seven years old, and top vintages reward cellaring for at least a decade. The 2000 (★★★★☆) is a blend of Cabernet Sauvignon (69 per cent), Merlot (20 per cent) and Cabernet Franc (11 per cent), cropped at an average of below 5 tonnes per hectare. Deep but not dense in colour, it's a very complete, finely balanced wine with strong blackcurrant, plum, green-leaf and spice flavours, good complexity and ripe tannins. It's a forward vintage, already highly approachable. There is no 2001.

Vintage	01	00	99	98	97	96	95	94
WR	NM	7	7	7	7	7	6	7
Drink	NM	03-10	03-11	03-08	03-10	03-05	03-05	03-08

DRY $69 -V
🍇🍇🍇

Goldwater Wood's Hill Cabernet/Merlot (★★★☆)

Showing good concentration and complexity, the 2002 vintage (★★★☆) was made from grapes off young vines and others not selected for the top label (above). Estate-grown on Waiheke Island and matured for a year in French and American oak casks (50 per cent new), it's a blend of Cabernet Sauvignon (69 per cent) and Merlot (31 per cent). Full-coloured, with cassis, green-leaf and spice aromas, it's a full-bodied wine with strong blackcurrant-like flavours, nutty oak and firm tannins. Best drinking 2004–06.

Vintage 02
WR 6
Drink 03-09

DRY $29 -V

Himmelsfeld Moutere Cabernet Sauvignon ★★★☆

Grown on a north-facing clay slope, this Upper Moutere, Nelson red is typically a sturdy, characterful, full-coloured wine with a slightly leafy bouquet, good body and depth of blackcurrant, plum and spice flavours and a firm tannin grip. The boldly coloured 2001 vintage (★★★★) is the finest yet. Fragrant, with blackcurrant and herb aromas, it's a substantial, rich wine with deep cassis, plum and spice characters, the herbal twist of Cabernet Sauvignon and a solid foundation of tannin. One of the region's best Cabernet Sauvignons to date, it's a good drink-now or cellaring proposition.

DRY $28 -V

Hitchen Road
Cabernet Sauvignon/Cabernet Franc/Merlot (★★)

Grown above Pokeno township, in the north Waikato, the 1999 vintage (★★) was aged for 14 months in French oak casks (half new). Showing fullish, developed colour, it's a leathery, slightly leafy red, now past its best.

DRY $17 -V

Hyperion Kronos Cabernet/Merlot ★★★☆

Grown at Matakana, north of Auckland, the 2000 vintage (★★★☆) is a blend of Cabernet Sauvignon (80 per cent) and Merlot (20 per cent), matured for a year in French and American oak casks. The colour is full and youthful; the palate is flavoursome and firm, with some fruit sweetness, good density and the distinctive earthiness of Auckland reds.

Vintage	00	99	98
WR	6	6	7
Drink	04-08	P	P

DRY $32 -V

Hyperion Millennios Cabernet Sauvignon ★★☆

The 2000 vintage (★★☆) of this Matakana red is an unblended Cabernet Sauvignon, oak-aged for a year. Fullish in colour, it's a characterful, flavoursome wine, savoury, leafy and spicy, with some complexity, but it lacks full ripeness, with a slightly green finish.

Vintage	00	99	98
WR	3	5	4
Drink	03-05	P	P

DRY $22 -V

Hyperion The Titan Cabernet Sauvignon (★★★★)

It's not as gigantic as the term 'titan' suggests, but the debut 2002 vintage (★★★★) of this Matakana red is deeply coloured and fragrant, with strong, well-ripened blackcurrant and spice flavours, free of undue herbaceousness. Brambly, with sweet-fruit characters, it's a strongly varietal wine, already a pleasure to drink.

DRY $40 -V

Isola Estate Cabernet Sauvignon/Merlot (★★☆)

Grown on Waiheke Island, the 2002 vintage (★★☆) is full-coloured, with a spicy, slightly leafy bouquet. It's a plummy, reasonably flavoursome wine but also shows a slight lack of warmth, with a crisp, minty finish.

DRY $30 -V

Kemblefield The Reserve Cabernet Sauvignon (★★★☆)

The debut 2000 vintage (★★★☆) was estate-grown at Mangatahi, in Hawke's Bay, and matured for 15 months in French oak casks. Full but not dense in colour, with the slightly leafy aromas of cool-climate Cabernet Sauvignon, it's a full-bodied, mellow, well-rounded wine, already highly approachable, with strong blackcurrant and plum flavours, some green, herbal notes and savoury, spicy complexities.

DRY $36 -V

Kemblefield Winemakers Signature Cabernet Sauvignon/Merlot ★★☆

The 2002 vintage (★★) was estate-grown at Mangatahi, in Hawke's Bay, and French oak-aged. A blend of Cabernet Sauvignon (50 per cent), Merlot (35 per cent) and Cabernet Franc (15 per cent), it shows lightish colour, with slightly leafy aromas. It's a medium-bodied, slightly rustic wine with moderate depth of red-berry and herb flavours and a crisp finish.

DRY $17 -V

Kennedy Point Vineyard Cabernet Sauvignon ★★★★

The 2000 vintage (★★★☆) is a very good Waiheke Island red. Cabernet Sauvignon-based (75 per cent), with 17 per cent Merlot and splashes of Cabernet Franc and Malbec, it was matured for 16 months in French oak barriques (60 per cent new). Boldly coloured, it has a spicy, nutty, slightly herbal bouquet, leading into a firm, well-structured palate. A strongly oaked wine with concentrated blackcurrant, green-leaf and spice flavours, it's well worth cellaring.

Vintage 00 99
WR 6 6
Drink 03-10 03-10

DRY $39 -V

Kerr Farm Kumeu Cabernet Sauvignon ★★★

This is typically a solid West Auckland red with berryish, spicy, slightly leafy flavours. The 2001 vintage (★★★) was matured for a year in French and American oak casks. Deeply coloured, with slightly leafy aromas and some cedary oak adding complexity, it has berry and plum flavours showing some richness, but finishes with green-edged tannins.

Vintage 01 00
WR 7 7
Drink 04-07 03-05

DRY $22 -V

Kingsley Estate Cabernet Sauvignon/Merlot ★★★★☆

The 2000 vintage (★★★★☆) was grown organically in Gimblett Road, Hawke's Bay, and matured for 20 months in French oak barriques (one-third new). A blend of Cabernet Sauvignon (67 per cent), Merlot (30 per cent) and Malbec (3 per cent), it was bottled without fining and with minimal filtration. It makes no concessions to drink-young appeal. Dark, with a spicy, leathery, oaky bouquet, it's a complex style with firm tannins bracing its strong, well-ripened, blackcurrant, plum and spice flavours. A serious wine, it's built for cellaring; open 2004+.

Vintage 00
WR 6
Drink 03-07

DRY $39 -V

Kingsley Estate Gimblett Gravels Cabernet/Malbec (★★★★)

The gutsy, ripe 2001 vintage (★★★★) is a 60/40 blend, grown in three vineyards in the Gimblett Gravels district of Hawke's Bay. Deep and youthful in colour, with a brambly, earthy, spicy bouquet, it's a powerful and concentrated wine with blackcurrant and nut flavours and the slight rusticity typical of Malbec. It's a complex, well-structured red, for drinking now or cellaring.

Vintage 01
WR 6
Drink 03-08

DRY $39 -V

Lake Chalice Platinum Cabernet Sauvignon ★★★☆
The 2001 vintage (★★★☆) of this Marlborough red was estate-grown in the Falcon vineyard and matured for a year in French and American oak casks. It's a full-coloured, crisp wine with strong blackcurrant and red-berry flavours, a hint of mint and firm tannins.

Vintage	01	00	99	98
WR	7	6	6	7
Drink	03-08	03-06	03-06	03-05

DRY $28 -V

Lincoln Heritage Collection Petar Cabernet/Merlot ★★☆
Named after the founder, Petar Fredatovich, the 2000 vintage (★★☆) is a blend of Te Kauwhata Cabernet Sauvignon (60 per cent) and Gisborne Merlot (40 per cent). Fullish in colour, it shows solid depth of fresh, plummy, berryish flavours, but slightly lacks warmth and softness.

Vintage	00	99	98
WR	5	5	6
Drink	03-04	P	P

DRY $17 -V

Linden Estate Dam Block Cabernet/Malbec/Merlot ★★★★
A single-vineyard Hawke's Bay wine, grown in the Esk Valley, the 2000 vintage (★★★★) is a blend of Cabernet Sauvignon (70 per cent), Malbec (20 per cent) and Merlot (10 per cent), matured in French oak barriques (30 per cent new). Richly coloured, with a perfumed bouquet, it's a generous, supple and harmonious wine with strong, plummy, sweetly oaked flavours, good complexity and a lingering finish. Highly attractive drinking now onwards.

Vintage	00
WR	6
Drink	03-06

DRY $36 -V

Linden Estate Two Valleys Cabernet/Malbec/Merlot (★★☆)
Lightish in colour, the 2001 vintage (★★☆) was grown in the Esk and Dartmoor valleys of Hawke's Bay. It's a solid quaffer, with a slightly herbaceous thread on the nose and palate. Berryish and spicy, with some savoury, earthy touches and a slightly high-acid finish, it lacks real depth. Drink 2003–04.

DRY $19 -V

Lombardi Reserve Cabernet/Merlot/Franc (★★★★☆)
The richly coloured, finely fragrant 2000 vintage (★★★★☆) was estate-grown at Havelock North, in Hawke's Bay and matured in French oak barriques (30 per cent new). A blend of Cabernet Sauvignon (50 per cent), Merlot (33 per cent) and Cabernet Franc (17 per cent), it's a vibrantly fruity wine with ripe cassis/plum flavours showing excellent depth, sweet-fruit characters and well-integrated oak. A subtle, classy wine, it's a strong candidate for cellaring.

Vintage	00
WR	6
Drink	03-06

DRY $32 AV

Longview Estate Scarecrow Cabernet Sauvignon ★★★☆
From a small, terraced vineyard south of Whangarei flows this rare Northland red, at its best crammed with ripe, brambly, spicy flavour. The easy-drinking 2000 vintage (★★★☆) is an unblended Cabernet Sauvignon, matured for 14 months in French and American oak casks. Full but not dense in colour, with a spicy, slightly smoky bouquet, it's a full-bodied, ripe, plummy and berryish red with oak complexity, good depth and gentle tannins.

DRY $21 AV

Loopline Cabernet (★★★)

Purple-flushed, the 2002 vintage (★★★) is a blend of Cabernet Sauvignon (67 per cent), Cabernet Franc (28 per cent) and Merlot (5 per cent), grown at Opaki, north of Masterton, in the Wairarapa, and matured for a year in French oak barriques (one-third new). It's a buoyantly fruity, distinctly cool-climate style of red with the fresh, raspberry and plum flavours characteristic of Cabernet Franc. It's still youthful; open mid-2004+.

Vintage 02
WR 6
Drink 04-09

DRY $29 -V

Lucknow Estate Cabernets/Merlot ★★★

The 2002 vintage (★★★) of this Hawke's Bay red is a blend of Cabernet Franc, Merlot and Cabernet Sauvignon. Full and youthful in colour, with berry, plum and herb flavours and a touch of spicy oak, it's a fresh and vibrant, fruit-driven style with moderate tannins and very decent depth.

DRY $19 AV

Mahurangi Estate Selection Gimblett Gravels Cabernet Sauvignon/Merlot (★★★☆)

Likely to be long-lived, the 2000 vintage (★★★☆) is still youthful in colour, with fresh, strong, red-berry, plum and spice flavours, oak complexity and firm, grippy tannins. Evolving slowly, it's a tautly structured Hawke's Bay red, best opened 2005+.

DRY $24 AV

Margrain Cabernet Sauvignon/Merlot/Cabernet Franc (★★★)

The deeply coloured 2001 vintage (★★★) was grown in Martinborough and matured for 10 months in French oak barriques. A blend of 65 per cent Cabernet Sauvignon, 30 per cent Merlot and 5 per cent Cabernet Franc, it shows good intensity of blackcurrant and plum flavours, wrapped in fine-quality oak, crisp, slightly unripe herbal characters and a firm tannin grip.

Vintage 01
WR 7
Drink 03-08

DRY $38 -V

Matariki Reserve Hawke's Bay Cabernet Sauvignon ★★★★

The 2000 vintage (★★★★☆), an unblended Cabernet Sauvignon, was grown in Gimblett Road, matured for a year in seasoned oak casks and then aged for a further eight months in new French oak barriques. Dark, it's a highly concentrated wine with blackcurrant, plum and mint flavours, cedary, nutty oak adding complexity and a firm tannin grip. A worthy effort from a difficult year, the 2001 (★★★☆) is deeply coloured, with a fragrant bouquet of herbs and nuts. It's a weighty wine, slightly high in acidity, with very good depth of blackcurrant, plum and spice flavours, quality oak and tight tannins. Open 2005+.

Vintage 01 00
WR 6 7
Drink 04-09 03-12

DRY $40 -V

Matawhero Cabernet/Merlot (★★★☆)

Fullish and developed in colour, the 1999 vintage (★★★☆) of this Gisborne red is mellow and flavoursome, with the savoury, leathery characters you'd normally expect in a much older wine. It's a sturdy red, full of character, but ready now.

DRY $32 -V

Matua Valley Ararimu Cabernet Sauvignon/Merlot (★★★☆)

Most recent vintages of Matua's flagship red have been Merlot-predominant, but the 2001 (★★★☆) was blended from Cabernet Sauvignon (55 per cent), Merlot (38 per cent) and Malbec (7 per cent). Matured for over a year in all-new French (80 per cent) and American oak barriques, it's a full-coloured Hawke's Bay red with strong blackcurrant and plum flavours and some leathery, savoury complexity. However, it lacks the notable power and concentration of this label at its best and is probably only for short-term cellaring.

DRY $40 -V

Matua Valley Hawke's Bay Cabernet Sauvignon/Merlot ★★☆

An easy-drinking red. The 2002 vintage (★★☆) is a blend of Cabernet Sauvignon (53 per cent) and Merlot (47 per cent), matured in one, two and three-year-old French and American oak casks. Fullish in colour, it offers decent depth of plum, spice and green-leaf flavours, but there's a slight lack of warmth and softness on the finish.

DRY $18 -V

Matua Valley Matheson Cabernet/Merlot ★★★☆

Grown in the Ngatarawa district of Hawke's Bay and matured in French and American oak casks (half new), the 2002 vintage (★★★) is a richly coloured, distinctly herbal blend of Cabernet Sauvignon (80 per cent) and Merlot. Balanced for easy drinking, it possesses strong, vibrantly fruity blackcurrant and spice flavours, leafy, minty characters and a very smooth finish.

Vintage	02	01
WR	6	6
Drink	03-05	03-04

DRY $21 AV

McCashin's Hawke's Bay Cabernet Sauvignon (★★☆)

Still youthful in colour, the 2000 vintage (★★☆) was matured for 10 months in American oak casks. It's a distinctly herbaceous wine with fresh, blackcurrant-like flavours of decent depth, but lacks real warmth and roundness.

DRY $21 -V

Mebus Dakins Road Cabernet/Merlot/Malbec (★★★)

I disagree with the back label description of the 2000 vintage (★★★) as 'great wine'. Grown in the Wairarapa and matured in all-new oak barrels, it has deep colour, with a slightly herbaceous bouquet. The palate is smooth, vibrantly fruity and green-edged, with plenty of flavour.

DRY $27 -V

Mills Reef Elspeth Cabernet/Merlot ★★★★★

Grown in the company's stony, close-planted Mere Road vineyard, near Hastings, this is a consistently outstanding Hawke's Bay red. The 2000 vintage (★★★★★) is crying out for more time. The colour is very bold and purple-flushed; the bouquet is fragrant, with sweet, ripe blackberry aromas. It's a tight, highly concentrated wine with rich, vibrant cassis, plum, spice and cedary oak flavours, a hint of dark chocolate and powerful tannins. The 2001 (★★★★) is dark, with deep blackcurrant, plum and spice flavours showing a slight herbal influence. A generous, supple wine, it should be drinking well from mid-2004 onwards.

Vintage	01	00	99	98	97	96	95	94
WR	6	7	6	7	7	NM	7	7
Drink	03-06	03-05	03-04	03-04	P	NM	P	P

DRY $40 AV

284   RED WINES

Mills Reef Elspeth Cabernet Sauvignon ★★★★★

Grown in the company's shingly vineyard at Mere Road, near Hastings, the 2000 vintage (★★★★☆) is based entirely on Cabernet Sauvignon. Densely coloured, it's a natural candidate for cellaring, with substantial body (14 per cent alcohol), good fruit sweetness, a seasoning of fine-quality French oak and bold, youthful, concentrated flavours, spicy, nutty and tannic. The 2001, tasted just prior to bottling (and so not rated), was deeply coloured, with spicy French oak aromas. It's a relatively forward vintage, supple and not hugely concentrated, but still showing rich blackcurrant, plum and herb flavours, nutty and complex.

Vintage	01	00	99	98	97
WR	6	7	6	7	7
Drink	03-06	03-05	03-04	03-04	P

DRY $40 AV

Mills Reef Reserve Cabernet/Merlot ★★★☆

The 2001 vintage (★★★☆) of this French oak-matured, Hawke's Bay red is full-coloured, with strong blackcurrant, plum, green-leaf and spice flavours, nutty oak and a firm tannin grip. The 2002 (★★★★) is a substantial, tightly structured wine. Dark and youthful in colour, it is fragrant and spicy, warm and complex, with excellent depth of blackcurrant and plum flavours, hints of coffee and spice, and the potential to mature well.

Vintage	02	01
WR	7	7
Drink	04-07	03-06

DRY $25 AV

Mission Gimblett Road Cabernet/Merlot ★★★☆

The 2000 vintage (★★★) is a blend of Cabernet Sauvignon (77 per cent) and Merlot (23 per cent), matured for 15 months in French oak casks (half new). It's a concentrated, spicy, nutty and firmly structured Hawke's Bay wine, but too green-leafy to rate more highly.

Vintage	00	99	98
WR	6	6	6
Drink	03-10	03-10	03-07

DRY $28 -V

Mission Hawke's Bay Cabernet/Merlot ★★☆

The 'Cabernet' on the label of the 2002 vintage (★★☆) refers to Cabernet Sauvignon (34 per cent) and Cabernet Franc (33 per cent), with Merlot making up the rest of the blend. Matured for six months in French and American oak, it's a deeply coloured wine with a spicy, herbaceous bouquet and flavours, showing decent depth.

DRY $15 AV

Mission Hawke's Bay Cabernet Sauvignon ★★☆

In favourable vintages, this reasonably priced Hawke's Bay red can offer very appealing value; in lesser years it is light and leafy. Partly oak-aged, with 12 per cent Cabernet Franc and 8 per cent Merlot, the 2002 vintage (★★☆) is richly coloured, but strongly herbaceous on the nose and palate, with blackcurrant-like flavours and a slightly high-acid finish.

DRY $15 AV

Mission Reserve Cabernet Sauvignon ★★★

Grown in Gimblett Road, Hawke's Bay, and matured in French oak casks, the 2000 vintage (★★★) is richly coloured but herbaceous, with good depth of cassis and green-leaf flavours and a smooth finish. The herbaceous 2001 (★★★☆), which includes 14 per cent Syrah, was matured in French oak casks (half new). It's a full-flavoured wine, but too leafy and high-acid to rate more highly.

Vintage	01	00	99
WR	5	5	7
Drink	P	03-08	03-10

DRY $22 -V

Mount Cass Vineyards Waipara Valley Cabernet Sauvignon (★★☆)

Not released until mid-2003, the 2000 vintage (★★☆) is fullish in colour, with plenty of raspberry and herb flavour in a firm, distinctly cool-climate Cabernet style that lacks real ripeness.

Vintage	01
WR	5
Drink	04-06

DRY $19 -V

Mount Riley Marlborough Cabernet/Merlot/Malbec ★★★

The richly coloured 2001 vintage (★★★☆) is a blend of Cabernet Sauvignon grown in the Wairau Valley, and Merlot and Malbec from the company's Seventeen Valley vineyard, south of Blenheim. French and American oak-aged for eight months, it's a smooth, fruit-packed wine, plummy, spicy and gently wooded, with soft tannins. Good drinking now onwards.

DRY $19 AV

Moutere Hills Nelson Cabernet/Merlot ★★☆

Estate-grown at Upper Moutere, this is typically a berryish, slightly herbal, middleweight red. The 2001 vintage (★★☆), matured in an even split of French and American oak casks, offers lots of fresh, berryish, plummy flavour in a very fruit-driven style with a crisp finish. Verging on three-star quality.

Vintage	01	00	99	98	97
WR	5	5	5	4	5
Drink	03-04	03-05	P	P	P

DRY $22 -V

Mudbrick Vineyard Cabernet/Malbec/Syrah (★★★☆)

Brambly, spicy and gamey on the nose, the 2002 vintage (★★★☆) is a Waiheke Island blend of Cabernet Sauvignon (76 per cent), Malbec (12 per cent) and Syrah (12 per cent), matured for a year in French and American oak barriques (30 per cent new). Richly coloured, with a strong, sweet oak influence, it's forward in its appeal, with loads of berryish, spicy flavour, the rustic character of Malbec, and slightly chewy tannins.

DRY $25 AV

Mudbrick Vineyard Reserve Cabernet/Merlot (★★★)

Grown on Waiheke Island, the 2002 vintage (★★★) is a blend of Cabernet Sauvignon (72 per cent) and Merlot (28 per cent). Matured for a year in French oak barriques (30 per cent new), it's a boldly coloured wine with a spicy bouquet. It was clearly too young when tasted in mid-2003, with a strong oak influence and taut raspberry and spice flavours that needed a year or two to soften.

DRY $38 -V

Nautilus Marlborough Cabernet Sauvignon/Merlot ★★★★

Cabernet Sauvignon has struggled to succeed in Marlborough, but Nautilus is keeping the flag flying. Deeply coloured, the 1999 vintage (★★★☆) is a blend of Cabernet Sauvignon (64 per cent) and Merlot (36 per cent), matured in French and American oak casks. It's a generous, distinctly cool-climate style of Cabernet/Merlot, fresh and crisp, with green-leaf aromas, very good depth of blackcurrant, herbal and plum flavours, oak complexity and plenty of body.

Vintage	99	98	97	96	95	94
WR	6	7	6	5	4	5
Drink	03-04	P	P	P	P	P

DRY $30 AV

Newton/Forrest Cornerstone Cabernet/Merlot/Malbec ★★★★★

Grown in the Cornerstone Vineyard, on the junction of Gimblett Road and State Highway 50, in Hawke's Bay, this is a consistently distinguished wine. The impressively dark and concentrated 2000 vintage (★★★★☆) is a blend of Cabernet Sauvignon (41 per cent), Merlot (32 per cent), Malbec (20 per cent) and Cabernet Franc (7 per cent), matured in French (principally) and American oak barriques. Built to last, it's a very generous wine with noble colour, bold blackcurrant, plum, mint and spice flavours, the meaty, gamey characters typical of Malbec, a firm foundation of tannin and a rich finish. (The 1998 vintage [★★★★★] was recently re-released at $90. It's still amazingly youthful, with dense, purple-flushed colour and a lovely array of blackcurrant, plum, spice and coffee flavours, seductively rich and smooth.)

Vintage	01	00	99	98
WR	4	7	6	7
Drink	04-05	05-10	03-05	03-10

DRY $40 AV

Newton Forrest Cornerstone Cabernet Sauvignon (★★★★★)

The strapping 1998 vintage (★★★★★) is a straight Cabernet Sauvignon, grown in Gimblett Road and matured in all French oak barriques. Showing huge colour, it's firm and still youthful, with a powerful wood influence, big tannins and great density of plum/spice flavours.

Vintage	98
WR	6
Drink	05-08

DRY $55 AV

Ngatarawa Glazebrook Cabernet Sauvignon ★★★★

The 2001 vintage (★★★☆) is the first since the bold, lovely 1998 (★★★★★). Attractive in its youth, it was matured in American oak casks (70 per cent new) and blended with 15 per cent Merlot. It's a full-coloured Hawke's Bay red with fairly rich, plummy flavours showing a slight herbal streak, a sweet oak influence and gentle tannins. Drink now or cellar. (Sold only at the cellar door.)

DRY $25 AV

Ngatarawa Stables Cabernet/Merlot ★★★

Typically a sturdy Hawke's Bay red with drink-young appeal and lots of flavour. Due to the devastating frost of November 2000, which decimated the crop, the 2001 vintage (★★★) is a blend of Australian (55 per cent) and New Zealand wine. Principally Cabernet Sauvignon (80 per cent), with Merlot (13 per cent) and Cabernet Franc (7 per cent), it's a full-coloured, flavoursome, fresh and supple wine, marrying the relatively herbaceous characters of New Zealand Cabernet Sauvignon with the riper, softer flavours of Australia.

Vintage	01	00	99	98	97	96
WR	6	6	5	7	6	7
Drink	03-05	03-04	P	P	P	P

DRY $17 AV

Nobilo Icon Cabernet/Merlot (★★★)

The fresh, vibrant 2001 vintage (★★★) is a Marlborough blend of equal parts of Cabernet Sauvignon and Merlot, matured for a year in French and American oak casks (new and seasoned). It's a boldly coloured wine with herbal characters, plenty of blackcurrant, plum and spice flavour, some oak complexity and a slightly green, high-acid finish.

DRY $23 -V

Odyssey Hawke's Bay Cabernet Sauvignon ★★★

The 2002 vintage (★★★) was grown in the Dartmoor Valley and matured for a year in French and American oak casks (half new). Full-coloured, with a leafy bouquet, it's full-bodied, flavoursome and firm, with some complexity, but also shows a slight lack of ripeness and warmth.

Vintage	02
WR	5
Drink	03-08

DRY $20 AV

Odyssey Kumeu Cabernet Sauvignon (★★☆)

The 2002 vintage (★★☆), matured in seasoned oak casks, is a flavoursome red but lacks full ripeness, with green, leafy characters to the fore.

DRY $18 -V

Okahu Estate Kaz Cabernet ★★★★

Recently released, the 1998 vintage (★★★★) is a complex, still youthful Northland red, estate-grown near Kaitaia and matured in French and American oak casks (half new). Full and bright in colour, with a warm, nutty, savoury palate, cedary and spicy, it shows good concentration and should be long-lived.

Vintage	98
WR	6
Drink	03-09

DRY $45 -V

Okahu Estate Ninety Mile
Cabernet Sauvignon/Cabernet Franc/Merlot ★★★☆

At its best this is an excellent red, fleshy, with lots of savoury, spicy flavour. The 2000 vintage (★★★☆) marries Cabernet Sauvignon, Cabernet Franc and Merlot, grown in the estate vineyard at Kaitaia, Northland, with Cabernet Franc from Clevedon, in South Auckland, and Merlot from Hawke's Bay. Matured in French and American oak casks (20 per cent new), it has a fragrant, berryish bouquet, with integrated oak. The palate is fresh and supple, with blackcurrant and plum flavours, slightly savoury and earthy touches and gentle tannins. It's not a blockbuster, but quietly satisfying.

Vintage	00	99	98	97	96
WR	6	5	6	6	5
Drink	03-08	03-08	03-06	03-05	P

DRY $24 AV

Onetangi Road
Cabernet Sauvignon/Merlot/Franc/Malbec (★★)

The 2001 vintage (★★) is far inferior to the reserve model from 2000 (below). Showing moderate depth of colour, with some development, it's an under-ripe, very green and herbaceous Waiheke Island red, with a high-acid finish.

DRY $20 -V

Onetangi Road Reserve Cabernet Sauvignon/Merlot/Malbec ★★★★

Grown on Waiheke Island, the 2000 vintage (★★★★☆) is a densely coloured, seductively soft and warm red, blended from Cabernet Sauvignon (46 per cent), Merlot (33 per cent), Malbec (14 per cent) and Cabernet Franc (7 per cent). It's a rich, complex wine with deliciously concentrated blackcurrant/plum flavours wrapped in quality oak.

DRY $39 -V

Peacock Ridge Cabernet Sauvignon/Malbec/Merlot/Cabernet Franc (★★★☆)

Grown at Onetangi, on Waiheke Island, the 2002 vintage (★★★☆) is a promising debut. Based principally on Cabernet Sauvignon (70 per cent), with equal minor portions of Malbec, Merlot and Cabernet Franc, it was matured for 14 months in French and American oak casks. Deeply coloured, with a leafy bouquet, it has concentrated cassis and herb flavours, spicy, nutty characters and a firm underlay of tannin. It needs more time; open 2005+.

DRY $35 -V

Pegasus Bay Cabernet/Merlot ★★★★

Grown at Waipara, this is one of the best claret-style reds to flow from Canterbury. The 2001 vintage (★★★★) is a blend of Cabernet Sauvignon, Merlot, Malbec and Cabernet Franc, matured for 18 months in French and American oak casks (30 per cent new) and bottled unfiltered. It's a dark, substantial and complex wine with satisfyingly rich, spicy, plummy, brambly flavours and hints of dark chocolate and mint. Firmly structured, it needs another two years to reach its peak; open 2005+.

Vintage	01	00	99	98	97	96	95
WR	6	5	6	7	5	6	6
Drink	03-10	03-05	03-05	03-11	P	03-04	03-04

DRY $27 AV

Peninsula Estate Oneroa Bay Cabernet/Syrah/Merlot ★★★☆

This sturdy Waiheke red is Peninsula Estate's second-tier, claret-style red. It lacks the lush, sweet-fruit characters of the island's top reds, but is typically savoury and spicy, with some warmth and complexity and firm tannins.

DRY $30 -V

Phoenix Cabernet/Merlot/Franc ★★★

The 2001 vintage (★★★) was estate-grown at Henderson, in West Auckland. A blend of Cabernet Sauvignon (74 per cent), Merlot (20 per cent) and Cabernet Franc (6 per cent), it was matured for six months in French (60 per cent) and American oak casks. It's a full-coloured wine with blackcurrant and herbal notes in a slightly rustic style with drying tannins.

Vintage	01	00
WR	5	5
Drink	03+	P

DRY $15 AV

Pleasant Valley Auckland Cabernet Sauvignon (★★☆)

The 2001 vintage (★★☆), grown at Kumeu, is a full-coloured wine with fresh, vibrant plum/berry flavours and a slightly high-acid finish.

DRY $19 -V

Quarry Road Cabernet Sauvignon/Merlot ★★★

Deeply coloured, the 2000 vintage (★★★) is a Waikato red, estate-grown at Te Kauwhata. It's a full-flavoured wine, berryish and spicy, with well-balanced tannins and a slightly chocolatey richness.

DRY $15 AV

Ransom Dark Summit Cabernet Sauvignon ★★★☆

Grown at Mahurangi, north of Auckland, and oak-aged for 21 months, the 2000 vintage (★★★★) is the best yet. It's a dark, weighty wine with concentrated cassis, plum, herbal and spice flavours, quality oak, leathery, savoury touches adding complexity and a firm tannin grip. Drink now or cellar.

Vintage	00	99	98
WR	6	NM	5
Drink	03-06	NM	P

DRY $26 -V

Ransom Mahurangi Cabernet/Merlot ★★★

Designed for earlier consumption than its Dark Summit stablemate (above), the 2000 vintage (★★★) was oak-aged for 21 months. Fullish in colour, it's an earthy, spicy, wholesome Auckland red, sturdy, with some complexity and firm underlying tannins. Good drinking now onwards.

Vintage	00
WR	6
Drink	03-06

DRY $20 AV

Riverside Dartmoor Cabernet/Merlot ★★☆

Grown in the Dartmoor Valley of Hawke's Bay and matured in French and American oak, this is typically a light, leafy red, lacking real ripeness and staying power. It's an easy-drinking style, green-edged, with moderate depth of plum, spice and red-berry flavours.

Vintage	01
WR	5
Drink	04-05

DRY $15 AV

Rongopai Vintage Reserve Cabernet Sauvignon/Merlot (★★★☆)

The 2000 vintage (★★★☆) is a blend of Hawke's Bay Cabernet Sauvignon (55 per cent) and Te Kauwhata Merlot and Malbec. Showing a strong, perfumed oak influence, it's a weighty wine (14 per cent alcohol) with plenty of blackcurrant/plum flavour, slightly earthy and nutty, good complexity and a smooth finish.

Vintage	00
WR	6
Drink	03-04

DRY $25 AV

St Francis Hawke's Bay Cabernet Sauvignon (★★☆)

Full-flavoured, the 2000 vintage (★★☆) was matured for 15 months in new and one-year-old American oak casks. Showing some development, it's a brambly, herbaceous wine with gentle tannins and a slightly high-acid finish.

Vintage	00
WR	5
Drink	03-06

DRY $25 -V

Sacred Hill Helmsman Cabernet/Merlot (★★★★☆)

The potent 2000 vintage (★★★★☆) is a Hawke's Bay blend of Cabernet Sauvignon (49 per cent), Merlot (38 per cent), Cabernet Franc (9 per cent) and Malbec (4 per cent), matured for 18 months in French oak barriques. Deep and still youthful in colour, it is fragrant and rich, with concentrated blackcurrant, mint and nut flavours, brambly and complex, and ripe, firm tannins. Lovely drinking now onwards.

Vintage 00
WR 7
Drink 03-08

DRY $35 AV

Saints Cabernet Sauvignon/Merlot ★★★☆

The 2001 vintage (★★★☆), blended by Montana from Hawke's Bay and South Australian wine, is full-coloured, fresh and smooth, with satisfying depth of blackcurrant and plum flavours and a touch of sweet oak. A finely balanced wine with good varietal characters, it's drinking well now.

DRY $18 V+

Sanderson Bellvine Cabernet/Merlot (★★☆)

Showing a lack of real ripeness and softness, the 2000 vintage (★★☆) is a full-coloured blend of Cabernet Sauvignon (68 per cent), Merlot (16 per cent), Malbec (8 per cent) and Syrah (8 per cent), matured for a year in one-year-old French oak casks. It's a relatively lightweight Hawke's Bay red with crisp acidity and plummy, green-edged flavours.

Vintage 00
WR 6
Drink 03-06

DRY $20 -V

Schubert Hawke's Bay Cabernet Sauvignon ★★★★

From a Wairarapa-based company, the 2001 vintage (★★★★) is a Gimblett Road, Hawke's Bay red, matured for over two years in French oak casks (75 per cent new). It's a boldly coloured wine, sturdy (14.5 per cent alcohol), slightly minty and leafy, but with highly concentrated blackcurrant, plum and spice flavours, seasoned with fine-quality oak. It's less striking than the opulent 1999 vintage (★★★★★), but should mature well for several years.

Vintage 01 00 99
WR 6 7 6
Drink 03-10 03-10 03-09

DRY $45 -V

Schubert Wairarapa Cabernet Sauvignon/Merlot ★★★☆

Harvested in May, the 2001 vintage (★★★★) is a 50/50 blend of Cabernet Sauvignon and Merlot, matured for over two years in French oak casks (75 per cent new). Densely coloured, it's a powerful red (14 per cent alcohol) with fresh blackcurrant, plum, mint and nut flavours, concentrated and youthful. Well worth cellaring.

Vintage 01 00
WR 6 6
Drink 03-11 03-10

DRY $38 -V

Seifried Nelson Cabernet Sauvignon ★★☆

Grown at Appleby, the 2002 vintage (★★☆) shows moderate colour intensity. Berryish and spicy, with a leafy streak, it's a gently oaked wine with decent flavour depth and a crisp finish.

DRY $19 -V

Selaks Premium Selection Cabernet Sauvignon ★★

Typically a plain, green-edged wine. Grown in Marlborough and Hawke's Bay, the 2002 vintage (★★☆) is full-coloured, with a leafy bouquet. A fruity wine with very little oak showing, it offers reasonable depth of blackcurrant, red-berry and herb flavours and a slightly high-acid finish.

Vintage 02
WR 6
Drink 03-05

MED/DRY $15 -V

Soljans Hawke's Bay Cabernet/Merlot ★★☆

The 2001 vintage (★★☆) is a smooth, easy-drinking style. Fullish in colour, with a leafy, herbaceous bouquet, it's a plummy, spicy, lightly oaked wine with gentle tannins, but lacks real warmth and stuffing. (The 2002 is a blend of 70 per cent Cabernet Franc and 30 per cent Merlot.)

DRY $18 -V

Solstone Wairarapa Valley Cabernet/Merlot Reserve (★★★)

Made from 20-year-old vines at Masterton, matured for 16 months in French oak casks (25 per cent new) and bottled unfiltered, the 2000 vintage (★★★) is gutsy and firm, with full colour. It's a flavoursome, spicy and leathery wine, tightly structured, with a slight lack of warmth and roundness, but the likelihood of a long life ahead.

Vintage 00
WR 6
Drink 03-09

DRY $40 -V

Squawking Magpie Cabernet Sauvignon/Merlot ★★★★

The dark, tautly structured 2000 vintage (★★★★☆) is a single-vineyard wine, grown in Gimblett Road, Hawke's Bay, and matured in new French oak barriques. The colour is bold and youthful; the palate is serious and concentrated, with fresh, rich cassis, plum and spice flavours seasoned with cedary oak and a firm tannin grip. Still youthful, the 2001 (★★★☆) is deeply coloured, fresh and vibrant, with rich blackcurrant, plum and green-leaf flavours and a firm finish. It's a slightly more herbaceous wine than its stablemate from 2002 (below).

DRY $35 -V

Squawking Magpie The Cabernets (★★★★★)

The beautifully ripe and intense 2002 vintage (★★★★★) is a blend of Cabernet Sauvignon, Merlot and Cabernet Franc, grown in Gimblett Road, Hawke's Bay. A single-vineyard red, it is densely coloured and warm, with highly concentrated blackcurrant, spice and nut flavours, complex and long. It's a firmly structured wine, built to last, yet already accessible and full of personality.

DRY $37 AV

Stony Bay Cabernet/Merlot (★★☆)

From the Matariki winery, the 2001 vintage (★★☆) is a Hawke's Bay blend of Cabernet Sauvignon (84 per cent) and Merlot (16 per cent). It's a solid quaffer with fullish colour, leafy aromas and decent depth of plummy, green-edged flavour.

Vintage 01 00
WR 5 6
Drink 03-05 03-05

DRY $20 -V

Stonyridge Larose Cabernets ★★★★★

Typically a stunning Waiheke wine. Dark and seductively perfumed, with smashing fruit flavours, it is a magnificently concentrated red that matures superbly for a decade or longer, acquiring great complexity. The vines, grown in poor clay soils threaded with rotten rock, a kilometre from the sea at Onetangi, are extremely low-yielding. The wine is matured for a year in French (80 per cent) and American oak barriques; in a top year, 80 per cent of the casks are new or freshly shaved. The wine is sold largely on an 'en primeur' basis, whereby the customers, in return for paying for their wine about nine months in advance of its delivery, secure a substantial price reduction. The 2001 (★★★★), from a difficult season, is full, fragrant, fruit-packed and supple, but a lightweight by Stonyridge's illustrious standards, with slightly higher acid than usual and mid-term cellaring potential. The 2002 (★★★★☆) is a blend of Cabernet Sauvignon (51 per cent), Malbec (27 per cent), Petit Verdot (11 per cent), Merlot (8 per cent) and Cabernet Franc (4 per cent). That these figures total 101 per cent is understandable, given that the wine is Larose! It's a densely coloured, purple-black wine with a fragrant bouquet of spice, blackcurrants, eucalypt and berries and rich, ripe, concentrated flavours. It's a fruit bomb (as Robert Parker would put it), but with such a high Malbec content, does it have the breed – the sheer class – of past Laroses?

Vintage	02	01	00	99	98	97	96	95	94	93
WR	7	6	7	7	6	7	7	6	7	5
Drink	05-15	04-10	04-13	03-11	03-10	03-12	03-14	03-05	03-10	03-05

DRY $125 -V 🍇🍇🍇

Sunset Valley Vineyard Cabernet Sauvignon ★★☆

Grown organically at Upper Moutere, in Nelson, the 2001 vintage (★★☆) is a deeply coloured red, French oak-aged, with a slightly leafy bouquet and plenty of fresh blackcurrant and plum flavour. It's a substantial wine, but lacks real ripeness and roundness.

Vintage	01	00
WR	5	5
Drink	04	P

DRY $23 -V

Te Awa Farm Longlands Cabernet Sauvignon/Merlot ★★★★

The Lawson family's vineyard in the Gimblett Road area of Hawke's Bay yields consistently impressive reds. The 2000 vintage (★★★★) is a blend of Cabernet Sauvignon (70 per cent) and Merlot (30 per cent), matured in French and American oak casks. It's a stylish, full-coloured wine, warm and ripe, with strong blackcurrant, plum and spice flavours, finely integrated oak and supple tannins.

Vintage	00	99	98	97	96	95	94
WR	7	6	7	5	6	6	5
Drink	03-05	03-04	03-04	P	P	P	P

DRY $25 AV

Te Awa Farm Zone 10 Cabernet Sauvignon (★★★★★)

This very classy Hawke's Bay red comes from part of the vineyard that 'ripens behind other zones', giving grapes 'with more generosity and less austerity than other Cabernet Sauvignon plantings'. The 2000 vintage (★★★★★) was matured for 18 months in French oak barriques (half new). Deeply coloured, with a totally non-herbaceous bouquet, it's a highly concentrated wine with cassis, plum, spice and nut flavours, a hint of dark mint chocolate and ripe tannins. It's not a blockbuster, but rich, delicate and stylish.

Vintage	00
WR	7
Drink	03-08

DRY $65 -V

Te Kairanga Castlepoint Cabernet Sauvignon/Merlot ★★

The 2001 (★★), a straight Cabernet Sauvignon, lacks colour, body, ripeness and richness. The equally disappointing 2002 vintage (★★) is a blend of Cabernet Sauvignon (75 per cent) and Merlot, grown in the Hawke's Bay (principally), Wairarapa and Gisborne regions, and matured for six months in French oak. It's a simple, under-ripe wine, herbaceous and high in acidity.

DRY $17 -V

Te Mata Awatea Cabernet/Merlot ★★★★★

Positioned slightly below its Coleraine stablemate in the Te Mata red-wine hierarchy, Awatea was once a top single-vineyard Hawke's Bay red, but since the 1989 vintage has been a blend of wines from several of Te Mata's original vineyards in the Havelock North hills, combined with more recent plantings in the 'Ngatarawa triangle'. Compared to Coleraine, in its youth Awatea is more seductive, more perfumed, and tastes more of sweet, ripe fruit, but is more forward and slightly less concentrated. It is typically a blend of about 55 per cent Cabernet Sauvignon, 35 per cent Merlot and 10 per cent Cabernet Franc. Maturation is in French oak barriques, typically one-half new. The wine can mature gracefully for many years, but is also delicious at two years old. The 2001 vintage (★★★★☆) is a blend of Cabernet Sauvignon (54 per cent), Merlot (30 per cent), Cabernet Franc (14 per cent) and Petit Verdot (2 per cent), matured for 18 months in new and seasoned French oak barriques. A very tightly structured wine, spicy, slightly leafy, nutty and complex, it's a strong candidate for cellaring. Richly coloured, with a well-spiced, slightly herbaceous bouquet, excellent flavour concentration and firm tannins, it's recommended by the winery for longer cellaring than usual; open 2005+.

Vintage	01	00	99	98	97	96	95	94
WR	6	7	6	7	5	6	7	6
Drink	05-08	04-10	04-06	03-12	03-05	03-04	03-07	P

DRY $38 AV

Te Mata Coleraine Cabernet/Merlot ★★★★★

Breed, rather than brute power, is the hallmark of Coleraine, which since its first vintage in 1982 has carved out a reputation second-to-none among New Zealand's reds, although it does show marked vintage variation. At its best (as in 1991, 1998 and 2000) it is a magical wine, with an intensity, complexity and subtlety on the level of a top-class Bordeaux. A single-vineyard Hawke's Bay red from 1982 to 1988, since 1989 Coleraine has been blended from several sites (including the original Coleraine vineyard) at Havelock North. Compared with its Awatea stablemate (above), Coleraine is more strongly influenced by new oak, more concentrated and more slowly evolving. The wine is matured for 18 to 20 months in French oak barriques, typically 70 per cent new. The 2001 vintage (★★★★★) is a blend of Cabernet Sauvignon (55 per cent), Merlot (29 per cent) and Cabernet Franc (16 per cent). It's a notably concentrated wine, richly coloured, with lovely depth of plummy, spicy flavour, hints of herbs and dark chocolate and a firm, chewy finish. Deep, complex and tightly structured, it's built for cellaring.

Vintage	01	00	99	98	97	96	95	94
WR	6	7	6	7	6	6	7	6
Drink	07-13	05-15	06-09	04-20	03-10	03-08	03-10	03-06

DRY $62 AV

Te Mata Estate Woodthorpe Cabernet/Merlot ★★★☆

Up to and including the 2000 vintage, this Hawke's Bay red was called Te Mata Cabernet/Merlot (the name change reflects its origin in the company's Woodthorpe Terraces vineyard in the Dartmoor Valley). Not to be confused with its Coleraine and Awatea big brothers, it can still be an impressive mouthful. Matured in new and seasoned oak barrels, the 2002 vintage (★★★★) is a blend of Cabernet Sauvignon (54 per cent), Merlot (33 per cent) and Cabernet Franc (13 per cent). Promisingly deep in colour, it is fragrant and full-bodied, with a slightly leafy bouquet, but good density of cassis, plum and spice flavours, finely integrated oak and fairly firm tannins. Best drinking 2004–05.

Vintage	02	01	00
WR	7	7	6
Drink	05-07	04-06	03-05

DRY $20 AV

Te Motu Cabernet/Merlot ★★★★☆

The Dunleavy family's flagship Waiheke Island red is grown at Onetangi (over the fence from Stonyridge) and matured in French and American oak barriques. The 1994 vintage (★★★★★) is the star to date – dark, intense and chewy – followed by the elegant, scented and savoury 1996 (★★★★☆), but the wine is not consistently brilliant, and so struggles to justify its super-high price. The 1999 vintage (★★★★☆) is one of the best – generous, mouthfilling and complex, with strong blackcurrant, plum and spice flavours, warm, leathery and savoury. Deeply coloured, with a fragrant, welcoming bouquet, it's a wine of style and complexity rather than brute power. Already delicious, it's also worth cellaring.

Vintage	99	98	97	96	95	94	93
WR	7	7	6	7	6	7	5
Drink	03-06	03-04	P	03-05	P	03-04	P

DRY $80 -V

Te Whare Ra Henrietta Cabernet Sauvignon/Merlot (★★★☆)

Estate-grown at Renwick, in Marlborough, the 2002 vintage (★★★☆) is a robust wine (14 per cent alcohol) with deep, inky colour and a bouquet of blackcurrants and herbs. A fruit bomb with strong cassis, plum and spice flavours, a hint of dark chocolate and gentle tannins, it works well as a fresh, vibrant, drink-young style.

Vintage	02	01
WR	5	6
Drink	03-09	03-08

DRY $19 V+

Thornbury Hawke's Bay Cabernet Sauvignon (★★★☆)

The full-coloured, purple-flushed 2000 vintage (★★★☆) was grown in Gimblett Road and matured for 15 months in French oak barriques. It's a strongly varietal wine with blackcurrant, spice and green-leaf flavours, showing very good depth, mouthfilling body and a firm, tightly structured finish. Open 2004+.

DRY $28 -V

Torlesse Cabernet/Merlot ★★★

Grown at Waipara and oak-aged for 18 months, the 2001 vintage (★★★☆) is a generous red, blended from Cabernet Sauvignon (85 per cent), Merlot (10 per cent) and Cabernet Franc (5 per cent). There's a herbal thread running through its plum and red-berry flavours, but it shows very good depth. The 2002 (★★☆) is a blend of Waipara and Marlborough grapes. Fresh and vibrantly fruity, it has fullish colour, berryish, slightly leafy flavours and a slightly high-acid finish.

Vintage	02
WR	7
Drink	03-06

DRY $18 AV

Trinity Hill Gimblett Road Cabernet Sauvignon/Merlot ★★★★

In top years, this is a finely balanced Hawke's Bay wine in the classic claret style, with intense cassis, plum and spice flavours and finely integrated oak. It is matured for up to 20 months in French oak barriques, typically 30 per cent new. Superior to the slightly austere 2000 vintage (★★★☆), the 2001 (★★★★) is full-coloured, with spicy French oak aromas. It offers well-concentrated cassis, plum and spice flavours, showing good ripeness, depth and complexity, and the structure to age well.

Vintage	02	01	00	99	98	97
WR	7	6	5	6	6	5
Drink	04-12	04-09	03-09	03-08	03-05	03-05

DRY $30 AV

Vidal Joseph Soler Cabernet Sauvignon (★★★★★)

Still youthful, the 1998 (★★★★★) is a powerful Hawke's Bay red that reflects the quality of the exceptionally hot, dry vintage. Launched in late 2002, it's a densely coloured, single-vineyard wine, grown in the Gimblett Gravels district and matured for 21 months in French and American oak barriques. It shows great depth and structure, with strikingly concentrated blackcurrant and nut, slightly chocolatey flavours and a firm tannin grip. It needs more time to unfold its full potential; open 2005 onwards. (There is no 1999, 2000 or 2001.)

Vintage	98
WR	7
Drink	04-10

DRY $89 -V

Vidal Reserve Cabernet Sauvignon ★★★★★

This Hawke's Bay label has a distinguished show track record, stretching back over more than a decade to the gloriously deep-scented, flavour-packed and complex 1990. The 2000 vintage (★★★★☆) was matured for the unusually long period of 20 months in French and American oak barriques. Still unfolding, it has rich, vibrant plum and spice flavours, slightly chewy tannins and a long finish. Open 2005+.

Vintage	01	00	99	98	97	96	95	94
WR	NM	7	NM	NM	6	NM	6	6
Drink	NM	05-10	NM	NM	03-04	NM	P	P

DRY $44 AV

Villa Maria Cellar Selection Cabernet Sauvignon/Merlot (★★★★☆)

The 2001 vintage (★★★★☆) is a great buy. Densely coloured, it's a youthful and complex wine, grown in the company's Ngakirikiri vineyard in the Gimblett Gravels district of Hawke's Bay and matured for 18 months in new and used French and American oak. Concentrated, with sweet-fruit characters, deep cassis, plum and spice flavours seasoned with toasty oak and a lasting finish, it should be at its best from 2004–05 onwards. Although not quite as good as the delicious Cellar Selection Merlot/Cabernet Sauvignon 2000 (Best Buy of the Year in the 2003 *Buyer's Guide*), it's still a bargain.

Vintage	01
WR	6
Drink	03-07

DRY $22 V+

Villa Maria Reserve Cabernet Sauvignon/Merlot ★★★★★
Past vintages have been outstanding, but the 2001 (★★★★★) is the first since 1997. Grown in the company's Ngakirikiri vineyard in the Gimblett Gravels district of Hawke's Bay and matured for 18 months in new French and American oak barriques, it's a powerful, dark wine, crammed with cassis, plum and spice flavours, slightly chocolatey, nutty and firm. Drink 2005 onwards.

Vintage 01
WR 7
Drink 05-10

DRY $40 AV

Voss Waihenga Cabernet/Merlot – see the Cabernet Franc section

Waimea Estates Nelson Cabernet/Merlot ★★☆
The 2002 vintage (★★☆) is a blend of Cabernet Sauvignon (62 per cent), Merlot (29 per cent) and Cabernet Franc (9 per cent), matured in French and American oak casks. It's a full-coloured wine with a herbaceous bouquet. The palate is fresh and crisp, with decent depth of raspberry, green-leaf and plum flavours, but it lacks real ripeness and roundness. Overpriced.

DRY $21 -V

Waimea Estates The Hill Cabernet Sauvignon/Cabernet Franc (★★★★)
The well-ripened 2001 vintage (★★★★) was made from 10-year-old, low-cropping vines on a north-facing slope in Nelson and matured in French and American oak. Offering strong berry, spice and mint flavours, with nutty oak and some savoury complexity, it shows good weight, roundness and sheer drinkability.

DRY $34 -V

Waipara Springs Cabernet Sauvignon (★★★)
A middleweight style, the 2001 vintage (★★★) is based on 12-year-old vines at Waipara. Blended with 10 per cent Merlot and French oak-aged for 10 months, it's fullish in colour, with decent depth of ripe, plummy, spicy flavours and a smooth finish.

Vintage 02
WR 5
Drink 03-05

DRY $20 AV

Weeping Sands Waiheke Cabernet/Merlot (★★★★)
This is the second label of Obsidian, grown at Onetangi ('weeping sands'). Matured for a year in American oak casks (a third new), the 2000 vintage (★★★★) has deep, youthful colour. Plummy, spicy and berryish, with firm tannins and sweet wood adding complexity, it's a rich and stylish wine with a long finish.

Vintage 00
WR 6
Drink 03-05

DRY $29 AV

West Brook Blue Ridge Cabernet Sauvignon ★★★

The Blue Ridge label is reserved for the top wines from the small West Brook winery in West Auckland. The 2000 vintage (★★★) is a smooth, flavoursome Hawke's Bay blend of Cabernet Sauvignon (80 per cent) and Cabernet Franc (20 per cent). Medium-full in colour, with plummy, slightly herbal characters, it's a forward, easy-drinking style.

Vintage	00
WR	5
Drink	03-05

DRY $23 -V

Winslow Petra Cabernet ★★★★

Winslow's 100 per cent Cabernet Sauvignon is a less 'complete' Martinborough wine than its blended stablemate (below), but is still a delicious mouthful and consistently one of the region's top claret-style reds. Drenched with colour, the 2001 vintage (★★★★) was matured for a year in French and American oak casks. It's a powerful, mouthfilling wine (14 per cent alcohol), with a streak of mint running through its highly concentrated cassis, plum and spice flavours, which are braced by firm tannins.

Vintage	01	00	99	98	97	96	95	94
WR	7	6	NM	NM	4	7	5	6
Drink	04-11	03-10	NM	NM	P	03-05	03-04	P

DRY $35 -V

Winslow Turakirae Reserve Cabernet Sauvignon/Franc ★★★★☆

This very powerful Martinborough blend is typically riper and more complex than its Petra stablemate (above), with deep, vibrant, blackcurrant-like flavours. A blend of Cabernet Sauvignon (principally) and smaller proportions of Cabernet Franc and Merlot, the 2001 vintage (★★★★★) was ultra low-cropped (3 tonnes per hectare) and matured for a year in French oak barriques (25 per cent new). Densely coloured, it is built to last, with highly concentrated blackcurrant and spice flavours seasoned with toasty oak and a backbone of firm, chewy tannins. Open 2004+.

Vintage	01	00	99	98	97	96	95	94
WR	7	NM	6	7	4	7	5	6
Drink	04-10	NM	03-05	03-06	P	03-05	03-04	P

DRY $65 -V

Chambourcin

Chambourcin is one of the more highly rated French hybrids, well known in Muscadet for its good disease resistance and bold, crimson hue. Rare in New Zealand, it is principally used as a blending variety, to add colour.

Marsden Estate Chambourcin ★★★☆

The 2000 vintage (★★★★) is a dark, supple Northland red, sturdy and concentrated, with ripe, sweet-fruit characters and loads of blackcurrant, spice and plum flavour. Barrel-aged for 16 months, the 2001 (★★★) is richly coloured and mouthfilling, with strong raspberry and plum flavours, a sweet oak influence and the slightly rustic character typical of Chambourcin. It's less warm and intense than the 2000, but still appealing.

Vintage	01	00
WR	4	6
Drink	03-06	03-06

DRY $26 -V

Gamay Noir

Gamay Noir is single-handedly responsible for the seductively scented and soft red wines of Beaujolais. The grape is still rare in New Zealand, although the area of bearing vines will rise between 2002 and 2005 from 6 to 10 hectares. In the Omaka Springs vineyard in Marlborough, Gamay ripened later than Cabernet Sauvignon (itself an end-of-season ripener), with higher levels of acidity than in Beaujolais, but at Te Mata's Woodthorpe Terraces vineyard in Hawke's Bay, the 2002 crop was picked as early as 15 March.

Lucknow Estate QBV Gamay Noir ★★★

The 2002 vintage (★★★) is a Hawke's Bay red 'that takes fun seriously'. Grown in the Quarry Bridge Vineyard at Maraekakaho and not oak-aged, it's a ruby-hued, vibrantly fruity wine with lots of fresh, red-berry and plum flavour and a slightly spicy, refreshingly crisp finish.

DRY $20 AV

Monarch Te Horo Gamay Beaujolais (★★)

Grown on the Kapiti Coast, the 2001 vintage (★★) is ruby-hued, with herbaceous aromas and flavours that lack varietal character, ripeness and suppleness.

DRY $16 -V

Te Awa Farm Longlands Gamay (★★★☆)

Light pink/red, the highly attractive 2002 vintage (★★★☆) was grown in Hawke's Bay and not oak-aged. It's a supple, raspberryish, gently spicy wine with light tannins and acids well under control, giving excellent lunchtime drinking.

DRY $18 V+

Te Mata Estate Woodthorpe Gamay Noir ★★★☆

Ruby-hued, with raspberryish aromas, the 2002 vintage (★★★☆) is a single-vineyard Hawke's Bay wine, whole-bunch fermented (in the traditional Beaujolais manner) and oak-aged for four months. Fresh, ripe, berryish and smooth, it's less immediately seductive than a top Beaujolais, but hits the target as an enjoyable light red. The 2003 (★★★★) is delicious in its youth. Bright ruby, with an enticingly floral bouquet, it has sweet-fruit characters, fresh, strong raspberry and spice flavours and gentle tannins.

DRY $19 V+

Grenache

Grenache, the world's second most extensively planted grape variety, thrives in the hot, dry vineyards of Spain and southern France. It is starting to yield some exciting wines in Australia, especially from old, unirrigated, bush-pruned vines, but is exceedingly rare in New Zealand.

Matua Valley Innovator Grenache ★★★★

Grown in the Ngatarawa district of Hawke's Bay, the 2000 vintage (★★★☆) is ruby-hued, with a peppery bouquet. It's a medium-weight wine with fresh, ripe plum and pepper flavours (quite Syrah-like), oak complexity and firm but not excessive acidity. The 2002 (★★★★) was made from the ripest grapes the winery has seen since the outstanding, sturdy, sweet-fruited 1998. Matured for 10 months in French oak barriques (40 per cent new), it's a fresh, vibrantly fruity wine with acids under control and strong, plummy, spicy flavours.

DRY $29 AV

Malbec

With a leap from 20 hectares of bearing vines in 1997 to 163 hectares in 2004, this old Bordeaux variety is starting to make its presence felt in New Zealand, where two-thirds of all plantings are clustered in Hawke's Bay. It is typically used as a blending variety, adding brilliant colour and rich, sweet-fruit flavours to its blends with Merlot, Cabernet Sauvignon and Cabernet Franc. Several unblended Malbecs have also been released recently, possessing loads of flavour and often the slight rusticity typical of the variety.

Arahura Malbec ★★★★☆

Grown at Clevedon in South Auckland, the 2002 vintage (★★★★☆) was matured in French and American oak barriques. A worthy follow-up to the dark, concentrated 1999 Arahura Malbec/Franc (★★★★☆), it's a densely coloured wine, rich, vibrant and supple, with lovely depth of plum and spice flavours, oak complexity and loads of character. Drink now or cellar.

Vintage 02
WR 6
Drink 03-05

DRY $30 AV

Collards Shanty Block Malbec ★★★★

The 2002 vintage (★★★★) was made from second-crop vines in the estate vineyard at Henderson and oak-aged. One of the country's most enjoyable Malbecs, it's richly coloured, with a fragrant bouquet of raspberry, plum and spice. Warm and supple, slightly earthy and chocolatey, with sweet-fruit characters and gentle tannins, it shows good ripeness, complexity and depth.

DRY $25 AV

Delegat's Gimblett Gravels Malbec (★★★★☆)

Still very youthful, the 2000 vintage (★★★★☆) was grown in Hawke's Bay and matured for two years in French oak barriques (new and one-year-old). It's a boldly coloured wine with sweet, ripe-fruit characters and rich flavours of plums and spice, seasoned with fine-quality oak. One of the classiest Malbecs on the market.

DRY $? V?

Fromm La Strada Malbec Reserve ★★★★☆

Grown in Marlborough and matured for 15–18 months in French oak casks (30 per cent new), the 2001 vintage (★★★★) is a strapping (14 per cent alcohol), boldly coloured wine with fragrant, red-berry aromas. It's a very generous red with rich, berryish, spicy flavours and firm tannins. Still youthful, it should be at its best from 2005 onwards, when winemaker Hatsch Kalberer suggests drinking it with 'a large piece of wild venison'.

Vintage 02 01 00 99 98
WR 6 7 5 6 7
Drink 05-12 04-11 03-08 03-09 03-10

DRY $48 -V

Mills Reef Elspeth Malbec ★★★★★

The densely coloured 2001 vintage (★★★★★) was grown in Mere Road, in the Gimblett Gravels district of Hawke's Bay, and French oak-aged for 18 months. It's a dark, warm, spicy, gamey, nutty red with a wild, slightly jammy and rustic bouquet, a soft entry, sweet-fruit characters, great flavour concentration and a firm finish. What more can you ask from Malbec? The opaque, very youthful 2002 (★★★★★) has very spicy, plummy aromas leading into a blockbuster palate with gobs of plum, spice and raspberry fruit, quality oak and powerful tannins. It's a powerful brute, likely to be at its best from 2005 onwards.

Vintage	01	00
WR	7	7
Drink	03-06	03-05

DRY $40 AV

Moana Park Malbec (★★★)

Grown in the Dartmoor Valley, Hawke's Bay, the 2000 vintage (★★★) is still youthful and vibrantly fruity. It's a flavoursome but not very complex wine with plummy, spicy flavours and a crisp finish that shows a slight lack of warmth and softness.

DRY $30 -V

Monarch Te Horo Malbec (★★☆)

Deeply coloured, with a herbaceous bouquet, the 2001 vintage (★★☆) was grown on the Kapiti Coast. It's a fruit-driven style, fresh, plummy and berryish, but simple, with a high-acid finish.

DRY $16 -V

Rongopai Reserve Malbec (★★★☆)

Grown in the Waikato and oak-aged for a year, the 2002 vintage (★★★☆) is a buoyantly fruity red with deep, purple-flushed colour and fresh, plum and black pepper aromas. It shows good ripeness and depth, with strong raspberry, plum and spice flavours, subtle oak and a slightly chewy finish.

DRY $22 AV

West Brook Estate Range Malbec (★★★☆)

The debut 2002 vintage (★★★☆) was picked from first-crop vines in the estate vineyard at Waimauku, in West Auckland. Matured for 14 months in a 50/50 split of American and French oak barriques, it's a deeply coloured, purple-flushed wine with a highly scented, floral rather than gamey bouquet. Gutsy, with sweet-fruit characters and plenty of spicy, slightly pruney and herbal flavour, it has firm tannins and lots of character.

DRY $33 -V

Merlot

After judging at the 2003 New Zealand Wine Society Royal Easter Wine Show, the influential Australian critic, James Halliday, was highly enthusiastic about New Zealand Merlots. 'New Zealand as a whole will often, although not always, produce a superior wine to Australia. The trophy-winning Merlot [Villa Maria Reserve Hawke's Bay Merlot 2001] is a lovely wine with lots of varietal flavour, a lot of complexity and great structure.'

Over the past decade, Merlot has replaced Cabernet Sauvignon as our principal variety for claret-style reds, with a host of new releases and the restructuring of some previous Cabernet/Merlot blends as Merlot/Cabernets.

Excitement is especially high in Hawke's Bay about this most extensively cultivated red-wine grape in Bordeaux. Everywhere in Bordeaux – the world's greatest red-wine region – except in the Médoc and Graves districts, the internationally much higher-profile Cabernet Sauvignon variety plays second fiddle to Merlot. The elegant, fleshy wines of Pomerol and St Émilion bear delicious testimony to Merlot's capacity to produce great, yet relatively early-maturing, reds.

In New Zealand, after decades of preoccupation with the more austere and slowly evolving Cabernet Sauvignon, the rich, persistent flavours and (more practically) earlier-ripening ability of Merlot are now fully appreciated. Poor set can be a major drawback with the older clones, reducing yields, but Merlot ripens ahead of Cabernet Sauvignon, a major asset in cooler wine regions, especially in vineyards with colder clay soils. Merlot grapes are typically lower in tannin and higher in sugar than Cabernet Sauvignon's; its wines are thus silkier and a shade stronger in alcohol.

Hawke's Bay has over 70 per cent of New Zealand's Merlot vines; the rest are clustered in Marlborough, Auckland and Gisborne. The country's fourth most extensively planted grape variety, Merlot has knocked Cabernet Sauvignon into fifth spot. Between 2000 and 2005, the total area of bearing Merlot vines will more than double.

Merlot's key role in New Zealand was traditionally that of a minority blending variety, bringing a soft, mouthfilling richness and floral, plummy fruitiness to its marriages with the predominant Cabernet Sauvignon. With the fast-rising stream of straight Merlots and Merlot-predominant blends, this aristocratic grape has now been fully recognised as a top-flight wine in its own right.

Alpha Domus Hawke's Bay Merlot ★★★

The 2002 vintage (★★★) is a light, drink-young style of Hawke's Bay red, oak-aged for five months. It's a full-coloured wine with fresh, berryish, plummy flavours, gentle tannins and a smooth finish.

Vintage 02
WR 7
Drink 03-07

DRY $18 AV

Alpha Domus Merlot/Cabernet ★★★☆

This Hawke's Bay label is designed for early drinking. The 2001 vintage (★★★☆), which includes some Cabernet Franc and Malbec, is an honest Bordeaux style, green-edged but showing some good, savoury, earthy complexity. Oak-matured for a year, the deeply coloured 2002 (★★★☆) is full-flavoured and supple, with cassis, plum and green-leaf characters and a hint of sweet oak.

Vintage	02	01	00	99	98
WR	6	6	6	5	7
Drink	04-09	03-07	03-06	03-05	03-04

DRY $19 V+

Arahura Merlot/Cabernet Sauvignon (★★★★)

The 1999 vintage (★★★★) is made from estate-grown, Clevedon (South Auckland) grapes, matured for a year in French and American oak barriques (30 per cent new). A blend of Merlot (66 per cent), Cabernet Sauvignon (31 per cent) and Cabernet Franc (3 per cent), it is warm, rich and smooth, with berry, plum and spice flavours and a lovely suppleness of texture. A savoury, Bordeaux-like wine.

Vintage	00	99	98	97
WR	5	6	NM	6
Drink	03-04	03-04	NM	P

DRY $23 V+

Arahura Merlot/Malbec (★★★★)

The stylish 2000 vintage (★★★★) was grown at Clevedon, in South Auckland, and matured for a year in French and American oak casks. It's a fragrant, spicy, dark, youthful wine, still purple-flushed, with finely integrated oak and fresh, rich flavours of plums and spice. Worth cellaring.

Vintage	00
WR	6
Drink	04-06

DRY $30 AV

Artisan Riverstone Vineyard Merlot ★★★

Grown in Omahu Road, in the Gimblett Gravels district of Hawke's Bay, the 2001 vintage (★★★☆) shows promisingly deep colour. Matured in French oak barriques (30 per cent new), it has a slight lack of softness on the finish, but very good depth of blackcurrant, spice and herb flavours, with oak complexity and hints of coffee and nuts. Drink now to 2005.

DRY $23 -V

Ascension Matakana Merlot (★★☆)

The 2002 vintage (★★☆) is a solid wine, but too herbaceous to rate higher. Matured in French and American oak, it shows fresh, berryish, leafy characters and some earthy, spicy complexity. A drink-young style.

DRY $22 -V

Ascension The Ascent Merlot/Malbec/Cabernet Sauvignon ★★★

Estate-grown at Matakana, the 2002 vintage (★★★☆) is a blend of Merlot (68 per cent), Malbec (22 per cent) and Cabernet Sauvignon (10 per cent), matured for over a year in French and American oak casks (half new). It's an elegant, youthful wine with ripe, spicy fruit aromas and concentrated flavours showing slightly high acidity, but also good structure and length.

DRY $30 -V

Babich Winemakers Reserve Merlot ★★★☆

Grown in Gimblett Road, Hawke's Bay, the 2001 (★★★) is full but not densely coloured, with berryish, plummy, spicy, slightly earthy flavours. It's a moderately complex, gently oaked wine, not highly concentrated but showing decent depth and balanced for easy drinking. The 2002 vintage (★★★☆) has youthful, purple/red colour of good depth. It offers fresh, vibrantly fruity berry and plum flavours, with a subtle oak influence and gentle tannins.

Vintage	02	01	00
WR	7	6	7
Drink	03-08	03-07	03-06

DRY $22 AV

Black Barn Merlot/Cabernet Sauvignon/Cabernet Franc (★★★)

Hill-grown at Havelock North, the debut 2001 vintage (★★★) is a Merlot-based red (54 per cent), blended with Cabernet Sauvignon (30 per cent) and Cabernet Franc (16 per cent). It's a fresh, vibrantly fruity wine with plenty of plummy, spicy flavour, some oak complexity and a slightly crisp finish. Re-tasted in August 2003, it's still youthful and maturing solidly.

DRY $23 -V

Black Barn Reserve Hawke's Bay Merlot (★★★★☆)

Grown on a north-facing slope at Havelock North, the debut 2001 vintage (★★★★☆) includes minor portions of Cabernet Sauvignon (10 per cent) and Cabernet Franc (5 per cent). Matured in French oak barriques (35 per cent new), it's an elegant, richly coloured Hawke's Bay red, still youthful, with excellent depth of ripe, plummy, spicy flavour, considerable complexity and a lasting, well-rounded finish. Re-tasted in August 2003, it's aging beautifully.

DRY $36 -V

Borthwick Wairarapa Merlot (★★★)

For drinking now or cellaring, the 2001 vintage (★★★) was grown near Masterton and matured for 18 months in oak casks (90 per cent new). It's a richly coloured wine with a leafy bouquet and concentrated plum, spice and herb flavours, but shows a slight lack of full ripeness.

DRY $30 -V

Brajkovich Merlot – see Kumeu River Village Merlot

Brightwater Vineyards Nelson Merlot ★★★

Matured for a year in mostly French oak, the 2001 vintage (★★★☆) is clearly superior to the slightly high-acid 2000 (★★☆). Deeply coloured, it's a fruit-packed wine, brambly, plummy and spicy, with cool-climate freshness, very good concentration and a well-rounded finish.

Vintage	01	00	99
WR	7	5	4
Drink	03-07	03-04	P

DRY $28 -V

Cable Bay Five Hills Merlot/Malbec/Cabernet Sauvignon (★★★☆)

Grown on five hillside sites on Waiheke Island and matured in French oak barriques, the debut 2002 vintage (★★★☆) is a full-coloured wine with plum and spice aromas. Fresh and youthful, with good ripeness and flavour depth, some savoury complexity and firm tannins, it should be at its best from 2005 onwards.

DRY $35 -V

Canterbury House Waipara Merlot (★★★)

Grown at Waipara, the 2001 vintage (★★★) is full-coloured, with floral, berryish aromas. It's an easy-drinking style with ripe, gently oaked raspberry and plum flavours, showing decent depth.

DRY $22 -V

Charles Wiffen Marlborough Merlot (★★★)

The 2002 vintage (★★★) is a sweetly oaked wine with plum and red-berry flavours, fresh and vibrantly fruity, and a smooth finish. An enjoyable drink-young style.

DRY $25 -V

Charles Wiffen Reserve Marlborough Merlot ★★★☆

A very good claret-style red by the region's standards, the 2001 vintage (★★★☆) was grown in the Wairau Valley and matured in new French oak barriques. Fresh and fruit-crammed, it's a full-coloured wine with good concentration of vibrant, plummy, spicy flavours seasoned with fine-quality oak, but also a slightly high-acid finish.

DRY $35 -V

Church Road Merlot/Cabernet (★★★☆)

The 2002 vintage (★★★☆) is the first of Montana's Church Road reds (apart from the reserve) to be merlot-predominant. Deeply coloured, with a slightly herbal bouquet, it's a blend of Merlot (61 per cent), Cabernet Sauvignon (26 per cent) and Malbec (12 per cent), matured for 14 months in French oak barriques (43 per cent new). It shows good body and flavour depth, with blackcurrant, herb and spice flavours, savoury, nutty complexities and a smooth finish.

Vintage 02
WR 6
Drink 04-08

DRY $23 AV

Church Road Reserve Merlot/Cabernet ★★★★☆

Released after four years' maturation in barrel and bottle, the 1999 (★★★★) is a good but not great vintage of Montana's Hawke's Bay red. Full-bodied and richly flavoured, it's a deliciously well-rounded wine with leathery, nutty characters and strong drink-now appeal. A blend of 84 per cent Merlot, 7 per cent Cabernet Sauvignon, 7 per cent Malbec and 2 per cent Cabernet Franc, the 1999 was matured for 16 months in mainly new French oak barriques. Clearly superior, the 2000 vintage (★★★★★) is dark, with beautifully rich blackcurrant, plum and spice flavours and chocolatey, leathery characters. It's an impressively complex wine with the power to age, but you can drink it with pleasure now.

Vintage 99
WR 7
Drink 03-08

DRY $35 AV

C.J. Pask Gimblett Road Merlot ★★★★

Matured for over a year in French and American oak casks, the 2000 vintage (★★★★☆) is highly impressive for a non-reserve wine. Grown in Gimblett Road, Hawke's Bay, it is full-coloured, with a spicy bouquet. Warm and supple, it's a rather Bordeaux-like wine with deliciously sweet fruit characters and well-integrated oak. Offering good complexity, it's an elegant, finely structured wine, already delicious.

Vintage 00 99 98 97 96 95
WR 7 6 7 6 6 7
Drink 03-06 03-04 03-04 P P P

DRY $28 AV

C.J. Pask Reserve Merlot ★★★★★

Following on from the memorable 1998 (★★★★★) and 1999 (★★★★★) vintages, the 2000 (★★★★★) is the most distinguished Hawke's Bay Merlot on the market. Based on the company's oldest, ungrafted vines in Gimblett Road (low-cropping at 6.5 tonnes/hectare), and matured for 16 months in all-new French and American oak barriques, it is dark and notably ripe, with layers of cassis, spice, nut and coffee flavours. A magical wine, built for the long haul, it proves the great complexity and concentration of which Merlot is capable. Best drinking 2005+.

Vintage	00	99	98	97
WR	7	6	7	6
Drink	03-07	03-05	03-05	P

DRY $55 AV

Clearview Estate Cape Kidnappers Merlot ★★★

The 2002 vintage (★★★) is a full-coloured Hawke's Bay red with a slightly rustic bouquet. Gutsy and chewy, it offers plenty of spicy, slightly leafy and nutty flavour, with some complexity and a firm tannin grip.

Vintage	02
WR	5
Drink	03-05

DRY $22 -V

Clearview Estate Reserve Merlot/Malbec ★★★★★

Dark, mouthfilling and crammed with ripe-fruit characters, this is a serious yet sensuous Hawke's Bay red, with a seductive intensity of spicy, vibrant, almost sweet-tasting flavour. Grown in a mix of clay and stone at Te Awanga, where the vines yield only 5 to 6 tonnes per hectare, it is matured for 18 months in French (80 per cent) and American oak (20 per cent); about 70 per cent of the barrels are new each year. The 2000 vintage (★★★★☆) is a blend of Merlot (50 per cent), Malbec (28 per cent), Cabernet Franc (12 per cent) and Cabernet Sauvignon (10 per cent). Purple-flushed, it is plump and deep, with concentrated blackcurrant, plum and spice flavours, chocolatey, gamey nuances and a lasting finish.

Vintage	00	99	98	97	96	95	94
WR	7	6	7	6	5	6	6
Drink	03-06	03-05	03-05	P	P	P	P

DRY $40 AV

Collards Hawke's Bay Merlot ★★★

From the West Auckland winery that in 1980 made New Zealand's first straight Merlot, the 2000 vintage (★★★) was grown in the shingly Gimblett Road area of Hawke's Bay. Medium-full in colour, it's a middleweight style with good varietal character, fresh acidity and decent depth of plummy, spicy flavour.

Vintage	01	00	99	98	97
WR	7	6	7	7	6
Drink	03-06	03-05	03-04	P	P

DRY $19 AV

Coopers Creek Hawke's Bay Merlot ★★★

This is Coopers Creek's most popular red wine. The ruby-hued 2002 vintage (★★★) is based mainly on Havelock North grapes and was matured for six months in American and French oak casks. Raspberry and spice aromas lead into a fresh, vibrantly fruity wine with good depth of berryish, spicy flavours, a gentle oak influence and smooth finish. As a drink-young style, this works well.

Vintage	02	01	00	99	98
WR	6	5	6	5	7
Drink	03-05	03-04	03-04	P	P

DRY $17 AV

Coopers Creek Reserve The Gardener
Huapai Merlot/Cabernet Sauvignon ★★★☆

The flavoursome 2000 vintage (★★★☆) is a West Auckland red, blended from two-thirds Merlot and one-third Cabernet Sauvignon, and matured in American and French oak casks (mostly new). Drinking well now, it offers berry, plum and spice flavours, showing some warmth and savoury, earthy complexity, and fairly firm tannins. There is no 2001, but 'the 2002 vintage is better than the 2000', says winemaker Simon Nunns.

Vintage	02	01	00
WR	6	NM	6
Drink	04-08	NM	03-06

DRY $30 -V

Corazon The Collective Merlot/Malbec (★★★☆)

Fleshy and tightly structured, the debut 2002 vintage (★★★☆) is a single-vineyard red, grown at Waiohika Estate in Gisborne and matured for 10 months in French oak casks (one-third new). A blend of 60 per cent Merlot and 40 per cent Malbec, it has spicy, distinctly Malbec aromas and a youthful palate, showing good concentration and length. Full-coloured, gutsy and characterful, it's already drinking well but worth cellaring.

Vintage	02
WR	6
Drink	03-07

DRY $28 -V

Corbans Private Bin
Hawke's Bay Merlot/Cabernet Sauvignon (★★★★)

Here's a great opportunity to buy an aged Hawke's Bay red, maturing well. Released in mid-2003, the 1999 vintage (★★★★) is a full but not densely coloured blend of Merlot (68 per cent) and Cabernet Sauvignon (32 per cent), grown in the Gimblett Gravels district and matured for 14 months in French oak barriques (30 per cent new). Brambly and spicy, with hints of coffee, leather and herbs, it's drinking well now, with loads of character.

Vintage	99
WR	5
Drink	03-06

DRY $22 V+

Crab Farm Reserve Merlot (★★★)

Hand-picked in Hawke's Bay and matured for 15 months in new French oak casks, the 2002 vintage (★★★) has deep, youthful, purple-flushed colour. Chewy and tannic, it has buckets of plummy, berryish fruit, but at this stage impresses more with its intensity than fragrance or finesse. Still youthful and raw, it needs time; open 2005 onwards.

Vintage	02
WR	6
Drink	05-06

DRY $25 -V

Craggy Range Gimblett Gravels Vineyard Merlot (★★★★☆)

Densely coloured, with leathery, nutty complexities and fine-grained tannins, the 2001 vintage (★★★★☆) is an unusually classy and characterful Hawke's Bay wine for its price. Harvested at over 24 brix, matured for 19 months in French oak barriques (65 per cent new) and bottled unfiltered, it's a fragrant red with concentrated blackcurrant, plum, herb and spice flavours, good complexity and a slightly chewy finish.

Vintage	01
WR	6
Drink	06-09

DRY $25 V+

Craggy Range Seven Poplars Vineyard Merlot ★★★★★

Still opening out, the 2001 vintage (★★★★★) was grown in stony soils at the Dolbel Estate vineyard in the lower Dartmoor Valley, picked at 23.8 brix, matured for a year in French oak casks (80 per cent new), and then aged for another nine months in two-year-old barrels before bottling. Fragrant, spicy and brambly on the nose, with rich, purple-flushed colour, it's a very generous red. The flavours are rich and plummy, with a spicy Malbec influence (9 per cent of the blend) and hints of coffee and nuts. It's a highly concentrated wine, warm and supple, with lovely mouthfeel and texture.

Vintage	01	00	99
WR	6	6	6
Drink	05-08	03-07	03-05

DRY $40 AV

Crossroads Destination Series Merlot/Cabernet Sauvignon (★★★)

The 2001 vintage (★★★) is a moderately ripe Hawke's Bay red with plummy, spicy, slightly leafy flavours, a sweet oak influence and gentle tannins.

Vintage	01
WR	6
Drink	03-06

DRY $25 -V

Delegat's Gimblett Gravels Merlot (★★★★☆)

To be released in late 2003, the 2000 vintage (★★★★☆) is a boldly coloured Hawke's Bay red, matured for two years in French oak barriques (new and one-year-old). Still youthful, it shows beautifully ripe, sweet-fruit characters and highly concentrated blackcurrant, plum and spice flavours.

DRY $? V?

Delegat's Reserve Merlot ★★★★

Perfumed, with plum and chocolate aromas, the 2001 vintage (★★★★) was grown in the Ngatarawa and Gimblett Gravels districts of Hawke's Bay and matured for a year in new and one-year-old French oak barriques. Plummy, with ripe tannins and lush, sweet-fruit characters, it's a vibrantly fruity wine, still youthful. Tasted as a barrel sample (and so not rated), the 2002 was promisingly dark, with buckets of ripe blackcurrant, plum and chocolate flavour.

Vintage	02	01	00	99	98	97
WR	6	6	6	6	7	6
Drink	03-05	03-04	03-04	P	P	P

DRY $20 V+

Drylands Marlborough Merlot ★★☆

The 2002 vintage (★★★) from Nobilo was matured in American and French oak barriques. It's a fruit-driven, lightly wooded style, fresh and plummy, with good depth and a slightly leafy, spicy finish.

Vintage	02	01
WR	7	7
Drink	03-06	03-04

DRY $20 -V

Equinox Hawke's Bay Merlot/Cabernet Sauvignon (★★★)

A middleweight style, offering smooth, easy drinking, the 2000 vintage (★★★) is a French and American oak-aged red, blended from Merlot (67 per cent), Cabernet Sauvignon (25 per cent) and Malbec (8 per cent). Fullish in colour, it possesses decent depth of plummy, spicy flavours, showing some complexity.

Vintage	00
WR	4
Drink	03-04

DRY $19 AV

Esk Valley Hawke's Bay Merlot ★★★★☆

The 2002 vintage (★★★★) of this consistently excellent wine was grown in the Dartmoor Valley, Puketapu and Gimblett Road districts and matured for a year in French and American oak barriques. It's a muscular wine (14.5 per cent alcohol), densely coloured and very fragrant, with bold, vibrant fruit flavours of blackcurrants and plums, a hint of dark chocolate and firm tannins. Powerful, with a chewy finish, it should mature well for several years.

Vintage	02	01	00	99	98	97	96
WR	7	NM	6	NM	7	5	6
Drink	03-07	NM	03-05	NM	03-05	P	P

DRY $23 V+

Esk Valley Merlot/Cabernet Sauvignon/Malbec ★★★★

This Hawke's Bay winery specialises in Merlot-based reds. Grown in the Gimblett Gravels and Dartmoor Valley districts, the 2002 vintage (★★★★) is a blend of Merlot (58 per cent), Cabernet Sauvignon (27 per cent), Malbec (13 per cent) and Cabernet Franc (2 per cent), matured for a year in French and American oak casks. Weighty, concentrated and fruit-packed, it possesses deep, bright colour, a spicy, sweet oak influence and excellent depth of ripe blackcurrant, plum and spice flavours.

Vintage	02	01	00
WR	7	6	6
Drink	03-08	03-05	03-05

DRY $23 AV

Esk Valley Reserve Merlot/Cabernet Sauvignon/Malbec ★★★★★

Dark, vibrantly fruity and bursting with ripe, sweet-tasting blackcurrant, plum and French oak flavours, this is one of the country's classiest claret-style reds. Its superb quality, even in cooler years, makes it an important signpost to the future of Hawke's Bay reds. Since 1995, the grapes have come largely 'off the stones' – the company-owned Ngakirikiri vineyard, near Gimblett Road, and neighbouring sites. The fermenting juice is hand-plunged and the wine is matured for a long period in French oak barriques (new and one-year-old). The 2001 vintage (★★★★★), labelled Merlot/Cabernet Sauvignon (no Malbec), is a densely coloured, generous red with warm blackcurrant, spice and oak flavours showing great intensity, sweet-fruit characters and ripe tannins in a deliciously soft, forward style. The 2002 is a blend of Merlot (58 per cent), Cabernet Sauvignon (27 per cent), Malbec (13 per cent) and Cabernet Franc (2 per cent). Tasted as a barrel sample (and so not rated), it was inky-black, with super-charged flavour.

Vintage	02	01	00	99	98	97	96	95	94
WR	7	6	7	7	7	6	7	6	5
Drink	03-10	03-06	03-08	03-08	03-08	P	P	P	P

DRY $50 AV

Forrest Estate Marlborough Merlot ★★★☆

Boldly coloured, the 2001 vintage (★★★☆) is a very smooth, American oak-aged red with strong blackcurrant/plum flavours and hints of dark chocolate and herbs. Fractional sweetness (4 grams/litre of sugar) gives a delicious drink-young style. (The 2002 is a Merlot/Malbec.)

Vintage	02	01
WR	4	5
Drink	04-05	04-07

DRY $24 AV

Framingham Marlborough Merlot/Malbec (★★★☆)

The 2001 vintage (★★★☆) is a 60/40 blend, matured in French and American oak casks (30 per cent new). Purple-flushed, with fresh, red-berry aromas, it is smooth, vibrantly fruity, ripe and plummy in a moderately complex style with very good flavour depth.

DRY $24 AV

Fromm La Strada Marlborough Merlot/Malbec ★★★★

Both the 2000 (★★★☆) and 2001 (★★★★) vintages include all the grapes from the Fromm Vineyard that in warmer years would have been reserved for the Merlot Reserve label (not made in 2000 or 2001). Matured in seasoned oak casks, the 2000 is a sturdy, deeply coloured, strongly flavoured wine, spicy and gamey, with a slight herbal edge, chewy tannins and loads of character. More youthful in colour, the 2001 is a full-flavoured, slightly riper wine, vibrant, plummy, spicy and firm, with good aging potential.

Vintage	02	01	00	99
WR	5	5	5	5
Drink	04-08	03-07	03-06	03-05

DRY $28 AV

Gladstone Merlot/Cabernet Sauvignon (★★★)

The full-flavoured 2001 vintage (★★★) is a blend of estate-grown Merlot (50 per cent) and Cabernet Franc (5 per cent) with Cabernet Sauvignon (45 per cent) from another vineyard at Gladstone, in the Wairarapa. Matured for a year in French (two-thirds) and American oak casks, it is deeply coloured, with a leafy, spicy bouquet. Vibrantly fruity, with strong flavours of plums and herbs, it shows a slight lack of full ripeness, but good intensity and some savoury complexity.

DRY $29 -V

Gladstone Reserve Merlot ★★★

Grown at two sites in the Wairarapa (the home vineyard at Gladstone and at Opaki, north of Masterton), the 2001 vintage (★★☆) was matured for nine months in one to three-year-old French oak casks. Full-coloured, with a green-edged bouquet, it's a fresh wine with plenty of blackcurrant, plum and green-leaf flavours, but too herbaceous to rate more highly.

DRY $30 -V

Goldridge Estate Premium Reserve Hawke's Bay Merlot (★★★)

The 2000 vintage (★★★) doesn't measure up to the overkill on the back label, but is still a decent red. A single-vineyard wine, matured in new and one-year-old French oak casks, it's full-coloured, with strong blackcurrant/plum flavours in a vibrantly fruity and smooth, moderately complex style.

Vintage	00
WR	5
Drink	03-05

DRY $20 AV

Goldwater Esslin Merlot ★★★★☆

Grown in the Esslin Vineyard on Waiheke Island, the 1999 vintage (★★★★☆) is savoury and supple, with complex flavours of spice, plum and chocolate and gentle tannins. The 2000 (★★★★☆), from a 'very good' season, was harvested at 24 brix and matured for 15 months in French oak barriques (80 per cent new). Full but not dense in colour, with a hint of development, it is leathery, spicy and gamey, with impressive depth, warmth and complexity. Compared to Hawke's Bay Merlots, it is less vibrantly fruity, more earthy and savoury, and already highly enjoyable.

Vintage	00	99	98	97	96
WR	7	7	7	7	7
Drink	03-10	03-10	03-07	03-05	03-05

DRY $90 -V

Grove Mill Marlborough Merlot ★★★★

The 1999 vintage (★★★★) was French oak-matured for 20 months. Richly coloured, mouthfilling, fruity and firm, it's a concentrated, finely balanced wine, similar to the 1998, with impressive complexity, warmth and depth.

Vintage	00	99	98	97
WR	6	7	6	5
Drink	03-05	03-04	03	P

DRY $30 AV

Gunn Estate Merlot/Cabernet (★★☆)

From the Sacred Hill winery, the 2002 vintage (★★☆) is a lightly oaked blend of Merlot (58 per cent), Cabernet Sauvignon (32 per cent) and Malbec (8 per cent), with minor portions of Pinot Noir and Cabernet Franc. A medium-bodied Hawke's Bay red, fresh, berryish and spicy, it offers enjoyable drinking in its youth and is verging on three-star quality.

Vintage	02
WR	6
Drink	03-05

DRY $15 AV

Harrier Rise Bigney Coigne Merlot – see Harrier Rise Bigney Coigne in the Branded and Other Reds section

Harrier Rise Uppercase Merlot – see Harrier Rise Uppercase in the Branded and Other Reds section

Heron's Flight La Cerise Merlot/Sangiovese ★★★

In the past this was usually an unblended Merlot, but since 1999 Sangiovese – the great grape of Chianti – has been part of the blend. Estate-grown at Matakana and oak-aged, it is designed as 'a light style red, perfect for drinking with lunch or light evening meals'. It's typically a ruby-hued, medium-bodied wine with plenty of fresh, vibrant, plummy, cherryish flavour.

DRY $22 -V

312   RED WINES

Herzog Spirit of Marlborough Merlot/Cabernet Sauvignon ★★★★★

Grown on the banks of the Wairau River and matured for two years in new French oak barriques, the 1999 vintage (★★★★★) is a densely coloured, statuesque red, overflowing with blackcurrant, plum, spice and new oak flavours, braced by chewy tannins. A blend of Merlot (60 per cent), Cabernet Sauvignon (15 per cent), Cabernet Franc (15 per cent) and Malbec (10 per cent), bottled without fining or filtration, it's an exciting mouthful, and the region's boldest claret-style red.

Vintage 99
WR 6
Drink 03-15

DRY $56 AV

Hinchco Matakana Merlot (★★★)

The deeply coloured 2002 vintage (★★★) is a French and American oak-matured red with a leafy streak running through its berry, spice and plum flavours, which show satisfying depth.

DRY $25 -V

Huapai Estate Merlot/Cabernet Franc (★★☆)

Grown in the Huapai vineyard once known as Bazzard Estate, the 2002 vintage (★★☆) is a solid debut. French oak-aged for 11 months, it's a full-coloured, medium-bodied wine with fresh, berryish flavours, the earthiness typical of Auckland reds and a slightly high-acid finish. Verging on three stars.

DRY $20 -V

Huntaway Reserve Hawke's Bay Merlot/Cabernet Sauvignon ★★★

Full but not densely coloured, the 2000 vintage (★★★) from Montana is a middleweight, vibrantly fruity style with plenty of plummy, spicy, slightly toasty flavour.

Vintage 00
WR 6
Drink 03+

DRY $20 AV

Hunter's Marlborough Merlot ★★★

Top vintages are warm and spicy, with cassis, plum and green-leaf flavours showing very good depth. In cooler years, the wine offers reasonable depth of blackcurrant/plum flavours in a smooth, undemanding style.

Vintage 01   00   99 98
WR   5   4   4   5
Drink   05   03-04 P   P

DRY $22 -V

Hyperion Gaia Merlot ★★★☆

Grown at Matakana, north of Auckland, the charming 2000 vintage (★★★☆) is fullish in colour, with raspberry/plum flavours showing good depth, a sweet oak influence and moderate complexity. The 2002 (★★★☆), oak-aged for 14 months, is a full-coloured, plummy and berryish, sweetly oaked wine with savoury, earthy characters adding complexity, very good flavour depth and moderately firm tannins. Drink mid-2004 onwards.

Vintage 00   99 98
WR   7   NM 6
Drink   04-08 NM P

DRY $40 -V

Isola Estate Merlot (★★☆)

Grown on Waiheke Island, the 2002 vintage (★★☆) was aged for 14 months in French and American oak barriques (30 per cent new). Bright and youthful in colour, with a perfumed, sweetly oaked bouquet, it's a fruity, spicy, plummy wine that lacks a bit of ripeness and warmth, with a slightly high-acid finish.

DRY $30 -V

Kemblefield The Distinction Merlot ★★★

This Hawke's Bay red is estate-grown at Mangatahi. The 2000 vintage (★★★) includes 15 per cent Cabernet Sauvignon and Cabernet Franc, and was matured for 14 months in French oak casks. Medium-full in colour, berryish and spicy, with some complexity, a distinctly leafy streak and smooth tannins, it's an easy-drinking and slightly rustic wine, with character.

DRY $22 -V

Kennedy Point Vineyard Merlot (★★★★)

Distinctly Bordeaux-like, the 2002 vintage (★★★★) of this Waiheke Island red is a blend of Merlot (77 per cent), Cabernet Franc (18 per cent) and Malbec (5 per cent), French oak-aged for over a year. It avoids the leafiness that detracted slightly from the vineyard's earlier, Cabernet Sauvignon-based reds, showing good warmth and concentration of plummy, spicy flavours. It's a firmly structured wine, well worth cellaring to at least 2005.

Vintage 02
WR 6
Drink 04-10

DRY $35 -V

Kim Crawford Te Awanga Vineyard Merlot ★★★

The 2002 vintage (★★★) of this Hawke's Bay red was matured for 10 months in oak casks (half new). Full and bright in colour, it has strong blackcurrant, mint and plum flavours, with firm acidity and a slightly leafy streak. Pricey.

Vintage 02
WR 6
Drink 06-08

DRY $30 -V

Kingsley Estate Merlot ★★★★☆

Grown organically in Gimblett Road, Hawke's Bay, and matured for 20 months in French oak barriques (one-third new), the 2000 vintage (★★★★☆) is a blend of Merlot (86 per cent) and Malbec (14 per cent). Densely coloured, it is firm and concentrated, with rich plummy, spicy flavours, a hint of mint chocolate and a long, firm, tight-knit finish. It needs time; open mid-2004+.

Vintage 00
WR 7
Drink 04-10

DRY $49 -V

Kumeu River Kumeu Merlot (★★★★)

The 2000 vintage (★★★★), oak-aged for 18 months, is the first wine under this label since the gold medal 1983. Deeply coloured, it's from a great year that winemaker Michael Brajkovich reports yielded 'an abundance of riches. Grapes of this quality would normally have gone into our top Melba label.' A delicious wine with very good intensity of berry, plum and spice flavours, sweet-fruit characters and good tannin backbone, it's well worth cellaring and bargain-priced. There is no 2001, 2002 or 2003.

Vintage	03	02	01	00
WR	NM	NM	NM	7
Drink	NM	NM	NM	03-08

DRY $20 V+

Kumeu River Village Merlot ★★★

In the past sold under the Brajkovich brand, this West Auckland red is grown at Kumeu and matured for up to a year in old French oak barrels. It is typically spicy, berryish and firm. The 2000 vintage (★★★) has a spicy, slightly earthy bouquet and firm palate with plenty of red-berry, plum and spice flavour, now showing some savoury, leathery complexity. Drink now to 2004.

DRY $15 V+

Kumeu River Village Merlot/Malbec (★★★☆)

There's an instant appeal about the bargain-priced 1999 vintage (★★★☆) of this West Auckland red. French oak-matured for eight months, with 30 per cent Malbec in the blend, it's a fleshy, sweetly-fruited wine with plummy, spicy, savoury characters in a rather Bordeaux-like mould showing good complexity. Drink now onwards. An excellent buy.

DRY $15 V+

Lake Chalice Black Label Vineyard Selection Merlot ★★☆

The 2002 vintage (★★☆), grown in Marlborough and Hawke's Bay, is a Merlot-based red (85 per cent) with smaller portions of Cabernet Franc and Cabernet Sauvignon. Matured briefly (for four months) in French and American oak casks, it is fullish in colour, with raspberryish, leafy aromas. Fresh, simple and smooth, it's a fruit-driven style with moderately firm tannins.

Vintage	02
WR	6
Drink	03-06

DRY $20 -V

Lake Chalice Platinum Merlot ★★★★

The excellent 2001 vintage (★★★★☆) was harvested at 24.5 brix in the company-owned Falcon Vineyard and the nearby Parata Vineyard, in the Rapaura district of Marlborough, and barrique-aged for a year. Boldly coloured, with dense cassis, plum and spice flavours, it is ripe and concentrated, complex and firm. Built to last, it's a highly impressive wine and decidedly superior to most of the region's claret-style reds. Matured for a year in oak casks (half new), the 2002 (★★★☆) is boldly coloured, with fresh plum and spice flavours showing very good depth, a seasoning of sweet oak and firm tannins. It's less striking than the 2001, but still worth cellaring.

Vintage	01	00	99	98
WR	7	7	7	7
Drink	03-07	03-06	03-05	03-04

DRY $28 AV

Le Grys Marlborough Merlot ★★☆

The smooth, easy-drinking 2001 vintage (★★☆) is a single-vineyard wine, grown at Rapaura and lightly oaked (one-half of the final blend was matured for 11 months in French oak casks). It's a full-coloured, moderately complex wine with raspberryish aromas and berry/plum flavours offering decent depth. Verging on three stars.

Vintage	01	00
WR	5	6
Drink	03-06	P

DRY $19 -V

Lincoln Heritage Merlot (★★☆)

Grown in Gisborne, the 2001 vintage (★★☆) was matured for a year in mostly American oak casks (25 per cent new). It offers decent depth of plum and red-berry flavours, but the tannins are a bit green and hard.

Vintage	01
WR	6
Drink	03-06

DRY $19 -V

Lincoln Winemakers Series Gisborne Merlot ★★★

This affordable red is typically plummy and slightly spicy in a medium-bodied style with lifted fruit characters, a bouquet of fresh raspberries and smooth red-berry/plum flavours. Handled entirely in stainless steel tanks, it's an ideal lunch red in the Beaujolais mould, simple but enjoyable.

DRY $14 V+

Linden Estate Hawke's Bay Merlot ★★★

Grown in the Esk Valley, the 2000 vintage (★★★) includes 15 per cent Malbec and was matured for a year in American (80 per cent) and French oak casks. Fragrant and full-coloured, it's a mouthfilling wine with plenty of firm, plummy, strongly spicy flavour. The 2001 (★★★), which includes 5 per cent Malbec, was matured in French oak casks (15 per cent new). It's a full-coloured wine with good depth of fresh, plummy, spicy flavours, oak complexity and a slightly crisp finish.

Vintage	00	99	98	97	96	95
WR	6	5	7	5	4	5
Drink	03-06	P	03-04	P	P	P

DRY $23 -V

Linden Estate Two Valleys Merlot/Malbec/Cabernet (★★☆)

The 'two valleys' referred to on the label are the Esk and Dartmoor, in Hawke's Bay. The 2001 vintage (★★☆), a blend of Merlot (43 per cent), Malbec (37 per cent) and Cabernet Sauvignon (20 per cent), is an easy-drinking red with a hint of sweet oak, gentle tannins and moderate depth of flavour, berryish, plummy and smooth.

DRY $19 -V

Longridge Hawke's Bay Merlot/Cabernet ★★★

Showing good colour depth, the 2002 vintage (★★☆) from Montana is a blend of Merlot (60 per cent), Cabernet Sauvignon (27 per cent) and Cabernet Franc (13 per cent), matured for nine months in a 3:1 mix of French and American oak casks (15 per cent new). It possesses plenty of blackcurrant, green-leaf and mint flavour, but slightly lacks warmth and roundness. Still, the price is right.

Vintage	02	01	00
WR	5	6	6
Drink	03-06	03+	P

DRY $15 AV

Longview Estate Gumdiggers Merlot/Cabernet Sauvignon/Cabernet Franc (★★)

This Northland winery has made some impressive reds in the past, but the 2000 vintage (★★) is disappointing. Matured for 16 months in French oak casks, it's a lightly coloured, leafy, vegetative wine in the old New Zealand style, lacking ripeness, richness and roundness. Ready.

DRY $25 -V

Longview Estate Mario's Merlot ★★★☆

Drinking well now, the 2000 vintage (★★★☆) was estate-grown just south of Whangarei, in Northland, and French oak-aged for 15 months. It's a vibrantly fruity and supple wine with very good depth of plum, red-berry and green-leaf flavours, integrated spicy oak and well-balanced tannins.

DRY $26 -V

Loopline Vineyard Wairarapa Reserve Merlot (★★★)

The 2001 vintage was grown on the Opaki Plains, north of Masterton, and aged for nine months in French oak casks (one-third new). Fullish in colour, with berryish, slightly leafy aromas, it offers fresh, vibrant berry/plum flavours with a restrained oak influence and gentle tannins. Drink now onwards.

Vintage 01
WR 6
Drink 03-08

DRY $29 -V

Lucknow Estate Quarry Bridge Vineyard Merlot ★★☆

The 2001 vintage (★★★) is a Hawke's Bay red, matured for 22 months in American oak casks (30 per cent new). Fullish in colour, with toasty oak aromas, it's a characterful wine with a slightly leafy, vegetal streak but also some spicy, nutty complexity. An honest, flavoursome and firmly structured wine, it offers decent drinking from now onwards.

Vintage 01
WR 7
Drink 05-06

DRY $22 -V

Lynskeys Wairau Peaks Marlborough Merlot (★★★★)

Densely coloured, with a perfumed, spicy bouquet, the 2001 vintage (★★★★) was matured for 15 months in new American (30 per cent) and older French oak casks. Packed with blackcurrant, spice and mint flavours, it's a bold, impressively concentrated red, with ripe-fruit characters seasoned with sweet, nutty oak and chewy tannins. Made in a very upfront style, it's not the ultimate in style, but if you love big Aussie reds, you'll enjoy this.

Vintage 01
WR 7
Drink 03-06

DRY $42 -V

Margrain Martinborough Merlot ★★★☆

French oak-matured for 10 months, the 2002 vintage (★★★☆) is deeply coloured, with a slightly leafy bouquet. It's a full-bodied, generous wine with strong blackcurrant, red-berry and herb flavours, fresh and vibrantly fruity, with well-integrated oak and the potential to age well.

Vintage 02 01 00 99 98
WR 7 7 6 6 7
Drink 04-08 03-06 03-06 03-05 03-06

DRY $32 -V

Marsden Bay of Islands Merlot (★★★)

Grown at Kerikeri, in Northland, the 2000 vintage (★★★) has medium-full colour, light for Merlot. Oak-aged for 16 months, it is fruity, berryish, plummy and supple, with some earthy, spicy, savoury complexity.

Vintage 00
WR 6
Drink 03-06

DRY $24 -V

Matariki Reserve Merlot (★★★★)

The graceful, supple 2000 vintage (★★★★) was grown in Gimblett Road, Hawke's Bay, and matured for 20 months in French oak barriques (new and seasoned). Boldly coloured, it's a rich wine, fresh and vibrant, with oodles of blackcurrant and plum flavour, warm and rounded. It should reward lengthy cellaring.

Vintage 00
WR 7
Drink 03-10

DRY $40 -V

Matua Valley Ararimu Merlot/Syrah/Cabernet Sauvignon ★★★★★

Matua's flagship Hawke's Bay red from 2000 (★★★★★) is a strikingly rich blend of Merlot (52 per cent), Cabernet Sauvignon (45 per cent) and Malbec (3 per cent), matured in all-new French (60 per cent) and American oak barriques. Dark and highly fragrant, it is crammed with beautifully ripe blackcurrant, red-berry and spice flavour, showing lovely balance and length. A generous, highly concentrated and finely textured wine, with gentle tannins, it offers great drinking over the next several years. The 2001 (★★★☆) is a Cabernet Sauvignon/Merlot (see Cabernet Sauvignon and Cabernet-predominant Blends). The 2002 vintage (★★★★★) is a different blend again – Merlot (50 per cent), Syrah (25 per cent), Cabernet Sauvignon (20 per cent) and Malbec (5 per cent). Matured for a year entirely in French oak barriques (75 per cent new), it possesses noble colour and very rich blackcurrant, plum and pepper flavours. A beautifully vibrant wine, crammed with fruit and already showing savoury, gamey complexities, it looks like an outstanding vintage.

Vintage 00
WR 7
Drink 03-08

DRY $40 AV

Matua Valley Bullrush Vineyard Merlot ★★★★

The 2002 vintage (★★★★) is a single-vineyard Hawke's Bay wine, grown in the Ngatarawa district and matured in French and American oak casks (70 per cent new). Fruity and full-flavoured, with raspberry, plum and spice characters showing excellent ripeness and warmth, it's a richly coloured wine with good tannin backbone and the depth and structure to mature well.

Vintage 02   01
WR 7   7
Drink 03-09 03-08

DRY $29 AV

Matua Valley Hawke's Bay Merlot ★★★

The 2001 vintage (★★☆), grown principally in the Dartmoor Valley and matured in one and two-year-old American and French oak casks, has medium-full colour, with plummy, spicy, leafy flavours, crisp acidity and a sliver of sweetness to smooth the finish.

Vintage 01
WR 4
Drink P

DRY $18 AV

Melness Marlborough Merlot/Cabernet ★★★☆

Still on the market, the 2000 vintage (★★★) was matured for 18 months in French oak barriques (one-third new). It's a perfumed, savoury wine, plummy and spicy, with soft tannins. Mellow and flavoursome, it's drinking well now.

Vintage	00
WR	6
Drink	03-08

DRY $24 AV

Miller's Merlot (★★★☆)

From a challenging season, the 2001 vintage (★★★☆) is on a slightly lower plane than the excellent 2000 (★★★★), which included Cabernet Franc and was labelled Miller's Serious One. Grown on the Awhitu Peninsula, in South Auckland, it has fullish colour, showing some development, generous, berryish, earthy, spicy flavours, seasoned with quality oak, slightly high acidity and moderate tannins. It shows lots of character, but is best drunk during 2004.

DRY $45 -V

Mill Road Hawke's Bay Merlot/Cabernet ★★☆

From Morton Estate, this is typically a fresh, uncomplicated style with moderate depth of red-berry/plum flavours, a hint of American oak and a smooth, off-dry finish.

MED/DRY $13 AV

Mills Reef Elsepth Merlot ★★★★☆

Grown in the company's Mere Road vineyard, near Hastings, the 2000 vintage (★★★★☆) is deeply coloured, with a fragrant bouquet of red berries, spices and cedary oak. A very elegant and approachable wine, it has concentrated plum and red-berry flavours, lovely fruit sweetness, a strong nutty oak influence and a powerful finish. Tasted just prior to bottling (and so not rated), the 2001 was full-coloured, with a spicy, leathery bouquet showing good complexity. Full-bodied, with fresh, plummy, spicy, savoury characters and firm tannins, it's a good but not great vintage, for drinking now onwards.

Vintage	01	00	99	98
WR	6	7	7	7
Drink	03-06	03-05	P	03-04

DRY $40 -V

Mills Reef Merlot/Cabernet ★★★

The fresh, lightly wooded 2001 vintage (★★☆) is a Hawke's Bay blend of Merlot (55 per cent) and Cabernet Sauvignon (45 per cent). Full-coloured, with leafy, spicy aromas, it's a fruit-driven style, crisp and vibrant, with blackcurrant and plum flavours showing moderate ripeness. Clearly superior, the 2002 (★★★☆) has a bouquet of ripe fruit and toasty oak. A blend of 80 per cent Merlot and 20 per cent Cabernet Sauvignon, matured for seven months in French oak, it's a good-value red with lots of plum, spice and raspberry flavour and a firm, tannic finish.

Vintage	02	01	00
WR	7	6	6
Drink	03-06	03-05	P

DRY $18 AV

Mills Reef Reserve Cooks Beach Merlot (★★★☆)

Fragrant, with full but not dense colour, the 2001 vintage was grown on the Coromandel Peninsula, in the Waikato. Fresh, plummy and spicy, it's a ripe-tasting wine with firm tannins, oak complexity and very satisfying flavour depth.

DRY $25 AV

Mills Reef Reserve Merlot ★★★★

The 2002 (★★★★☆) is a top vintage of this Hawke's Bay red. French oak-matured for 14 months, it's a serious wine with deep, youthful, purple-flushed colour and a highly fragrant bouquet of cassis, coffee and spice. The flavours are warm and deliciously concentrated, with oak complexity, a firm underlay of tannin and a long finish. A strong candidate for cellaring.

Vintage	02	01	00	99	98	97	96
WR	7	6	7	7	NM	7	5
Drink	03-07	03-06	04	P	NM	P	P

DRY $25 AV

Mills Reef Reserve Merlot/Cabernet ★★★★

The 2000 vintage (★★★★), grown in Hawke's Bay, has bold colour. It's an impressively concentrated wine, rich, plummy and soft, with hints of tobacco, good structure and length. There is no 2001. The 2002 (★★★★) is full of promise, showing good ripeness and complexity. It's a deeply coloured and fragrant wine with sweet-fruit characters, strong, plummy, spicy, slightly minty flavours, savoury, leathery touches and a firm tannin grip. Open mid-2004+.

Vintage	02	01	00
WR	7	NM	6
Drink	04-07	NM	04

DRY $25 AV

Mission Hawke's Bay Merlot ★★★

The 2002 vintage (★★☆) is an easy-drinking red, matured for six months in French and American oak. Full-coloured, it offers smooth raspberry, plum and green-leaf flavours, with a slightly high-acid finish.

DRY $15 AV

Moana Park Pascoe Series Merlot/Cabernet (★★★)

Made in a 'fruit-driven' style, the 2002 vintage (★★★) was grown in the Dartmoor Valley of Hawke's Bay and blended principally from Merlot (64 per cent) and Cabernet Sauvignon (22 per cent), with small amounts of Cabernet Franc and Malbec. The colour is full and vibrant; the bouquet is fresh, berryish and slightly herbal. It's a flavoursome wine with a seasoning of spicy, sweet oak and a well-rounded finish.

DRY $17 AV

Montana Barrique Matured Reserve Merlot ★★★☆

The 2001 vintage (★★★☆) is a blend of Marlborough and Hawke's Bay grapes, matured in French and American oak barriques (one-third new). It's a full-coloured, brambly, plummy, spicy wine, slightly herbaceous, with plenty of flavour, oak complexity and chewy tannins.

Vintage	01	00	99	98
WR	6	6	6	7
Drink	03-08	03-07	03-06	03-05

DRY $20 AV

Montana Fairhall Estate Merlot/Cabernet Sauvignon (★★★☆)

Montana's top Marlborough red from the 1999 vintage (★★★☆) was matured entirely in French oak barriques (58 per cent new). It shows good concentration of blackcurrant and nutty oak flavours, with green olive and fennel characters reflecting its cool-climate origin, good complexity and firm tannins.

Vintage	99
WR	6
Drink	03-06

DRY $29 V

320   RED WINES

Morton Estate Black Label
Hawke's Bay Merlot/Cabernet ★★★★☆
Grown at the Riverview vineyard and matured for two years in new French and American oak barriques, the 1998 vintage (★★★★★) is drinking superbly now. Boldly coloured, with a perfumed bouquet, it is a blend of Merlot (55 per cent) and Cabernet Sauvignon (45 per cent). Impressively concentrated and weighty, it is savoury, brambly, leathery, nutty and complex, with richness through the palate and a rounded, lasting finish. In the view of winemaker Evan Ward, it's the best red he has ever made.

Vintage	98	97	96
WR	7	6	7
Drink	03-09	03-05	03-05

DRY $60 -V

Moteo Terroire Merlot/Cabernet Sauvignon/Franc ★★★
Grown in Hawke's Bay, the 2001 vintage (★★★) is a full-coloured blend of Merlot (75 per cent) with Cabernet Sauvignon and Cabernet Franc, matured in French oak casks (half new). It's a gutsy, tannic red, slightly rustic but flavoursome, with plummy, berryish, nutty characters and some complexity.

DRY $20 AV

Mount Riley Merlot/Cabernet Franc (★★☆)
A drink-young style, the 2001 vintage (★★☆) was grown in the Gimblett Road area of Hawke's Bay and 60 per cent of the blend was matured for eight months in French and American oak casks. It's a fruity, smooth wine with crisp, fairly simple berry/plum flavours.

DRY $19 -V

Mud House Marlborough Merlot ★★★☆
The richly coloured 2001 vintage (★★★★) was matured for a year in French oak barriques. It's a finely balanced, ripe-tasting wine with good complexity and excellent depth of vibrant, plummy, spicy flavour, concentrated and firm. One of the region's finest Merlots, it should reward cellaring.

Vintage	01
WR	7
Drink	03-07

DRY $28 -V

Ngatarawa Alwyn Reserve Merlot/Cabernet ★★★★☆
The dark, rich 2000 vintage (★★★★☆) is a blend of Merlot (60 per cent) and Cabernet Sauvignon (40 per cent), matured for a year in new French and American oak barriques, then blended and returned to oak for a further six months before bottling. Purple/black, it's a real fruit bomb, bursting with blackcurrant, plum and mint fruit characters, deliciously vibrant and fresh. You can drink it now for its exuberant fruit characters, or keep it to develop savoury, aged complexities.

Vintage	01	00	99	98
WR	NM	7	NM	7
Drink	NM	03-10	NM	03-08

DRY $45 -V

Ngatarawa Glazebrook Merlot ★★★★
Richly coloured and fragrant, with aromas of plums, spice and sweet oak, the 2000 vintage (★★★★) of this Hawke's Bay red includes 20 per cent Cabernet Sauvignon. Still quite youthful, it's a supple wine with strong blackcurrant, plum and spice flavours and some gamey complexities emerging. There is no 2001.

DRY $25 AV

Ngatarawa Glazebrook Merlot/Cabernet ★★★★

The 2001 vintage (★★★☆) of this Hawke's Bay red is a blend of Merlot (55 per cent), Cabernet Sauvignon (37 per cent) and Malbec (8 per cent). For drinking now or cellaring, it's a deeply coloured, slightly herbaceous wine with rich blackcurrant, plum and spice flavours seasoned with sweet oak and moderate tannins.

Vintage	01	00	99	98
WR	6	6	6	7
Drink	03-09	03-07	03-06	03-08

DRY $25 AV

Nikau Point Hawke's Bay Merlot/Cabernet (★★★)

Made for early drinking, the 2002 vintage (★★★) from One Tree Hill Vineyards (a division of Morton Estate) was matured for several months in American oak. It's a full-bodied wine, fresh and vibrant, with plummy fruit characters, hints of chocolate and mint and a smooth, off-dry finish.

Vintage	02
WR	6
Drink	03-04

MED/DRY $16 AV

Nobilo Merlot ★★★

The 2002 vintage (★★★) is a blend of Hawke's Bay, Gisborne and Marlborough grapes, French and American oak-matured. It's a slightly rustic and earthy, characterful wine with good colour depth, plenty of berry, plum and spice flavour and firm tannins.

Vintage	02	01
WR	7	7
Drink	03-06	03-04

DRY $16 AV

Odyssey Kumeu Merlot (★★★☆)

The full-coloured, vibrantly fruity 2002 vintage (★★★☆) is a West Auckland red, matured in French oak casks (50 per cent new). Firm, with plum and spice flavours showing considerable concentration, warmth and complexity, it's well worth cellaring.

Vintage	02
WR	6
Drink	03-08

DRY $25 AV

Ohinemuri Estate Hawke's Bay Merlot ★★★

Drinking well from now onwards, the 2001 vintage (★★★☆) is a warm, plummy, spicy, slightly earthy and leathery wine, full-coloured and flavoursome, with considerable complexity.

Vintage	01	00
WR	6	6
Drink	03-07	03-05

DRY $21 –V

Okahu Shipwreck Bay Merlot/Chambourcin/Pinotage ★★★

This is the Northland winery's bottom-tier red, but it's often full of character. The 2001 vintage (★★★), blended from Hawke's Bay, Auckland and Northland grapes, was matured for a year in one to three-year-old barrels, mostly American. It has a slight lack of fruit sweetness and warmth, but the blackcurrant, plum and spice flavours also show good depth.

Vintage	01	00	99	98
WR	6	5	5	6
Drink	03-06	03-07	03-05	03-04

DRY $17 AV

Omaka Springs Merlot ★★★

The 2001 vintage (★★★☆), grown in Marlborough, was matured for a year in American oak casks and bottled unfiltered. It has deep colour and strong cassis/plum flavours. A mouthfilling, youthful wine with a hint of mint chocolate and spicy oak adding complexity, it's worth cellaring; open 2004+.

DRY $16 AV

Passage Rock Merlot (★★★★)

Perfumed and concentrated, the 2002 vintage (★★★★) of this Waiheke Island red was grown at three sites and matured for 15 months in American and French oak barriques (40 per cent new). Youthful and deeply coloured, it's rich, brambly and spicy, with nutty oak adding complexity and a firm underlay of tannin. Open mid-2004+.

DRY $35 -V

Peacock Ridge Reserve Merlot (★★★★☆)

A highly impressive debut, the 2002 vintage (★★★★☆) was grown at Onetangi, Waiheke Island, and matured for a year in French and American oak casks. It's a dark, warm and concentrated wine with rich, brambly, spicy flavours, a hint of dark chocolate, good complexity and a firmly structured finish. It's built to last; open 2005+.

DRY $37 -V

Ponder Estate Artist's Reserve Marlborough Merlot ★★★★

Full of character, the 2001 vintage (★★★★) was grown in the Val-De-Merlot vineyard and aged in French and American oak for eight months. Richly coloured, it is impressively weighty and deep, with fresh, vibrant blackcurrant, herb, spice and plum flavours, oak complexity and finely balanced tannins.

Vintage	01	00
WR	7	7
Drink	03-08	03-07

DRY $30 AV

Redmetal Basket Press Merlot/Franc ★★★★★

This Maraekakaho, Hawke's Bay blend of Merlot and Cabernet Franc is a sophisticated, beautifully rich and supple wine, weighty and bursting with ripe blackcurrant/plum flavours. Still purple-flushed, the 2000 vintage (★★★★★) is richly coloured, plump and well-rounded, with a wealth of cassis, plum and mint flavours, a silky texture and long finish. With bottle-age, it's starting to develop real complexity. There is no 2001 vintage.

Vintage	02	01	00	99	98
WR	6	NM	7	5	7
Drink	04-10	NM	03-09	03-06	03-10

DRY $40 AV

Redmetal Merlot/Cabernet Franc ★★★★

This Hawke's Bay red is made for early drinking. A 2:1 blend, grown at Maraekakaho and matured for a year in French and American oak casks, the 2002 (★★★★) is the first vintage to exclude Cabernet Sauvignon. It's a skilfully crafted wine, fragrant, with very good depth of ripe-berry and plum flavours, a sweet, coconutty oak influence and strong drink-young appeal.

Vintage	02	01	00	99	98
WR	6	NM	6	5	6
Drink	04-06	NM	03-04	P	P

DRY $24 V+

Redmetal The Merlot ★★★★★

A statuesque Hawke's Bay wine, the 1998 vintage (★★★★★) is an inky brute with enormous concentration. Matured for 14 months in French (80 per cent) and American oak casks (80 per cent new), it shows great all-round power, with savoury, spicy, nutty, chocolatey complexities developing with bottle-age. The 2000 (★★★★★) is more approachable in its infancy than the 1998, but still needs more time. The colour is dark and dense; the palate is supple and weighty, with deep blackcurrant/plum flavours wrapped in spicy oak and a long, rounded finish. There is no 2001.

DRY $90 -V

Vintage	01	00	99	98
WR	NM	6	NM	7
Drink	NM	03-10	NM	04-10

Riverside Dartmoor Merlot ★★☆

This Dartmoor Valley, Hawke's Bay red is typically berryish and herbal, fresh and crisp. It is matured in French and American oak, but tends to lack ripeness and depth.

Vintage	02
WR	5
Drink	03-05

DRY $15 AV

Rongopai Merlot/Malbec (★★★)

Made for early consumption, the 2002 vintage (★★★) has fullish, purple-flushed colour and the meaty, savoury, earthy aromas of Malbec. Fresh and supple, it's a very fruit-driven style with plum and red-berry flavours, gentle tannins and a smooth finish.

DRY $16 AV

Rongopai Reserve Merlot (★★★★)

Offering fine value, the 2002 vintage (★★★★) is a gutsy, single-vineyard Gisborne red, oak-aged for a year. Boldly coloured, with a gamey, spicy bouquet, sweet-fruit characters and lots of brambly, spicy, plummy, slightly chocolately flavour, it's still youthful and well worth cellaring to 2005+.

DRY $20 V+

Rongopai Reserve Merlot/Malbec ★★★

The moderately ripe 2001 vintage (★★☆) is a blend of Merlot (55 per cent) and Malbec, grown in Te Kauwhata and Hawke's Bay. French oak-matured for 14 months, it's a full-coloured red, berryish, plummy and slightly gamey, with firm tannins and plenty of flavour, but also a slight lack of complexity, ripeness and warmth.

DRY $25 -V

St Helena Marlborough Merlot (★★☆)

Made in a 'fruit-driven' style with 'light oak', the 2002 vintage (★★☆) is medium-full in colour, with a herbaceous bouquet. Balanced for easy drinking, it offers plum, spice and green-leaf flavours, with gentle tannins giving a smooth finish.

Vintage	02
WR	5
Drink	03-05

DRY $22 -V

Sacred Hill Basket Press Merlot
★★★★

The 2001 vintage (★★★★) is a full-coloured Hawke's Bay blend of Merlot (86 per cent), with 12 per cent Malbec and a splash of Cabernet Sauvignon, oak-aged for a year. Firm, with ripe tannins and finely integrated oak, it has excellent depth of blackcurrant, plum and spice flavours, developing considerable savoury, earthy complexity.

Vintage	01	00	99
WR	6	7	6
Drink	03-08	03-04	03-05

DRY $25 AV

Sacred Hill Basket Press Merlot/Malbec
(★★★☆)

Densely coloured, the 2002 vintage (★★★☆) offers loads of fresh, ripe spice and plum flavour. Grown in Hawke's Bay and oak-aged for a year, it's a blend of Merlot (57 per cent) and Malbec (28 per cent) principally, with smaller portions of Cabernet Sauvignon and Cabernet Franc. Vibrantly fruity, it has lots of drink-young charm.

Vintage	02
WR	7
Drink	03-08

DRY $25 AV

Sacred Hill Brokenstone Merlot
★★★★☆

The 2000 vintage (★★★★★) is a densely coloured Hawke's Bay red, crammed with cassis, plum, spice and nut flavours. A blend of Merlot (85 per cent), Malbec (11 per cent) and Cabernet Franc (4 per cent), matured for 18 months in French oak casks (new and one-year-old), it's a generous, concentrated wine with beautifully rich, sweet-fruit characters and silky tannins. Delicious drinking from now onwards.

DRY $40 -V

Sacred Hill Whitecliff Estate Merlot
★★★☆

This Hawke's Bay red is typically delicious in its youth – fragrant and vibrantly fruity, with plenty of blackcurrant/plum flavour, fresh, ripe and smooth. The 2002 vintage (★★★) is already attractive, with good colour depth, ripe-fruit flavours, hints of herbs and chocolate and moderate tannins.

DRY $16 V+

Saint Clair Marlborough Merlot
★★☆

Matured for five months in seasoned oak casks, the 2002 vintage (★★☆) is a fruit-driven, easy-drinking style, ruby-hued, with fresh, raspberryish, slightly leafy flavours and a very smooth finish.

Vintage	02	01	00
WR	6	6	6
Drink	03-05	03-04	P

DRY $19 -V

Saint Clair Rapaura Road Reserve Marlborough Merlot
★★★☆

This is a more oak-influenced style than its stablemate (above), in warm years showing deep colour and ripe-fruit characters. The 2001 vintage (★★★★), matured for a year in new and seasoned American oak casks, is a complex style, still developing. Showing bold, youthful, purple-flushed colour, it is warm and ripe, with rich blackcurrant and spice flavours strongly seasoned with cedary oak.

Vintage	01	00	99	98
WR	7	6	7	7
Drink	03-06	03-06	03-05	P

DRY $28 -V

Selaks Founders Reserve
Hawke's Bay Merlot/Cabernet Franc ★★★★

The 2001 vintage (★★★☆) under the Founders Reserve label is an unblended Marlborough Merlot, dark and youthful, with substantial body, very good depth of blackcurrant/plum flavours and slightly chewy tannins. In 2002 (★★★★☆), the region of origin switched to Hawke's Bay and Cabernet Franc was added to the recipe. Harvested in the Ngatarawa district at over 24 brix and matured for 14 months in new and one-year-old French oak casks, it's a highly attractive wine, very elegant, concentrated and supple, with impressive depth of fully ripe blackcurrant and plum flavours, good balance and complexity.

Vintage	02	01	00	99
WR	7	7	NM	6
Drink	03-07	03-04	NM	P

DRY $27 AV

Shepherds Point Merlot/Cabernet/Syrah (★★★★☆)

The powerful 2002 vintage (★★★★☆) was grown at Onetangi, on Waiheke Island, and matured for a year in French oak barriques (30 per cent new). Densely coloured, with buckets of fruit and intense blackcurrant, plum and pepper flavours, it's a complex, firmly structured wine, full of potential. Open 2005 onwards.

DRY $38 -V

Sileni Cellar Selection Merlot/Cabernet Franc ★★★☆

Released within six months of the harvest, the 2002 (★★★) is a Hawke's Bay blend of Merlot (60 per cent), Cabernet Franc (32 per cent), Malbec (5 per cent) and Cabernet Sauvignon (3 per cent), briefly matured in French and American oak. It's a fruit-driven style, enjoyable from the start, with fresh berryish aromas, mouthfilling body, vibrant plum and red-berry flavours and gentle tannins.

Vintage	02	01	00
WR	5	NM	6
Drink	03-06	NM	03-06

DRY $24 AV

Sileni Estate Selection Merlot/Cabernets ★★★★☆

The generous and very harmonious 2000 vintage (★★★★☆) of this Hawke's Bay red is a blend of Merlot (75 per cent), Malbec (8 per cent), Cabernet Franc (13 per cent) and Cabernet Sauvignon (4 per cent), matured for a year in French (principally) and American oak casks. Its rich, deep cassis, plum and spice flavours are seasoned with slightly sweet oak, with good density through the palate, complex, savoury, leathery touches emerging and a smooth, rich finish. Re-tasted in 2003, it is maturing very gracefully.

Vintage	00	99	98
WR	6	5	7
Drink	03-09	03-08	03-10

DRY $34 AV

Sileni EV Merlot ★★★★★

'EV' stands for 'exceptional vintage', and the debut 1998 (★★★★★), labelled EV Merlot/Cabernets, lives up to its billing. Based on the best blocks of fruit, in the Ngatarawa triangle and the Dartmoor Valley, it is an 80/20 blend of Merlot and Cabernet Franc, matured for 14 months in French (90 per cent) and American oak barriques (80 per cent new). Beautifully dark, it has a voluminous bouquet, spicy and cedary. Packed with rich, brambly fruit, it's a more forward wine than the Cabernet Sauvignon-based reds of the vintage, warm, savoury, leathery and notably complex. There is no 1999. The 2000 vintage (★★★★★) is a straight Merlot. Warm and rich, it's a sweet-fruited wine with deep plum, blackcurrant and coffee flavours, braced by supple yet firm tannins. Already dangerously drinkable, but built for the long haul, it should be at its best from 2004 onwards.

Vintage	00	99	98
WR	5	NM	5
Drink	04-12	NM	03-18

DRY $95 -V

Soljans Barrique Reserve Merlot ★★★

Grown in Hawke's Bay, the 2002 vintage (★★★) has lots of drink-young charm. Fresh and supple, with full, bright colour, it's a buoyantly fruity wine with red-berry and plum flavours, some spicy oak and a gentle underlay of tannin.

DRY $20 AV

Solstone Wairarapa Valley Merlot ★★★

Rich and youthful in colour, the 2001 vintage (★★★☆) of this Masterton red offers rich blackcurrant and plum flavours, with a slightly leafy bouquet. French oak-aged for 16 months, it's a generous wine with firm, balanced tannins and considerable complexity.

Vintage	01
WR	6
Drink	03-05

DRY $23 -V

Spy Valley Marlborough Merlot (★★★★)

The deeply coloured 2001 vintage (★★★★) was harvested at 25 brix in the Waihopai Valley and matured in French oak casks. Fleshy, forward and smooth, it's crammed with berry, plum and mint chocolate flavours, with an almost Malbec-like richness.

Vintage	02	01	00
WR	5	6	5
Drink	03-06	03-06	03-04

DRY $20 V+

Stonecutter Martinborough Merlot ★★★

The ruby-hued 2002 vintage (★★★) is an attractive middleweight. Fruity and smooth, with sweet-fruit characters and plummy, spicy flavours, it's already drinking well.

DRY $28 -V

Stoneleigh Marlborough Merlot (★★★☆)

The debut 2002 vintage (★★★☆) from Montana was French oak-aged for nine months. It's a richly coloured, vibrantly fruity wine with strong plum/spice flavours in a moderately complex style with firm tannins.

DRY $20 AV

Te Awa Farm Longlands Merlot ★★★★

The 2000 vintage (★★★☆) is a blend of Merlot (85 per cent), Malbec (11 per cent) and Cabernet Franc (4 per cent), matured in American and French oak barrels (15 per cent new). It's a spicy, warm red, full-coloured, with good concentration of plum, blackcurrant and slightly chocolatey flavours, oak complexity and smooth tannins.

Vintage	00	99	98	97	96
WR	7	6	7	5	6
Drink	03-05	03-04	P	P	P

DRY $20 V+

Te Kairanga Gisborne Merlot (★★★)

French oak-aged for 10 months, the 2002 vintage (★★★) has a slightly earthy bouquet and full, bright, youthful colour. It's a full-bodied wine, cherryish, plummy and spicy, with sweet-fruit characters, moderate complexity and a firm finish. Best drinking 2004–05.

DRY $20 AV

Te Whau The Point Merlot/Cabernet Sauvignon/Cabernet Franc/Malbec – see Te Whau The Point in the Branded and Other Reds section

Te Whau Vineyard Single Barrel Merlot (★★★★★)

From 'a great Merlot year on Waiheke Island', the 2002 vintage (★★★★★) is a selection of the best of 12 barrels, bottled without fining or filtering. Only 300 bottles were produced. Matured in French oak for 15 months, it's a very savoury, gamey, earthy and spicy wine, warm and complex, with a firm tannin backbone. Drink now or cellar.

Vintage	02
WR	7
Drink	04-08

DRY $43 AV

Torlesse Waipara Merlot (★★★★)

One of the best claret-style reds from the region, the fragrant and generous 2001 vintage (★★★★) was grown in two sites at Waipara and French oak-aged for a year. Full but not dark in colour, with a fleshy mid-palate and firm finish, it has plum, spice and slight coffee flavours, seasoned with nutty oak, and very good depth, ripeness and complexity.

Vintage	01
WR	7
Drink	03-07

DRY $30 AV

Trinity Hill Gimblett Road Merlot ★★★★☆

The classy 2001 vintage (★★★★☆) of this Hawke's Bay red was matured for 16 months in French oak barriques (60 per cent new) and blended with a small proportion of Cabernet Franc 'to add an aromatic lift'. Boldly coloured, it has beautifully ripe blackcurrant and plum flavours, spicy oak and firm but supple tannins. Still youthful, with sweet-fruit characters and good, savoury complexity, it's an elegant and harmonious wine with strong cellaring potential.

Vintage	02	01	00	99	98	97
WR	7	6	5	6	6	5
Drink	03-10	03-09	03-09	03-09	03-06	03-04

DRY $30 AV

Trinity Hill Shepherds Croft Merlot/Cabernets/Syrah ★★★

The 2002 vintage (★★★) is a Hawke's Bay blend of Merlot, Cabernet Franc, Syrah and Cabernet Sauvignon. Grown in the Ngatarawa and Gimblett Gravels districts, it was matured for 16 months in seasoned oak casks. It's a vibrantly fruity, berryish, gently oaked wine, showing a slight lack of warmth and softness, but very fresh and flavoursome. Attractive drinking through 2004–05.

Vintage	02	01	00	99	98	97	96
WR	6	5	5	4	7	4	6
Drink	04-08	03-07	03-04	P	P	P	P

DRY $20 AV

Vidal Estate Merlot/Cabernet Sauvignon (★★★★)

Offering top value, the 2001 vintage (★★★★) is a youthful, dark Hawke's Bay red, blended from 56 per cent Merlot, 33 per cent Cabernet Sauvignon and 11 per cent Malbec. Matured for a year in French and American oak barriques, it has concentrated blackcurrant, plum and chocolate flavours, seasoned with spicy oak, and slightly chewy tannins.

Vintage	02	01	00
WR	7	6	NM
Drink	03-07	03-05	NM

DRY $19 V+

Vidal Reserve Merlot/Cabernet Sauvignon (★★★★★)

The serious yet beautiful 2000 vintage (★★★★★) is a single-vineyard red from the Gimblett Gravels district, matured for 20 months in French and American oak casks. A blend of Merlot (54 per cent), Cabernet Sauvignon (37 per cent) and Malbec (9 per cent), it is deeply coloured and fragrant, with firm, ripe tannins and concentrated cassis, plum and spice flavours in a classic claret style with lovely warmth, depth and structure. Already highly approachable, this is Hawke's Bay red at its finest.

Vintage	01	00	99	98
WR	NM	7	7	NM
Drink	NM	05-10	03-07	NM

DRY $39 AV

Villa Maria Private Bin
East Coast Merlot/Cabernet Sauvignon ★★★

The flavourful 2002 vintage (★★★) was matured for 15 months in French and American oak barriques (30 per cent new). A full-bodied wine with some complexity, it displays very good depth of plum, blackcurrant and green-leaf flavours, seasoned with sweet, coconutty oak.

Vintage	02
WR	7
Drink	03-06

DRY $17 AV

Villa Maria Reserve Hawke's Bay Merlot ★★★★★

The 2000 vintage (★★★★★) is a generous, highly concentrated Hawke's Bay red, grown in the company's Ngakirikiri vineyard in the Gimblett Gravels district and matured in French (principally) and American oak barriques. Brilliantly deep and youthful in colour, it has an abundance of sweet-fruit characters, balanced tannins and intense plummy, spicy flavours, warm, savoury and complex. The 2001 (★★★★★) is equally striking. Also grown at Ngakirikiri, it is highly fragrant and densely coloured, with intense blackcurrant, berry, plum and spice flavours, strongly seasoned with toasty oak. Firmly structured and concentrated, it should be very long-lived.

Vintage	01	00	99	98	97	96	95
WR	7	7	7	7	NM	6	7
Drink	04-12	03-10	03-05	03-06	NM	P	P

DRY $40 AV

Villa Maria Reserve Merlot/Cabernet Sauvignon ★★★★★

Grown at the stony Ngakirikiri Vineyard, in the Gimblett Gravels district of Hawke's Bay, and matured in French (principally) and American oak casks, the very stylish 2000 vintage (★★★★★) is boldly coloured, warm and rounded, with sweet, concentrated fruit characters of cassis, plums and spice. A blend of Merlot (54 per cent), Cabernet Sauvignon (39 per cent) and Malbec (7 per cent), it is densely packed, fleshy and supple, with power right through the palate. Re-released in early 2003, the 1999 vintage (★★★★☆) is deeply coloured, with a hint of development. The bouquet is fragrant and complex, spicy and leathery; the palate is concentrated, with cassis, coffee and spice flavours, highly reminiscent of a fine-quality Bordeaux. Ready.

Vintage	00	99	98	97	96	95
WR	7	7	7	NM	NM	7
Drink	03-10	03-07	03-07	NM	NM	P

DRY $40 AV

West Brook Merlot/Shiraz/Cabernet (★★★)

The moderately concentrated 2000 vintage (★★★) is a blend of Merlot (42 per cent), Syrah (38 per cent) and Cabernet Sauvignon (20 per cent), grown in Hawke's Bay (mostly) and Auckland. Matured in French and American oak casks, it's a medium to full-bodied style with berryish, spicy flavours showing good depth and some savoury complexity.

DRY $18 AV

Wishart Basket Press Merlot ★★★☆

The 2000 vintage (★★★) is plummy, peppery and minty, with good depth. Grown at Bay View, in Hawke's Bay, and matured for 10 months in French and American oak casks, the 2001 vintage (★★★★) is a smooth, savoury red with a floral, berryish bouquet, good palate sweetness and excellent flavour depth.

Vintage	01	00
WR	6	6
Drink	03-06	03-05

DRY $24 AV

Wishart Reserve Hawke's Bay Merlot (★★★★☆)

The fruit-packed 2001 vintage (★★★★☆) was grown at Bay View and matured in French and American oak casks. Deeply coloured, it is warm and concentrated, with lovely depth of cassis, plum and spice flavours, the earthy richness of Malbec (10 per cent) and well-rounded tannins.

Vintage	01
WR	6
Drink	03-08

DRY $28 V+

Montepulciano

Montepulciano is widely planted across central Italy, yielding deeply coloured, ripe wines with good levels of alcohol, extract and flavour. In the Abruzzi, it is the foundation of the often superb-value Montepulciano d'Abruzzo, and in the Marches it is the key ingredient in the noble Rosso Conero.

In New Zealand, Montepulciano is still a rarity and there has been confusion between the Montepulciano and Sangiovese varieties. Some wines may have been incorrectly labelled. According to the latest national vineyard survey, by 2005 New Zealand will have 4 hectares of bearing Montepulciano vines and 7 hectares of Sangiovese.

Herzog Marlborough Montepulciano ★★★★★

Typically a giant of a red, overflowing with sweet, ripe flavours of plum, liquorice and spice. The 2001 vintage (★★★★★), which includes 15 per cent Cabernet Franc, was matured for two years in new French oak barriques and bottled without fining or filtration. It's a strikingly rich wine, strapping (14.4 per cent alcohol), with bold, youthful colour. Absolutely crammed with flavour, it's a firmly structured, tannic wine with great warmth and complexity and loads of everything. It should be very long-lived.

Vintage	01	00
WR	7	6
Drink	03-15	03-10

DRY $59 -V

Pinotage

Pinotage lives in the shadow of Pinot Noir, Merlot and Cabernet Sauvignon in New Zealand. Plantings are expanding slowly, and having been passed during the past decade by Cabernet Franc, Syrah and Malbec, Pinotage now ranks as the country's seventh most extensively planted red-wine variety.

Pinotage is a cross of the great Burgundian grape, Pinot Noir, and Cinsaut, a heavy-cropping variety popular in the south of France. Cinsaut's typically 'meaty, chunky sort of flavour' (in Jancis Robinson's words) is also characteristic of Pinotage. Valued for its reasonably early-ripening and disease-resistant qualities, and good yields, Pinotage has long been a favourite in Auckland (which still has heavier plantings than any other region). Its plantings are mostly in the North Island (Auckland, Hawke's Bay and Gisborne), with a significant pocket in Marlborough.

A well-made Pinotage displays a slightly gamey bouquet and a smooth, berryish, peppery palate that can be reminiscent of a southern Rhône. It matures swiftly and usually peaks within two or three years of the vintage.

Amor-Bendall Pinotage Reserve (★★★★)

Showing a Syrah-like spiciness, the 2002 vintage (★★★★) is an impressive Gisborne red. Deeply coloured, it is mouthfilling and warm, with excellent depth of plummy, peppery flavour.

DRY $22 AV

Ascension Matakana Pinotage ★★★

'Line it up against a $20 Pinot Noir and let the customer decide!' says winemaker Darryl Soljan, promoting his 2002 vintage (★★★☆). It's a full-coloured, oak-aged style with a gamey bouquet and strong, berryish, spicy, slightly earthy flavours, showing some complexity.

DRY $20 -V

Babich East Coast Pinotage/Cabernet ★★★

Over more than three decades, this smooth but fully dry, moderately priced red has built up a strong following. The 2002 vintage (★★★) is a blend of Pinotage (90 per cent) and Cabernet Sauvignon, grown in Gisborne and West Auckland. It's a fresh, crisp, Beaujolais-style red (no longer oak-aged), with vibrant, ripe raspberry and spice flavours and good varietal character.

DRY $13 V+

Babich Winemakers Reserve Pinotage ★★★★☆

This is one of the country's finest Pinotages – arguably the finest. Grown in Gimblett Road, Hawke's Bay, harvested at over 25 brix and matured for a year in new and seasoned French and American oak casks, the 2002 vintage (★★★★☆) is richly coloured and supple, with sweet-fruit delights and strong, plummy, spicy, gamey flavours. It's a delightful red, for drinking now onwards.

Vintage	02	01	00	99
WR	7	7	6	7
Drink	03-08	03-07	03-05	03-04

DRY $20 V+

Kerr Farm Kumeu Pinotage ★★★☆

This is Kerr Farm's most consistently impressive wine. Estate-grown in West Auckland and matured in seasoned French and American oak barriques, the 2001 vintage (★★★) is fresh and flavoursome, with full, bright colour, strong berry/spice characters and a touch of toasty oak. Still youthful, it's a well-structured wine, for drinking now or moderate cellaring.

Vintage 01
WR 6
Drink 03-05

DRY $18 V+

Lincoln Winemakers Series Gisborne Pinotage (★★★☆)

The gutsy, richly coloured, buoyantly fruity 2002 vintage (★★★☆) has the gamey, meaty aromas of Pinotage. Fresh, berryish and spicy, with earthy, savoury characters adding interest, it's an unoaked style with loads of body (14.5 per cent alcohol) and flavour. Excellent value.

Vintage 02
WR 6
Drink 03-05

DRY $15 V+

Matua Valley Settler Pinotage/Cabernet Sauvignon ★★☆

This is one of Matua's most popular wines, especially in supermarkets. The 2002 vintage (★★☆) is a blend of Pinotage (55 per cent) and Cabernet Sauvignon (45 per cent), grown in Gisborne and Hawke's Bay. It's a simple but generous wine, richly coloured, with plenty of raspberry/spice flavour.

DRY $13 AV

Muddy Water Waipara Pinotage (★★★★☆)

The 2000 vintage (★★★★☆) is the finest South Island Pinotage I've tasted – full and smooth, with warm, rich, slightly raisiny flavour and spicy, nutty oak adding complexity. Harvested at a super-ripe 27 brix, the 2002 (tasted as a barrel sample, and so not rated) revealed the variety's typical earthiness, with sweet-fruit characters, good body and loads of berryish, gamey flavour.

Vintage 02　01　00
WR 6　NM　7
Drink 03-08　NM　03-06

DRY $25 AV

Park Estate Pinotage (★★☆)

The light, developed 2001 vintage (★★☆), which includes 10 per cent Cabernet Franc, was grown in Hawke's Bay and not oak-aged. Plummy, spicy and slightly gamey, it's a smooth, easy-drinking style with moderate depth. Ready.

Vintage 01
WR 7
Drink P

DRY $15 -V

Pleasant Valley Signature Selection Auckland Pinotage ★★★☆

Hill-grown in the Henderson Valley of West Auckland, this is a highly characterful, smooth red made for early drinking, but it can also mature well. Still on sale, the full-coloured 2000 (★★★★) is a top vintage, oak-aged for nine months, with strong, ripe raspberry, cherry and spice flavours and slightly earthy, savoury touches adding complexity.

Vintage 00
WR 6
Drink 03-04

DRY $18 V+

Riverside Stirling Reserve Pinotage (★★★☆)

Promisingly deep in colour, the 2000 vintage (★★★☆) was grown in the Dartmoor Valley of Hawke's Bay. One of Riverside's finest reds yet, it's a full-bodied, raspberry/plum-flavoured wine, less gamey and earthy than many Pinotages, with ripe, vibrant fruit characters and a well-rounded finish. Verging on four stars.

Vintage 01 00
WR 6 5
Drink 04-05 03-04

DRY $20 AV

Saints Pinotage ★★★★

If you haven't discovered the delights of Pinotage, try this. The 2001 (★★★★), grown in Marlborough, is deeply coloured, with a strong surge of plum, raspberry and spice flavours, oak complexity and ripe, supple tannins. The 2002 vintage (★★★★) is a Hawke's Bay wine, matured in American (55 per cent) and French oak casks. Grown in Montana's vineyard at Korokipo, it's full-coloured and crammed with warm, ripe, brambly, spicy flavour, with moderately firm tannins and rich varietal character.

Vintage 02 01
WR 6 6
Drink 03-08 04+

DRY $18 V+

Sanctuary Marlborough Pinotage/Pinot Noir ★★★

Made by Grove Mill, this is an attractive style for early drinking. The vibrantly fruity 2001 vintage (★★★) has plum/spice flavours, restrained oak (French and American) and a fresh, firm finish. The ruby-hued 2002 (★★★) has the berryish, gamey and earthy characters of Pinotage in a smooth, fruit-driven style with good warmth and depth.

Vintage 02 01 00
WR 7 7 6
Drink 03-05 03-04 P

DRY $17 AV

Soljans Auckland Pinotage ★★★★

This small winery has a long history of satisfying West Auckland Pinotages. Grown in the Henderson Valley and at Kumeu, blended with 5 per cent Malbec (for 'colour and length'), and matured for three months in seasoned oak casks, the 2002 vintage (★★★★) is a full-bodied, sweet-fruited wine with cherry, plum and spice flavours, gamey varietal character and excellent depth.

DRY $17 V+

Soljans Vineyard Selection Pinotage ★★★☆

The small West Auckland winery has a long-standing reputation for characterful Pinotages. Grown in Gisborne, the 2002 vintage (★★★☆) is full-coloured, with the distinctive berryish, earthy aromas of Pinotage. It's a supple, ripe-tasting wine with berryish, plummy flavours showing good depth.

DRY $16 V+

Te Awa Farm Longlands Pinotage ★★★★

The excellent 2001 vintage (★★★★) was grown in the Gimblett Gravels district of Hawke's Bay and matured for 15 months in French oak casks. Full and youthful in colour, it is fresh and supple, with strong cherry and plum flavours, the distinctive gamey character of Pinotage and a spicy, very harmonious finish. It's a richly varietal and charming wine, offering top drinking from now onwards.

Vintage	01	00	99	98
WR	7	7	6	7
Drink	04-07	03-06	03-04	03-04

DRY $26 -V

Yelas Winemaker's Reserve Auckland Pinotage ★★★★

Estate-grown at Henderson and oak-matured for nine months, the 2002 vintage (★★★☆) is a medium to full-bodied red with gamey, earthy touches, attractive berry and plum flavours and a firm tannin grip. A good food wine with the structure to age, it should be at its best during 2004–05.

Vintage	02
WR	7
Drink	03-06

DRY $22 AV

Pinot Noir

The rising quality of New Zealand Pinot Noir attracted significant overseas acclaim in the past year. At the 2003 Sydney International Wine Competition, the trophy for champion Pinot Noir was awarded to Te Kairanga Reserve Pinot Noir 2001 and the joint runners-up were also New Zealand wines – Gibbston Valley Central Otago Pinot Noir 2001 and Martinborough Vineyard Pinot Noir 2001.

Yet the picture is not entirely rosy for the country's burgeoning output of Pinot Noir. After tasting over 60 wines, prominent UK wine writer Jancis Robinson declared in the *Financial Times* (March 8, 2003) that 'quality is definitely improving, but there is a long way to go... New Zealand Pinots that are genuinely savoury, interesting and nuanced in the way that the finest Pinot Noir can be are in a small minority ... too many of them are just pleasant red wines.'

The 2003 vintage yielded 9402 tonnes of Pinot Noir grapes, well ahead of Merlot with 4957 tonnes and Cabernet Sauvignon with 3201 tonnes. The vine is spreading like wildfire. Between 2000 and 2005, New Zealand's area of bearing Pinot Noir vines will almost triple, from 1126 hectares to 3282 hectares.

Pinot Noir is the princely grape variety of red Burgundy. Cheaper wines typically display light, raspberry-evoking flavours that lack the velvety riches of classic Burgundy. Great red Burgundy has substance, suppleness and a gorgeous spread of flavours: cherries, fruit cake, spice and plums.

Pinot Noir over the past decade has become New Zealand's most internationally acclaimed red-wine style. The vine is by far our most widely planted red grape, and is our third most commonly planted variety overall, trailing only Sauvignon Blanc and Chardonnay. Over 40 per cent of the vines are concentrated in Marlborough (where 12 per cent of the crop is reserved for bottle-fermented sparkling wine), and the variety is also well established in Central Otago, Canterbury, the Wairarapa, Hawke's Bay, Gisborne and Nelson.

Yet Pinot Noir is a frustrating variety to grow. Because it buds early, it is vulnerable to spring frosts; its compact bunches are also very prone to rot. One crucial advantage is that it ripens early, well ahead of Cabernet Sauvignon. Low cropping and the selection of superior clones are essential aspects of the production of fine wine.

The Wairarapa and Central Otago have been the capitals of New Zealand Pinot Noir during the past decade, but the total supply of each region's wine has been tiny. In the year to June 2003, New Zealand exported 139,188 cases of Pinot Noir (4.5 per cent of all wine exports). Currently Marlborough's potential for the production of much larger volumes of Pinot Noir is being explored.

Akarua Central Otago Pinot Noir ★★★★

The 2001 (★★★★) was grown at Bannockburn, picked at over 24 brix and matured for 10 months in French oak barriques (60 per cent new). Full-coloured, with a fragrant, plummy, spicy bouquet, it's an exuberantly fruity wine with ripe-cherry and red-berry fruit flavours, fresh and vibrant, seasoned with French oak. The densely coloured 2002 vintage (★★★★☆) is deliciously soft and rich, with loads of sweet, ripe cherry, plum and spice flavour. A muscular wine (14.5 per cent alcohol), vibrant and youthful, it should be at its best around 2005.

Vintage	02	01	00	99
WR	7	6	6	5
Drink	03-10	03-07	03-07	03-04

DRY $40 AV

Akarua The Gullies Pinot Noir ★★★☆

Showing a Beaujolais-like freshness and charm, the 2001 vintage (★★★☆) was made from grapes off young Bannockburn, Central Otago vines, harvested at over 24 brix. Matured for 10 months in French oak barriques (20 per cent new), it's a ruby-hued red with strong, ripe raspberry, cherry and plum fruit flavours to the fore, subtle oak and gentle tannins. The 2002 (★★★★) is much bolder. Richly coloured, with fragrant cherry and spice aromas, it shows very good concentration of warm, ripe flavour, with oak complexity and plenty of muscle (14.5 per cent alcohol).

Vintage	02	01	00
WR	7	6	5
Drink	03-10	03-07	P

DRY $30 AV

Alana Estate Pinot Noir ★★★★

This Martinborough red is typically full of charm – fragrant and supple, with strong, sweet cherry/plum flavours, integrated oak and easy tannins. The 2001 vintage (★★★★), matured in French oak barriques (25 per cent new), is an elegant wine, ruby-hued, with vibrant cherry and plum flavours, fresh and strong, a subtle seasoning of oak and good weight and depth. The 2002 (★★★★) has a fragrant, complex bouquet, with warm, ripe cherry/plum flavours, savoury, spicy, nutty characters and a relatively firm tannin grip. Best drinking 2005–06.

Vintage	01	00	99	98
WR	7	6	6	7
Drink	03-07	03-05	03-05	03-05

DRY $44 -V

Alan McCorkindale Waipara Valley Pinot Noir (★★★★)

The powerful, weighty, firmly structured 2001 vintage (★★★★) is built to last. Grown in the Montserrat vineyard, it has berryish, spicy aromas leading into a sturdy palate with fresh cherry, strawberry and spice flavours, well-integrated oak, some savoury notes and firm tannins. It's well worth cellaring to 2005.

DRY $43 -V

Alexander Martinborough Pinot Noir ★★★☆

The 2001 vintage (★★★☆), which for the first time includes new Dijon clones, was matured for a year in French oak barriques (25 per cent new). Still youthful, it shows good concentration of ripe, plummy flavour, savoury, spicy characters and firm tannins.

Vintage	01	00
WR	5	5
Drink	03-05	03-04

DRY $29 AV

Alexandra Wine Company Crag an Oir Pinot Noir (★★★★)

The youthful, warm 2002 vintage (★★★★) is a single-vineyard Central Otago red, matured for 11 months in French oak casks (35 per cent new). It's a generous and fragrant wine with sweet, ripe-fruit flavours of plums, cherries and spice, good oak handling, gentle tannins and excellent depth and drinkability. Instantly likeable, with great texture, it's a drink-now or cellaring proposition.

Vintage 02
WR 6
Drink 04-06

DRY $32 AV

Alexandra Wine Company Davishon Pinot Noir ★★★★

Grown in the Davishon vineyard at Alexandra in Central Otago, the 2002 vintage (★★★★☆) is weighty and rich, with good complexity. Matured for 11 months in French oak barriques (35 per cent new), it is ruby-hued, warm, savoury and supple, with strong cherry, raspberry and spice flavours and good power through the palate. Slightly bolder than its Crag an Oir stablemate (above), it's well worth keeping to 2005.

Vintage 02 01 00 99
WR 6 6 7 7
Drink 04-06 03-05 03-04 03-04

DRY $32 AV

Allan Scott Joshua Pinot Noir (★★☆)

Named after Marlborough winemaker Joshua ('Josh') Scott and bottled unfiltered, the 2001 vintage (★★☆) is disappointingly light, green-edged and simple, lacking the warmth and stuffing you'd expect in its price range.

DRY $32 -V

Allan Scott Marlborough Pinot Noir ★★★

The mouthfilling, supple 2001 vintage (★★★) was matured in French oak barriques, new and old. Fresh plum/spice aromas lead into a weighty but green-edged wine with some savoury complexity and good flavour depth.

Vintage 02 01
WR 4 7
Drink 03-05 03-04

DRY $25 -V

Alpha Domus Pinot Noir ★★★☆

The 2002 vintage (★★★) is a full-coloured Hawke's Bay red, oak-aged for a year. Youthful, it has strong cherry and plum flavours, showing some fruit sweetness, and a firm finish. Open mid-2004+.

Vintage 02
WR 7
Drink 03-08

DRY $28 AV

Amisfield Central Otago Pinot Noir (★★★★☆)

Jeff Sinnott made top-flight Pinot Noirs at Isabel Estate in Marlborough, so it's no surprise his first Amisfield red is highly impressive. The warm, seriously structured 2002 vintage (★★★★☆) was estate-grown at the foot of the Pisa Range, in the Cromwell Basin, picked at 24.8 brix and fermented with cultured and indigenous yeasts. It's a complex wine with a lovely array of cherry, raspberry and spice flavours, seasoned with nutty oak, and a long finish with fine-grained tannins. A label to watch.

DRY $40 AV

Anthony James Central Otago Pinot Noir ★★☆

Grown at Alexandra, the 2001 vintage (★★☆) is youthful in colour, with simple, red-berry flavours that lack any real subtlety and richness.

DRY $28 -V

Ashwell Pinot Noir ★★★

The quality of this Martinborough red has been inconsistent, although the 1997 (★★★★★) was very generous and silky. The 2000 vintage (★★☆) is ruby-hued, berryish and plummy, but also green-edged, with a slightly high-acid finish. The 2001 (★★★), French oak-aged for 18 months, shows good concentration of cherry, spice and nut flavours, but again a touch of greenness detracts.

DRY $40 -V

Ata Rangi Pinot Noir ★★★★★

One of the greatest of all New Zealand wines, this stunning Martinborough red is powerfully built and concentrated, yet seductively fragrant and supple. 'Intense, opulent fruit with power beneath' is winemaker Clive Paton's goal. 'Complexity comes with time.' The grapes are drawn from numerous sites, including the estate vineyard, planted in 1980. The wine is fermented in small batches, with up to 15 per cent whole-bunch fermentation giving 'stalk-derived spiciness and tautness', and maturation is for a year in French oak barriques, typically 25 per cent new. At a vertical tasting held in mid-2003, the 1994 to 1996 vintages were mature, but the younger wines are still developing, demonstrating that Ata Rangi responds well to at least five years' cellaring; even more for the best vintages. The 2002 (★★★★★) is deep ruby, with a notably complex bouquet – gamey, spicy, nutty. Weighty and warm, with great presence in the mouth, it's a finely structured wine with rich cherry and spice flavours, already very complex and savoury, and loads of personality.

Vintage	02	01	00	99	98	97	96	95	94
WR	6	7	7	7	6	7	7	6	7
Drink	03-07	03-06	03-05	03-04	03-05	03-04	P	P	P

DRY $60 AV 🍇🍇🍇

Ata Rangi Young Vines Pinot Noir ★★★☆

Based on young vines in Martinborough and the Petrie vineyard, south of Masterton, this briefly oak-aged red is a drink-young style. The 2002 vintage (★★★☆) was matured for four months in French oak barriques (25 per cent new). Ruby-hued, weighty and rounded, with excellent depth of raspberry, plum and spice flavours, it's deliciously fresh and crisp, with greater complexity than you'd expect. However, this label has recently been replaced by Walnut Ridge Pinot Noir (see that entry).

Vintage	02	01	00	99	98
WR	6	7	6	6	6
Drink	P	03-04	P	P	P

DRY $25 AV

Babich East Coast Pinot Noir ★★☆

This blend of Hawke's Bay, West Auckland and (to a lesser extent) Marlborough grapes has replaced Babich's former Henderson Valley Pinot Noir. The 2002 vintage (★★☆), matured for six months in old French oak casks, is a ruby-hued, light-bodied wine with moderately ripe, strawberryish, spicy flavours and a rounded finish.

DRY $18 AV

Babich Winemakers Reserve Pinot Noir ★★★☆

The 2002 vintage (★★★☆) was grown at three sites in the Wairau Valley and matured for nine months in French oak casks. Ruby-hued, with a fragrant, cherryish, toasty bouquet, it is harmonious and supple, although not concentrated, with ripe cherry and plum flavours and good balance and complexity. Drink now onwards.

Vintage 02 01 00
WR 7 7 6
Drink 03-07 03-05 03-04

DRY $29 AV

Bald Hills Estate Central Otago Pinot Noir (★★★★)

Still very youthful, the debut 2002 vintage (★★★★) was grown in the Hunt family's vineyard at Bannockburn and matured for nine months in French oak barriques (50 per cent new). Purple-flushed, with good colour depth, it's a buoyantly fruity red, packed with fresh plum and cherry flavours. Tightly structured, with oak complexity and a long finish, it's worth cellaring to 2005+.

DRY $42 -V

Bilancia Hawke's Bay Pinot Noir (★★★☆)

The elegant and supple 2002 vintage (★★★☆) was grown at Glencoe Station, in the slightly cooler hill country south of the Heretaunga Plains, and matured for 11 months in mostly new French oak barriques. Ruby-hued, it's a middleweight style with ripe cherry, plum and raspberry flavours, a layer of toasty oak and some earthy, forest floor notes. Lots of drink-young charm.

Vintage 02
WR 6
Drink 03-06

DRY $25 AV

Black Estate Waipara Pinot Noir ★★★★

This single-vineyard, North Canterbury label is consistently satisfying. The 2001 vintage (★★★★☆) is full-coloured and fragrant, with impressive richness through the palate and a savoury, spicy complexity. From a wetter, higher-yielding season, the 2002 (★★★☆) is lighter in colour, with a slightly earthy bouquet. Matured for a year in French oak barriques (one-third new), it shows good complexity, with savoury, cherryish, spicy characters and moderately firm tannins. Drink now or cellar.

Vintage 02 01
WR 5 6
Drink 04-10 03-08

DRY $38 AV

Black Ridge Pinot Noir ★★★☆

This Alexandra, Central Otago red is typically sturdy, vibrantly fruity and supple. The 2001 vintage (★★★☆), matured in French oak barriques (25 per cent new), is maturing well, with a youthful, ruby hue and ripe cherry/plum flavours, developing savoury, spicy complexities with bottle-age. A supple but not intense wine, it shows good varietal character and is drinking well now.

DRY $37 -V

Borthwick Wairarapa Valley Pinot Noir ★★★☆

Estate-grown near Masterton and matured in French oak casks (25 per cent new), the 2001 vintage (★★★) shows strawberry/cherry characters and spicy oak, but a green-edged finish. It's a middleweight style with slightly high acidity but some elegance.

DRY $30 AV

Bunny Martinborough Pinot Noir (★★★☆)

Gentle, velvety, warm and harmonious, the 2001 vintage (★★★☆) has more muscle than its lightish colour suggests. Grown at Te Rehua Vineyard, in Huangarua Road, it has sweet-fruit delights and good depth of cherry and plum flavours. It's drinking well right now.

DRY $30 AV

Burnt Spur Martinborough Pinot Noir ★★★☆

The 2002 vintage (★★★☆) is ruby-hued and fragrant, with cherryish, spicy flavours and firm tannins. It's a middleweight style showing a slight lack of fruit sweetness, but also some savoury, earthy complexity. It should age solidly; open 2005+.

Vintage 01
WR 7
Drink 03-06

DRY $39 -V

Cairnbrae Marlborough Pinot Noir ★★★☆

The 2001 vintage (★★★☆) was matured for 14 months in French oak barriques. Developing well, it's still youthful in colour, with plenty of cherryish, spicy flavour, good complexity and moderately firm tannins. A good buy.

Vintage 01 00
WR 6   7
Drink 03-05 03-06

DRY $22 V+

Canterbury House Pinot Noir ★★☆

The Pinot Noirs from this North Canterbury producer have typically been plain. Grown at Waipara, the 2001 vintage (★★☆) is medium-full ruby, with crisp, strawberryish, green-edged flavours. It's a solid wine, but lacks real weight, ripeness and depth.

DRY $20 -V

Cape Campbell Blenheim Point Marlborough Pinot Noir (★★★☆)

Full and youthful in colour, the 2001 vintage (★★★☆) has strong fruit flavours, with some savoury, spicy characters and a slightly high-acid finish. It's a firm, tight wine with good complexity.

DRY $30 AV

Cape Campbell Marlborough Pinot Noir (★★★)

The charming 2001 vintage (★★★) was grown at Rapaura, in the Wairau Valley. French oak-aged for a year, it's a lightly wooded style, not complex but fruity, with cherry and plum flavours and a smooth finish.

DRY $24 AV

Cape Campbell Reserve Marlborough Pinot Noir (★★★☆)

Named after the cape at the southern entrance to Cook Strait, the 2001 vintage (★★★☆) is a single-vineyard wine, grown at Rapaura and was matured for a year in French oak casks. Purple-flushed, it is fruit-crammed and supple, in a moderately complex style with good weight, fresh, vibrant fruit characters and strong cherry/plum flavours.

DRY $34 -V

Carrick Central Otago Pinot Noir ★★★★☆

Built for cellaring, the powerful 2002 vintage (★★★★★) was grown at Bannockburn and matured for a year in French oak barriques (35 per cent new). Richly coloured and fragrant, it's a highly concentrated wine with cherryish, spicy, slightly nutty flavours. Sturdy and complex, with a firm backbone of tannin, it offers excellent potential; open 2005+.

Vintage	02	01
WR	7	7
Drink	05+	03+

DRY $38 V+

Chard Farm Finla Mor Pinot Noir ★★★★

Rob Hay's second-tier Central Otago red typically has strong raspberry and cherry flavours, with finely integrated wood. The 2002 vintage (★★★★) was grown in three districts in the Cromwell Basin – Cairnmuir, Bannockburn and Parkburn – and matured for 11 months in French oak barriques. A sweetly fruited, richly coloured and fragrant wine, it offers deep, ripe flavours of cherry, raspberry and spice, seasoned with toasty oak. With its moderately firm tannins and good intensity, it should age well.

Vintage	02	01	00	99
WR	7	6	5	6
Drink	04-08	03-05	P	P

DRY $38 AV

Chard Farm Red Gate Vineyard Pinot Noir ★★★☆

This single-vineyard Central Otago red is grown at Parkburn, in the Cromwell Basin. The 2001 (★★★) is a ruby-hued, moderately complex wine with fresh acidity and strong cherry/plum flavours. Bottled unfined and unfiltered, the 2002 vintage (★★★★) is dark and exuberantly fruity. Crammed with sweet, ripe-fruit flavours of plums and cherries, it's a supple, deliciously well-rounded but still very youthful wine that needs a lot more time to show its best; open 2005+.

DRY $52 -V

Chard Farm River Run Pinot Noir ★★★☆

The 2001 vintage (★★★☆) is a floral, fruit-driven style with lots of drink-young charm. The 2002 (★★★☆) is equally attractive. A blend of Central Otago (Gibbston district) and Nelson grapes, French oak-aged, it is full-coloured and vibrant, with strong cherry, plum and spice flavours, sweet-fruit characters and gentle tannins. Drink now onwards.

Vintage	02	01	00
WR	7	6	5
Drink	03-05	03-04	P

DRY $28 AV

C.J. Pask Gimblett Road Pinot Noir ★★★☆

This Hawke's Bay wine is typically less scented and lush than southern styles, more weighty and firm. Richly coloured, with a spicy, fragrant bouquet, the 2000 vintage (★★★☆) is warm and oaky (after a year in new and one-year-old French barrels), firm and complex, in a serious style for cellaring.

Vintage	00	99	98	97	96
WR	7	6	7	NM	6
Drink	03-06	03-05	03-05	NM	P

DRY $30 AV

Cloudy Bay Pinot Noir ★★★★

Cloudy Bay a few years ago successfully switched its red-wine focus from Cabernet/Merlot blends to Pinot Noir. The 2001 vintage (★★★★) was grown in the lower Brancott and Fairhall districts of the Wairau Valley, fermented with indigenous yeasts and matured for 11 months in French oak barriques (50 per cent new). Savoury and complex, with strawberry and spice flavours showing very good but not great depth, it's a very appealing and stylish wine but, like the 2000 vintage (★★★★), lacks the power and richness of Marlborough's finest Pinot Noirs.

Vintage	01	00	99	98	97	96	95	94
WR	6	6	6	5	6	5	NM	4
Drink	03-05	03-04	03-04	P	P	P	NM	P

DRY $40 AV

Collards Queen Charlotte Marlborough Pinot Noir ★★★

The 2000 vintage (★★★☆) is an elegant, supple wine with fragrant, strawberry/spice aromas leading into a full-bodied, lightly wooded wine with gentle tannins. It's now savoury and mellow. (There are no subsequent vintages.)

Vintage	03	02	01	00	99
WR	NM	NM	NM	7	6
Drink	NM	NM	NM	03-04	P

DRY $19 AV

Coney Pizzicato Pinot Noir ★★★★

Full of drink-young charm, the 2001 vintage (★★★★) of this Martinborough red is full-coloured and fragrant, with ripe raspberry/plum flavours, a subtle oak influence and gentle tannins. The 2002 (★★★☆) is an enjoyable middleweight with good depth of cherryish, plummy flavours, spicy oak and a rounded finish. Silky elegance is the theme.

Vintage	02	01
WR	5	6
Drink	03-06	03-06

DRY $34 AV

Coopers Creek Marlborough Pinot Noir ★★★☆

The delicious 2002 vintage (★★★★) was grown at four sites on the Wairau Plains and in the Brancott Valley and matured in French oak casks (33 per cent new). Supple and vibrantly fruity, with gentle tannins, finely integrated oak and rich, plummy flavours, it's a floral, sweet-fruited wine, ready to roll.

Vintage	02	01
WR	6	6
Drink	03-05	03-04

DRY $20 V+

Coopers Creek Pinot Noir (★★★)

The affordably priced 2002 vintage (★★★) is a blend of Hawke's Bay (60 per cent) and Marlborough grapes, intended as an 'easy drinking, fruit-driven style'. Light/medium ruby, with decent depth of ripe raspberry and spice flavours and gentle tannins, it's a clearly varietal wine, immediately appealing.

Vintage	02	01
WR	6	6
Drink	03-04	P

DRY $17 V+

Coopers Creek Reserve Marlborough Pinot Noir (★★★★☆)

The lovely 2002 vintage (★★★★☆) is a single-vineyard wine, grown near Blenheim and matured for 10 months in new and one-year-old French oak barriques. Ruby-hued, with a delicious spread of raspberry, cherry and plum flavours, it's a ripe and supple, notably harmonious wine, with smoky oak adding complexity. Winemaker Simon Nunns likens it to a premier cru of Burgundy – and fair enough.

DRY $27 V+

Corbans Cottage Block Marlborough Pinot Noir (★★★★★)

The deep ruby 2002 vintage (★★★★★) is Montana's finest Pinot Noir to date. The richly fragrant bouquet of cherries and spice leads into a serious, concentrated yet supple wine with lovely fruit sweetness and notable complexity. Very savoury, spicy and nutty, it's already delicious, yet also has good cellaring potential.

DRY $35 V+

Corbans Private Bin Marlborough Pinot Noir (★★★★)

Showing good complexity, the 2001 vintage (★★★★) was matured in French oak barriques (40 per cent new). Fragrant and ruby-hued, it offers strong plum, cherry and spice flavours, with fairly firm tannins.

Vintage 01
WR 5
Drink 03-06

DRY $25 V+

Covell Estate Pinot Noir ★☆

Grown against the flanks of the Ureweras at Galatea, near Murupara, in the inland Bay of Plenty, this has typically been a light, mellow wine, lacking real richness and stuffing. Tasted in 2003, the 1999 vintage (–) was tawny and badly faded.

DRY $20 -V

Crab Farm Pinot Noir ★★★

The 2000 vintage (★★☆) was grown in Hawke's Bay and matured for 16 months in French oak casks (30 per cent new). Deeply coloured, it is mouthfilling and tannic, brambly and spicy. As a gutsy, flavoursome red, it works well, but it shows only limited varietal character.

Vintage 00
WR 6
Drink 03-05

DRY $25 -V

Crossings, The, Marlborough Pinot Noir ★★★

Grown at elevation in the Awatere Valley, the 2001 vintage (★★★) is an elegant middleweight with moderately complex, plummy flavours and gentle tannins. The 2002 (★★★), French oak-aged for 10 months, is firm and mouthfilling, with plum and cherry flavours showing good depth, but a crisp, green-edged finish.

DRY $24 AV

Crossroads Destination Series Pinot Noir (★★★)

The debut 2002 vintage (★★★) of this Hawke's Bay red was oak-matured for seven months. It's a lightish but attractive wine with ripe raspberry and cherry flavours, some savoury, spicy notes and gentle tannins.

Vintage 02
WR 6
Drink 03-04

DRY $25 -V

Crossroads Reserve Pinot Noir (★★★★)

The 2000 vintage (★★★★) is a bold, mouthfilling Hawke's Bay red with good colour and well-defined varietal character. Based on young vines and matured in French oak casks (25 per cent new), it has warm, sweet-fruit flavours of cherry and spice and a lasting, rounded finish. One of the best Hawke's Bay Pinots yet.

Vintage 00
WR 6
Drink 03-04

DRY $32 AV

Daniel Schuster Omihi Hills Vineyard Selection Pinot Noir ★★★★☆

Canterbury winemaker Danny Schuster's pride and joy is made from a 'selection of the best fruit from the Omihi Vineyard at Waipara, aged in a mixture of new and older Tronçais oak'. The powerful 2001 vintage (★★★★★) is the best yet. Based on 16-year-old, unirrigated, very low-yielding vines (2.5 to 3.5 tonnes/hectare), it was matured for 15 months in French oak barriques (30 per cent new) and bottled without fining or filtration. Deeply coloured, it is very generous, sweet-fruited and savoury, with deep plum, berry and spice flavours and lots of early complexity. A substantial (14 per cent alcohol), well-structured wine, it should mature well for several years, but as Schuster puts it, 'will make a lot of people happy early on'. Tasted as a barrel sample (and so not rated), the 2002 vintage was deliciously sweet-fruited, silky and charming, but not powerful (in Schuster's words: 'Not dramatic'). There is no 2003.

Vintage 03 02 01 00 99 98
WR NM 6 7 6 NM 7
Drink NM 05-08 06-09 03-06 NM 03-06

DRY $60 -V

Daniel Schuster Twin Vineyards Pinot Noir ★★★☆

Danny Schuster's regional blend is designed for earlier drinking than the top label (above). The 2002 vintage (★★★☆) is a blend of grapes from the Petrie vineyard near Rakaia, south of Christchurch, and the Omihi Hills vineyard at Waipara. Matured for a year in seasoned French oak casks, it's a ruby-hued wine with fresh raspberry, cherry and spice aromas leading into a middleweight palate, sweet-fruited, ripe and supple, with some savoury complexity. Drink now on.

Vintage 03 02 01 00
WR 6 6 6 6
Drink 04-06 03-06 03-05 P

DRY $27 AV

Dashwood Marlborough Pinot Noir ★★★

Designed for early drinking, the 2002 vintage (★★★☆) from Vavasour was hand-picked in the Wairau and Awatere valleys. Offering great drink-young charm, it is fresh and vibrant, with ripe, sweet-fruit flavours of plums and cherries and a silky-smooth finish. It's not a complex style, but immensely drinkable.

Vintage 02 01
WR 7 6
Drink 03-05 P

DRY $20 AV

Domaine Georges Michel Golden Mile Pinot Noir ★★☆

The 2002 vintage (★★☆) was grown in the Rapaura district of Marlborough and French oak-aged for eight months. It's a solid but unexciting wine with smoky aromas, straightforward raspberry and cherry flavours and a slightly green, stalky finish.

Vintage 02 01
WR 6 5
Drink 03-07 03-06

DRY $28 -V

Domaine Georges Michel Petit Pinot ★★

Designed as a Beaujolais-style red for easy, luncheon drinking, the 2001 vintage (★★) of this Marlborough red was French oak-matured for seven months. Ruby-hued, it shows simple, high-acid, raspberryish flavours that lack real ripeness, richness and roundness – and so lacks the easy-drinking charm the label sets out to offer.

Vintage	01	00
WR	5	5
Drink	03-05	03-04

DRY $18 -V

Dry Gully Pinot Noir ★★★★

Grown at Alexandra, in Central Otago, the 2002 vintage (★★★★☆) is a top buy. Matured for 10 months in French oak barriques (20 per cent new), it's a serious wine with a long future. Full-coloured and richly scented, with enticing raspberry and herb aromas, it has loads of sweet fruit on the palate, with good savoury, spicy complexity and a firm, lingering finish.

Vintage	02	01	00	99	98	97
WR	7	7	5	5	5	6
Drink	03-07	03-07	03-04	03-05	03-05	03-04

DRY $29 V+

Drylands Marlborough Pinot Noir ★★☆

The 2002 vintage (★★☆) from Nobilo is a drink-young style. Matured in new and seasoned French oak casks, it's a relatively light wine with cherryish, slightly nutty flavours and a crisp, faintly sweet finish.

Vintage	02	01
WR	7	7
Drink	03-06	03-04

DRY $20 -V

Dry River Pinot Noir ★★★★★

Dark, robust and densely flavoured, this Martinborough red ranks among New Zealand's greatest Pinot Noirs. Its striking depth, says winemaker Neil McCallum, comes from 'getting the grapes really ripe' and 'keeping the vines' crops below 2.5 tonnes per acre'. Matured for a year in French oak barriques (25 to 30 per cent new), it is a slower developing wine than other New Zealand Pinot Noirs, but matures superbly. The 2002 vintage (★★★★★) is a wine of enormous power. Boldly coloured, with a voluminous bouquet, it is lush and silky on the palate, with super-ripe flavours of plums, spice, even liquorice and prunes (the last two fruit characters not seen in other New Zealand Pinot Noirs), and firm supporting tannins. Hugely concentrated, with a rich, complex, resounding finish, it's already dangerously drinkable, but best cellared to at least 2005.

Vintage	02	01	00	99	98	97	96	95	94
WR	7	7	7	7	6	7	7	5	7
Drink	03-10	03-09	03-08	03-07	03-08	03-04	03-04	P	03-05

DRY $65 AV

Escarpment Vineyard Martinborough Pinot Noir ★★★★☆

The debut 2001 vintage (★★★★★) from Larry McKenna makes a strong style statement. Made from 12-year-old vines in the Cleland vineyard, it's a serious, firmly structured, savoury and complex wine, built for cellaring rather than instant seduction. The 2002 (★★★★☆) is similar – sturdy (14.5 per cent alcohol) and tannic, with a very spicy fragrance and strong, savoury, spicy, nutty flavours. It's a tautly structured and notably complex wine, worth laying down to at least 2005.

Vintage	02	01
WR	6	5
Drink	06-07	05-06

DRY $45 AV

Fairhall Downs Marlborough Pinot Noir ★★★★

Grown in the Brancott Valley, the 2001 vintage (★★★★☆) is a fine debut – mouthfilling, warm, cherryish, plummy and savoury, with plenty of spicy oak, good complexity and fairly firm tannins. The 2002 (★★★☆) is full-coloured, with raspberry, cherry and spice flavours in a moderately complex style with some savoury, nutty oak and a firm, slightly chewy finish. It's less compelling than the 2001, but still developing; open 2005+.

DRY $39 AV

Fairmont Estate Block One Pinot Noir (★★★★☆)

The 2001 vintage (★★★★☆) is one of the finest wines I've tasted from this small producer at Gladstone, in the Wairarapa. Lush and supple, with a welcoming bouquet and generous palate, it offers strong cherry and plum flavours, with good complexity and power.

DRY $30 V+

Fairmont Estate Pinot Noir ★★★

Grown in the Wairarapa, the 2001 vintage (★★★) is ruby-hued, with slightly herbal fruit and highish acidity, but also well-integrated oak and some gamey complexity.

DRY $25 -V

Felton Road Block 3 Pinot Noir ★★★★★

Grown at Bannockburn, this is a majestic Central Otago wine, among the finest Pinot Noirs in the country. Cultivated in a section of the vineyard where the clay content is relatively high, giving 'dried herbs and ripe fruit' characters, in barrel tastings the wine from Block 3 'always shows greater concentration and complexity', says winemaker Blair Walter. French oak-aged for a year, the 2002 vintage (★★★★★) is stunning in its youth – powerful, with noble, deep colour and a lovely fragrance. It offers exceptional depth of black fruit, plum and spice flavours, braced by firm, ripe, supple tannins. The masses of sweet fruit give drink-young appeal, but the wine's great concentration and structure indicate a long future.

Vintage	02	01	00	99	98	97
WR	7	7	7	7	7	7
Drink	03-10	03-07	03-06	03-04	P	P

DRY $54 AV

Felton Road Block 5 Pinot Noir ★★★★★

The authoritative, weighty and complex 2001 vintage (★★★★★) was grown in a single block in the vineyard at Bannockburn, in Central Otago, and French oak-aged for 18 months. Deeply coloured, it's powerful, rich and firmly structured, with a lovely generosity of plum, herb and cherry flavours, warm and spicy. A savoury, multi-faceted wine, still developing, it should be at its best from 2005 onwards.

Vintage	01	00	99
WR	7	7	7
Drink	03-09	03-08	03-05

DRY $54 AV

Felton Road Pinot Noir ★★★★

The Bannockburn, Central Otago winery's 'standard' Pinot Noir is made with 'restrained' use of oak. The lovely 2002 vintage (★★★★☆) is the best yet. French oak-aged for a year, it's a full-coloured wine with raspberry and herb aromas leading into a sweet-fruited palate with loads of fresh cherry, raspberry and spice flavour, gently seasoned with oak. It's already delicious, but worth cellaring for at least a year or two.

Vintage	02	01	00	99	98	97
WR	7	6	7	6	6	6
Drink	03-09	03-06	03-06	03-04	03	P

DRY $40 AV

Fiddler's Green Waipara Pinot Noir ★★★☆

The 2001 vintage (★★★★) is boldly coloured, sturdy and crammed with sweet, ripe, plummy fruit flavours. Matured for 10 months in French oak barriques (30 per cent new), the 2002 (★★★☆) is slightly lighter than its predecessor. An elegant style with raspberry, plum and spice flavours, toasty oak and fairly firm tannins, it's still youthful and should reward cellaring; open 2005+.

Vintage	02	01	00
WR	6	6	6
Drink	04-07	03-06	P

DRY $39 -V

Firstland Pinot Noir ★★★

The 2001 vintage (★★★) is a blend of Marlborough (principally), Hawke's Bay and Waikato fruit, matured in French oak casks (40 per cent new). Medium to full-bodied, it is ripely flavoured, savoury and supple, in a forward style, ready now.

DRY $26 -V

Floating Mountain Waipara Pinot Noir ★★★☆

Grown in the Mark Rattray Vineyard, the 2001 vintage (★★★★) is fleshy and firm, with well-ripened cherry, plum and spice flavours showing excellent depth. From a higher-yielding season, the 2002 (★★★☆) is fragrant and supple, with good but not great flavour depth, gentle tannins and strong drink-young appeal.

Vintage	02	01
WR	5	6
Drink	03-04	03-08

DRY $30 AV

Forrest Marlborough Pinot Noir ★★★

Full-bodied, the 2001 vintage (★★★☆) is a ruby-hued red, balanced for easy drinking. It shows very good depth of cherry, raspberry and spice flavours, with toasty oak adding complexity and a sliver of sweetness (4 grams/litre of sugar) to smooth the finish. Drink now onwards.

Vintage	02	01	00
WR	5	4	4
Drink	04-05	P	P

DRY $24 AV

Fossil Ridge Pinot Noir (★★★)

The debut 2001 vintage (★★★) was hill-grown on the outskirts of Richmond, in Nelson. Ruby-hued, it is tight and youthful, fresh and bright, with good depth of raspberry and strawberry flavours and some savoury, spicy complexity.

DRY $28 -V

Foxes Island Pinot Noir ★★★★☆

Showing significant quality advances in recent vintages, John Belsham's Marlborough red is grown in the 'Home Block' at Rapaura and matured in French oak barriques (60 per cent new). The 2001 (★★★★☆) has excellent concentration, ripeness and complexity. A very graceful wine with full, bright colour and a fragrant, smoky bouquet, it possesses strong, sweet, cherry and plum fruit flavours, finely balanced oak and a solid foundation of tannin.

Vintage	01	00	99	98
WR	6	6	5	5
Drink	04-06	03-05	03-04	P

DRY $39 V+

Framingham Marlborough Pinot Noir ★★★☆

The 2002 vintage (★★★☆) has strong drink-young appeal. Matured in French oak casks (25 per cent new), it is ruby-hued, with attractive raspberry and spice aromas. A graceful, supple wine, it is moderately concentrated, with sweet, ripe flavours of berries and spice and a gentle seasoning of oak.

Vintage	02	01	00	99
WR	6	5	4	6
Drink	03-06	03-04	P	P

DRY $29 AV

Fromm La Strada Clayvin Vineyard Pinot Noir ★★★★★

This powerful, muscular but not tough Marlborough red is grown at the hillside Clayvin site in the Brancott Valley. Matured for 14 months in French oak barriques (20 per cent new), and bottled without fining or filtering, the 2001 vintage (★★★★★) is notably sturdy, warm and concentrated, with rich red-berry and plum flavours, savoury, spicy, nutty complexities and firm underlying tannins. It's a wine of great depth and structure, likely to reward lengthy cellaring.

Vintage	02	01	00
WR	6	6	6
Drink	04-10	03-09	03-08

DRY $52 AV

Fromm La Strada Fromm Vineyard Pinot Noir ★★★★★

Winemaker Hatsch Kalberer describes this majestic Marlborough red, first made in 1996, as 'not a typical New World style, but the truest expression of *terroir* you could find'. Estate-grown between Woodbourne and Renwick, in the heart of the Wairau Valley, it is matured in French oak barriques (25 per cent new). The firmly structured 2001 vintage (★★★★★) is typically robust, warm and concentrated. Richly coloured and strongly spicy, with densely packed cherry, plum and nut flavours and a firm tannin grip, it's still very youthful, and should blossom for many years.

Vintage	02	01	00	99	98	97	96
WR	6	6	6	7	6	7	7
Drink	05-12	04-11	03-08	03-07	03-06	03-09	03-10

DRY $60 AV

Fromm La Strada Pinot Noir ★★★★☆

The Fromm Pinot Noir style is distinctive – powerful, warm, meaty and firm. Grown at two sites (one is the Clayvin Vineyard) in the Brancott Valley of Marlborough and matured in French oak casks (only 10 per cent new), the 2001 vintage (★★★★★) is arguably the best yet, and superior to most producers' top labels. It's a very weighty and generous wine with rich, complex flavours, subtle oak, firm but not grippy tannins and great mouthfeel. It's less of a crime to drink this wine young than its stablemates (above), but it still shows obvious cellaring potential.

Vintage	02	01	00	99	98	97	96	95	94
WR	6	6	6	6	6	5	5	6	5
Drink	04-08	03-07	03-06	03-05	03-04	P	P	P	P

DRY $42 AV

Gibbston Valley Central Otago Pinot Noir ★★★☆

Typically a strongly varietal, middleweight style, but the denser, riper 2002 vintage (★★★★) is by far the best yet. French oak-matured for 11 months, it is richly coloured, with lots of warm, ripe cherry, plum and spice flavour. Sturdy, with a smoky bouquet and good complexity, it should win a lot of friends.

Vintage	02	01	00	99	98	97	96
WR	7	6	6	6	6	5	5
Drink	05-12	03-09	03-08	03-05	03-04	P	P

DRY $39 -V

Gibbston Valley Gold River Pinot Noir ★★☆

This is the Central Otago winery's 'lighter' red. The 2002 vintage (★★☆), oak-aged for six months, is light/medium ruby, with ripe, cherry and herb flavours and very gentle tannins. It's not rich, but enjoyably fresh and smooth.

DRY $26 -V

Gibbston Valley Reserve Pinot Noir ★★★★★

This multiple gold medal and trophy-winning Central Otago red is typically mouthfilling and savoury, with a superb concentration of sweet-tasting, plummy fruit and lovely harmony. Winemaker Grant Taylor is after a 'tannic, powerful style'. The wine is typically matured in French oak barriques, 100 per cent new, for between 12 and 18 months. The 1998 vintage sold at $48; the 1999 at $55, the 2000 at $65, the 2001 at $75 and the 2002 has been released at $90. The 2002 vintage (★★★★★) is richly fragrant, with red-berry and herb aromas, and deep, purple-flushed colour. Bursting with ripe plum and cherry flavours, it's a beautifully harmonious, exceptionally rich wine with silky tannins. A fruit bomb in its youth, yet to develop secondary, bottle-aged characters, it needs time; open 2006+.

Vintage	02	01	00	99	98	97	96
WR	7	7	7	6	7	6	6
Drink	06-15	04-15	03-12	03-10	03-15	03-10	03-05

DRY $90 -V

Giesen Marlborough Pinot Noir (★★★)

A very fruit-driven style, the 2001 vintage (★★★) has good colour depth, with fresh, berryish aromas. A youthful wine with fresh acidity, it offers good depth of raspberryish, plummy flavour.

Vintage	01
WR	5
Drink	03-04

DRY $21 AV

Giesen Reserve Barrel Selection Canterbury Pinot Noir ★★★★

The 2001 vintage (★★★★) is a strong candidate for cellaring. Boldly coloured, it is packed with cherryish, plummy flavour, seasoned with spicy oak. A youthful, firmly structured wine, it should be at its best from 2005 onwards.

Vintage	01	00	99	98	97	96
WR	7	7	7	6	5	6
Drink	03-13	03-07	03-05	03-07	03-05	03-05

DRY $50 -V

Giesen Reserve Barrel Selection Marlborough Pinot Noir ★★★☆

An elegant wine, built to last, the 2000 (★★★★) is full-coloured and scented, with strong raspberry and spice flavours, oak complexity and a firmly structured finish. Still very fresh and youthful, the 2001 vintage (★★★☆) reveals deep, bright colour and strong raspberry, strawberry and spice flavours. It's a moderately complex wine with potential; open mid-2004+.

Vintage	01	00
WR	7	7
Drink	03-08	03-05

DRY $35 -V

Gladstone Wairarapa Pinot Noir ★★★

The debut 2001 vintage (★★★) was grown at Gladstone and matured for nine months in one and two-year-old French oak casks. It's a moderately complex wine, ruby-hued, vibrantly fruity and soft, with ripe, plummy, cherryish flavours, some spicy, savoury characters and gentle tannins. The 2002 (★★★) is fresh and lively, but not highly complex, with cherry, plum and herb flavours and light tannins in a forward, easy-drinking style.

DRY $32 -V

350   RED WINES

Glenmark Pinot Noir (★★★)

Grown at Waipara, in North Canterbury, the 2000 vintage (★★★) is still on the market. It's a middleweight style with some fruit sweetness, decent depth of raspberryish, strawberryish flavour and firm tannins. Drink 2003–04.

DRY $25 ·V

Glover's Moutere Pinot Noir Front Block ★★★

Upper Moutere winemaker Dave Glover keeps to one side the grapes from the cooler block in front of the winery, which produce a slightly more floral and supple style than the wine from the hotter Back Block. However, the 2001 vintage (★★) shows stalky, green-edged, high-acid characters that lack softness and charm.

DRY $40 ·V

Greenhough Hope Vineyard Pinot Noir ★★★★★

One of Nelson's finest wines. The 2001 vintage (★★★★☆) was harvested at a very ripe 24.8 to 25.6 brix and matured in French oak barriques (25 per cent new). Delicious from the start, it's a very refined wine, full-coloured, with sweet-fruit characters, strong, fresh, vibrant cherry, plum and spice flavours and a silky texture. The 2002 (★★★★★) is notably complex. Full-coloured, it is a less buoyantly fruity style than most of the region's reds, placing its accent on savoury, spicy, gamey, nutty characters. Firmly structured, it offers extremely satisfying drinking from 2004 onwards.

Vintage	02	01	00	99	98	97
WR	7	6	6	6	5	6
Drink	03-07	03-06	03-05	03-04	P	P

DRY $38 V+

Greenhough Nelson Pinot Noir ★★★☆

This wine is handled in a similar way to its Hope Vineyard stablemate (above), but without the contribution of as much new oak or fruit from the oldest vines. The 2001 vintage (★★★☆) was hand-harvested at 24.5 brix from young, close-planted vines in the Moutere hills and matured for eight months in French oak barriques (10 per cent new). Fresh, berryish aromas lead into a supple wine with good depth of raspberry and strawberry flavours, some spicy oak and a well-rounded finish. As a drink-young style, it works well.

Vintage	01	00	99	98	97	96
WR	5	NM	NM	5	5	4
Drink	03-04	NM	NM	P	P	P

DRY $26 AV

Grove Mill Marlborough Pinot Noir ★★★★

The 2001 vintage (★★★) was hand-picked from low-cropping vines in the Wairau Valley and matured for nine months in French oak barriques (40 per cent new). It's a full-coloured wine with strong cherry, herb and spice flavours and firm tannins. From an even lower-yielding season (4 tonnes/ha), the 2002 (★★★★☆) is deeply coloured, with a complex, ripe bouquet. Robust and rounded, with deep, well-ripened plum and spice flavours, earthy, gamey characters, gentle acidity and a solid underlay of tannins, it's a bold and highly complex wine, for drinking now or cellaring.

Vintage	02	01	00	99
WR	7	6	5	5
Drink	04-09	03-06	03-04	P

DRY $35 AV

Hanmer Junction, The, South Island Pinot Noir (★★★)

A fruit-driven style, the 2001 vintage (★★★) was blended from Waipara (65 per cent) and Marlborough grapes, French oak-aged for 10 months. Fresh, raspberryish aromas lead into a berry and plum-flavoured wine with a restrained oak influence and gentle tannins. It's drinking well now, with attractive bottle-aged characters.

Vintage 01
WR 6
Drink 03-05

DRY $19 AV

Hawkdun Rise Redbarnais Pinot Noir ★★★☆

Grown on the northern outskirts of Alexandra, in Central Otago, the 2001 vintage (★★★) is a single-vineyard red, made from low-cropping vines (5 tonnes/ha). Ruby-hued, it shows some fruit sweetness, with plenty of flavour and a green-edged, slightly high-acid finish. The superior 2002 (★★★★) is a full-coloured red with a scented bouquet of raspberries and herbs. Elegant, with strong, sweet cherry, plum and spice flavours and smooth, ripe tannins, it shows good warmth, depth and complexity.

Vintage 02
WR 6
Drink 05-07

DRY $36 -V

Herzog Marlborough Pinot Noir ★★★★☆

The majestic 2001 vintage (★★★★★) was picked at 25 brix, matured for a year in new French oak barriques and bottled without fining or filtration. It is bold, deeply coloured and weighty (14.3 per cent alcohol), with beautifully sweet, plum and cherry fruit characters and notable concentration and harmony of flavour. A powerful, supple wine with firm supporting tannins, it is flourishing with bottle-age.

Vintage 01
WR 7
Drink 03-10

DRY $48 -V

Highfield Marlborough Pinot Noir ★★★☆

The 2000 vintage (★★★☆) is a mouthfilling wine (14 per cent alcohol) with good depth of berry/spice flavours, a strong, cedary oak influence and firm tannins. The 2001 (★★★☆) is ruby-hued, with a hint of development. The bouquet is fragrant, smoky and savoury; the palate is firm, spicy and nutty, with some herbal notes but considerable complexity. Drink 2003–04.

Vintage 01 00 99
WR 7 6 6
Drink 04-06 03-04 03-05

DRY $44 -V

Huia Marlborough Pinot Noir ★★★☆

The 2001 vintage (★★★★) is a blend of eight clones grown in four vineyards, matured for 15 months in new and one-year-old French oak puncheons. Ruby-hued, full-bodied and supple, with warm berry/plum characters, some gamey, earthy elements and silky tannins, it is currently drinking very well.

Vintage 01 00 99
WR 6 6 5
Drink 03-05 03-05 03-04

DRY $35 -V

Hunter's Marlborough Pinot Noir ★★★☆

Easy to enjoy, the 2001 vintage (★★★☆) was matured for nine months in French oak casks (20 per cent new). Ruby-hued, fresh and ripe, with cherry, raspberry and spice flavours, deft oak handling and firm tannins, it's a moderately concentrated, moderately complex wine, priced right.

Vintage	01	00	99	98	97	96
WR	6	6	6	6	6	6
Drink	03-05	03-04	P	P	P	P

DRY $27 AV

Hyperion Eos Pinot Noir ★★☆

Estate-grown at Matakana, north of Auckland, and French oak-matured for a year, this is one of New Zealand's northernmost Pinot Noirs. From a challenging season, the 2001 (★★☆) is light and developed in colour, with strawberryish, slightly earthy and spicy flavours that lack real freshness and depth. The 2002 vintage (★★★) is a good effort. A clearly varietal wine with bright, ruby colour and attractive, ripe, cherry and spice flavours, it shows good freshness and liveliness, with some savoury elements and gentle tannins.

DRY $27 -V

Isabel Marlborough Pinot Noir ★★★★★

This outstanding red is grown in a single, close-planted vineyard near Renwick and matured in French oak casks (20 per cent new). Already offering great pleasure, the beautifully rich, fruit-crammed 2001 vintage (★★★★★) was made from nine Pinot Noir clones, harvested ripe at 23.7 to 26.6 brix, vinified separately and blended just before bottling. Deeply coloured, it is youthful, warm and supple, with very sweet fruit characters of cherries and plums, French oak complexity and lovely harmony.

Vintage	02	01	00	99	98	97	96	95	94
WR	6	7	6	6	5	5	4	NM	6
Drink	04-10	03-09	03-08	03-06	03-05	P	P	NM	P

DRY $42 V+

Jackson Estate Pinot Noir ★★★

The 2001 (★★★) was matured in an equal split of new, one-year-old and two-year-old French oak barrels. Ruby-hued, smooth and berryish, it's a sweet-fruited wine with ripe strawberry and spice flavours, not intense but offering plenty of drink-young charm. The 2002 (★★★) is vibrantly fruity, with fresh, strong cherry and spice aromas. It's a moderately oaked wine with gentle tannins and ripe cherry and plum flavours of good depth.

Vintage	02	01	00	99	98
WR	6	5	6	6	5
Drink	03-05	03-04	03-05	03-04	P

DRY $25 -V

Johanneshof Marlborough Pinot Noir ★★☆

French oak-matured for 10 months, the 2001 vintage (★★☆) is ruby-hued, with some colour development, and a slightly leafy bouquet. A mellow wine with berryish, herbal flavours and firm tannins, it tastes ready.

DRY $21 -V

Jules Taylor Marlborough Pinot Noir (★★★)

Showing a Beaujolais-like freshness, fruitiness and charm, the debut 2002 vintage (★★★) was hand-picked in the Omaka Valley and matured for 11 months in French oak casks (40 per cent new). It's a vibrantly fruity wine with gentle tannins and attractive raspberry/plum flavours, fresh and smooth.

DRY $28 -V

Kaikoura Pinot Noir (★★★)

There's no region stated on the label, but the 2002 vintage (★★★) was grown in Canterbury. Matured in new to four-year-old French oak casks, it's a fruity, easy-drinking style with ripe, raspberry and cherry characters, a restrained wood influence and a smooth finish.

DRY $24 AV

Kaimira Estate Brightwater Pinot Noir ★★★☆

Estate-grown at Brightwater, in Nelson, and matured for a year in French oak casks (30 per cent new), the 2001 vintage (★★★☆) is ruby-hued, with a spicy fragrance. A moderately concentrated and supple wine, warm, raspberryish and savoury, it shows good varietal character and complexity.

Vintage	02	01	00	99
WR	NM	5	5	6
Drink	NM	03-07	03-05	03-04

DRY $28 AV

Kaituna Valley The Awatere Vineyard Pinot Noir ★★★★★

This show-stopping red is crammed with fruit. The 2001 (★★★★★), matured for 14 months in French oak barriques (50 per cent new) and bottled unfiltered, is very generous and warm, with the cherryish, gamey bouquet of classic Pinot Noir. It has a commanding mouthfeel (14.5 per cent alcohol), notable complexity in its youth, gentle acidity and a delicious, velvety texture. Deeply coloured and richly scented, with a clear herbal influence, the 2002 vintage (★★★★☆) is vibrant and harmonious, with lovely weight and depth of cherry, herb and spice flavours and silky tannins.

Vintage	01	00
WR	7	7
Drink	03-06	03-05

DRY $47 AV

Kaituna Valley The Kaituna Vineyard Pinot Noir ★★★★★

This consistently superb Canterbury red flows from a close-planted, low-yielding vineyard on Banks Peninsula, first planted in the late 1970s, and is matured for over a year in French oak casks (60 to 70 per cent new). The 2001 vintage (★★★★★) is densely coloured, tannic and chock full of very ripe, plummy, spicy flavour. The 2002 (★★★★★) reveals impressive depth of colour and a highly fragrant bouquet of cherries, raspberries and spice. Very youthful, fresh and vibrant, it is weighty and concentrated, with a lingering finish, but needs time; open 2005+.

Vintage	01	00	99	98	97	96	95	94
WR	7	7	7	7	6	6	NM	6
Drink	04-09	03-06	03-07	03-06	P	P	NM	P

DRY $47 AV

Kawarau Estate Pinot Noir ★★★

A fresh, lightly oaked style, grown organically at Lowburn, near Cromwell in Central Otago. Typically medium-bodied, ripe and supple, it's a drink-young style, but can show some funky, earthy characters.

DRY $27 -V

Kawarau Estate Reserve Pinot Noir ★★★★

Grown organically at Lowburn in Central Otago, at its best this is a notably classy, powerful and complex wine. The 2002 vintage (★★★★☆) is highly impressive. Matured in French oak barriques (20 per cent new), it offers lovely depth of cherry, raspberry and spice flavours, with finely integrated oak. Still purple-flushed, with deep colour and a scented bouquet, it is fresh, ripe and concentrated, with good weight and savoury, complex characters that will intensify with bottle-age. Drink mid-2004+.

Vintage	02	01	00	99	98
WR	6	6	6	5	5
Drink	03-06	03-05	03-04	P	P

DRY $36 AV

Kim Crawford Anderson Vineyard Marlborough Pinot Noir (★★★★)

Grown in the Anderson Vineyard, in the Brancott Valley, the 2001 vintage (★★★★) is deeply coloured and richly flavoured, with ripe, plummy fruit seasoned with toasty oak (French, one-third new). It's a very well-structured wine with good, savoury complexity.

Vintage	02
WR	6
Drink	06-08

DRY $40 AV

Kim Crawford Marlborough Pinot Noir ★★★

A fruit-driven style, only 50 per cent wood-aged (in older American oak barrels). The 2001 vintage (★★★) is full-bodied, fruity and smooth, with ripe, raspberry and plum flavours and gentle tannins in an enjoyable, drink-young style.

DRY $20 AV

Konrad & Co Pinot Noir ★★★☆

Supple and harmonious, the 2002 vintage (★★★☆) was matured in French oak casks (new and old). Ruby-hued, it is full-bodied, with warm cherry and plum flavours, oak complexity, some savoury, earthy characters and a well-rounded finish. Drink now onwards. The 2001 (★★★☆) is similar, with some substance, ripe, finely balanced flavours, gentle tannins and great drinkability.

Vintage	02
WR	5
Drink	03-08

DRY $35 -V

Koura Bay Blue Duck Pinot Noir ★★★★

Estate-grown in the Awatere Valley, the 2001 vintage (★★★★) of this Marlborough red has a lovely, spicy bouquet of fruit and oak. Still unfolding, with a firm tannin backbone, it's an elegant wine with cherry and plum flavours showing good warmth and complexity. The equally stylish 2002 (★★★★) is promisingly full in colour, with fresh, raspberry and spice aromas. Worth cellaring, it is vibrantly fruity, with strong, ripe flavours showing considerable complexity and firm tannins.

Vintage	01
WR	5
Drink	04-05

DRY $36 AV

Kumeu River Kumeu Pinot Noir ★★★★

This West Auckland red is typically markedly different to the perfumed, vibrantly fruity reds grown in the south – less intensely varietal, more earthy and 'red-winey'. Now at its peak, the 2000 (★★★★) is very savoury and gamey, with coffee and spice characters and balanced tannins. The 2002 vintage (tasted just prior to bottling, and so not rated), is fragrant, with strong, vibrant cherry, plum and spice flavours, a distinctly gamey character and a firm tannin underlay. It needs time; open mid-2004+.

Vintage	03	02	01	00	99	98	97
WR	7	7	6	6	5	5	4
Drink	05-10	04-08	04-06	03-05	P	P	P

DRY $36 AV

Kumeu River Village Pinot Noir (NR)

Tasted prior to bottling (and so not rated), the 2002 vintage was grown at Kumeu, in West Auckland, and oak-aged for a year. It offers plenty of fresh, plummy, spicy flavour and a firm tannin structure.

DRY $19 V?

Lake Chalice Marlborough Pinot Noir (★★☆)

The 2002 vintage (★★☆) was grown in the Rapaura district (although not estate-grown) and matured for 11 months in French oak barriques (25 per cent new). Medium ruby, it offers reasonable depth of plummy, raspberryish flavours, fresh, lively and smooth, but lacks real complexity.

Vintage 02
WR 6
Drink 04

DRY $25 -V

Lake Hayes Central Otago Pinot Noir ★★★

Still available, the 2000 vintage (★★★) was grown at Gibbston and Lake Hayes, matured for a year in French oak barriques (partly new), and bottled unfined and unfiltered. Ruby-hued, with a hint of development, it's a slightly herbaceous wine with some mature, savoury, bottle-aged characters, fresh acidity and plenty of flavour. Drink 2003–04.

DRY $30 -V

Lawson's Dry Hills Marlborough Pinot Noir ★★★☆

The latest releases are the best. Grown at several sites around the Wairau Valley, the 2002 vintage (★★★☆) was fermented mainly with indigenous ('wild', rather than cultured) yeasts and matured in new to four-year-old French oak casks. Ruby-hued, with fragrant raspberry and spice aromas, it's full-bodied, fresh and supple, with well-ripened, vibrant fruit characters, gentle tannins and some savoury complexity. It's not highly concentrated, but instantly appealing.

Vintage 02 01 00
WR 6 6 5
Drink 04-07 03-06 P

DRY $27 AV

Le Grys Marlborough Pinot Noir (★★★☆)

Estate-grown and French oak-aged for a year, the 2001 vintage (★★★☆) has a full ruby hue, with floral and red-berry aromas. A vibrantly fruity wine with sweet-fruit characters of plums and cherries and fresh acidity, it's a moderately complex style with subtle oak and fairly firm tannins.

Vintage 01
Drink 03-07

DRY $38 -V

Lincoln Heritage Pinot Noir ★★☆

Pinot Noir is a rare beast in the Waikato, but the 2002 vintage (★★★) of this Te Kauwhata red shows decent varietal character. Blended with 10 per cent Malbec and matured in French oak casks (30 per cent new), it's a full-coloured wine with strong, raspberryish, spicy, slightly raisined and nutty flavours.

Vintage 02 01
WR 6 5
Drink 03-06 03-04

DRY $20 AV

Loopline Vineyard Wairarapa Pinot Noir ★★★☆

The ruby-hued 2001 vintage (★★★☆), grown on the Opaki Plains, north of Masterton, has fresh cherry and spice aromas and flavours, a subtle oak influence, sweet-fruit characters and gentle tannins. It's delicious in its youth. The very similar 2002 (★★★☆) was matured for 10 months in French oak barriques (50 per cent new). Light/medium ruby, with fresh, berryish aromas, it shows good ripeness, with raspberry/cherry flavours, some savoury complexity and a well-rounded finish.

Vintage	02	01	00
WR	7	6	5
Drink	04-09	03-06	03-05

DRY $29 AV

Loopline Vineyard Wairarapa Reserve Pinot Noir ★★★☆

Grown north of Masterton and matured for 10 months in French oak barriques (50 per cent new), the 2001 vintage (★★★☆) is a full-bodied, moderately complex style, ruby-hued, with good depth of ripe raspberryish and cherryish flavours and a smooth, well-rounded finish. The 2002 (★★★☆) is full ruby, with a spicy, raspberryish bouquet. Still coming together in mid-2003, it is full-bodied and sweet-fruited, with cherry and plum flavours showing some toasty complexity. Open mid-2004+.

Vintage	02	01
WR	7	6
Drink	04-09	03-08

DRY $39 -V

Lynskeys Wairau Peaks Marlborough Pinot Noir ★★★☆

The powerful 2001 (★★★★) is warm, complex and supple, with very ripe, cherryish, plummy fruit flavours seasoned with nutty oak and substantial body. Matured in French oak barriques (half new), the less concentrated, easy-drinking 2002 vintage (★★★) is smooth and fruity, with slightly earthy aromas and plenty of berryish, moderately complex flavour.

Vintage	02	01	00	99	98
WR	7	7	6	7	7
Drink	04-06	03-05	03-04	P	P

DRY $38 -V

Mahi Bryne Vineyard Pinot Noir (★★★★☆)

Mahi is the personal label of Brian Bicknell, winemaker at Seresin Estate. The bold, tightly structured 2001 vintage (★★★★☆) was grown in a vineyard at Conders Bend, near Renwick, in Marlborough, French oak-aged for 16 months and bottled unfiltered. Deep and youthful in colour, it's built for the long haul, with sweet-fruit characters and layers of plum, cherry and spice flavours, showing excellent complexity. Firm, with loads of personality and a lasting finish, it's a serious wine for cellaring; open 2005+.

Vintage	01
WR	6
Drink	04-09

DRY $35 V+

Main Divide Pinot Noir ★★★☆

A great buy. The 2001 vintage (★★★☆) has rich colour and ripe raspberry and plum aromas. It's a softly mouthfilling, moderately complex wine with a gentle oak influence and strong cherry, red berry and plum flavours. The 2002 (★★★☆) was grown in Canterbury and matured for 18 months in seasoned French oak casks. Full ruby, with fragrant raspberry and spice aromas, it's satisfyingly weighty, warm and supple, with ripe-fruit flavours of plums and cherries, subtle oak and very gentle tannins. Delicious in its youth.

Vintage	02	01	00
WR	5	7	6
Drink	03-04	03-05	03-04

DRY $24 V+

Margrain Petit Pinot Noir (★★★☆)

'Barrel selected for its smoothness and early drinking charm', the 2002 vintage (★★★☆) was grown in Martinborough and oak-aged for eight months. Ruby-hued, with a spicy, smoky bouquet, it shows good depth of savoury, cherryish, spicy flavours, with moderately firm tannins. It's a more serious and complex style than most 'petit' pinot noirs, for drinking now to 2005.

Vintage	02
WR	5
Drink	03-06

DRY $30 AV

Margrain Vineyard Pinot Noir ★★★★☆

This is a consistently rewarding Martinborough red. French oak-matured for 15 months and bottled without filtering, the 2002 vintage (★★★★☆) is coming together well. Deep ruby, with a gamey, spicy bouquet, it's a muscular wine with warm, concentrated cherry, spice and nut flavours, showing a high degree of complexity. It's a powerful wine for drinking mid-2004 onwards.

Vintage	02	01	00	99	98	97	96	95
WR	6	6	6	7	7	5	6	4
Drink	04-08	03-08	03-06	03-05	03-04	P	P	P

DRY $45 AV

Martinborough Vineyard Pinot Noir ★★★★★

This was the first consistently distinguished Pinot Noir made in New Zealand. An intensely varietal wine, it is typically fragrant, with sweet-tasting fruit and cherryish, spicy, slightly smoky flavours. In the past, it impressed principally with fragrance and finesse, rather than sheer scale, but in recent years (especially since the phasing out of the magisterial Reserve Pinot Noir, last seen from the 1998 vintage), the wine has become markedly bolder. Most (but not all) of the grapes are grown on the shingly Martinborough Terrace and the wine is matured for a year in French oak barriques (30 per cent new, the rest one and two-year-old). The youthful 2001 vintage (★★★★★) is full-coloured, with a fragrant bouquet of cherries and spice. Weighty, warm and savoury, with rich cherry, plum and spice flavours seasoned with smoky oak, it's a complex style for cellaring; open mid-2004+.

Vintage	01	00	99	98	97	96	95	94
WR	7	7	7	7	6	7	7	7
Drink	04-06	03-05	03-04	03-04	P	P	P	P

DRY $60 AV

🍇🍇🍇

358   RED WINES

Martinborough Vineyard Te Tera Pinot Noir (★★★★)

Te Tera ('the other') is designed as 'a more accessible wine, approachable earlier' than its famous big brother (above). Based on young and old vines grown in Martinborough and French oak-matured for a year, the 2002 vintage (★★★★) is a ruby-hued wine with a spicy, gamey, savoury fragrance and a core of warm cherry and spice flavours. A medium to full-bodied style with no shortage of character, it offers much more complexity than most Pinot Noirs in its price bracket, and is already highly enjoyable.

DRY $28 V+

Martinus Estate Martinborough Pinot Noir ★★★

The debut 2001 (★★★★) is an exuberantly fruity wine with deep, cherryish, plummy flavours, finely integrated oak and a rounded finish. However, the 2002 (★★☆), matured in French oak casks (25 per cent new), lacks the generosity and ripeness of the 2001, with slightly austere, green-edged flavours and a high-acid finish.

Vintage	02	01
WR	5	7
Drink	04-06	03-06

DRY $35 -V

Matariki Pinot Noir ★★★☆

For drinking now or cellaring, the 2001 vintage (★★★☆) was grown in the siltiest (coolest) soils in the company's vineyard in Gimblett Road, Hawke's Bay, and matured in French oak casks. Showing good varietal character, it is fresh, vibrant and supple, with cherry and spice aromas and flavours and a firm, distinctly spicy finish.

Vintage	01
WR	5
Drink	03-06

DRY $30 AV

Matawhero Pinot Noir (★☆)

Bottled in mid-2002 after the exceptionally long period of three years in oak, the 1999 vintage (★☆) of this Gisborne red has lost its fruit characters and is dull and tired.

DRY $32 -V

Matua Valley Shingle Peak Marlborough Pinot Noir ★★★

The 2002 vintage (★★★) was matured for six months in new and older oak casks, French and American. Light-medium ruby, with a floral, raspberryish, slightly spicy bouquet, it's a supple, lightly wooded wine, made in an attractive, drink-young style.

Vintage	02	01	00	99
WR	6	5	5	4
Drink	03-06	03-04	03-04	P

DRY $21 AV

Matua Valley Wairarapa Pinot Noir ★★★★

Here's proof you don't have to pay $35 or more for an excellent New Zealand Pinot Noir. Grown in the Petrie vineyard, south of Masterton, the powerful 2001 vintage (★★★★), matured for 11 months in French oak barriques (30 per cent new), is a strapping (14.5 per cent alcohol) wine with strong, ripe cherry, plum and spice flavours, oak complexity and a smooth, rich finish. The 2002 (★★★★) is a less alcoholic wine (13 per cent) with full colour and complex cherry and spice aromas. Smoky and firm, with tight cherry, plum, spice and coffee flavours, it's a seriously structured wine that should cellar well (better than the 2001, according to the winery).

Vintage	02	01	00	99	98
WR	6	6	6	NM	5
Drink	03-07	03-04	03-06	NM	03-04

DRY $28 V+

McCashin's Nelson Pinot Noir (★★☆)

The 2001 vintage (★★☆) is the first Pinot Noir from McCashin's made solely from Nelson grapes. Matured in predominantly new French oak barriques, it offered some drink-young charm, but with bottle-age is revealing some green, unripe characters, with a high-acid finish.

DRY $25 -V

Melness Paton Pinot Noir (★★★★)

Grown in two Canterbury vineyards (at Cust, near Rangiora, and Burnham, south-west of Christchurch), and French oak-aged for 10 months, the 2001 vintage (★★★★) is a good drink-now or cellaring proposition. Full-coloured, with a youthful, purplish hue, it is attractively ripe and savoury, with loads of plummy, cherryish flavour, oak complexity and a seductively smooth finish.

Vintage 01
WR 7
Drink 03-06

DRY $33 AV

Mills Reef Cooks Beach Pinot Noir ★★☆

Grown on the Coromandel Peninsula, the 2000 vintage (★★★) is a soft, slightly jammy wine – reflecting the warm northern climate – with plenty of raspberry, strawberry and spice flavour and gentle tannins. The 2002 (★★☆), French oak-aged for seven months, shows some colour development and green-edged, slightly rustic flavours.

DRY $18 AV

Millton Clos de Ste Anne Naboth's Vineyard Pinot Noir ★★★★

This single-vineyard Gisborne red is one of the country's northernmost quality Pinot Noirs. The 2002 vintage (★★★★) was fermented with indigenous yeasts, matured for a year in French oak barriques and bottled without filtration. Described as 'masculine' by winemaker James Millton, it is deep and youthful in colour, with a tight tannin grip. Very fresh and vibrant, with strong, ripe cherry, raspberry and spice flavours and considerable earthy, savoury complexity, it should be long-lived.

Vintage 02 01 00 99 98
WR 6 NM NM 5 5
Drink 04-09 NM NM 03-05 03-04

DRY $47 -V

Montana Marlborough Pinot Noir ★★★

As an 'entry level' Pinot Noir, this large-volume red works well, smelling and tasting like Pinot Noir in a medium-bodied style that offers very easy drinking. The 2002 vintage (★★★) was matured in a mix of French oak barriques and 10,000-litre oak cuves. Full-coloured, it offers plenty of ripe, cherryish, spicy flavour (more than you'd expect for $16), with a smooth, slightly off-dry finish.

Vintage 02 01 00
WR 5 6 6
Drink 03-06 03+ P

MED/DRY $16 V+

Montana Reserve Marlborough Pinot Noir ★★★★

This is consistently a finely structured, harmonious wine, bargain-priced. The 2001 vintage (★★★☆), matured in French oak barriques (40 per cent new), is spicy and tannic, with some complexity, but it also shows a slight lack of fruit sweetness. The 2002 (★★★★) is very warm and satisfying, with deep, well-ripened, cherry and spice flavours and a savoury, nutty complexity. A top vintage, it should be at its best during 2004–05.

Vintage 01
WR 5
Drink 04-07

DRY $22 V+

Morton Estate Black Label Hawke's Bay Pinot Noir ★★★☆

Grown at the Riverview vineyard in Hawke's Bay and matured for 19 months in French oak casks (40 per cent new), the 1998 vintage (★★★☆) has more body and flavour than its light colour suggests. Mellow, savoury and spicy, it's a clearly varietal wine with ripe, cherryish fruit characters, a strong, nutty oak influence and firm tannins. The 1999 vintage (tasted in 2000 as a barrel sample, and so not rated), looked more powerful than the 1998, with substantial body and concentrated plum and cherry flavours.

Vintage 99 98 97 96 95 94
WR 6 5 NM 6 NM 7
Drink 03-06 03-04 NM 03-04 NM P

DRY $35 -V

Morton Estate Stone Creek Marlborough Pinot Noir (★★☆)

The 2000 vintage (★★☆) is fungal, vegetal, savoury and spicy. However, when re-tasted in 2003, it looked and tasted very mature and is now past its best.

Vintage 01
WR 6
Drink 03-06

DRY $21 -V

Morton Estate White Label Hawke's Bay Pinot Noir ★★★

French oak-matured for a year, the 2001 vintage (★★☆) was grown in the company's coolest vineyards, Riverview and Colefield. It's a pleasant, ruby-hued wine, berryish and smooth, with herbal, mushroomy characters and drink-young appeal.

Vintage 02 01 00 99 98
WR 7 6 7 5 5
Drink 04-07 03-06 03-06 03-04 P

DRY $18 V+

Morton Estate White Label Marlborough Pinot Noir (★★★)

The 2001 vintage (★★★) has the quality edge on its Hawke's Bay stablemate (above). Ruby-hued, it's a full-bodied wine with good depth of raspberry, plum and spice flavours and a firm backbone of tannin. It's worth cellaring to 2004.

Vintage 01
WR 6
Drink 03-06

DRY $19 AV

Morworth Estate Canterbury Pinot Noir ★★★

Estate-grown on the outskirts of Christchurch, the 2001 vintage (★★★) has good drink-young appeal. Ruby-hued, fresh and supple, it has berry, plum and spice flavours in a moderately complex style, ripe and rounded.

DRY $22 AV

Mount Cass Waipara Valley Pinot Noir (★★★)

French oak-matured for 15 months, the 2001 vintage (★★★) offers raspberry and plum flavours, with a restrained wood influence and a slightly high-acid finish. It's not a highly complex style, but full-flavoured.

Vintage 01
WR 5
Drink 03-04

DRY $28 -V

Mount Edward Central Otago Pinot Noir ★★★★☆

Alan Brady aims for 'elegance, fine texture and an enduring structure' – and hits the target with his 2002 vintage (★★★★☆). A blend of grapes from the Gibbston (70 per cent) and Alexandra sub-regions, matured for a year in French oak barriques (30 per cent new), it caresses the mouth with its abundance of sweet-fruit characters. A graceful and complex wine, cherryish and very savoury, it certainly has the structure to age, with a persistent, moderately firm finish.

Vintage 02 01 00 99 98
WR   7   6   6   6   6
Drink   04-10 03-08 03-07 03-07 03-07

DRY $42 AV

Mountford Pinot Noir ★★★★☆

From a small hillside vineyard at Waipara, Mountford produces bold, rich Pinot Noirs, full of personality. The outstanding 2001 vintage (★★★★★) is a voluptuous, silky red. Richly coloured, it is plump, deeply flavoured and supple, with intense cherry and plum characters, good savoury, mushroomy complexity, a backbone of ripe tannins and a lasting finish. Highly seductive in its youth, it's best cellared for at least a couple of years. The 2002 (★★★★☆) is slightly lighter, but beautifully fragrant and savoury, with moderately firm tannins and impressive warmth, depth and complexity. Drink 2004–05.

DRY $52 -V

Mount Maude Central Otago Pinot Noir ★★★☆

The 2000 vintage (★★★☆) was grown on steep slopes in the Maungawera Valley, between Lakes Wanaka and Hawea. Full-coloured, it possesses good weight, plummy, spicy, faintly herbal flavours showing good concentration, oak complexity and a finely balanced finish. Deep and youthful in colour, the 2002 (★★★☆) has strong plum, cherry and spice flavours, braced by firm tannins. It needs time; open mid-2004+.

DRY $38 -V

Mount Michael Pinot Noir ★★★☆

Grown at Cromwell, in Central Otago, the 2001 vintage (★★★☆) is a floral, charming wine with some complexity and a well-rounded finish. Matured in French oak barriques (35 per cent new), the 2002 (★★★☆) is full-coloured and fragrant, with raspberry and herb aromas. Buoyantly fruity, with fresh, strong cherry, plum and spice flavours and firm tannins, it's a youthful wine with good aging potential.

Vintage 02 01 00
WR   6   6   7
Drink   03-07 03-04 03-04

DRY $32 -V

Mount Riley Marlborough Pinot Noir ★★★☆

The 2002 vintage (★★★☆) is a tightly structured wine with warm, cherryish flavours that unfold well through the palate and savoury, smoky, slightly earthy complexities from eight months' aging in French and American oak. It should develop well.

DRY $22 V+

Mount Riley Seventeen Valley Marlborough Pinot Noir ★★★★

The 2000 vintage (★★★★☆) is a single-vineyard wine, grown south of Blenheim. A sturdy, powerful red, it is fragrant, plummy, cherryish and spicy, with sweet-fruit charm, savoury characters and good cellaring potential. The 2001 (★★★☆) is deeply coloured, with strong, spicy, slightly herbal flavours, well seasoned with smoky oak (French and American).

DRY $35 AV

Moutere Hills Nelson Pinot Noir ★★★

The 2001 vintage (★★★), matured in French oak casks, is a charming, supple wine with full ruby colour and raspberry and spice aromas. Forward in its appeal, it has good depth of ripe strawberry and spice flavours, with restrained oak adding a touch of complexity and gentle tannins.

Vintage	01	00	99	98
WR	5	5	6	4
Drink	03-06	P	03-05	03-04

DRY $24 AV

Mt Difficulty Pinot Noir ★★★★

Grown at Bannockburn, in Central Otago, the 2001 (★★★★) has a complex bouquet with barnyard characters and smoky oak. It offers strong cherry and spice flavours, with sweet fruit, a rich mid-palate and a firm foundation of tannin. The robust 2002 vintage (★★★★☆) is deeply coloured, with concentrated, ripe cherry and plum flavours. A muscular wine (14.5 per cent alcohol), it is vibrantly fruity, with finely integrated oak and a firm, long finish. It should mature well; open mid-2004+.

DRY $40 AV

Muddy Water Waipara Pinot Noir ★★★★

The ruby-hued 2001 vintage (★★★★) has a beguiling fragrance of strawberries and smoky oak. Hand-picked at 24 to 25 brix, it was fermented with indigenous yeasts, matured for a year in French oak barriques (20 per cent new) and bottled without filtration. A mouthfilling, warm wine that seduces with its grace, charm and suppleness rather than sheer power, it is finely balanced, well-rounded and harmonious, although slightly less concentrated than in top vintages.

Vintage	02	01	00	99	98	97
WR	6	5	6	5	5	5
Drink	03-06	03-08	03-05	03-04	P	P

DRY $39 AV

Mud House Black Swan Reserve Pinot Noir ★★★☆

The 2001 vintage (★★★☆) is a single-vineyard Marlborough wine, French oak-aged for a year. Showing some funky elements on the nose, with full, youthful colour, it's a warm and concentrated wine with strong cherry and plum, slightly earthy flavours, quality oak and a firm, tight finish.

Vintage	01
WR	6
Drink	03-07

DRY $40 -V

Mud House Marlborough Vineyard Selection Pinot Noir (★★★)

The 2002 vintage (★★★) was French oak-aged for 10 months. Bright ruby-red, with fresh raspberry, cherry and plum flavours, slightly spicy and nutty, and firm tannins, it's a moderately complex style, likely to be at its best from mid-2004 onwards.

DRY $20 AV

Murdoch James Blue Rock Pinot Noir ★★★★

The 2001 (★★★★★), estate-grown just south of Martinborough, is fragrant and fleshy, with an array of savoury, spicy, nutty flavours. It's a powerful wine with strong, sweet-fruit characters, seasoned with smoky oak, and impressive ripeness and richness. The 2002 vintage (★★★★) is a full-coloured, youthful red, matured in French oak barriques (30 per cent new). A graceful wine with strong cherry and plum flavours, it is vibrantly fruity, with fresh acidity and a smooth finish.

Vintage	02	01	00	99
WR	6	7	6	5
Drink	03-06	03-06	03-05	03-04

DRY $55 -V

Murdoch James Fraser Pinot Noir ★★★★

Grown in the Fraser vineyard, on the Martinborough Terrace, the full-coloured 2001 vintage (★★★★) has substantial body (14.5 per cent alcohol), sweet-fruit characters and cherry, plum and nut flavours, showing considerable complexity. Powerful, ripe and fleshy, it should mature well. The 2002 (★★★★), matured in French oak barriques (30 per cent new), shows good weight, ripeness and roundness, with fresh, strong cherry/plum flavours, finely integrated oak and good aging potential.

Vintage	02	01	00	99	98	97	96
WR	6	7	6	6	5	6	6
Drink	04-08	04-07	03-06	03-06	03-04	P	P

DRY $60 -V

Murdoch James Waiata Pinot Noir ★★★

The 2002 vintage (★★★) of this single-vineyard Martinborough red was matured in seasoned French oak barriques (one to four-year-old). Robust (14.5 per cent alcohol), it's a soft, full-coloured wine with strong, ripe, plummy flavours, sweetish fruit characters and a very smooth finish. Drink 2003–04.

DRY $40 -V

Nautilus Marlborough Pinot Noir ★★★★

The 2001 vintage (★★★☆) is a blend of seven clones grown at six sites, hand-picked and matured for 11 months in French oak barriques (30 per cent new). Supple, with good weight and intensity of cherry, raspberry and spice fruit characters, it shows a slight lack of fruit sweetness, but is an elegant wine with the structure to mature well.

Vintage	02	01	00	99	98	97
WR	7	7	6	5	NM	6
Drink	04-07	03-05	03-06	03-05	NM	03-04

DRY $37 AV

Neudorf Moutere Home Vineyard Pinot Noir ★★★★★

Neudorf's flagship Pinot Noir. Estate-grown at Upper Moutere, in Nelson, the 2001 vintage (★★★★★) was based principally on older, clone 5 ('Pommard') vines. Matured for a year in French oak barriques (44 per cent new), it is powerful, fleshy and flavour-crammed, with a beguiling fragrance of cherries, raspberries, spice and smoky oak and a rich, savoury, velvety palate. A wonderfully refined and concentrated wine, it should develop well for several years.

Vintage	02	01
WR	6	6
Drink	03-12	03-08

DRY $56 AV

Neudorf Moutere Pinot Noir ★★★★★

Typically a very classy Nelson red. The generous 2001 vintage (★★★★★) is robust and richly flavoured, with savoury, nutty complexities and a firm but supple, lingering finish. The 2002 (★★★★★) is a blend of grapes harvested at over 24 brix in the home vineyard and from mature, low-cropping vines in the Neudorf-managed Pomona vineyard, overlooking Tasman Bay. Fermented with indigenous yeasts, matured for a year in French oak barriques (44 per cent new) and bottled without fining or filtering, it's a highly complex wine, deep ruby, with substantial body (14 per cent alcohol) and very concentrated flavours, cherryish, nutty and spicy. Built to last, with a firm tannin grip, it's clearly a great vintage, best cellared to at least 2005.

Vintage	02	01	00	99	98	97	96
WR	6	7	6	6	NM	7	6
Drink	05-12	03-08	03-05	03-04	NM	03-04	P

DRY $48 AV

Nevis Bluff Pinot Noir ★★★☆

Grown in the Nevis Bluff estate vineyard and the neighbouring Pociecha block at Gibbston, and matured in French oak casks (20 per cent new), the 2002 vintage (★★★★) of this Central Otago red is one of the best yet. Boldly coloured, it is fragrant and exuberantly fruity, with concentrated, ripe flavours of cherries and plums and finely integrated oak. A powerful, youthful wine, it's worth cellaring.

Vintage	02	01	00
WR	6	5	5
Drink	04-07	03-06	P

DRY $36 -V

Nga Waka Pinot Noir ★★★☆

Typically a graceful rather than highly concentrated Martinborough red, scented and supple. French oak-aged, the 2001 vintage (★★★☆) has fragrant, red-berry aromas leading into a moderately concentrated palate with ripe cherry/plum flavours, vibrant and well-rounded. An elegant wine, forward in its appeal, it's now developing some savoury, bottle-aged complexities.

Vintage	01	00	99	98
WR	6	7	6	6
Drink	03-05	03-04	P	P

DRY $40 -V

Nobilo Fall Harvest Pinot Noir (★★)

A blend of Australian and New Zealand wine, the 2002 vintage (★★) is a ripe, slightly raisiny red with plum and raspberry flavours and a very smooth finish. It's a solid quaffer, but shows limited varietal character.

DRY $12 AV

Nobilo Icon Pinot Noir ★★★

Showing lots of drink-young charm, the debut 2001 vintage (★★★☆) is a fruit-driven style, grown in Central Otago, with strong, raspberryish, cherryish flavours and gentle tannins. For 2002 (★★★), the grape supply switched to Marlborough. French oak-aged, it's an elegant middleweight with ripe cherry and spice characters, enough complexity and tannin to be interesting and some aging potential.

Vintage	02	01
WR	7	7
Drink	03-05	03-04

DRY $24 AV

Northrow Marlborough Pinot Noir (★★★★)

Northrow is a new range from Villa Maria, aimed at the restaurant trade. The 2002 vintage (★★★★) is full-coloured and fragrant, with cherry and spice aromas, ripe-fruit characters and good complexity. It's an intensely varietal wine with moderate tannins and strong drink-young appeal.

DRY $30 AV

Olssen's Jackson Barry Pinot Noir ★★★★

From the 2002 vintage onwards, this is the Bannockburn, Central Otago winery's 'mainstream' red; Slapjack Creek (below) is the reserve. Showing the concentration and structure to age well, the 2002 (★★★★☆) was estate-grown in The Garden Vineyard and matured in French oak barriques (35 per cent new). Vivid, purple-red, with floral, red-berry aromas, it is finely scented and mouthfilling, fleshy and sweet-fruited, with rich cherry and plum flavours, spicy oak and firm tannins. Open mid-2004+.

Vintage	02	01
WR	7	5
Drink	03-10	03-08

DRY $38 AV

Olssen's of Bannockburn Pinot Noir ★★★☆

This Central Otago red has been consistently good, but the 2001 vintage is the last. Matured for a year in French oak casks (25 per cent new), the 2001 (★★★☆) is floral, nutty and spicy, with good balance, depth, warmth and complexity.

Vintage	01	00	99	98
WR	5	6	5	6
Drink	03-06	03-04	P	P

DRY $34 V

Olssen's Slapjack Creek Reserve Pinot Noir ★★★★☆

The top label from the Bannockburn, Central Otago winery is 'made from a careful selection of barrels in those years when the wine is of distinctly superior quality'. The 2001 vintage (★★★★☆) is deliciously plump, rich and rounded. The 2002 vintage (★★★★★) is boldly coloured, with a rich, spicy bouquet. Powerful and robust, it is packed with cherry, plum and spice flavours, seasoned with fine-quality oak (French, 60 per cent new). Showing lovely concentration and warmth, with a firm foundation of tannin and a lasting finish, it should offer outstanding drinking around 2005.

Vintage	02	01	00	99	98
WR	7	6	NM	6	5
Drink	04-08	03-06	NM	03-05	P

DRY $45 AV

Omaka Springs Marlborough Pinot Noir (★★★☆)

Offering fine value, the 2001 vintage (★★★☆) is densely coloured and firmly structured, with well-ripened plum/spice flavours seasoned with oak and very good depth. It's a youthful wine with some cellaring potential.

Vintage	01
WR	6
Drink	03-04

DRY $22 V+

Opihi Pinot Noir ★★☆

Grown in South Canterbury, the 2001 vintage (★★★) was matured for 10 months in French oak casks. It's a middleweight style, light/medium ruby, with fresh raspberry and strawberry flavours seasoned with toasty oak. Firm and ripe, with some complexity, it's worth short-term cellaring.

Vintage 01
WR 6
Drink 03-07

`DRY $24 –V`

Oyster Bay Marlborough Pinot Noir ★★★★

The generous, velvety 2001 vintage (★★★★) from Delegat's is a softly seductive, mouthfilling and very harmonious wine, still youthful, with vibrant, plummy flavours and gentle tannins. Matured for 10 months in French oak barriques (25 per cent new), the 2002 (★★★★) is more savoury, spicy and gamey than the 2001, with cherryish, sweet-fruit characters in a supple, elegant, richly varietal style, already delicious.

Vintage 02   01
WR   7   7
Drink 03-05 03-06

`DRY $30 AV`

Palliser Estate Pinot Noir ★★★★★

A richly perfumed, notably elegant and harmonious Martinborough red, concentrated, supple and attractively priced (reflecting its relatively large volume.) Wood maturation is for a year in French oak barriques (25 per cent new). The 2001 vintage (★★★★★) is a generous wine (14 per cent alcohol), full-coloured and ripely fragrant, with sweet-fruit delights, rich raspberry, plum and spice flavours, smoky oak adding complexity, firm underlying tannins and a lasting finish. Offering substance and charm, it should be at its best in 2004+. The 2002 (★★★★) is medium-full ruby, with sweet, ripe-plum and cherry flavours and firm tannins. It's an impressively complex wine with savoury, spicy, nutty characters, but less lush and concentrated than the best of past vintages, and more forward; drink 2004–05.

Vintage 01   00   99   98   97   96   95   94
WR   7   7   7   7   7   7   5   5
Drink 03-08 03-07 03-06 03-05 03-05 03-04 P   P

`DRY $38 V+` 🍇🍇

Palliser Pencarrow Martinborough Pinot Noir ★★★★

The 2001 vintage (★★★★) is Palliser Estate's second-tier label, but it's still an impressive wine and better than many company's top reds. Matured in French oak barriques (25 per cent new), it has a spicy, smoky bouquet, leading into a full-bodied, raspberry and spice-flavoured palate with excellent depth and a smooth finish. It's already delicious. The 2002 (★★★☆) has sweet, ripe-fruit characters, with cherry and spice flavours showing greater depth than its lightish colour suggests. Savoury and supple, it's a forward vintage, for drinking during 2004.

`DRY $26 V+`

Pegasus Bay Pinot Noir ★★★★★

This Waipara red is one of Canterbury's greatest Pinot Noirs, typically very rich in body and flavour. Matured for 18 months in French oak barriques (30 per cent new) and bottled unfiltered, the 2001 vintage (★★★★★) is deep and youthful in colour. Crammed with fruit and potentially very complex, it is concentrated and smooth, with substantial body (14 per cent alcohol), deep cherry, plum and spice flavours and fine, supple tannins. It's still very youthful; open mid-2004+.

Vintage 02   01   00   99
WR   5   7   5   7
Drink 03-08 03-10 03-05 03-08

`DRY $43 V+` 🍇🍇

Pegasus Bay Prima Donna Pinot Noir ★★★★★

For its reserve Waipara Pinot Noir, Pegasus Bay wants 'a heavenly voice, a shapely body and a velvety nose'. Harvested 'after an amazing Indian summer', the 2001 vintage (★★★★★) was matured for 18 months in Burgundy oak barriques (30 per cent new). Powerful, weighty and youthful, with rich colour, it is firm and highly concentrated, but crying out for more time. Its bold, warm cherry, plum and spice flavours build to a rich, tightly structured, lasting finish. It should be a great bottle around 2005.

Vintage	01	00	99	98	97	96
WR	7	NM	6	7	NM	5
Drink	03-12	NM	03-10	03-10	NM	03-04

DRY $75 AV

Peregrine Pinot Noir ★★★★★

The 2001 vintage (★★★★★) of this bold, richly flavoured Central Otago red was outstanding in mid-late 2003 – deep and youthful in colour, with concentrated, plummy, spicy flavours, firm, ripe and complex. The 2002 (★★★★★) is also notably intense. Matured in French oak barriques (30 per cent new), it is dark and highly fragrant, with raspberry, herb and cherry aromas. Showing lovely warmth and flavour density, it is vibrantly fruity and supple, with savoury, earthy notes adding complexity and finely balanced tannins. A great buy, it's already hard to resist.

Vintage	02
WR	7
Drink	03-08

DRY $35 V+

Peregrine Wentworth Pinot Noir (★★★★☆)

Estate-grown in the Wentworth Vineyard, at Gibbston, in Central Otago, the debut 2002 vintage (★★★★☆) was matured for 10 months in French oak barriques (30 per cent new). Boldly coloured, it's deliciously mouthfilling and supple, with concentrated plum, cherry and spice flavours, hints of coffee and herbs, firm tannins and a long, rich finish. Still in its infancy, it's currently more restrained than its lower-priced stablemate (above) and needs time; open late 2004+.

Vintage	02
WR	7
Drink	03-10

DRY $50 -V

Pisa Range Estate Black Poplar Block Pinot Noir ★★★★

Grown at Pisa Flats, north of Cromwell, in Central Otago, the 2001 (★★★★) is enticingly scented and supple. It's a ruby-hued wine with mouthfilling body, sweet-fruit characters, plum, cherry and herb flavours seasoned with spicy oak, good complexity and gentle tannins. The 2002 vintage (★★★★☆) was matured for a year in French oak barriques (one-third new). Crammed with dark plum and cherry fruit characters, it's a substantial, supple wine, best kept for a year or two, but already hugely drinkable.

DRY $37 AV

Porters Martinborough Pinot Noir ★★★★

The 2001 vintage (★★★★) is a deeply coloured wine with a fragrant, plummy, spicy bouquet. Weighty and supple, it's a generous red with sweet, ripe cherry and plum characters, well-integrated oak and some savoury complexity. Drink now onwards.

Vintage	02	01	00	99	98
WR	6	7	7	7	6
Drink	03-06	03-07	03-06	03-04	P

DRY $49 -V

Pukawa Lake Taupo Pinot Noir ★★★

Grown on the southern shores of the lake, the 2001 (★★★) is fullish in colour, spicy, cherryish and slightly vegetal, with some fruit sweetness, toasty French oak adding complexity and a crisp finish. French oak-aged for 10 months, the 2002 vintage (★★★☆) is full-coloured, with a spicy, almost peppery fragrance. Tightly structured, with strong cherry and spice flavours and nutty oak, it's a serious wine for cellaring. There's a slight lack of ripeness here, but it's a quality wine nevertheless.

DRY $30 -V

Putiki Bay Pinot Noir ★★☆

Grown on Waiheke Island (where Pinot Noir vines are a rare sight) and French oak-aged for a year, the 2000 vintage (★★☆) has light, developed colour. Savoury and firm, it lacks the perfume and opulence of more southern Pinot Noirs, but shows quite well-defined coffee and spice varietal characters in a light style. Ready.

DRY $27 -V

Quartz Reef Bendigo Estate Vineyard Pinot Noir (★★★★★)

Sold only in 1.5-litre magnums, the 2002 vintage (★★★★★) of Rudi Bauer's Central Otago red was grown in the company's 'seriously warm' vineyard at the north-east end of Lake Dunstan, at Bendigo Station. Exceptionally rich in colour, it is still very youthful, with super-charged cherry, raspberry and plum flavours, seasoned with spicy, nutty oak, and some gamey elements. A splendidly ripe wine, muscular and firm, it needs time to unfold; open 2005+.

Vintage	02
WR	6
Drink	03-07

DRY $150 (1.5L) AV

Quartz Reef Pinot Noir ★★★★☆

A classy, intensely varietal Central Otago red, always very graceful and complex. The 2002 vintage (★★★★☆) is a blend of grapes from Pisa Range Estate, near Lowburn, north of Cromwell (80 per cent), and the company's own vineyard at Bendigo (20 per cent). Boldly coloured and fragrant, it is weighty and supple, with loads of cherry, plum and herb flavour. Beautifully ripe, with some savoury complexity and great drink-young charm, it also has the power to age; open 2004+.

Vintage	02	01	00	99	98
WR	7	6	6	7	6
Drink	03-09	03-06	03-07	03-07	03-05

DRY $42 AV

Richmond Plains Nelson Pinot Noir ★★★

Grown organically and matured in a 50/50 split of tanks and barriques, the generous 2001 vintage (★★★☆) is full-coloured, fresh and mouthfilling, with plenty of plummy, spicy flavour and some oak complexity.

DRY $22 AV

Richmond Plains Reserve Pinot Noir ★★★☆

Grown in the stoniest part of the vineyard and matured in all-new French oak barriques, the 2001 vintage (★★★★) of this bold Nelson red is full-coloured and sweet-fruited, with rich flavours of plums and cherries. A fragrant, generous, vibrantly fruity and supple wine, it's deliciously fleshy, soft and forward.

DRY $28 AV

Rimu Grove Nelson Pinot Noir (★★★☆)

Showing good cellaring potential, the 2001 vintage (★★★☆) was hand-harvested in the Moutere hills, matured for nine months in French oak barriques and bottled unfiltered. Full and youthful in colour, with raspberry and plum flavours showing good density, sweet fruit and good body, it's a moderately complex, firmly structured wine; open 2004+.

DRY $38 -V

Rippon Pinot Noir ★★★★

A scented, vibrantly fruity Lake Wanaka, Central Otago red with plenty of body and smooth, cherryish flavours (green-edged in cool seasons). The charming 2001 vintage (★★★★) is one of the best. Ruby-hued, it's a middleweight style but elegant, intensely varietal and supple, with cherry and spice flavours showing good complexity, gentle tannins and a finely balanced, lingering finish.

Vintage	01	00	99	98	97	96	95	94
WR	7	6	5	5	6	5	6	5
Drink	03-07	03-06	03-04	P	P	P	P	P

DRY $39 AV

Riverby Estate Marlborough Pinot Noir (★★★)

Deep and youthful in colour, the 2001 vintage (★★★) has strong raspberry, dark cherry and plum flavours, still developing, and a firm finish.

DRY $29 -V

Rockburn Central Otago Pinot Noir ★★★★

Coming together well, the 2001 vintage (★★★★) of this Central Otago red has fragrant, cherry and herb aromas, full, youthful colour and warm, spicy, nutty flavours, savoury, complex and well-rounded. The sturdy 2002 (★★★★☆) is a blend of Lowburn, Cromwell Basin (82 per cent), Gibbston (10 per cent) and Lake Hayes (8 per cent) grapes, matured in French oak barriques (one-third new). Deep ruby, it is generous and concentrated, with lovely cherry, plum and spice flavours and firm supporting tannins. Showing good fruit sweetness and complexity, it's a sophisticated wine, still youthful but already a delight to drink.

DRY $35 AV

Rossendale Canterbury Pinot Noir ★★☆

Estate-grown at Halswell, on the outskirts of Christchurch, the lightly oaked 2001 (★★☆) is ruby-hued, fruity and plummy in a simple, drink-young, Beaujolais style with some sweet-fruit charm. The 2002 vintage (★★☆) has slightly herbal aromas, fresh, plummy flavours and a slightly high-acid finish.

DRY $20 -V

St Helena Canterbury Pinot Noir ★★☆

Robin Mundy's Belfast red set the Canterbury wine scene on fire with the 1982's gold medal success, but the wine now lacks its old notable power and flavour richness. At its best, it has cherryish, savoury, spicy, nutty characters and decent depth, but other years are smooth, strawberryish, green-edged and simple. The 2001 vintage (★★) is light in colour, with simple, berryish, slightly spicy flavours and a smooth finish.

Vintage 01
WR 5
Drink 03-04

`DRY $24 -V`

St Helena Reserve Pinot Noir ★★★

The 2002 vintage (★★★) is labelled as being of South Island, rather than entirely Canterbury, origin. Matured in French oak casks (25 per cent new), it is lightish in colour, with spicy, slightly leafy flavours showing good depth. It's not especially ripe or concentrated, but offers some savoury complexity.

Vintage 02
WR 6
Drink 04-07

`DRY $34 -V`

Saint Clair Doctor's Creek Marlborough Pinot Noir ★★★☆

Grown mainly in the company's Doctors Creek vineyard in the Wairau Valley, the 2001 vintage (★★★☆) was matured for 11 months in French oak casks (35 per cent new). A smooth, flavoursome wine with an easy-drinking charm, it is full-coloured and fruity, with plum and cherry characters in a gently wooded, moderately complex style with a long, rounded finish.

Vintage 01
WR 6
Drink 03-05

`DRY $24 V+`

Saint Clair Omaka Reserve Marlborough Pinot Noir ★★★☆

The deeply coloured 2001 vintage (★★★★) was grown in the Omaka Valley, hand-picked and matured for 12 months in a mix of new French (35 per cent) and older American oak casks. Still developing, it's a warm, generous wine with a strong bouquet of cherries and smoky bacon and plummy, spicy flavours, firm and youthful.

Vintage 01 00
WR 6 6
Drink 03-06 03-05

`DRY $29 AV`

Saint Clair Vicar's Choice Marlborough Pinot Noir (★★★)

A fruit-driven style, the 2002 vintage (★★★) was handled mostly in tanks, but 25 per cent spent eight months in new and used French oak casks. Fresh and vibrant, with ripe-fruit aromas, it has berryish, plummy fruit characters to the fore, with gentle tannins and good drink-young charm.

Vintage 02
WR 6
Drink 03-05

`DRY $19 AV`

Schubert Marion's Vineyard Pinot Noir (★★★☆)

Schubert's lower-tier Pinot Noir has lots of character. The 2002 vintage (★★★☆) was grown in the Wairarapa and matured for over a year in French oak barriques (60 per cent new). Sturdy and concentrated, it's a full-coloured wine with fragrant spice, herb and nut aromas. Firm and slightly oaky in its youth, it needs more time; open 2005 onwards.

Vintage 02
WR 5
Drink 03-07

DRY $30 AV

Schubert Wairarapa Pinot Noir ★★★★

Based mainly on first-crop vines at East Taratahi, near Masterton, the sturdy 2001 vintage (★★★★☆) is drenched with ripe plum/cherry flavours, seasoned with spicy French oak. The 2002 (★★★★) was matured for over a year in French oak barriques (60 per cent new). It's a powerful wine, robust (14.5 per cent alcohol), with sweet-fruit characters and strong cherry and spice flavours, already quite savoury, nutty and complex. A firm wine with loads of character, it will probably be at its best during 2004–06.

Vintage 02 01
WR 6 6
Drink 03-12 03-11

DRY $45 -V

Seifried Nelson Pinot Noir ★★☆

A middleweight style. Matured for nine months in oak, with some whole-berry fermentation, the 2001 (★★☆) is light-medium ruby in colour, with spicy, nutty flavours and slightly green tannins. Grown at Appleby, the 2002 vintage (★★☆) has raspberry, spice and herb flavours, with moderate depth and a slightly hard finish.

Vintage 01 00 99 98 97 96
WR 6 6 5 5 5 5
Drink 03-05 03-06 03-05 P P P

DRY $21 -V

Seifried Winemakers Collection Pinot Noir ★★★

Grown in Nelson, the 2001 (★★☆) was matured for nine months in oak casks (80 per cent new). Ruby-hued, it is berryish and ripely flavoured, but lacks real freshness and vibrancy. Slightly earthy and rustic, with a bouquet of mushrooms and herbs, the 2002 vintage (★★★) has some fruit sweetness, plenty of flavour and a firm backbone of tannin.

Vintage 01
WR 7
Drink 03-07

DRY $35 -V

Selaks Founders Reserve Marlborough Pinot Noir (★★★☆)

Strongly wood-influenced, the 2002 vintage (★★★☆) is a single-vineyard red, harvested at over 24 brix and matured for 14 months in all-new French oak barriques. It's a youthful wine, warm, spicy and supple, with ripe plum and spice flavours, gentle tannins and a smooth finish.

Vintage 02
WR 7
Drink 03-06

DRY $33 -V

Seresin Marlborough Pinot Noir ★★★★★

Top vintages are crammed with dark cherry, spice and nut flavours, very warm, complex and rich. Grown at Renwick, fermented with indigenous ('wild') yeasts, matured for 15 months in French oak barriques and bottled unfiltered, the 2001 (★★★★☆) is deeply coloured and fragrant, with sweet-fruit delights and rich cherry, raspberry and spice flavours. Slightly less complex in its youth than the outstanding 2000 (★★★★★), it is firmly structured and still youthful; open mid-2004+.

Vintage	01	00	99	98
WR	6	6	6	6
Drink	04-08	03-09	03-09	03-07

DRY $38 V+

Sherwood Estate Pinot Noir ★★★

One of the better sub-$20 Pinot Noirs, the 2002 vintage (★★★) is a briefly oak-aged blend of Marlborough and Canterbury grapes. Full ruby, with mouthfilling body, fresh, strong strawberry and spice flavours and a rounded finish, it's drinking well now but should also offer enjoyable drinking during 2004–05.

DRY $19 AV

Sherwood Estate Reserve Pinot Noir ★★★☆

A single-vineyard Marlborough wine, the 2002 vintage was tasted prior to bottling (and so not rated). Boldly coloured, it has mouthfilling body and strong, ripe, plum and cherry flavours, very fresh and vibrant.

DRY $32 -V

Shingle Peak Marlborough Pinot Noir – see Matua Valley Shingle Peak Marlborough Pinot Noir

Sileni Cellar Selection Pinot Noir (★★★)

Made for early consumption, the charming 2002 vintage (★★★) was based on first-crop vines at the company's elevated, relatively cool Plateau Vineyard, between Maraekakaho and Mangatahi, in Hawke's Bay. French oak-aged for nine months, it is light in colour, with ripe cherry and plum flavours, some earthy, spicy touches and soft tannins. Drink 2004. (Cellar door sales only.)

Vintage	02
WR	5
Drink	04-07

DRY $27 -V

Sleeping Dogs Pinot Noir (★★★☆)

Grown on the slopes of Mount Rosa, in the Gibbston district, the 2002 vintage (★★★☆) of Roger Donaldson's Central Otago red is rich in colour, with fresh, strong plum and spice flavours. An exuberantly fruity, moderately complex wine with firm tannins, it's still very youthful and worth cellaring.

DRY $30 AV

Solstone Wairarapa Valley Pinot Noir ★★★

Grown at Masterton and French oak-aged for 10 months, the 2001 vintage (★★★) is a middleweight style, ruby-hued, with strawberry and spice flavours, some savoury complexity and a fresh, crisp finish.

Vintage	01	00
WR	6	6
Drink	03-05	03-04

DRY $31 -V

Springvale Estate Pinot Noir ★★★

The 2000 (★★★★) is an aromatic, mouthfilling Alexandra, Central Otago red with rich colour and generous raspberry, plum and spice flavours. On a lower plane, the 2001 (★★☆) is light and berryish, with a crisp, green-edged finish.

Vintage	01	00	99
WR	5	6	4
Drink	03-06	P	P

DRY $27 -V

Spy Valley Marlborough Pinot Noir ★★★☆

Grown in the Waihopai Valley, the 2001 (★★★☆) has raspberry and spice flavours showing good depth, some gamey, toasty complexity and firm tannins. The full-bodied 2002 vintage (★★★☆), matured for a year in French oak barriques (30 per cent new), has fragrant, fresh raspberry and spice aromas leading into a vibrantly fruity wine with berryish, plummy flavours, a seasoning of toasty oak and a smooth finish.

Vintage	02	01	00
WR	6	6	6
Drink	03-07	03-06	03-05

DRY $29 AV

Squawking Magpie The Mudlark Martinborough Pinot Noir (★★☆)

Described as a 'notably bold style', the 2002 vintage (★★☆) is a single-vineyard red, French oak-aged. Lightish in colour, with mellow, cherryish flavours and a hint of herbs, it's a forward style with moderate depth.

DRY $27 -V

Staete Landt Marlborough Pinot Noir ★★★☆

In the graceful mould of Volnay or Santenay, the debut 2001 (★★★★) is a single-vineyard red with sweet-fruit charms, ripe-cherry and red-berry flavours, good complexity and velvety tannins. The 2002 vintage (★★★☆) was harvested at 24 to 25 brix and matured in French oak barriques (25 per cent new). Only moderately concentrated but very charming, it displays ripe cherry and raspberry flavours mingled with spicy oak and a well-rounded finish. Drink 2004–05.

Vintage	02
WR	6
Drink	04-06

DRY $36 -V

Stonecutter Martinborough Pinot Noir ★★★☆

The 2002 vintage (★★★☆) is light/medium ruby, with a youthful, vibrantly fruity palate. It's a moderately concentrated wine with ripe cherry, plum and spice flavours showing some savoury, nutty complexity and balanced tannins.

DRY $35 -V

Stoneleigh Marlborough Pinot Noir ★★★☆

Gone are the days when you couldn't buy a decent Pinot Noir for under $20. The 2002 vintage (★★★☆) from Montana was matured for 10 months in French oak casks (30 per cent new). Deep ruby, with a smoky, toasty bouquet, it is warm, spicy and flavoursome, with fairly firm tannins. Still youthful, it's well worth cellaring to at least 2005.

Vintage	02	01	00	99	98	97
WR	6	6	7	6	5	4
Drink	03-10	04+	03+	P	P	P

DRY $20 V+

Stoneleigh Vineyards Rapaura Series Marlborough Pinot Noir ★★★★

The 2001 vintage (★★★★) is a firmly structured, mouthfilling wine, full-coloured, with strong cherry and spice flavours, savoury, complex characters and slightly chewy tannins. Matured for a year in French oak barriques (30 per cent new), the mouthfilling 2002 (★★★★) is full ruby, with strong fruit flavours of cherry and spice. Showing good fruit sweetness, depth and complexity, it should age well and offers fine value.

Vintage	02	01	00
WR	6	7	7
Drink	03-10	04+	P

DRY $27 V+

Stratford Martinborough Pinot Noir ★★★★★

The 2001 vintage (★★★★★) shows lovely warmth and roundness. Richly fragrant, with ripe-fruit and toasty oak aromas, deep colour and strong cherry, plum and spice flavours, it's an impressively concentrated wine. The 2002 (★★★★☆) was matured for 10 months in French oak barriques. It's a complex style with rich cherry and spice flavours, nutty and savoury, and a firm tannin grip. Built to last, it needs time; open 2005+.

Vintage	02	01	00	99	98	97
WR	5	6	6	7	6	5
Drink	04-10	03-07	03-06	03-06	03-05	P

DRY $44 AV

Sunset Valley Vineyard Reserve Pinot Noir (★★★★)

Grown organically in the Upper Moutere hills, the 2002 vintage (★★★★) was matured for 10 months in new French oak casks. Full-coloured, with excellent depth of plummy, earthy and spicy flavours showing considerable complexity, it's a ripe, youthful wine with firm tannins and good cellaring potential.

Vintage	02
WR	6
Drink	04+

DRY $28 V+

Tasman Bay Nelson Pinot Noir ★★☆

The 2002 vintage (★★☆) is a ruby-hued, medium-bodied wine with strawberryish, green-edged flavours and a slightly crisp finish. It's a drink-young style, lacking any real complexity.

Vintage	01	00	99
WR	6	6	5
Drink	03-05	03-05	03-04

DRY $20 -V

Tasman Bay Vintage Special Selection Pinot Noir (★★☆)

Designed as a 'soft, fruit-driven' style, the 2002 vintage (★★☆) is a blend of grapes from five regions: Hawke's Bay, Martinborough, Nelson, Marlborough and Canterbury. Ruby-hued, with strawberry and spice flavours, it's an easy-drinking, light to medium-bodied wine, quite developed for its age, with some savoury characters and gentle tannins. Drink now to 2004.

DRY $19 -V

Te Hera Estate Martinborough Pinot Noir (★★☆)

First planted in 1996, Te Hera ('The Sail') Estate was the first commercial vineyard founded in the Te Muna Road district, a few kilometres south of Martinborough. The debut 2001 vintage (★★☆), matured for a year in French oak barriques (one-third new), is still purple-flushed, with berryish aromas. Still youthful, it has strong cherry and plum flavours, but lacks real complexity and warmth, with a slightly high-acid finish.

DRY $29 -V

Te Kairanga Martinborough Pinot Noir ★★★★

This Martinborough red is consistently attractive and the 2001 vintage (★★★★) is a top drink-young style. Fresh, lifted raspberry and spice aromas lead into a deeply coloured, strongly flavoured wine. Harvested at an average of 24 brix and matured for 10 months in French oak barriques (20 per cent new), the 2002 (★★★☆) is medium ruby, with cherry and spice flavours and gentle tannins. It shows good but not great flavour depth, with some complexity and plenty of drink-young charm.

Vintage	02	01	00	99	98	97
WR	7	7	7	7	7	6
Drink	03-07	03-06	03-05	03-04	P	P

DRY $35 AV

Te Kairanga Reserve Pinot Noir ★★★★

Based on a vineyard selection by 'vine age and specific flavours', the sturdy 2001 vintage (★★★★) of this Martinborough red is a notably bold style of Pinot Noir. Full-coloured and robust (14.5 per cent alcohol), rich and firm, it is crammed with warm, plummy, spicy flavours, seasoned with quality oak (French, 30 per cent new). It's quite developed for its age; drink now to 2004. There is no 2002.

Vintage	02	01	00	99	98	97	96	95	94
WR	NM	7	7	6	6	5	5	5	5
Drink	NM	03-08	03-06	03-06	03-05	P	P	P	P

DRY $45 -V

Te Mania Nelson Pinot Noir ★★★★

From a small winery on the Waimea Plains, this wine offers consistently good value. The 2001 (★★★★) is impressively dense and powerful, with bold, rich colour and concentrated flavours, spicy and firm. The 2002 vintage (★★★★), partly oak-aged, has lots of personality. Full and youthful in colour, it is fragrant, full-bodied, fresh and vibrantly fruity, placing its accent on beautifully ripe cherry and plum flavours. A delicious drink-young style.

Vintage	02	01	00	99	98
WR	6	6	5	6	5
Drink	04-06	03-05	P	03-04	P

DRY $25 V+

Te Mania Reserve Pinot Noir (★★★★★)

The top-flight 2001 vintage (★★★★★) is a highly concentrated Nelson red, low-cropped (at below 5 tonnes/hectare) and matured for 10 months in French oak barriques (half new). Bold and youthful in colour, with rich, sweet-fruit characters and firm tannins, it is powerful, structured and long, but needs time; open mid-2003+.

Vintage	02	01
WR	6	7
Drink	04-07	03-06

DRY $30 V+

Terrace Downs Central Otago Pinot Noir (★★☆)

Produced and bottled for CK Wines, an Auckland-based wine distributor, the 2001 vintage (★★☆) was grown at Alexandra. Light ruby-hued, with fresh, smooth, cherry and plum flavours of moderate depth, it shows only limited varietal character and is highly over-priced.

DRY $35 -V

Terrace Road Marlborough Pinot Noir ★★★

Past vintages were plain, but Cellier Le Brun's red took a giant step forward in 2002 (★★★★). Offering outstanding value, it was matured for 10 months in French oak barriques (25 per cent new). Fullish in colour, it is warm, ripe, full-flavoured and firm, with attractive cherry and spice characters, toasty oak adding complexity and slightly chewy tannins. Put simply, it's the best sub-$20 Pinot Noir on the market.

DRY $20 AV

Thornbury Marlborough Pinot Noir ★★★

The mouthfilling, fruit-crammed 2001 (★★★☆) was made from young vines at Rapaura and oak-aged for a year. The colour is rich and youthful; the bouquet is fresh and berryish; the palate is moderately complex, with subtle oak, fairly firm tannins and strong, vibrant cherry/plum flavours. The 2002 vintage (★★☆) was disappointing in mid-late 2003. Deeply coloured, with a charry bouquet, it's a gutsy, powerful wine, but slightly rustic, chewy and extractive, lacking any real finesse.

Vintage	02	01
WR	6	6
Drink	04-09	03-07

DRY $38 -V

Tohu Marlborough Pinot Noir ★★★☆

Hand-picked and French oak-matured, the 2001 vintage (★★★☆) is highly attractive in its youth. Full ruby in hue, it is vibrantly fruity, with gentle tannins, well-integrated oak and good depth of plum, cherry, spice and nut flavours. The 2002 (★★★☆) is very similar, with sweet-fruit charms, cherry, raspberry and herb flavours, moderate complexity and good harmony.

Vintage	02
WR	4
Drink	03-05

DRY $26 AV

Torlesse Canterbury Pinot Noir (★★☆)

Fresh, lively and supple, the 2002 vintage (★★☆) is a blend of grapes grown at Waipara (50 per cent), Swannanoa and West Eyreton. Ruby-hued, it's a middleweight style with slightly spicy, green-edged flavours and some drink-young charm.

Vintage	02
WR	7
Drink	03-06

DRY $19 -V

Torlesse Waipara Pinot Noir ★★★☆

Supple and forward, the 2001 vintage (★★★☆) of this North Canterbury red is ruby-hued, with strawberry and spice aromas. It's a smooth, weighty, moderately concentrated wine with sweet, ripe-fruit characters and some savoury, nutty complexity.

Vintage	01
WR	7
Drink	03-06

DRY $30 AV

Trinity Hill Hawke's Bay Pinot Noir (★★★)

Priced right, the 2002 vintage (★★★) is an attractive drink-young style. Grown at two sites, at Te Awanga and in the hill country south of the Heretaunga Plains, it was matured for eight months in one-year-old French oak casks and bottled without filtration. Ruby-hued, with clearly varietal, strawberry and spice aromas and flavours, it's not highly concentrated but warm, spicy and savoury, with a rounded finish.

DRY $20 AV

Trinity Hill Hill Country Pinot Noir (★★★★)

Grown at Glencoe Station, in Central Hawke's Bay, the 2002 vintage (★★★★) was matured for 10 months in new French oak barriques. Weighty, warm and supple, with strawberry, plum and spice aromas and flavours, sweet-fruit delights and complex, earthy and gamey characters, it's one of the most convincing Hawke's Bay Pinot Noirs yet.

Vintage	03	02
WR	6	5
Drink	03-08	03-06

DRY $39 AV

Trinity Hill Te Awanga Pinot Noir ★★★★

The 2001 vintage (★★★★☆) is very successful. Rich and supple, it was grown in a relatively cool coastal area of Hawke's Bay and matured for a year in new French oak barriques. A stylish wine with good potential, it is full-coloured and flavoursome, with sweet-fruit characters of cherries and plums, spicy oak and a rounded finish.

Vintage	01	00
WR	5	6
Drink	03-04	03-05

DRY $39 AV

Twin Islands Marlborough Pinot Noir ★★★

Negociants' red offers good value in an easy-drinking style. The lightly oaked 2002 vintage (★★★) is more complex than most wines in its price category, with mouthfilling body (13.5 per cent alcohol), some savoury touches and good depth of plum, cherry and spice flavours. It's a warm, supple wine with considerable grace and charm.

Vintage	02	01	00	99	98
WR	7	6	6	6	5
Drink	03-05	03-04	P	P	P

DRY $20 AV

Two Paddocks Pinot Noir ★★★★

Sam Neill's Central Otago red has shown good form since the perfumed, weighty and supple 1999 (★★★★). Promoted as the 'first true vintage from our two paddocks', the 2001 (★★★☆) is a 50/50 blend of Gibbston and Earnscleugh (near Alexandra) grapes. Full ruby, with slightly developed colour and a fragrant, spicy and mushroomy, complex bouquet, it's not highly concentrated, but seamless and silky, with sweet-fruit charms and gentle tannins. Drink 2003–04. (The 2002 vintage has produced two single-vineyard wines, First Paddock, grown at Gibbston, and The Last Chance, from Earnscleugh.)

Vintage	01	00
WR	5	6
Drink	03-09	03-08

DRY $36 AV

Valli Bannockburn Vineyard Pinot Noir (★★★★★)

The power-packed 2002 vintage (★★★★★) was grown in the same vineyard as Valli's splendid Bald Hills Pinot Noir 2001 (★★★★★). French oak-aged for 10 months, it is much more tannic than its Gibbston Vineyard stablemate from 2002 (see below). Deeply coloured and sturdy, it is bold and ripe, with a rich array of cherry, spice and nut flavours and a lasting finish. It's a seriously structured wine for cellaring; open 2005+.

Vintage	02
WR	6
Drink	04-10

DRY $45 AV

Valli Gibbston Vineyard Pinot Noir (★★★★★)

The 2002 vintage (★★★★★) was grown in the same block as Valli's lovely Colleen's Vineyard Pinot Noir 2001 (★★★★★). Finely scented, it is rich and rounded, with an abundance of sweet, ripe cherry, plum and spice flavours and gentle tannins. It should reward lengthy cellaring, but is delicious in its youth.

Vintage 02
WR 7
Drink 04-10

DRY $45 AV

Vavasour Marlborough Pinot Noir ★★★☆

The 2001 vintage (★★★☆) is a blend of Wairau Valley (57 per cent) and Awatere Valley (43 per cent) grapes, matured for nine months in French oak casks (35 per cent new). Harvested at 24 to 25 brix, it is full and fresh, with smoky, toasty aromas and strong raspberry, cherry and spice flavours. Showing finely balanced tannins and good complexity, it's worth cellaring for a year or two.

Vintage 02 01 00 99
WR   7   7   6   6
Drink 04-07 03-04 P   P

DRY $30 AV

Vidal Estate Hawke's Bay Pinot Noir (★★★★)

Robust (14.5 per cent alcohol), with excellent flavour depth, the 2002 vintage (★★★★) was matured for 10 months in French oak casks. Dark and concentrated, with cherry and spice characters, it is warm and savoury, with good complexity and moderately firm tannins. A good buy.

Vintage 02
WR 6
Drink 04-06

DRY $25 V+

Vidal Estate Marlborough Pinot Noir ★★★★

An elegant wine, opening out well with bottle-age, the 2001 vintage (★★★★☆) is a blend of fruit from young vines in the Wairau Valley (principally) and the Awatere Valley. French oak-matured for 10 months, it's deeply coloured, with ripe plum and cherry flavours, spicy oak and a rich, rounded finish. The 2002 (★★★★) again shows excellent depth, with cherry and spice flavours seasoned with toasty oak, strong colour and a fragrant, welcoming bouquet.

Vintage 02 01 00 99
WR   6   6   6   5
Drink 04-06 03-05 03-05 P

DRY $30 AV

Vidal Estate Stopbank Pinot Noir (★★★★☆)

Richly coloured and highly fragrant, the 2002 vintage (★★★★☆) was grown in the Keltern Vineyard in Hawke's Bay. It's a mouthfilling wine with lovely softness through the palate, warm, ripe cherry and spice flavours and savoury, slightly earthy and chocolatey characters adding complexity.

Vintage 02
WR 7
Drink 04-07

DRY $30 V+

Villa Maria Cellar Selection Marlborough Pinot Noir ★★★★☆

At just under $30, this consistently delightful wine is a match for many, much higher-priced Pinot Noirs. The 2002 vintage (★★★★☆) was grown in the Awatere and Wairau valleys and matured for nine months in French oak casks (30 per cent new). Soft, rich and savoury, with deep colour, it offers strong, ripe cherry and spice flavours, substantial body (14 per cent alcohol) and excellent complexity. Drink now onwards.

Vintage	02	01	00	99
WR	7	6	7	5
Drink	03-07	03-06	03-06	P

DRY $30 V+

Villa Maria Reserve Marlborough Pinot Noir ★★★★★

Launched from 2000, this label has swiftly won recognition as one of the region's boldest, lushest reds. The 2001 (★★★★☆) is an 'iron fist in a velvet glove' – strapping, rich and supple, with lovely intensity of plummy, cherryish, spicy flavours and even a hint of liquorice. But it's not the ultimate in style, with a soaring alcohol level (15 per cent) and less finesse than the country's greatest Pinot Noirs. Matured for nine months in French oak barriques (40 per cent new), the 2002 vintage (★★★★★) is richly coloured and highly fragrant. Substantial (14 per cent alcohol), with lovely, sweet-fruit characters and complex cherry and spice flavours, it's a superior wine to the 2001, more savoury and intensely varietal.

Vintage	02	01	00
WR	7	6	7
Drink	04-09	03-06	03-06

DRY $50 AV

Voss Estate Pinot Noir ★★★★

Voss is a tiny Martinborough winery with a big, instantly likeable Pinot Noir. The 2002 vintage (★★★★), matured for a year in French oak barriques, is still youthful, with full ruby colour, strong flavours of cherries, plums and spice and French oak complexity. Showing good concentration, sweet-fruit characters and a firm underlay of tannin, it should unfold well during 2004–05.

Vintage	02	01	00	99	98	97	96
WR	5	6	6	7	7	6	6
Drink	03-06	03-06	03-05	03-04	03-04	P	03-04

DRY $37 AV

Vynfields Martinborough Pinot Noir (★★★)

Grown organically, the 2002 vintage (★★★) is a fruit-driven style with fresh, red-berry aromas, ripe, slightly spicy flavours and a smooth finish.

DRY $32 -V

Waimea Estates Bolitho Reserve Pinot Noir (★★★★)

Fragrant and rich, the 2001 vintage (★★★★) was made from low-cropped (below 5 tonnes/hectare) Nelson vines, matured in French oak casks (a third new) and bottled unfiltered. It's a powerful wine with an attractive bouquet of cherries, spice and oak, and a bold, spicy, complex palate with sweet-fruit characters, good concentration and firm tannins. Open 2004–05.

DRY $35 AV

Waimea Estates Nelson Pinot Noir ★★★

The powerful 2002 vintage (★★★☆) is a full-coloured, concentrated red. Hand-picked at six sites in the region at an average of 24.6 brix, it's a gently oaked wine with sweet, ripe-fruit characters, youthful cherry and spice flavours and a firm tannin structure. Good cellaring potential.

Vintage	01	00	99
WR	6	4	5
Drink	03-05	P	P

DRY $24 AV

Waipara Downs Pinot Noir ★★★

The latest vintages of this North Canterbury wine are the best. The 2001 (★★★), matured in French oak barriques (10 per cent new), has full colour and berryish, spicy, distinctly plummy flavours. It's a well-balanced wine, although not highly concentrated. For the 2002 (★★★), the new oak influence rose to 25 per cent. The bouquet is floral and berryish; the palate is fresh and vibrantly fruity, with raspberry and plum flavours and moderately firm tannins. Priced right.

DRY $19 AV

Waipara Hills Canterbury Pinot Noir (★★☆)

The 2002 vintage (★★☆) was grown in Canterbury, but not at Waipara. French oak-aged for nine months, it has light-medium colour, with slightly leafy and vegetal aromas. A light-bodied wine with cherryish, raspberryish, green-edged flavours and a crisp finish, it's a drink-young style.

Vintage	02
WR	6
Drink	03-07

DRY $22 -V

Waipara Hills Marlborough Pinot Noir (★★★)

A 'fruit-driven' style, the 2002 vintage (★★★) has the edge on its Canterbury stablemate (above). French oak-aged for six months, it is light ruby, with sweet, ripe cherry and plum flavours and a silky-smooth finish. It's not concentrated, but a graceful, finely balanced wine for current consumption.

Vintage	02
WR	5
Drink	03-07

DRY $22 AV

Waipara Hills Marlborough Simmonds Vineyard Pinot Noir (★★★★)

Still unfolding, the 2002 vintage (★★★★) is a youthful, sweet-fruited red. Grown in Dog Point Road, adjacent to the Omaka River, it was matured for a year in all-new French oak casks. Ruby-hued, it's a generous wine with good concentration of raspberry, cherry and plum flavours, spicy oak and ripe, supple tannins.

Vintage	02
WR	7
Drink	04-14

DRY $50 -V

Waipara Hills Reserve Pinot Noir (★★★★☆)

Grown at West Melton, near Christchurch, rather than Waipara, the 2001 vintage (★★★★☆) was matured for a year in French oak casks (50 per cent new). Delicious in its youth, it's a generous, full-coloured wine with rich, well-ripened cherry and spice flavours, good fruit/oak balance and a rounded finish.

DRY $37 AV

Waipara Springs Pinot Noir ★★★☆

The charming 2001 vintage (★★★★) was made from low-yielding, young vines at Waipara and matured for 10 months in well-seasoned French oak barrels. Scented, with sweet-fruit characters, excellent depth of raspberry/plum flavours, subtle oak and a soft finish, it's delightful in its youth. The 2002 (★★★) is less concentrated, but still attractive. Matured in older oak casks, it's a supple, easy-drinking wine with fresh, vibrant, red-berry and plum aromas and flavours.

Vintage	02	01
WR	6	7
Drink	03-05	03-06

DRY $25 AV

Waipara Springs Reserve Pinot Noir ★★★★

The 2001 vintage (★★★★☆) was made from Waipara vines (mostly 18 to 20-year-old), matured for over a year in French oak barriques (40 per cent new) and bottled unfiltered. Showing concentrated, sweet, well-ripened fruit characters, it's a full-coloured wine with strong raspberry, plum and cherry flavours, good, savoury, nutty complexity and a well-rounded finish. Drink now onwards.

Vintage	02	01
WR	6	6
Drink	03-05	03-06

DRY $38 AV

Waipara West Pinot Noir ★★★★

This is a small-volume red (340 cases in 2001), mostly exported to the UK. The stylish 2001 vintage (★★★★) was harvested at 24.8 brix from very low-cropping vines (4.3 tonnes/hectare) and matured for 11 months in French oak barriques (30 per cent new). Full ruby, with fragrant, raspberry and spice aromas, it's a finely structured wine with ripe cherry and plum flavours, well integrated oak and savoury, spicy characters adding complexity. Slower to mature than some Waipara reds, it's sure to reward cellaring; open mid-2004+.

Vintage	01	00	99	98
WR	6	6	6	7
Drink	03-05	P	P	P

DRY $39 AV

Waitiri Creek Pinot Noir ★★★

This red has the herbal character often found in Pinot Noirs from Gibbston, one of the cooler sub-regions of Central Otago. Hand-picked from 19 April to 10 May and matured in French oak barriques, the 2002 vintage (★★★☆) is one of the best. Richly coloured, with very good concentration of plum and herb flavours, it's a moderately complex wine, worth cellaring for a year or two.

DRY $35 -V

Waiwera Estate Pinot Noir ★★★☆

Grown at Golden Bay, in Nelson, the 2001 vintage (★★★★) is a fleshy, deeply coloured wine with a fragrant, warm and spicy bouquet. Matured for 15 months in two-year-old French oak casks, it's a generous, smooth wine with sweet-fruit delights, concentrated plum/spice flavours, oak complexity and loads of character. Re-tasted in mid-2003, it's still youthful and getting better and better with age.

DRY $26 AV

Walnut Ridge Pinot Noir ★★★★★

Bill Brink, the founder of this tiny Martinborough winery, died in 2002, leaving a rich legacy of lush, opulent, single-vineyard Pinot Noirs. The land was soon after sold to neighbouring Ata Rangi, who completed and bottled the 2001 vintage (★★★★). Full-coloured, with a hint of development, it's a warm, mellow wine with savoury, spicy, complex flavours and substantial body. Rich and firm, it should be at its best during 2003–05. (From the 2003 vintage onwards, Walnut Ridge will be a blend of grapes from several Martinborough sites, including Walnut Ridge and younger vineyards.)

Vintage	01	00	99	98	97	96	95	94
WR	6	7	7	6	7	6	5	6
Drink	03-05	03-08	03-07	03-06	03-05	P	P	P

DRY $42 AV

Whitehaven Pinot Noir ★★★☆

Matured in French oak barriques (40 per cent new), the 2001 (★★★) is a vibrantly fruity wine with decent depth of cherryish, slightly nutty and spicy flavours and firm tannins. The 2002 vintage (★★★), French oak-aged, has red-berry and slightly herbal aromas leading into a moderately firm wine with fresh acidity and good depth of plummy, spicy flavour. Drink 2004.

Vintage	02	01	00
WR	6	6	5
Drink	03-06	03-04	03-05

DRY $30 AV

Whitestone Waipara Pinot Noir (★★★)

A drink-young style, the 2002 vintage (★★★) is rare – only 60 cases were made. Matured in new French oak casks, it's a middleweight style with ripe cherry and spice flavours, some savoury complexity and moderate tannins.

DRY $30 -V

William Hill Pinot Noir ★★★

This small Alexandra, Central Otago winery typically makes an attractive, cherry and plum-flavoured wine in a moderately complex style with gentle tannins. The 2001 vintage (★★☆) was hand-picked at 24 brix and matured for 11 months in new to three-year-old French oak casks. Cherry and raspberryish, with some funky, earthy characters, it's a moderately varietal wine, lacking the fragrance and charm of this label at its best. (I have also tasted a fresh, vibrantly fruity, plummy and spicy, but only moderately complex 2001 vintage [★★★] Reserve Pinot Noir.)

Vintage	01	00	99
WR	5	6	5
Drink	03-07	03-06	03-06

DRY $32 -V

Winslow Colton Reserve Pinot Noir ★★☆

Ensconsed in a claret-style bottle – unusual for Pinot Noir – the 2001 vintage (★★☆) of this Martinborough red is deeply coloured, with fresh, strong, berryish flavours, but it shows limited varietal character. The 2002 (★★☆), based on low-cropping vines (3.5 tonnes/hectare) and French oak-matured for nine months, is a medium-bodied style with green-edged flavours.

DRY $32 -V

Wishart Basket Press Pinot Noir (★★★)

The fresh, supple 2002 vintage (★★★) was grown in Hawke's Bay, harvested at 23 brix and matured for eight months in seasoned French oak casks. It's a full-bodied wine with good varietal character and depth of raspberry, plum and spice flavours in a slightly earthy, moderately complex style.

DRY $25 -V

Wishart Reserve Pinot Noir (★★★☆)

The substantial, warm and spicy 2001 vintage (★★★☆) was grown at Bay View, on the Hawke's Bay coast, and matured for 18 months in French oak casks. Full and youthful in colour, with ripe, spicy aromas, it is sturdy and supple, with cherryish, plummy, slightly earthy flavours, savoury and nutty. It's a less intensely varietal wine than more southern styles, but generous and concentrated.

DRY $39 -V

Wither Hills Marlborough Pinot Noir ★★★★★

Built to last, the 2001 vintage (★★★★★) is one of the region's most multi-faceted Pinot Noirs. Matured for 14 months in French oak barriques (60 per cent new), it's a full-coloured wine with a savoury, smoky bouquet, ripe, sweet plum, berry and spice flavours, showing excellent density, and a firm finish. The 2002 (★★★★★) is full ruby, with a complex bouquet, spicy, earthy and savoury. Showing excellent warmth and depth, it possesses rich cherry, plum and spice flavours, braced by firm tannins. Already delicious, it offers very classy drinking from now onwards.

Vintage	02	01	00	99	98	97
WR	7	7	7	7	7	6
Drink	03-07	03-07	03-06	03-05	03-04	03-04

DRY $47 AV

Woollaston Estates Nelson Pinot Noir (★★★★)

The bold, chewy 2002 vintage (★★★★) was based on extremely low-yielding vines (below 2.5 tonnes/hectare) and matured for 10 months in French oak barriques. Deeply coloured, it's a powerful wine with very ripe, almost Syrah-like flavours of raspberry and spice. It needs cellaring and could be very long-lived.

DRY $29 V+

Sangiovese

Sangiovese is Italy's most extensively planted red-wine variety, but a rarity in New Zealand. Cultivated as a workhorse grape throughout central Italy, in Tuscany it is the foundation of such famous reds as Chianti and Brunello di Montalcino. Here, Sangiovese is sometimes confused with Montepulciano, and the seven hectares of bearing vines in 2002 are not projected to expand by 2005.

Borthwick Estate Wairarapa Valley Sangiovese (★★☆)

Grown near Masterton and matured for nine months in old oak barrels, the 2000 vintage (★★☆) is a vibrantly fruity wine with plum and red-berry flavours threaded with high acidity. The 2001 (★★☆) is fresh and flavoursome, with cherry, plum and spice characters, but again lacks real ripeness and warmth, with a slightly green finish. Both wines are well made, but the Wairarapa may simply be too cool for Sangiovese.

DRY $27 -V

Heron's Flight Matakana Sangiovese (★★★★☆)

North of Auckland, David Hoskins and Mary Evans have staked their future on Sangiovese. At its best, as in the 1999 vintage (★★★★☆) it is purple-black, with highly concentrated plum/spice flavours, strongly seasoned with new French oak, some savoury elements and a firm foundation of tannin. (The cheapest way to try this rare, high-priced wine is at the winery – $12 per glass on weekends and holidays.)

DRY $50 -V

Matariki Sangiovese (★★★☆)

The promising 2001 vintage (★★★☆) was grown in the Gimblett Gravels district of Hawke's Bay and blended with 25 per cent Cabernet Sauvignon. It tastes like Sangiovese, with fresh, vibrant cherry, plum and spice flavours and a crisp but not over-acid finish. Deeply coloured and mouthfilling, with well-integrated oak, it's an attractive wine, drinking well now.

Vintage 01
WR 5
Drink 04-08

DRY $40 -V

Vin Alto Sangiovese (★★☆)

Grown at Clevedon, in South Auckland, and oak-matured for two years, the 1999 vintage (★★☆) has fullish colour, showing some development. It's a firmly structured wine with cherry, raspberry and spice flavours and oak complexity, but lacks real ripeness and roundness.

Vintage 99
WR 4
Drink 06

DRY $28 -V

Syrah (Shiraz)

The 'Syrah' of the Rhône Valley, in France, and the 'Shiraz' of the Barossa Valley in South Australia – they're the same grape variety. On the rocky, baking slopes of the upper Rhône Valley, and in several Australian states, this noble grape yields red wines renowned for their outstanding depth of cassis, plum and black-pepper flavours.

In New Zealand, interest in the classic variety has been stirring for a decade. Dozens of labels are now on the market, and the results to date are extremely promising. After judging at the 2003 New Zealand Wine Society Royal Easter Wine Show, Australian wine writer James Halliday declared that the 'outstanding class of the show was undoubtedly Syrah/Shiraz… The great thing about this [Hawke's Bay] style is that it is ripe. There's no hint of green or minty or other unripe flavours, yet it also keeps those wonderful spice, liquorice, black-pepper characters which are at the riper end of the cool-climate spectrum. So it beautifully straddles the two. It is definitely different in style from Australian shiraz, notwithstanding its diversity within Australia.'

Syrah was well known in New Zealand a century ago. Government viticulturist S.F. Anderson wrote in 1917 that Shiraz was being 'grown in nearly all our vineyards [but] the trouble with this variety has been an unevenness in ripening its fruit'. For today's winemakers, the problem has not changed: Syrah has never favoured a too-cool growing environment. Having said that, it thrives in poor soils and ripens ahead of Cabernet Sauvignon.

The latest national vineyard survey showed that 117 hectares of Syrah were bearing in 2002 – only 3 per cent of the total area of red-wine varieties, but almost double the 62 hectares bearing in 2000. By 2004, 153 hectares will be in production. Over 70 per cent of the vines are in Hawke's Bay, with smaller pockets in Auckland and Marlborough. Syrah's potential in this country's warmer vineyard sites is finally being tapped.

Ata Rangi Syrah ★★★★☆

After repeated urgings by its customers to release Syrah (a key component of its blended red, Célèbre) as a varietal wine, Ata Rangi leased a block of Syrah in the Arapoff vineyard, at Martinborough. The second release, from the 2002 vintage (★★★★☆) was matured for 18 months in French and American oak barriques (25 per cent new). It's a weighty, warm wine with deep, youthful colour and bold, black-pepper aromas, unmistakably Syrah. It shows good aging potential, with very concentrated cassis, plum and black-pepper flavours, complexity and a very persistent finish.

Vintage	02	01
WR	6	6
Drink	03-06	03-06

DRY $40 -V

Babich Winemakers Reserve Syrah ★★★★

One of New Zealand's few mid-priced Syrahs. Grown in Gimblett Road, Hawke's Bay, and matured for a year in American oak casks, the youthful 2002 vintage (★★★★) is sure to reward cellaring, with deep, purple-flushed colour and a fragrant, peppery, toasty bouquet. It's a warm, elegant wine with strong, vibrant plum and black-pepper flavours, finely integrated oak and firm tannins. Open 2005+.

Vintage	02	01	00	99	98
WR	7	6	6	7	7
Drink	03-09	03-07	03-07	03-07	03-06

DRY $25 AV

Bilancia Hawke's Bay Syrah ★★★★

The highly concentrated 2001 vintage (★★★★) is a densely coloured wine with good varietal character and excellent fruit depth. The 2002 (★★★★☆) is a blend of grapes from vineyards in the Gimblett Gravels district (80 per cent) and the company's own block, La Collina, on Roys Hill. Matured for 17 months in French (predominantly) and American oak barriques, it's a dark, weighty wine with black pepper aromas and powerful, plummy, spicy flavours, intense and chewy. Still very youthful, it's a firm, concentrated wine with the structure to age well for several years.

Vintage 02 01
WR 7 6
Drink 04-10 03-08

DRY $34 -V

Brookfields Reserve Vintage Hillside Syrah ★★★★☆

Grown on a sheltered slope between Maraekakaho and Bridge Pa in Hawke's Bay (described by winemaker Peter Robertson as 'surreal – a chosen site'), the debut 2000 vintage (★★★★☆) was matured in new American oak casks. Almost opaque, it's a stylish rather than blockbuster red, warm, plummy and spicy, with impressive ripeness and concentration, some gamey touches and a long finish. The 2001 (★★★★☆) is also impressive, with fresh, deep, intensely varietal plum/spice flavours, showing a strong toasty oak influence, and good fruit sweetness and complexity.

Vintage 01 00
WR 7 7
Drink 07-10 04-12

DRY $40 -V

C.J. Pask Gimblett Road Syrah (★★★☆)

Full-coloured, with strong peppery aromas, the 2001 vintage (★★★☆) is a Hawke's Bay wine, matured for 16 months in new French oak. Based on young, second-crop vines, it's a strongly varietal wine with good weight, plum/pepper flavours that show a slight lack of softness, finely balanced oak and gentle tannins. A decent Rhône style, it is developing complexity with bottle-age and drinking well now.

DRY $25 AV

C.J. Pask Reserve Syrah (★★★★)

The 2000 vintage (★★★★) was based on first-crop vines in Gimblett Road and matured for 16 months in all-new French oak barriques. Deeply coloured, with an assertive, toasty oak influence, it has ripe, concentrated plum and black-pepper fruit flavours and firm tannins.

DRY $30 AV

Craggy Range Gimblett Gravels Vineyard Block 14 Syrah (★★★★)

Dark, with intensely peppery aromas and deep blackcurrant/spice flavours, the 2001 vintage (★★★★) is a youthful, tightly structured wine. Fermented with indigenous yeasts, it was matured for 18 months in French oak barriques (35 per cent new) and bottled unfined and unfiltered. Bold and tight-knit, with impressive concentration, it needs time to soften; open 2005+.

Vintage 01
WR 7
Drink 05-09

DRY $30 AV

Craggy Range Le Sol Syrah (★★★★★)

The super-charged 2001 vintage (★★★★★) of this Gimblett Gravels, Hawke's Bay red was harvested at 26.4 brix, when the grapes were shrunken and dehydrated, matured for 19 months in French oak barriques (40 per cent new), and bottled without fining or filtering. Opaque, with a very rich fragrance of plums and spice, it's a statuesque wine (14.7 per cent alcohol) that simply overflows with intensely varietal, cassis and black-pepper flavours, framed by firm tannins. It's a great red on the rise; open 2006+.

Vintage 01
WR 7
Drink 06-16

DRY $70 AV

Crossroads Destination Series Syrah (★★★☆)

Grown in Hawke's Bay, the 2002 vintage (★★★☆) is full-bodied and smooth, with purple-flushed colour and a peppery, earthy bouquet. It's a strongly varietal wine with sweet-fruit characters, raspberry, plum and pepper flavours showing very good depth, a seasoning of toasty oak and a lasting finish.

DRY $25 AV

Delegat's Gimblett Gravels Syrah (★★★☆)

The refined 2000 vintage (★★★☆) was made from Hawke's Bay vines that have since been replaced with a superior clone of Syrah. Barrique-aged for two years, it's a warm, rounded wine, not hugely concentrated, but ripe and clearly varietal, with great drinkability.

DRY $35 -V

Dry River Syrah ★★★★☆

The tautly structured 2001 vintage (★★★★☆), labelled 'Arapoff', needs another two or three years to unfold. Grown in Martinborough, it was matured for a year in French oak barriques (30 per cent new). Deep and very youthful in colour, with rich, black-pepper and plum aromas and flavours, it's very fresh and vibrant, with a firm backbone of tannin and a long, spicy finish. A distinctly cool-climate style, it's well worth cellaring to at least 2005.

Vintage 01 00 99 98 97
WR 7 7 6 7 7
Drink 03-11 03-11 03-10 03-05 03-10

DRY $55 -V

Fromm La Strada Reserve Syrah ★★★★★

Delicious already, the 2001 vintage (★★★★☆) was blended with a 'homoeopathic' amount of Viognier (less than 1 per cent) and matured for 16 months in French oak casks (30 per cent new). Densely coloured, rich and supple, it's a concentrated wine with brambly, plummy, spicy flavours and firm, ripe tannins, but also lots of drink-young charm. (The 1999 vintage, tasted in late 2003, is still developing with impressively deep, peppery, gamey, firm flavours.)

Vintage 02 01 00 99 98 97 96
WR 6 6 NM 6 7 7 6
Drink 04-10 03-09 NM 03-07 03-10 03-09 03-06

DRY $48 AV

Goldridge Estate Matakana Shiraz/Merlot/Cabernet (★★☆)

Estate-grown and matured for nine months in mostly French oak casks, the 2001 vintage (★★☆) is a light to medium-bodied red (11 per cent alcohol) with fullish colour and sweet oak aromas. A leafy, herbaceous wine with firm acidity, it clearly reflects the difficult season and it is unfortunate that the back label superlatives stretch credibility beyond breaking point.

Vintage 01
WR 5
Drink 03-05

DRY $16 -V

Holmes Nelson Shiraz (★★★★)

The intensely varietal 2001 vintage (★★★★) is a top buy. Grown in a clay, hillside vineyard and matured in American oak barriques, it is boldly coloured, with a powerful bouquet of plums and black pepper. An exuberantly fruity red, it is warm and concentrated, with loads of plummy, spicy flavour, finely balanced oak and firm, ripe tannins.

DRY $20 V+

Kingsley Estate Gimblett Gravels Syrah (★★★★☆)

Due to devastating frosts, the classy 2001 vintage (★★★★☆) was not grown organically at the estate vineyard, but based on grapes from three other vineyards in the Gimblett Gravels area of Hawke's Bay. A blend of Syrah (76 per cent), Cabernet Sauvignon (12 per cent) and Malbec (12 per cent), it was matured in French oak barriques (45 per cent new). Densely coloured, with buckets of sweet fruit, strong blackcurrant and spice flavours and a rich finish, it's a complex wine that should age well, but is already highly satisfying.

Vintage 01
WR 7
Drink 03-08

DRY $39 -V

Longview Estate Syrah (NR)

Like a decent Côtes-du-Rhône, the 2002 vintage (tasted prior to bottling, and so not rated) offers good depth of warm, plum and spice flavours. Matured in a 50/50 split of French and American oak casks, it's a full-coloured Northland red with a fragrant, clearly varietal bouquet of plums and pepper. Ripely flavoured, with a toasty oak influence and gentle acidity and tannins, it's a very promising debut.

DRY $25 V?

Marsden Bay of Islands Syrah (★★☆)

Oak-aged for 15 months, the 2001 vintage (★★☆) of this Northland red is fullish in colour, with berryish, slightly spicy flavours and a sweet wood influence. However, it lacks real ripeness and richness.

Vintage 01
WR 3
Drink 03-05

DRY $20 -V

Matakana Estate Syrah ★★★★

The estate-grown 2000 vintage (★★★★) is an elegant red with good intensity and rich colour, showing some development. Matured for a year in predominantly new French oak barriques, it has ripe blackcurrant, plum and black-pepper flavours seasoned with toasty oak, considerable savoury complexity and a firm backbone of tannin.

Vintage 00 99
WR 6 6
Drink 06-07 05-06

DRY $35 -V

Matariki Hawke's Bay Syrah ★★★☆

Showing some earthy rusticity, the 2001 vintage (★★★) is a full-coloured Hawke's Bay red, weighty and moderately ripe, with firm tannins, fresh acidity and good depth of plum and spice flavours.

Vintage 01
WR 6
Drink 04-08

DRY $30 -V

Matariki Reserve Syrah (★★★★)

Grown in Gimblett Road, Hawke's Bay, and matured for 15 months in French and American oak casks (40 per cent new), the 2000 vintage (★★★★) is dark, warm and generous. Peppery, slightly earthy and smoky, it is complex and concentrated, with well-defined varietal characters, fine, supple tannins and a rich finish.

Vintage 00
WR 7
Drink 03-07

DRY $40 -V

Matua Valley Innovator Bullrush Vineyard Syrah (★★★★☆)

Concentrated by the 'saignee' (bleeding) technique, whereby a portion of the juice is drawn off at the start of ferment to concentrate the remaining juice, the 2002 vintage (★★★★☆) is a densely coloured Hawke's Bay red, matured in French and American oak barriques (half new). It's a bold, powerful, mouthfilling wine with warm plum, black-pepper and dark chocolate flavours, rich, nutty and tannic.

Vintage 02
WR 6
Drink 03-07

DRY $29 V+

Matua Valley Matheson Syrah (★★★)

Grown at the Matheson Vineyard, in the 'Ngatarawa Triangle', the 2002 vintage (★★★) is a boldly coloured Hawke's Bay wine. Matured in American and French oak casks (50 per cent new), it shows good varietal character, with fresh, vibrant plum and black-pepper flavours, gentle tannins and a distinctly spicy finish.

Vintage 02
WR 5
Drink 03-06

DRY $20 AV

Mills Reef Elspeth Syrah ★★★★★

New Zealand Syrah at its greatest. Estate-grown in the company's Mere Road vineyard, near Hastings, in Hawke's Bay, the 2001 vintage (★★★★★) is dark and rich, with concentrated cassis and black-pepper flavours and nutty, spicy oak. It's a dense, firmly structured wine, sure to be long-lived. The 2002 vintage (★★★★★) is exceptional. Showing astonishingly deep, purple/black colour, it's a super-rich wine, overflowing with ripe cassis, black-pepper and nut flavours. Strapping, with bold tannins in balance with its enormously concentrated fruit, it's a sort of New Zealand version of Penfolds Grange. Don't open it until 2005 onwards, maybe 2010 onwards.

Vintage 01 00 99 98
WR 7 7 7 7
Drink 03-06 03-05 03-04 03-04

DRY $45 AV

Mission Jewelstone Syrah ★★★★

Rich and still youthful in colour, the 2001 vintage (★★★☆) was grown at Gimblett Road, in Hawke's Bay, and matured in French oak barriques (half new). It's a slightly high-acid red with a very spicy nose, black-pepper flavours and firm but not excessive tannin.

Vintage 01 00 99
WR 5 NM 7
Drink 03-08 NM 03-10

DRY $35 -V

Mission Reserve Syrah (★★★☆)

Still on the market, the 2000 vintage (★★★☆) was made from low-cropping (5 tonnes/hectare) vines at Gimblett Road, in Hawke's Bay, and matured for a year in French oak barriques (40 per cent new). Deeply coloured and weighty, it offers strong blackcurrant, plum, herb and spice flavours, with a slightly high-acid finish.

Vintage	00
WR	6
Drink	03-10

DRY $28 -V

Morton Estate Black Label Hawke's Bay Syrah (★★★☆)

Showing good complexity but also a slight lack of warmth and softness, the 2001 vintage (★★★☆) was matured for a year in American oak casks. It's a savoury, earthy wine with strong cassis and black-pepper flavours and a firm finish.

Vintage	01
WR	6
Drink	03-08

DRY $35 -V

Mudbrick Vineyard Reserve Syrah (★★☆)

The 2002 vintage (★★☆) of this Waiheke Island red was matured for a year in French oak barriques (30 per cent new). It's a full-coloured wine with firm acidity woven through its plum and black-pepper flavours. When tasted in mid-2003, it lacked real warmth and softness, but will probably improve with time.

DRY $38 -V

Murdoch James Syrah ★★★

This Martinborough producer makes a characterful Syrah (prior to the 2001 vintage labelled Shiraz), but its quality has varied. The 2002 vintage (★★★) was harvested at over 25 brix and matured for 11 months in French oak casks (30 per cent new). Deep and youthful in colour, it has strong, black-pepper aromas. Fresh, smooth and vibrantly fruity, with plum and spice flavours, it's a moderately complex wine, but less ripe-tasting and intense than the top Hawke's Bay Syrahs.

Vintage	01	00	99	98
WR	6	7	6	4
Drink	04-07	03-07	03-07	P

DRY $35 -V

Newton Forrest Estate Cornerstone Syrah (★★★★)

Still unfolding, the 2001 vintage (★★★★) is a dark, chewy Gimblett Road, Hawke's Bay red. Purple-flushed, it has fresh, strong cassis, plum and black-pepper flavours, seasoned with sweet, spicy oak, and a firm, tannic finish. Open mid-2004 onwards.

Vintage	01
WR	5
Drink	05-07

DRY $50 -V

Okahu Estate Kaz Shiraz ★★★★

Estate-grown at Kaitaia, this is a consistently impressive Northland wine, ripe and rich. Fragrant, warm and supple, the 2000 vintage (★★★★) was matured for 18 months in American (60 per cent) and French oak casks (half new). Plummy and spicy, with full, youthful colour and perfumed, sweet oak aromas, it offers excellent flavour depth, varietal character and complexity.

Vintage	00	99	98
WR	7	NM	7
Drink	03-12	NM	03-10

DRY $55 -V

Okahu Estate Ninety Mile Shiraz/Cabernet (★★★☆)

Estate-grown near Kaitaia, the 2001 vintage (★★★☆) is a blend of 60 per cent Shiraz, 34 per cent Cabernet Sauvignon and 6 per cent Merlot, matured for a year in new and older French and American oak casks. There's a slight lack of warmth and softness on the finish, but it's a full-coloured wine with berryish, plummy, strongly peppery flavours. An honest, earthy, firm red, it shows lots of character.

Vintage 01
WR 6
Drink 03-07

DRY $27 -V

Passage Rock Syrah ★★★★☆

A robust Waiheke Island red, dark and complex, with a powerful presence in the mouth. Matured in French and American oak barriques (60 per cent new), the 2002 vintage (★★★★☆) is an intensely varietal wine with fragrant, black-pepper aromas leading into a warm, spicy, nutty, firm palate with excellent depth and structure and a lasting finish. Drink now or cellar.

Vintage 01
WR 6
Drink 03-10

DRY $40 -V

Schubert Syrah ★★★★☆

The bold, purple-black 2001 vintage (★★★★☆) is a blend of Wairarapa and Hawke's Bay grapes. (For the first time, most of the fruit came from the Wairarapa and, from 2002 onwards, it's entirely Wairarapa-grown.) Harvested in early May and matured for over two years in French oak barriques (half new), it's a highly concentrated, peppery, plummy, nutty wine with ripe, almost stewed fruit characters, hints of liquorice and prunes and very firm tannins.

Vintage 01 00 99
WR 7 7 6
Drink 03-11 03-10 03-09

DRY $45 -V

Stonecroft Syrah ★★★★★

With an arresting series of bold, dark, flavour-drenched reds, Alan Limmer was the first winemaker in this country to consistently produce a top-flight Syrah. The early vintages were grown entirely in Stonecroft's stony, arid vineyard in Mere Road, west of Hastings, but the 1998 introduced grapes from the newer Tokarahi vineyard at the foot of Roys Hill, which is contributing 'denser, more intense flavours'. Maturation is for 18 months in French oak barriques (50 per cent new). The 2001 vintage (★★★★☆) impresses with complexity rather than sheer power. Fullish, not dense, in colour, it has a complex, earthy, peppery bouquet that is classic Syrah. A forward vintage, it has strong, warm flavours of plums and pepper, oak complexity, spicy, savoury complexities and slightly higher acidity than usual. It's already delicious.

Vintage 01 00 99 98 97 96
WR 6 NM 6 6 6 6
Drink 04-10 NM 03-10 03-10 03-08 03-06

DRY $45 AV

Te Awa Farm Longlands Syrah ★★★

Grown at Roys Hill, in Hawke's Bay, and matured for 15 months in French oak barriques, the 2001 vintage (★★★) is a flavoursome wine with full, youthful colour and fragrant, black-pepper aromas. Spicy and earthy, it's a moderately ripe-tasting wine with good complexity and a slightly high-acid finish.

Vintage 01 00 99
WR 6 6 6
Drink 03-05 03-05 P

DRY $20 AV

Te Mata Estate Bullnose Syrah ★★★★★

Grown in the Bullnose vineyard, in the Ngatarawa district of Hawke's Bay, this very classy red is matured for 16 months in French oak barriques, new and one-year-old. The 2001 vintage (★★★★☆) is slightly less intense than the benchmark 2000 vintage (★★★★★) but unusually savoury and complex, with plum, black-pepper and nutty oak flavours, noble tannins and a long, spicy finish.

Vintage	02	01	00	99	98	97	96	95
WR	7	7	7	6	7	7	6	6
Drink	05-09	04-07	03-06	03-05	03-04	P	P	P

DRY $38 AV

Te Mata Estate Woodthorpe Syrah/Viognier (★★★★)

Delicious drinking from now on, the 2002 vintage (★★★★) was made by co-fermenting Syrah with a small amount of Viognier (a traditional technique of the northern Rhône Valley, designed to add 'a perfumed, floral aroma'). French oak-aged for 15 months, it's a richly coloured Hawke's Bay wine with lifted, cracked-pepper aromas. Intensely varietal, warm and concentrated, with cassis, pepper and slightly dark chocolate flavours, it has a well-rounded, spicy finish.

Vintage	02
WR	6
Drink	04-06

DRY $25 AV

Trinity Hill Gimblett Road Syrah ★★★★

The sophisticated 2001 vintage (★★★★) was matured for 16 months in French and American oak barriques (25 per cent new). Deeply coloured, fresh and vibrant, it shows good intensity of plum and black-pepper flavours, with a hint of sweet oak, firm, chewy tannins and a strongly spicy finish.

Vintage	02	01	00	99	98	97
WR	7	6	5	6	5	6
Drink	04-10	03-09	03-07	03-07	03-04	03-05

DRY $30 AV

Vidal Estate Soler Syrah (★★★★)

The generous, richly varietal 2001 vintage (★★★★) was grown in the Gimblett Gravels district of Hawke's Bay and matured for 18 months in French and American oak. Dark, with sweet-fruit characters of cassis, plum and black pepper, it's a muscular (14 per cent alcohol) yet highly approachable wine with impressive depth and rounded tannins. Tasted as a barrel sample (and so not rated), the 2002 vintage looked even better, with notable warmth and concentration.

Vintage	01
WR	6
Drink	05

DRY $30 AV

Vidal Estate Syrah (NR)

Showing striking depth for a non-reserve label, the 2002 vintage of this Hawke's Bay red was tasted as a barrel sample, and so not rated. Densely coloured, with a peppery fragrance, it's highly concentrated, warm and tannic, with loads of character.

DRY $25 V?

Wishart Reserve Hawke's Bay Syrah ★★★★

Grown on the beach gravels at Bay View, the 2001 vintage (★★★★) is an excellent debut. French oak-aged for a year, it is dark and fragrant, with highly concentrated flavours of blackcurrants, plums and spice and oak complexity. Rich and fairly ripe, yet with firm acidity, it's a sophisticated wine, still unfolding.

Vintage 01
WR 6
Drink 03-08

DRY $45 -V

Zinfandel

In California, where it is extensively planted, Zinfandel produces muscular, heady reds that can approach a dry port style. It is believed to be identical to the Primitivo variety, which yields highly characterful, warm, spicy reds in southern Italy. There are only four hectares of bearing Zinfandel vines in New Zealand, but Alan Limmer, of the Stonecroft winery in Hawke's Bay, believes 'Zin' has potential here, 'if you can stand the stress of growing a grape that falls apart at the first sign of a dubious weather map!'

Kemblefield The Reserve Zinfandel (★★★★)

Only the second 'commercial' release of 'Zin' in New Zealand, the 2000 vintage (★★★★) of this Hawke's Bay red was estate-grown at Mangatahi and matured for 15 months in French oak casks. Full, although not dense, in colour, with berry fruits and a hint of pepper on the nose, it's a brambly wine with smooth raspberry and spice flavours and good concentration and complexity.

DRY $50 -V

Stonecroft Zinfandel ★★★☆

The first 'commercial' release of Zinfandel grown in New Zealand was the 1999 vintage (★★★☆), a Hawke's Bay red with moderately ripe, plummy, spicy flavours and firm acidity. The 2000 (★★★☆) is similar – fullish in colour, with crisp acidity woven through its fresh, berryish, slightly peppery flavours. There was no 2001, but 'watch for the 2002' says winemaker Alan Limmer.

DRY $25 AV

Index of Wine Brands

This index should be especially useful when you are visiting wineries as a quick way to find the reviews of each company's range of wines. It also provides links between different wine brands made by the same producer (for example Matua Valley and Shingle Peak).

125 Gimblett Road 35

Akarua 35, 128, 336
Alana 35, 144, 175, 336
Alan McCorkindale 128, 145, 224, 239, 336
Alexander 267, 271, 336
Alexandra Wine Company 36, 145, 337
Alexia 36, 145, 175
Allan Scott 36, 145, 175, 240, 337
Alpha Domus 36, 37, 175, 218, 224, 254, 302, 303, 337
Amisfield 129, 176, 337 (*see also* Arcadia, Lake Hayes)
Amor-Bendall 114, 129, 145, 331
Anthony James 338
Aquila 240
Arahura 300, 303
Arcadia 240
Archipelago 271
Artisan 37, 114, 176, 254, 303
Ascension 37, 129, 145, 222, 303, 331
Ashwell 176, 271
Askerne 37, 114, 145, 176, 219, 225, 271
Ata Rangi 37, 38, 129, 176, 225, 249, 254, 338, 385
Awarua Terraces 176, 219, 271

Babich 30, 38, 115, 129, 146, 177, 222, 225, 272, 304, 331, 338, 339, 385
Bald Hills 129, 339
Benfield & Delamare 255
Bernadino 240
Bilancia 39, 130, 255, 339, 386
Black Barn 39, 177, 304 (*see also* Lombardi)
Black Estate 39, 339
Black Ridge 30, 39, 115, 146, 339
Bladen 115, 130, 146, 177
Borthwick 39, 146, 272, 304, 339, 384
Brajkovich 40, 304
Brick Bay 130, 255

Brightwater 40, 146, 177, 304
Brookfields 40, 115, 130, 146, 272, 273, 386
Bunny 340
Burnt Spur 40, 41, 147, 177, 340

Cable Bay 41, 178, 304
Cairnbrae 41, 178, 225, 340 (*see also* Gunn Estate, Sacred Hill)
Canadoro 41, 273
Canterbury House 41, 130, 147, 178, 226, 240, 305, 340
Cape Campbell 41, 147, 178, 340
Carrick 42, 131, 147, 178, 341
Cat's Pee on a Gooseberry Bush 178
Chancellor 226 (*see also* Hanmer Junction, The)
Chard Farm 42, 115, 131, 147, 341
Charles Wiffen 42, 147, 179, 226, 305
Christina 148, 249, 255
Church Road 42, 43, 179, 226, 273, 305 (*see also* Montana)
C.J. Pask 43, 44, 179, 256, 273, 305, 306, 341, 386
Claddagh 179
Clearview 44, 115, 179, 219, 226, 250, 256, 267, 274, 306
Clifford Bay 44, 148, 179
Cloudy Bay 30, 45, 116, 180, 227, 342 (*see also* Pelorus)
Collards 45, 112, 116, 180, 222, 227, 274, 300, 306, 342
Coney 148, 342
Coniglio 45
Coopers Creek 46, 47, 116, 131, 148, 180, 222, 227, 240, 274, 306, 307, 342, 343 (*see also* Cat's Pee, Fat Cat)
Corazon 47, 307
Corbans 47, 48, 125, 131, 148, 149, 181, 241, 275, 307, 343
Cottle Hill 48, 181, 227, 250
Covell 48, 343

INDEX OF WINE BRANDS

Crab Farm 48, 116, 181, 267, 275, 307, 343
Craggy Range 31, 49, 149, 182, 256, 307, 308, 386, 387 (*see also* Red Rock, White Rock)
Crossings The 182, 343
Crossroads 49, 50, 116, 149, 183, 256, 276, 308, 343, 344, 387

D 242
Daniel Le Brun 241, 242 (*see also* Terrace Road)
Daniel Schuster 50, 344
Darjon 149
Dashwood 50, 183, 276, 344
De Gyffarde 183
Delegat's 50, 183, 276, 300, 308, 387(*see also* Oyster Bay)
De Redcliffe 276 (*see also* Firstland)
Deutz 242
Dog Rock 257
Domaines Georges Michel 51, 184, 344, 345
Dry Gully 345
Drylands 51, 131, 149, 184, 308, 345 (*see also* Nobilo, Selaks)
Dry River 51, 116, 132, 149, 184, 227, 228, 345, 387
Dunleavy 277

Elstree 242
Equinox 52, 184, 309
Escarpment 132, 345
Eskdale 52, 116
Esk Valley 52, 112, 132, 150, 184, 221, 250, 257, 309 (*see also* Vidal, Villa Maria)

Fairhall Downs 52, 132, 185, 346
Fairmont 53, 150, 185, 346
Fat Cat 53
Felton Road 53, 228, 250, 346
Fenton 150, 257, 277
Ferryman 277
Fiddler's Green 54, 150, 185, 347
Firstland 228, 277, 347 (*see also* De Redcliffe)
Floating Mountain 54, 347
Forefathers 185
Foreman's Vineyard 277
Forrest 54, 113, 117, 151, 185, 228, 250, 310, 347 (*see also* Newton/Forrest)

Fossil Ridge 54, 347
Foxes Island 55, 347
Framingham 55, 117, 133, 151, 186, 228, 310, 348
Fromm 55, 117, 151, 229, 300, 310, 348, 387
Fusion 243

Gibbston Valley 56, 127, 133, 152, 186, 250, 348, 349
Giesen 56, 152, 186, 229, 349 (*see also* Voyage)
Gladstone 56, 133, 152, 186, 310, 349
Glenmark 31, 117, 152, 257, 350
Glover's 152, 186, 229, 257, 277, 350
Goldridge 133, 186, 278, 310, 387
Goldwater 56, 57, 187, 278, 311
Gravitas 57, 187
Greenhough 57, 152, 187, 278, 311
Grove Mill 58, 117, 133, 153, 173, 187, 311, 350 (*see also* Sanctuary)
Gunn Estate 58, 188, 311

Hanmer Junction 58, 134, 153, 351
Harrier Rise 258
Hatton 31, 258
Hawkdun Rise 351
Hay's Lake 134
Heron's Flight 59, 243, 311, 384
Herzog 59, 134, 223, 312, 330, 351
Highfield 59, 153, 188, 351 (*see also* Elstree)
Himmelsfeld 59, 188, 278
Hinchco 312
Hitchen Road 279
Huapai 312
Huia 60, 118, 134, 153, 188, 243, 351
Holmes 388
Huntaway 60, 118, 134, 312
Hunter's 33, 60, 118, 154, 188, 189, 230, 243, 312, 352
Hurunui River 154, 189
Huthlee 189
Hyperion 60, 134, 279, 312, 352

Inverness 61, 219, 268
Isabel 61, 135, 154, 190, 352
Isola 279, 313

Jackman Ridge 125, 190
Jackson 61, 154, 190, 230, 352
Johanneshof 61, 135, 154, 190, 230, 243, 352

Judge Valley 268
Jules Taylor 154, 352

Kahurangi 62, 118, 155, 190, 230 (*see also* Trout Valley)
Kaikoura 62, 118, 190, 353
Kaimira 62, 155, 191, 353
Kaituna Valley 63, 191, 353
Karaka Point 63
Kawarau 63, 353
Kemblefield 64, 118, 191, 279, 280, 313, 393
Kennedy Point 191, 280, 313
Kerr Farm 64, 191, 219, 280, 332
Kim Crawford 31, 64, 65, 135, 156, 192, 230, 258, 268, 313, 354
Kingsley 280, 313, 388
Konrad 192, 230, 354
Koura Bay 65, 135, 156, 192, 354
Kumeu River 65, 66, 135, 259, 314, 354, 355 (*see also* Brajkovich)

Lake Chalice 66, 156, 192, 193, 230, 251, 281, 314, 355
Lake Hayes 156, 193, 355
Langdale 67
Laverique 243
Lawson's Dry Hills 67, 118, 136, 156, 193, 231, 355
Leaning Rock 119, 156, 231
Le Brun 244
Le Grys 67, 157, 193, 315, 355
Lincoln 67, 68, 193, 194, 231, 281, 315, 332, 355
Lindauer 244, 245
Linden 68, 157, 194, 251, 281, 315
Lombardi 281
Longridge 68, 119, 194, 315
Longview 68, 119, 281, 316, 388
Loopline 68, 136, 157, 282, 316, 356
Lucknow 69, 136, 157, 268, 282, 298, 316
Lynskeys 69, 119, 194, 316, 356

Mad Red 259
Mahi 194, 356
Mahurangi 69, 157, 194, 282
Main Divide 69, 195, 357
Margrain 69, 113, 119, 136, 157, 231, 251, 259, 282, 316, 357 (*see also* Mad Red)
Marsden 69, 70, 136, 251, 298, 317, 388
Martinborough Vineyard 70, 136, 158, 195, 231, 251, 357, 358
Martinus 358
Matakana Estate 70, 137, 220, 268, 388 (*see also* Goldridge)
Matariki 70, 195, 232, 259, 282, 317, 358, 384, 388, 389 (*see also* Stony Bay)
Matawhero 71, 120, 195, 282, 358
Matua Valley 71, 72, 137, 158, 195, 196, 232, 293, 299, 317, 332, 358, 389 (*see also* Shingle Peak)
McCashin's 72, 158, 196, 283, 359
Mebus 196, 282
Melness 72, 158, 196, 318, 359
Miller's 259, 318
Mill Road 72, 318
Mills Reef 73, 120, 137, 158, 159, 196, 197, 251, 260, 268, 282, 284, 301, 318, 319, 359, 389
Millton 73, 74, 113, 120, 159, 223, 251, 359
Mission 74, 75, 120, 137, 159, 197, 232, 269, 284, 285, 319, 389, 390
Moana Park 75, 159, 197, 269, 301, 319
Monarch 298, 301
Montana 75, 76, 120, 159, 160, 197, 198, 220, 232, 319, 359, 360 (*see also* Aquila, Bernadino, Church Road, Corbans, Deutz, Huntaway, Jackman Ridge, Lindauer, Longridge, Murray Ridge, Robard & Butler, Saints, Stoneleigh, Timara, Tom, Verde, Wohnsiedler)
Morton 76, 77, 137, 160, 198, 233, 245, 260, 320, 360, 390 (*see also* Coniglio, Mill Road, Nikau Point)
Morworth 77, 120, 160, 360
Moteo 78, 320
Mount Cass 78, 160, 198, 233, 285, 361
Mount Edward 160, 361
Mountford 78, 361
Mount Maude 121, 161, 361
Mount Michael 78, 361
Mount Nelson 199
Mount Riley 78, 161, 199, 245, 285, 320, 362
Moutere Hills 79, 161, 285, 362
Mt Difficulty 79, 138, 161, 362
Mudbrick 79, 161, 285, 390 (*see also* Shepherd's Point)
Muddy Water 79, 161, 162, 260, 332, 362
Mud House 79, 162, 199, 320, 362, 363 (*see also* Le Grys)

INDEX OF WINE BRANDS

Murdoch James 79, 80, 137, 162, 199, 269, 363, 390
Murray Ridge 199
Mystery Creek 80

Naked 17 80
Nautilus 80, 138, 200, 245, 286, 363 (*see also* Twin Islands)
Neudorf 80, 81, 138, 162, 200, 252, 363, 364
Nevis Bluff 81, 138, 364
Newton/Forrest 286, 390
Ngatarawa 81, 200, 233, 234, 286, 320, 321
Nga Waka 82, 163, 200, 364
Nikau Point 82, 201, 321
Nobilo 82, 83, 201, 260, 287, 321, 364 (*see also* Drylands, Selaks, White Cloud)

Obsidian 261 (*see also* Weeping Sands)
Odyssey 83, 201, 287, 321
Ohinemuri 83, 121, 163, 321
Okahu 84, 202, 220, 234, 252, 287, 321, 390, 391
Old Coach Road 84, 202
Olssen's 85, 121, 163, 202, 234, 261, 365
Omaka Springs 85, 138, 163, 202, 322, 365
Onetangi Road 287, 288
Opihi 85, 125, 139, 163, 366
Origin 202
Oyster Bay 86, 202, 366

Palliser 86, 139, 163, 202, 203, 245, 366
Park 86, 164, 246, 332
Passage Rock 86, 87, 223, 261, 322, 391
Peacock Ridge 288, 322
Pegasus Bay 87, 164, 203, 234, 261, 288, 366, 367 (*see also* Main Divide)
Pelorus 246
Peninsula 87, 262, 288
Peregrine 87, 121, 139, 164, 203, 367
Phoenix 87, 121, 164, 288
Pisa Range 367
Pleasant Valley 88, 121, 203, 288, 332 (*see also* Yelas)
Pleiades 262
Ponder 322
Porters 139, 368
Providence 262
Pukawa 368
Pukeora 88, 165

Putiki Bay 252, 368

Quarry Road 203, 288
Quartz Reef 139, 246, 368

Ra Nui 203
Ransom 88, 139, 288
Redmetal 252, 322, 323
Revington 122
Richmond Plains 88, 204, 234, 262, 368, 369 (*see also* Holmes)
Ridgeview 88, 140
Rimu Grove 88, 89, 369
Rippon 31, 89, 127, 165, 204, 262, 369
Riverby 165, 204, 369
Riverside 89, 204, 252, 289, 323, 333
Robard & Butler 89, 204
Rockburn 89, 140, 165, 204, 369
Rongopai 89, 204, 205, 235, 289, 301, 323
Rossendale 122, 165, 205, 369
Ruben Hall 205
Rymer's Change 90, 253

St Aubyns 32, 246, 247
St Francis 90, 140, 165, 205, 289
St Helena 32, 140, 165, 205, 323, 370
Sacred Hill 90, 140, 166, 205, 206, 235, 290, 324 (*see also* Cairnbrae, Gunn Estate)
Saint Clair 90, 91, 140, 141, 166, 206, 324, 370
Saints 91, 122, 206, 235, 290, 333
Sanctuary 91, 166, 207, 333
Sanderson 91, 220, 290
Schubert 32, 92, 207, 235, 290, 371, 391
Seifried 92, 122, 166, 207, 235, 290, 371 (*see also* Old Coach Road)
Selaks 92, 93, 167, 207, 208, 236, 247, 291, 325, 371 (*see also* Drylands, Nobilo, White Cloud)
Seresin 93, 141, 167, 208, 247, 372
Shepherd's Point 93, 325
Sherwood 93, 167, 208, 372 (*see also* Laverique)
Shingle Peak 94, 141, 167, 208
Sienna 247
Sileni
Soljans 94, 123, 167, 247, 291, 326, 333 (*see also* Sienna)
Solstone 94, 168, 208, 263, 269, 291, 326, 372
Spencer Hill 95 (*see also* Tasman Bay)

Springvale 95, 373
Spy Valley 95, 123, 141, 168, 208, 326, 373
Squawking Magpie 95, 209, 291, 373
Staete Landt 96, 141, 209, 373
Stonecroft 96, 123, 263, 391, 393
Stonecutter 32, 142, 326, 373
Stoneleigh 96, 168, 209, 326, 373, 374
Stony Bay 96, 209, 291
Stonyridge 97, 292
Stratford 97, 168, 236, 374
Sunset Valley 97, 210, 292, 374

Tasman Bay 97, 142, 210, 374 (see also Spencer Hill)
Te Awa Farm 97, 98, 210, 263, 292, 298, 326, 334, 391
Te Hera 374
Te Kairanga 98, 168, 210, 253, 293, 326, 375
Te Mania 99, 211, 264, 375
Te Mata 99, 211, 223, 293, 294, 298, 392 (see also Rymer's Change)
Te Motu 294 (see also Dunleavy)
Terrace Downs 375
Terrace Heights 211
Terrace Road 99, 113, 211, 247, 376
Te Whare Ra 100, 123, 168, 221, 264, 294
Te Whau 100, 264, 327
Thornbury 100, 211, 294, 376
Three Sisters 100, 142, 169, 212
Timara 101, 169
Tiritiri 101
Tohu 101, 212, 376
Tom 264
Torlesse 101, 102, 123, 142, 169, 212, 236, 294, 327, 376
Trinity Hill 102, 142, 169, 212, 253, 295, 327, 376, 377, 392
Trout Valley 102, 169
TW 102, 103, 223, 237, 265
Twin Islands 103, 212, 377
Two Paddocks 377

Unison 253, 265

Valli 377, 378
Vavasour 103, 142, 212, 213, 378 (see also Dashwood)
Verde 247
Vidal 103, 170, 213, 295, 328, 378, 392 (see also Esk Valley, Villa Maria)

Vilagrad 103, 104
Villa Maria 104, 105, 106, 107, 123, 124, 126, 143, 170, 213, 214, 237, 295, 296, 328, 329, 379 (see also Esk Valley, Ruben Hall, St Aubyns, Vidal)
Vin Alto 107, 143, 265, 266, 384
Voss 107, 170, 237, 269, 296, 379
Voyage 248
Vynfields 379

Waimarie 107, 266
Waimea Estates 107, 108, 143, 170, 171, 214, 215, 237, 296, 379, 380
Waipara Downs 108, 380
Waipara Hills 108, 124, 127, 143, 171, 215, 253, 380 (see also Langdale)
Waipara Springs 109, 109, 171, 215, 238, 296, 381
Waipara West 109, 171, 215, 266, 381
Wairau River 109, 124, 143, 171, 215, 216, 238
Waitiri Creek 109, 124, 381
Waiwera 381
Walnut Ridge 382
Weeping Sands 296
West Brook 109, 110, 172, 216, 238, 269, 297, 301, 329
White Cloud 32, 110, 248
Whitehaven 110, 124, 172, 216, 238, 382
White Rock 216
Whitestone 382
William Hill 110, 124, 172, 382
Winslow 110, 172, 253, 297, 382
Wishart 111, 216, 329, 383, 393
Wither Hills 111, 217, 383
Wohnsiedler 126
Woollaston 111, 172, 217, 383

Yelas 334

Michael Cooper is New Zealand's most acclaimed wine writer, with 25 books, hundreds of magazine and newspaper articles, and several major literary awards to his credit.

The wine columnist for the *Sunday Star-Times*, he is the New Zealand editor of Australia's *Winestate* magazine and chairman of its New Zealand tasting panel.

In 1977 he obtained a Master of Arts degree from the University of Auckland with a thesis entitled 'The Wine Lobby: Pressure Group Politics and the New Zealand Wine Industry'. The marketing manager for Babich Wines from 1980 to 1990, he has been a full-time wine writer since 1991, and is a senior judge in New Zealand wine competitions.

As a consultant to Foodstuffs, New Zealand's largest grocery retailer, he selects the Wine of the Week for New World and Pak 'N Save supermarkets throughout the upper North Island and South Island, and was chairman of judges at the inaugural New World Wine Awards in 2003.

His authoritative and lavishly illustrated *Wine Atlas of New Zealand* (2002) won the coveted Montana Medal for the supreme work of non-fiction at the 2003 Montana New Zealand Book Awards. His other works include *Pocket Guide To Wines of New Zealand* (second edition, 2000), *Classic Wines of New Zealand* (1999), and the multiple prize-winning *The Wines and Vineyards of New Zealand* (fifth edition, 1996). He is also the New Zealand consultant for Hugh Johnson's annual *Pocket Wine Book* and *World Atlas of Wine*.

Wine Atlas of New Zealand

Winner of the Montana Medal for Non-Fiction 2003

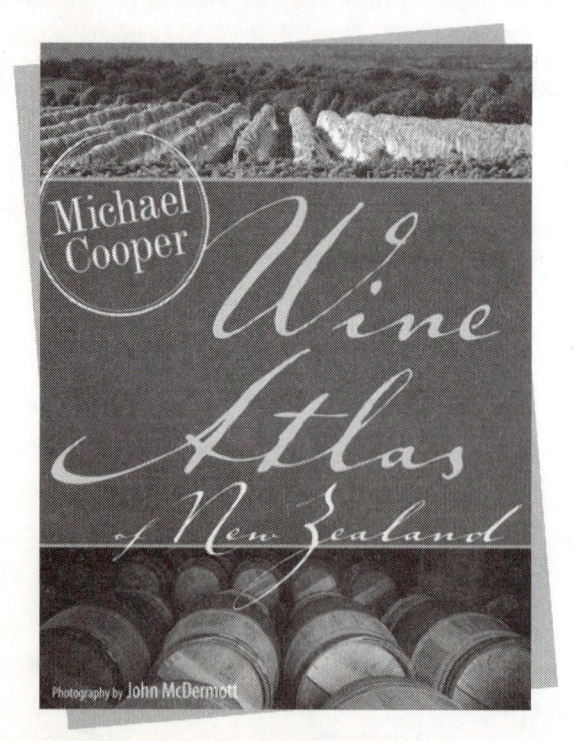

A visually stunning and comprehensive overview of the wine industry in New Zealand, Michael Cooper's *Wine Atlas of New Zealand* offers buyers, for the first time, an opportunity to own the ultimate reference book on the subject.